Human Anatomy
Laboratory Manual

WITH CAT DISSECTIONS

Fifth Edition

Elaine N. Marieb, R.N., Ph.D.
Holyoke Community College

PEARSON

Benjamin
Cummings

San Francisco Boston New York
Cape Town Hong Kong London Madrid Mexico City
Montreal Munich Paris Singapore Sydney Tokyo Toronto

Editor-in-Chief: Serina Beauparlant
Associate Project Editor: Sabrina Larson
Development Manager: Claire Alexander
Managing Editor: Wendy Earl
Production Supervisor: Michele Mangelli
Editorial Assistant: Annie Bleecker
Copy Editor: Anita Wagner
Text and Cover Designer: Yvo Riezebos
Cover Image: Mehau Kulyk/Photo Researchers, Inc.
Senior Manufacturing Buyer: Stacey Weinberger
Marketing Manager: Gordon Lee

Credits appear after the Appendices.

The Author and Publisher believe that the lab experiments described in this publication, when
conducted in conformity with the safety precautions described herein and according to the
school's laboratory safety procedures, are reasonably safe for the students to whom this lab
manual is directed. Nonetheless, many of the described experiments are accompanied by some
degree of risk, including human error, the failure or misuse of laboratory or electrical
equipment, mismeasurement, spills of chemicals, and exposure to sharp objects, heat, bodily
fluids, blood, or other biologics. The Author and Publisher disclaim any liability arising from
such risks in connection with any of the experiments contained in this manual. If students have
any questions or problems with materials, procedures, or instructions, on any experiment, they
should *always* ask their instructor for help before proceeding.

ISBN: 0-8053-3856-X
ISBN: 978-0-8053-3856-0

2 3 4 5 6 7 8 9 10—CRK—11 10 09 08 07

www.aw-bc.com

Contents

THE CIRCULATORY SYSTEM

THE RESPIRATORY SYSTEM

THE DIGESTIVE SYSTEM

THE URINARY SYSTEM

THE REPRODUCTIVE SYSTEM

SURFACE ANATOMY

Preface for the Instructor

The philosophy behind the fifth edition of this manual mirrors that of earlier editions. It reflects a still-developing sensibility for the way teachers teach and students learn, engendered by years of teaching the subject and by listening to the suggestions of other instructors as well as those of students enrolled in multifaceted health-care programs. *Human Anatomy Laboratory Manual with Cat Dissections* was originally developed to facilitate and enrich the laboratory experience of both teachers and students. This edition retains those same goals.

This manual, intended for students in introductory human anatomy courses, presents a wide range of anatomical laboratory experiences for students concentrating in nursing, physical therapy, dental hygiene, pharmacology, respiratory therapy, health and physical education, as well as biology and premedical programs. This manual studies anatomy of the human specimen in particular, but the cat and isolated animal organs are also used in the dissection experiments.

BASIC PEDAGOGICAL APPROACH

The organization and scope of this laboratory manual lend themselves to use in the one-term human anatomy course. The variety of anatomical studies enables instructors to gear their courses to specific academic programs or to their own teaching preferences. Although the main textbook, *Human Anatomy,* Fifth Edition (Elaine N. Marieb, Jon Mallatt, and Patricia Brady Wilhelm, Benjamin Cummings, © 2008), provided the impetus for this revision, the laboratory manual, as in previous editions, is based largely upon exercises developed for use independent of any textbook. It contains all the background discussion and terminology necessary to perform all manipulations effectively and eliminates the need for students to bring a textbook into the laboratory.

The laboratory manual is comprehensive and balanced enough to be flexible and is carefully written so that students can successfully complete each of its 30 exercises with little supervision. The manual begins with an exercise on anatomical terminology and an orientation to the human body. The second exercise provides the necessary tools for studying the various body systems. Succeeding exercises on the microscope, the cell, and tissues lay the groundwork for a study of each body system from the cellular to the organ level. Exercises 6 through 29 explore the anatomy of organ systems in detail, and Exercise 30 provides experience with the clinically valuable study of surface anatomy.

Homeostasis is continually emphasized as a requirement for optimal health. Pathological conditions are viewed as a loss of homeostasis. These discussions can be recognized by the homeostatic imbalance logo within the descriptive material of each exercise. This holistic approach encourages an integrated understanding of the human body.

FEATURES AND CHANGES

In this revision, I tried to respond to the feedback of reviewers and users concerning trends that are having an impact on the anatomical laboratory experience, most importantly:

- The declining popularity of animal dissection exercises
- The increased use of multimedia in the laboratory
- The ever-increasing computer literacy of our students
- The visual nature of today's students engendered by the advent of television and computer games

Changes made in each of these areas are described next.

Pedagogy

Organization Changes
A major change for this edition of the lab manual is to move the Review Sheets for each exercise from the back of the manual to conveniently follow each exercise. As in previous editions, the Histology Atlas and Human Anatomy Atlas follow Exercise 30.

Art and Photo Improvements
A completely revitalized art program is offered with this new edition. Several new figures have been added, and many illustrations have been revised for more detail, improved line quality, and stronger color. The muscle art has been enhanced with a richer, more realistic color. All of the bone art has been rerendered for incredibly realistic, 3-D texture. New photomicrographs are offered through the main exercises and in the vastly revised Histology Atlas. Many line drawings in the Review Sheets have been rerendered for clarity. Finally, this lab manual features 24 superb, brand-new cat dissection photographs.

Content Changes
Activities that have proven to be of limited pedagogical value because of unpredictability of results, difficult implementation, or general unpopularity have been deleted from this lab manual.

A number of new activities, many of which depend on student-student interaction, have been added to this edition. The following are representative of these additions:

- Examining shoulder actions in Exercise 12
- Testing for binocular vision in Exercise 18
- Two new activities on taste and smell in Exercise 20
- Using the heart model to study cardiac circulation in Exercise 23

Updated Anatomical Terminology
The anatomical terminology in this fifth edition has been updated to match that in *Human Anatomy,* Fifth Edition (main text authored by Marieb, Mallatt, and Wilhelm).

Design Enhancements

In response to complaints that students often spend lab time reading descriptive material (much better read before the lab), thus delaying the actual hands-on lab experience, the manual now has turquoise activity headings to alert the student that "this is the place" they get actively involved in their learning. Each activity within an exercise is numbered sequentially for easy assignment and reference. Additionally, sections that entail dissection of isolated organs are heralded by a dissection logo and an orange dissection heading. The end of such sections is indicated by a colored block of the same hue. Essentially, all diagrams and photographs in the Exercise sections are now in full color—a pedagogical plus for enhancing the interest of today's visually oriented students.

SPECIAL FEATURES RETAINED

Virtually all the special features appreciated by the adopters of the last edition are retained.

* Each exercise begins with learning objectives.

* Key terms appear in boldface print, and each term is defined when introduced.

* Illustrations are large and of exceptional quality. Full-color photographs and drawings highlight and differentiate important structures, and focus student attention on them.

* Body structures are studied from simple to complex levels, and physiological experiments allow ample opportunity for student observation and manipulation.

* The realism of several aspects of anatomy is enhanced by the use of additional full-color photographs and illustrations. Color is used pedagogically; that is, the structures and systems are color-coded to facilitate identification. Exercises are embellished with full color. The art program features many illustrations from the recently revised *Human Anatomy,* Fifth Edition (Marieb/Mallatt/Wilhelm). Photographs were carefully selected from the Stanford Bassett Collection and the Marieb/Mallatt/Wilhelm textbook.

* All laboratory instructions and procedures incorporate the latest precautions as recommended by the Centers for Disease Control and Prevention (CDC); these are reinforced by the laboratory safety procedures described inside the front cover and in the front section of the *Instructor Guide.* These procedures can be easily photocopied and posted in the lab.

* Clinical information is scattered throughout the exercises to point out how systems behave when structural abnormalities occur. It is identifiable by the symbol shown here.

* Laboratory Review Sheets at the end of each exercise require students to label diagrams and answer multiple-choice, short-answer, and essay questions. Every attempt has been made to achieve an acceptable balance between explanatory and recognition questions.

* The well-received Histology Atlas now has 55 color photomicrographs. The photomicrographs selected correspond closely to slides typically viewed in the lab. Most such tissues are stained with hematoxylin and eosin (H & E),

but a few depicted in the Histology Atlas are stained with differential stains to allow selected cell populations to be identified in a given tissue. Line drawings, corresponding exactly to selected plates in the Histology Atlas, appear in appropriate places within the text and add to the utility and effectiveness of the atlas. These diagrams can be colored by the student to duplicate the stains of the slides they are viewing, thus providing a valuable learning aid. Purple-colored page edges allow the Histology Atlas to be located quickly.

* Appendix B correlates some of the required anatomical laboratory observations with the corresponding sections of A.D.A.M.® Interactive Anatomy (AIA). Using AIA software to complement the printed manual descriptions of anatomical structures provides an extremely useful study method for visually oriented students.

* Four icons alert students to special features or instructions:

 The dissection scissors icon appears at the beginning of activities that entail the dissection of the cat as well as isolated animal organs.

 The homeostatic imbalance icon directs the student's attention to conditions representing a loss of homeostasis.

A safety icon notifies students that specific safety precautions are to be observed when using certain equipment or conducting particular lab procedures (for example, when handling body fluids such as blood, urine, and saliva).

 The AIA icon indicates where use of A.D.A.M.® Interactive Anatomy would enhance the study and comprehension of the laboratory topics.

SUPPLEMENTS

Instructor Guide

The *Instructor Guide* that accompanies the *Human Anatomy Laboratory Manual* contains a wealth of information. The guide includes help in anticipating pitfalls and problem areas, directions for lab setup, a complete materials list for each lab, and answers to the lab manual questions. The probable in-class time required for each lab is indicated by a clock icon. (ISBN 0-8053-9579-2)

Anatomy Atlas

The Bassett Atlas of Human Anatomy (ISBN 0-8053-0118-6)

MULTIMEDIA

Human Anatomy & Physiology Videotapes

These videotapes are available free of charge to qualified adopters. Produced by University Media Services and scripted by Rose Leigh Vines, Rosalee Carter, and Ann Motekaitis of California State University, Sacramento, these excellent videotapes reinforce many of the concepts covered in this manual and will represent a valuable addition to any multimedia library.

- *Selected Actions of Hormones and Other Chemical Messengers* videotape by Rose Leigh Vines and Juantia Barrena (0-8053-4155-2)

- *Human Musculature* videotape by Rose Leigh Vines and Allan Hinderstein (ISBN 0-8053-0106-2)

- *The Human Cardiovascular System: The Heart* videotape by Rose Leigh Vines and Rosalee Carter, University Media Services, California State University, Sacramento (ISBN 0-8053-4289-3)

- *The Human Cardiovascular System: The Blood Vessels* videotape by Rose Leigh Vines and Rosalee Carter, University Media Services, California State University, Sacramento (ISBN 0-8053-4297-4)

- *The Human Nervous System: Human Brain and Cranial Nerves* videotape by Rose Leigh Vines and Rosalee Carter, University Media Services, California State University, Sacramento (ISBN 0-8053-4012-2)

- *The Human Nervous System: The Spinal Cord and Nerves* videotape by Rose Leigh Vines and Rosalee Carter, University Media Services, California State University, Sacramento (ISBN 0-8053-4013-0)

- *The Human Respiratory System* videotape by Rose Leigh Vines and Ann Motekaitis (ISBN 0-8053-4822-0)

- *The Human Digestive System* videotape by Rose Leigh Vines and Ann Motekaitis (ISBN 0-8053-4823-9)

- *The Human Urinary System* videotape by Rose Leigh Vines and Ann Motekaitis (ISBN 0-8053-4915-4)

- *The Human Reproductive Systems* videotape by Rose Leigh Vines and Ann Motekaitis (ISBN 0-8053-4914-6)

- *Student Video Series Vol. I* (ISBN 0-8053-4110-2)

- *Student Video Series Vol. II* (ISBN 0-8053-6115-4)

Available for purchase from Benjamin Cummings to enhance student learning are the following:

Practice Anatomy Lab™

Practice Anatomy Lab™ is an interactive, visually engaging study and lab assessment tool that gives students 24/7 access to a rich array of anatomy lab specimens including human cadavers, anatomical models, histology slides, cat dissections, and fetal pig dissections.

Each module includes hundreds of images and quiz questions as well as interactive tools for reviewing the specimens and taking practice quizzes and simulated lab practical exams. Features include:

- Rich variety of quizzes to test students' recall of anatomical structures as well as their understanding of functional anatomy and clinical application

- Built-in audio pronunciation of hundreds of key anatomical terms

- Gradable lab practical exams (ISBN 0-8053-9432-X)

A.D.A.M.® Interactive Anatomy

A.D.A.M.® Interactive Anatomy Student Package, Third Edition, by Mark Lafferty and Sam Panella, with Windows DVD (ISBN 0-8053-7232-6) or with Windows CD-ROM (0-8053-9574-1).

A.D.A.M.® Interactive Anatomy Student Lab Guide, Third Edition, by Mark Lafferty and Sam Panella (ISBN 0-8053-5911-7)

Answer key to A.D.A.M.® Interactive Anatomy Student Lab Guide, Third Edition (ISBN 0-8053-7346-2). Available to instructors only.

Contact your Benjamin Cummings sales representative for more information on these titles, or visit our web site at www.aw-bc.com.

ACKNOWLEDGMENTS

Many thanks to the Benjamin Cummings editorial team: Serina Beauparlant, Editor-in-Chief; Sabrina Larson, Associate Project Editor; Claire Alexander, Development Manager; and Annie Bleecker, Editorial Assistant. Thanks also to Stacey Weinberger, Senior Manufacturing Buyer, and Gordon Lee, Marketing Manager. Kudos as usual to Wendy Earl and her production team; to Michele Mangelli, my production editor for this project, to Yvo Riezebos for a beautiful cover and interior design, and, as always, to my incredibly conscientious copyeditor Anita Wagner.

Last but not least, a huge thank you to Shawn Miller and Mark Nielsen, the cat dissectionist and photographer team who produced the fabulous new cat dissection photos found in this lab manual.

As always, I invite users of this edition to send me their comments and suggestions for subsequent editions.

Elaine N. Marieb
Benjamin Cummings
1301 Sansome Street
San Francisco, CA 94111

Hopefully, your laboratory experiences will be exciting times for you. As with any unfamiliar experience, it really helps if you know in advance what to expect and what will be expected of you.

LABORATORY ACTIVITIES

The laboratory exercises in this manual are designed to help you gain a broad understanding of anatomy. You can anticipate that you will be examining models, dissecting isolated animal organs, and using a microscope to look at tissue slides (anatomical approaches). You will also investigate a limited selection of physiological phenomena (conduct visual tests, plot sensory receptor locations, and so forth) to make your anatomy studies more meaningful.

A.D.A.M.® INTERACTIVE ANATOMY

If the A.D.A.M.® Interactive Anatomy CD-ROM software is available for your use, Appendix B, which correlates the various laboratory topics with specific frames of the A.D.A.M.® software, will provide an invaluable resource to help you in your studies.

ICONS/VISUAL MNEMONICS

I have tried to make this manual easy for you to use, and to this end two colored section heads and four different icons (visual mnemonics) are used throughout:

 The new **Dissection** head is orange and is accompanied by the **dissection scissors icon** at the beginning of activities that require you to dissect the cat organs.

The new **Activity** head is turquoise. Because most exercises have some explanatory background provided before the experiment(s), this visual cue alerts you that your lab involvement is imminent.

The **homeostatic imbalance icon** appears where a clinical disorder is described to indicate what happens when there is a structural abnormality or physiological malfunction, that is, a loss of homeostasis.

A **safety icon** notifies you that specific safety precautions are to be observed when using certain equipment or conducting particular lab procedures (for example, when working with ether a hood is to be used or when handling body fluids such as blood, urine, or saliva, gloves are to be worn).

 The **AIA icon** alerts you where the use of A.D.A.M.® Interactive Anatomy would enhance your laboratory experience.

HINTS FOR SUCCESS IN THE LABORATORY

With the possible exception of those who have photographic memories, most students can use helpful hints and guidelines to ensure that they have successful lab experiences.

1. Perhaps the best bit of advice is to attend all your scheduled labs and to participate in all the assigned exercises. Learning is an *active* process.

2. Scan the scheduled lab exercise and the questions in the Review Sheet at the end of the exercise *before* going to lab.

3. Be on time. Most instructors explain what the lab is about, pitfalls to avoid, and the sequence or format to be followed at the beginning of the lab session. If you are late, not only will you miss this information, you will not endear yourself to the instructor.

4. Review your lab notes after completing the lab session to help you focus on and remember the important concepts.

5. Keep your work area clean and neat. This reduces confusion and accidents.

6. Assume that all lab chemicals and equipment are sources of potential danger to you. Follow directions for equipment use and observe the laboratory safety guidelines provided inside the front cover of this manual.

7. Keep in mind the real value of the laboratory experience—a place for you to observe, manipulate, and experience hands-on activities that will dramatically enhance your understanding of the lecture presentations.

I really hope that you enjoy your A&P laboratories and that this lab manual makes learning about intricate structures and functions of the human body a fun and rewarding process. I'm always open to constructive criticism and suggestions for improvement in future editions. If you have any, please write to me in care of Benjamin Cummings.

Elaine N. Marieb

Elaine N. Marieb
Benjamin Cummings
1301 Sansome Street
San Francisco, CA 94111

The Language of Anatomy

O B J E C T I V E S

1. To describe the anatomical position verbally or by demonstration, and to explain its importance.
2. To use proper anatomical terminology to describe body directions, planes, and surfaces.
3. To name the body cavities and indicate the important organs in each.

Most of us are naturally curious about our bodies. This fact is amply demonstrated by infants, who are fascinated with their own waving hands or their mother's nose. Unlike the infant, however, the student of anatomy must learn to observe and identify the dissectible body structures formally.

When beginning the study of any science, the student is often initially overcome by jargon unique to the subject. The study of anatomy is no exception. But without this specialized terminology, confusion is inevitable. For example, what do *over, on top of, superficial to, above,* and *behind* mean in reference to the human body? Anatomists have an accepted set of reference terms that are universally understood. These allow body structures to be located and identified with a minimum of words and a high degree of clarity.

This exercise presents some of the most important anatomical terminology used to describe the body and introduces you to basic concepts of **gross anatomy,** the study of body structures visible to the naked eye.

Anatomical Position

When anatomists or doctors refer to specific areas of the human body, they do so in accordance with a universally accepted standard position called the **anatomical position.** It is essential to understand this position because much of the body terminology employed in this book refers to this body positioning, regardless of the position the body happens to be in. In the anatomical position the human body is erect, with the feet only slightly apart, head and toes pointed forward, and arms hanging at the sides with palms facing forward (Figure 1.1).

• Assume the anatomical position, and notice that it is not particularly comfortable. The hands are held unnaturally forward rather than hanging partially cupped toward the thighs.

Surface Anatomy

Body surfaces provide a wealth of visible landmarks for study of the body (Figure 1.1).

Axial: Relating to head, neck, and trunk, the axis of the body

Appendicular: Relating to limbs and their attachments to the axis

Anterior Body Landmarks

Note the following regions in Figure 1.2a:

Abdominal: Pertaining to the anterior body trunk region inferior to the ribs

Acromial: Pertaining to the point of the shoulder

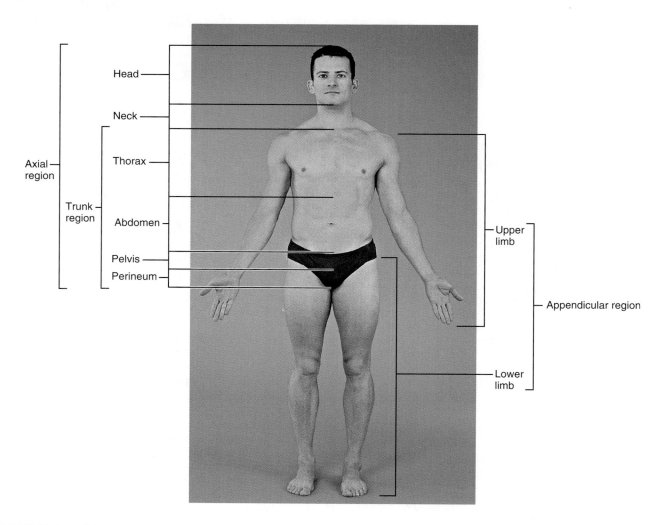

FIGURE 1.1 Anatomical position.

Antebrachial: Pertaining to the forearm

Antecubital: Pertaining to the anterior surface of the elbow

Axillary: Pertaining to the armpit

Brachial: Pertaining to the arm

Buccal: Pertaining to the cheek

Carpal: Pertaining to the wrist

Cervical: Pertaining to the neck region

Coxal: Pertaining to the hip

Crural: Pertaining to the leg

Digital: Pertaining to the fingers or toes

Femoral: Pertaining to the thigh

Fibular (peroneal): Pertaining to the side of the leg

Frontal: Pertaining to the forehead

Hallux: Pertaining to the great toe

Inguinal: Pertaining to the groin

Mammary: Pertaining to the breast

Mental: Pertaining to the chin

Nasal: Pertaining to the nose

Oral: Pertaining to the mouth

Orbital: Pertaining to the bony eye socket (orbit)

Palmar: Pertaining to the palm of the hand

Patellar: Pertaining to the anterior knee (kneecap) region

Pedal: Pertaining to the foot

Pelvic: Pertaining to the pelvis region

Pollex: Pertaining to the thumb

Pubic: Pertaining to the genital region

Sternal: Pertaining to the region of the breastbone

Tarsal: Pertaining to the ankle

Thoracic: Pertaining to the chest

Umbilical: Pertaining to the navel

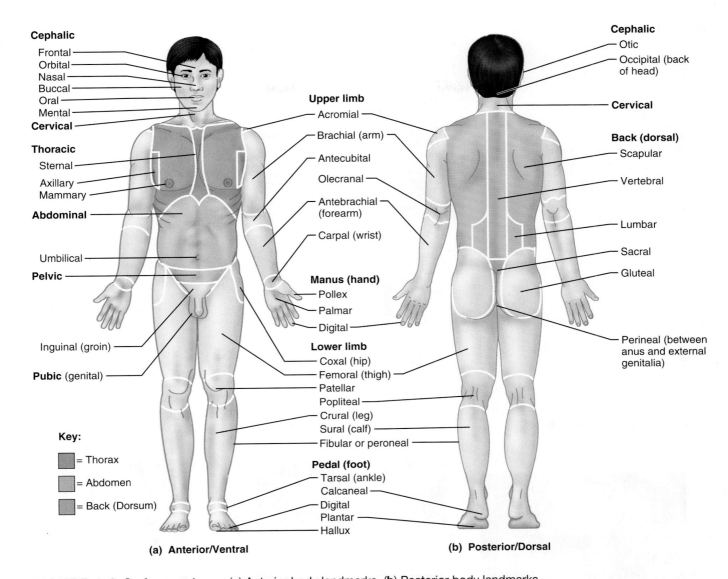

FIGURE 1.2 Surface anatomy. (a) Anterior body landmarks. (b) Posterior body landmarks.

Posterior Body Landmarks

Note the following body surface regions in Figure 1.2b:

Acromial: Pertaining to the point of the shoulder

Brachial: Pertaining to the arm

Calcaneal: Pertaining to the heel of the foot

Cephalic: Pertaining to the head

Dorsum: Pertaining to the back

Femoral: Pertaining to the thigh

Gluteal: Pertaining to the buttocks or rump

Lumbar: Pertaining to the area of the back between the ribs and hips; the loin

Manus: Pertaining to the hand

Occipital: Pertaining to the posterior aspect of the head or base of the skull

Olecranal: Pertaining to the posterior aspect of the elbow

Otic: Pertaining to the ear

Perineal: Pertaining to the region between the anus and external genitalia

Plantar: Pertaining to the sole of the foot

Popliteal: Pertaining to the back of the knee

Sacral: Pertaining to the region between the hips (overlying the sacrum)

Scapular: Pertaining to the scapula or shoulder blade area

Sural: Pertaining to the calf or posterior surface of the leg

Vertebral: Pertaining to the area of the spinal column

ACTIVITY 1

Locating Body Regions

Locate the anterior and posterior body landmarks on yourself, your lab partner, and a human torso model before continuing. ▮

FIGURE 1.3 **Planes of the body.**

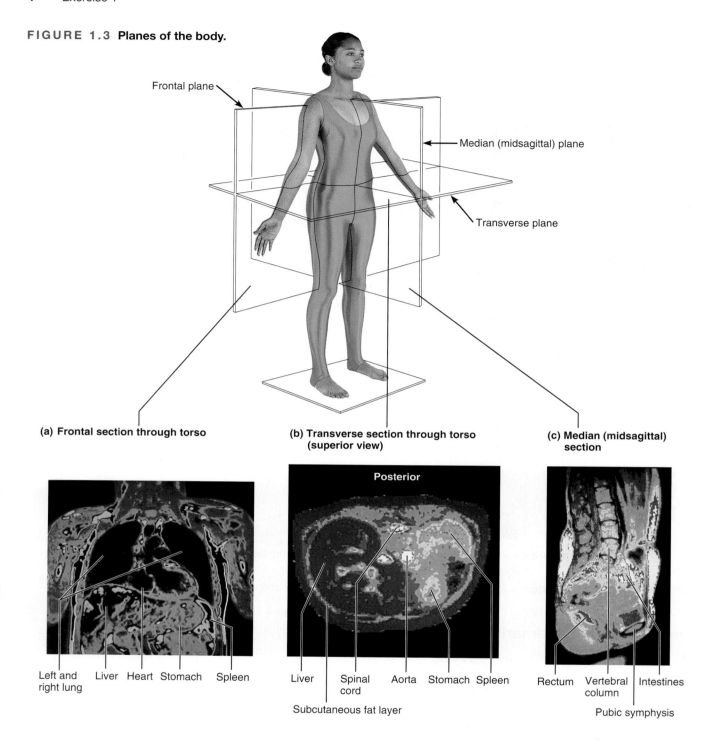

Frontal plane

Median (midsagittal) plane

Transverse plane

(a) Frontal section through torso

(b) Transverse section through torso (superior view)

(c) Median (midsagittal) section

Posterior

Left and right lung   Liver   Heart   Stomach   Spleen

Liver   Spinal cord   Aorta   Stomach   Spleen

Subcutaneous fat layer

Rectum   Vertebral column   Intestines

Pubic symphysis

Body Planes and Sections

The body is three-dimensional; and, in order to observe its internal structures, it is often helpful and necessary to make use of a **section,** or cut. When the section is made through the body wall or through an organ, it is made along an imaginary surface or line called a **plane.** Anatomists commonly refer to three planes (Figure 1.3), or sections, that lie at right angles to one another.

Sagittal plane: A plane that runs longitudinally and divides the body into right and left parts is referred to as a sagittal plane. If it divides the body into equal parts, right down the median plane of the body, it is called a **median,** or **midsagittal, plane.** All other sagittal planes are referred to as **parasagittal planes.**

Frontal plane: Sometimes called a **coronal plane,** the frontal plane is a longitudinal plane that divides the body (or an organ) into anterior and posterior parts.

Transverse plane: A transverse plane runs horizontally, dividing the body into superior and inferior parts. When organs are sectioned along the transverse plane, the sections are commonly called **cross sections.**

On microscope slides, the abbreviation for a longitudinal section (sagittal or frontal) is l.s. Cross sections are abbreviated x.s. or c.s.

As shown in Figure 1.4, a sagittal or frontal plane section of any nonspherical object, be it a banana or a body organ, provides quite a different view than a transverse section. Parasagittal sections provide still different views.

ACTIVITY 2

Observing Sectioned Specimens

1. Go to the demonstration area and observe the transversely and longitudinally cut organ specimens (kidneys). Pay close attention to the different structural details in the samples because you will need to draw these views in the Review Sheet at the end of this exercise.

2. After completing instruction 1, obtain a gelatin-spaghetti mold and a scalpel and bring them to your laboratory bench. (Essentially, this is just cooked spaghetti added to warm gelatin, which is then allowed to gel.)

3. Cut through the gelatin-spaghetti mold along any plane, and examine the cut surfaces. You should see spaghetti strands that have been cut transversely (x.s.), some cut longitudinally, and some cut obliquely.

4. Draw the appearance of each of these spaghetti sections below, and verify the accuracy of your section identifications with your instructor.

Transverse cut   Longitudinal cut   Oblique cut ▭

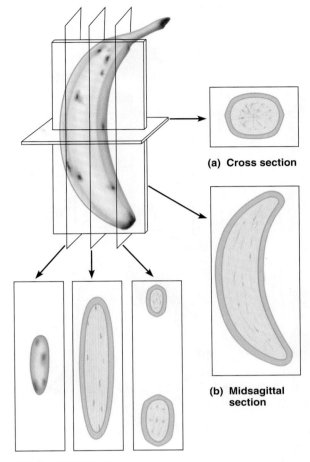

(a) Cross section

(b) Midsagittal section

(c) Frontal sections

FIGURE 1.4 Objects can look odd when viewed in section. This banana has been sectioned in three different planes (**a–c**), and only in one of these planes (b) is it easily recognized as a banana. In order to recognize human organs in section, one must anticipate how the organs will look when cut that way. If one cannot recognize a sectioned organ, it is possible to reconstruct its shape from a series of successive cuts, as from the three serial sections in (c).

Body Orientation and Direction

Study the terms that follow, referring to Figure 1.5. Notice that certain terms have a different meaning for a four-legged animal (quadruped) than they do for a human (biped).

Superior/inferior (*above/below*): These terms refer to placement of a structure along the long axis of the body. Superior structures always appear above other structures, and inferior structures are always below other structures. For example, the nose is superior to the mouth, and the abdomen is inferior to the chest.

Anterior/posterior (*front/back*): In humans the most anterior structures are those that are most forward—the face, chest, and abdomen. Posterior structures are those toward the backside of the body. For instance, the spine is posterior to the heart.

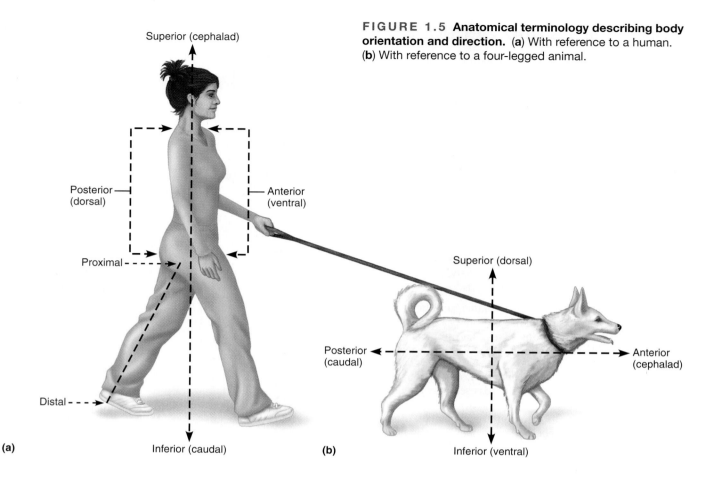

FIGURE 1.5 Anatomical terminology describing body orientation and direction. (a) With reference to a human. (b) With reference to a four-legged animal.

Medial/lateral (*toward the midline/away from the midline or median plane*): The sternum (breastbone) is medial to the ribs; the ear is lateral to the nose.

The terms of position described previously assume the person is in the anatomical position. The next four term pairs are more absolute. Their applicability is not relative to a particular body position, and they consistently have the same meaning in all vertebrate animals.

Cephalad (cranial)/caudal (*toward the head/toward the tail*): In humans these terms are used interchangeably with *superior* and *inferior,* but in four-legged animals they are synonymous with *anterior* and *posterior,* respectively.

Dorsal/ventral (*backside/belly side*): These terms are used chiefly in discussing the comparative anatomy of animals, assuming the animal is standing. *Dorsum* is a Latin word meaning "back." Thus, *dorsal* refers to the animal's back or the *back*side of any other structures; for example, the posterior surface of the human leg is its dorsal surface. The term *ventral* derives from the Latin term *venter,* meaning "belly," and always refers to the belly side of animals. In humans the terms *ventral* and *dorsal* are used interchangeably with the terms *anterior* and *posterior,* but in four-legged animals *ventral* and *dorsal* are synonymous with *inferior* and *superior,* respectively.

Proximal/distal (*nearer the trunk or attached end/farther from the trunk or point of attachment*): These terms are used primarily to locate various areas of the body limbs. For example, the fingers are distal to the elbow; the knee is proximal to the toes. However, these terms may also be used to

indicate regions (closer to or farther from the head) of internal tubular organs.

Superficial (external)/deep (internal) (*toward or at the body surface/away from the body surface*): These terms locate body organs according to their relative closeness to the body surface. For example, the skin is superficial to the skeletal muscles, and the lungs are deep to the rib cage.

A C T I V I T Y   3

Practicing Using Correct Anatomical Terminology

Before continuing, use a human torso model, a human skeleton, or your own body to specify the relationship between the following structures when the body is in the anatomical position.

1. The wrist is _____ to the hand.

2. The trachea (windpipe) is _____ to the spine.

3. The brain is _____ to the spinal cord.

4. The kidneys are _____ to the liver.

5. The nose is _____ to the cheekbones.

6. The thumb is _____ to the ring finger.

7. The thorax is _____ to the abdomen.

8. The skin is _____ to the skeleton. ▪

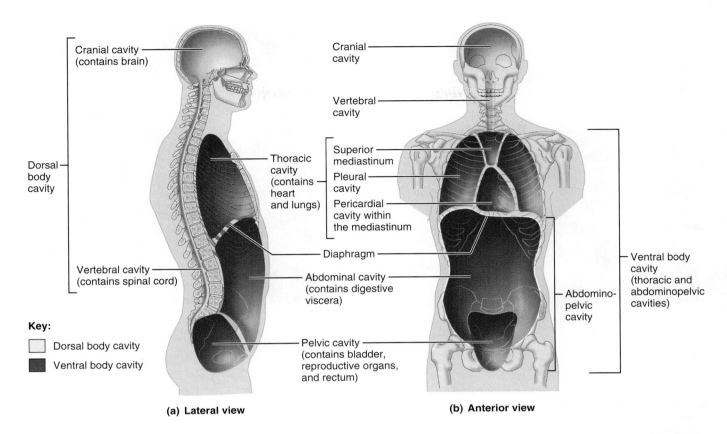

Key:

☐ Dorsal body cavity

■ Ventral body cavity

(a) Lateral view

(b) Anterior view

FIGURE 1.6 Body cavities and their subdivisions.

Body Cavities

The axial portion of the body has two large cavities that provide different degrees of protection to the organs within them (Figure 1.6).

Dorsal Body Cavity

The dorsal body cavity can be subdivided into the **cranial cavity,** in which the brain is enclosed within the rigid skull, and the **vertebral** (or **spinal**) **cavity,** within which the delicate spinal cord is protected by the bony vertebral column. Because the spinal cord is a continuation of the brain, these cavities are continuous with each other.

Ventral Body Cavity

Like the dorsal cavity, the ventral body cavity is subdivided. The superior **thoracic cavity** is separated from the rest of the ventral cavity by the dome-shaped diaphragm. The heart and lungs, located in the thoracic cavity, are afforded some measure of protection by the bony rib cage. The cavity inferior to the diaphragm is often referred to as the **abdominopelvic cavity.** Although there is no further physical separation of the ventral cavity, some prefer to describe the abdominopelvic cavity in terms of a superior **abdominal cavity,** the area that houses the stomach, intestines, liver, and other organs, and an inferior **pelvic cavity,** the region that is partially enclosed by the bony pelvis and contains the reproductive organs, bladder, and rectum. Notice in Figure 1.6 that the abdominal and pelvic

cavities are not continuous with each other in a straight plane but that the pelvic cavity is tipped away from the perpendicular.

Serous Membranes of the Ventral Body Cavity

The walls of the ventral body cavity and the outer surfaces of the organs it contains are covered with an exceedingly thin, double-layered membrane called the serosa, or serous membrane. The part of the membrane lining the cavity walls is referred to as the parietal serosa, and it is continuous with a similar membrane, the visceral serosa, covering the external surface of the organs within the cavity. These membranes produce a thin lubricating fluid that allows the visceral organs to slide over one another or to rub against the body wall without friction. Serous membranes also compartmentalize the various organs so that infection of one organ is prevented from spreading to others.

The specific names of the serous membranes depend on the structures they envelop. Thus the serosa lining the abdominal cavity and covering its organs is the **peritoneum,** that enclosing the lungs is the **pleura,** and that around the heart is the **pericardium** (see Figure 7.1c, p. 94).

Abdominopelvic Quadrants and Regions   Because the abdominopelvic cavity is quite large and contains many organs, it is helpful to divide it up into smaller areas for discussion or study.

A scheme, used by most physicians and nurses, divides the abdominal surface (and the abdominopelvic cavity deep to it) into four approximately equal regions called **quadrants.** These quadrants are named according to their relative

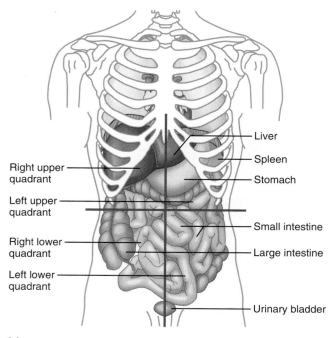

(a)

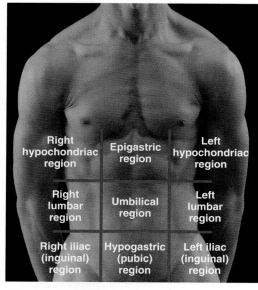

(b)

FIGURE 1.7 Abdominopelvic surface and cavity. (a) The four quadrants, showing superficial organs in each quadrant. (b) Nine regions delineated by four planes. The superior horizontal plane is just inferior to the ribs; the inferior horizontal plane is at the superior aspect of the hip bones. The vertical planes are just medial to the nipples. (c) Anterior view of the abdominopelvic cavity showing superficial organs.

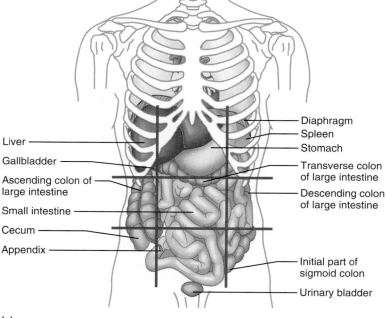

(c)

position—that is, *right upper quadrant, right lower quadrant, left upper quadrant,* and *left lower quadrant* (see Figure 1.7a). Note that the terms left and right refer to the left and right of the body shown, not your own. The left and right of the body viewed are referred to as **anatomical left and right.**

Identifying Organs in the Abdominopelvic Cavity

Examine the torso model to respond to the following directions and questions.

Name two organs found in the left upper quadrant.

_____ and _____

Name two organs found in the right lower quadrant.

_____ and _____

What organ (Figure 1.7a) is divided into identical halves by

the median plane line? _____

A different scheme commonly used by anatomists divides the abdominal surface and abdominopelvic cavity into nine separate regions by four planes, as shown in Figure 1.7b.

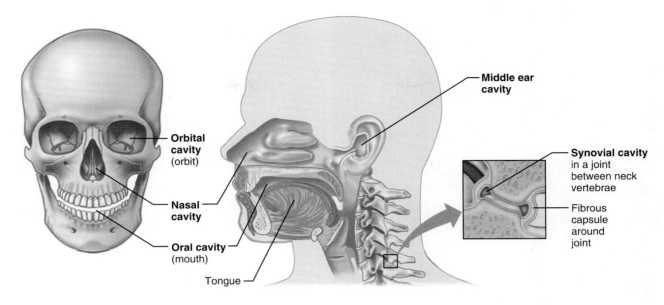

FIGURE 1.8 Other body cavities. The oral, nasal, orbital, and middle ear cavities are located in the head and open to the body exterior. Synovial cavities are found in joints between many bones such as the vertebrae of the spine, and at the knee, shoulder, and hip.

Although the names of these nine regions are unfamiliar to you now, with a little patience and study they will become easier to remember. As you read through the descriptions of these nine regions and locate them in Figure 1.7b, also look at Figure 1.7c to note the organs the regions contain.

Umbilical region: The centermost region, which includes the umbilicus

Epigastric region: Immediately superior to the umbilical region; overlies most of the stomach

Hypogastric (pubic) region: Immediately inferior to the umbilical region; encompasses the pubic area

Iliac (inguinal) regions: Lateral to the hypogastric region and overlying the superior parts of the hip bones

Lumbar regions: Between the ribs and the flaring portions of the hip bones; lateral to the umbilical region

Hypochondriac regions: Flanking the epigastric region laterally and overlying the lower ribs

ACTIVITY 5

Locating Abdominal Surface Regions

Locate the regions of the abdominal surface on a human torso model and on yourself before continuing. ▨

Other Body Cavities

Besides the large, closed body cavities, there are several types of smaller body cavities (Figure 1.8). Many of these are in the head, and most open to the body exterior.

Oral cavity: The oral cavity, commonly called the mouth, contains the tongue and teeth. It is continuous with the rest of the digestive tube, which opens to the exterior at the anus.

Nasal cavity: Located within and posterior to the nose, the nasal cavity is part of the passages of the respiratory system.

Orbital cavities: The orbital cavities (orbits) in the skull house the eyes and present them in an anterior position.

Middle ear cavities: Each middle ear cavity lies just medial to an eardrum and is carved into the bony skull. These cavities contain tiny bones that transmit sound vibrations to the organ of hearing in the inner ears.

Synovial (sĭ-no′ve-al) **cavities:** Synovial cavities are joint cavities—they are enclosed within fibrous capsules that surround the freely movable joints of the body, such as those between the vertebrae and the knee and hip joints. Like the serous membranes of the ventral body cavity, membranes lining the synovial cavities secrete a lubricating fluid that reduces friction as the enclosed structures move across one another.

NAME _____

LAB TIME/DATE _____

The Language of Anatomy

Surface Anatomy

1. For each of the numbered descriptions, write the equivalent key term or its letter in front of the description.

Key: a. buccal   c. cephalic   e. patellar
     b. calcaneal   d. digital   f. scapular

_____ 1. cheek

_____ 2. pertaining to the fingers

_____ 3. shoulder blade region

_____ 4. anterior aspect of knee

_____ 5. heel of foot

_____ 6. pertaining to the head

2. Indicate the following body areas on the accompanying diagram by placing the correct key letter at the end of each line.

Key:

a. abdominal
b. antecubital
c. axillary
d. brachial
e. cervical
f. crural
g. femoral
h. fibular
i. gluteal
j. inguinal
k. lumbar
l. occipital
m. oral
n. popliteal
o. pubic
p. sural
q. thoracic
r. umbilical

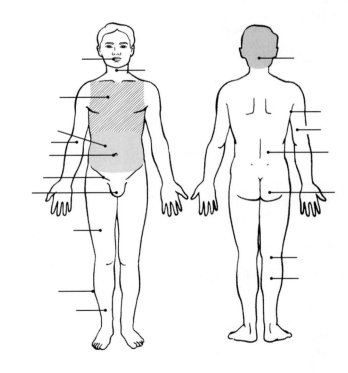

3. Classify each of the terms in the key of question 2 above into one of the large body regions indicated below. Insert the appropriate key letters on the answer blanks.

_____ 1. appendicular

_____ 2. axial

Body Orientation, Direction, Planes, and Sections

4. Describe completely the standard human anatomical position. _____

_____

5. Define *section.* _____

6. Several incomplete statements are listed below. Correctly complete each statement by choosing the appropriate anatomical term from the key. Record the key letters and/or terms on the correspondingly numbered blanks below.

Key: a. anterior   d. inferior   g. posterior   j. superior
      b. distal   e. lateral   h. proximal   k. transverse
      c. frontal   f. medial   i. sagittal

   In the anatomical position, the face and palms are on the _1_ body surface; the buttocks and shoulder blades are on the _2_ body surface; and the top of the head is the most _3_ part of the body. The ears are _4_ and _5_ to the shoulders and _6_ to the nose. The heart is _7_ to the vertebral column (spine) and _8_ to the lungs. The elbow is _9_ to the fingers but _10_ to the shoulder. The abdominopelvic cavity is _11_ to the thoracic cavity and _12_ to the spinal cavity. In humans, the dorsal surface can also be called the _13_ surface; however, in quadruped animals, the dorsal surface is the _14_ surface.

   If an incision cuts the heart into right and left parts, the section is a _15_ section; but if the heart is cut so that superior and inferior portions result, the section is a _16_ section. You are told to cut a dissection animal along two planes so that both kidneys are observable in each section. The two sections that will always meet this requirement are the _17_ and _18_ sections. A section that demonstrates the continuity between the spinal and cranial cavities is a _19_ section.

1. _____   8. _____   14. _____

2. _____   9. _____   15. _____

3. _____   10. _____   16. _____

4. _____   11. _____   17. _____

5. _____   12. _____   18. _____

6. _____   13. _____   19. _____

7. _____

7. Correctly identify each of the body planes by inserting the appropriate term for each on the answer line below the drawing.

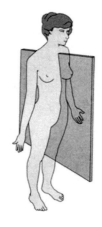

(a)

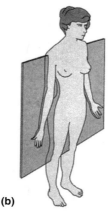

(b)

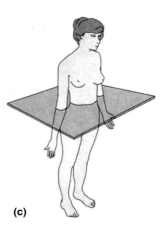

(c)

_____   _____   _____

8. Draw a kidney as it appears when sectioned in each of the three different planes.

Transverse section	Sagittal section	Frontal section

9. Correctly identify each of the nine areas of the abdominal surface by inserting the appropriate term for each of the letters indicated in the drawing.

a. _____

b. _____

c. _____

d. _____

e. _____

f. _____

g. _____

h. _____

i. _____

(a)
(b)
(c)
(d)
(e)
(f)
(g)
(h)
(i)

Body Cavities

10. Which body cavity would have to be opened for the following types of surgery or procedures? (Insert letter of key choice in same-numbered blank. More than one choice may apply.)

Key: a. abdominopelvic   c. dorsal   e. thoracic
       b. cranial   d. spinal   f. ventral

_____ 1. surgery to remove a cancerous lung lobe   _____ 4. appendectomy

_____ 2. removal of the uterus, or womb   _____ 5. stomach ulcer operation

_____ 3. removal of a brain tumor   _____ 6. delivery of preoperative "saddle" anesthesia

11. Name the muscle that subdivides the ventral body cavity. _____

12. What are the bony landmarks of the abdominopelvic cavity? _____

_____

13. Which body cavity affords the least protection to its internal structures? _____

14. What is the function of the serous membranes of the body? _____

_____

15. A nurse informs you that she is about to take blood from the antecubital region. What portion of your body should you present

to her? _____

16. Using the key choices, identify the small body cavities described below.

Key: a. middle ear cavity   c. oral cavity   e. synovial cavity
     b. nasal cavity   d. orbital cavity

_____ 1. holds the eyes in an anterior-facing position   _____ 4. contains the tongue

_____ 2. houses three tiny bones involved in hearing   _____ 5. lines a joint cavity

_____ 3. contained within the nose

17. On the incomplete flowchart provided below:

- Fill in the cavity names as appropriate to boxes 3–8.
- Then, using either the name of the cavity or the box numbers, identify the descriptions in the list that follows.

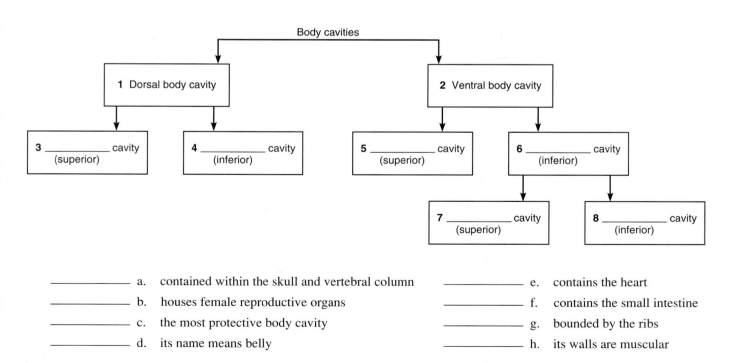

_____ a. contained within the skull and vertebral column   _____ e. contains the heart

_____ b. houses female reproductive organs   _____ f. contains the small intestine

_____ c. the most protective body cavity   _____ g. bounded by the ribs

_____ d. its name means belly   _____ h. its walls are muscular

Organ Systems Overview

O B J E C T I V E S

1. To name the human organ systems and indicate the major functions of each.
2. To identify these organs in a dissected rat or human cadaver or on a dissectible human torso model.
3. To identify the correct organ system for each organ when presented with a list of organs (as studied in the laboratory).

The basic unit or building block of all living things is the **cell.** Cells fall into four different categories according to their structures and functions. Each of these corresponds to one of the four tissue types: epithelial, muscular, nervous, and connective. A **tissue** is a group of cells that are similar in structure and function. An **organ** is a structure composed of two or more tissue types that performs a specific function for the body. For example, the small intestine, which digests and absorbs nutrients, is composed of all four tissue types.

An **organ system** is a group of organs that act together to perform a particular body function. For example, the organs of the digestive system work together to break down foods moving through the digestive system and absorb the end products into the bloodstream to provide nutrients and fuel for all the body's cells. In all, there are 11 organ systems, which are described in Table 2.1. The lymphatic system also encompasses a *functional system* called the immune system, which is composed of an army of mobile *cells* that act to protect the body from foreign substances.

Read through this summary of the body's organ systems before beginning your rat dissection or examination of the predissected human cadaver. If a human cadaver is not available, selected views in Figures 2.3 through 2.6 will serve as a partial replacement.

DISSECTION AND IDENTIFICATION:
The Organ Systems of the Rat

Many of the external and internal structures of the rat are quite similar in structure and function to those of the human, so a study of the gross anatomy of the rat should help you understand our own physical structure. The following instructions complement and direct your dissection and observation of a rat, but the descriptions for organ observations in Activity 4 ("Examining the Ventral Body Cavity," which begins on p. 18) also apply to superficial observations of a previously dissected human cadaver. In addition, the general instructions for observing external structures can easily be extrapolated to serve human cadaver observations. The photographs in Figures 2.3 to 2.6 will provide visual aids.

Note that four of the organ systems listed in Table 2.1 will not be studied at this time (integumentary, skeletal, muscular, and nervous), as they require microscopic study or more detailed dissection.

TABLE 2.1	Overview of Organ Systems of the Body	
Organ system	Major component organs	Function
Integumentary (Skin)	Epidermal and dermal regions; cutaneous sense organs and glands	• Protects deeper organs from mechanical, chemical, and bacterial injury, and desiccation (drying out) • Excretes salts and urea • Aids in regulation of body temperature • Produces vitamin D
Skeletal	Bones, cartilages, tendons, ligaments, and joints	• Body support and protection of internal organs • Provides levers for muscular action • Cavities provide a site for blood cell formation
Muscular	Muscles attached to the skeleton	• Primary function is to contract or shorten; in doing so, skeletal muscles allow locomotion (running, walking, etc.), grasping and manipulation of the environment, and facial expression • Generates heat
Nervous	Brain, spinal cord, nerves, and sensory receptors	• Allows body to detect changes in its internal and external environment and to respond to such information by activating appropriate muscles or glands • Helps maintain homeostasis of the body via rapid transmission of electrical signals
Endocrine	Pituitary, thymus, thyroid, parathyroid, adrenal, and pineal glands; ovaries, testes, and pancreas	• Helps maintain body homeostasis, promotes growth and development; produces chemical "messengers" (hormones) that travel in the blood to exert their effect(s) on various "target organs" of the body
Cardiovascular	Heart, blood vessels, and blood	• Primarily a transport system that carries blood containing oxygen, carbon dioxide, nutrients, wastes, ions, hormones, and other substances to and from the tissue cells where exchanges are made; blood is propelled through the blood vessels by the pumping action of the heart • Antibodies and other protein molecules in the blood act to protect the body
Lymphatic/ Immunity	Lymphatic vessels, lymph nodes, spleen, thymus, tonsils, and scattered collections of lymphoid tissue	• Picks up fluid leaked from the blood vessels and returns it to the blood • Cleanses blood of pathogens and other debris • Houses lymphocytes that act via the immune response to protect the body from foreign substances (antigens)
Respiratory	Nasal passages, pharynx, larynx, trachea, bronchi, and lungs	• Keeps the blood continuously supplied with oxygen while removing carbon dioxide • Contributes to the acid-base balance of the blood via its carbonic acid–bicarbonate buffer system.
Digestive	Oral cavity, esophagus, stomach, small and large intestines, and accessory structures (teeth, salivary glands, liver, and pancreas)	• Breaks down ingested foods to minute particles, which can be absorbed into the blood for delivery to the body cells • Undigested residue removed from the body as feces
Urinary	Kidneys, ureters, bladder, and urethra	• Rids the body of nitrogen-containing wastes (urea, uric acid, and ammonia), which result from the breakdown of proteins and nucleic acids by body cells • Maintains water, electrolyte, and acid-base balance of blood
Reproductive	Male: testes, prostate, scrotum, penis, and duct system, which carries sperm to the body exterior	• Provides germ cells (sperm) for perpetuation of the species
	Female: ovaries, uterine tubes, uterus, mammary glands, and vagina	• Provides germ cells (eggs); the female uterus houses the developing fetus until birth; mammary glands provide nutrition for the infant

Observing External Structures

1. If your instructor has provided a predissected rat, go to the demonstration area to make your observations. Alternatively, if you and/or members of your group will be dissecting the specimen, obtain a preserved or freshly killed rat (one for every two to four students), a dissecting tray, dissecting pins or twine, scissors, probe, forceps, and disposable gloves, and bring them to your laboratory bench.

If a predissected human cadaver is available, obtain a probe, forceps, and disposable gloves before going to the demonstration area.

! 2. Don the gloves before beginning your observations. This precaution is particularly important when handling freshly killed animals, which may harbor internal parasites.

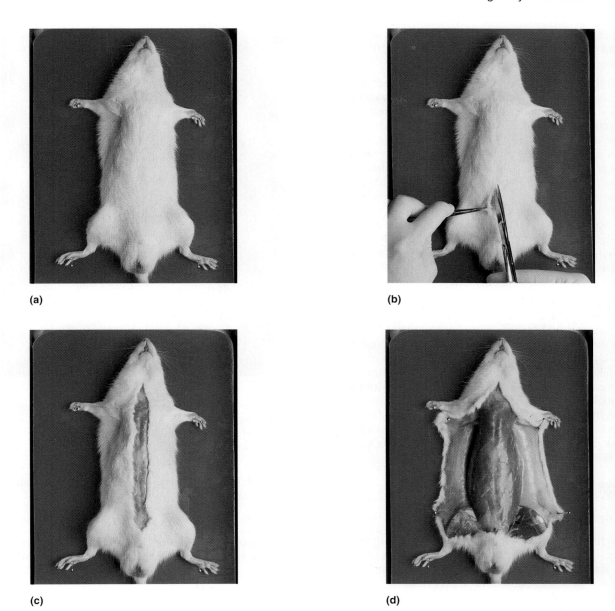

(a)

(b)

(c)

(d)

FIGURE 2.1 Rat dissection: Securing for dissection and the initial incision. (**a**) Securing the rat to the dissection tray with dissecting pins. (**b**) Using scissors to make the incision on the median line of the abdominal region. (**c**) Completed incision from the pelvic region to the lower jaw. (**d**) Reflection (folding back) of the skin to expose the underlying muscles.

3. Observe the major divisions of the body—head, trunk, and extremities. If you are examining a rat, compare these divisions to those of humans. ▇

Examining the Oral Cavity

Examine the structures of the oral cavity. Identify the teeth and tongue. Observe the extent of the hard palate (the portion underlain by bone) and the soft palate (immediately posterior to the hard palate, with no bony support). Notice that the posterior end of the oral cavity leads into the throat, or pharynx,

a passageway used by both the digestive and respiratory systems. ▇

Opening the Ventral Body Cavity

1. Pin the animal to the wax of the dissecting tray by placing its dorsal side down and securing its extremities to the wax with large dissecting pins as shown in Figure 2.1a.

If the dissecting tray is not waxed, you will need to secure the animal with twine as follows. (Some may prefer this method in any case.) Obtain the roll of twine. Make a loop knot around one upper limb, pass the twine under the tray, and secure the opposing limb. Repeat for the lower extremities.

2.   Lift the abdominal skin with a forceps, and cut through it with the scissors (Figure 2.1b). Close the scissor blades and insert them flat under the cut skin. Moving in a cephalad direction, open and close the blades to loosen the skin from the underlying connective tissue and muscle. Now cut the skin along the body midline, from the pubic region to the lower jaw (Figure 2.1c). Finally, make a lateral cut about halfway down the ventral surface of each limb. Complete the job of freeing the skin with the scissor tips, and pin the flaps to the tray (Figure 2.1d). The underlying tissue that is now exposed is the skeletal musculature of the body wall and limbs. It allows voluntary body movement. Notice that the muscles are packaged in sheets of pearly white connective tissue (fascia), which protect the muscles and bind them together.

3.   Carefully cut through the muscles of the abdominal wall in the pubic region, avoiding the underlying organs. Remember, to *dissect* means "to separate"—not mutilate! Now, hold and lift the muscle layer with a forceps and cut through the muscle layer from the pubic region to the bottom of the rib cage. Make two lateral cuts through the rib cage (Figure 2.2). A thin membrane attached to the inferior boundary of the rib cage should be obvious; this is the **diaphragm,** which separates the thoracic and abdominal cavities. Cut the diaphragm where it attaches to the ventral ribs to loosen the rib cage. You can now lift the ribs to view the contents of the thoracic cavity. ▬

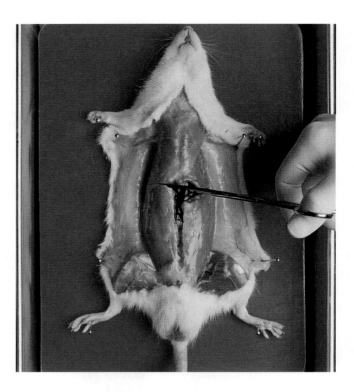

FIGURE 2.2 Rat dissection: Making lateral cuts at the base of the rib cage.

ACTIVITY 4

Examining the Ventral Body Cavity

1.   Starting with the most superficial structures and working deeper, examine the structures of the thoracic cavity. Refer to Figure 2.3, which shows the superficial organs, as you work. Choose the appropriate view depending on whether you are examining a rat (a) or a human cadaver (b).

Thymus: An irregular mass of glandular tissue overlying the heart (not illustrated in the human cadaver photograph).

With the probe, push the thymus to the side to view the heart.

Heart: Medial oval structure enclosed within the pericardium (serous membrane sac).

Lungs: Flanking the heart on either side.

Now observe the throat region to identify the trachea.

Trachea: Tubelike "windpipe" running medially down the throat; part of the respiratory system.

Follow the trachea into the thoracic cavity; notice where it divides into two branches. These are the bronchi.

Bronchi: Two passageways that plunge laterally into the tissue of the two lungs.

To expose the esophagus, push the trachea to one side.

Esophagus: A food chute; the part of the digestive system that transports food from the pharynx (throat) to the stomach.

Diaphragm: A thin muscle attached to the inferior boundary of the rib cage; separates the thoracic and abdominal cavities.

Follow the esophagus through the diaphragm to its junction with the stomach.

Stomach: A curved organ important in food digestion and temporary food storage.

2.   Examine the superficial structures of the abdominopelvic cavity. Lift the **greater omentum,** an extension of the peritoneum that covers the abdominal viscera. Continuing from the stomach, trace the rest of the digestive tract (Figure 2.4).

Small intestine: Connected to the stomach and ending just before the saclike cecum.

Large intestine: A large muscular tube connected to the small intestine and ending at the anus.

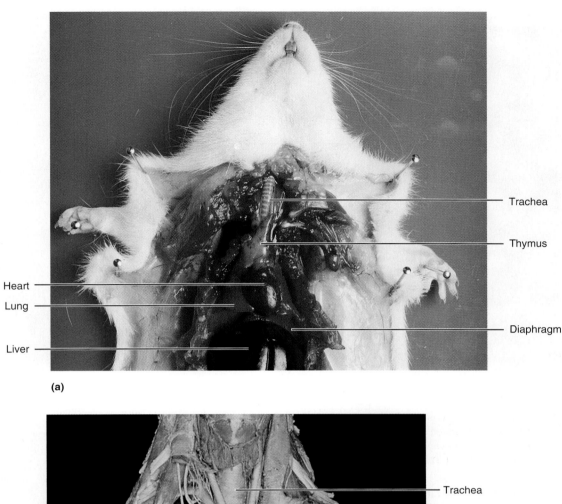

Trachea

Thymus

Heart

Lung

Diaphragm

Liver

(a)

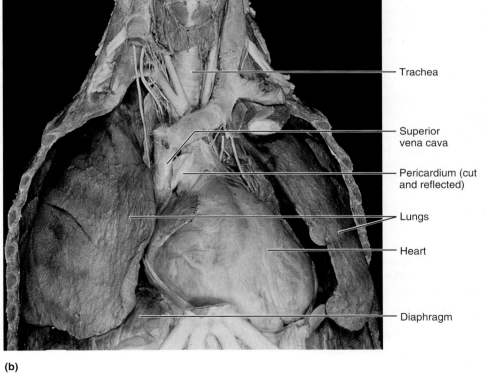

Trachea

Superior
vena cava

Pericardium (cut
and reflected)

Lungs

Heart

Diaphragm

(b)

FIGURE 2.3 Superficial organs of the thoracic cavity. (**a**) Dissected rat. (**b**) Human cadaver.

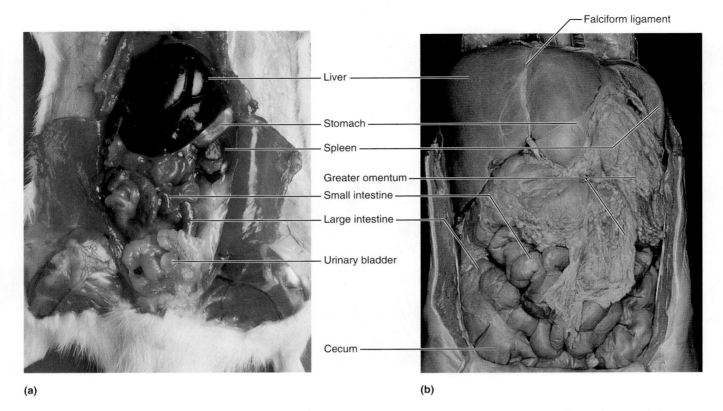

(a)

(b)

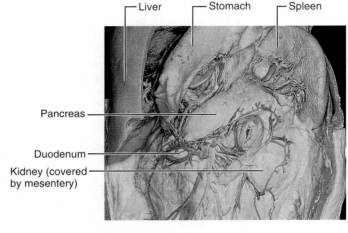

(c)

FIGURE 2.4 Abdominal organs. (a) Dissected rat, superficial view. **(b)** Human cadaver, superficial view. **(c)** Human cadaver, intermediate view. Stomach reflected superiorly to reveal the pancreas, spleen, and duodenum.

Cecum: The initial portion of the large intestine.

Follow the course of the large intestine to the rectum, which is partially covered by the urinary bladder (Figures 2.4 and 2.5).

Rectum: Terminal part of the large intestine; continuous with the anal canal (not visible in this dissection).

Anus: The opening of the digestive tract (through the anal canal) to the exterior.

Now lift the small intestine with the forceps to view the mesentery.

Mesentery: An apronlike serous membrane; suspends many of the digestive organs in the abdominal cavity. Notice that it is heavily invested with blood vessels and, more likely than not, riddled with large fat deposits.

Locate the remaining abdominal structures.

Pancreas: A diffuse gland; rests dorsal to and in the mesentery between the first portion of the small intestine and the stomach. You will need to lift the stomach to view the pancreas.

Spleen: A dark red organ curving around the left lateral side of the stomach; considered part of the lymphatic system and often called the red blood cell graveyard.

Liver: Large and brownish red; the most superior organ in the abdominal cavity, directly beneath the diaphragm.

3.   To locate the deeper structures of the abdominopelvic cavity, move the stomach and the intestines to one side with the probe.

Examine the posterior wall of the abdominal cavity to locate the two kidneys (Figure 2.5).

Kidneys: Bean-shaped organs; retroperitoneal (behind the peritoneum).

Adrenal glands: Large endocrine glands that sit astride the superior margin of each kidney; considered part of the endocrine system.

Carefully strip away part of the peritoneum with forceps and attempt to follow the course of one of the ureters to the bladder.

Ureter: Tube running from the indented region of a kidney to the urinary bladder.

Urinary bladder: The sac that serves as a reservoir for urine.

Right   Left

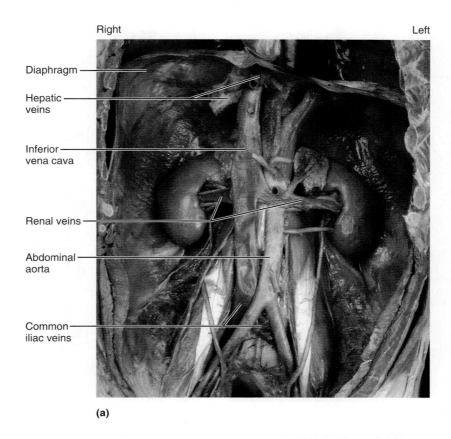

Diaphragm

Hepatic
veins

Inferior
vena cava

Renal veins

Abdominal
aorta

Common
iliac veins

(a)

FIGURE 2.5 Deep structures of the abdominopelvic cavity. (a) Human cadaver.

4.   In the midline of the body cavity lying between the kidneys are the two principal abdominal blood vessels. Identify each.

Inferior vena cava: The large vein that returns blood to the heart from the lower regions of the body.

Descending aorta: Deep to the inferior vena cava; the largest artery of the body; carries blood away from the heart down the midline of the body.

5.   Only a cursory examination of reproductive organs will be done. If you are working with a rat, first determine if the animal is a male or female. Observe the ventral body surface beneath the tail. If a saclike scrotum and an opening for the anus are visible, the animal is a male. If three body openings—urethral, vaginal, and anal—are present, it is a female.

Male Animal

Make a shallow incision into the **scrotum.** Loosen and lift out one oval **testis.** Exert a gentle pull on the testis to identify the slender **ductus deferens,** or **vas deferens,** which carries sperm from the testis superiorly into the abdominal cavity and joins with the urethra. The urethra runs through the penis of the male and carries both urine and sperm out of the body. Identify the **penis,** extending from the bladder to the ventral body wall. Figure 2.5b indicates other glands of the male rat's reproductive system, but they need not be identified at this time.

Female Animal

Inspect the pelvic cavity to identify the Y-shaped **uterus** lying against the dorsal body wall and beneath the bladder (Figure 2.5c). Follow one of the uterine horns superiorly to identify an **ovary,** a small oval structure at the end of the uterine

horn. (The rat uterus is quite different from the uterus of a human female, which is a single-chambered organ about the size and shape of a pear.) The inferior undivided part of the rat uterus is continuous with the **vagina,** which leads to the body exterior. Identify the **vaginal orifice** (external vaginal opening).

If you are working with a human cadaver, proceed as indicated next.

Male Cadaver

Make a shallow incision into the **scrotum** (Figure 2.6a). Loosen and lift out the oval **testis.** Exert a gentle pull on the testis to identify the slender **ductus (vas) deferens,** which carries sperm from the testis superiorly into the abdominal cavity (Figure 2.6b) and joins with the urethra. The urethra runs through the penis of the male and carries both urine and sperm out of the body. Identify the **penis,** extending from the bladder to the ventral body wall.

Female Cadaver

Inspect the pelvic cavity to identify the pear-shaped **uterus** lying against the dorsal body wall and beneath the bladder. Follow one of the **uterine tubes** superiorly to identify an **ovary,** a small oval structure at the end of the uterine tube (Figure 2.6c). The inferior part of the uterus is continuous with the **vagina,** which leads to the body exterior. Identify the **vaginal orifice** (external vaginal opening).

6.   When you have finished your observations, rewrap or store the dissection animal or cadaver according to your instructor's directions. Wash the dissecting tools and equipment with laboratory detergent. Dispose of the gloves. Then wash

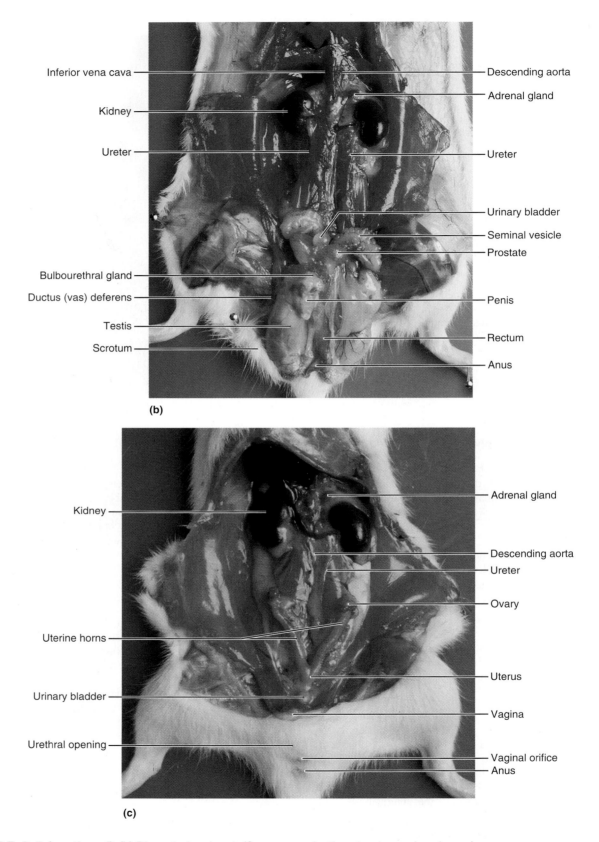

(b)

(c)

FIGURE 2.5 (*continued*) (b) Dissected male rat. (Some reproductive structures also shown.) (c) Dissected female rat. (Some reproductive structures also shown.)

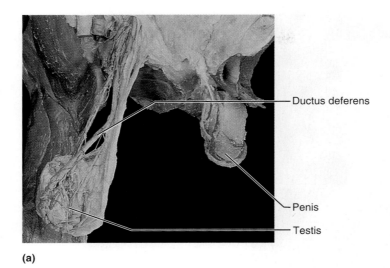

(a)

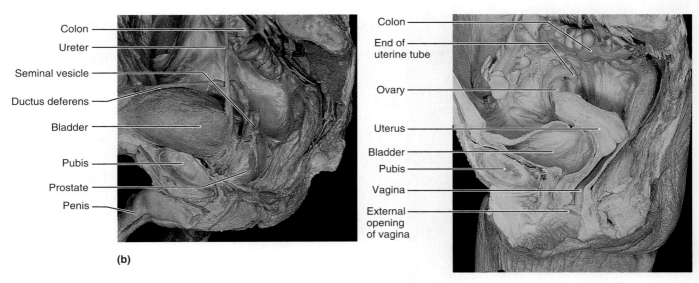

(b)

(c)

FIGURE 2.6 Human reproductive organs. (**a**) Male external genitalia.
(**b**) Sagittal section of the male pelvis. (**c**) Sagittal section of the female pelvis.

and dry your hands before continuing with the examination of the human torso model. ▮▮

ACTIVITY 5

Examining the Human Torso Model

1.   Examine a human torso model to identify the organs listed on p. 24. If a torso model is not available, Figure 2.7 may be used for this part of the exercise. Some model organs will have to be removed to see the deeper organs.

2.   Using the terms to the right of 2.7, label each organ supplied with a leader line in Figure 2.7.

3.   Place each of the organs listed in the correct body cavity or cavities. For organs found in the abdominopelvic cavity, also indicate which quadrant they occupy.

Dorsal body cavity _____

Thoracic cavity _____

_____

Abdominopelvic cavity _____

_____

_____

4.   Determine which organs are found in each abdominopelvic region and record below.

Umbilical region: _____

Epigastric region: _____

Hypogastric region: _____

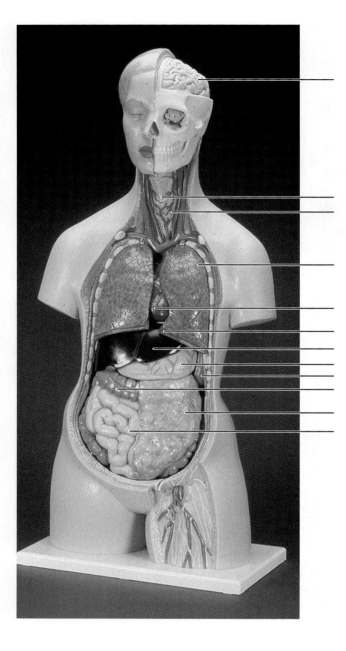

FIGURE 2.7 Human torso model.

Adrenal gland
Aortic arch
Brain
Bronchi
Descending aorta
Diaphragm
Esophagus
Greater omentum
Heart
Inferior vena cava
Kidneys
Large intestine
Liver
Lungs
Pancreas
Rectum
Small intestine
Spinal cord
Spleen
Stomach
Thyroid gland
Trachea
Ureters
Urinary bladder

Urinary: _____

_____

Cardiovascular: _____

_____

Endocrine: _____

_____

Reproductive: _____

_____

Respiratory: _____

_____

Lymphatic/Immunity: _____

_____

Right iliac region: _____

Left iliac region: _____

Right lumbar region: _____

Left lumbar region: _____

Right hypochondriac region: _____

Left hypochondriac region: _____

Now, assign each of the organs just identified to one of the organ system categories listed below.

Digestive: _____

_____

Nervous: _____

_____

Organ Systems Overview

1. Use the key below to indicate the body systems that perform the following functions for the body. Then, circle the organ systems (in the key) that are present in all subdivisions of the ventral body cavity.

Key: a. cardiovascular   d. integumentary   g. nervous   j. skeletal
       b. digestive   e. lymphatic/immunity   h. reproductive   k. urinary
       c. endocrine   f. muscular   i. respiratory

_____ 1. rids the body of nitrogen-containing wastes

_____ 2. is affected by removal of the thyroid gland

_____ 3. provides support and levers on which the muscular system acts

_____ 4. includes the heart

_____ 5. protects underlying organs from drying out and from mechanical damage

_____ 6. protects the body; destroys bacteria and tumor cells

_____ 7. breaks down ingested food into its building blocks

_____ 8. removes carbon dioxide from the blood

_____ 9. delivers oxygen and nutrients to the tissues

_____ 10. moves the limbs; facilitates facial expression

_____ 11. conserves body water or eliminates excesses

_____ and _____ 12. facilitate conception and childbearing

_____ 13. controls the body by means of chemical molecules called hormones

_____ 14. is damaged when you cut your finger or get a severe sunburn

2. Using the above key, choose the *organ system* to which each of the following sets of organs or body structures belongs.

_____ 1. thymus, spleen, lymphatic vessels   _____ 5. epidermis, dermis, and cutaneous glands

_____ 2. bones, cartilages, tendons   _____ 6. testis, ductus deferens, urethra

_____ 3. pancreas, pituitary, adrenals   _____ 7. esophagus, large intestine, rectum

_____ 4. trachea, bronchi, alveoli   _____ 8. arteries, veins, heart

3. Using the key below, place the following organs in their proper body cavity.

Key:

a. abdominopelvic   b. cranial   c. spinal   d. thoracic

_____ 1. stomach   _____ 4. liver   _____ 7. heart

_____ 2. esophagus   _____ 5. spinal cord   _____ 8. trachea

_____ 3. large intestine   _____ 6. urinary bladder   _____ 9. rectum

4. Using the organs listed in question 3 above, record, by number, which would be found in the abdominal regions listed below.

_____ 1. hypogastric region   _____ 4. epigastric region

_____ 2. right lumbar region   _____ 5. left iliac region

_____ 3. umbilical region   _____ 6. left hypochondriac region

5. The levels of organization of a living body are chemicals, _____, _____,

_____, _____, and organism.

6. Define *organ.*_____

_____

7. Using the terms provided, correctly identify all of the body organs provided with leader lines in the drawings below. Then name the organ systems by entering the name of each on the answer blank below each drawing.

Key: blood vessels   heart   nerves   spinal cord   urethra
       brain   kidney   sensory receptor   ureter   urinary bladder

a. _____   b. _____   c. _____

8. Why is it helpful to study the external and internal structures of the rat? _____

_____

The Microscope

MATERIALS

☐ Compound microscope

☐ Millimeter ruler

☐ Prepared slides of the letter *e* or newsprint

☐ Immersion oil

☐ Lens paper

☐ Prepared slide of grid ruled in millimeters (grid slide)

☐ Prepared slide of three crossed colored threads

☐ Clean microscope slide and coverslip

☐ Toothpicks (flat-tipped)

☐ Physiologic saline in a dropper bottle

☐ Iodine or methylene blue stain (dilute) in a dropper bottle

☐ Filter paper or paper towels

☐ Beaker containing fresh 10% household bleach solution for wet mount disposal

☐ Disposable autoclave bag

☐ Prepared slide of cheek epithelial cells

Note to the Instructor: The slides and coverslips used for viewing cheek cells are to be soaked for 2 hours (or longer) in 10% bleach solution and then drained. The slides and disposable autoclave bag (containing coverslips, lens paper, and used toothpicks) are to be autoclaved for 15 min at 121°C and 15 pounds pressure to ensure sterility. After autoclaving, the disposable autoclave bag may be discarded in any disposal facility and the slides and glassware washed with laboratory detergent and reprepared for use. These instructions apply as well to any bloodstained glassware or disposable items used in other experimental procedures.

OBJECTIVES

1. To identify the parts of the microscope and list the function of each.
2. To describe and demonstrate the proper techniques for care of the microscope.
3. To define *total magnification* and *resolution*.
4. To demonstrate proper focusing technique.
5. To define *parfocal*, *field*, and *depth of field*.
6. To estimate the size of objects in a field.

With the invention of the microscope, biologists gained a valuable tool to observe and study structures (like cells) that are too small to be seen by the unaided eye. The information gained helped in establishing many of the theories basic to the understanding of biological sciences. This exercise will familiarize you with the workhorse of microscopes—the compound microscope—and provide you with the necessary instructions for its proper use.

Care and Structure of the Compound Microscope

The **compound microscope** is a precision instrument and should always be handled with care. *At all times you must observe the following rules for its transport, cleaning, use, and storage:*

• When transporting the microscope, hold it in an upright position with one hand on its arm and the other supporting its base. Avoid swinging the instrument during its transport and jarring the instrument when setting it down.

• Use only special grit-free lens paper to clean the lenses. Use a circular motion to wipe the lenses, and clean all lenses before and after use.

• Always begin the focusing process with the lowest-power objective lens in position, changing to the higher-power lenses as necessary.

• Use the coarse adjustment knob only with the lowest-power lens.

• Always use a coverslip with temporary (wet mount) preparations.

• Before putting the microscope in the storage cabinet, remove the slide from the stage, rotate the lowest-power objective lens into position, wrap the cord neatly around the base, and replace the dust cover or return the microscope to the appropriate storage area.

• Never remove any parts from the microscope; inform your instructor of any mechanical problems that arise.

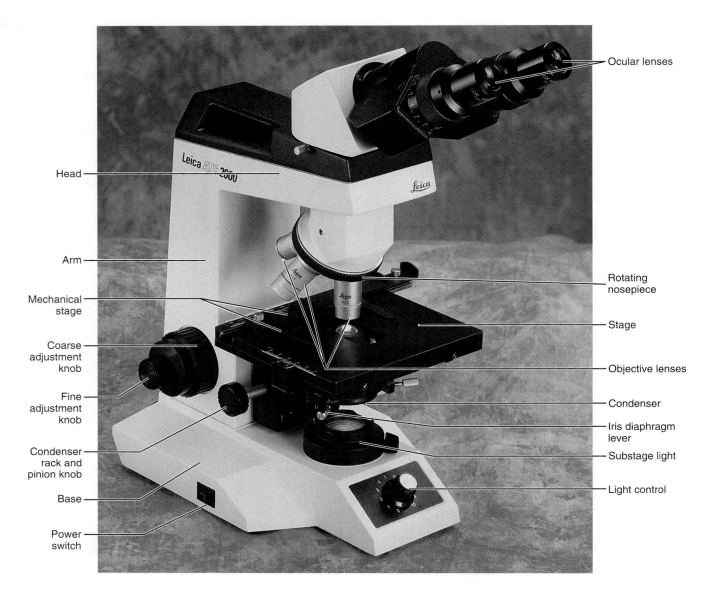

FIGURE 3.1 Compound microscope and its parts.

Identifying the Parts of a Microscope

1.   Obtain a microscope and bring it to the laboratory bench. (Use the proper transport technique!)

•   Record the number of your microscope in the summary chart on p. 30.

Compare your microscope with the illustration in Figure 3.1 and identify the following microscope parts:

Base: Supports the microscope. (**Note:** Some microscopes are provided with an inclination joint, which allows the instrument to be tilted backward for viewing dry preparations.)

Substage light or **mirror:** Located in the base. In microscopes with a substage light source, the light passes directly upward through the microscope: light controls are located on the microscope base. If a mirror is used, light must be reflected from a separate free-standing lamp.

Stage: The platform the slide rests on while being viewed. The stage has a hole in it to permit light to pass through both it and the specimen. Some microscopes have a stage equipped with *spring clips;* others have a clamp-type *mechanical stage* as shown in Figure 3.1. Both hold the slide in position for viewing; in addition, the mechanical stage has two adjustable knobs that control precise movement of the specimen.

Condenser: Small substage lens that concentrates the light on the specimen. The condenser may have a rack and pinion knob that raises and lowers the condenser to vary light delivery. Generally, the best position for the condenser is close to the inferior surface of the stage.

Iris diaphragm lever: Arm attached to the base of the condenser that regulates the amount of light passing through the condenser. The iris diaphragm permits the best possible contrast when viewing the specimen.

Coarse adjustment knob: Used to focus on the specimen.

Fine adjustment knob: Used for precise focusing once coarse focusing has been completed.

Head or **body tube:** Supports the objective lens system (which is mounted on a movable nosepiece) and the ocular lens or lenses.

Arm: Vertical portion of the microscope connecting the base and head.

Ocular (or *eyepiece*): Depending on the microscope, there are one or two lenses at the superior end of the head or body tube. Observations are made through the ocular(s). An ocular lens has a magnification of 10×. (It increases the apparent size of the object by ten times, or ten diameters.) If your microscope has a **pointer** (used to indicate a specific area of the viewed specimen), it is attached to one ocular and can be positioned by rotating the ocular lens.

Nosepiece: Rotating mechanism at the base of the head. Generally carries three or four objective lenses and permits sequential positioning of these lenses over the light beam passing through the hole in the stage. Use the nosepiece to change the objective lenses. Do not directly grab the lenses.

Objective lenses: Adjustable lens system that permits the use of a **scanning lens,** a **low-power lens,** a **high-power lens,** or an **oil immersion lens.** The objective lenses have different magnifying and resolving powers.

2.   Examine the objective lenses carefully; note their relative lengths and the numbers inscribed on their sides. On many microscopes, the scanning lens, with a magnification between 4× and 5×, is the shortest lens. If there is no scanning lens, the low-power objective lens is the shortest and typically has a magnification of 10×. The high-power objective lens is of intermediate length and has a magnification range from 40× to 50×, depending on the microscope. The oil immersion objective lens is usually the longest of the objective lenses and has a magnifying power of 95× to 100×. Some microscopes lack the oil immersion lens.

•   Record the magnification of each objective lens of your microscope in the first row of the chart on p. 30. Also, cross out the column relating to a lens that your microscope does not have. Plan on using the same microscope for all microscopic studies.

3.   Rotate the lowest-power objective lens until it clicks into position, and turn the coarse adjustment knob about 180 degrees. Notice how far the stage (or objective lens) travels during this adjustment. Move the fine adjustment knob 180 degrees, noting again the distance that the stage (or the objective lens) moves. ▬

Magnification and Resolution

The microscope is an instrument of magnification. In the compound microscope, magnification is achieved through the interplay of two lenses—the ocular lens and the objective lens. The objective lens magnifies the specimen to produce a **real image** that is projected to the ocular. This real image is magnified by the ocular lens to produce the **virtual image** seen by your eye (Figure 3.2).

The **total magnification** (TM) of any specimen being viewed is equal to the power of the ocular lens multiplied by the power of the objective lens used. For example, if the ocular lens magnifies 10× and the objective lens being used magnifies 45×, the total magnification is 450× (or 10 × 45).

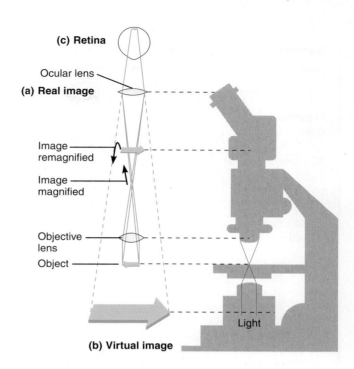

FIGURE 3.2 Image formation in light microscopy. **(a)** Light passing through the objective lens forms a real image. **(b)** The real image serves as the object for the ocular lens, which remagnifies the image and forms the virtual image. **(c)** The virtual image passes through the lens of the eye and is focused on the retina.

•   Determine the total magnification you can achieve with each of the objectives on your microscope, and record the figures on the second row of the chart.

The compound light microscope has certain limitations. Although the level of magnification is almost limitless, the **resolution** (or resolving power), that is, the ability to discriminate two close objects as separate, is not. The human eye can resolve objects about 100 μm apart, but the compound microscope has a resolution of 0.2 μm under ideal conditions. Objects closer than 0.2 μm are seen as a single fused image.

Resolving power is determined by the amount and physical properties of the visible light that enters the microscope. In general, the more light delivered to the objective lens, the greater the resolution. The size of the objective lens aperture (opening) decreases with increasing magnification, allowing less light to enter the objective. Thus, you will probably find it necessary to increase the light intensity at the higher magnifications.

ACTIVITY 2

Viewing Objects Through the Microscope

1.   Obtain a millimeter ruler, a prepared slide of the letter *e* or newsprint, a dropper bottle of immersion oil, and some lens paper. Adjust the condenser to its highest position and switch on the light source of your microscope. (If the light

Summary Chart for Microscope # _____

	Scanning	Low power	High power	Oil immersion
Magnification of objective lens	_____ ×	_____ ×	_____ ×	_____ ×
Total magnification	_____ ×	_____ ×	_____ ×	_____ ×
Working distance	_____ mm	_____ mm	_____ mm	_____ mm
Detail observed Letter *e*				
Field size (diameter)	____mm ____μm	____mm ____μm	____mm ____μm	____mm ____μm

source is not built into the base, use the curved surface of the mirror to reflect the light up into the microscope.)

2.   Secure the slide on the stage so that you can read the slide label and the letter *e* is centered over the light beam passing through the stage. If you are using a microscope with spring clips, make sure the slide is secured at both ends. If your microscope has a mechanical stage, open the jaws of its slide retainer (holder) by using the control lever (typically) located at the rear left corner of the mechanical stage. Insert the slide squarely within the confines of the slide retainer. Check to see that the slide is resting on the stage (and not on the mechanical stage frame) before releasing the control lever.

3.   With your lowest-power (scanning or low-power) objective lens in position over the stage, use the coarse adjustment knob to bring the objective lens and stage as close together as possible.

4.   Look through the ocular lens and adjust the light for comfort using the iris diaphragm. Now use the coarse adjustment knob to focus slowly away from the *e* until it is as clearly focused as possible. Complete the focusing with the fine adjustment knob.

5.   Sketch the letter *e* in the circle on the summary chart just as it appears in the **field** (the area you see through the microscope).

What is the total magnification? _____ ×

How far is the bottom of the objective lens from the specimen? In other words, what is the **working distance**? Use a millimeter ruler to make this measurement. _____ mm

Record the TM detail observed and the working distance in the summary chart.

How has the apparent orientation of the *e* changed top to bottom, right to left, and so on?

_____

_____

6.   Move the slide slowly away from you on the stage as you view it through the ocular lens. In what direction does the image move?

_____

Move the slide to the left. In what direction does the image move?

_____

At first this change in orientation may confuse you, but with practice you will learn to move the slide in the desired direction with no problem.

7.   Today most good laboratory microscopes are **parfocal;** that is, the slide should be in focus (or nearly so) at the higher magnifications once you have properly focused. *Without touching the focusing knobs,* increase the magnification by rotating the next higher magnification lens (low-power or high-power) into position over the stage. Make sure it clicks into position. Using the fine adjustment only, sharpen the focus.* Note the decrease in working distance. As you can see, focusing with the coarse adjustment knob could drive the

*If you are unable to focus with a new lens, your microscope is not parfocal. Do not try to force the lens into position. Consult your instructor.

objective lens through the slide, breaking the slide and possibly damaging the lens. Sketch the letter *e* in the summary chart (p. 30). What new details become clear?

_____

_____

What is the total magnification now? _____ ×

Record the TM, detail observed, and working distance in the summary chart.

As best you can, measure the distance between the objective and the slide (the working distance), and record it on the chart (p. 30).

Is the image larger or smaller? _____

Approximately how much of the letter *e* is visible now?

_____

Is the field larger or smaller? _____

Why is it necessary to center your object (or the portion of the slide you wish to view) before changing to a higher power?

_____

Move the iris diaphragm lever while observing the field. What happens?

_____

Is it more desirable to increase *or* decrease the light when changing to a higher magnification?

_____ Why? _____

_____

8.   If you have just been using the low-power objective, repeat the steps given in direction 7 using the high-power objective lens.

Record the TM, detail observed, and working distance in the summary chart (p. 30).

9.   Without touching the focusing knob, rotate the high-power lens out of position so that the area of the slide over the opening in the stage is unobstructed. Place a drop of immersion oil over the *e* on the slide and rotate the oil immersion lens into position. Set the condenser at its highest point (closest to the stage), and open the diaphragm fully. Adjust the fine focus and fine-tune the light for the best possible resolution.

Note: If for some reason the specimen does not come into view after adjusting the fine focus, do not go back to the 40× lens to recenter. You do not want oil from the oil immersion

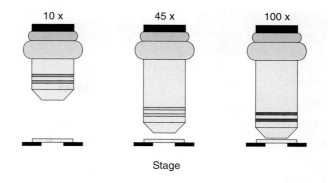

FIGURE 3.3 Relative working distances of the 10×, 45×, and 100× objectives.

lens to cloud the 40× lens. Turn the revolving nosepiece in the other direction to the low-power lens and recenter and refocus the object. Then move the immersion lens back into position, again avoiding the 40× lens.

Is the field again decreased in size? _____

What is the total magnification with the oil immersion lens?

_____ ×

Is the working distance less *or* greater than it was when the high-power lens was focused?

_____

Compare your observations on the relative working distances of the objective lenses with the illustration in Figure 3.3. Explain why it is desirable to begin the focusing process in the lowest power.

_____

_____

_____

10. Rotate the oil immersion lens slightly to the side and remove the slide. Clean the oil immersion lens carefully with lens paper, and then clean the slide in the same manner with a fresh piece of lens paper. ▪

The Microscope Field

By this time you should know that the size of the microscope field decreases with increasing magnification. For future microscope work, it will be useful to determine the diameter of each of the microscope fields. This information will allow you to make a fairly accurate estimate of the size of the objects you view in any field. For example, if you have calculated the field diameter to be 4 mm and the object being observed extends across half this diameter, you can estimate the length of the object to be approximately 2 mm.

TABLE 3.1	Comparison of Metric Units of Length	
Metric unit	**Abbreviation**	**Equivalent**
Meter	m	(about 39.3 in.)
Centimeter	cm	10^{-2} m
Millimeter	mm	10^{-3} m
Micrometer (or micron)	μm (μ)	10^{-6} m
Nanometer (or millimicrometer or millimicron)	nm (mμ)	10^{-9} m
Ångstrom	Å	10^{-10} m

Microscopic specimens are usually measured in micrometers and millimeters, both units of the metric system. You can get an idea of the relationship and meaning of these units from Table 3.1. A more detailed treatment appears in Appendix A.

ACTIVITY 3

Estimating the Diameter of the Microscope Field

1. Obtain a grid slide (a slide prepared with graph paper ruled in millimeters). Each of the squares in the grid is 1 mm on each side. Use your lowest-power objective to bring the grid lines into focus.

2. Move the slide so that one grid line touches the edge of the field on one side, and then count the number of squares you can see across the diameter of the field. If you can see only part of a square, as in the accompanying diagram, estimate the part of a millimeter that the partial square represents.

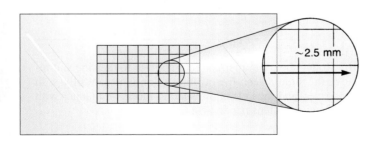

~2.5 mm

Record this figure in the appropriate space marked "field size" on the summary chart (p. 30). (If you have been using the scanning lens, repeat the procedure with the low-power objective lens.)

Complete the chart by computing the approximate diameter of the high-power and oil immersion fields. The general formula for calculating the unknown field diameter is:

$$\text{Diameter of field } A \times \text{total magnification of field } A =$$
$$\text{diameter of field } B \times \text{total magnification of field } B$$

where A represents the known or measured field and B represents the unknown field. This can be simplified to

Diameter of field B =

$$\frac{\text{diameter of field } A \times \text{total magnification of field } A}{\text{total magnification of field } B}$$

For example, if the diameter of the low-power field (field A) is 2 mm and the total magnification is 50×, you would compute the diameter of the high-power field (field B) with a total magnification of 100× as follows:

Field diameter B = (2 mm × 50)/100

Field diameter B = 1 mm

3. Estimate the length (longest dimension) of the following microscopic objects. *Base your calculations on the field sizes you have determined for your microscope.*

a. Object seen in low-power field:

approximate length:

_____ mm

b. Object seen in high-power field:

approximate length:

_____ mm

or _____ μm

c. Object seen in oil immersion field:

approximate length:

_____ μm

4. If an object viewed with the oil immersion lens looked as it does in the field depicted just below, could you determine its approximate size from this view?

If not, then how could you determine it? _____

_____

_____

_____

Perceiving Depth

Any microscopic specimen has depth as well as length and width; it is rare indeed to view a tissue slide with just one layer of cells. Normally you can see two or three cell thicknesses. Therefore, it is important to learn how to determine relative depth with your microscope. In microscope work the **depth of field** (the depth of the specimen clearly in focus) is greater at lower magnifications.

Perceiving Depth

1. Obtain a slide with colored crossed threads. Focusing at low magnification, locate the point where the three threads cross each other.

2. Use the iris diaphragm lever to greatly reduce the light, thus increasing the contrast. Focus down with the coarse adjustment until the threads are out of focus, then slowly focus upward again, noting which thread comes into clear focus first. (You will see two or even all three threads, so you must be very careful in determining which one first comes into clear focus.) Observe: As you rotate the adjustment knob forward (away from you), does the stage rise or fall? If the stage rises, then the first clearly focused thread is the top one; the last clearly focused thread is the bottom one.

If the stage descends, how is the order affected? _____

_____

Record your observations as to which color of thread is uppermost, in the middle, or lowest:

Top thread _____

Middle thread _____

Bottom thread _____ ▮

Viewing Cells Under the Microscope

There are various ways to prepare cells for viewing under a microscope. Cells and tissues can look very different with different stains and preparation techniques. One method of preparation is to mix the cells in physiologic saline (called a wet mount) and stain them with methylene blue stain.

If you are not instructed to prepare your own wet mount, obtain a prepared slide of epithelial cells to make the observations in step 10 of Activity 5.

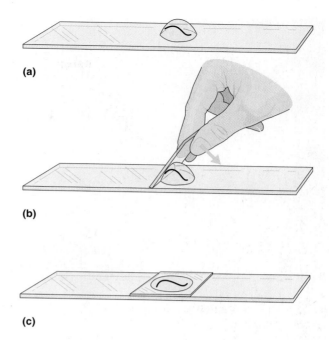

FIGURE 3.4 Procedure for preparation of a wet mount. (a) The object is placed in a drop of water (or saline) on a clean slide, **(b)** a coverslip is held at a 45° angle with the fingertips, and **(c)** it is lowered carefully over the water and the object.

Preparing and Observing a Wet Mount

1. Obtain the following: a clean microscope slide and coverslip, two flat-tipped toothpicks, a dropper bottle of physiologic saline, a dropper bottle of iodine or methylene blue stain, and filter paper (or paper towels). Handle only your own slides throughout the procedure.

2. Place a drop of physiologic saline in the center of the slide. Using the flat end of the toothpick, *gently* scrape the inner lining of your cheek. Transfer your cheek scrapings to the slide by agitating the end of the toothpick in the drop of saline (Figure 3.4a).

⚠ *Immediately* discard the used toothpick in the disposable autoclave bag provided at the supplies area.

3. Add a tiny drop of the iodine or methylene blue stain to the preparation. (These epithelial cells are nearly transparent and thus difficult to see without the stain, which colors the nuclei of the cells and makes them look much darker than the cytoplasm.) Stir again.

⚠ *Immediately* discard the used toothpick in the disposable autoclave bag provided at the supplies area.

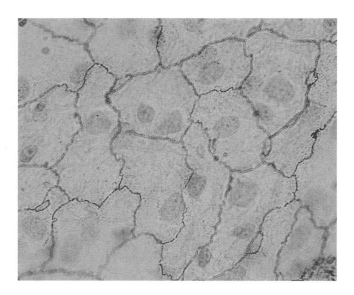

FIGURE 3.5 Epithelial cells of the cheek cavity. (Surface view, 400×.)

4. Hold the coverslip with your fingertips so that its bottom edge touches one side of the fluid drop (Figure 3.4b), then *carefully* lower the coverslip onto the preparation (Figure 3.4c). *Do not just drop the coverslip,* or you will trap large air bubbles under it, which will obscure the cells. *A coverslip should always be used with a wet mount* to prevent soiling the lens if you should misfocus.

5. Examine your preparation carefully. The coverslip should be closely apposed to the slide. If there is excess fluid around its edges, you will need to remove it. Obtain a piece of filter paper, fold it in half, and use the folded edge to absorb the excess fluid. (You may use a twist of paper towel as an alternative.)

! Before continuing, discard the filter paper in the disposable autoclave bag.

6. Place the slide on the stage, and locate the cells in low power. You will probably want to dim the light with the iris diaphragm to provide more contrast for viewing the lightly stained cells. Furthermore, a wet mount will dry out quickly in bright light because a bright light source is hot.

7. Cheek epithelial cells are very thin, six-sided cells. In the cheek, they provide a smooth, tilelike lining, as shown in Figure 3.5. Move to high power to examine the cells more closely.

8. Make a sketch of the epithelial cells that you observe.

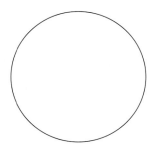

Use information on your summary chart (p. 30) to estimate the diameter of cheek epithelial cells.

_____ mm

Why do *your* cheek cells look different than those illustrated in Figure 3.5? (Hint: What did you have to *do* to your cheek to obtain them?)

_____

_____

! 9. When you complete your observations of the wet mount, dispose of your wet mount preparation in the beaker of bleach solution, and put the coverslips in an autoclave bag.

10. Obtain a prepared slide of cheek epithelial cells, and view them under the microscope.

Estimate the diameter of one of these cheek epithelial cells using information from the summary chart (p. 30).

_____ mm

Why are these cells more similar to those seen in Figure 3.5 and easier to measure than those of the wet mount?

_____

_____

11. Before leaving the laboratory, make sure all other materials are properly discarded or returned to the appropriate laboratory station. Clean the microscope lenses and put the dust cover on the microscope before you return it to the storage cabinet. ▮

NAME _____

LAB TIME/DATE _____

The Microscope

Care and Structure of the Compound Microscope

1. Label all indicated parts of the microscope.

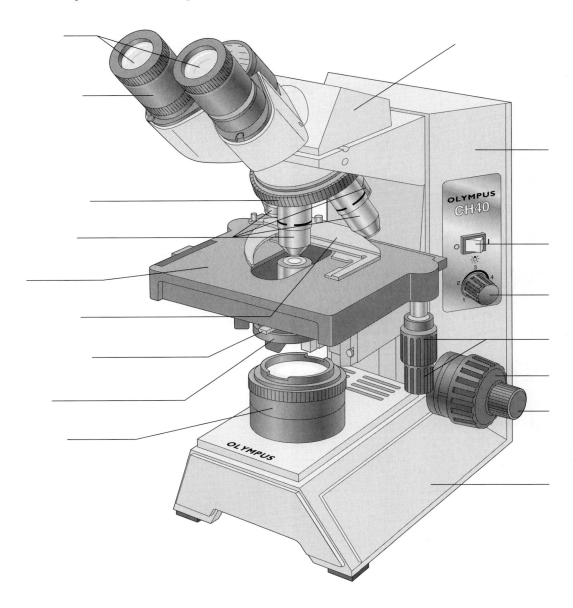

2. Determine whether each of the following statements is true or false. If it is true, write *T* on the answer blank. If it is false, correct the statement by writing on the blank the proper word or phrase to replace the one that is underlined.

_____ 1.   The microscope lens may be cleaned <u>with any soft tissue</u>.

_____ 2.   The microscope should be stored with the <u>oil immersion</u> lens in position over the stage.

_____ 3.   When beginning to focus, the <u>lowest-power</u> lens should be used.

_____ 4.   When focusing, always focus <u>toward</u> the specimen.

_____ 5.   A coverslip should always be used <u>with wet mounts and the high-power and oil lenses</u>.

3. Match the microscope structures given in column B with the statements in column A that identify or describe them.

Column A

_____ 1.   platform on which the slide rests for viewing

_____ 2.   lens located at the superior end of the body tube

_____ 3.   secure(s) the slide to the stage

_____ 4.   delivers a concentrated beam of light to the specimen

_____ 5.   used for precise focusing once initial focusing has been done

_____ 6.   carries the objective lenses; rotates so that the different objective lenses can be brought into position over the specimen

_____ 7.   used to increase the amount of light passing through the specimen

Column B

a.   coarse adjustment knob

b.   condenser

c.   fine adjustment knob

d.   iris diaphragm

e.   mechanical stage or spring clips

f.   movable nosepiece

g.   objective lenses

h.   ocular

i.   stage

4. Explain the proper technique for transporting the microscope.

_____

_____

5. Define the following terms.

real image: _____

_____

resolution: _____

Viewing Objects Through the Microscope

6. Complete, or respond to, the following statements:

_____ 1. The distance from the bottom of the objective lens in use to the specimen is called the _____.

_____ 2. Assume there is an object on the left side of the field that you want to bring to the center (that is, toward the apparent right). In what direction would you move your slide?

_____ 3. The area of the specimen seen when looking through the microscope is the _____.

_____ 4. If a microscope has a 10× ocular and the total magnification at a particular time is 950×, the objective lens in use at that time is _____×.

_____ 5. Why should the light be dimmed when looking at living (nearly transparent) cells?

_____ 6. If, after focusing in low power, only the fine adjustment need be used to focus the specimen at the higher powers, the microscope is said to be _____.

_____ 7. If, when using a 10× ocular and a 15× objective, the field size is 1.5 mm, the approximate field size with a 30× objective is _____ mm.

_____ 8. If the size of the high-power field is 1.2 mm, an object that occupies approximately a third of that field has an estimated diameter of _____ mm.

7. You have been asked to prepare a slide with the letter _k_ on it (as shown below). In the circle below, draw the _k_ as seen in the low-power field.

k

8. The numbers for the filed sizes below are too large to represent the typical compound microscope lens system, but the relationships depicted are accurate. Figure out the magnification of fields 1 and 3, and the field size of 2. (_Hint:_ Use your ruler.)

5 mm   _____ mm   0.5 mm

1. →○←   2. →○←   3. →∘←

_____×   100×   _____×

9. Say you are observing an object in the low-power field. When you switch to high-power, it is no longer in your field of view.

Why might this occur? _____

_____

What should be done initially to prevent this from happening? _____

_____

10. Do the following factors increase or decrease as one moves to higher magnifications with the microscope?

resolution: _____ amount of light needed: _____

working distance: _____ depth of field: _____

11. A student has the high-dry lens in position and appears to be intently observing the specimen. The instructor, noting a working distance of about 1 cm, knows the student isn't actually seeing the specimen.

How so? _____

12. Describe the proper procedure for preparing a wet mount.

_____

_____

_____

13. Give two reasons why the light should be dimmed when viewing living or unstained material.

_____

_____

14. Indicate the probable cause of the following situations arising during use of a microscope.

a. Only half of the field is illuminated: _____

_____

b. Field does not change as mechanical stage is moved: _____

_____

The Cell: Anatomy and Division

O B J E C T I V E S

1. To define *cell, organelle,* and *inclusion.*
2. To identify on a cell model or diagram the following cellular regions and to list the major function of each: nucleus, cytoplasm, and plasma membrane.
3. To identify and list the major functions of the various organelles studied.
4. To compare and contrast specialized cells with the concept of the "generalized cell."
5. To define *interphase, mitosis,* and *cytokinesis.*
6. To list the stages of mitosis and describe the events of each stage.
7. To identify the mitotic phases on slides or appropriate diagrams.
8. To explain the importance of mitotic cell division and its product.

The **cell,** the structural and functional unit of all living things, is a complex entity. The cells of the human body are highly diverse, and their differences in size, shape, and internal composition reflect their specific roles in the body. Nonetheless, cells do have many common anatomical features, and all cells must carry out certain functions to sustain life. For example, all cells can maintain their boundaries, metabolize, digest nutrients and dispose of wastes, grow and reproduce, move, and respond to a stimulus. Most of these functions are considered in detail in later exercises. This exercise focuses on structural similarities that typify the "composite," or "generalized," cell and considers only the function of cell reproduction (cell division).

Anatomy of the Composite Cell

In general, all cells have three major regions, or parts, that can readily be identified with a light microscope: the *nucleus,* the *plasma membrane,* and the *cytoplasm.* The nucleus is typically a round or oval structure near the center of the cell. It is surrounded by cytoplasm, which in turn is enclosed by the plasma membrane. Since the advent of the electron microscope, even smaller cell structures—organelles—have been identified. Figure 4.1a is a diagrammatic representation of the fine structure of the composite cell; Figure 4.1b depicts cellular structure (particularly that of the nucleus) as revealed by the electron microscope.

Nucleus

The **nucleus** contains the genetic material, DNA, sections of which are called "genes." Often described as the control center of the cell, the nucleus is necessary for cell reproduction. A cell that has lost or ejected its nucleus (for whatever reason) is literally programmed to die.

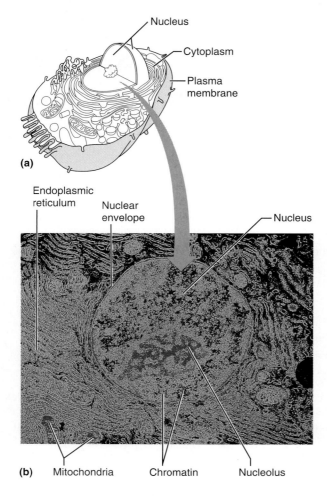

FIGURE 4.1 Anatomy of the composite animal cell.
(**a**) Diagrammatic view. (**b**) Transmission electron micrograph
(6000×).

When the cell is not dividing, the genetic material is loosely dispersed throughout the nucleus in a threadlike form called **chromatin.** When the cell is in the process of dividing to form daughter cells, the chromatin coils and condenses, forming dense, darkly staining rodlike bodies called **chromosomes**—much in the way a stretched spring becomes shorter and thicker when it is released. (Cell division is discussed later in this exercise.) Carefully note the appearance of the nucleus—it is somewhat nondescript when a cell is

healthy. When the nucleus appears dark and the chromatin becomes clumped, this is an indication that the cell is dying and undergoing degeneration.

The nucleus also contains one or more small round bodies, called **nucleoli,** composed primarily of proteins and ribonucleic acid (RNA). The nucleoli are assembly sites for ribosomal particles (particularly abundant in the cytoplasm), which are the actual protein-synthesizing "factories."

The nucleus is bound by a double-layered porous membrane, the **nuclear envelope.** The nuclear envelope is similar in composition to other cellular membranes, but it is distinguished by its large **nuclear pores.** Although they are spanned by diaphragms, these pores permit easy passage of protein and RNA molecules.

ACTIVITY 1

Identifying Parts of a Cell

As able, identify the nuclear envelope, chromatin, nucleolus, and the nuclear pores in Figure 4.1a and b and Figure 4.3 on p. 43. ■

Plasma Membrane

The **plasma membrane** separates cell contents from the surrounding environment. Its main structural building blocks are phospholipids (fats) and globular protein molecules, but some of the externally facing proteins and lipids have sugar (carbohydrate) side chains attached to them that are important in cellular interactions (Figure 4.2). Described by the fluid mosaic model, the membrane is a bilayer of phospholipid molecules in which the protein molecules float. Occasional cholesterol molecules dispersed in the fluid phospholipid bilayer help stabilize it.

Besides providing a protective barrier for the cell, the plasma membrane plays an active role in determining which substances may enter or leave the cell and in what quantity. Because of its molecular composition, the plasma membrane is selective about what passes through it. It allows nutrients to enter the cell but keeps out undesirable substances. By the same token, valuable cell proteins and other substances are kept within the cell, and excreta or wastes pass to the exterior. This property is known as **selective permeability.** Transport through the plasma membrane occurs in two basic ways. In *active transport,* the cell must provide energy (adenosine triphosphate, ATP) to power the transport process. In *passive transport,* the transport process is driven by concentration or pressure differences.

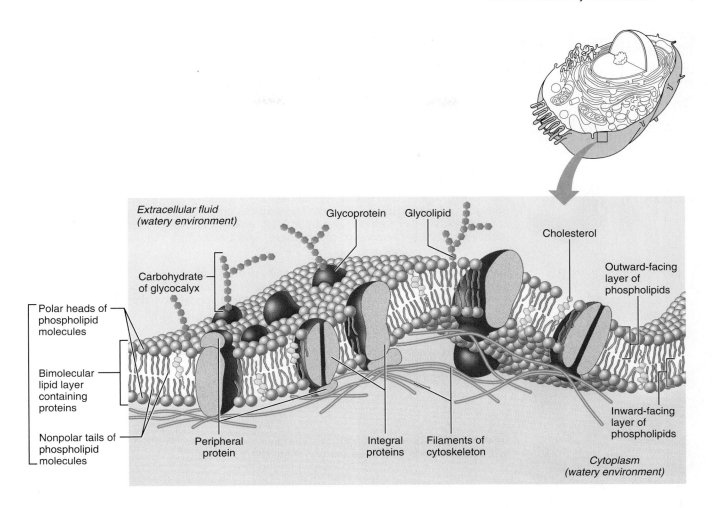

FIGURE 4.2 Structural details of the plasma membrane.

Additionally, the plasma membrane maintains a resting potential that is essential to normal functioning of excitable cells, such as neurons and muscle cells, and plays a vital role in cell signaling and in cell-to-cell interactions. In some cells the membrane is thrown into minute fingerlike projections or folds called **microvilli** (see Figure 4.3). Microvilli greatly increase the surface area of the cell available for absorption or passage of materials and for the binding of signaling molecules.

ACTIVITY 2

Identifying Components of a Plasma Membrane

Identify the phospholipid and protein portions of the plasma membrane in Figure 4.2. Also locate the sugar (*glyco* = carbohydrate) side chains and cholesterol molecules. Identify the microvilli in the diagram at the top of Figure 4.2 and in Figure 4.3.

Cytoplasm and Organelles

The **cytoplasm** consists of the cell contents outside the nucleus. It is the major site of most activities carried out by the cell. Suspended in the **cytosol,** the fluid cytoplasmic material, are many small structures called **organelles** (literally, "small organs"). The organelles are the metabolic machinery of the cell, and they are highly organized to carry out specific functions for the cell as a whole. The organelles include the ribosomes, endoplasmic reticulum, Golgi apparatus, lysosomes, peroxisomes, mitochondria, cytoskeletal elements, and centrioles.

ACTIVITY 3

Locating Organelles

Each organelle type is summarized in Table 4.1 and described briefly below. Read through this material and then, as best you can, locate the organelles in both Figures 4.1b and 4.3.

• **Ribosomes** are densely staining, roughly spherical bodies composed of RNA and protein. They are the actual sites of protein synthesis. They are seen floating free in the cytoplasm or attached to a membranous structure. When they are attached, the whole ribosome-membrane complex is called the *rough endoplasmic reticulum.*

TABLE 4.1	Cytoplasmic Organelles
Organelle	**Location and function**
Ribosomes	Tiny spherical bodies composed of RNA and protein; floating free or attached to a membranous structure (the rough ER) in the cytoplasm. Actual sites of protein synthesis.
Endoplasmic reticulum (ER)	Membranous system of tubules that extends throughout the cytoplasm. Two varieties—rough ER is studded with ribosomes (tubules of the rough ER provide an area for storage and transport of the proteins made on the ribosomes to other cell areas; external face synthesizes phospholipids and cholesterol) and smooth ER, which has no function in protein synthesis (rather it is a site of steroid and lipid synthesis, lipid metabolism, and drug detoxification).
Golgi apparatus	Stack of flattened sacs with bulbous ends and associated small vesicles; found close to the nucleus. Plays a role in packaging proteins or other substances for export from the cell or incorporation into the plasma membrane and in packaging lysosomal enzymes.
Lysosomes	Various-sized membranous sacs containing digestive enzymes (acid hydrolases). Function to digest worn-out cell organelles and foreign substances that enter the cell; have the capacity of total cell destruction if ruptured.
Peroxisomes	Small lysosome-like membranous sacs containing oxidase enzymes that detoxify alcohol, hydrogen peroxide, and other harmful chemicals.
Mitochondria	Generally rod-shaped bodies with a double-membrane wall; inner membrane is thrown into folds, or cristae. Contain enzymes that oxidize foodstuffs to produce cellular energy (ATP); often referred to as "powerhouses of the cell."
Centrioles	Paired, cylindrical bodies lie at right angles to each other, close to the nucleus. Direct the formation of the mitotic spindle during cell division; form the bases of cilia and flagella.
Cytoskeletal elements: microfilaments, intermediate filaments, and microtubules	Provide cellular support; function in intracellular transport. Microfilaments are formed largely of actin, a contractile protein, and thus are important in cell mobility (particularly in muscle cells). Intermediate filaments are stable elements composed of a variety of proteins and resist mechanical forces acting on cells. Microtubules form the internal structure of the centrioles and help determine cell shape.

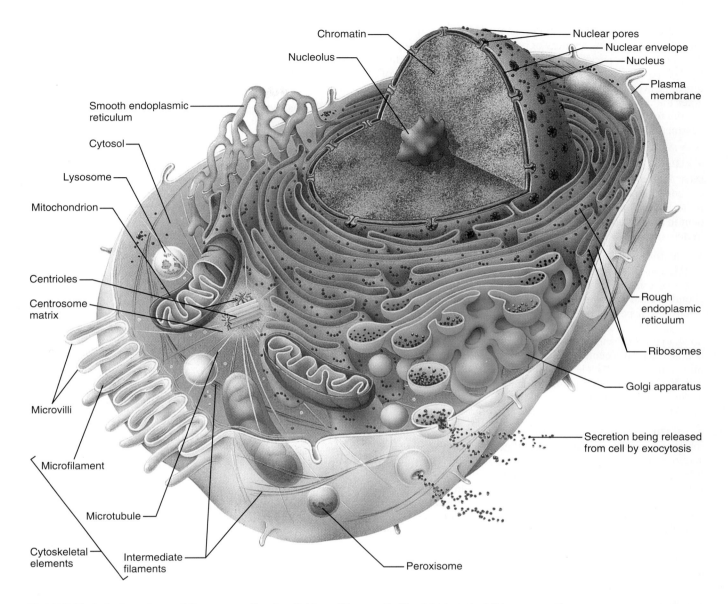

FIGURE 4.3 Structure of the generalized cell. No cell is exactly like this one, but this composite illustrates features common to many human cells. Note that not all organelles are drawn to the same scale in this illustration.

• The **endoplasmic reticulum (ER)** is a highly folded system of membranous tubules and cisternae (sacs) that extends throughout the cytoplasm. The ER is continuous with the nuclear envelope. Thus, it is assumed that the ER provides a system of channels for the transport of cellular substances (primarily proteins) from one part of the cell to another. The ER exists in two forms; a particular cell may have both or only one, depending on its specific functions. The **rough ER,** as noted earlier, is studded with ribosomes. Its cisternae modify and store the newly formed proteins and dispatch them to other areas of the cell. The external face of the rough ER is involved in phospholipid and cholesterol synthesis. The amount of rough ER is closely correlated with the amount of protein a cell manufactures and is especially abundant in cells that make protein products for export—for example, the pancreas cells that produce digestive enzymes destined for the small intestine.

The **smooth ER** does not participate in protein synthesis but is present in conspicuous amounts in cells that produce steroid-based hormones—for example, the interstitial cells of the testes, which produce testosterone. Smooth ER is also abundant in cells that are active in lipid metabolism and drug detoxification activities—liver cells, for instance.

• The **Golgi apparatus** is a stack of flattened sacs with bulbous ends that is generally found close to the nucleus. Within its cisternae, the proteins delivered to it by transport vesicles from the rough ER are modified (by attachment of sugar groups), segregated, and packaged into membranous vesicles that ultimately (1) are incorporated into the plasma membrane, (2) become secretory vesicles that release their contents from the cell, or (3) become lysosomes.

• **Lysosomes,** which appear in various sizes, are membrane-bound sacs containing an array of powerful digestive enzymes. A product of the packaging activities of the Golgi apparatus, the lysosomes contain *acid hydrolases,* enzymes capable of digesting worn-out cell structures and foreign substances that enter the cell via vesicle formation through phagocytosis or endocytosis. Because they have the capacity of total cell destruction, the lysosomes are often referred to as the "suicide sacs" of the cell.

• **Peroxisomes,** like lysosomes, are enzyme-containing sacs. However, their *oxidases* have a different task. Using oxygen, they detoxify a number of harmful substances, most importantly free radicals. Peroxisomes are particularly abundant in kidney and liver cells, cells that are actively involved in detoxification.

• **Mitochondria** are generally rod-shaped bodies with a double-membrane wall; the inner membrane is thrown into folds, or *cristae.* Oxidative enzymes on or within the mitochondria catalyze the reactions of the citric acid cycle and the electron transport chain (collectively called oxidative respiration), in which the end products of food digestion are broken down to produce energy. The released energy is captured in the bonds of ATP molecules, which are then transported out of the mitochondria to provide a ready energy supply to power the cell. Every living cell requires a constant supply of ATP for its many activities. Because the mitochondria provide the bulk of this ATP, they are referred to as the "powerhouses" of the cell.

• **Cytoskeletal elements** ramify throughout the cytoplasm, forming an internal scaffolding called the *cytoskeleton* that supports and moves substances within the cell. The **microtubules** are slender tubules formed of proteins called *tubulins,* which have the ability to aggregate and then disaggregate spontaneously. Microtubules organize the cytoskeleton and direct formation of the spindle formed by the centrioles during cell division. They also act in the transport of substances down the length of elongated cells (such as neurons), suspend organelles, and help maintain cell shape by providing rigidity to the soft cellular substance. **Intermediate filaments** are *stable* proteinaceous cytoskeletal elements that act as internal guy-wires to resist mechanical (pulling) forces acting on cells. **Microfilaments,** ribbon or cordlike elements, are formed of contractile proteins, primarily *actin.* Because of their ability to shorten and then relax to assume a more elongated form, these are important in cell mobility and are conspicuous in cells that are specialized to contract (such as muscle cells). A cross-linked network of *lamin* microfilaments braces and strengthens the internal face of the plasma membrane.

The cytoskeletal structures are changeable and minute. With the exception of the microtubules of the spindle, which are obvious during cell division (see pp. 46–47), and the microfilaments of skeletal muscle cells (see Figure 13.1 on p. 176), they are rarely seen, even in electron micrographs, and are not visible in Figure 4.1b. However, special stains can reveal the plentiful supply of these important organelles.

• The paired **centrioles** lie close to the nucleus in all animal cells capable of reproducing themselves. They are rod-shaped bodies that lie at right angles to each other. Internally each centriole is composed of nine triplets of microtubules. During cell division, the centrioles direct the formation of the mitotic spindle. Centrioles also form the basis for cell projections called cilia and flagella.

The cell cytoplasm contains various other substances and structures, including stored foods (glycogen granules and lipid droplets), pigment granules, crystals of various types, water vacuoles, and ingested foreign materials. However, these are not part of the active metabolic machinery of the cell and are therefore called **inclusions.**

ACTIVITY 4

Examining the Cell Model

Once you have located all of these structures in Figure 4.3, examine the cell model (or cell chart) to repeat and reinforce your identifications. ■

Differences and Similarities in Cell Structure

ACTIVITY 5

Observing Various Cell Structures

1.   Obtain a compound microscope and prepared slides of simple squamous epithelium, smooth muscle cells (teased), human blood, and sperm.

2.   Observe each slide under the microscope, carefully noting similarities and differences in the cells. (The oil immersion lens will be needed to observe blood and sperm.) Distinguish the limits of the individual cells, and notice the shape and position of the nucleus in each case. When you look at the human blood smear, direct your attention to the red blood cells, the pink-stained cells that are most numerous. The color photomicrographs illustrating a blood smear (Plate 50) and sperm (Plate 47) that appear in the Histology Atlas may be helpful in this cell structure study. Sketch your observations in the circles provided on p. 45.

**Simple squamous
epithelium**

Diameter _____

Sperm cells

Length _____

Diameter _____

**Human red
blood cells**

Diameter _____

**Teased smooth
muscle cells**

Length _____

Diameter _____

3. Measure the length and/or diameter of each cell, and record below the appropriate sketch.

4. How do these four cell types differ in shape and size?

_____

_____

_____

_____

How might cell shape affect cell function?

_____

_____

_____

_____

Which cells have visible projections?

_____

How do these projections relate to the function of these cells?

_____

_____

_____

Do any of these cells lack a plasma membrane? _____

A nucleus? _____

In the cells with a nucleus, can you discern nucleoli?

_____

Were you able to observe any of the organelles in these cells?

_____ Why or why not? _____

_____

_____

_____

Cell Division: Mitosis and Cytokinesis

A cell's *life cycle* is the series of changes it goes through from the time it is formed until it reproduces itself. It encompasses two stages—**interphase,** the longer period during which the cell grows and carries out its usual activities (Figure 4.4a), and **cell division,** when the cell reproduces itself by dividing. In an interphase cell about to divide, the genetic material (DNA) is replicated (duplicated exactly). Once this important event has occurred, cell division ensues.

Cell division in all cells other than bacteria consists of a series of events collectively called mitosis and cytokinesis. **Mitosis** is nuclear division; **cytokinesis** is the division of the cytoplasm, which begins after mitosis is nearly complete. Although mitosis is usually accompanied by cytokinesis, in some instances cytoplasmic division does not occur, leading to the formation of binucleate (or multinucleate) cells. This is relatively common in the human liver.

The product of **mitosis** is two daughter nuclei that are genetically identical to the mother nucleus. This distinguishes mitosis from **meiosis,** a specialized type of nuclear division that occurs only in the reproductive organs (testes or ovaries). Meiosis, which yields four daughter nuclei that differ genetically in composition from the mother nucleus, is used only for the production of gametes (eggs and sperm) for sexual reproduction. The function of cell division, including mitosis and cytokinesis in the body, is to increase the number of cells for growth and repair while maintaining their genetic heritage.

The stages of mitosis illustrated in Figure 4.4 include the following events:

Prophase (Figure 4.4b and c): At the onset of cell division, the chromatin threads coil and shorten to form densely staining, short, barlike **chromosomes.** By the middle of prophase the chromosomes appear as double-stranded structures (each strand is a **chromatid**) connected by a small median body called a **centromere** and an adhesive protein called *cohesin.* The centrioles separate from one another and act as focal points for the assembly of two systems of microtubules: the **mitotic spindle,** which forms between the centrioles, and the **asters** ("stars"), which radiate outward from the ends of the spindle and anchor it to the plasma membrane. The spindle acts as a scaffolding for the attachment and movement of the chromosomes during later mitotic stages. Meanwhile, the nuclear envelope and the nucleolus break down and disappear.

Metaphase (Figure 4.4d): A brief stage, during which the chromosomes migrate to the central plane or equator of the spindle and align along that plane in a straight line (the so-called *metaphase plate*) from the superior to the inferior region of the spindle (lateral view). Viewed from the poles of the cell (end view), the chromosomes appear to be arranged in a "rosette," or circle, around the widest dimension of the spindle.

Anaphase (Figure 4.4e): At the beginning of anaphase, the enzyme *separase* cleaves cohesin and the centromeres split. The chromatids (now called chromosomes again) separate from one another and then progress slowly toward opposite ends of the cell. The chromosomes are pulled by the kinetochore

microtubules attached to their centromeres, their "arms" dangling behind them. Anaphase is complete when poleward movement ceases.

Telophase (Figure 4.4f): During telophase, the events of prophase are essentially reversed. The chromosomes clustered at the poles begin to uncoil and resume the chromatin form, the spindle breaks down and disappears, a nuclear envelope forms around each chromatin mass, and nucleoli appear in each of the daughter nuclei.

Mitosis is essentially the same in all animal cells, but depending on the tissue, it takes from 5 minutes to several hours to complete. In most cells, centriole replication occurs during interphase of the next cell cycle.

Cytokinesis, or the division of the cytoplasmic mass, begins during telophase (Figure 4.4f) and provides a good guide for where to look for the mitotic figures of telophase. In animal cells, a *cleavage furrow* begins to form approximately over the spindle equator and eventually splits or pinches the original cytoplasmic mass into two portions. Thus at the end of cell division, two daughter cells exist—each with a smaller cytoplasmic mass than the mother cell but genetically identical to it. The daughter cells grow and carry out the normal spectrum of metabolic processes until it is their turn to divide.

Cell division is extremely important during the body's growth period. Most cells divide until puberty, when normal body size is achieved and overall body growth ceases. After this time in life, only certain cells carry out cell division routinely—for example, cells subjected to abrasion (epithelium of the skin and lining of the gut). Other cell populations—such as liver cells—stop dividing but retain this ability should some of them be removed or damaged. Skeletal muscle, cardiac muscle, and mature neurons almost completely lose this ability to divide and thus are severely handicapped by injury. Throughout life, the body retains its ability to repair cuts and wounds and to replace some of its aged cells.

ACTIVITY 6

Identifying the Mitotic Stages

1. Watch a video presentation of mitosis (if available).

2. Using the three-dimensional models of dividing cells provided, identify each of the mitotic states described above.

3. Obtain a prepared slide of whitefish blastulae to study the stages of mitosis. The cells of each *blastula* (a stage of embryonic development consisting of a hollow ball of cells) are at approximately the same mitotic stage, so it may be necessary to observe more than one blastula to view all the mitotic stages. A good analogy for a blastula is a soccer ball in which each leather piece making up the ball's surface represents an embryonic cell. The exceptionally high rate of mitosis observed in this tissue is typical of embryos, but if it occurs in specialized tissues it can indicate cancerous cells, which also have an extraordinarily high mitotic rate. Examine the slide carefully, identifying the four mitotic stages and the process of cytokinesis. Compare your observations with Figure 4.4, and verify your identifications with your instructor. ▪

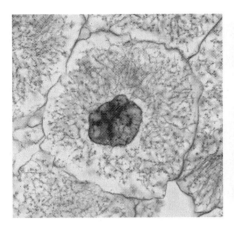
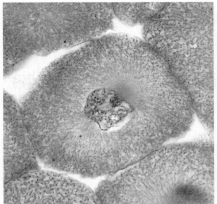
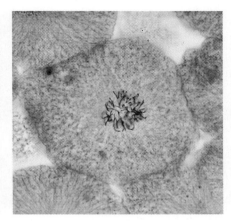

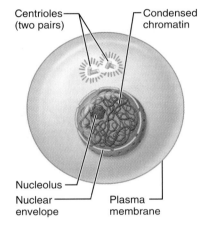
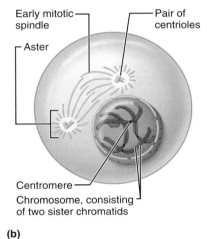
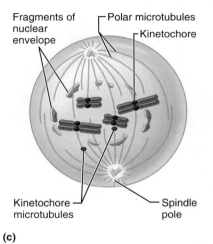

(a)

Centrioles (two pairs) — Condensed chromatin

Nucleolus

Nuclear envelope — Plasma membrane

(b)

Early mitotic spindle — Pair of centrioles

Aster

Centromere

Chromosome, consisting of two sister chromatids

(c)

Fragments of nuclear envelope — Polar microtubules

Kinetochore

Kinetochore microtubules — Spindle pole

Interphase

Interphase is the period of a cell's life when it is carrying out its normal metabolic activities and growing. During interphase, the chromosomal material is seen in the form of extended and condensed chromatin, and the nuclear membrane and nucleolus are intact and visible. Microtubule arrays (asters) are seen extending from the centrosomes. During various periods of this phase, the centrioles begin replicating (G_1 through G_2), DNA is replicated (S), and the final preparations for mitosis are completed (G_2). The centriole pair finishes replicating into two pairs during G_2.

Early prophase

As mitosis begins, microtubule arrays called *asters* ("stars") are seen extending from the centrosome matrix around the centrioles. Early in *prophase,* the first and longest phase of mitosis, the chromatin threads coil and condense, forming barlike *chromosomes* that are visible with a light microscope. Since DNA replication has occurred during interphase, each chromosome is actually made up of two identical chromatin threads, now called *chromatids*. The chromatids of each chromosome are held together by a small, buttonlike body called a *centromere* and a protein complex called cohesin. After the chromatids separate, each is considered a new chromosome.

As the chromosomes appear, the nucleoli disappear, and the cytoskeletal microtubules disassemble. The centriole pairs separate from one another. The centrioles act as focal points for growth of a new assembly of microtubules called the *mitotic spindle.* As these microtubules lengthen, they push the centrioles farther and farther apart, propelling them toward opposite ends (poles) of the cell.

Late prophase

While the centrioles are still moving away from each other, the nuclear envelope fragments, allowing the spindle to occupy the center of the cell and to interact with the chromosomes. Meanwhile, some of the growing spindle microtubules attach to special protein–DNA complexes, called *kinetochores* (ki-ne′to-korz), on each chromosome's centromere. Such microtubules are called *kinetochore microtubules.* The remaining spindle microtubules, which do not attach to any chromosomes, are called *polar microtubules.* The tips of the polar microtubules are linked near the center; these push against each other forcing the poles apart. The kinetochore microtubules, on the other hand, pull on each chromosome from both poles, resulting in a tug-of-war that ultimately draws the chromosomes in a jerky march to the middle of the cell.

FIGURE 4.4 The interphase cell and the stages of mitosis. The cells shown are from an early embryo of a whitefish. Photomicrographs are above; corresponding diagrams are below. (Micrographs approximately 600×.)

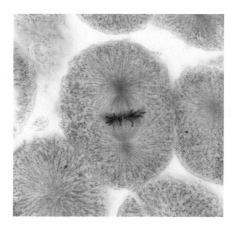
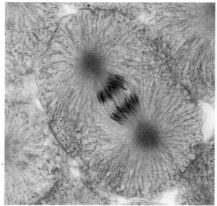
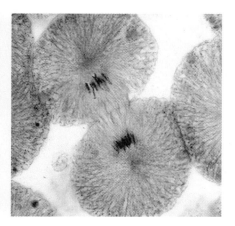

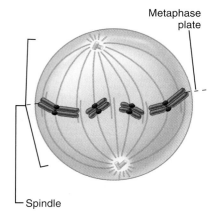
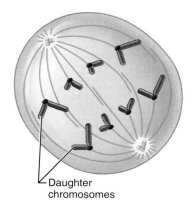
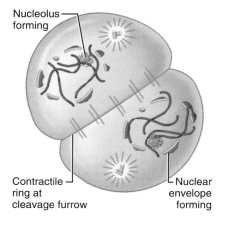

Metaphase plate

Spindle

Daughter chromosomes

Nucleolus forming

Contractile ring at cleavage furrow

Nuclear envelope forming

(d)

Metaphase

Metaphase is the second phase of mitosis. The chromosomes cluster at the middle of the cell, with their centromeres precisely aligned at the exact center, or *equator,* of the spindle. This arrangement of the chromosomes along a plane midway between the poles is called the *metaphase plate.*

An enzyme called *separase* cleaves cohesin, triggering separation of the chromatids at the metaphase–anaphase transition.

(e)

Anaphase

Anaphase, the third phase of mitosis, begins abruptly as the centromeres of the chromosomes split, and each chromatid now becomes a chromosome in its own right. The kinetochore fibers, moved along by motor proteins in the kinetochores, rapidly disassemble at their kinetochore ends by removing tubulin subunits and gradually pull each chromosome toward the pole it faces. By contrast the polar microtubules slide past each other and lengthen (a process presumed to be driven by kinesin motor molecules) and push the two poles of the cell apart, causing the cell to elongate. Anaphase is easy to recognize because the moving chromosomes look V-shaped. The centromeres, which are attached to the kinetochore microtubules, lead the way, and the chromosomal "arms" dangle behind them. Anaphase is the shortest stage of mitosis; it typically lasts only a few minutes.

This process of moving and separating the chromosomes is helped by the fact that the chromosomes are short, compact bodies. Diffuse threads of extended chromatin would tangle, trail, and break, which would damage the genetic material and result in its imprecise "parceling out" to the daughter cells.

(f)

Telophase and cytokinesis

Telophase begins as soon as chromosomal movement stops. This final phase is like prophase in reverse. The identical sets of chromosomes at the opposite poles of the cell uncoil and resume their threadlike extended-chromatin form. A new nuclear envelope, derived from components of the original nuclear envelope stored in the rough ER, reforms around each chromatin mass. Nucleoli reappear within the nuclei, and the spindle breaks down and disappears. Mitosis is now ended. The cell, for just a brief period, is binucleate (has two nuclei), and each new nucleus is identical to the original mother nucleus.

As a rule, as mitosis draws to a close, *cytokinesis* completes the division of the cell into two daughter cells. Cytokinesis occurs as a contractile ring of peripheral microfilaments forms at the *cleavage furrow* and squeezes the cells apart. Cytokinesis actually begins during late anaphase and continues through and beyond telophase.

FIGURE 4.4 *(continued)* **The stages of mitosis.**

NAME_____

LAB TIME/DATE_____

The Cell: Anatomy and Division

Anatomy of the Composite Cell

1. Define the following terms:

organelle: _____

_____

cell: _____

2. Although cells have differences that reflect their specific functions in the body, what functions do they have in common?

_____

3. Identify the following cell parts:

_____ 1. external boundary of cell; regulates flow of materials into and out of the cell; site of cell signaling

_____ 2. contains digestive enzymes of many varieties; "suicide sac" of the cell

_____ 3. scattered throughout the cell; major site of ATP synthesis

_____ 4. slender extensions of the plasma membrane that increase its surface area

_____ 5. stored glycogen granules, crystals, pigments, and so on

_____ 6. membranous system consisting of flattened sacs and vesicles; packages proteins for export

_____ 7. control center of the cell; necessary for cell division and cell life

_____ 8. two rod-shaped bodies near the nucleus; direct formation of the mitotic spindle

_____ 9. dense, darkly staining nuclear body; packaging site for ribosomes

_____ 10. contractile elements of the cytoskeleton

_____ 11. membranous system; involved in intracellular transport of proteins and synthesis of membrane lipids

_____ 12. attached to membrane systems or scattered in the cytoplasm; synthesize proteins

_____ 13. threadlike structures in the nucleus; contain genetic material (DNA)

_____ 14. site of free-radical detoxification

4. In the following diagram, label all parts provided with a leader line.

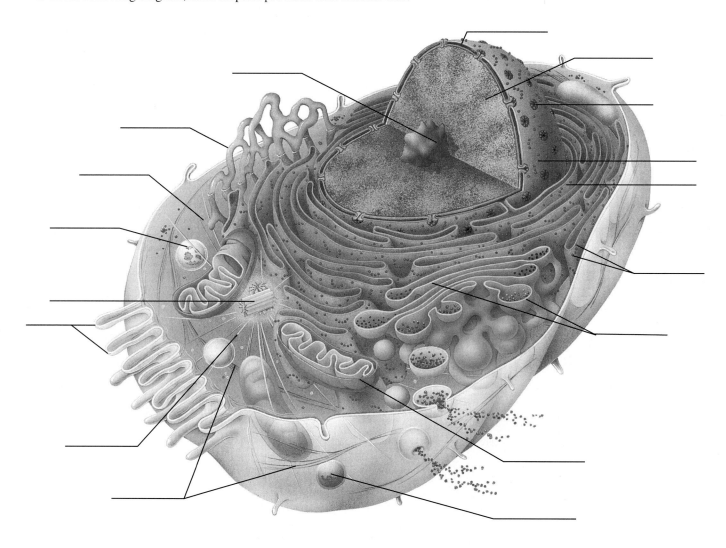

Differences and Similarities in Cell Structure

5. For each of the following cell types, list (a) *one* important structural characteristic observed in the laboratory, and (b) the function that the structure complements or ensures.

squamous epithelium   a. _____

                       b. _____

sperm   a. _____

                       b. _____

smooth muscle   a. _____

                       b. _____

red blood cells a. _____

b. _____

6. What is the significance of the red blood cell being anucleate (without a nucleus)? _____

_____

Did it ever have a nucleus? _____ If so, when? _____

7. Of the four cells observed microscopically (squamous epithelial cells, red blood cells, smooth muscle cells, and sperm) which has the smallest diameter? _____ Which is the longest? _____

Cell Division: Mitosis and Cytokinesis

8. Identify the three phases of mitosis in the following photomicrographs.

a. _____   b. _____   c. _____

9. What is the importance of mitotic cell division? _____

_____

10. Complete or respond to the following statements:

Division of the __1__ is referred to as mitosis. Cytokinesis is division of the __2__. The major structural difference between chromatin and chromosomes is that the latter is __3__. Chromosomes attach to the spindle fibers by undivided structures called __4__. If a cell undergoes mitosis but not cytokinesis, the product is __5__. The structure that acts as a scaffolding for chromosomal attachment and movement is called the __6__. __7__ is the period of cell life when the cell is not involved in division. Two cell populations in the body that do not undergo cell division are __8__ and __9__. The implication of an inability of a cell population to divide is that when some of its members die, they are replaced by __10__.

1. _____
2. _____
3. _____
4. _____
5. _____
6. _____
7. _____
8. _____
9. _____
10. _____

11. Draw the phases of mitosis for a cell with a chromosome number of 4.

12. Using the key, categorize each of the events described below according to the phase in which it occurs.

   Key: a.   anaphase   b.   interphase   c.   metaphase   d.   prophase   e.   telophase

   _____   1. Chromatin coils and condenses, forming chromosomes.

   _____   2. The chromosomes are V-shaped.

   _____   3. The nuclear membrane re-forms.

   _____   4. Chromosomes stop moving toward the poles.

   _____   5. Chromosomes line up in the center of the cell.

   _____   6. The nuclear membrane fragments.

   _____   7. The mitotic spindle forms.

   _____   8. DNA synthesis occurs.

   _____   9. Centrioles replicate.

   _____   10. Chromosomes first appear to be duplex structures.

   _____   11. Chromosomal centromeres are attached to the kinetochore fibers.

   _____   12. Cleavage furrow forms.

   _____ and _____   13. The nuclear membrane(s) is absent.

13. What is the physical advantage of the chromatin coiling and condensing to form short chromosomes at the onset of mitosis?

   _____

   _____

Classification of Tissues

O B J E C T I V E S

1. To name the four major types of tissues in the human body and the major subcategories of each.
2. To identify the tissue subcategories through microscopic inspection or inspection of an appropriate diagram or projected slide.
3. To state the location of the various tissue types in the body.
4. To list the general functions and structural characteristics of each of the four major tissue types.

Exercise 4 describes cells as the building blocks of life and the all-inclusive functional units of unicellular organisms. However, in higher organisms, cells do not usually operate as isolated, independent entities. In humans and other multicellular organisms, cells depend on one another and cooperate to maintain homeostasis in the body.

With a few exceptions, even the most complex animal starts out as a single cell, the fertilized egg, which divides almost endlessly. The trillions of cells that result become specialized for a particular function; some become supportive bone, others the transparent lens of the eye, still others skin cells, and so on. Thus a division of labor exists, with certain groups of cells highly specialized to perform functions that benefit the organism as a whole. Cell specialization carries with it certain hazards, because when a small specific group of cells is indispensable, any inability to function on its part can paralyze or destroy the entire body.

Groups of cells that are similar in structure and function are called **tissues.** The four primary tissue types—epithelium, connective tissue, nervous tissue, and muscle—have distinctive structures, patterns, and functions. The four primary tissues are further divided into subcategories, as described shortly.

To perform specific body functions, the tissues are organized into **organs** such as the heart, kidneys, and lungs. Most organs contain several representatives of the primary tissues, and the arrangement of these tissues determines the organ's structure and function. Thus **histology,** the study of tissues, complements a study of gross anatomy and provides the structural basis for a study of organ physiology.

The main objective of this exercise is to familiarize you with the major similarities and dissimilarities of the primary tissues, so that when the tissue composition of an organ is described, you will be able to more easily understand (and perhaps even predict) the organ's major function. Because epithelium and some types of connective tissue will not be considered again, they are emphasized more than muscle, nervous tissue, and bone (a connective tissue), which are covered in more depth in later exercises.

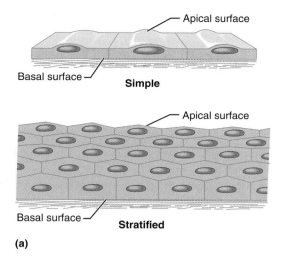

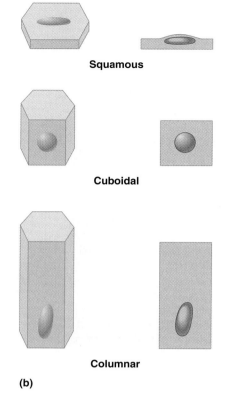

FIGURE 5.1 Classification of epithelia. (a) Classification on the basis of arrangement (relative number of layers). **(b)** Classification on the basis of cell shape. For each category, a whole cell is shown on the left and a longitudinal section is shown on the right.

Epithelial Tissue

Epithelial tissue, or **epithelium,** covers surfaces. For example, epithelium covers the external body surface (as the epidermis), lines its cavities and tubules, and generally marks off our "insides" from our outsides. Since the various endocrine (hormone-producing) and exocrine glands of the body almost invariably develop from epithelial membranes, glands, too, are logically classed as epithelium.

Epithelial functions include protection, absorption, filtration, excretion, secretion, and sensory reception. For example, the epithelium covering the body surface protects against bacterial invasion and chemical damage; that lining the respiratory tract is ciliated to sweep dust and other foreign particles away from the lungs. Epithelium specialized to absorb substances lines the stomach and small intestine. In the kidney tubules, the epithelium absorbs, secretes, and filters. Secretion is a specialty of the glands.

The following characteristics distinguish epithelial tissues from other types:

- Polarity. The membranes always have one free surface, called the *apical surface,* and typically that surface is significantly different from the *basal surface.*

- Cellularity and specialized contacts. Cells fit closely together to form membranes, or sheets of cells, and are bound together by specialized junctions.

- Supported by connective tissue. The cells are attached to and supported by an adhesive **basement membrane,** which is an amorphous material secreted partly by the epithelial cells (*basal lamina*) and connective tissue cells (*reticular lamina*) that lie adjacent to each other.

- Avascularity. Epithelial tissues have no blood supply of their own (are avascular), but instead depend on diffusion of nutrients from the underlying connective tissue. (Glandular epithelia, however, are very vascular.)

- Regeneration. If well nourished, epithelial cells can easily regenerate themselves. This is an important characteristic because many epithelia are subjected to a good deal of friction.

The covering and lining epithelia are classified according to two criteria—arrangement or relative number of layers and cell shape (Figure 5.1). On the basis of arrangement, there are **simple** epithelia, consisting of one layer of cells attached to the basement membrane, and **stratified** epithelia, consisting of two or more layers of cells. The general types based on shape are **squamous** (scalelike), **cuboidal** (cubelike), and **columnar** (column-shaped) epithelial cells. The terms denoting shape and arrangement of the epithelial cells are combined to describe the epithelium fully. *Stratified epithelia are named according to the cells at the apical surface of the epithelial membrane,* not those resting on the basement membrane.

There are, in addition, two less easily categorized types of epithelia. **Pseudostratified epithelium** is actually a simple columnar epithelium (one layer of cells), but because its cells vary in height and their nuclei lie at different levels above the basement membrane, it gives the false appearance of being stratified. This epithelium is often ciliated.

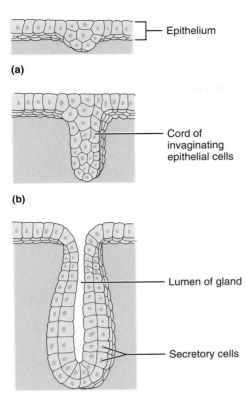

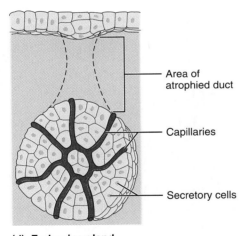

(a)

— Epithelium

(b)

— Cord of
invaginating
epithelial cells

(c) Exocrine gland

— Lumen of gland

— Secretory cells

(d) Endocrine gland

— Area of
atrophied duct

— Capillaries

— Secretory cells

FIGURE 5.2 Formation of endocrine and exocrine glands from epithelial sheets. (a) Epithelial cells grow and push into the underlying tissue. (b) A cord of epithelial cells forms. (c) In an exocrine gland, a lumen (cavity) forms. The inner cells form the duct, the outer cells produce the secretion. (d) In a forming endocrine gland, the connecting duct cells atrophy, leaving the secretory cells with no connection to the epithelial surface. However, they do become heavily invested with blood and lymphatic vessels that receive the secretions.

Transitional epithelium is a rather peculiar stratified squamous epithelium formed of rounded, or "plump," cells with the ability to slide over one another to allow the organ to be stretched. Transitional epithelium is found only in urinary system organs subjected to periodic distension, such as the bladder. The superficial cells are flattened (like true squamous cells) when the organ is distended and rounded when the organ is empty.

Epithelial cells forming glands are highly specialized to remove materials from the blood and to manufacture them into new materials, which they then secrete. There are two types of glands, as shown in Figure 5.2. **Endocrine glands** lose their surface connection (duct) as they develop; thus they are referred to as ductless glands. Their secretions (all hormones) are extruded directly into the blood or the lymphatic vessels that weave through the glands. **Exocrine glands** retain their ducts, and their secretions empty through these ducts to an epithelial surface. The exocrine glands—including the sweat and oil glands, liver, and pancreas—are both external and internal; they will be discussed in conjunction with the organ systems to which their products are functionally related.

The most common types of epithelia, their characteristic locations in the body, and their functions are described in Figure 5.3.

ACTIVITY 1

Examining Epithelial Tissue Under the Microscope

Obtain slides of simple squamous, simple cuboidal, simple columnar, pseudostratified ciliated columnar, stratified squamous (nonkeratinized), stratified cuboidal, stratified columnar, and transitional epithelia. Examine each carefully, and notice how the epithelial cells fit closely together to form intact sheets of cells, a necessity for a tissue that forms linings or covering membranes. Scan each epithelial type for modifications for specific functions, such as cilia (motile cell projections that help to move substances along the cell surface), and microvilli, which increase the surface area for absorption. Also be alert for goblet cells, which secrete lubricating mucus (see Plate 1 of the Histology Atlas). Compare your observations with the descriptions and photomicrographs in Figure 5.3.

While working, check the questions in Review Sheet 5 at the end of this exercise. A number of the questions there refer to some of the observations you are asked to make during your microscopic study. ▪

(a) Simple squamous epithelium

Description: Single layer of flattened cells with disc-shaped central nuclei and sparse cytoplasm; the simplest of the epithelia.

Function: Allows passage of materials by diffusion and filtration in sites where protection is not important; secretes lubricating substances in serosae.

Location: Kidney glomeruli and corpuscles; air sacs of lungs; lining of heart, blood vessels, and lymphatic vessels; lining of ventral body cavity (serosae).

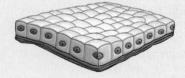

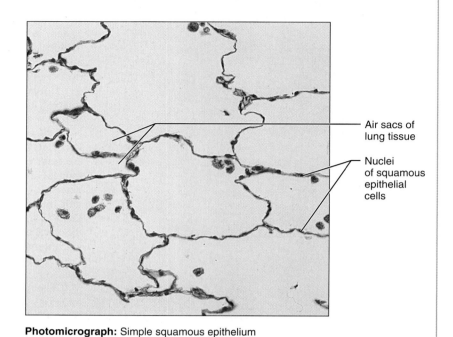

Air sacs of lung tissue

Nuclei of squamous epithelial cells

Photomicrograph: Simple squamous epithelium forming part of the alveolar (air sac) walls (400×).

(b) Simple cuboidal epithelium

Description: Single layer of cubelike cells with large, spherical central nuclei.

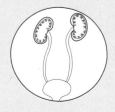

Function: Secretion and absorption.

Location: Kidney tubules; ducts and secretory portions of small glands; ovary surface.

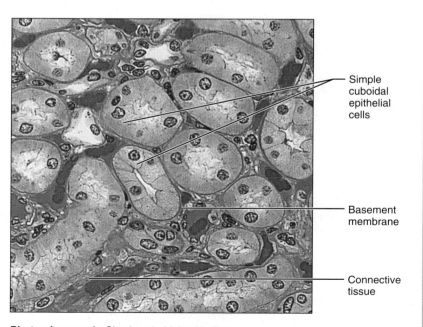

Simple cuboidal epithelial cells

Basement membrane

Connective tissue

Photomicrograph: Simple cuboidal epithelium in kidney tubules (400×).

FIGURE 5.3 Epithelial tissues. Simple epithelia (**a** and **b**).

(c) Simple columnar epithelium

Description: Single layer of tall cells with *round* to *oval* nuclei; some cells bear cilia; layer may contain mucus-secreting unicellular glands (goblet cells).

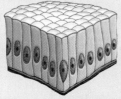

Function: Absorption; secretion of mucus, enzymes, and other substances; ciliated type propels mucus (or reproductive cells) by ciliary action.

Location: Nonciliated type lines most of the digestive tract (stomach to anal canal), gallbladder, and excretory ducts of some glands; ciliated variety lines small bronchi, uterine tubes, and some regions of the uterus.

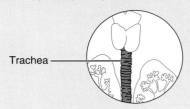

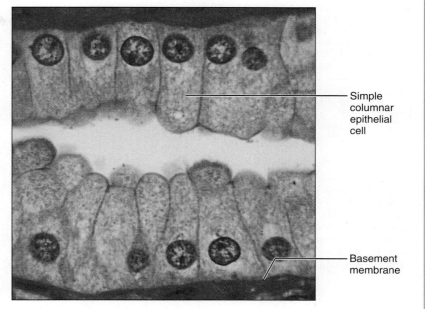

Simple columnar epithelial cell

Basement membrane

Photomicrograph: Simple columnar epithelium of the stomach mucosa (1300×).

(d) Pseudostratified columnar epithelium

Description: Single layer of cells of differing heights, some not reaching the free surface; nuclei seen at different levels; may contain goblet cells and bear cilia.

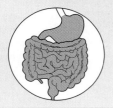

Function: Secretion, particularly of mucus; propulsion of mucus by ciliary action.

Location: Nonciliated type in male's sperm-carrying ducts and ducts of large glands; ciliated variety lines the trachea, most of the upper respiratory tract.

Trachea

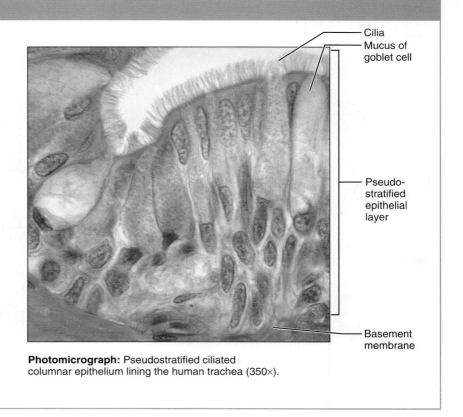

Cilia

Mucus of goblet cell

Pseudostratified epithelial layer

Basement membrane

Photomicrograph: Pseudostratified ciliated columnar epithelium lining the human trachea (350×).

FIGURE 5.3 *(continued)* Simple epithelia (**c** and **d**).

(e) Stratified squamous epithelium

Description: Thick membrane composed of several cell layers; basal cells are cuboidal or columnar and metabolically active; surface cells are flattened (squamous); in the keratinized type, the surface cells are full of keratin and dead; basal cells are active in mitosis and produce the cells of the more superficial layers.

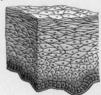

Function: Protects underlying tissues in areas subjected to abrasion.

Location: Nonkeratinized type forms the moist linings of the esophagus, mouth, and vagina; keratinized variety forms the epidermis of the skin, a dry membrane.

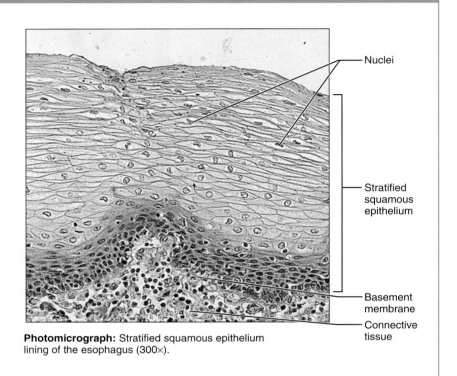

Nuclei

Stratified squamous epithelium

Basement membrane

Connective tissue

Photomicrograph: Stratified squamous epithelium lining of the esophagus (300×).

(f) Stratified cuboidal epithelium

Description: Generally two layers of cubelike cells.

Function: Protection

Location: Largest ducts of sweat glands, mammary glands, and salivary glands.

Basement membrane

Cuboidal epithelial cells

Duct lumen

Photomicrograph: Stratified cuboidal epithelium forming a salivary gland duct (300×).

FIGURE 5.3 *(continued)* **Epithelial tissues.** Stratified epithelia (**e** and **f**).

(g) Stratified columnar epithelium

Description: Several cell layers; basal cells usually cuboidal; superficial cells elongated and columnar.

Function: Protection; secretion.

Location: Rare in the body; small amounts in male urethra and in large ducts of some glands.

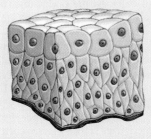

Urethra

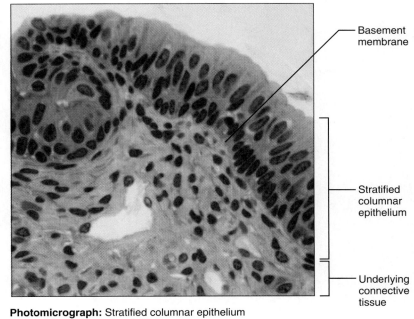

Basement membrane

Stratified columnar epithelium

Underlying connective tissue

Photomicrograph: Stratified columnar epithelium lining of the male urethra (460×).

(h) Transitional epithelium

Description: Resembles both stratified squamous and stratified cuboidal; basal cells cuboidal or columnar; surface cells dome shaped or squamouslike, depending on degree of organ stretch.

Function: Stretches readily and permits distension of urinary organ by contained urine.

Location: Lines the ureters, bladder, and part of the urethra.

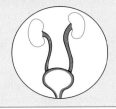

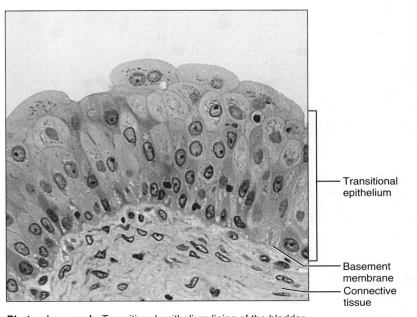

Transitional epithelium

Basement membrane

Connective tissue

Photomicrograph: Transitional epithelium lining of the bladder, relaxed state (500×); note the bulbous, or rounded, appearance of the cells at the surface; these cells flatten and become elongated when the bladder is filled with urine.

FIGURE 5.3 *(continued)* Stratified epithelia (**g** and **h**).

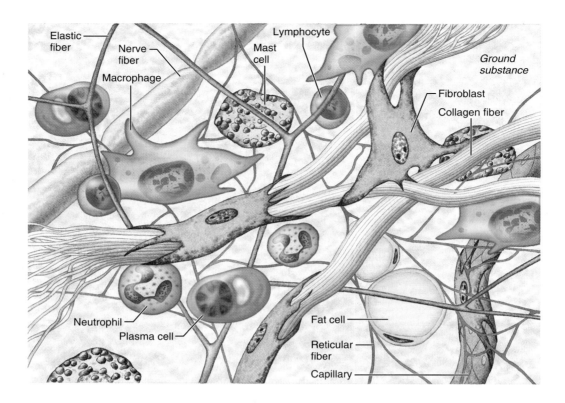

FIGURE 5.4 Areolar connective tissue: A prototype (model) connective tissue. This tissue underlies epithelia and surrounds capillaries. Note the various cell types and the three classes of fibers (collagen, reticular, elastic) embedded in the ground substance.

Connective Tissue

Connective tissue is found in all parts of the body as discrete structures or as part of various body organs. It is the most abundant and widely distributed of the tissue types.

Connective tissues perform a variety of functions, but they primarily protect, support, and bind together other tissues of the body. For example, bones are composed of connective tissue (**bone,** or **osseous tissue**), and they protect and support other body tissues and organs. The ligaments and tendons (**dense connective tissue**) bind the bones together or bind skeletal muscles to bones.

Areolar connective tissue (Figure 5.4) is a soft packaging material that cushions and protects body organs. **Adipose** (fat) tissue provides insulation for the body tissues and a source of stored food. Blood-forming (**hematopoietic**) tissue replenishes the body's supply of red blood cells. Connective tissue also serves a vital function in the repair of all body tissues since many wounds are repaired by connective tissue in the form of scar tissue.

The characteristics of connective tissue include the following:

• With a few exceptions (cartilages, which are avascular, and tendons and ligaments, which are poorly vascularized), connective tissues have a rich supply of blood vessels.

• Connective tissues are composed of many types of cells.

• There is a great deal of noncellular, nonliving material (matrix) between the cells of connective tissue.

The nonliving material between the cells—the **extracellular matrix**—deserves a bit more explanation because it distinguishes connective tissue from all other tissues. It is produced by the cells and then extruded. The matrix is primarily responsible for the strength associated with connective tissue, but there is variation. At one extreme, adipose tissue is composed mostly of cells. At the opposite extreme, bone and cartilage have few cells and large amounts of matrix.

The matrix has two components—ground substance and fibers. The **ground substance** is composed chiefly of interstitial fluid, cell adhesion proteins, and proteoglycans. Depending on its specific composition, the ground substance may be liquid, semisolid, gel-like, or very hard. When the matrix is firm, as in cartilage and bone, the connective tissue cells reside in cavities in the matrix called *lacunae*. The fibers, which provide support, include **collagen** (white) **fibers, elastic** (yellow) **fibers,** and **reticular** (fine collagen) **fibers.** Of these, the collagen fibers are most abundant.

Generally speaking, the ground substance functions as a molecular sieve, or medium, through which nutrients and other dissolved substances can diffuse between the blood capillaries and the cells. The fibers in the matrix hinder diffusion somewhat and make the ground substance less pliable. The properties of the connective tissue cells and the makeup and arrangement of their matrix elements vary tremendously, accounting for the amazing diversity of this tissue type. Nonetheless, the connective tissues have a common structural plan seen best in *areolar connective tissue* (Figure 5.4), a soft packing tissue that occurs throughout the body. Since all other connective tissues are variations of areolar, it is considered the model or prototype of the connective tissues. Notice in Figure 5.4 that areolar tissue has all three varieties of fibers, but they are sparsely arranged in its transparent gel-like ground substance. The cell type that secretes its matrix is the *fibroblast,* but a wide variety of other cells including phagocytic cells like macrophages and certain white blood cells and mast cells that act in the inflammatory response are present as well. The more durable connective tissues, such as bone, cartilage, and the dense fibrous varieties, characteristically have a firm ground substance and many more fibers.

There are four main types of adult connective tissue, all of which typically have large amounts of matrix. These are **connective tissue proper** (which includes areolar, adipose, reticular, and dense [fibrous] connective tissues), **cartilage, bone,** and **blood.** All of these derive from an embryonic tissue called *mesenchyme.* Figure 5.5 lists the general characteristics, location, and function of some of the connective tissues found in the body.

ACTIVITY 2

Examining Connective Tissue Under the Microscope

Obtain prepared slides of mesenchyme; of areolar, adipose, reticular, and dense irregular and regular connective tissue; of hyaline and elastic cartilage and fibrocartilage; of osseous connective tissue (bone); and of blood. Compare your observations with the views illustrated in Figure 5.5.

Distinguish between the living cells and the matrix and pay particular attention to the denseness and arrangement of the matrix. For example, notice how the matrix of the dense fibrous connective tissues, making up tendons and the dermis of the skin, is packed with collagen fibers, and that in the *regular* variety (tendon), the fibers are all running in the same direction, whereas in the dermis (a dense *irregular* connective tissue) they appear to be running in many directions.

While examining the areolar connective tissue, notice how much empty space there appears to be (*areol* = small empty space), and distinguish between the collagen fibers and the coiled elastic fibers. Identify the starlike fibroblasts. Also, try to locate a **mast cell,** which has large, darkly staining granules in its cytoplasm (*mast* = stuffed full of granules). This cell type releases histamine that makes capillaries

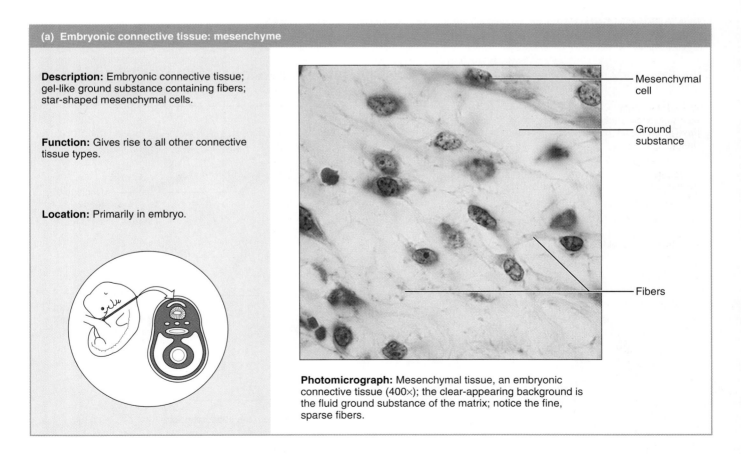

(a) Embryonic connective tissue: mesenchyme

Description: Embryonic connective tissue; gel-like ground substance containing fibers; star-shaped mesenchymal cells.

Function: Gives rise to all other connective tissue types.

Location: Primarily in embryo.

Mesenchymal cell

Ground substance

Fibers

Photomicrograph: Mesenchymal tissue, an embryonic connective tissue (400×); the clear-appearing background is the fluid ground substance of the matrix; notice the fine, sparse fibers.

FIGURE 5.5 Connective tissues. Embryonic connective tissue **(a)**.

(b) Connective tissue proper: loose connective tissue, areolar

Description: Gel-like matrix with all three fiber types; cells: fibroblasts, macrophages, mast cells, and some white blood cells.

Function: Wraps and cushions organs; its macrophages phagocytize bacteria; plays important role in inflammation; holds and conveys tissue fluid.

Location: Widely distributed under epithelia of body, e.g. forms lamina propria of mucous membranes; packages organs; surrounds capillaries.

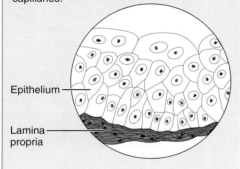

Epithelium

Lamina propria

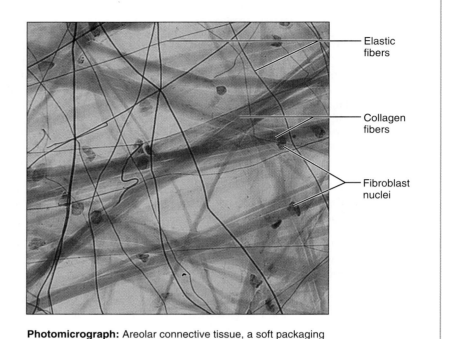

Elastic fibers

Collagen fibers

Fibroblast nuclei

Photomicrograph: Areolar connective tissue, a soft packaging tissue of the body (400×).

(c) Connective tissue proper: loose connective tissue, adipose

Description: Matrix as in areolar, but very sparse; closely packed adipocytes, or fat cells, have nucleus pushed to the side by large fat droplet.

Function: Provides reserve food fuel; insulates against heat loss; supports and protects organs.

Location: Under skin in the hypodermis; around kidneys and eyeballs; within abdomen; in breasts.

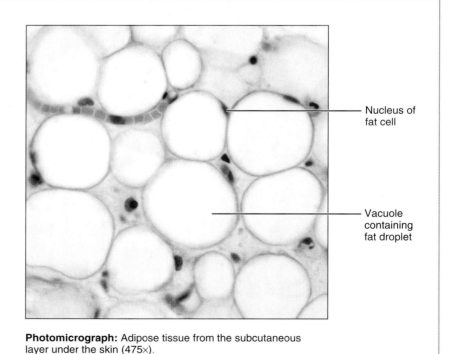

Nucleus of fat cell

Vacuole containing fat droplet

Photomicrograph: Adipose tissue from the subcutaneous layer under the skin (475×).

FIGURE 5.5 (continued) Connective tissues. Connective tissue proper (**b** and **c**).

(d) Connective tissue proper: loose connective tissue, reticular

Description: Network of reticular fibers in a typical loose ground substance; reticular cells lie on the network.

Function: Fibers form a soft internal skeleton (stroma) that supports other cell types including white blood cells, mast cells, and macrophages.

Location: Lymphoid organs (lymph nodes, bone marrow, and spleen).

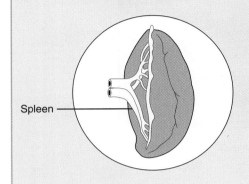

Spleen

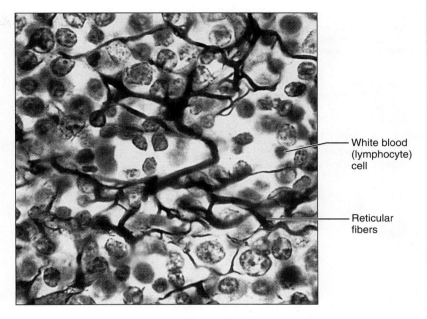

White blood (lymphocyte) cell

Reticular fibers

Photomicrograph: Dark-staining network of reticular connective tissue fibers forming the internal skeleton of the spleen (350×).

(e) Connective tissue proper: dense connective tissue, dense irregular

Description: Primarily irregularly arranged collagen fibers; some elastic fibers; major cell type is the fibroblast.

Function: Able to withstand tension exerted in many directions; provides structural strength.

Location: Dermis of the skin; submucosa of digestive tract; fibrous capsules of organs and of joints.

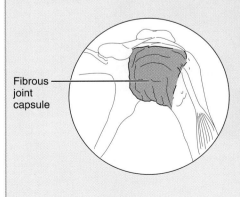

Fibrous joint capsule

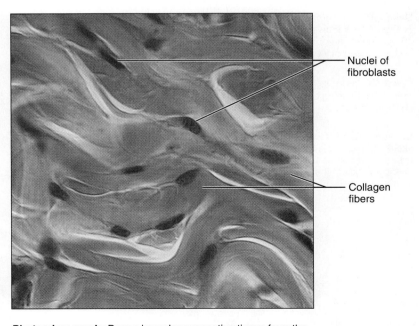

Nuclei of fibroblasts

Collagen fibers

Photomicrograph: Dense irregular connective tissue from the dermis of the skin (400×).

FIGURE 5.5 (continued) Connective tissue proper (**d** and **e**).

(f) Connective tissue proper: dense connective tissue, dense regular

Description: Primarily parallel collagen fibers; a few elastic fibers; major cell type is the fibroblast. Fibroblast nuclei are aligned parallel to the collagen fibers.

Function: Attaches muscles to bones or to muscles; attaches bones to bones; withstands great tensile stress when pulling force is applied in one direction.

Location: Tendons, most ligaments, aponeuroses.

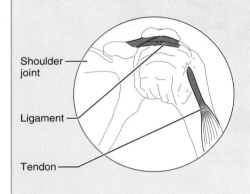

Shoulder joint

Ligament

Tendon

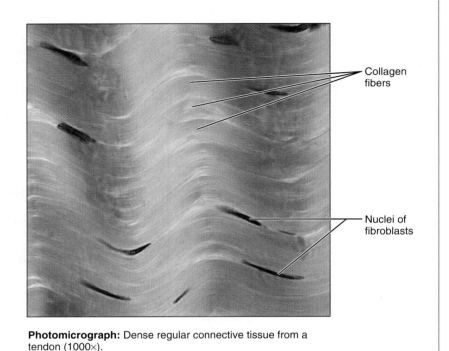

Collagen fibers

Nuclei of fibroblasts

Photomicrograph: Dense regular connective tissue from a tendon (1000×).

(g) Cartilage: hyaline

Description: Amorphous but firm matrix; collagen fibers form an imperceptible network; chondroblasts produce the matrix and when mature (chondrocytes) lie in lacunae.

Function: Supports and reinforces; has resilient cushioning properties; resists compressive stress.

Location: Forms most of the embryonic skeleton; covers the ends of long bones in joint cavities; forms costal cartilages of the ribs; cartilages of the nose, trachea, and larynx.

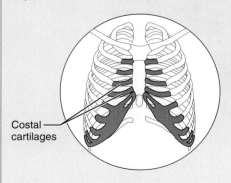

Costal cartilages

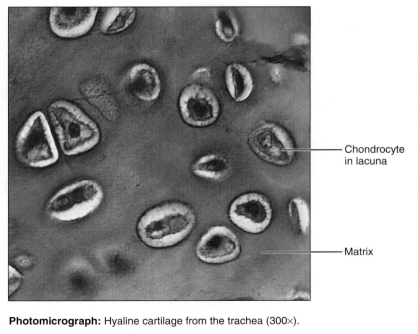

Chondrocyte in lacuna

Matrix

Photomicrograph: Hyaline cartilage from the trachea (300×).

FIGURE 5.5 (continued) Connective tissues. Connective tissue proper (**f** and **g**).

(h) Cartilage: elastic

Description: Similar to hyaline cartilage, but more elastic fibers in matrix.

Function: Maintains the shape of a structure while allowing great flexibility.

Location: Supports the external ear (pinna); epiglottis.

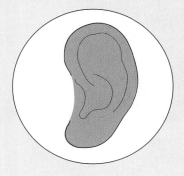

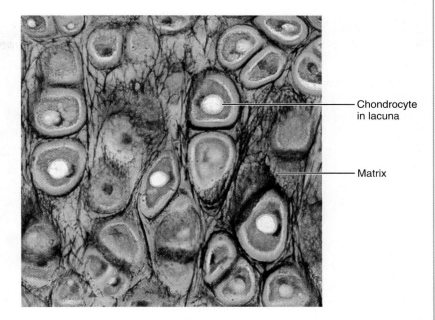

Chondrocyte in lacuna

Matrix

Photomicrograph: Elastic cartilage from the human ear pinna; forms the flexible skeleton of the ear (640×).

(i) Cartilage: fibrocartilage

Description: Matrix similar to but less firm than that in hyaline cartilage; thick collagen fibers predominate.

Function: Tensile strength with the ability to absorb compressive shock.

Location: Intervertebral discs; pubic symphysis; discs of knee joint.

Intervertebral discs

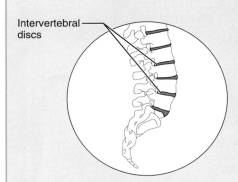

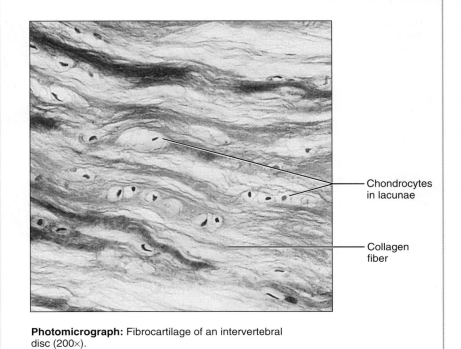

Chondrocytes in lacunae

Collagen fiber

Photomicrograph: Fibrocartilage of an intervertebral disc (200×).

FIGURE 5.5 *(continued)* Cartilage (**h** and **i**).

(j) Bone (osseous tissue)

Description: Hard, calcified matrix containing many collagen fibers; osteocytes lie in lacunae. Very well vascularized.

Function: Bone supports and protects (by enclosing); provides levers for the muscles to act on; stores calcium and other minerals and fat; marrow inside bones is the site for blood cell formation (hematopoiesis).

Location: Bones

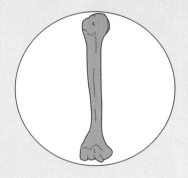

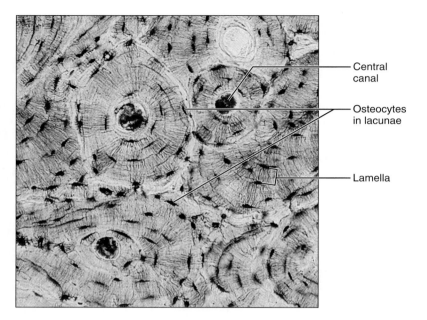

Photomicrograph: Cross-sectional view of bone (70×).

Central canal

Osteocytes in lacunae

Lamella

(k) Blood

Description: Red and white blood cells in a fluid matrix (plasma).

Function: Transport of respiratory gases, nutrients, wastes and other substances.

Location: Contained within blood vessels.

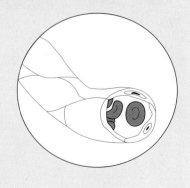

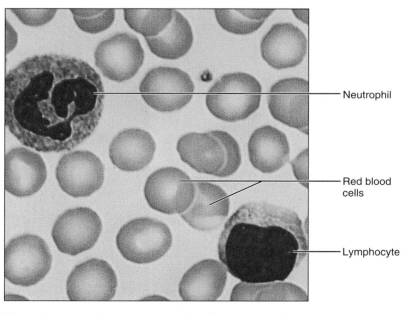

Photomicrograph: Smear of human blood (1500×); two white blood cells (neutrophil in upper left and lymphocyte in lower right) are seen surrounded by red blood cells.

Neutrophil

Red blood cells

Lymphocyte

FIGURE 5.5 *(continued)* Bone (**j**) and blood (**k**).

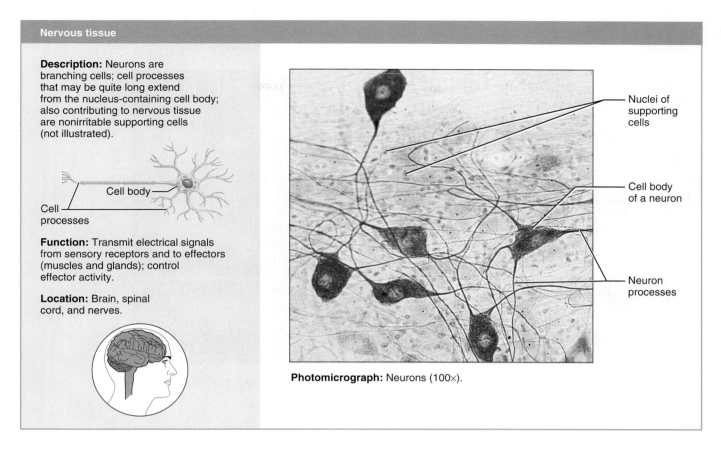

Nervous tissue

Description: Neurons are branching cells; cell processes that may be quite long extend from the nucleus-containing cell body; also contributing to nervous tissue are nonirritable supporting cells (not illustrated).

Cell body

Cell processes

Function: Transmit electrical signals from sensory receptors and to effectors (muscles and glands); control effector activity.

Location: Brain, spinal cord, and nerves.

Nuclei of supporting cells

Cell body of a neuron

Neuron processes

Photomicrograph: Neurons (100×).

FIGURE 5.6 Nervous tissue.

more permeable during inflammatory reactions and allergies and thus is partially responsible for that "runny nose" of some allergies.

In adipose tissue, locate a "signet ring" cell, a fat cell in which the nucleus can be seen pushed to one side by the large, fat-filled vacuole that appears to be a large empty space. Also notice how little matrix there is in adipose (fat) tissue. Distinguish between the living cells and the matrix in the dense fibrous, bone, and hyaline cartilage preparations.

Scan the blood slide at low and then high power to examine the general shape of the red blood cells. Then, switch to the oil immersion lens for a closer look at the various types of white blood cells. How does blood differ from all other connective tissues?

Nervous Tissue

Nervous tissue is composed of two major cell populations. The **neuroglia** are special supporting cells that protect, support, and insulate the more delicate neurons. The

neurons are highly specialized to receive stimuli (irritability) and to conduct waves of excitation, or impulses, to all parts of the body (conductivity). They are the cells that are most often associated with nervous system functioning.

The structure of neurons is markedly different from that of all other body cells. They all have a nucleus-containing cell body, and their cytoplasm is drawn out into long extensions (cell processes)—sometimes as long as 1 m (about 3 feet), which allows a single neuron to conduct an impulse over relatively long distances. More detail about the anatomy of the different classes of neurons and neuroglia appears in Exercise 15.

ACTIVITY 3

Examining Nervous Tissue Under the Microscope

Obtain a prepared slide of a spinal cord smear. Locate a neuron and compare it to Figure 5.6. Keep the light dim—this will help you see the cellular extensions of the neurons. See also Plates 5 and 6 in the Histology Atlas. ■

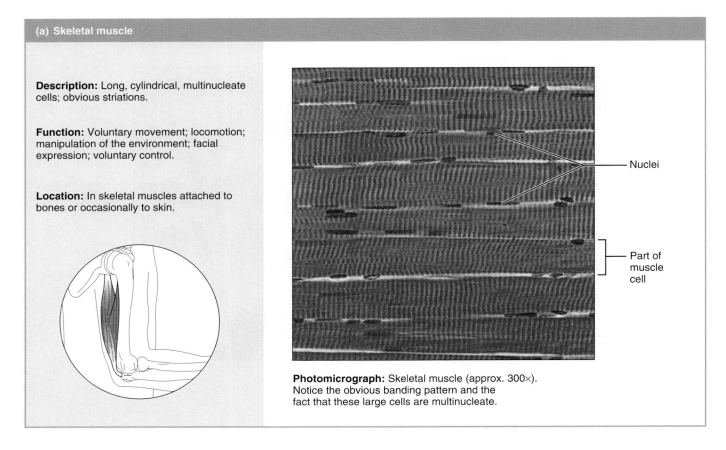

(a) Skeletal muscle

Description: Long, cylindrical, multinucleate cells; obvious striations.

Function: Voluntary movement; locomotion; manipulation of the environment; facial expression; voluntary control.

Location: In skeletal muscles attached to bones or occasionally to skin.

Nuclei

Part of muscle cell

Photomicrograph: Skeletal muscle (approx. 300×). Notice the obvious banding pattern and the fact that these large cells are multinucleate.

FIGURE 5.7 Muscle tissues. Skeletal muscle (**a**).

Muscle Tissue

Muscle tissue (Figure 5.7) is highly specialized to contract and produces most types of body movement. As you might expect, muscle cells tend to be elongated, providing a long axis for contraction. The three basic types of muscle tissue are described briefly here. Cardiac and skeletal muscles are treated more completely in later exercises.

Skeletal muscle, the "meat," or flesh, of the body, is attached to the skeleton. It is under voluntary control (consciously controlled), and its contraction moves the limbs and other external body parts. The cells of skeletal muscles are long, cylindrical, and multinucleate (several nuclei per cell), with the nuclei pushed to the periphery of the cells; they have obvious *striations* (stripes).

Cardiac muscle is found only in the heart. As it contracts, the heart acts as a pump, propelling the blood into the blood vessels. Cardiac muscle, like skeletal muscle, has striations, but cardiac cells are branching uninucleate cells that interdigitate (fit together) at junctions called **intercalated discs.** These structural modifications allow the cardiac muscle to act as a unit. Cardiac muscle is under involuntary control, which means that we cannot voluntarily or consciously control the operation of the heart.

Smooth muscle, or *visceral muscle,* is found mainly in the walls of hollow organs (digestive and urinary tract organs, uterus, blood vessels). Typically it has two layers that run at right angles to each other; consequently its contraction can constrict or dilate the lumen (cavity) of an organ and propel substances along predetermined pathways. Smooth muscle cells are quite different in appearance from those of skeletal or cardiac muscle. No striations are visible, and the uninucleate smooth muscle cells are spindle-shaped.

ACTIVITY 4

Examining Muscle Tissue Under the Microscope

Obtain and examine prepared slides of skeletal, cardiac, and smooth muscle. Notice their similarities and dissimilarities in your observations and in the illustrations in Figure 5.7. Teased smooth muscle shows individual cell shape clearly (see Plate 3, Histology Atlas). ▪

(b) Cardiac muscle

Description: Branching, striated, generally uninucleate cells that interdigitate at specialized junctions (intercalated discs).

Function: As it contracts, it propels blood into the circulation; involuntary control.

Location: The walls of the heart.

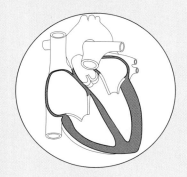

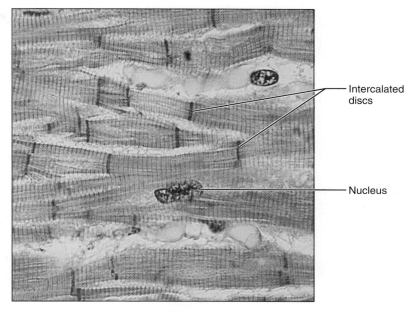

Intercalated discs

Nucleus

Photomicrograph: Cardiac muscle (800×); notice the striations, branching of cells, and the intercalated discs.

(c) Smooth muscle

Description: Spindle-shaped cells with central nuclei; no striations; cells arranged closely to form sheets.

Function: Propels substances or objects (foodstuffs, urine, a baby) along internal passageways; involuntary control.

Location: Mostly in the walls of hollow organs.

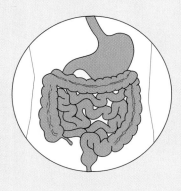

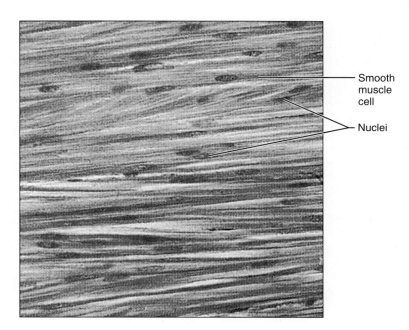

Smooth muscle cell

Nuclei

Photomicrograph: Sheet of smooth muscle (approx. 600×).

FIGURE 5.7 *(continued)* Cardiac (**b**) and smooth (**c**) muscles.

NAME _____

LAB TIME/DATE _____

Classification of Tissues

Tissue Structure and Function—General Review

1. Define *tissue*. _____

_____

2. Use the key choices to identify the major tissue types described below.

Key: a.   connective tissue   b. epithelium   c. muscle   d. nervous tissue

_____ 1.   lines body cavities and covers the body's external surface

_____ 2.   pumps blood, flushes urine out of the body, allows one to swing a bat

_____ 3.   transmits electrochemical impulses

_____ 4.   anchors, packages, and supports body organs

_____ 5.   cells may absorb, secrete, and filter

_____ 6.   most involved in regulating and controlling body functions

_____ 7.   major function is to contract

_____ 8.   synthesizes hormones

_____ 9.   the most durable tissue type

_____ 10.   abundant nonliving extracellular matrix

_____ 11.   most widespread tissue in the body

_____ 12.   forms nerves and the brain

Epithelial Tissue

3. Describe five general characteristics of epithelial tissue. _____

_____

_____

_____

4. On what basis are epithelial tissues classified? _____

5. List five major functions of epithelium in the body, and give examples of each. _____

Function 1: _____ Example: _____

Function 2: _____ Example: _____

Function 3: _____ Example: _____

Function 4: _____ Example: _____

Function 5: _____ Example: _____

6. How does the function of stratified epithelium differ from the function of simple epithelium? _____

_____

_____

7. Where is ciliated epithelium found? _____

_____

What role does it play? _____

_____

_____

8. Transitional epithelium is actually stratified squamous epithelium, but there is something special about it.

How does it differ structurally from other stratified squamous epithelia? _____

_____

How does the structural difference support its function in the body? _____

_____

_____

9. How do the endocrine and exocrine glands differ in structure and function? _____

_____

_____

_____

10. Respond to the following with the key choices.

Key: a. pseudostratified ciliated columnar   c. simple cuboidal   e. stratified squamous
      b. simple columnar   d. simple squamous   f. transitional

_____ 1. lining of the esophagus

_____ 2. lining of the stomach

_____ 3. alveolar sacs of lungs

_____ 4. tubules of the kidney

_____ 5. epidermis of the skin

_____ 6. lining of bladder; peculiar cells that have the ability to slide over each other

_____ 7. forms the thin serous membranes; a single layer of flattened cells

Connective Tissue

11. What are three general characteristics of connective tissues? _____

_____

_____

12. What functions are performed by connective tissue? _____

_____

13. How are the functions of connective tissue reflected in its structure? _____

_____

_____

14. Using the key, choose the best response to identify the connective tissues described below.

_____ 1. attaches bones to bones and muscles to bones

_____ 2. acts as a storage depot for fat

_____ 3. the dermis of the skin

_____ 4. makes up the intervertebral discs

_____ 5. forms the hip bone

_____ 6. composes basement membranes; a soft packaging tissue with a jellylike matrix

_____ 7. forms the larynx, the costal cartilages of the ribs, and the embryonic skeleton

_____ 8. provides a flexible framework for the external ear

_____ 9. firm, structurally amorphous matrix heavily invaded with fibers; appears glassy and smooth

_____ 10. matrix hard owing to calcium salts; provides levers for muscles to act on

_____ 11. insulates against heat loss

Key: a. adipose connective tissue
b. areolar connective tissue
c. dense fibrous connective tissue
d. elastic cartilage
e. fibrocartilage
f. hematopoietic tissue
g. hyaline cartilage
h. osseous tissue

15. Why do adipose cells remind people of a ring with a single jewel? _____

_____

Nervous Tissue

16. What two physiological characteristics are highly developed in neurons (nerve cells)? _____

_____

17. In what ways are neurons similar to other cells? _____

_____

How are they different? _____

18. Describe how the unique structure of a neuron relates to its function in the body. _____

_____

Muscle Tissue

19. The three types of muscle tissue exhibit similarities as well as differences. Check the appropriate space in the chart to indicate which muscle types exhibit each characteristic.

Characteristic	Skeletal	Cardiac	Smooth
Voluntarily controlled			
Involuntarily controlled			
Striated			
Has a single nucleus in each cell			
Has several nuclei per cell			
Found attached to bones			
Allows you to direct your eyeballs			
Found in the walls of the stomach, uterus, and arteries			
Contains spindle-shaped cells			
Contains branching cylindrical cells			
Contains long, nonbranching cylindrical cells			
Has intercalated discs			
Concerned with locomotion of the body as a whole			
Changes the internal volume of an organ as it contracts			
Tissue of the heart			

For Review

20. Label the tissue types illustrated here and on the next pages, and identify all structures provided with leader lines.

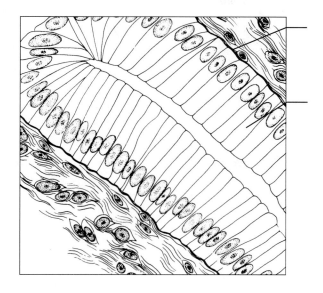

(a) _____

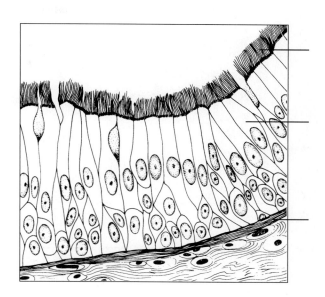

(b) _____

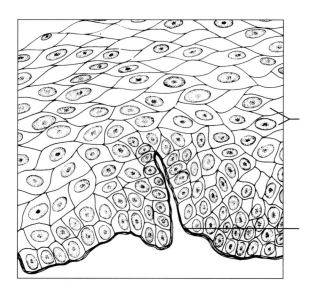

(c) _____

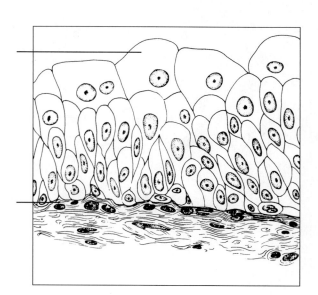

(d) _____

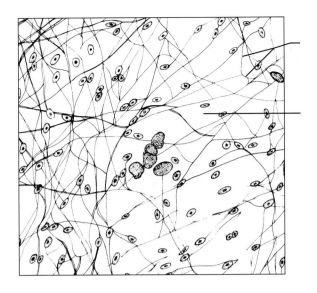

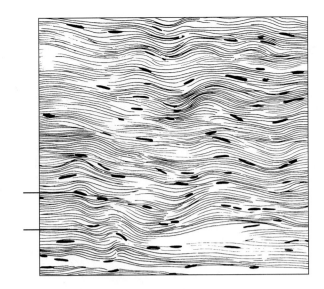

(e) _____

(f) _____

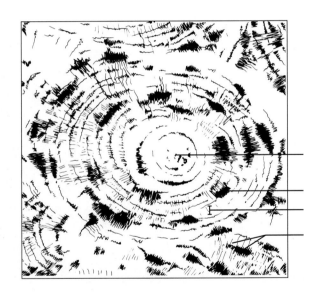

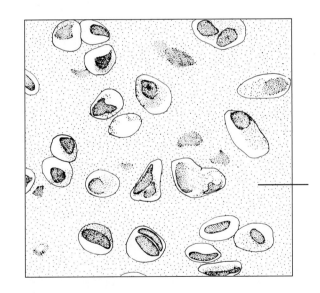

(g) _____

(h) _____

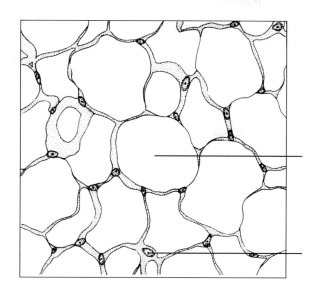

(i) _____

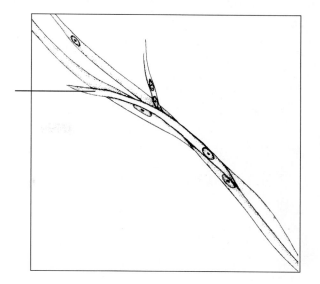

(j) _____

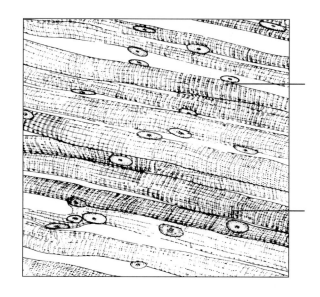

(k) _____

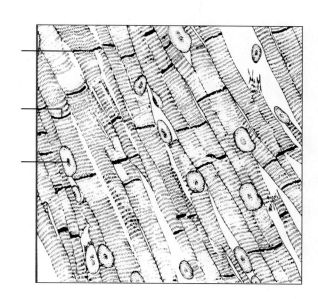

(l) _____

The Integumentary System

MATERIALS

- ☐ Skin model (three-dimensional, if available)
- ☐ Compound microscope
- ☐ Prepared slide of human scalp
- ☐ Prepared slide of skin of palm or sole
- ☐ Sheet of 20# bond paper ruled to mark off 1-cm^2 areas
- ☐ Scissors
- ☐ Betadine swabs, or Lugol's iodine and cotton swabs
- ☐ Adhesive tape
- ☐ Disposable gloves
- ☐ Data collection sheet for plotting distribution of sweat glands
- ☐ Porelon fingerprint pad or portable inking foils
- ☐ Ink cleaner towelettes
- ☐ Index cards (4 in. × 6 in.)
- ☐ Magnifying glasses

OBJECTIVES

1. To list several important functions of the skin, or integumentary system.
2. To recognize and name during observation of an appropriate model, diagram, projected slide, or microscopic specimen the following skin structures: epidermis, dermis (papillary and reticular layers), hair follicles and hair, sebaceous glands, and sweat glands.
3. To name the layers of the epidermis and describe the characteristics of each.
4. To compare the properties of the epidermis to those of the dermis.
5. To describe the distribution and function of the skin derivatives— sebaceous glands, sweat glands, and hairs.
6. To differentiate between eccrine and apocrine sweat glands.
7. To enumerate the factors determining skin color.
8. To describe the function of melanin.
9. To identify the major regions of nails.

The **skin,** or **integument,** is considered an organ system because of its extent and complexity. It is much more than an external body covering; architecturally the skin is a marvel. It is tough yet pliable, a characteristic that enables it to withstand constant insult from outside agents.

The skin has many functions, most (but not all) concerned with protection. It insulates and cushions the underlying body tissues and protects the entire body from mechanical damage (bumps and cuts), chemical damage (acids, alkalis, and the like), thermal damage (heat), and bacterial invasion (by virtue of its acid mantle and continuous surface). The hardened uppermost layer of the skin (the cornified layer) helps prevent water loss from the body surface. The skin's abundant capillary network (under the control of the nervous system) plays an important role in regulating heat loss from the body surface.

The skin has other functions as well. For example, it acts as a mini excretory system; urea, salts, and water are lost through the skin pores in sweat. The skin also has important metabolic duties. For example, like liver cells, it carries out some chemical conversions that activate or inactivate certain drugs and hormones, and it is the site of vitamin D synthesis for the body. Finally, the cutaneous sense organs are located in the dermis.

Basic Structure of the Skin

The skin has two distinct regions—the superficial *epidermis* composed of epithelium and an underlying connective tissue *dermis* (Figure 6.1). These layers are firmly "cemented" together along an undulating border. But friction, such as the rubbing of a poorly fitting shoe, may cause them to separate, resulting in a blister. Immediately deep to the dermis is the **hypodermis,** or **superficial fascia** (primarily adipose tissue), which is not considered part of the skin. The main skin areas and structures are described next.

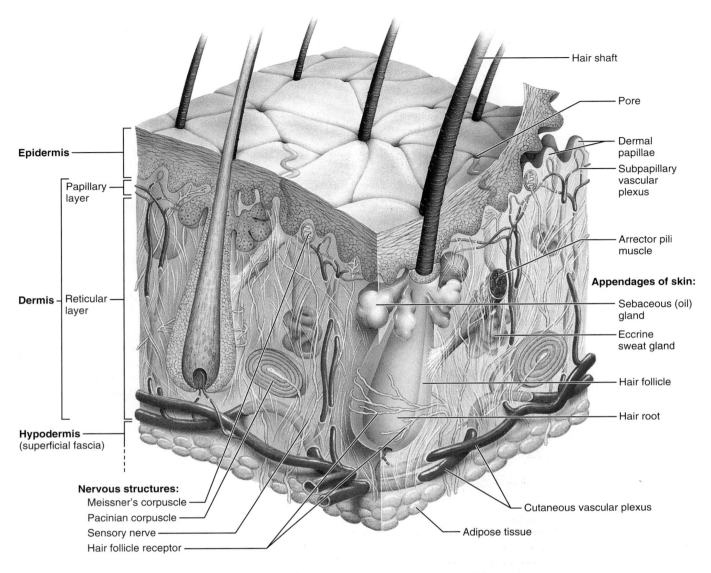

Hair shaft

Pore

Dermal papillae

Subpapillary vascular plexus

Arrector pili muscle

Appendages of skin:

Sebaceous (oil) gland

Eccrine sweat gland

Hair follicle

Hair root

Cutaneous vascular plexus

Adipose tissue

Epidermis

Papillary layer

Dermis — Reticular layer

Hypodermis (superficial fascia)

Nervous structures:

Meissner's corpuscle

Pacinian corpuscle

Sensory nerve

Hair follicle receptor

FIGURE 6.1 Skin structure. Three-dimensional view of the skin and the underlying hypodermis. The epidermis and dermis have been pulled apart at the right corner to reveal the dermal papillae.

ACTIVITY 1

Locating Structures on a Skin Model

As you read, locate the following structures in Figure 6.1 and on a skin model. ▬

Epidermis

Structurally, the avascular epidermis is a keratinized stratified squamous epithelium consisting of four distinct cell types and four or five distinct layers.

Cells of the Epidermis

• **Keratinocytes** (literally, keratin cells): The most abundant epidermal cells, they function mainly to produce keratin fibrils. **Keratin** is a fibrous protein that gives the epidermis its durability and protective capabilities. Keratinocytes are tightly connected to each other by desmosomes.

Far less numerous are the following types of epidermal cells (Figure 6.2):

• **Melanocytes:** Spidery black cells that produce the brown-to-black pigment called **melanin.** The skin tans because melanin production increases when the skin is exposed to sunlight. The melanin provides a protective pigment umbrella over the nuclei of the cells in the deeper epidermal layers, thus shielding their genetic material (deoxyribonucleic acid, DNA) from the damaging effects of ultraviolet radiation. A concentration of melanin in one spot is called a *freckle.*

• **Langerhans cells:** Also called *epidermal dendritic cells,* these phagocytic cells (macrophages) play a role in immunity.

• **Merkel cells:** Occasional spiky hemispheres that, in conjunction with sensory nerve endings, form sensitive touch receptors called *Merkel discs* located at the epidermal-dermal junction.

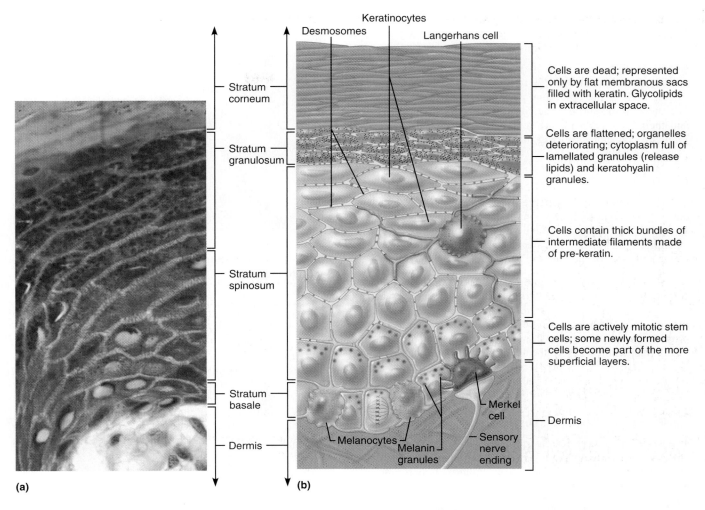

Keratinocytes
Desmosomes
Langerhans cell

Stratum corneum

Cells are dead; represented only by flat membranous sacs filled with keratin. Glycolipids in extracellular space.

Stratum granulosum

Cells are flattened; organelles deteriorating; cytoplasm full of lamellated granules (release lipids) and keratohyalin granules.

Cells contain thick bundles of intermediate filaments made of pre-keratin.

Stratum spinosum

Cells are actively mitotic stem cells; some newly formed cells become part of the more superficial layers.

Stratum basale

Merkel cell

Dermis

Dermis

Melanocytes

Melanin granules

Sensory nerve ending

(a)   (b)

FIGURE 6.2 The main structural features in epidermis of thin skin. (a) Photomicrograph depicting the four major epidermal layers. **(b)** Diagram showing the layers and relative distribution of the different cell types. Keratinocytes (tan) form the bulk of the epidermis. Melanocytes (gray) produce the pigment melanin. Langerhans cells (blue) function as macrophages. A Merkel cell (purple) associates with a sensory nerve ending (yellow) that extends from the dermis to form a Merkel disc (touch receptor). Notice that the keratinocytes, but not the other cell types, are joined by numerous desmosomes. Only a portion of the stratum corneum is illustrated in each case.

Layers of the Epidermis The epidermis consists of four layers in thin skin, which covers most of the body. Thick skin, found on the palms of the hands and soles of the feet, contains a fifth layer, the stratum lucidum. From deep to superficial, the layers of the epidermis are the stratum basale, stratum spinosum, stratum granulosum, stratum lucidum, and stratum corneum (Figure 6.2).

•   **Stratum basale** (basal layer): A single row of cells immediately adjacent to the dermis. Its cells are constantly undergoing mitotic cell division to produce millions of new cells daily, hence its alternate name *stratum germinativum*. From 10% to 25% of the cells in this layer are melanocytes, which thread their processes through this and the adjacent layers of keratinocytes (see Figure 6.2).

•   **Stratum spinosum** (spiny layer): A stratum consisting of several cell layers immediately superficial to the basal layer. Its cells contain thick weblike bundles of intermediate

filaments made of a pre-keratin protein. The stratum spinosum cells appear spiky (hence their name) because as the skin tissue is prepared for histological examination, they shrink but their desmosomes hold tight. Cells divide fairly rapidly in this layer, but less so than in the stratum basale. Cells in the basal and spiny layers are the only ones to receive adequate nourishment via diffusion of nutrients from the dermis. So as their daughter cells are pushed upward and away from the source of nutrition, they gradually die.

•   **Stratum granulosum** (granular layer): A thin layer named for the abundant granules its cells contain. These granules are of two types: (1) *lamellated granules,* which contain a waterproofing glycolipid that is secreted into the extracellular space; and (2) *keratohyalin granules,* which combine with the intermediate filaments in the more superficial layers to form the keratin fibrils. At the upper border of this layer, the cells are beginning to die.

- **Stratum lucidum** (clear layer): A very thin translucent band of flattened dead keratinocytes with indistinct boundaries. It is not present in regions of thin skin.

- **Stratum corneum** (horny layer): This outermost epidermal layer consists of some 20 to 30 cell layers, and accounts for the bulk of the epidermal thickness. Cells in this layer, like those in the stratum lucidum (where it exists), are dead and their flattened scalelike remnants are fully keratinized. They are constantly rubbing off and being replaced by division of the deeper cells.

Dermis

The dense irregular connective tissue making up the dermis consists of two principal regions—the papillary and reticular areas. Like the epidermis, the dermis varies in thickness. For example, the skin is particularly thick on the palms of the hands and soles of the feet and is quite thin on the eyelids.

- **Papillary layer:** The more superficial dermal region composed of areolar connective tissue. It is very uneven and has fingerlike projections from its superior surface, the **dermal papillae,** which attach it to the epidermis above. These projections lie on top of the larger dermal ridges. In the palms of the hands and soles of the feet, they produce the *fingerprints,* unique patterns of *epidermal ridges* that remain unchanged throughout life. The abundant capillary networks in the papillary layer furnish nutrients for the epidermal layers and allow heat to radiate to the skin surface. The pain and touch receptors (**Meissner's corpuscles**) are also found here.

- **Reticular layer:** The deepest skin layer. It is composed of dense irregular connective tissue and contains many arteries and veins, sweat and sebaceous glands, and pressure receptors (**Pacinian corpuscles**).

Both the papillary and reticular layers are heavily invested with collagenic and elastic fibers. The elastic fibers give skin its exceptional elasticity in youth. In old age, the number of elastic fibers decreases and the subcutaneous layer loses fat, which leads to wrinkling and inelasticity of the skin. Fibroblasts, adipose cells, various types of macrophages (which are important in the body's defense), and other cell types are found throughout the dermis.

The abundant dermal blood supply, consisting mainly of the deep *cutaneous vascular plexus* (between the dermis and hypodermis) and the *subpapillary vascular plexus* (located just deep to the dermal papillae), allows the skin to play a role in the regulation of body temperature. When body temperature is high, the arterioles serving the skin dilate, and the capillary network of the dermis becomes engorged with the heated blood. Thus body heat is allowed to radiate from the skin surface. If the environment is cool and body heat must be conserved, the arterioles constrict so that blood bypasses the dermal capillary networks temporarily.

Any restriction of the normal blood supply to the skin results in cell death and, if severe enough, skin ulcers (Figure 6.3). **Bedsores (decubitus ulcers)** occur in bedridden patients who are not turned regularly enough. The weight

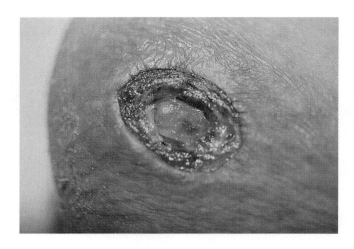

FIGURE 6.3 Photograph of a deep (stage III) decubitus ulcer.

of the body exerts pressure on the skin, especially over bony projections (hips, heels, etc.), which leads to restriction of the blood supply and tissue death.

The dermis is also richly provided with lymphatic vessels and a nerve supply. Many of the nerve endings bear highly specialized receptor organs that, when stimulated by environmental changes, transmit messages to the central nervous system for interpretation. Some of these receptors—free nerve endings (pain receptors), a Meissner's corpuscle, a Pacinian corpuscle, and a hair follicle receptor (also called a *root hair plexus*)—are shown in Figure 6.1.

Skin Color

Skin color is a result of the relative amount of melanin in skin, the relative amount of carotene in skin, and the degree of oxygenation of the blood. People who produce large amounts of melanin have brown-toned skin. In light-skinned people, who have less melanin pigment, the dermal blood supply flushes through the rather transparent cell layers above, giving the skin a rosy glow. *Carotene* is a yellow-orange pigment present primarily in the stratum corneum and in the adipose tissue of the hypodermis. Its presence is most noticeable when large amounts of carotene-rich foods (carrots, for instance) are eaten.

Skin color may be an important diagnostic tool. For example, flushed skin may indicate hypertension, fever, or embarrassment, whereas pale skin is typically seen in anemic individuals. When the blood is inadequately oxygenated, as during asphyxiation and serious lung disease, both the blood and the skin take on a bluish or cyanotic cast. **Jaundice,** in which the tissues become yellowed, is almost always diagnostic for liver disease, whereas a bronzing of the skin hints that a person's adrenal cortex is hypoactive (**Addison's disease**).

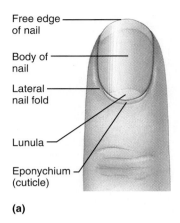

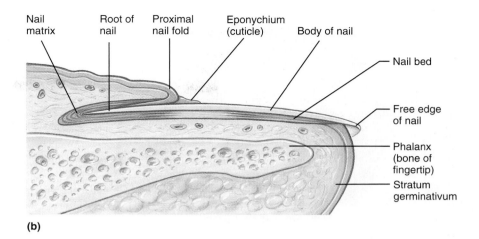

FIGURE 6.4 Structure of a nail. (**a**) Surface view of the distal part of a finger showing nail parts. The nail matrix that forms the nail lies beneath the lunula; the epidermis of the nail bed underlies the nail. (**b**) Sagittal section of the fingertip.

Accessory Organs of the Skin

The accessory organs of the skin—cutaneous glands, hair, and nails—are all derivatives of the epidermis, but they reside in the dermis. They originate from the stratum basale and grow downward into the deeper skin regions.

Nails

Nails are hornlike derivatives of the epidermis (Figure 6.4). Their named parts are:

- **Body:** The visible attached portion.

- **Free edge:** The portion of the nail that grows out away from the body.

- **Root:** The part that is embedded in the skin and adheres to an epithelial nail bed.

- **Nail folds:** Skin folds that overlap the borders of the nail.

- **Eponychium:** The thick proximal nail fold commonly called the cuticle.

- **Nail bed:** Extension of the stratum basale beneath the nail.

- **Nail matrix:** The thickened proximal part of the nail bed containing germinal cells responsible for nail growth. As the matrix produces the nail cells, they become heavily keratinized and die. Thus nails, like hairs, are mostly nonliving material.

- **Lunula:** The proximal region of the thickened nail matrix, which appears as a white crescent. Everywhere else, nails are transparent and nearly colorless, but they appear pink because of the blood supply in the underlying dermis. When someone is cyanotic due to a lack of oxygen in the blood, the nail beds take on a blue cast.

ACTIVITY 2

Identifying Nail Structures

Identify the nail structures shown in Figure 6.4 on yourself or your lab partner. ■

Hairs and Associated Structures

Hairs, enclosed in hair follicles, are found all over the entire body surface, except for thick-skinned areas (the palms of the hands and the soles of the feet), parts of the external genitalia, the nipples, and the lips.

- **Hair:** A structure consisting of three parts: a *medulla,* which is the central region, surrounded first by the *cortex* and then by a protective *cuticle* (Figure 6.5). Abrasion of the cuticle results in split ends. Hair color is a manifestation of the amount and kind of melanin pigment within the hair cortex. The portion of the hair enclosed within the follicle is called the **root;** that portion projecting from the scalp surface is called the **shaft.** The **hair bulb** is a collection of well-nourished germinal epithelial cells at the basal end of the follicle. As the daughter cells are pushed farther away from the growing region, they die and become keratinized; thus the bulk of the hair shaft, like the bulk of the epidermis, is dead material.

- **Follicle:** A structure formed from both epidermal and dermal cells (see Figure 6.5). Its inner epithelial root sheath, with two parts (internal and external), is enclosed by a thickened basement membrane, the glassy membrane, and a connective tissue root sheath, which is essentially dermal tissue.

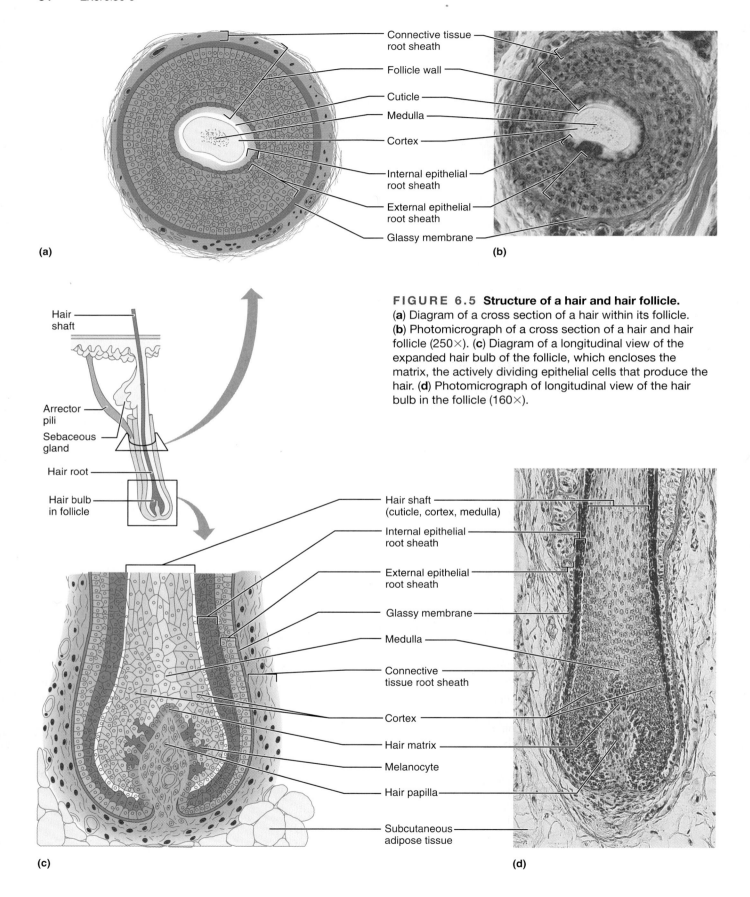

(a)

(b)

Connective tissue root sheath
Follicle wall
Cuticle
Medulla
Cortex
Internal epithelial root sheath
External epithelial root sheath
Glassy membrane

Hair shaft
Arrector pili
Sebaceous gland
Hair root
Hair bulb in follicle

FIGURE 6.5 Structure of a hair and hair follicle.
(**a**) Diagram of a cross section of a hair within its follicle.
(**b**) Photomicrograph of a cross section of a hair and hair follicle (250×). (**c**) Diagram of a longitudinal view of the expanded hair bulb of the follicle, which encloses the matrix, the actively dividing epithelial cells that produce the hair. (**d**) Photomicrograph of longitudinal view of the hair bulb in the follicle (160×).

Hair shaft (cuticle, cortex, medulla)
Internal epithelial root sheath
External epithelial root sheath
Glassy membrane
Medulla
Connective tissue root sheath
Cortex
Hair matrix
Melanocyte
Hair papilla
Subcutaneous adipose tissue

(c)

(d)

A small nipple of dermal tissue that protrudes into the hair bulb from the connective tissue sheath and provides nutrition to the growing hair is called the **papilla.**

• **Arrector pili muscle:** Small bands of smooth muscle cells connecting each hair follicle to the papillary layer of the dermis (Figures 6.1 and 6.5). When these muscles contract (during cold or fright), the slanted hair follicle is pulled up-right, dimpling the skin surface with goose bumps. This phe-nomenon is especially dramatic in a scared cat, whose fur ac-tually stands on end to increase its apparent size. The activity of the arrector pili muscles also exerts pressure on the seba-ceous glands surrounding the follicle, causing a small amount of sebum to be released.

ACTIVITY 3

Comparing Hairy and Relatively Hair-Free Skin Microscopically

While thick skin has no hair follicles or sebaceous (oil) glands, thin skin typical of most of the body has both. The scalp, of course, has the highest density of hair follicles.

1. Obtain a prepared slide of the human scalp, and study it carefully under the microscope. Compare your tissue slide to the view shown in Figure 6.6a, and identify as many of the structures diagrammed in Figure 6.1 as possible.

How is this stratified squamous epithelium different from that observed in Exercise 5?

_____

_____

How do these differences relate to the functions of these two similar epithelia?

_____

_____

_____

2. Obtain a prepared slide of hairless skin of the palm or sole (Figure 6.6b). Compare the slide to Figure 6.6a. In what ways does the thick skin of the palm or sole differ from the thin skin of the scalp?

_____

_____

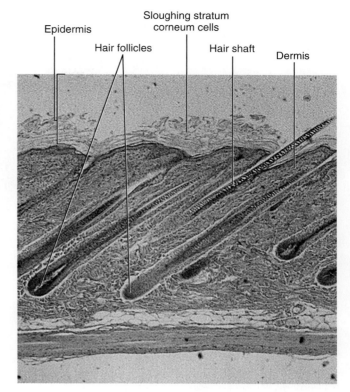

(a)

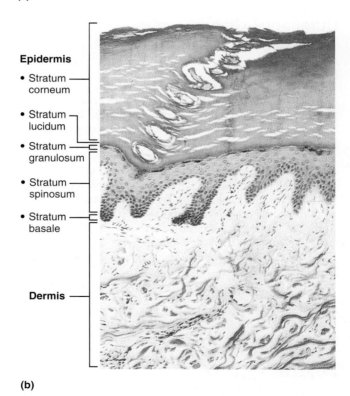

(b)

FIGURE 6.6 Photomicrographs of skin. (a) Thin skin with hairs (34×). **(b)** Thick hairless skin (400×).

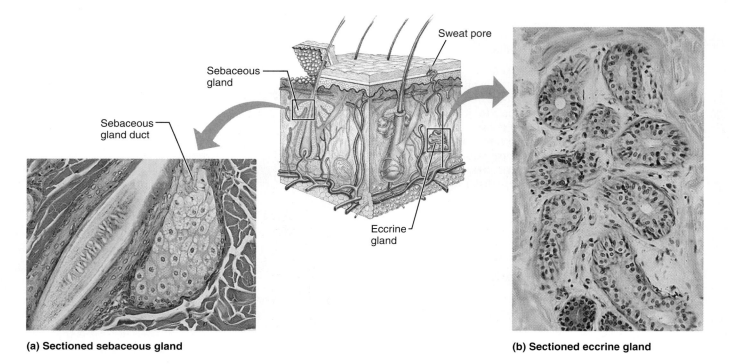

(a) Sectioned sebaceous gland

(b) Sectioned eccrine gland

FIGURE 6.7 **Cutaneous glands.** (**a**) Photomicrograph of a sebaceous gland (160×).
(**b**) Photomicrograph of eccrine sweat gland (250×).

Cutaneous Glands

The cutaneous glands fall primarily into two categories: the sebaceous glands and the sweat glands (Figure 6.1 and Figure 6.7).

Sebaceous (Oil) Glands   The sebaceous glands are found nearly all over the skin, except for the palms of the hands and the soles of the feet. Their ducts usually empty into a hair follicle, but some open directly on the skin surface.

Sebum is the product of sebaceous glands. It is a mixture of oily substances and fragmented cells that acts as a lubricant to keep the skin soft and moist (a natural skin cream) and keeps the hair from becoming brittle. The sebaceous glands become particularly active during puberty when more male hormones (androgens) begin to be produced; thus the skin tends to become oilier during this period of life.

Blackheads are accumulations of dried sebum, bacteria, and melanin from epithelial cells in the oil duct. **Acne** is an active infection of the sebaceous glands. ●

Sweat (Sudoriferous) Glands   These exocrine glands are widely distributed all over the skin. Outlets for the glands are epithelial openings called *pores*. Sweat glands are categorized by the composition of their secretions.

•   **Eccrine glands:** Also called **merocrine sweat glands,** these glands are distributed all over the body. They produce clear perspiration consisting primarily of water, salts (mostly NaCl), and urea. Eccrine sweat glands, under the control of the nervous system, are an important part of the body's heat-regulating apparatus. They secrete perspiration when the external temperature or body temperature is high. When this water-based substance evaporates, it carries excess body heat with it. Thus evaporation of greater amounts of perspiration provides an efficient means of dissipating body heat when the capillary cooling system is not sufficient or is unable to maintain body temperature homeostasis.

•   **Apocrine glands:** Found predominantly in the axillary and genital areas, these glands secrete a milky protein- and fat-rich substance (also containing water, salts, and urea) that is an excellent nutrient medium for the microorganisms typically found on the skin. Because these glands enlarge and recede with the phases of a women's menstrual cycle, the apocrine glands may be analogous to the pheromone-producing scent glands of other animals.

ACTIVITY 4

Differentiating Sebaceous and Sweat Glands Microscopically

Using the slide *thin skin with hairs*, and Figure 6.7 as a guide, identify sebaceous and eccrine sweat glands. What characteristics relating to location or gland structure allow you to differentiate these glands?

_____

_____

_____

Plotting the Distribution of Sweat Glands

1.   Form a hypothesis about the relative distribution of sweat glands on the palm and forearm. Justify your hypothesis.

2.   For this simple experiment you will need two squares of bond paper (each 1 cm × 1 cm), adhesive tape, and a Betadine (iodine) swab *or* Lugol's iodine and a cotton-tipped swab. (The bond paper has been preruled in cm^2—put on disposable gloves and cut along the lines to obtain the required squares.)

3.   Paint an area of the medial aspect of your left palm (avoid the crease lines) and a region of your left forearm with the iodine solution, and allow it to dry thoroughly. The painted area in each case should be slightly larger than the paper squares to be used.

4.   Have your lab partner *securely* tape a square of bond paper over each iodine-painted area, and leave them in place for 20 minutes. (If it is very warm in the laboratory while this test is being conducted, good results may be obtained within 10 to 15 minutes.)

5.   After 20 minutes, remove the paper squares, and count the number of blue-black dots on each square. The presence of a blue-black dot on the paper indicates an active sweat gland. (The iodine in the pore is dissolved in the sweat and reacts chemically with the starch in the bond paper to produce the blue-black color.) Thus "sweat maps" have been produced for the two skin areas.

6.   Which skin area tested has the greater density of sweat glands?

_____

_____

7.   Tape your results (bond paper squares) to a data collection sheet labeled "palm" and "forearm" at the front of the lab. Be sure to put your paper squares in the correct columns on the data sheet.

8.   Once all the data has been collected, review the class results. ▮

Dermography: Fingerprinting

As noted on p. 82, each of us has a unique, genetically determined set of fingerprints. Because of the usefulness of fingerprinting for identifying and apprehending criminals, most people associate this craft solely with criminal investigations. However, civil fingerprints are invaluable in quickly identifying amnesia victims, missing persons, and unknown deceased such as those killed in major disasters.

The friction ridges responsible for fingerprints appear in several patterns, which are clearest when the fingertips are inked and then pressed against white paper. Impressions are also made when perspiration or any foreign material such as blood, dirt, or grease adheres to the ridges and the fingers are then pressed against a smooth, nonabsorbent surface. The three most common patterns are *arches, loops,* and *whorls* (Figure 6.8). The *pattern area* in loops and whorls is the only area of the print used in identification, and it is delineated by

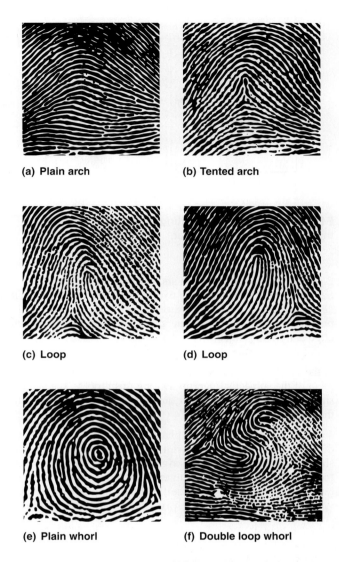

(a) Plain arch   (b) Tented arch

(c) Loop   (d) Loop

(e) Plain whorl   (f) Double loop whorl

FIGURE 6.8 Main types of fingerprint patterns. (**a**–**b**) Arches. (**c**–**d**) Loops. (**e**–**f**) Whorls.

the *type lines*—specifically the two innermost ridges that start parallel, diverge, and/or surround or tend to surround the pattern area.

Taking and Identifying Inked Fingerprints

For this activity, you will be working as a group with your lab partners. Though the equipment for professional fingerprinting is fairly basic, consisting of a glass or metal inking plate, printer's ink (a heavy black paste), ink roller, and standard 8 in. × 8 in. cards, you will be using supplies that are even easier to handle. Each student will prepare two index cards, each bearing his or her thumbprint and index fingerprint of the right hand.

1.   Obtain the following supplies and bring them to your bench: two 4 in. × 6 in. index cards per student, Porelon fingerprint pad or portable inking foils, ink cleaner towelettes, and a magnifying glass.

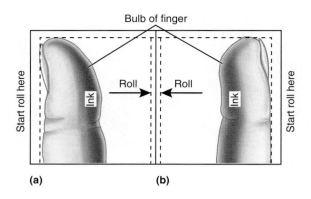

FIGURE 6.9 **Finger printing.** Method of inking (**a**) the thumb and (**b**) the index finger.

2.   The subject should wash and dry the hands. Open the ink pad or peel back the covering over the ink foil, and position it close to the edge of the laboratory bench. The subject should position himself or herself at arm's length from the bench edge and inking object.

3.   A second student, called the *operator,* will stand to the left of the subject and with two hands will hold and direct the movement of the subject's fingertip. During this process, the subject should look away, try to relax, and refrain from trying to help the operator.

4.   The thumbprint is to be placed on the left side of the index card, the index fingerprint on the right. The operator should position the subject's right thumb or index finger on the side of the bulb of the finger in such a way that the area to be inked spans the distance from the fingertip to just beyond the first joint, and then roll the finger lightly across

the inked surface until its bulb faces in the opposite direction. To prevent smearing, the thumb is rolled away from the body midline (from left to right as the subject sees it; see Figure 6.9) and the index finger is rolled toward the body midline (from right to left). The same ink foil can be reused for all the students at the bench; the ink pad is good for thousands of prints. Repeat the procedure (still using the subject's right hand) on the second index card.

5.   If the prints are too light, too dark, or smeary, repeat the procedure.

6.   While subsequent members are making clear prints of their thumb and index finger, those who have completed that activity should clean their inked fingers with a towelette and attempt to classify their own prints as arches, loops, or whorls. Use the magnifying glass as necessary to see ridge details.

7.   When all members at a bench have completed the above steps, they are to write their names on the backs of their index cards, then combine their cards and shuffle them before transferring them to the bench opposite for classification of pattern and identification of prints made by the same individuals.

How difficult was it to classify the prints into one of the three

categories given? _____

Why do you think this is so? _____

Was it easy or difficult to identify the prints made by the same

individual? _____

Why do you think this was so? _____

_____

NAME _____

LAB TIME/DATE _____

The Integumentary System

Basic Structure of the Skin

1. Complete the following statements by writing the appropriate word or phrase on the correspondingly numbered blank:

   The two basic tissues of which the skin is composed are dense irregular connective tissue, which makes up the dermis, and __1__, which forms the epidermis. The tough protective protein found in the epidermal cells is called __2__. The pigments melanin and __3__ contribute to skin color. A localized concentration of melanin is referred to as a __4__.

   1. _____

   2. _____

   3. _____

   4. _____

2. Four protective functions of the skin are:

   a. _____   b. _____

   c. _____   d. _____

3. Using the key choices, choose all responses that apply to the following descriptions.

   Key: a. stratum basale   d. stratum lucidum   g. reticular layer
           b. stratum corneum   e. stratum spinosum   h. epidermis as a whole
           c. stratum granulosum   f. papillary layer   i. dermis as a whole

   _____ 1. translucent cells containing keratin fibrils in thick skin

   _____ 2. dead cells

   _____ 3. dermal layer responsible for fingerprints

   _____ 4. vascular region

   _____ 5. major skin area that produces derivatives (nails and hair)

   _____ 6. epidermal region exhibiting the most rapid cell division

   _____ 7. scalelike dead cells, full of keratin, that constantly slough off

   _____ 8. mitotic cells filled with intermediate filaments

   _____ 9. has abundant elastic and collagenic fibers

   _____ 10. location of melanocytes and Merkel cells

   _____ 11. area where weblike pre-keratin filaments first appear

   _____ 12. region of areolar connective tissue

4. Label the skin structures and areas indicated in the accompanying diagram of thin skin. Then, complete the statements that follow.

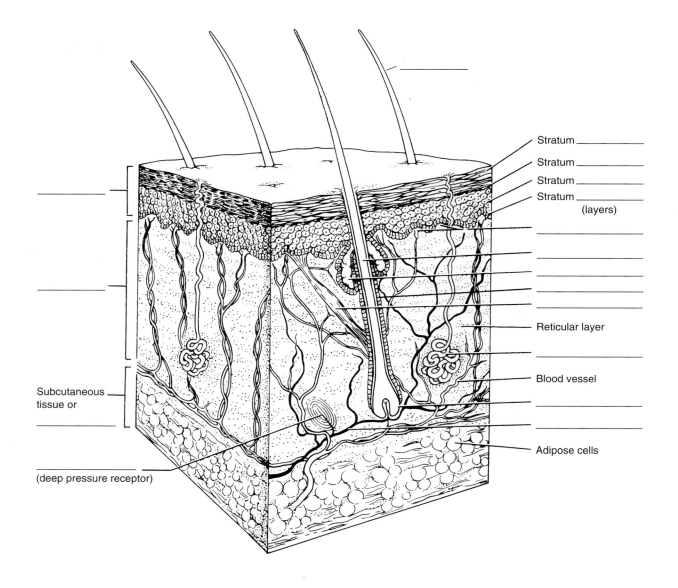

Stratum _____

Stratum _____

Stratum _____

Stratum _____
(layers)

_____

_____

_____

_____

Reticular layer

_____

Blood vessel

_____

_____

Adipose cells

Subcutaneous tissue or _____

_____

_____
(deep pressure receptor)

a. _____ granules extruded from the keratinocytes prevent water loss by diffusion through the epidermis.

b. Fibers in the dermis are produced by _____.

c. Glands that respond to rising androgen levels are the _____ glands.

d. Phagocytic cells that occupy the epidermis are called _____.

e. A unique touch receptor formed from a stratum basale cell and a nerve fiber is a _____.

f. What layer is present in thick skin but not in thin skin? _____

g. What cell-to-cell structures hold the cells of the stratum spinosum tightly together? _____

5. What substance is manufactured in the skin (but is not a secretion) to play a role elsewhere in the body?

_____

6. List the sensory receptors found in the dermis of the skin. _____

_____

_____

7. A nurse tells a doctor that a patient is cyanotic. Define *cyanosis*. _____

What does its presence imply? _____

8. What is a bedsore (decubitus ulcer) ? _____

Why does it occur? _____

_____

Accessory Organs of the Skin

9. Match the key choices with the appropriate descriptions.

Key: a. arrector pili
  b. cutaneous receptors
  c. hair

  d. hair follicle
  e. nail
  f. sebaceous gland

  g. sweat gland—apocrine
  h. sweat gland—eccrine

_____ 1. produces an accumulation of oily material that is known as a blackhead

_____ 2. tiny muscles, attached to hair follicles, that pull the hair upright during fright or cold

_____ 3. perspiration gland with a role in temperature control

_____ 4. sheath formed of both epithelial and connective tissues

_____ 5. less numerous type of perspiration-producing gland; found mainly in the pubic and axillary regions

_____ 6. found everywhere on the body except the palms of hands and soles of feet

_____ 7. primarily dead/keratinized cells

_____ 8. specialized nerve endings that respond to temperature, touch, etc.

_____ 9. its secretion is a lubricant for hair and skin

_____ 10. "sports" a lunula and a cuticle

10. Describe two integumentary system mechanisms that help in regulating body temperature. _____

_____

_____

_____

11. Several structures or skin regions are listed below. Identify each by matching its letter with the appropriate area on the figure.

a. adipose cells

b. dermis

c. epidermis

d. hair follicle

e. hair shaft

f. sloughing stratum corneum cells

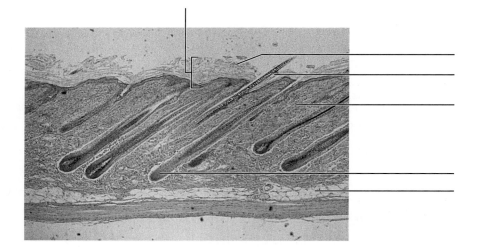

Plotting the Distribution of Sweat Glands

12. With what substance in the bond paper does the iodine painted on the skin react? _____

13. On the basis of class data, which skin area—the forearm or palm of hand—has more sweat glands?

_____

Was this an expected result? _____ Explain. _____

_____

Which other body areas would, if tested, prove to have a high density of sweat glands? _____

_____

14. What organ system controls the activity of the eccrine sweat glands? _____

Dermography: Fingerprinting

15. Why can fingerprints be used to identify individuals?

_____

16. Name the three common fingerprint patterns.

_____, _____, and _____

Classification of Covering and Lining Membranes

M A T E R I A L S

- ☐ Compound microscope
- ☐ Prepared slides of trachea (x.s.), esophagus (x.s.), and small intestine (x.s.)
- ☐ Prepared slide of serous membrane (for example, mesentery artery and vein [x.s.] or small intestine [x.s.])
- ☐ Longitudinally cut fresh beef joint (if available)

AIA   See Appendix B, Exercise 7 for links to A.D.A.M.® Interactive Anatomy.

O B J E C T I V E S

1. To compare the structure and function of the major membrane types.
2. To list the general functions of each membrane type and indicate its location in the body.
3. To recognize by microscopic examination cutaneous, mucous, and serous membranes.

The body membranes, which cover surfaces, line body cavities, and form protective (and often lubricating) sheets around organs, fall into two major categories. These are the so-called *epithelial membranes* and the *synovial membranes.*

Epithelial Membranes

Most of the covering and lining epithelia take part in forming one of the three common varieties of epithelial membranes: cutaneous, mucous, or serous. The term "epithelial membrane" is used in various ways. Here we will define an **epithelial membrane** as a simple organ consisting of an epithelial sheet bound to an underlying layer of connective tissue proper.

The **cutaneous membrane** (Figure 7.1a) is the skin, a dry membrane with a keratinizing epithelium (the epidermis). Since the skin is discussed in some detail in Exercise 6, the mucous and serous membranes will receive our attention here.

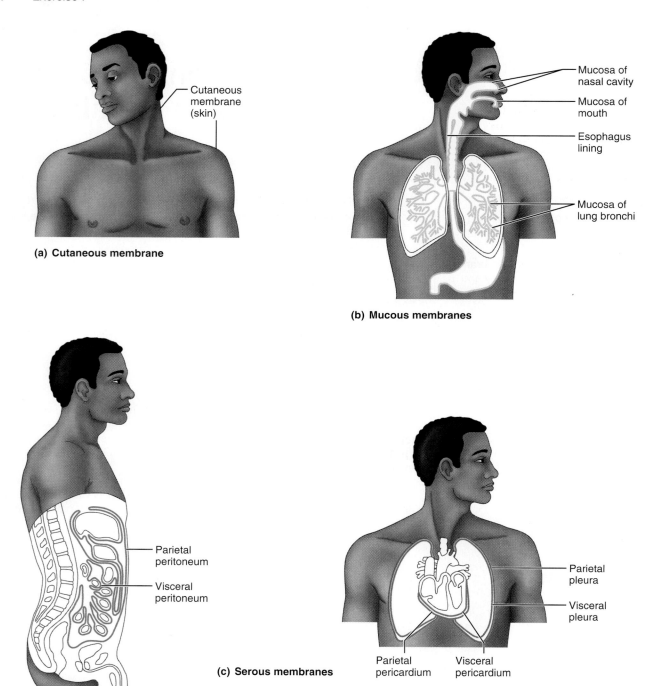

(a) Cutaneous membrane

Cutaneous membrane (skin)

Mucosa of nasal cavity

Mucosa of mouth

Esophagus lining

Mucosa of lung bronchi

(b) Mucous membranes

Parietal peritoneum

Visceral peritoneum

(c) Serous membranes

Parietal pleura

Visceral pleura

Parietal pericardium

Visceral pericardium

FIGURE 7.1 Epithelial membranes. Epithelial membranes are composite membranes with epithelial and connective tissue elements. (**a**) The cutaneous membrane, or skin, covers and protects the body surface. (**b**) Mucous membranes line body cavities (hollow organs) that open to the exterior. (**c**) Serous membranes line the closed ventral cavity of the body. Three examples, the peritonea, pericardia, and pleurae, are illustrated here.

Mucous Membranes

The **mucous membranes (mucosae)*** are composed of epithelial cells resting on a layer of loose connective tissue called the **lamina propria.** They line all body cavities that open to the body exterior—the respiratory, digestive (Figure 7.1b), and urogenital tracts. In most cases mucosae are "wet" membranes, which are continuously bathed by secretions (or,

in the case of urinary mucosa, urine). Although mucous membranes often secrete mucus, this is not a requirement. The mucous membranes of both the digestive and respiratory tracts secrete mucus; that of the urinary tract does not.

*Notice the spelling difference between *mucous,* an adjective describing the membrane type, and *mucus,* a noun indicating the product of glands.

Examining the Microscopic Structure of Mucous Membranes

Using Plates 27, 30, and 33 of the Histology Atlas as guides, examine slides made from cross sections of the trachea, esophagus, and small intestine. Draw the mucosa of each in the appropriate circle, and fully identify each epithelial type. Remember to look for the epithelial cells at the free surface. Also search the epithelial sheets for **goblet cells**—columnar epithelial cells with a large mucus-containing vacuole (goblet) in their apical cytoplasm.

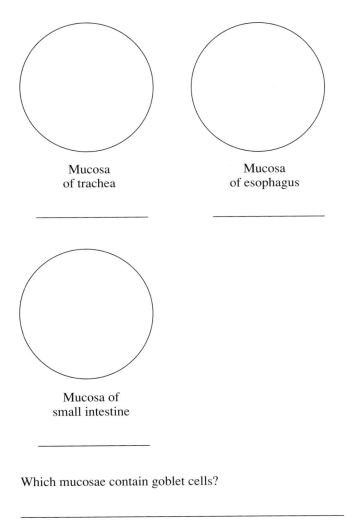

Mucosa
of trachea

Mucosa
of esophagus

_____   _____

Mucosa of
small intestine

_____

Which mucosae contain goblet cells?

_____

Compare and contrast the roles of these three mucous membranes.

_____

_____

_____

_____

Serous Membranes

The **serous membranes (serosae)** are also epithelial membranes (Figure 7.1c). They are composed of a layer of simple squamous epithelium on a scant amount of areolar connective tissue. The serous membranes generally occur in twos and are actually continuous. The *parietal layer* lines a body cavity, and the *visceral layer* covers the outside of the organs in that cavity. In contrast to the mucous membranes, which line open body cavities, the serous membranes line body cavities that are closed to the exterior (with the exception of the female peritoneal cavity and the dorsal body cavity). These double-layered serosae secrete a thin fluid (serous fluid) that lubricates the organs and body walls and thus reduces friction as the organs slide across one another and against the body cavity walls. Inflammation of these membranes typically results in less serous fluid being produced and excruciating pain.

A serous membrane also lines the interior of blood vessels (endothelium) and the heart (endocardium). In capillaries, the entire wall is composed of a serosa that serves as a selectively permeable membrane between the blood and the tissue fluid of the body.

Examining the Microscopic Structure of a Serous Membrane

Use Plate 33 of the Histology Atlas as a guide to examine a prepared slide of a serous membrane and diagram it in the circle provided here.

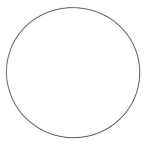

What are the specific names of the serous membranes covering the heart and lining the cavity in which it resides (respectively)?

_____ and _____

The abdominal viscera and visceral cavity (respectively)?

_____ and _____

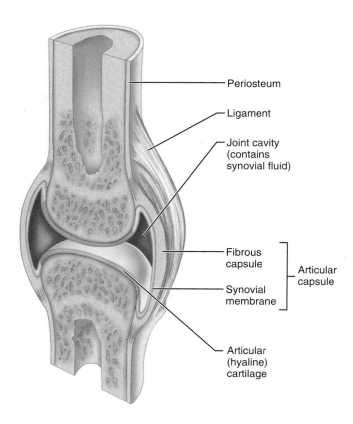

Periosteum

Ligament

Joint cavity
(contains
synovial fluid)

Fibrous
capsule

Articular
capsule

Synovial
membrane

Articular
(hyaline)
cartilage

FIGURE 7.2 General structure of a synovial joint. The joint cavity is lined with a synovial membrane, derived solely from connective tissue.

Synovial Membranes

Synovial membranes are composed entirely of connective tissue. Unlike mucous and serous membranes, they contain no epithelial cells. These membranes line the cavities surrounding the joints, providing a smooth surface and secreting a lubricating fluid. They also line smaller sacs of connective tissue (bursae and tendon sheaths), which cushion structures moving against each other, as during muscle activity. Figure 7.2 illustrates the position of a synovial membrane in the joint cavity.

ACTIVITY 3

Examining the Gross Structure of a Synovial Membrane

If a freshly sawed beef joint is available, visually examine the interior surface of the joint capsule to observe the smooth texture of the synovial membrane. A more detailed study of synovial membranes follows in Exercise 12. ■

NAME ______________________________

LAB TIME/DATE ______________________

REVIEW SHEET

EXERCISE 7

Classification of Covering and Lining Membranes

1. Complete the following chart.

Membrane	Tissue types: membrane composition (epithelial/connective)	Common locations	General functions
cutaneous			
mucous			
serous			
synovial			

2. Respond to the following statements by choosing an answer from the key.

Key: a. cutaneous b. mucous c. serous d. synovial

__________________ 1. membrane type in joints, bursae, and tendon sheaths

__________________ 2. epithelium of this membrane is always simple squamous epithelium

__________________, __________________ 3. membrane types *not* found in the ventral body cavity

__________________ 4. the only membrane type in which goblet cells are found

__________________ 5. the dry membrane with keratinizing epithelium

__________________ 6. "wet" membranes

__________________ 7. adapted for absorption and secretion

__________________ 8. has parietal and visceral layers

3. Using terms from the key above the figure, specifically identify the different types of body membranes (cutaneous, mucous, serous, and synovial) by writing in the terms at the end of the appropriate leader lines.

Key: a. cutaneous membrane (skin)
   b. esophageal mucosa
   c. gastric mucosa
   d. mucosa of lung bronchi
   e. nasal mucosa
   f. oral mucosa

   g. parietal pericardium
   h. parietal pleura
   i. synovial membrane of joint
   j. tracheal mucosa
   k. visceral pericardium
   l. visceral pleura

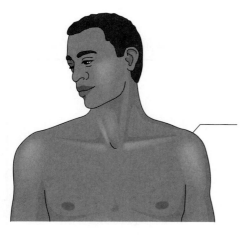
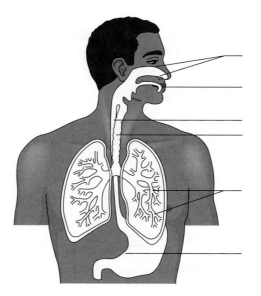
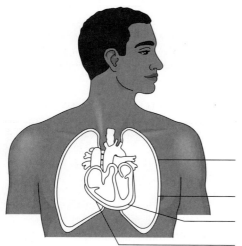
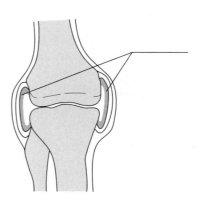

4. Knowing that *-itis* is a suffix meaning "inflammation of," what do peritonitis, pleurisy, and pericarditis (pathological conditions) have in common?

_____

5. Why are these conditions accompanied by a great deal of pain? _____

_____

Overview of the Skeleton: Classification and Structure of Bones and Cartilages

M A T E R I A L S

☐ Disarticulated bones (identified by number) that demonstrate classic examples of the four bone classifications (long, short, flat, and irregular)

☐ Long bone sawed longitudinally (beef bone from a slaughterhouse, if possible, or prepared laboratory specimen)

☐ Disposable gloves

☐ Long bone soaked in 10% hydrochloric acid (HCl) or vinegar until flexible

☐ Long bone baked at 250°F for more than 2 hours

☐ Compound microscope

☐ Prepared slide of ground bone (x.s.)

☐ Three-dimensional model of microscopic structure of compact bone

☐ Prepared slide of a developing long bone undergoing endochondral ossification

☐ Articulated skeleton

O B J E C T I V E S

1. To list five functions of the skeletal system.
2. To identify the four main groups of bones.
3. To identify surface bone markings and functions.
4. To identify the major anatomical areas on a longitudinally cut long bone (or diagram of one).
5. To identify the major regions and structures of an osteon in a histologic specimen of compact bone (or diagram of one).
6. To explain the role of the inorganic salts and organic matrix in providing flexibility and hardness to bone.
7. To locate and identify the three major types of skeletal cartilages.

The **skeleton,** the body's framework, is constructed of two of the most supportive tissues found in the human body—cartilage and bone. In embryos, the skeleton is predominantly composed of hyaline cartilage, but in the adult, most of the cartilage is replaced by more rigid bone. Cartilage persists only in such isolated areas as the external ear, bridge of the nose, larynx, trachea, joints, and parts of the rib cage (see Figure 8.5, p. 106).

Besides supporting and protecting the body as an internal framework, the skeleton provides a system of levers with which the skeletal muscles work to move the body. In addition, the bones store lipids and many minerals (most importantly calcium). Finally, the red marrow cavities of bones provide a site for hematopoiesis (blood cell formation).

The skeleton is made up of bones that are connected at *joints,* or *articulations.* The skeleton is subdivided into two divisions: the **axial skeleton** (those bones that lie around the body's center of gravity) and the **appendicular skeleton** (bones of the limbs, or appendages) (Figure 8.1).

Before beginning your study of the skeleton, imagine for a moment that your bones have turned to putty. What if you were running when this metamorphosis took place? Now imagine your bones forming a continuous metal framework within your body, somewhat like a network of plumbing pipes. What problems could you envision with this arrangement? These images should help you understand how well the skeletal system provides support and protection, as well as facilitating movement.

Classification of Bones

The 206 bones of the adult skeleton are composed of two basic kinds of osseous tissue that differ in their texture. **Compact bone** looks smooth and homogeneous; **spongy** (or *cancellous*) **bone** is composed of small *trabeculae* (bars) of bone and lots of open space.

Bones may be classified further on the basis of their relative gross anatomy into four groups: long, short, flat, and irregular bones.

Long bones, such as the femur and bones of the fingers (phalanges) (Figure 8.1), are much longer than they are wide, generally consisting of a shaft with heads at either end. Long bones are composed predominantly of compact bone. **Short**

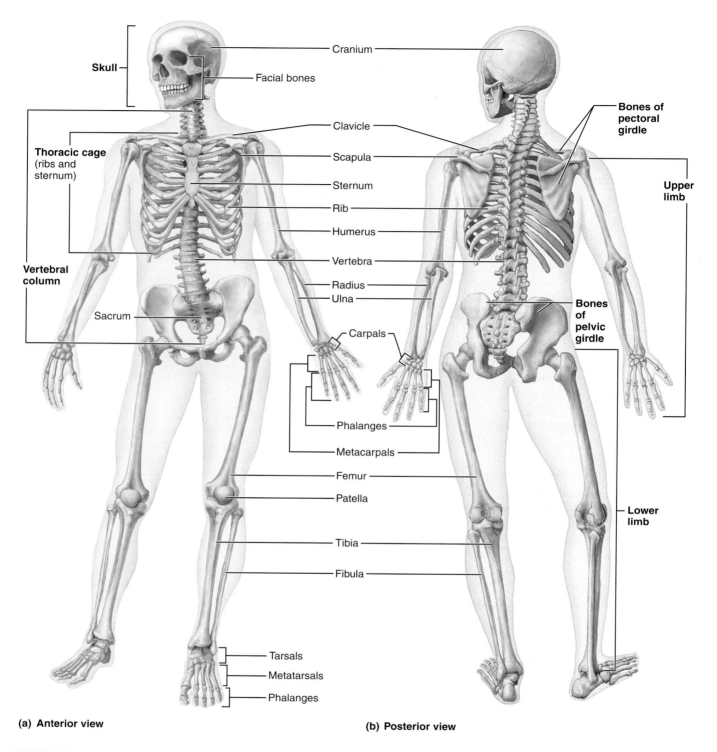

(a) **Anterior view**

(b) **Posterior view**

FIGURE 8.1 The human skeleton. The bones of the axial skeleton are colored green to distinguish them from the bones of the appendicular skeleton.

bones are typically cube-shaped, and they contain more spongy bone than compact bone. The tarsals and carpals in Figure 8.1 are examples.

Flat bones are generally thin, with two waferlike layers of compact bone sandwiching a layer of spongy bone between them. Although the name "flat bone" implies a structure that is level or horizontal, many flat bones are curved (for example, the bones of the skull). Bones that do not fall into one of the preceding categories are classified

as **irregular bones.** The vertebrae are irregular bones (see Figure 8.1).

Some anatomists also recognize two other subcategories of bones. **Sesamoid bones** are special types of short bones formed in tendons. The patellas (kneecaps) are sesamoid bones. **Wormian** or **sutural bones** are tiny bones between cranial bones. Except for the patellas, the sesamoid and Wormian bones are not included in the bone count of 206 because they vary in number and location in different individuals.

TABLE 8.1	Bone Markings	
Name of bone marking	Description	Illustration

Projections That Are Sites of Muscle and Ligament Attachment

Tuberosity (too"be-ros'ĭ-te)	Large rounded projection; may be roughened	
Crest	Narrow ridge of bone; usually prominent	
Trochanter (tro-kan'ter)	Very large, blunt, irregularly shaped process (the only examples are on the femur)	
Line	Narrow ridge of bone; less prominent than a crest	
Tubercle (too'ber-kl)	Small rounded projection or process	
Epicondyle (ep"ĭ-kon'dīl)	Raised area on or above a condyle	
Spine	Sharp, slender, often pointed projection	
Process	Any bony prominence	

Iliac crest

Trochanters — Intertrochanteri line

Ischial spine

Coxal bone — Ischial tuberosity

Vertebra

Femur of thigh

Adductor tubercle

Medial epicondyle

Spinous process

Surfaces That Form Joints

Head	Bony expansion carried on a narrow neck	
Facet	Smooth, nearly flat articular surface	
Condyle (kon'dīl)	Rounded articular projection, often articulates with a corresponding fossa	
Ramus (ra'mus)	Armlike bar of bone	

Head

Facets

Condyle

Ramus

Rib

Mandible

Depressions and Openings

For passage of vessels and nerves

Foramen (fo-ra'men)	Round or oval opening through a bone	
Groove	Furrow	
Fissure	Narrow, slitlike opening	
Notch	Indentation at the edge of a structure	

Others

Fossa (fos'ah)	Shallow basinlike depression in a bone, often serving as an articular surface	
Meatus (me-a'tus)	Canal-like passageway	
Sinus	Bone cavity, filled with air and lined with mucous membrane	

Meatus

Fossa

Notch

Groove

Sinus

Inferior orbital fissure

Foramen

Skull

Bone Markings

Even a casual observation of the bones will reveal that bone surfaces are not featureless smooth areas but are scarred with an array of bumps, holes, and ridges. These **bone markings** reveal where bones form joints with other bones, where muscles, tendons, and ligaments were attached, and where blood vessels and nerves passed. Bone markings fall into two categories: projections, or processes that grow out from the bone and serve as sites of muscle attachment or help form joints; and depressions or cavities, indentations or openings in the bone that often serve as conduits for nerves and blood vessels. The bone markings are summarized in Table 8.1.

ACTIVITY 1

Examining and Classifying Bones

Examine the isolated (disarticulated) bones on display to find specific examples of the bone markings described in Table 8.1. Then classify each of the bones into one of the four anatomical groups by recording its number in the accompanying chart. ▪

Long	Short	Flat	Irregular

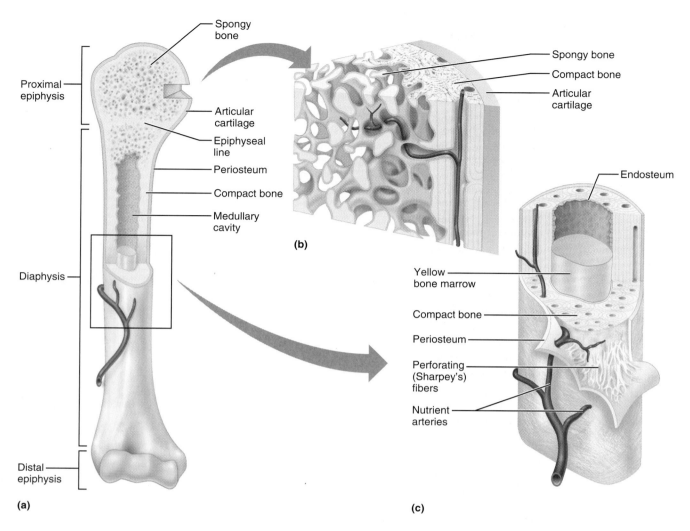

FIGURE 8.2 The structure of a long bone (humerus of the arm). (**a**) Anterior view with longitudinal section cut away at the proximal end. (**b**) Pie-shaped, three-dimensional view of spongy bone and compact bone of the epiphysis. (**c**) Cross section of diaphysis (shaft). Note that the external surface of the diaphysis is covered by a periosteum, but the articular surface of the epiphysis is covered with hyaline cartilage.

Gross Anatomy of the Typical Long Bone

ACTIVITY 2

Examining a Long Bone

1. Obtain a long bone that has been sawed along its longitudinal axis. If a cleaned dry bone is provided, no special preparations need be made.

! Note: If the bone supplied is a fresh beef bone, don disposable gloves before beginning your observations.

With the help of Figure 8.2, identify the **diaphysis** or shaft. Observe its smooth surface, which is composed of compact bone. If you are using a fresh specimen, carefully pull away the **periosteum,** or fibrous membrane covering, to view the bone surface. Notice that many fibers of the periosteum penetrate into the bone. These fibers are called **perforating**

(Sharpey's) fibers. Blood vessels and nerves travel through the periosteum and invade the bone. *Osteoblasts* (bone-forming cells) and *osteoclasts* (bone-destroying cells) are found on the inner, or osteogenic, layer of the periosteum.

2. Now inspect the **epiphysis,** the end of the long bone. Notice that it is composed of a thin layer of compact bone that encloses spongy bone.

3. Identify the **articular cartilage,** which covers the epiphyseal surface in place of the periosteum. Because it is composed of glassy hyaline cartilage, it provides a smooth surface to prevent friction at joint surfaces.

4. If the animal was still young and growing, you will be able to see the **epiphyseal plate,** a thin area of hyaline cartilage that provides for longitudinal growth of the bone during youth. Once the long bone has stopped growing, these areas are replaced with bone and appear as thin, barely discernible remnants—the **epiphyseal lines.**

5. In an adult animal, the central cavity of the shaft (*medullary cavity*) is essentially a storage region for adipose

tissue, or **yellow marrow.** In the infant, this area is involved in forming blood cells, and so **red marrow** is found in the marrow cavities. In adult bones, the red marrow is confined to the interior of the epiphyses, where it occupies the spaces between the trabeculae of spongy bone.

6.   If you are examining a fresh bone, look carefully to see if you can distinguish the delicate **endosteum** lining the shaft. The endosteum also covers the trabeculae of spongy bone and lines the canals of compact bone. Like the periosteum, the endosteum contains both osteoblasts and osteoclasts. As the bone grows in diameter on its external surface, it is constantly being broken down on its inner surface. Thus the thickness of the compact bone layer composing the shaft remains relatively constant.

7.   If you have been working with a fresh bone specimen, return it to the appropriate area and properly dispose of your gloves, as designated by your instructor. Wash your hands before continuing on to the microscope study.

Longitudinal bone growth at epiphyseal plates (growth plates) follows a predictable sequence and provides a reliable indicator of the age of children exhibiting normal growth. In cases in which problems of long-bone growth are suspected (for example, pituitary dwarfism), X rays are taken to view the width of the growth plates. An abnormally thin epiphyseal plate indicates growth retardation. ●

Chemical Composition of Bone

Bone is one of the hardest materials in the body. Although relatively light, bone has a remarkable ability to resist tension and shear forces that continually act on it. An engineer would tell you that a cylinder (like a long bone) is one of the strongest structures for its mass. Thus nature has given us an extremely strong, exceptionally simple (almost crude), and flexible supporting system without sacrificing mobility.

The hardness of bone is due to the inorganic calcium salts deposited in its ground substance. Its flexibility comes from the organic elements of the matrix, particularly the collagen fibers.

ACTIVITY 3

Examining the Effects of Heat and Hydrochloric Acid on Bones

Obtain a bone sample that has been soaked in hydrochloric acid (HCl) (or in vinegar) and one that has been baked. Heating removes the organic part of bone, whereas acid dissolves out the minerals. Do the treated bones retain the structure of untreated specimens?

_____

Gently apply pressure to each bone sample. What happens to the heated bone?

_____

What happens to the bone treated with acid?

_____

What does the acid appear to remove from the bone?

_____

What does baking appear to do to the bone?

_____

_____

In rickets, the bones are not properly calcified. Which of the demonstration specimens would more closely resemble the bones of a child with rickets?

_____

Microscopic Structure of Compact Bone

As you have seen, spongy bone has a spiky, open-work appearance, resulting from the arrangement of the **trabeculae** that compose it, whereas compact bone appears to be dense and homogeneous. However, microscopic examination of compact bone reveals that it is riddled with passageways carrying blood vessels, nerves, and lymphatic vessels that provide the living bone cells with needed substances and a way to eliminate wastes (see Figure 8.3). Indeed, bone histology is much easier to understand when you recognize that bone tissue is organized around its blood supply.

ACTIVITY 4

Examining the Microscopic Structure of Compact Bone

1.   Obtain a prepared slide of ground bone and examine it under low power. Using Figure 8.3 as a guide, focus on a central canal. The **central (Haversian) canal** runs parallel to the long axis of the bone and carries blood vessels, nerves, and lymphatic vessels through the bony matrix. Identify the **osteocytes** (mature bone cells) in **lacunae** (chambers), which are arranged in concentric circles (_concentric lamellae_) around the central canal. Because bone remodeling is going on all the time, you will also see some _interstitial lamellae,_ remnants of _circumferential lamellae_ (those at the circumference of the bony shaft) that have been broken down (Figure 8.3c).

A central canal and all the concentric lamellae surrounding it are referred to as an **osteon, or Haversian system.** Also identify **canaliculi,** tiny canals radiating outward from a central canal to the lacunae of the first lamella and then from lamella to lamella. The canaliculi form a dense transportation network through the hard bone matrix, connecting all the living cells of the osteon to the nutrient supply. The canaliculi allow each cell to take what it needs for nourishment and to pass along the excess to the next osteocyte. You may need a higher-power magnification to see the fine canaliculi.

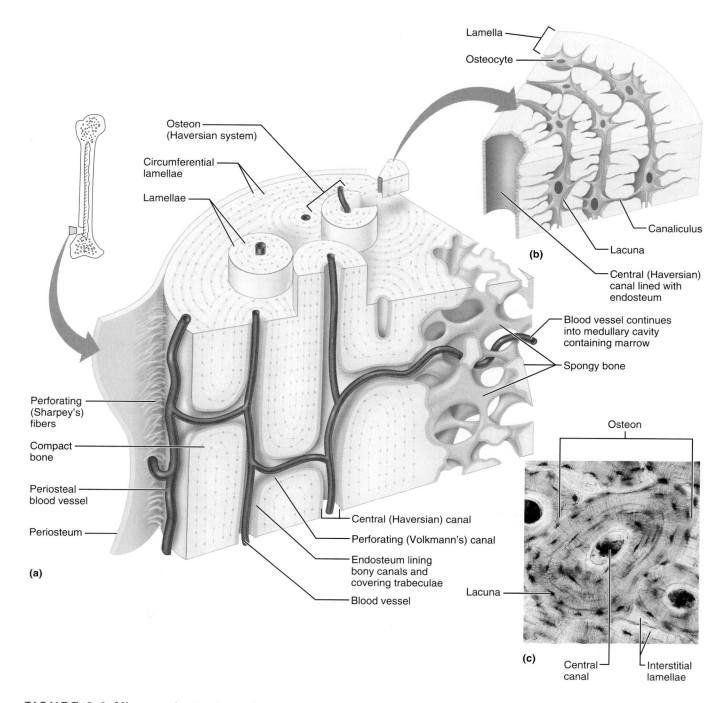

FIGURE 8.3 Microscopic structure of compact bone. (a) Diagrammatic view of a pie-shaped segment of compact bone, illustrating its structural units (osteons). (b) Higher magnification view of a portion of one osteon. Note the position of osteocytes in lacunae. (c) Photomicrograph of a cross-sectional view of an osteon (140×).

2. Also note the **perforating (Volkmann's) canals** in Figure 8.3. These canals run into the compact bone and marrow cavity from the periosteum, at right angles to the shaft. With the central canals, the perforating canals complete the communication pathway between the bone interior and its external surface.

3. If a model of bone histology is available, identify the same structures on the model.

Ossification: Bone Formation and Growth in Length

Except for the collarbones (clavicles), all bones of the body inferior to the skull form in the embryo by the process of **endochondral ossification,** which uses hyaline cartilage "bones" as patterns for bone formation. The major events of this process, which begins in the (primary ossification) center of the shaft of a developing long bone, are:

- The fibrous membrane covering the hyaline cartilage model is vascularized and converted to a periosteum.

- Osteoblasts at the inner surface of the periosteum secrete bone matrix around the hyaline cartilage model, forming a bone collar.

- Cartilage in the shaft center calcifies and then hollows out, forming an internal cavity.

A *periosteal bud* (blood vessels, nerves, red marrow elements, osteoblasts, and osteoclasts) invades the cavity, which becomes the medullary cavity.

This process proceeds in both directions from the *primary ossification center*. The medullary cavity gets larger and larger as chondroblasts lay down new cartilage matrix on the epiphyseal face of the epiphyseal plate, and it is eroded away and replaced by bony spicules on the side facing the medullary cavity. This process continues until late adolescence when the entire epiphyseal plate is replaced by bone.

ACTIVITY 5

Examination of the Osteogenic Epiphyseal Plate

Obtain a slide depicting endochondral ossification (cartilage bone formation) and bring it to your bench to examine under the microscope. Using Figure 8.4 as a reference, identify the hypertrophic, calcification, and ossification zones of the epiphyseal plate. Then, also identify the area of resting cartilage cells distal to the growth zone, some hypertrophied chondrocytes, bony spicules, the periosteal bone collar, and the medullary cavity. ▬

Cartilages of the Skeleton

Location and Basic Structure

As mentioned earlier, cartilaginous regions of the skeleton have a fairly limited distribution in adults (Figure 8.5). The most important of these skeletal cartilages are (1) **articular cartilages,** which cover the bone ends at movable joints; (2) **costal cartilages,** found connecting the ribs to the sternum (breastbone); (3) **laryngeal cartilages,** which largely construct the larynx (voice box); (4) **tracheal** and **bronchial cartilages,** which reinforce other passageways of the respiratory system; (5) **nasal cartilages,** which support the external nose; (6) **intervertebral discs,** which separate and cushion bones of the spine (vertebrae); and (7) the cartilage supporting the external ear.

The skeletal cartilages consist of some variety of *cartilage tissue,* which typically consists primarily of water and is fairly resilient. Cartilage tissues are also distinguished by the fact that they contain no nerves or blood vessels. Like bones, each cartilage is surrounded by a covering of dense connective tissue, called a *perichondrium* (rather than a periosteum). The perichondrium acts like a girdle to resist distortion of the cartilage when the cartilage is subjected to pressure. It also plays a role in cartilage growth and repair.

Classification of Cartilage

The skeletal cartilages have representatives from each of the three cartilage tissue types—hyaline, elastic, and fibrocarti-

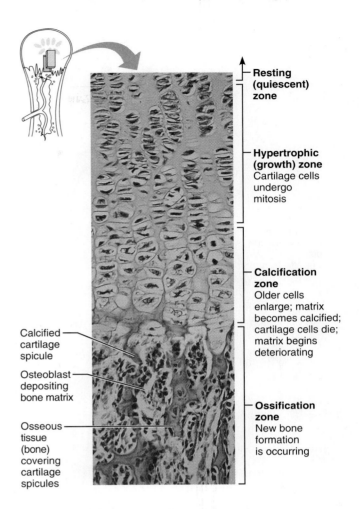

Resting (quiescent) zone

Hypertrophic (growth) zone Cartilage cells undergo mitosis

Calcification zone Older cells enlarge; matrix becomes calcified; cartilage cells die; matrix begins deteriorating

Ossification zone New bone formation is occurring

Calcified cartilage spicule

Osteoblast depositing bone matrix

Osseous tissue (bone) covering cartilage spicules

FIGURE 8.4 Endochondral ossification in a developing long bone.

lage. Since you have already studied cartilage tissues (Exercise 5), we will only briefly discuss that information here.

Hyaline Cartilage   **Hyaline cartilage** looks like frosted glass when viewed by the unaided eye. As easily seen in Figure 8.5, most skeletal cartilages are composed of hyaline cartilage. Hyaline cartilage provides sturdy support with some resilience or "give." Review Figure 5.5g, p. 64.

Elastic Cartilage   **Elastic cartilage** can be envisioned as "hyaline cartilage with more elastic fibers." Consequently, it is much more flexible than hyaline cartilage, and it tolerates repeated bending better. Essentially, only the cartilages of the external ear and the epiglottis (which flops over and covers the larynx when we swallow) are made of elastic cartilage. Review Figure 5.5h, p. 65.

Fibrocartilage   Fibrocartilage consists of rows of chondrocytes alternating with rows of thick collagen fibers. This tissue looks like a cartilage-dense regular connective tissue hybrid. Fibrocartilage has great tensile strength and can withstand heavy compression. Hence, its use to construct the intervertebral discs and the cartilages within the knee joint makes a lot of sense (see Figure 8.5). Review Figure 5.5i, p. 65. ▬

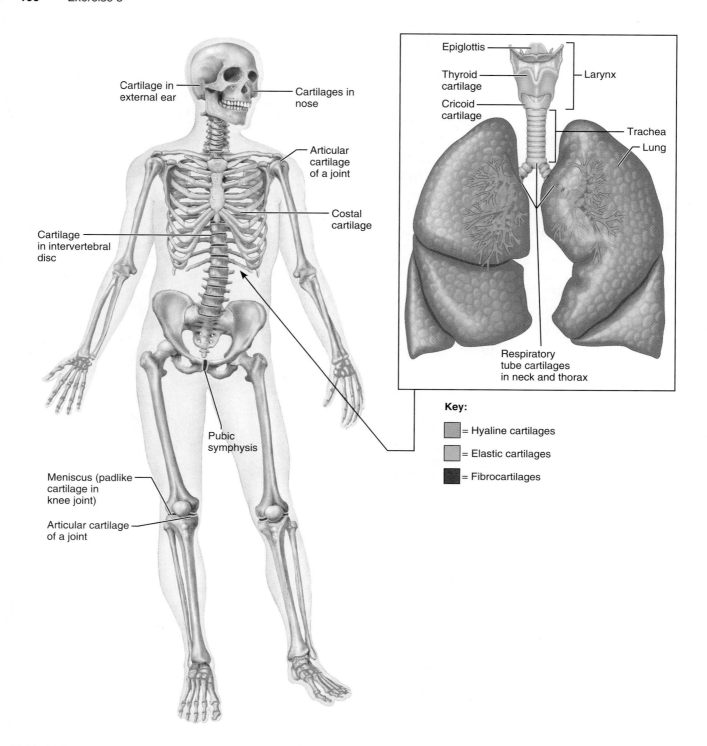

FIGURE 8.5 Cartilages in the adult skeleton and body. The cartilages that support the respiratory tubes and larynx are shown separately at the upper right.

NAME _____

LAB TIME/DATE _____

Overview of the Skeleton: Classification and Structure of Bones and Cartilages

Bone Markings

1. Match the terms in column B with the appropriate description in column A.

Column A

_____   1. sharp, slender process*

_____   2. small rounded projection*

_____   3. narrow ridge of bone*

_____   4. large rounded projection*

_____   5. structure supported on neck†

_____   6. armlike projection†

_____   7. rounded, convex projection†

_____   8. narrow opening‡

_____   9. canal-like structure‡

_____   10. round or oval opening through a bone‡

_____   11. shallow depression†

_____   12. air-filled cavity

_____   13. large, irregularly shaped projection*

_____   14. raised area on or above a condyle*

_____   15. projection or prominence

Column B

a.   condyle

b.   crest

c.   epicondyle

d.   fissure

e.   foramen

f.   fossa

g.   head

h.   meatus

i.   process

j.   ramus

k.   sinus

l.   spine

m.   trochanter

n.   tubercle

o.   tuberosity

* a site of muscle attachment
† takes part in joint formation
‡ a passageway for nerves or blood vessels

Classification of Bones

2. The four major anatomical classifications of bones are long, short, flat, and irregular. Which category has the least amount

   of spongy bone relative to its total volume? _____

3. Place the name of each labeled bone in Figure 8.1, p. 100, into the appropriate column of the chart below. Use appropriate references as necessary.

Long	Short	Flat	Irregular

Gross Anatomy of the Typical Long Bone

4. Use the terms below to identify the structures marked by leader lines and braces in the diagrams (some terms are used more than once).

Key: a. articular cartilage
b. compact bone
c. diaphysis
d. endosteum

e. epiphyseal line
f. epiphysis
g. medullary cavity
h. nutrient artery

i. periosteum
j. red marrow cavity
k. trabeculae of spongy bone
l. yellow marrow

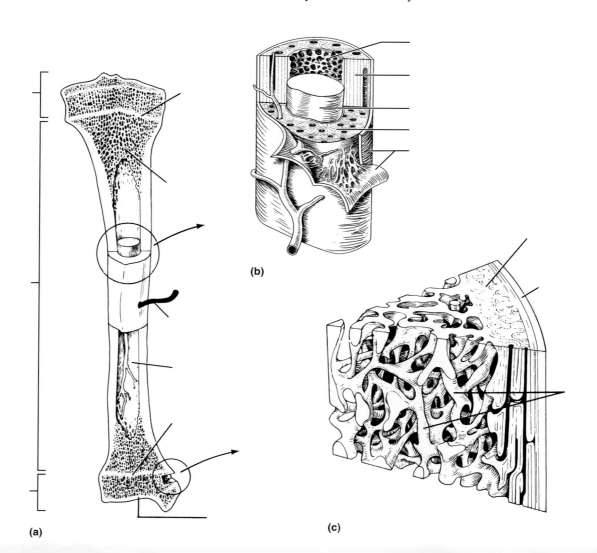

(a)

(b)

(c)

5. Match the letters of terms in question 4 with the information below.

_____ 1.   contains spongy bone in adults

_____ 2.   made of compact bone

_____ 3.   site of blood cell formation

_____, _____4.   major submembranous site of osteoclasts

_____ 5.   scientific term for bone shaft

_____ 6.   contains fat in adult bones

_____ 7.   growth plate remnant

_____ 8.   major submembranous site of osteoblasts

6. What differences between compact and spongy bone can be seen with the naked eye? _____

_____

7. What is the function of the periosteum? _____

Microscopic Structure of Compact Bone

8. Trace the route taken by nutrients through a bone, starting with the periosteum and ending with an osteocyte in a lacuna.

Periosteum $\xrightarrow{}$ _____ $\xrightarrow{}$ _____

_____ $\xrightarrow{}$ _____ $\xrightarrow{}$ ___ osteocyte

9. Several descriptions of bone structure are given below. Identify the structure involved by choosing the appropriate term from the key and placing its letter in the blank. Then, on the photomicrograph of bone on the right, identify all structures named in the key and bracket an osteon.

Key: a.   canaliculi   b.   central canal   c.   concentric lamellae   d.   lacunae   e.   matrix

_____ 1.   layers of bony matrix around a central canal

_____ 2.   site of osteocytes

_____ 3.   longitudinal canal carrying blood vessels, lymphatics, and nerves

_____ 4.   minute canals connecting osteocytes of an osteon

_____ 5.   inorganic salts deposited in organic ground substance

Ossification: Bone Formation and Growth in Length

10. Compare and contrast events occurring on the epiphyseal and diaphyseal faces of the epiphyseal plate.

Epiphyseal face: _____

Diaphyseal face: _____

_____

Chemical Composition of Bone

11. What is the function of the organic matrix in bone? _____

12. Name the important organic bone components. _____

13. Calcium salts form the bulk of the inorganic material in bone. What is the function of the calcium salts?

_____

14. Baking removes _____ from bone. Soaking bone in acid removes _____.

Cartilages of the Skeleton

15. Using the key choices, identify each type of cartilage described (in terms of its body location or function) below.

Key: a. elastic   b. fibrocartilage   c. hyaline

_____ 1. supports the external ear   _____ 6. meniscus in a knee joint

_____ 2. between the vertebrae   _____ 7. connects the ribs to the sternum

_____ 3. forms the walls of the   _____ 8. most effective at resisting
                              voice box (larynx)   compression

_____ 4. the epiglottis   _____ 9. most springy and flexible

_____ 5. articular cartilages   _____ 10. most abundant

16. Identify the two types of cartilage diagrammed below. On each, label the *chondrocytes in lacunae* and the *matrix*.

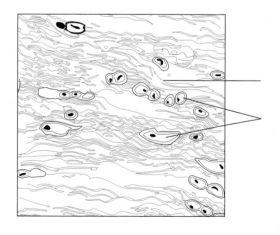

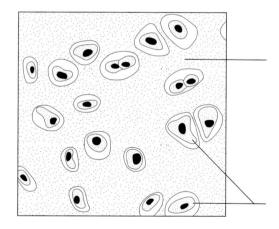

(a) _____   **(b)** _____

The Axial Skeleton

MATERIALS

☐ Intact skull and Beauchene skull

☐ X rays of individuals with scoliosis, lordosis, and kyphosis (if available)

☐ Articulated skeleton, articulated vertebral column, removable intervertebral discs

☐ Isolated cervical, thoracic, and lumbar vertebrae, sacrum, and coccyx

AIA See Appendix B, Exercise 9 for links to A.D.A.M.® Interactive Anatomy.

OBJECTIVES

1. To identify the three bone groups composing the axial skeleton.
2. To identify the bones composing the axial skeleton, either by examining isolated bones or by pointing them out on an articulated skeleton or a skull, and to name the important bone markings on each.
3. To distinguish the different types of vertebrae.
4. To discuss the importance of intervertebral discs and spinal curvatures.
5. To distinguish three abnormal spinal curvatures.

The **axial skeleton** (the green portion of Figure 8.1 on p. 100) can be divided into three parts: the skull, the vertebral column, and the thoracic cage.

The Skull

The **skull** is composed of two sets of bones. Those of the **cranium** enclose and protect the fragile brain tissue. The **facial bones** present the eyes in an anterior position and form the base for the facial muscles, which make it possible for us to present our feelings to the world. All but one of the bones of the skull are joined by interlocking joints called *sutures*. The mandible, or lower jawbone, is attached to the rest of the skull by a freely movable joint.

ACTIVITY 1

Identifying the Bones of the Skull

The bones of the skull, shown in Figures 9.1 through 9.7, are described below. As you read through this material, identify each bone on an intact (and/or Beauchene*) skull.

Note: Important bone markings are listed beneath the bones on which they appear. The color-coded dot before each bone name corresponds to the bone color in the figures. ▮▮

The Cranium

The cranium may be divided into two major areas for study—the **cranial vault** or **calvaria,** forming the superior, lateral, and posterior walls of the skull, and the **cranial floor** or **base,** forming the skull bottom. Internally, the cranial floor has three distinct concavities, the **anterior, middle,** and **posterior cranial fossae** (see Figure 9.3). The brain sits in these fossae, completely enclosed by the cranial vault.

Eight large flat bones construct the cranium. *With the exception of two paired bones (the parietals and the temporals), all are single bones.* Sometimes the six ossicles of the middle ear are also considered part of the cranium. Because the ossicles are functionally part of the hearing apparatus, their consideration is deferred to Exercise 19, Special Senses: Hearing and Equilibrium.

● *Frontal Bone*   See Figures 9.1, 9.3, and 9.6. Anterior portion of cranium; forms the forehead, superior part of the orbit, and floor of anterior cranial fossa.

*Two views (Plates A and B) of a Beauchene skull are provided in the Human Anatomy Atlas.

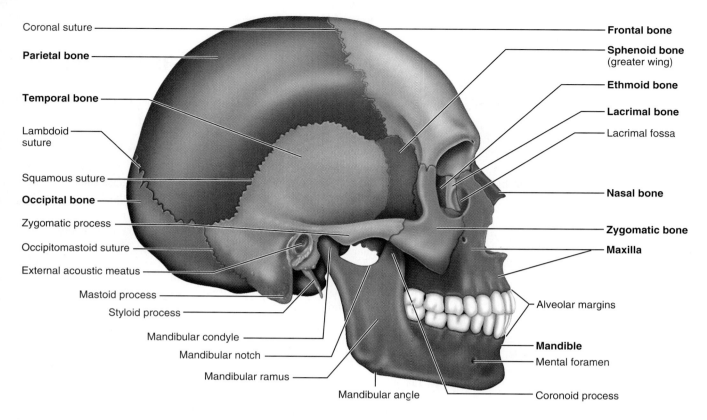

FIGURE 9.1 External anatomy of the right lateral aspect of the skull.

Supraorbital foramen (notch): Opening above each orbit allowing blood vessels and nerves to pass.

Glabella: Smooth area between the eyes.

● *Parietal Bone* See Figures 9.1 and 9.6. Posterolateral to the frontal bone, forming sides of cranium.

Sagittal suture: Midline articulation point of the two parietal bones.

Coronal suture: Point of articulation of parietals with frontal bone.

● *Temporal Bone* See Figures 9.1 through 9.3 and 9.6. Inferior to parietal bone on lateral skull. The temporals can be divided into four major parts: the **squamous region** abuts the parietals; the **tympanic region** surrounds the external ear opening; the **mastoid region** is the area posterior to the ear; and the **petrous part** forms the lateral portion of the skull base.

Important markings associated with the flaring squamous region (Figures 9.1 and 9.2) include:

Squamous suture: Point of articulation of the temporal bone with the parietal bone.

Zygomatic process: A bridgelike projection joining the zygomatic bone (cheekbone) anteriorly. Together these two bones form the *zygomatic arch.*

Mandibular fossa: Rounded depression on the inferior surface of the zygomatic process (anterior to the ear); forms the socket for the mandibular condyle, the point where the mandible (lower jaw) joins the cranium.

Tympanic region markings (Figures 9.1 and 9.2) include:

External acoustic meatus: Canal leading to eardrum and middle ear.

Styloid (*stylo*=stake, pointed object) **process:** Needle-like projection inferior to external acoustic meatus; attachment point for muscles and ligaments of the neck. This process is often broken off demonstration skulls.

Prominent structures in the mastoid region (Figures 9.1 and 9.2) are:

Mastoid process: Rough projection inferior and posterior to external acoustic meatus; attachment site for muscles.

The mastoid process, full of air cavities and so close to the middle ear—a trouble spot for infections—often becomes infected too, a condition referred to as **mastoiditis.** Because the mastoid area is separated from the brain by only a thin layer of bone, an ear infection that has spread to the mastoid process can inflame the brain coverings, or the meninges. The latter condition is known as **meningitis.** ●

Stylomastoid foramen: Tiny opening between the mastoid and styloid processes through which cranial nerve VII leaves the cranium.

The petrous part (Figures 9.2 and 9.3), which helps form the middle and posterior cranial fossae, exhibits several obvious foramina with important functions:

Jugular foramen: Opening medial to the styloid process through which the internal jugular vein and cranial nerves IX, X, and XI pass.

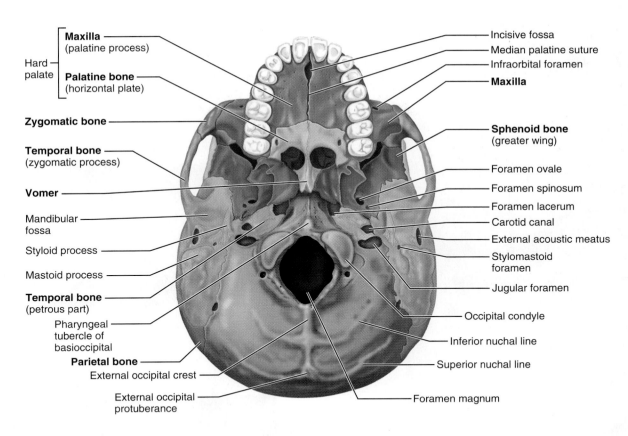

FIGURE 9.2 Inferior superficial view of the skull, mandible removed.

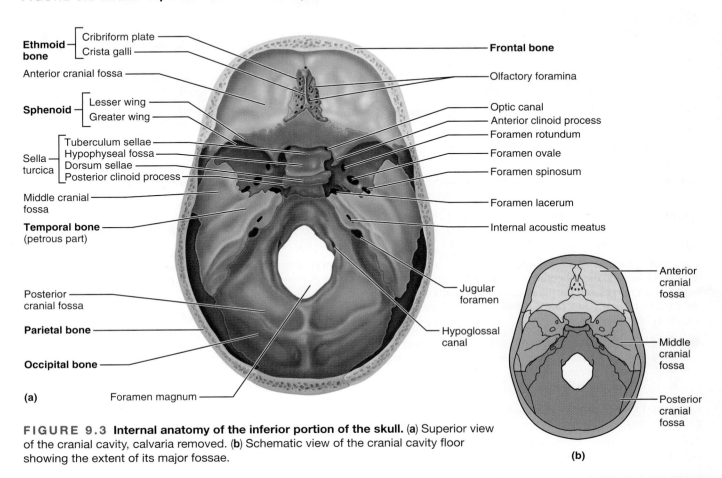

(a)

FIGURE 9.3 Internal anatomy of the inferior portion of the skull. (a) Superior view of the cranial cavity, calvaria removed. **(b)** Schematic view of the cranial cavity floor showing the extent of its major fossae.

(b)

FIGURE 9.4 **The sphenoid bone.**

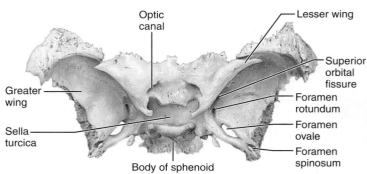

(a) Superior view

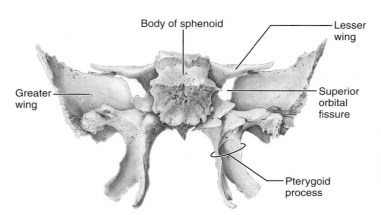

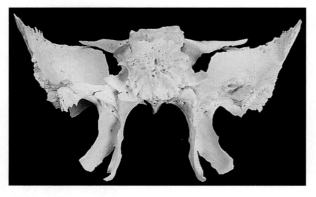

(b) Posterior view

Carotid canal: Opening medial to the styloid process through which the internal carotid artery passes into the cranial cavity.

Internal acoustic meatus: Opening on posterior aspect (petrous part) of temporal bone allowing passage of cranial nerves VII and VIII (Figure 9.3).

Foramen lacerum: A jagged opening between the petrous temporal bone and the sphenoid providing passage for a number of small nerves and for the internal carotid artery to enter the middle cranial fossa (after it passes through part of the temporal bone).

● ***Occipital Bone*** See Figures 9.1, 9.2, 9.3, and 9.6. Most posterior bone of cranium—forms floor and back wall. Joins sphenoid bone anteriorly via its narrow basioccipital region.

Lambdoid suture: Site of articulation of occipital bone and parietal bones.

Foramen magnum: Large opening in base of occipital, which allows the spinal cord to join with the brain.

Occipital condyles: Rounded projections lateral to the foramen magnum that articulate with the first cervical vertebra (atlas).

Hypoglossal canal: Opening medial and superior to the occipital condyle through which the hypoglossal nerve (cranial nerve XII) passes.

External occipital crest and protuberance: Midline prominences posterior to the foramen magnum.

● ***Sphenoid Bone*** See Figures 9.1 through 9.4 and 9.6. Bat-shaped bone forming the anterior plateau of the middle cranial fossa across the width of the skull.

Greater wings: Portions of the sphenoid seen exteriorly anterior to the temporal and forming a part of the eye orbits.

Superior orbital fissures: Jagged openings in orbits providing passage for cranial nerves III, IV, V, and VI to enter the orbit where they serve the eye.

The sphenoid bone can be seen in its entire width if the top of the cranium (calvaria) is removed (Figure 9.3).

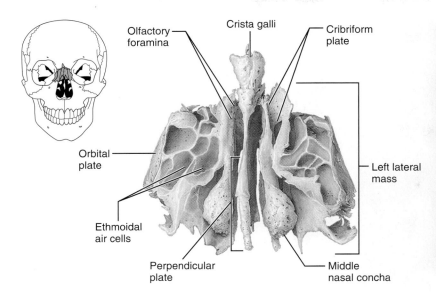

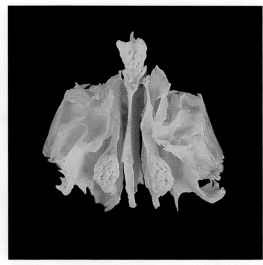

FIGURE 9.5 The ethmoid bone. Anterior view.

Sella turcica (Turk's saddle): A saddle-shaped region in the sphenoid midline which nearly encloses the pituitary gland. The pituitary gland sits in the **hypophyseal fossa** portion of the sella turcica, abutted fore and aft respectively by the **tuberculum sellae** and the **dorsum sellae**. The dorsum sellae terminates laterally in the **posterior clinoid processes.**

Lesser wings: Bat-shaped portions of the sphenoid anterior to the sella turcica. Posteromedially these terminate in the pointed **anterior clinoid processes,** which provide an anchoring site for the dura mater (outermost membrane covering of the brain).

Optic canals: Openings in the bases of the lesser wings through which the optic nerves enter the orbits to serve the eyes; these foramina are connected by the *chiasmatic groove.*

Foramen rotundum: Opening lateral to the sella turcica providing passage for a branch of the fifth cranial nerve. (This foramen is not visible on an inferior view of the skull.)

Foramen ovale: Opening posterior to the sella turcica that allows passage of a branch of the fifth cranial nerve.

● **Ethmoid Bone** See Figures 9.1, 9.3, 9.5, and 9.6. Irregularly shaped bone anterior to the sphenoid. Forms the roof of the nasal cavity, upper nasal septum, and part of the medial orbit walls.

Crista galli (cock's comb): Vertical projection providing a point of attachment for the dura mater, helping to secure the brain within the skull.

Cribriform plates: Bony plates lateral to the crista galli through which olfactory fibers pass to the brain from the nasal mucosa. Together the cribriform plates and the midline crista galli form the *horizontal plate* of the ethmoid bone.

Perpendicular plate: Inferior projection of the ethmoid that forms the superior part of the nasal septum.

Lateral masses: Irregularly shaped thin-walled bony regions flanking the perpendicular plate laterally. Their lateral surfaces (*orbital plates*) shape part of the medial orbit wall.

Superior and middle nasal conchae (turbinates): Thin, delicately coiled plates of bone extending medially from the

lateral masses of the ethmoid into the nasal cavity. The conchae make airflow through the nasal cavity more efficient and greatly increase the surface area of the mucosa that covers them, thus increasing the mucosa's ability to warm and humidify incoming air.

Facial Bones

Of the 14 bones composing the face, 12 are paired. *Only the mandible and vomer are single bones.* An additional bone, the hyoid bone, although not a facial bone, is considered here because of its location.

● **Mandible** See Figures 9.1, 9.6, and 9.7. The lower jawbone, which articulates with the temporal bones in the only freely movable joints of the skull.

Mandibular body: Horizontal portion; forms the chin.

Mandibular ramus: Vertical extension of the body on either side.

Mandibular condyle: Articulation point of the mandible with the mandibular fossa of the temporal bone.

Coronoid process: Jutting anterior portion of the ramus; site of muscle attachment.

Mandibular angle: Posterior point at which ramus meets the body.

Mental foramen: Prominent opening on the body (lateral to the midline) that transmits the mental blood vessels and nerve to the lower jaw.

Mandibular foramen: Open the lower jaw of the skull to identify this prominent foramen on the medial aspect of the mandibular ramus. This foramen permits passage of the nerve involved with tooth sensation (mandibular branch of cranial nerve V) and is the site where the dentist injects Novocain to prevent pain while working on the lower teeth.

Alveolar margin: Superior margin of mandible; contains sockets in which the teeth lie.

Mandibular symphysis: Anterior median depression indicating point of mandibular fusion.

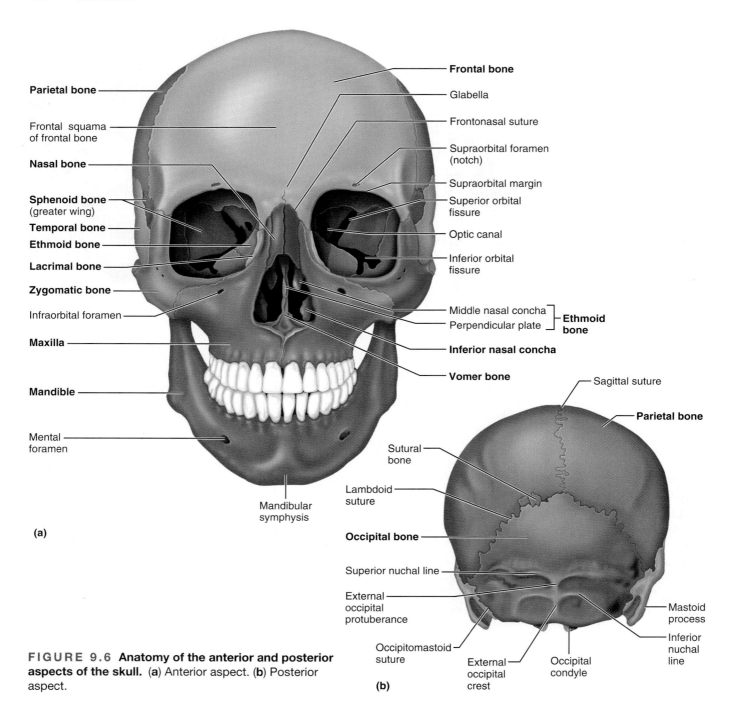

FIGURE 9.6 Anatomy of the anterior and posterior aspects of the skull. (a) Anterior aspect. **(b)** Posterior aspect.

● **Maxillae** See Figures 9.1, 9.2, 9.6, and 9.7. Two bones fused in a median suture; form the upper jawbone and part of the orbits. All facial bones, except the mandible, join the maxillae. Thus they are the main, or keystone, bones of the face.

Alveolar margin: Inferior margin containing sockets (alveoli) in which teeth lie.

Palatine processes: Form the anterior hard palate.

Infraorbital foramen: Opening under the orbit carrying the infraorbital nerves and blood vessels to the nasal region.

Incisive fossa: Large bilateral opening located posterior to the central incisor tooth of the maxilla and piercing the hard palate; transmits the nasopalatine arteries and blood vessels.

● **Palatine Bone** See Figure 9.2. Paired bones posterior to the palatine processes; form posterior hard palate and part of the orbit.

● **Zygomatic Bone** See Figures 9.1, 9.2, and 9.6a. Lateral to the maxilla; forms the portion of the face commonly called the cheekbone, and forms part of the lateral orbit. Its three processes are named for the bones with which they articulate.

● **Lacrimal Bone** See Figures 9.1 and 9.6a. Fingernail-sized bones forming a part of the medial orbit walls between the maxilla and the ethmoid. Each lacrimal bone is pierced by an opening, the **lacrimal fossa,** which serves as a passageway for tears (*lacrima* = "tear").

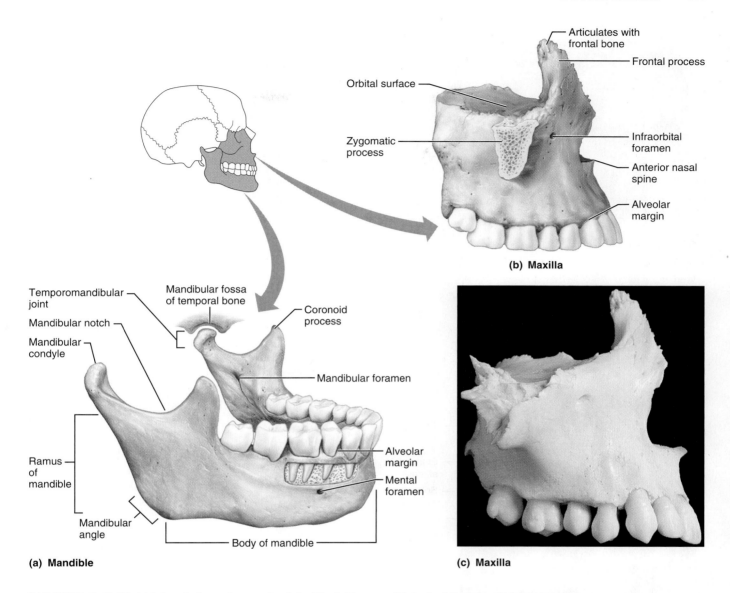

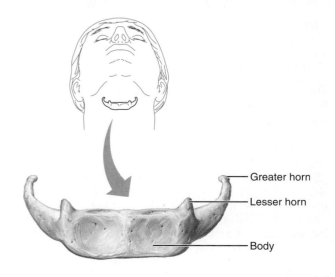

FIGURE 9.7 **Right lateral view of some isolated facial bones.** (Note that the mandible and maxilla are not drawn in proportion to each other.)

- *Nasal Bone* See Figures 9.1 and 9.6a. Small rectangular bones forming the bridge of the nose.

- *Vomer* (vomer = plow) See Figures 9.2 and 9.6. Blade-shaped bone in median plane of nasal cavity that forms the posterior and inferior nasal septum.

- *Inferior Nasal Conchae (Turbinates)* See Figure 9.6. Thin curved bones protruding medially from the lateral walls of the nasal cavity; serve the same purpose as the turbinate portions of the ethmoid bone (described earlier).

Hyoid Bone

Not really considered or counted as a skull bone, the hyoid bone is located in the throat above the larynx (Figure 9.8) where it serves as a point of attachment for many tongue and neck muscles. It does not articulate with any other bone and is thus unique. It is horseshoe-shaped with a body and two pairs of **horns,** or **cornua.**

FIGURE 9.8 Hyoid bone.

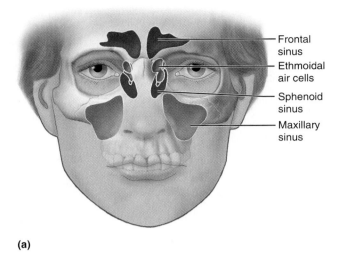

(a)

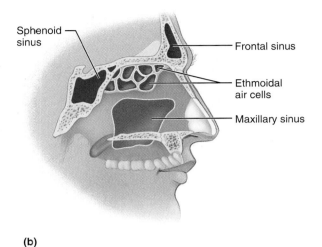

(b)

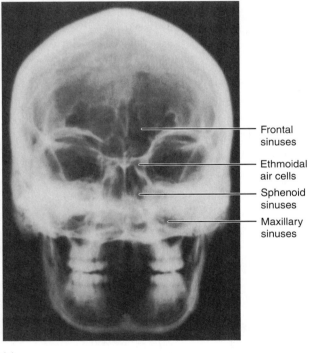

(c)

Frontal sinuses

Ethmoidal air cells

Sphenoid sinuses

Maxillary sinuses

FIGURE 9.9 Paranasal sinuses. (a) Anterior "see-through" view. **(b)** As seen in a sagittal section of the head. **(c)** Skull X ray showing the paranasal sinuses, anterior view.

Paranasal Sinuses

Four skull bones—maxillary, sphenoid, ethmoid, and frontal—contain sinuses (mucosa-lined air cavities), which lead into the nasal passages (see Figures 9.5 and 9.9). These paranasal sinuses lighten the facial bones and may act as resonance chambers for speech. The maxillary sinus is the largest of the sinuses found in the skull.

Sinusitis, or inflammation of the sinuses, sometimes occurs as a result of an allergy or bacterial invasion of the sinus cavities. In such cases, some of the connecting passageways between the sinuses and nasal passages may become blocked with thick mucus or infectious material. Then, as the air in the sinus cavities is absorbed, a partial vacuum forms. The result is a sinus headache localized over the inflamed sinus area. Severe sinus infections may require surgical drainage to relieve this painful condition. ●

ACTIVITY 2

Palpating Skull Markings

Palpate the following areas on yourself:

• Zygomatic bone and arch. (The most prominent part of your cheek is your zygomatic bone. Follow the posterior course of the zygomatic arch to its junction with your temporal bone.)

• Mastoid process (the rough area behind your ear).

• Temporomandibular joints. (Open and close your jaws to locate these.)

- Greater wing of sphenoid. (Find the indentation posterior to the orbit and superior to the zygomatic arch on your lateral skull.)

- Supraorbital foramen. (Apply firm pressure along the superior orbital margin to find the indentation resulting from this foramen.)

- Infraorbital foramen. (Apply firm pressure just inferior to the inferomedial border of the orbit to locate this large foramen.)

- Mandibular angle (most inferior and posterior aspect of the mandible).

- Mandibular symphysis (midline of chin).

- Nasal bones. (Run your index finger and thumb along opposite sides of the bridge of your nose until they "slip" medially at the inferior end of the nasal bones.)

- External occipital protuberance. (This midline projection is easily felt by running your fingers up the furrow at the back of your neck to the skull.)

- Hyoid bone. (Place a thumb and index finger beneath the chin just anterior to the mandibular angles, and squeeze gently. Exert pressure with the thumb, and feel the horn of the hyoid with the index finger.) ▬

The Vertebral Column

The **vertebral column,** extending from the skull to the pelvis, forms the body's major axial support. Additionally, it surrounds and protects the delicate spinal cord while allowing the spinal nerves to issue from the cord via openings between adjacent vertebrae. The term *vertebral column* might suggest a rather rigid supporting rod, but this is far from the truth. The vertebral column consists of 24 single bones called **vertebrae** and two composite, or fused, bones (the sacrum and coccyx) that are connected in such a way as to provide a flexible curved structure (Figure 9.10). Of the 24 single vertebrae, the seven bones of the neck are called *cervical vertebrae;* the next 12 are *thoracic vertebrae;* and the 5 supporting the lower back are *lumbar vertebrae.* Remembering common mealtimes for breakfast, lunch, and dinner (7 A.M., 12 noon, and 5 P.M.) may help you to remember the number of bones in each region.

The vertebrae are separated by pads of fibrocartilage, **intervertebral discs,** that cushion the vertebrae and absorb shocks. Each disc is composed of two major regions, a central gelatinous *nucleus pulposus* that behaves like a fluid, and an outer ring of encircling collagen fibers called the *anulus fibrosus* that stabilizes the disc and contains the pulposus.

As a person ages, the water content of the discs decreases (as it does in other tissues throughout the body), and the discs become thinner and less compressible. This situation, along with other degenerative changes such as weakening of the ligaments and muscle tendons associated with the vertebral column, predisposes older people to **ruptured discs.** In a ruptured disc, the nucleus pulposus herniates through the anulus portion and typically compresses adjacent nerves. ●

The presence of the discs and the S-shaped or spring-like construction of the vertebral column prevent shock to

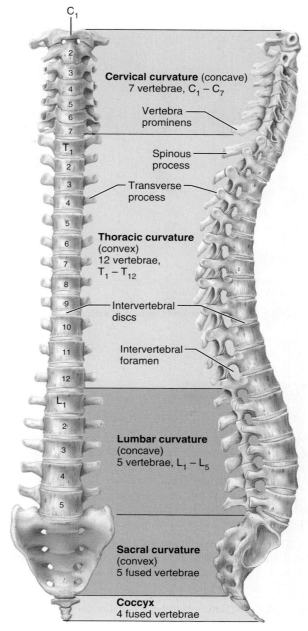

Anterior view   *Right lateral view*

FIGURE 9.10 The vertebral column. Notice the curvatures in the lateral view. (The terms *convex* and *concave* refer to the curvature of the posterior aspect of the vertebral column.)

the head in walking and running and provide flexibility to the body trunk. The thoracic and sacral curvatures of the spine are referred to as *primary curvatures* because they are present and well developed at birth. Later the *secondary curvatures* are formed. The cervical curvature becomes prominent when the baby begins to hold its head up independently, and the lumbar curvature develops when the baby begins to walk.

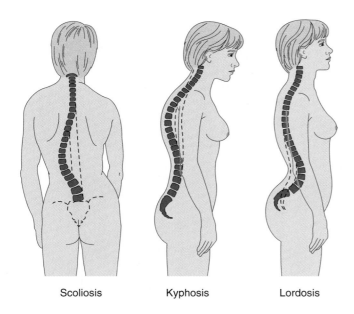

FIGURE 9.11 Abnormal spinal curvatures.

Scoliosis   Kyphosis   Lordosis

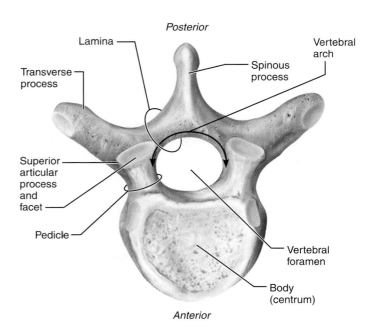

FIGURE 9.12 A typical vertebra, superior view. Inferior articulating surfaces not shown.

ACTIVITY 3

Examining Spinal Curvatures

1. Observe the normal curvature of the vertebral column in the articulated vertebral column or laboratory skeleton, and compare it to Figure 9.10. Then examine Figure 9.11, which depicts three abnormal spinal curvatures—*scoliosis, kyphosis,* and *lordosis.* These abnormalities may result from disease or poor posture. Also examine X rays, if they are available, showing these same conditions in a living patient.

2. Then, using the articulated vertebral column (or an articulated skeleton), examine the freedom of movement between two lumbar vertebrae separated by an intervertebral disc.

When the fibrous disc is properly positioned, are the spinal cord or peripheral nerves impaired in any way?

Remove the disc and put the two vertebrae back together. What happens to the nerve?

What would happen to the spinal nerves in areas of malpositioned or "slipped" discs?

Structure of a Typical Vertebra

Although they differ in size and specific features, all vertebrae have some features in common (Figure 9.12).

Body (or **centrum**): Rounded central portion of the vertebra, which faces anteriorly in the human vertebral column.

Vertebral arch: Composed of pedicles, laminae, and a spinous process, it represents the junction of all posterior extensions from the vertebral body.

Vertebral (spinal) foramen: Opening enclosed by the body and vertebral arch; a conduit for the spinal cord.

Transverse processes: Two lateral projections from the vertebral arch.

Spinous process: Single medial and posterior projection from the vertebral arch.

Superior and inferior articular processes: Paired projections lateral to the vertebral foramen that enable articulation with adjacent vertebrae. The superior articular processes typically face toward the spinous process (posteriorly), whereas the inferior articular processes face (anteriorly) away from the spinous process.

Intervertebral foramina: The right and left pedicles have notches (see Figure 9.14) on their inferior and superior surfaces that create openings, the intervertebral foramina, (see Figure 9.10), for spinal nerves to leave the spinal cord between adjacent vertebrae.

Figures 9.13 through 9.15 and Table 9.1 show how specific vertebrae differ; refer to them as you read the following sections.

Cervical Vertebrae

The seven cervical vertebrae (referred to as C_1 through C_7) form the neck portion of the vertebral column. The first two cervical vertebrae (atlas and axis) are highly modified to

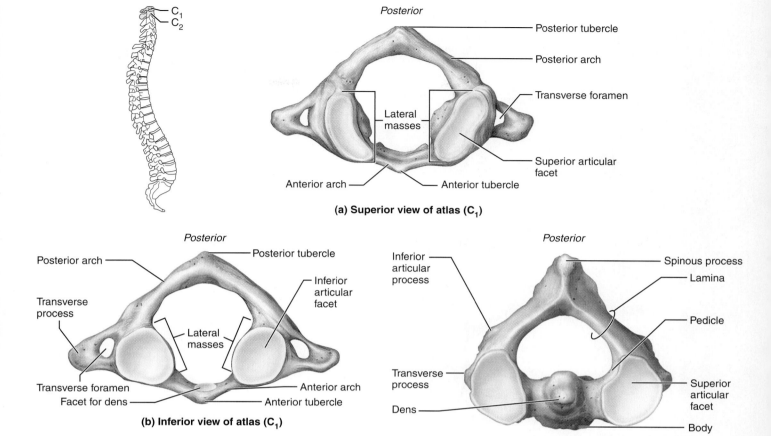

(a) **Superior view of atlas (C₁)**

(b) **Inferior view of atlas (C₁)**

FIGURE 9.13 Cervical vertebrae C₁ and C₂.

(c) **Superior view of axis (C₂)**

perform special functions (see Figure 9.13). The **atlas** (C_1) lacks a body, and its lateral processes contain large concave depressions on their superior surfaces that receive the occipital condyles of the skull. This joint enables you to nod "yes." The **axis** (C_2) acts as a pivot for the rotation of the atlas (and skull) above. It bears a large vertical process, the **dens,** that serves as the pivot point. The articulation between C_1 and C_2 allows you to rotate your head from side to side to indicate "no."

The more typical cervical vertebrae (C_3 through C_7) are distinguished from the thoracic and lumbar vertebrae by several features (see Table 9.1 and Figure 9.14). They are the smallest, lightest vertebrae, and the vertebral foramen is triangular. The spinous process is short and often bifurcated (divided into two branches). The spinous process of C_7 is not branched, however, and is substantially longer than that of the other cervical vertebrae. Because the spinous process of C_7 is visible through the skin, it is called the *vertebra prominens* (Figure 9.10) and is used as a landmark for counting the vertebrae. Transverse processes of the cervical vertebrae are wide, and they contain foramina through which the vertebral arteries pass superiorly on their way to the brain. Any time you see these foramina in a vertebra, you can be sure that it is a cervical vertebra.

• Palpate your vertebra prominens.

Thoracic Vertebrae

The 12 thoracic vertebrae (referred to as T_1 through T_{12}) may be recognized by the following structural characteristics. As shown in Figure 9.14, they have a larger body than the cervical vertebrae. The body is somewhat heart-shaped, with two small articulating surfaces, or **costal facets,** on each side (one superior, the other inferior) close to the origin of the vertebral arch. Sometimes referred to as *costal demifacets* because of their small size, these facets articulate with the heads of the corresponding ribs. The vertebral foramen is oval or round, and the spinous process is long, with a sharp downward hook. The closer the thoracic vertebra is to the lumbar region, the less sharp and shorter the spinous process. Articular facets on the transverse processes articulate with the tubercles of the ribs. Besides forming the thoracic part of the spine, these vertebrae form the posterior aspect of the bony thoracic cage (rib cage). Indeed, they are the only vertebrae that articulate with the ribs.

Lumbar Vertebrae

The five lumbar vertebrae (L_1 through L_5) have massive blocklike bodies and short, thick, hatchet-shaped spinous processes extending directly backward (see Table 9.1 and Figure 9.14). The superior articular facets face posteromedially; the inferior ones are directed anterolaterally. These

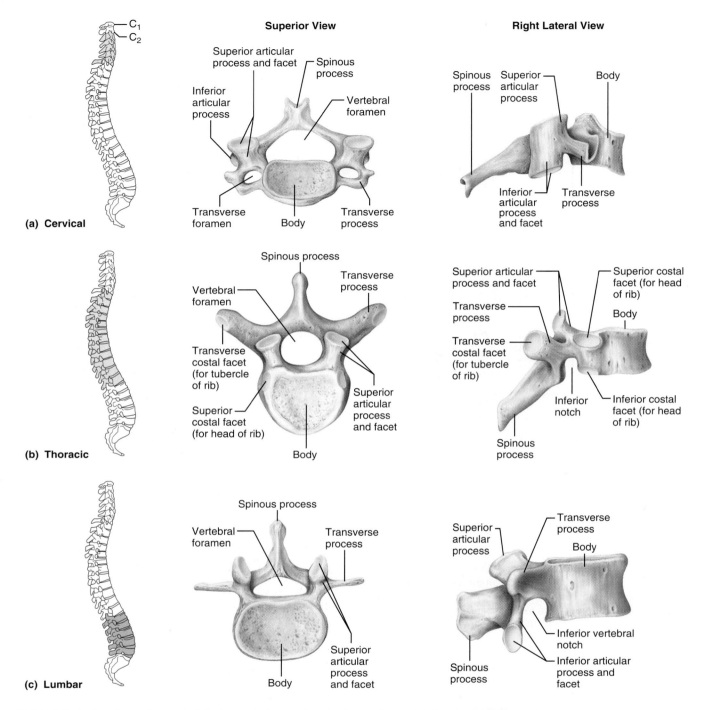

Superior View

Right Lateral View

(a) Cervical

Superior articular process and facet
Spinous process
Inferior articular process
Vertebral foramen
Transverse foramen
Body
Transverse process

Spinous process
Superior articular process
Body
Inferior articular process and facet
Transverse process

(b) Thoracic

Spinous process
Transverse process
Vertebral foramen
Transverse costal facet (for tubercle of rib)
Superior costal facet (for head of rib)
Body
Superior articular process and facet

Superior articular process and facet
Superior costal facet (for head of rib)
Transverse process
Body
Transverse costal facet (for tubercle of rib)
Inferior notch
Spinous process
Inferior costal facet (for head of rib)

(c) Lumbar

Spinous process
Vertebral foramen
Transverse process
Body
Superior articular process and facet

Transverse process
Superior articular process
Body
Inferior vertebral notch
Inferior articular process and facet
Spinous process

FIGURE 9.14 Superior and right lateral views of typical vertebrae. (a) Cervical. (b) Thoracic. (c) Lumbar.

structural features reduce the mobility of the lumbar region of the spine. Since most stress on the vertebral column occurs in the lumbar region, these are also the sturdiest of the vertebrae.

The spinal cord ends at the superior edge of L_2, but the outer covering of the cord, filled with cerebrospinal fluid, extends an appreciable distance beyond. Thus a *lumbar puncture* (for examination of the cerebrospinal fluid) or the administration of "saddle block" anesthesia for childbirth is normally done between L_3 and L_4 or L_4 and L_5, where there is little or no chance of injuring the delicate spinal cord.

The Sacrum

The **sacrum** (Figure 9.15) is a composite bone formed from the fusion of five vertebrae. Superiorly it articulates with L_5, and inferiorly it connects with the coccyx. The **median sacral crest** is a remnant of the spinous processes of the fused vertebrae. The winglike **alae,** formed by fusion of the transverse processes, articulate laterally with the hip bones. The sacrum is concave anteriorly and forms the posterior border of the pelvis. Four ridges (lines of fusion) cross the

TABLE 9.1	Regional Characteristics of Cervical, Thoracic, and Lumbar Vertebrae		
Characteristic	(a) Cervical (C₃–C₇)	(b) Thoracic	(c) Lumbar
Body	Small, wide side to side	Larger than cervical; heart-shaped; bears two costal facets	Massive; kidney-shaped
Spinous process	Short; bifid; projects directly posteriorly	Long; sharp; projects inferiorly	Short; blunt; projects directly posteriorly
Vertebral foramen	Triangular	Circular	Triangular
Transverse processes	Contain foramina	Bear facets for ribs (except T_{11} and T_{12})	Thin and tapered
Superior and inferior articulating processes	Superior facets directed superoposteriorly	Superior facets directed posteriorly	Superior facets directed posteromedially (or medially)
	Inferior facets directed inferoanteriorly	Inferior facets directed anteriorly	Inferior facets directed anterolaterally (or laterally)
Movements allowed	Flexion and extension; lateral flexion; rotation; the spine region with the greatest range of movement	Rotation; lateral flexion possible but limited by ribs; flexion and extension prevented	Flexion and extension; some lateral flexion; rotation prevented

FIGURE 9.15 **Sacrum and coccyx.**

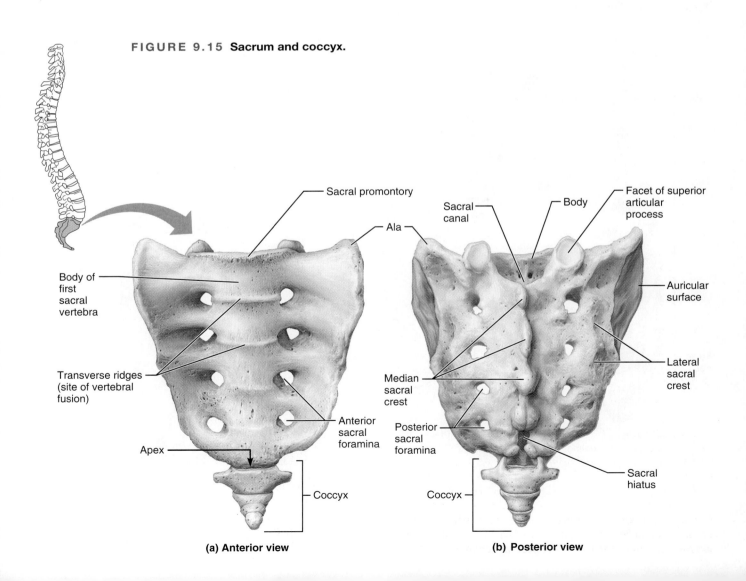

(a) Anterior view

(b) Posterior view

anterior part of the sacrum, and **sacral foramina** are located at either end of these ridges. These foramina allow blood vessels and nerves to pass. The vertebral canal continues inside the sacrum as the **sacral canal** and terminates near the coccyx via an enlarged opening called the **sacral hiatus.** The **sacral promontory** (anterior border of the body of S$_1$) is an important anatomical landmark for obstetricians.

• Attempt to palpate the median sacral crest of your sacrum. (This is more easily done by thin people and obviously in privacy.)

The Coccyx

The **coccyx** (see Figure 9.15) is formed from the fusion of three to five small irregularly shaped vertebrae. It is literally the human tailbone, a vestige of the tail that other vertebrates have. The coccyx is attached to the sacrum by ligaments.

ACTIVITY 4
Examining Vertebral Structure

Obtain examples of each type of vertebra and examine them carefully, comparing them to Figures 9.13, 9.14, 9.15 and Table 9.1, and to each other. ▬

The Thoracic Cage

The **thoracic cage,** or **bony thorax,** is composed of the sternum, ribs, and thoracic vertebrae (Figure 9.16). It is called a cage because of its appearance and because it forms a protective cone-shaped enclosure around the organs of the thoracic cavity (heart and lungs, for example).

The Sternum

The **sternum** (breastbone), a typical flat bone, is a result of the fusion of three bones—the manubrium, body, and xiphoid process. It is attached to the first seven pairs of ribs. The superiormost **manubrium** looks like the knot of a tie; it articulates with the clavicle (collarbone) laterally. The **body (gladiolus)** forms the bulk of the sternum. The **xiphoid process** constructs the inferior end of the sternum and lies at the level of the fifth intercostal space. Although it is made of hyaline cartilage in children, it is usually ossified in adults.

In some people, the xiphoid process projects dorsally. This may present a problem because physical trauma to the chest can push such a xiphoid into the heart or liver (both immediately deep to the process), causing massive hemorrhage. ●

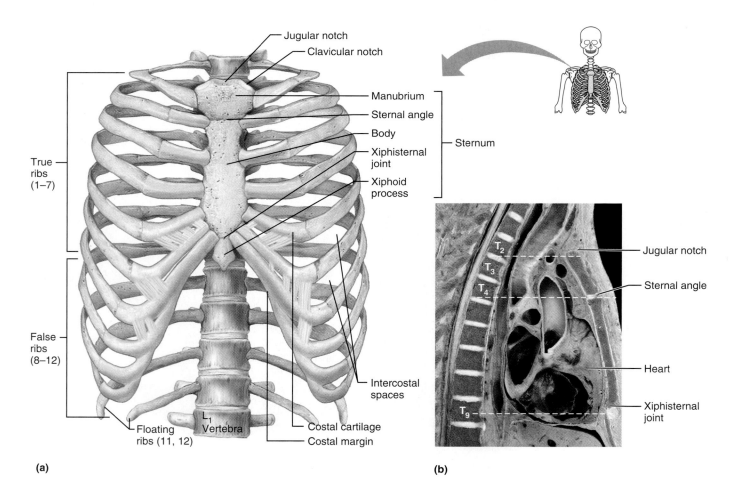

FIGURE 9.16 The thoracic cage. (a) Skeleton of the bony thorax, anterior view (costal cartilages are shown in blue). **(b)** Left lateral view of the thorax, illustrating the relationship of the surface anatomical landmarks of the thorax to the vertebral column (thoracic portion).

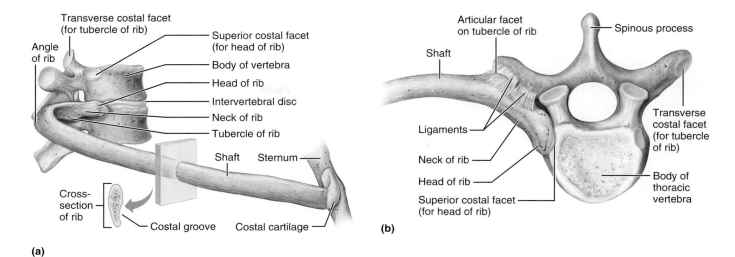

FIGURE 9.17 Structure of a "typical" true rib and its articulations. (a) Vertebral and sternal articulations of a typical true rib. (b) Superior view of the articulation between a rib and a thoracic vertebra, with costovertebral ligaments shown on left side only.

The sternum has three important bony landmarks—the jugular notch, the sternal angle, and the xiphisternal joint. The **jugular notch** (concave upper border of the manubrium) can be palpated easily; generally it is at the level of the third thoracic vertebra. The **sternal angle** is a result of the manubrium and body meeting at a slight angle to each other, so that a transverse ridge is formed at the level of the second ribs. It provides a handy reference point for counting ribs to locate the second intercostal space for listening to certain heart valves, and is an important anatomical landmark for thoracic surgery. The **xiphisternal joint,** the point where the sternal body and xiphoid process fuse, lies at the level of the ninth thoracic vertebra.

• Palpate your sternal angle and jugular notch.

Because of its accessibility, the sternum is a favored site for obtaining samples of blood-forming (hematopoietic) tissue for the diagnosis of suspected blood diseases. A needle is inserted into the marrow of the sternum and the sample withdrawn (sternal puncture).

The Ribs

The 12 pairs of **ribs** form the walls of the thoracic cage (see Figures 9.16 and 9.17). All of the ribs articulate posteriorly

with the vertebral column via their heads and tubercles and then curve downward and toward the anterior body surface. The first seven pairs, called the *true,* or *vertebrosternal, ribs,* attach directly to the sternum by their "own" costal cartilages. The next five pairs are called *false ribs;* they attach indirectly to the sternum or entirely lack a sternal attachment. Of these, rib pairs 8–10, which are also called *vertebrochondral ribs,* have indirect cartilage attachments to the sternum via the costal cartilage of rib 7. The last two pairs, called *floating,* or *vertebral, ribs,* have no sternal attachment.

ACTIVITY 5

Examining the Relationship Between Ribs and Vertebrae

First take a deep breath to expand your chest. Notice how your ribs seem to move outward and how your sternum rises. Then examine an articulated skeleton to observe the relationship between the ribs and the vertebrae.

Refer to Activity 3 ("Palpating Landmarks of the Trunk") and Activity 4 ("Palpating Landmarks of the Abdomen") in Exercise 30, Surface Anatomy Roundup (pp. 517–533). ■

NAME _____

LAB TIME/DATE _____

The Axial Skeleton

The Skull

1. Match the bone names in column B with the descriptions in column A.

Column A

_____ 1. forehead bone

_____ 2. cheekbone

_____ 3. lower jaw

_____ 4. bridge of nose

_____ 5. posterior bones of the hard palate

_____ 6. much of the lateral and superior cranium

_____ 7. most posterior part of cranium

_____ 8. single, irregular, bat-shaped bone forming part of the cranial floor

_____ 9. tiny bones bearing tear ducts

_____ 10. anterior part of hard palate

_____ 11. superior and medial nasal conchae formed from its projections

_____ 12. site of mastoid process

_____ 13. site of sella turcica

_____ 14. site of cribriform plate

_____ 15. site of mental foramen

_____ 16. site of styloid processes

_____, _____, _____, and_____ 17. four bones containing paranasal sinuses

_____ 18. condyles here articulate with the atlas _____ 19. foramen magnum contained here

_____ 20. small U-shaped bone in neck, where many tongue muscles attach

_____ 21. middle ear found here _____ 22. nasal septum

_____ 23. bears an upward protrusion, the "cock's comb," or crista galli

_____, _____ 24. contain alveoli that bear teeth

Column B

a. ethmoid

b. frontal

c. hyoid

d. lacrimal

e. mandible

f. maxilla

g. nasal

h. occipital

i. palatine

j. parietal

k. sphenoid

l. temporal

m. vomer

n. zygomatic

2. Using choices from the numbered key to the right, identify all bones and bone markings provided with leader lines in the two diagrams below.

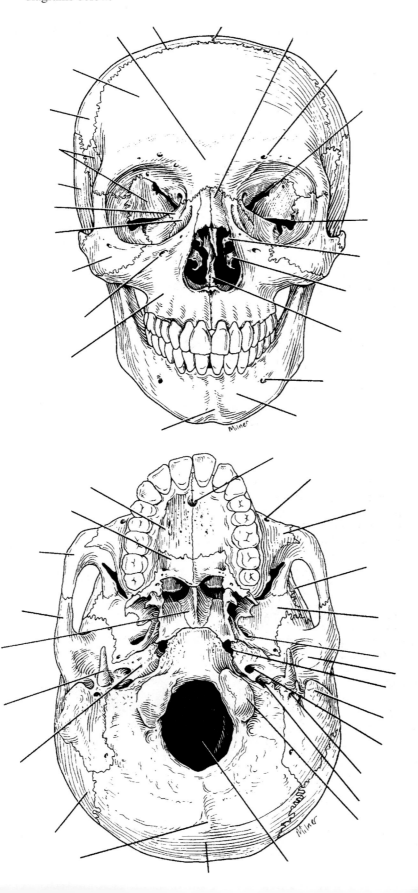

Key:
1. carotid canal
2. coronal suture
3. ethmoid bone
4. external occipital protuberance
5. foramen lacerum
6. foramen magnum
7. foramen ovale
8. frontal bone
9. glabella
10. incisive fossa
11. inferior nasal concha
12. inferior orbital fissure
13. infraorbital foramen
14. jugular foramen
15. lacrimal bone
16. mandible
17. mandibular fossa
18. mandibular symphysis
19. mastoid process
20. maxilla
21. mental foramen
22. middle nasal concha of ethmoid
23. nasal bone
24. occipital bone
25. occipital condyle
26. palatine bone
27. palatine process of maxilla
28. parietal bone
29. sagittal suture
30. sphenoid bone
31. styloid process
32. stylomastoid foramen
33. superior orbital fissure
34. supraorbital foramen
35. temporal bone
36. vomer bone
37. zygomatic bone
38. zygomatic process of temporal bone

3. Name the eight bones of the cranium.

_____ _____ _____ _____

_____ _____ _____ _____

4. Give two possible functions of the sinuses. _____

_____

5. What is the orbit? _____

What bones contribute to the formation of the orbit? _____

_____

6. Why can the sphenoid bone be called the keystone of the cranial floor? _____

_____

The Vertebral Column

7. The distinguishing characteristics of the vertebrae composing the vertebral column are noted below. Correctly identify each described structure/region by choosing a response from the key.

Key: a. atlas   d. coccyx   f. sacrum
     b. axis   e. lumbar vertebra   g. thoracic vertebra
     c. cervical vertebra—typical

_____ 1. vertebral type containing foramina in the transverse processes, through which the vertebral arteries ascend to reach the brain

_____ 2. dens here provides a pivot for rotation of the first cervical vertebra (C_1)

_____ 3. transverse processes faceted for articulation with ribs; spinous process pointing sharply downward

_____ 4. composite bone; articulates with the hip bone laterally

_____ 5. massive vertebrae; weight-sustaining

_____ 6. "tail bone"; vestigial fused vertebrae

_____ 7. supports the head; allows a rocking motion in conjunction with the occipital condyles

_____ 8. seven components; unfused

_____ 9. twelve components; unfused

8. Using the key, correctly identify the vertebral parts/areas described below. (More than one choice may apply in some cases.) Also use the key letters to correctly identify the vertebral areas in the diagram.

Key: a. body   d. pedicle   g. transverse process
     b. intervertebral foramina   e. spinous process   h. vertebral arch
     c. lamina   f. superior articular process   i. vertebral foramen

_____ 1. cavity enclosing the nerve cord

_____ 2. weight-bearing portion of the vertebra

_____ 3. provide levers against which muscles pull

_____ 4. provide an articulation point for the ribs

_____ 5. openings providing for exit of spinal nerves

_____ 6. structures that form an enclosure for the spinal cord

9. Describe how a spinal nerve exits from the vertebral column. _____

_____

10. Name two factors/structures that permit flexibility of the vertebral column.

_____ and _____

11. What kind of tissue composes the intervertebral discs? _____

12. What is a herniated disc? _____

What problems might it cause? _____

_____

13. Which two spinal curvatures are obvious at birth? _____ and _____

Under what conditions do the secondary curvatures develop? _____

_____

_____

14. On this illustration of an articulated vertebral column, identify each curvature indicated and label it as a primary or a secondary curvature. Also identify the structures provided with leader lines, using the letters of the terms listed in the key below.

Key: a.   atlas
b.   axis
c.   intervertebral disc
d.   sacrum
e.   two thoracic vertebrae
f.   two lumbar vertebrae
g.   vertebra prominens

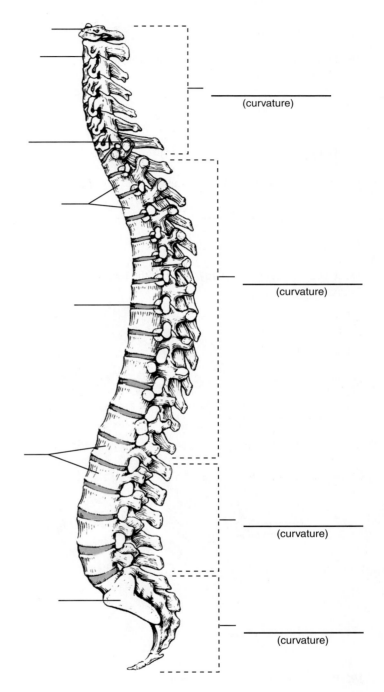

_____ (curvature)

_____ (curvature)

_____ (curvature)

_____ (curvature)

The Thoracic Cage

15. The major components of the thorax (excluding the vertebral column) are the _____

and the _____.

16. Differentiate between a true rib and a false rib. _____

_____

_____

Is a floating rib a true or a false rib? _____

17. What is the general shape of the thoracic cage? _____

_____

_____

18. Using the terms in the key, identify the regions and landmarks of the bony thorax.

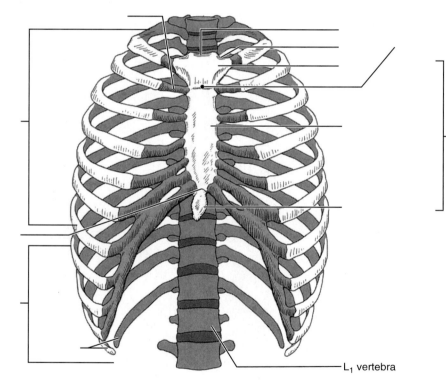

L₁ vertebra

Key: a. body

b. clavicular notch

c. costal cartilage

d. false ribs

e. floating ribs

f. jugular notch

g. manubrium

h. sternal angle

i. sternum

j. true ribs

k. xiphisternal joint

l. xiphoid process

19. Provide the more scientific name for the following rib types.

a. True ribs _____

b. False ribs (not including c) _____

c. Floating ribs _____

The Appendicular Skeleton

O B J E C T I V E S

1. To identify on an articulated skeleton the bones of the pectoral and pelvic girdles and their attached limbs.
2. To arrange unmarked, disarticulated bones in proper relative position to form the entire skeleton.
3. To differentiate between a male and a female pelvis.
4. To discuss the common features of the human appendicular girdles (pectoral and pelvic), and to note how their structure relates to their specialized functions.
5. To identify specific bone markings in the appendicular skeleton.

The **appendicular skeleton** (the gold-colored portion of Figure 8.1) is composed of the 126 bones of the appendages and the pectoral and pelvic girdles, which attach the limbs to the axial skeleton. Although the upper and lower limbs differ in their functions and mobility, they have the same fundamental plan, with each limb composed of three major segments connected together by freely movable joints.

A C T I V I T Y 1

Examining and Identifying Bones of the Appendicular Skeleton

Carefully examine each of the bones described throughout this exercise and identify the characteristic bone markings of each. The markings aid in determining whether a bone is the right or left member of its pair; for example, the glenoid cavity is on the lateral aspect of the scapula and the spine is on its posterior aspect. *This is a very important instruction because you will be constructing your own skeleton to finish this laboratory exercise.* Additionally, when corresponding X rays are available, compare the actual bone specimen to its X-ray image. ▬

Bones of the Pectoral Girdle and Upper Extremity

The Pectoral (Shoulder) Girdle

The paired **pectoral,** or **shoulder, girdles** (Figure 10.1) each consist of two bones—the anterior clavicle and the posterior scapula. The shoulder girdles function to attach the upper limbs to the axial skeleton, and serve as attachment points for many trunk and neck muscles.

The **clavicle,** or collarbone, is a slender, doubly curved bone—convex forward on its medial two-thirds and concave laterally. Its *sternal* (medial) *end,* which attaches to the sternal manubrium, is rounded or triangular in cross section. The sternal end projects above the manubrium and can be felt and (usually) seen forming the lateral walls of the *jugular notch* (see Figure 9.16, p. 124). The *acromial* (lateral) *end* of the clavicle is flattened where it articulates with the scapula to form part of the shoulder joint. On its posteroinferior surface is the prominent **conoid tubercle** (Figure 10.2b). This projection anchors a ligament and provides a handy landmark for determining whether a given clavicle is from the right or left side of the body. The clavicle serves as an anterior brace, or strut, to hold the arm away from the top of the thorax.

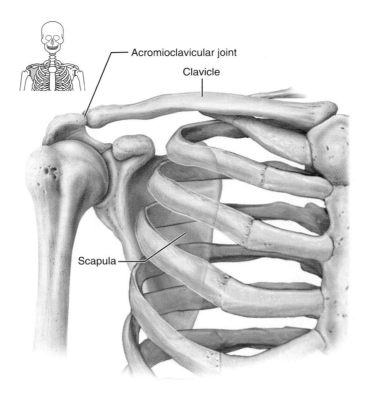

Acromioclavicular joint

Clavicle

Scapula

FIGURE 10.1 Articulated bones of the pectoral (shoulder) girdle. The right pectoral girdle is articulated to show the relationship of the girdle to the bones of the thorax and arm.

The **scapulae** (Figure 10.2c–e), or shoulder blades, are generally triangular and are commonly called the "wings" of humans. Each scapula has a flattened body and two important processes—the **acromion** (the enlarged end of the spine of the scapula) and the beaklike **coracoid process** (*corac* = crow, raven). The acromion connects with the clavicle; the coracoid process points anteriorly over the tip of the shoulder joint and serves as an attachment point for some of the upper limb muscles. The **suprascapular notch** at the base of the coracoid process allows nerves to pass. The scapula has no direct attachment to the axial skeleton but is loosely held in place by trunk muscles.

The scapula has three angles: superior, inferior, and lateral. The inferior angle provides a landmark for auscultating (listening to) lung sounds. The **glenoid cavity,** a shallow socket that receives the head of the arm bone (humerus), is located in the lateral angle. The scapula also has three named borders: superior, medial (vertebral), and lateral (axillary). Several shallow depressions (fossae) appear on both sides of the scapula and are named according to location; there are the anterior *subscapular fossa* and the posterior *infraspinous* and *supraspinous fossae.*

The shoulder girdle is exceptionally light and allows the upper limb a degree of mobility not seen anywhere else in the body. This is due to the following factors:

- The sternoclavicular joints are the *only* site of attachment of the shoulder girdles to the axial skeleton.

- The relative looseness of the scapular attachment allows it to slide back and forth against the thorax with muscular activity.

- The glenoid cavity is shallow and does little to stabilize the shoulder joint.

However, this exceptional flexibility exacts a price: The arm bone (humerus) is very susceptible to dislocation, and fracture of the clavicle disables the entire upper limb.

The Arm

The arm (Figure 10.3) consists of a single bone—the **humerus,** a typical long bone. Proximally its rounded *head* fits into the shallow glenoid cavity of the scapula. The head is separated from the shaft by the **anatomical neck** and by the more constricted **surgical neck,** which is a common site of fracture. Opposite the head are two prominences, the **greater** and **lesser tubercles** (from lateral to medial aspect), separated by a groove (the **intertubercular sulcus,** or *bicipital groove*) that guides the tendon of the biceps muscle to its point of attachment (the superior rim of the glenoid cavity). About midway down the lateral aspect of the shaft is a roughened area, the **deltoid tuberosity,** where the large fleshy shoulder muscle, the deltoid, attaches. Nearby, the **radial groove** descends obliquely, indicating the pathway of the radial nerve.

At the distal end of the humerus are two condyles—the medial **trochlea** (looking rather like a spool), which articulates with the ulna, and the lateral **capitulum,** which articulates with the radius of the forearm. This condyle pair is flanked medially by the **medial epicondyle** and laterally by the **lateral epicondyle.**

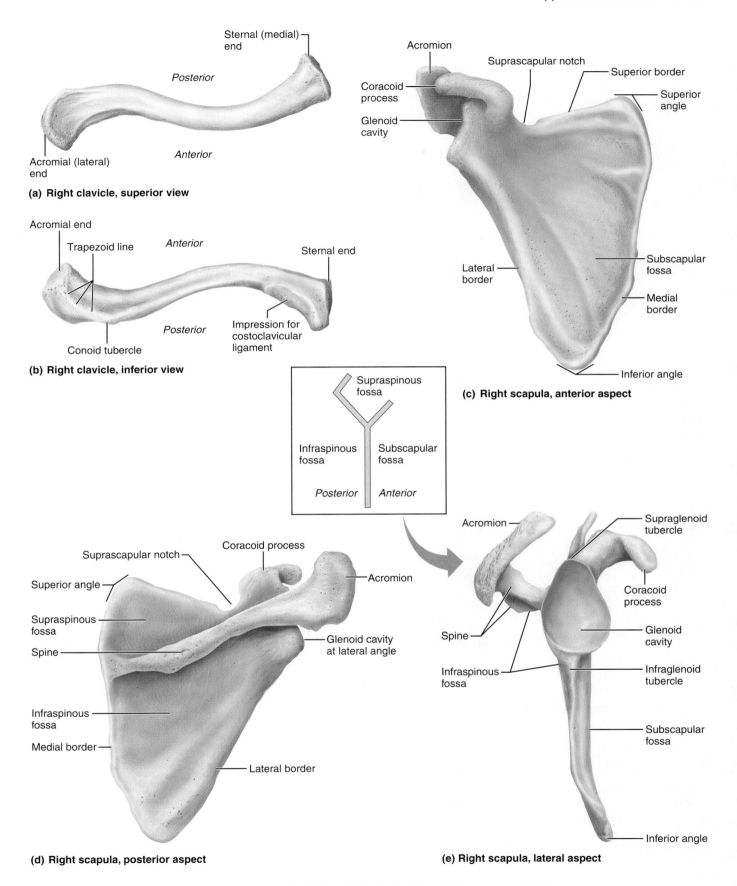

(a) **Right clavicle, superior view**

(b) **Right clavicle, inferior view**

(c) **Right scapula, anterior aspect**

(d) **Right scapula, posterior aspect**

(e) **Right scapula, lateral aspect**

FIGURE 10.2 Individual bones of the pectoral (shoulder) girdle. View (e) is accompanied by a schematic representation of its orientation.

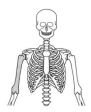

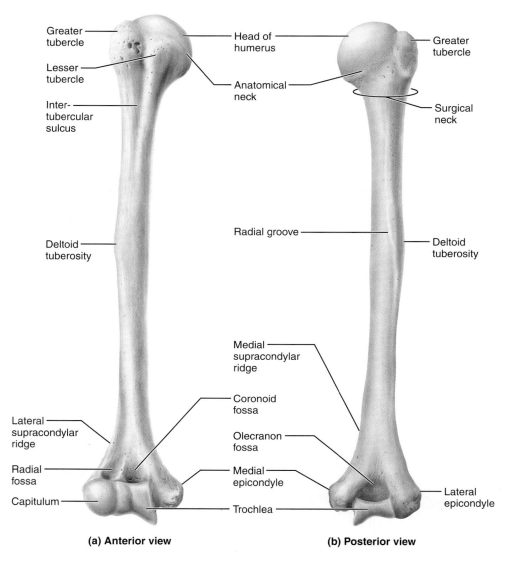

Greater tubercle

Head of humerus

Greater tubercle

Lesser tubercle

Anatomical neck

Surgical neck

Inter-tubercular sulcus

Radial groove

Deltoid tuberosity

Deltoid tuberosity

Medial supracondylar ridge

Coronoid fossa

Lateral supracondylar ridge

Olecranon fossa

Radial fossa

Medial epicondyle

Capitulum

Trochlea

Lateral epicondyle

(a) Anterior view

(b) Posterior view

FIGURE 10.3 Bone of the right arm. Humerus, (a) anterior view, (b) posterior view.

The medial epicondyle is commonly called the "funny bone." The ulnar nerve runs in a groove beneath the medial epicondyle, and when this region is sharply bumped, we are likely to experience a temporary, but excruciatingly painful, tingling sensation. This event is called "hitting the funny bone," a strange expression, because it is certainly *not* funny!

Above the trochlea on the anterior surface is the **coronoid fossa;** on the posterior surface is the **olecranon fossa.** These two depressions allow the corresponding processes of the ulna to move freely when the elbow is flexed and extended. The small **radial fossa,** lateral to the coronoid fossa, receives the head of the radius when the elbow is flexed.

The Forearm

Two bones, the radius and the ulna, compose the skeleton of the forearm, or antebrachium (see Figure 10.4). When the body is in the anatomical position, the **radius** is in the lateral position in the forearm, and the radius and ulna are parallel. Proximally, the disc-shaped head of the radius articulates with the capitulum of the humerus. Just below the head, on the medial aspect of the shaft, is a prominence called the **radial tuberosity,** the point of attachment for the tendon of the biceps muscle of the arm. Distally, the small **ulnar notch** reveals where it articulates with the end of the ulna.

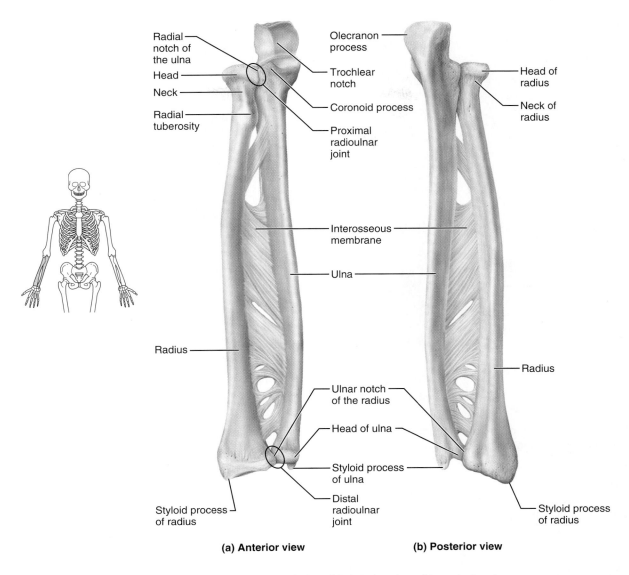

Radial notch of the ulna

Head

Neck

Radial tuberosity

Olecranon process

Trochlear notch

Coronoid process

Proximal radioulnar joint

Head of radius

Neck of radius

Interosseous membrane

Ulna

Radius

Radius

Ulnar notch of the radius

Head of ulna

Styloid process of ulna

Distal radioulnar joint

Styloid process of radius

Styloid process of radius

(a) Anterior view   **(b) Posterior view**

FIGURE 10.4 Bones of the right forearm. Radius and ulna, **(a)** anterior view, **(b)** posterior view.

The **ulna** is the medial bone of the forearm. Its proximal end bears the anterior **coronoid process** and the posterior **olecranon process,** which are separated by the **trochlear notch.** Together these processes grip the trochlea of the humerus in a plierslike joint. The small **radial notch** on the lateral side of the coronoid process articulates with the head of the radius. The slimmer distal end, the ulnar **head,** bears a small medial **styloid process,** which serves as a point of attachment for the ligaments of the wrist.

The Hand

The skeleton of the hand, or manus (Figure 10.5), includes three groups of bones, those of the carpus (wrist), the metacarpals (bones of the palm), and the phalanges (bones of the fingers).

The wrist is the proximal portion of the hand. It is referred to anatomically as the **carpus;** the eight marble-size bones composing it are the **carpals.** (So you actually wear your wristwatch over the distal part of your forearm.) The carpals are arranged in two irregular rows of four bones each, which

are illustrated in Figure 10.5. In the proximal row (lateral to medial) are the *scaphoid, lunate, triquetrum,* and *pisiform bones;* the scaphoid and lunate articulate with the distal end of the radius. In the distal row are the *trapezium, trapezoid, capitate,* and *hamate.* The carpals are bound closely together by ligaments, which restrict movements between them to allow only gliding movements. A mnemonic may help you to remember the names of the carpals in order from the lateral aspect of the proximal row and continuing with the distal row, lateral to medial: "**S**ally **L**eft **T**he **P**arty **T**o **T**ake **C**armen **H**ome."

The **metacarpals,** numbered 1 to 5 from the thumb side of the hand toward the little finger, radiate out from the wrist like spokes to form the palm of the hand. The *bases* of the metacarpals articulate with the carpals of the wrist; their more bulbous *heads* articulate with the phalanges of the fingers distally. When the fist is clenched, the heads of the metacarpals become prominent as the knuckles.

Like the bones of the palm, the fingers are numbered from 1 to 5, beginning from the thumb (*pollex*) side of the

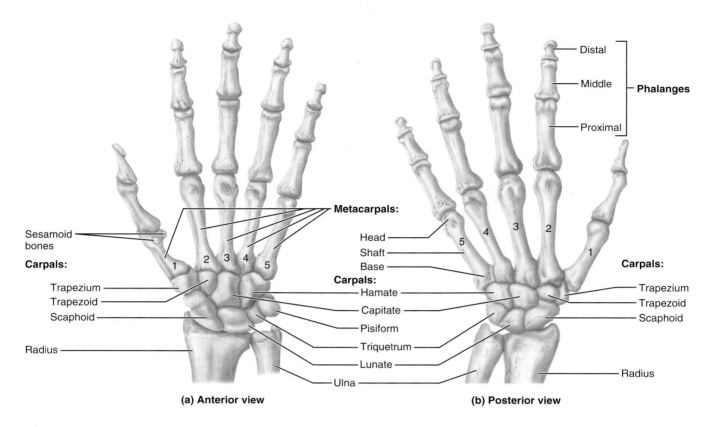

FIGURE 10.5 Bones of the right hand. **(a)** Anterior view showing the relationships of the carpals, metacarpals, and phalanges. **(b)** Posterior view.

hand. The 14 bones of the fingers, or digits, are miniature long bones, called **phalanges** (singular, *phalanx*) as noted above. Each finger contains three phalanges (proximal, middle, and distal) except the thumb, which has only two (proximal and distal).

ACTIVITY 2

Palpating the Surface Anatomy of the Pectoral Girdle and the Upper Limb

Before continuing on to study the bones of the pelvic girdle, take the time to identify the following bone markings on the skin surface of the upper limb. It is usually preferable to palpate the bone markings on your lab partner since many of these markings can only be seen from the dorsal aspect.

- Clavicle: Palpate the clavicle along its entire length from sternum to shoulder.

- Acromioclavicular joint: The high point of the shoulder, which represents the junction point between the clavicle and the acromion of the scapular spine.

- Spine of the scapula: Extend your arm at the shoulder so that your scapula moves posteriorly. As you do this, your scapular spine will be seen as a winglike protrusion on your dorsal thorax and can be easily palpated by your lab partner.

- Lateral epicondyle of the humerus: The inferiormost projection at the lateral aspect of the distal humerus. After you have located the epicondyle, run your finger posteriorly

into the hollow immediately dorsal to the epicondyle. This is the site where the extensor muscles of the hand are attached and is a common site of the excruciating pain of tennis elbow, a condition in which those muscles and their tendons are abused physically.

- Medial epicondyle of the humerus: Feel this medial projection at the distal end of the humerus.

- Olecranon process of the ulna: Work your elbow—flexing and extending—as you palpate its dorsal aspect to feel the olecranon process of the ulna moving into and out of the olecranon fossa on the dorsal aspect of the humerus.

- Styloid process of the ulna: With the hand in the anatomical position, feel out this small inferior projection on the medial aspect of the distal end of the ulna.

- Styloid process of the radius: Find this projection at the distal end of the radius (lateral aspect). It is most easily located by moving the hand medially at the wrist. Once you have palpated the styloid process, move your fingers just medially onto the anterior wrist. Press firmly and then let up slightly on the pressure. You should be able to feel your pulse at this pressure point, which lies over the radial artery (radial pulse).

- Pisiform: Just distal to the styloid process of the ulna, feel the rounded pealike pisiform bone.

- Metacarpophalangeal joints (knuckles): Clench your fist and find the first set of flexed-joint protrusions beyond the wrist—these are your metacarpophalangeal joints. ▪

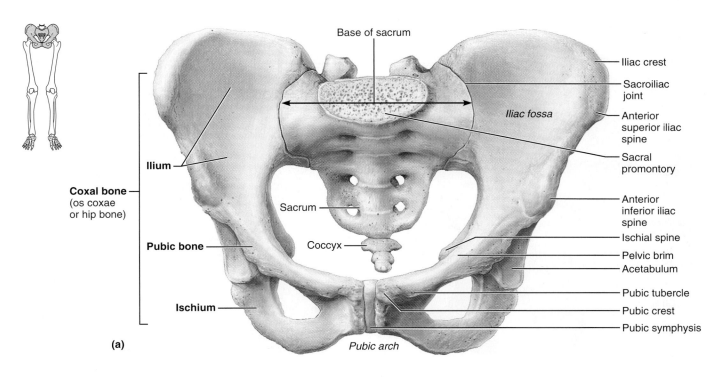

Base of sacrum

Iliac crest

Sacroiliac joint

Iliac fossa

Anterior superior iliac spine

Sacral promontory

Anterior inferior iliac spine

Ischial spine

Pelvic brim

Acetabulum

Pubic tubercle

Pubic crest

Pubic symphysis

Ilium

Coxal bone (os coxae or hip bone)

Sacrum

Pubic bone

Coccyx

Ischium

(a)

Pubic arch

FIGURE 10.6 Bones of the pelvic girdle. **(a)** Articulated bony pelvis, showing the two coxal bones, which together compose the pelvic girdle, the sacrum, and the coccyx.

Bones of the Pelvic Girdle and Lower Limb

The Pelvic (Hip) Girdle

As with the bones of the pectoral girdle and upper limb, pay particular attention to bone markings needed to identify right and left bones.

The **pelvic girdle,** or **hip girdle** (Figure 10.6), is formed by the two **coxal** (*coxa* = hip) **bones** (also called the **ossa coxae,** or hip bones). The two coxal bones together with the sacrum and coccyx form the **bony pelvis.** In contrast to the bones of the shoulder girdle, those of the pelvic girdle are heavy and massive, and they attach securely to the axial skeleton. The sockets for the heads of the femurs (thigh bones) are deep and heavily reinforced by ligaments to ensure a stable, strong limb attachment. The ability to bear weight is more important here than mobility and flexibility. The combined weight of the upper body rests on the pelvis (specifically, where the hip bones meet the sacrum).

Each coxal bone is a result of the fusion of three bones—the ilium, ischium, and pubis—which are distinguishable in the young child. The **ilium,** a large flaring bone, forms the major portion of the coxal bone. It connects posteriorly, via its **auricular surface,** with the sacrum at the **sacroiliac joint.** The superior margin of the iliac bone, the **iliac crest,** is rough; when you rest your hands on your hips, you are palpating your iliac crests. The iliac crest terminates anteriorly in the **anterior superior spine** and posteriorly in the **posterior superior spine.** Two inferior spines are located below these. The shallow **iliac fossa** marks its internal surface, and a prominent ridge, the **arcuate line,** outlines the pelvic inlet, or pelvic brim.

The **ischium** is the "sit-down" bone, forming the most inferior and posterior portion of the coxal bone. The most outstanding marking on the ischium is the rough **ischial tuberosity,** which receives the weight of the body when sitting. The **ischial spine,** superior to the ischial tuberosity, is an important anatomical landmark of the pelvic cavity (Figure 10.6). The obvious **lesser** and **greater sciatic notches** allow nerves and blood vessels to pass to and from the thigh. The sciatic nerve passes through the latter.

The **pubis,** or **pubic bone,** is the most anterior portion of the coxal bone. Fusion of the **rami** of the pubis anteriorly and the ischium posteriorly forms a bar of bone enclosing the **obturator foramen,** through which blood vessels and nerves run from the pelvic cavity into the thigh. The pubic bones of each hip bone meet anteriorly at the **pubic crest** to form a cartilaginous joint called the **pubic symphysis.** At the lateral end of the pubic crest is the *pubic tubercle* (see Figure 10.6c) to which the important *inguinal ligament* attaches.

The ilium, ischium, and pubis fuse at the deep hemispherical socket called the **acetabulum** (literally, "wine cup"), which receives the head of the thigh bone.

ACTIVITY 3

Observing Pelvic Articulations

Before continuing with the bones of the lower limbs, take the time to examine an articulated pelvis. Notice how each coxal bone articulates with the sacrum posteriorly and how the two coxal bones join at the pubic symphysis. The sacroiliac joint is a common site of lower back problems because of the pressure it must bear. ▪

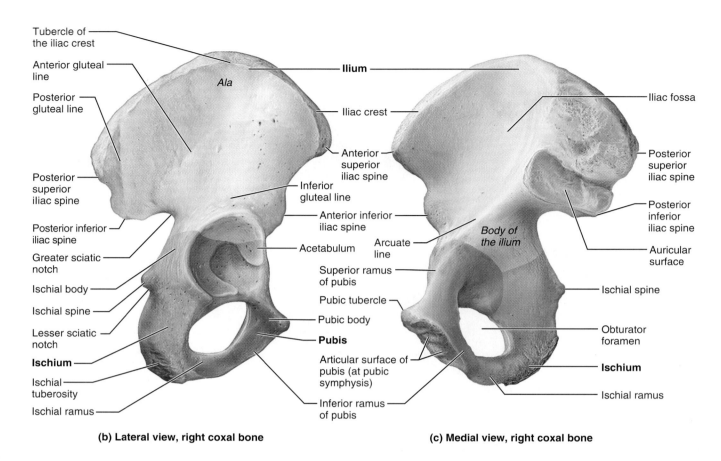

(b) Lateral view, right coxal bone

(c) Medial view, right coxal bone

FIGURE 10.6 (continued) Bones of the pelvic girdle. (b) Right coxal bone, lateral view, showing the point of fusion of the ilium, ischium, and pubic bones. **(c)** Right coxal bone, medial view.

Comparison of the Male and Female Pelves Although bones of males are usually larger, heavier, and have more prominent bone markings, the male and female skeletons are very similar. The exception to this generalization is pelvic structure.

The female pelvis reflects modifications for childbearing—it is wider, shallower, lighter, and rounder than that of the male. Not only must her pelvis support the increasing size of a fetus, but it must also be large enough to allow the infant's head (its largest dimension) to descend through the birth canal at birth.

To describe pelvic sex differences, we need to introduce a few more terms. The **false pelvis** is that portion superior to the arcuate line; it is bounded by the alae of the ilia laterally and the sacral promontory and lumbar vertebrae posteriorly. Although the false pelvis supports the abdominal viscera, it does not restrict childbirth in any way. The **true pelvis** is the region inferior to the arcuate line that is almost entirely surrounded by bone. Its posterior boundary is formed by the sacrum. The ilia, ischia, and pubic bones define its limits laterally and anteriorly.

The dimensions of the true pelvis, particularly its inlet and outlet, are critical if delivery of a baby is to be uncomplicated; and they are carefully measured by the obstetrician. The **pelvic inlet,** or **pelvic brim,** is the opening delineated by the sacral promontory posteriorly and the arcuate lines of the ilia anterolaterally. It is the superiormost margin of the true pelvis. Its widest dimension is from left to right, that is, along

the frontal plane. The **pelvic outlet** is the inferior margin of the true pelvis. It is bounded anteriorly by the pubic arch, laterally by the ischia, and posteriorly by the sacrum and coccyx. Since both the coccyx and the ischial spines protrude into the outlet opening, a sharply angled coccyx or large, sharp ischial spines can dramatically narrow the outlet. The largest dimension of the outlet is the anterior-posterior diameter.

The major differences between the male and female pelves are summarized in Table 10.1.

ACTIVITY 4

Comparing Male and Female Pelves

Examine male and female pelves for the following differences:

- The female inlet is larger and more circular.

- The female pelvis as a whole is shallower, and the bones are lighter and thinner.

- The female sacrum is broader and less curved, and the pubic arch is more rounded.

- The female acetabula are smaller and farther apart, and the ilia flare more laterally.

- The female ischial spines are shorter, farther apart, and everted, thus enlarging the pelvic outlet. ▪

TABLE 10.1	Comparison of the Male and Female Pelves	
Characteristic	Female	Male
General structure and functional modifications	Tilted forward; adapted for childbearing; true pelvis defines the birth canal; cavity of the true pelvis is broad, shallow, and has a greater capacity	Tilted less far forward; adapted for support of a male's heavier build and stronger muscles; cavity of the true pelvis is narrow and deep
Bone thickness	Less; bones lighter, thinner, and smoother	Greater; bones heavier and thicker, and markings are more prominent
Acetabula	Smaller; farther apart	Larger; closer
Pubic angle/arch	Broader (80°–290°); more rounded	More acute (50°–260°)
Anterior view		
Sacrum	Wider; shorter; sacrum is less curved	Narrow; longer; sacral promontory more ventral
Coccyx	More movable; straighter	Less movable; curves ventrally
Left lateral view		
Pelvic inlet (brim)	Wider; oval from side to side	Narrow; basically heart-shaped
Pelvic outlet	Wider; ischial spines shorter, farther apart, and everted	Narrower; ischial spines longer, sharper, and point more medially
Posteroinferior view		

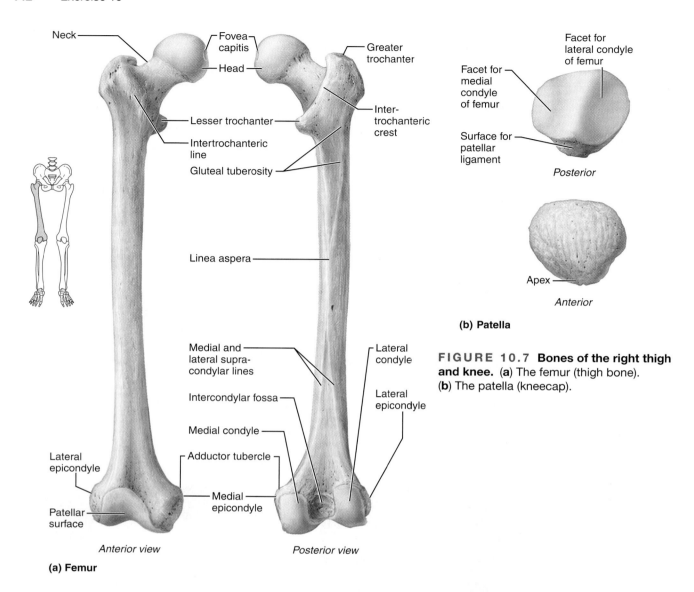

FIGURE 10.7 Bones of the right thigh and knee. (a) The femur (thigh bone). (b) The patella (kneecap).

(a) Femur

(b) Patella

The Thigh

The **femur,** or thigh bone (Figure 10.7a), is the sole bone of the thigh. It is the heaviest, strongest bone in the body. The ball-like head of the femur articulates with the hip bone via the deep, secure socket of the acetabulum. Obvious in the femur's head is a small central pit called the **fovea capitis** ("pit of the head") from which a small ligament runs to the acetabulum. The head of the femur is carried on a short, constricted *neck,* which angles laterally to join the shaft. The neck is the weakest part of the femur and is a common fracture site (an injury called a broken hip), particularly in the elderly. At the junction of the shaft and neck are the **greater** and **lesser trochanters** (separated posteriorly by the **intertrochanteric crest** and anteriorly by the **intertrochanteric line**). The trochanters and trochanteric crest, as well as the **gluteal tuberosity** and the **linea aspera** located on the shaft, are sites of muscle attachment.

The femur inclines medially as it runs downward to the leg bones; this brings the knees in line with the body's center of gravity, or maximum weight. The medial course of the femur is more noticeable in females because of the wider female pelvis.

Distally, the femur terminates in the **lateral and medial condyles,** which articulate with the tibia below, and the **patellar surface,** which forms a joint with the patella (kneecap) anteriorly. The **lateral** and **medial epicondyles,** just superior to the condyles, are separated by the **intercondylar fossa.** On the superior part of the medial epicondyle is a bump, the **adductor tubercle,** to which the large adductor magnus muscle attaches.

The **patella** (Figure 10.7b) is a triangular sesamoid bone enclosed in the (quadriceps) tendon that secures the anterior thigh muscles to the tibia. It guards the knee joint anteriorly and improves the leverage of the thigh muscles acting across the knee joint.

The Leg

Two bones, the tibia and the fibula, form the skeleton of the leg (see Figure 10.8). The **tibia,** or *shinbone,* is the larger and more medial of the two leg bones. At the proximal end, the **medial** and **lateral condyles** (separated by the **intercondylar eminence**) receive the distal end of the femur to form the knee joint. The **tibial tuberosity,** a roughened protrusion on the anterior tibial surface (just below the condyles), is the site

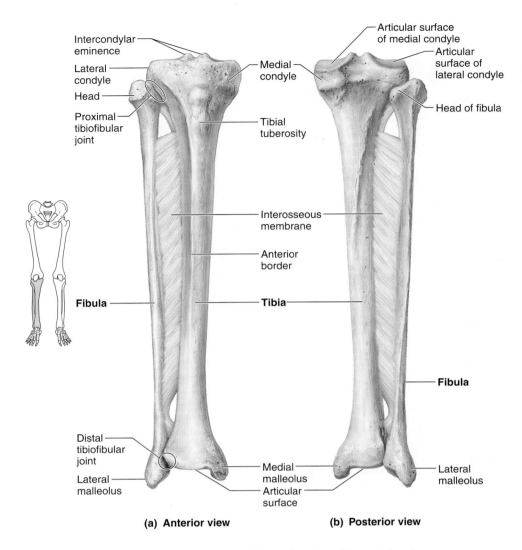

(a) Anterior view   (b) Posterior view

FIGURE 10.8 Bones of the right leg. Tibia and fibula, **(a)** anterior view, **(b)** posterior view.

of attachment of the patellar (kneecap) ligament. Small facets on its superior and inferior lateral surface articulate with the fibula. Distally, a process called the **medial malleolus** forms the inner (medial) bulge of the ankle, and the smaller distal end articulates with the talus bone of the foot. The anterior surface of the tibia bears a sharpened ridge that is relatively unprotected by muscles. This so-called **anterior border** is easily felt beneath the skin.

The **fibula,** which lies parallel to the tibia, takes no part in forming the knee joint. Its proximal head articulates with the lateral condyle of the tibia. The fibula is thin and sticklike with a sharp anterior crest. It terminates distally in the **lateral malleolus,** which forms the outer part, or lateral bulge, of the ankle.

The Foot

The bones of the foot include the 7 **tarsal** bones, 5 **metatarsals,** which form the instep, and 14 **phalanges,** which form the toes (see Figure 10.9). Body weight is concentrated on the two largest tarsals, which form the posterior aspect of the foot, the *calcaneus* (heel bone) and the *talus,* which lies between the tibia and the calcaneus. The other tarsals are named and identified in Figure 10.9. Like the fingers of the

hand, each toe has three phalanges except the great toe, which has two.

The bones in the foot are arranged to produce three strong arches—two longitudinal arches (medial and lateral) and one transverse arch (Figure 10.9b). Ligaments, binding the foot bones together, and tendons of the foot muscles hold the bones firmly in the arched position but still allow a certain degree of give. Weakened arches are referred to as fallen arches or flat feet.

ACTIVITY 5

Palpating the Surface Anatomy of the Pelvic Girdle and Lower Limb

Locate and palpate the following bone markings on yourself and/or your lab partner.

- Iliac crest and anterior superior iliac spine: Rest your hands on your hips—they will be overlying the iliac crests. Trace the crest as far posteriorly as you can and then follow it anteriorly to the anterior superior iliac spine. This latter bone

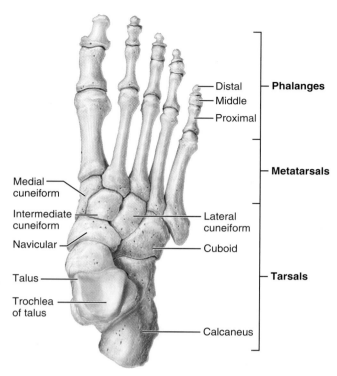

Phalanges
— Distal
— Middle
— Proximal

Metatarsals

Medial cuneiform

Intermediate cuneiform

Navicular

Lateral cuneiform

Cuboid

Tarsals

Talus

Trochlea of talus

Calcaneus

(a) Superior view

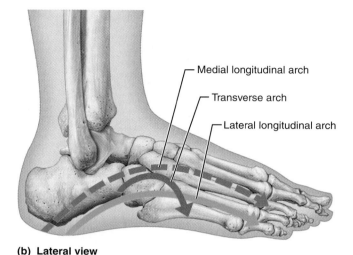

— Medial longitudinal arch
— Transverse arch
— Lateral longitudinal arch

(b) Lateral view

FIGURE 10.9 Bones of the right foot.
(**a**) Superior view. (**b**) Lateral view showing arches of the foot.

marking is easily felt in almost everyone, and is clearly visible through the skin (and perhaps the clothing) of very slim people. (The posterior superior iliac spine is much less obvious and is usually indicated only by a dimple in the overlying skin. Check it out in the mirror tonight.)

• Greater trochanter of the femur: This is easier to locate in females than in males because of the wider female pelvis; also it is more likely to be clothed by bulky muscles in males. Try to locate it on yourself as the most lateral point of the proximal femur. It typically lies about 6 to 8 inches below the iliac crest.

• Patella and tibial tuberosity: Feel your kneecap and palpate the ligaments attached to its borders. Follow the inferior patellar ligament to the tibial tuberosity.

• Medial and lateral condyles of the femur and tibia: As you move from the patella inferiorly on the medial (and then the lateral) knee surface, you will feel first the femoral and then the tibial condyle.

• Medial malleolus: Feel the medial protrusion of your ankle, the medial malleolus of the distal tibia.

• Lateral malleolus: Feel the bulge of the lateral aspect of your ankle, the lateral malleolus of the fibula.

• Calcaneus: Attempt to follow the extent of your calcaneus, or heel bone. ■

ACTIVITY 6

Constructing a Skeleton

1. When you finish examining yourself and the disarticulated bones of the appendicular skeleton, work with your lab partner to arrange the disarticulated bones on the laboratory bench in their proper relative positions to form an entire skeleton. Careful observation of bone markings should help you distinguish between right and left members of bone pairs.

2. When you believe that you have accomplished this task correctly, ask the instructor to check your arrangement to ensure that it is correct. If it is not, go to the articulated skeleton and check your bone arrangements. Also review the descriptions of the bone markings as necessary to correct your bone arrangement. ■

NAME _____

LAB TIME/DATE _____

The Appendicular Skeleton

Bones of the Pectoral Girdle and Upper Extremity

1. Match the bone names or markings in column B with the descriptions in column A.

Column A

Column B

_____ 1. raised area on lateral surface of humerus to which deltoid muscle attaches

_____ 2. arm bone

_____, _____ 3. bones of the shoulder girdle

_____, _____ 4. forearm bones

_____ 5. scapular region to which the clavicle connects

_____ 6. shoulder girdle bone that is unattached to the axial skeleton

_____ 7. shoulder girdle bone that transmits forces from the upper limb to the bony thorax

_____ 8. depression in the scapula that articulates with the humerus

_____ 9. process above the glenoid cavity that permits muscle attachment

_____ 10. the "collarbone"

_____ 11. distal condyle of the humerus that articulates with the ulna

_____ 12. medial bone of forearm in anatomical position

_____ 13. rounded knob on the humerus; adjoins the radius

_____ 14. anterior depression, superior to the trochlea, which receives part of the ulna when the forearm is flexed

_____ 15. forearm bone involved in formation of the elbow joint

_____ 16. wrist bones

_____ 17. finger bones

_____ 18. heads of these bones form the knuckles

_____, _____ 19. bones that articulate with the clavicle

a. acromion

b. capitulum

c. carpals

d. clavicle

e. coracoid process

f. coronoid fossa

g. deltoid tuberosity

h. glenoid cavity

i. humerus

j. metacarpals

k. olecranon fossa

l. olecranon process

m. phalanges

n. radial tuberosity

o. radius

p. scapula

q. sternum

r. styloid process

s. trochlea

t. ulna

2. Why is the clavicle at risk to fracture when a person falls on his or her shoulder? _____

_____

3. Why is it generally no problem for the arm to clear the widest dimension of the thoracic cage?

_____

_____

4. What is the total number of phalanges in the hand? _____

5. What is the total number of carpals in the wrist? _____

Name the carpals (medial to lateral) in the proximal row. _____

In the distal row, they are (medial to lateral) _____

6. Using items from the list at the right, identify the anatomical landmarks and regions of the scapula.

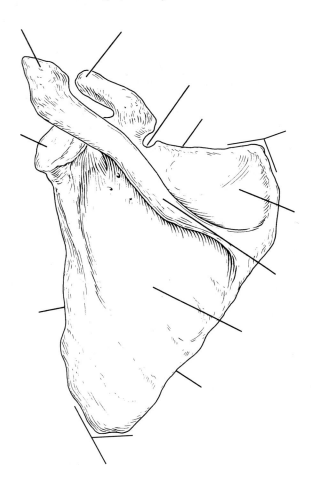

Key:

a. acromion

b. coracoid process

c. glenoid cavity

d. inferior angle

e. infraspinous fossa

f. lateral border

g. medial border

h. spine

i. superior angle

j. superior border

k. suprascapular notch

l. supraspinous fossa

7. Match the terms in the key with the appropriate leader lines on the drawings of the humerus and the radius and ulna. Also decide whether the bones shown are right or left bones.

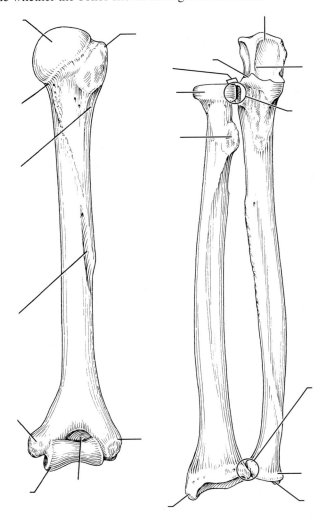

Key:

a.   anatomical neck

b.   coronoid process

c.   distal radioulnar joint

d.   greater tubercle

e.   head of humerus

f.   head of radius

g.   head of ulna

h.   lateral epicondyle

i.   medial epicondyle

j.   olecranon fossa

k.   olecranon process

l.   proximal radioulnar joint

m.   radial groove

n.   radial notch

o.   radial tuberosity

p.   styloid process of radius

q.   styloid process of ulna

r.   surgical neck

s.   trochlea

t.   trochlear notch

Circle the correct term for each pair in parentheses:

The humerus is the (right/left) bone in (an anterior/a posterior) view. The radius and ulna are (right/left) bones in (an anterior/a posterior) view.

Bones of the Pelvic Girdle and Lower Limb

8. Compare the pectoral and pelvic girdles by choosing appropriate descriptive terms from the key.

Key: a.   flexibility most important
       b.   massive
       c.   lightweight

d.   insecure axial and limb attachments
e.   secure axial and limb attachments
f.   weight-bearing most important

Pectoral: _____, _____, _____   Pelvic: _____, _____, _____

9. What organs are protected, at least in part, by the pelvic girdle? _____

_____

10. Distinguish between the true pelvis and the false pelvis. _____

_____

11. Use letters from the key to identify the bone markings on this illustration of an articulated pelvis. Make an educated guess as to whether the illustration shows a male or female pelvis and provide two reasons for your decision.

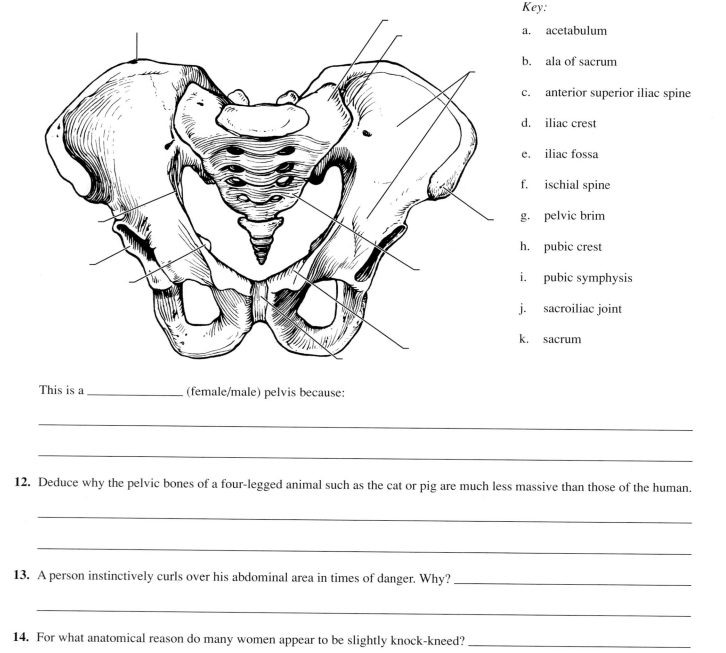

Key:

a.   acetabulum

b.   ala of sacrum

c.   anterior superior iliac spine

d.   iliac crest

e.   iliac fossa

f.   ischial spine

g.   pelvic brim

h.   pubic crest

i.   pubic symphysis

j.   sacroiliac joint

k.   sacrum

This is a _____ (female/male) pelvis because:

_____

_____

12. Deduce why the pelvic bones of a four-legged animal such as the cat or pig are much less massive than those of the human.

_____

_____

13. A person instinctively curls over his abdominal area in times of danger. Why? _____

_____

14. For what anatomical reason do many women appear to be slightly knock-kneed? _____

_____

_____

15. What does *fallen arches* mean? _____

_____

16. Match the bone names and markings in column B with the descriptions in column A.

Column A

_____, _____, and

_____ 1. fuse to form the coxal bone

_____ 2. inferoposterior "bone" of the coxal bone

_____ 3. point where the coxal bones join anteriorly

_____ 4. superiormost margin of the coxal bone

_____ 5. deep socket in the coxal bone that receives the head of the thigh bone

_____ 6. joint between axial skeleton and pelvic girdle

_____ 7. longest, strongest bone in body

_____ 8. thin lateral leg bone

_____ 9. heavy medial leg bone

_____, _____ 10. bones forming knee joint

_____ 11. point where the patellar ligament attaches

_____ 12. kneecap

_____ 13. shinbone

_____ 14. medial ankle projection

_____ 15. lateral ankle projection

_____ 16. largest tarsal bone

_____ 17. ankle bones

_____ 18. bones forming the instep of the foot

_____ 19. opening in hip bone formed by the pubic and ischial rami

_____ and _____ 20. sites of muscle attachment on the proximal femur

_____ 21. tarsal bone that "sits" on the calcaneus

_____ 22. weight-bearing bone of the leg

_____ 23. tarsal bone that articulates with the tibia

Column B

a. acetabulum

b. calcaneus

c. femur

d. fibula

e. gluteal tuberosity

f. greater and lesser trochanters

g. greater sciatic notch

h. iliac crest

i. ilium

j. ischial tuberosity

k. ischium

l. lateral malleolus

m. lesser sciatic notch

n. linea aspera

o. medial malleolus

p. metatarsals

q. obturator foramen

r. patella

s. pubic symphysis

t. pubis

u. sacroiliac joint

v. talus

w. tarsals

x. tibia

y. tibial tuberosity

17. Match the terms in the key with the appropriate leader lines on the drawings of the femur and the tibia and fibula. Also decide if these bones are right or left bones and whether it is their anterior or posterior view that is illustrated.

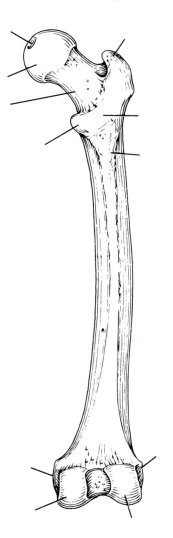
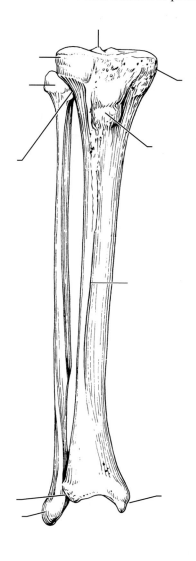

Key:

a.   distal tibiofibular joint

b.   fovea capitis

c.   gluteal tuberosity

d.   greater trochanter

e.   head of femur

f.   head of fibula

g.   intercondylar eminence

h.   intertrochanteric crest

i.   lateral condyle

j.   lateral epicondyle

k.   lateral malleolus

l.   lesser trochanter

m. medial condyle

n.   medial epicondyle

o.   medial malleolus

p.   neck of femur

q.   proximal tibiofibular joint

r.   tibial anterior border

s.   tibial tuberosity

The femur (the diagram on the ———————————— side) is the ———————————— member of the two femurs

illustrated in a(n) ———————————— view. The tibia and fibula (the diagram on the ———————————— side) are

———————————— bones illustrated in a(n) ———————————— view.

Summary of Skeleton

18. Identify all indicated bones (or groups of bones) in the diagram of the articulated skeleton on p. 151.

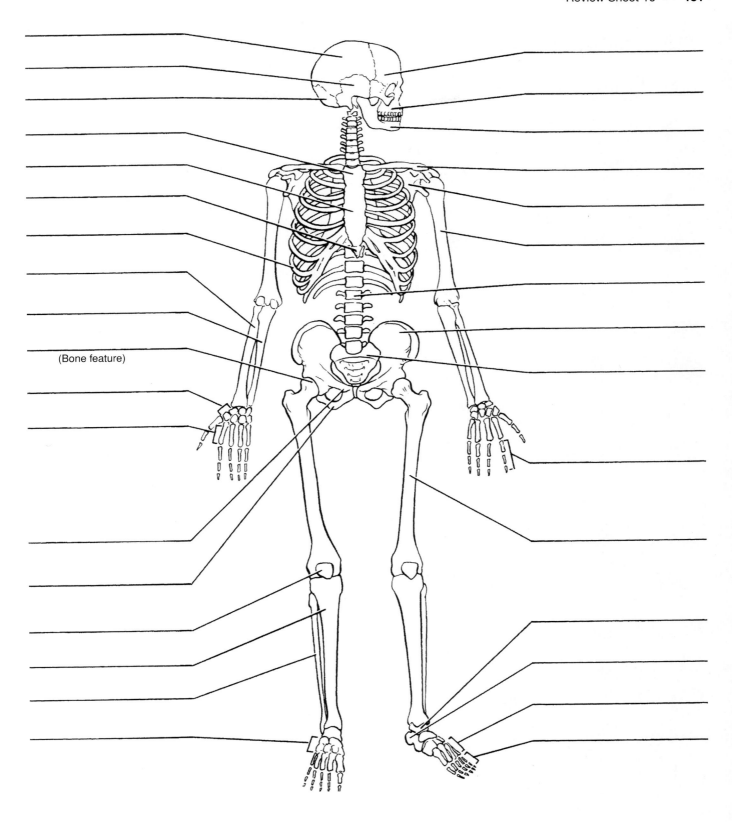

(Bone feature)

The Fetal Skeleton

OBJECTIVES

1. To demonstrate important differences between the fetal and adult skeletons.
2. To define *fontanelle* and discuss the function and fate of fontanelles in the fetus.

A human fetus about to be born has 275 bones, many more than the 206 bones found in the adult skeleton. This is because many of the bones described as single bones in the adult skeleton (for example, the coxal bone, sternum, and sacrum) have not yet fully ossified and fused in the fetus.

ACTIVITY

Examining a Fetal Skull and Skeleton

1. Obtain a fetal skeleton or use Figure 11.1, and examine it carefully, noting differences between it and an adult skeleton. Pay particular attention to the vertebrae, sternum, frontal bone of the cranium, patellae (kneecaps), coxal bones, carpals and tarsals, and rib cage.

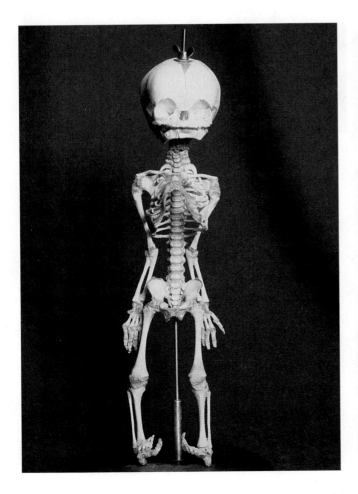 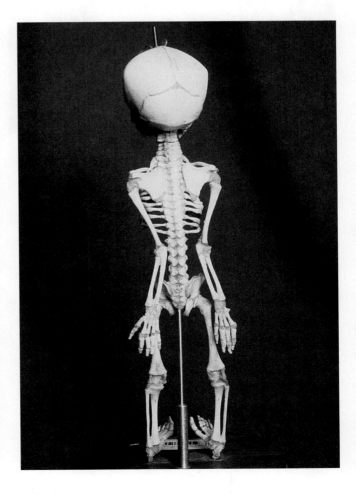

FIGURE 11.1 The fetal skeleton. Left, anterior view; right, posterior view.

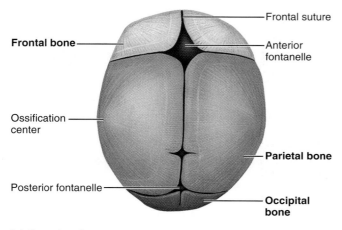

(a) Superior view

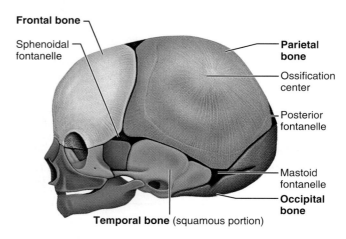

(b) Right lateral view

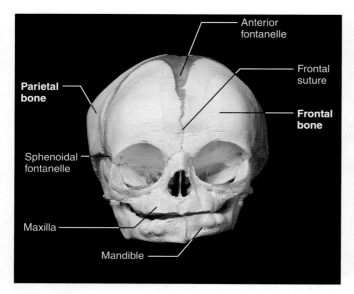

(c) Anterior view

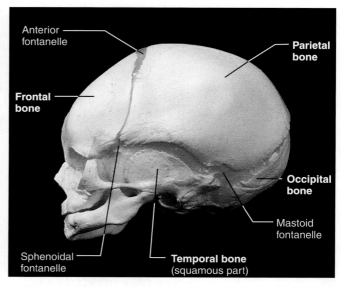

(d) Left lateral view

FIGURE 11.2 **The fetal skull.**

2. Obtain a fetal skull and study it carefully. Make observations as needed to answer the following questions.

• Does it have the same bones as the adult skull?

• How does the size of the fetal face relate to the cranium?

• How does this compare to what is seen in the adult?

3. Indentations between the bones of the fetal skull, called **fontanelles,** are fibrous membranes. These areas will become bony (ossify) as the fetus ages, completing the process by the age of 20 to 22 months. The fontanelles allow the fetal skull to be compressed slightly during birth and also allow for brain growth during late fetal life. Locate the following

fontanelles on the fetal skull with the aid of Figure 11.2: *anterior* (or *frontal*) *fontanelle, mastoid fontanelle, sphenoidal fontanelle,* and *posterior* (or *occipital*) *fontanelle.*

4. Notice that some of the cranial bones have conical protrusions. These are **ossification (growth) centers.** Notice also that the frontal bone is still bipartite, and the temporal bone is incompletely ossified, little more than a ring of bone.

5. Check the questions in the Review Sheet before completing this study to ensure that you have made all of the necessary observations. ■

NAME_____

LAB TIME/DATE _____

The Fetal Skeleton

1. Describe how the fetal skeleton compares with the adult skeleton in the following areas:

   vertebrae: _____

   _____

   ossa coxae: _____

   _____

   carpals and tarsals: _____

   sternum: _____

   frontal bone: _____

   patella: _____

   rib cage: _____

   _____

2. Are the same skull bones seen in the adult also found in the fetal skull? _____

3. How does the size of the fetal face compare to its cranium? _____

   _____

   How does this compare to the adult skull? _____

   _____

   _____

4. What are the outward conical projections on some of the fetal cranial bones? _____

5. What is a fontanelle? _____

   What is its fate? _____

   What is the function of the fontanelles in the fetal skull? _____

   _____

6. How does the size of the fetus's head compare to the size of its body? _____

_____

7. Using the terms listed, identify each of the fontanelles shown on the fetal skull below.

Key: a. anterior fontanelle   b. mastoid fontanelle   c. posterior fontanelle   d. sphenoidal fontanelle

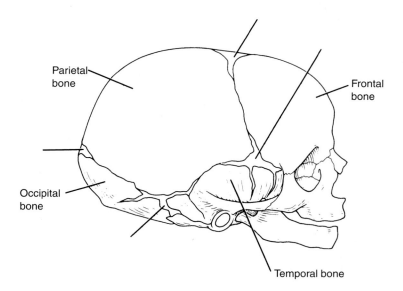

Parietal bone

Frontal bone

Occipital bone

Temporal bone

12

Articulations and Body Movements

O B J E C T I V E S

1. To name and describe the three functional categories of joints.

2. To name and describe the three structural categories of joints, and to compare their structure and mobility.

3. To identify the types of synovial joints.

4. To define *origin* and *insertion* for muscles.

5. To demonstrate or identify the various body movements.

With rare exceptions, every bone in the body is connected to, or forms a joint with, at least one other bone. **Articulations,** or joints, perform two functions for the body. They (1) hold the bones together and (2) allow the rigid skeletal system some flexibility so that gross body movements can occur.

Joints may be classified structurally or functionally. The structural classification is based on the presence of connective tissue fiber, cartilage, or a joint cavity between the articulating bones. Structurally, there are *fibrous, cartilaginous,* and *synovial joints.*

The functional classification focuses on the amount of movement allowed at the joint. On this basis, there are **synarthroses,** or immovable joints; **amphiarthroses,** or slightly movable joints; and **diarthroses,** or freely movable joints. Freely movable joints predominate in the limbs, whereas immovable and slightly movable joints are largely restricted to the axial skeleton, where firm bony attachments and protection of enclosed organs are a priority.

As a general rule, fibrous joints are immovable, and synovial joints are freely movable. Cartilaginous joints offer both rigid and slightly movable examples. Since the structural categories are more clear-cut, we will use the structural classification here and indicate functional properties as appropriate.

Fibrous Joints

In **fibrous joints,** the bones are joined by fibrous tissue. No joint cavity is present. The amount of movement allowed depends on the length of the fibers uniting the bones. Although some fibrous joints are slightly movable, most are synarthrotic and permit virtually no movement.

The two major types of fibrous joints are sutures and syndesmoses. In **sutures** (Figure 12.1d) the irregular edges of the bones interlock and are united by very short connective tissue fibers, as in most joints of the skull. In **syndesmoses** the articulating bones are connected by short ligaments of dense fibrous tissue; the bones do not interlock. The joint at the distal end of the tibia and fibula is an example of a syndesmosis (Figure 12.1e). Although this syndesmosis allows some give, it is classed functionally as a synarthrosis. Not illustrated here is a **gomphosis,** in which a tooth is secured in a bony socket by the periodontal ligament (see Figure 27.12, p. 467).

A C T I V I T Y   1

Identifying Fibrous Joints

Examine a human skull again. Notice that adjacent bone surfaces do not actually touch but are separated by fibrous connective tissue. Also examine a skeleton and anatomical chart of joint types and Table 12.1 on pp. 164 and 165 for examples of fibrous joints. ■

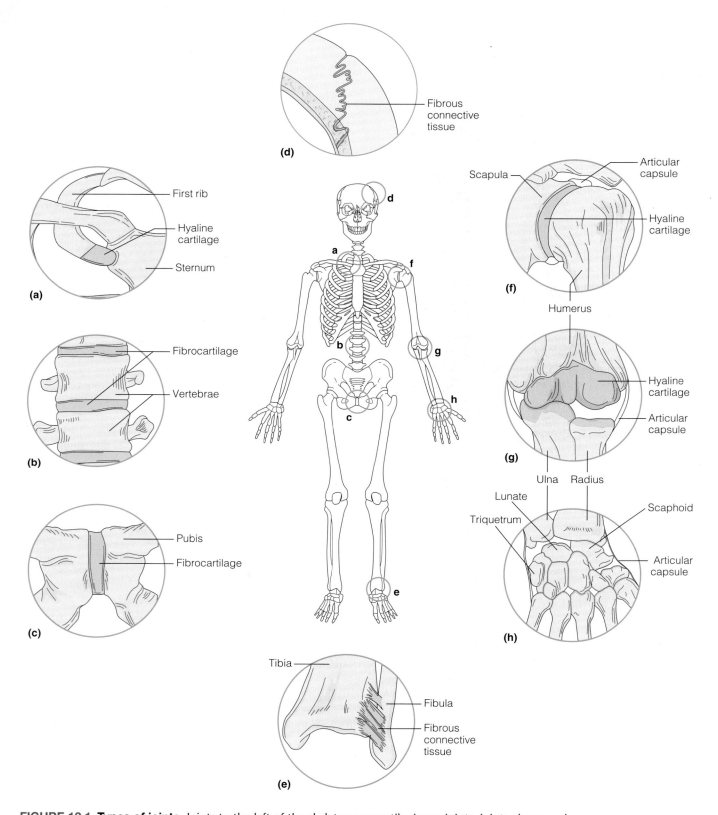

FIGURE 12.1 Types of joints. Joints to the left of the skeleton are cartilaginous joints; joints above and below the skeleton are fibrous joints; joints to the right of the skeleton are synovial joints. **(a)** Synchondrosis (joint between costal cartilage of rib 1 and the sternum). **(b)** Symphyses (intervertebral discs of fibrocartilage connecting adjacent vertebrae). **(c)** Symphysis (fibrocartilaginous pubic symphysis connecting the pubic bones anteriorly). **(d)** Suture (fibrous connective tissue connecting interlocking skull bones). **(e)** Syndesmosis (fibrous connective tissue connecting the distal ends of the tibia and fibula). **(f)** Synovial joint (multiaxial shoulder joint). **(g)** Synovial joint (uniaxial elbow joint). **(h)** Synovial joints (biaxial radiocarpal joint of the hand).

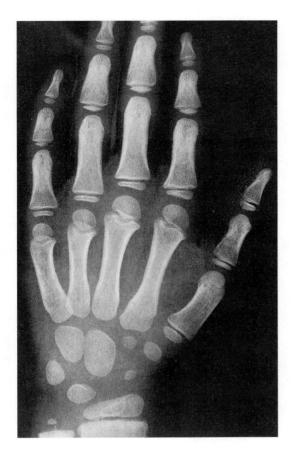

FIGURE 12.2 X ray of the hand of a child. Notice the cartilaginous epiphyseal plates, examples of temporary synchondroses.

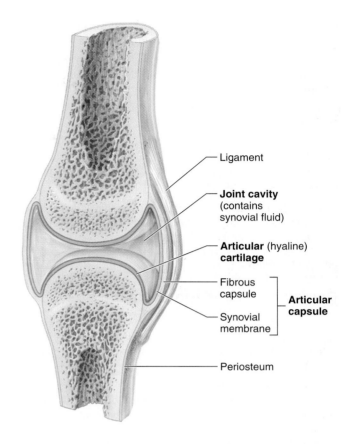

FIGURE 12.3 Major structural features of a synovial joint.

Cartilaginous Joints

In **cartilaginous joints,** the articulating bone ends are connected by a plate or pad of cartilage. No joint cavity is present. The two major types of cartilaginous joints are synchondroses and symphyses. Although there is variation, most cartilaginous joints are *slightly movable* (amphiarthrotic) functionally. In **symphyses** (*symphysis* = "a growing together"), the bones are connected by a broad, flat disc of fibrocartilage. The intervertebral joints and the pubic symphysis of the pelvis are symphyses (see Figure 12.1b and c). In **synchondroses** the bony portions are united by hyaline cartilage. The articulation of the costal cartilage of the first rib with the sternum (Figure 12.1a) is a synchondrosis, but perhaps the best examples of synchondroses are the epiphyseal plates seen in the long bones of growing children (Figure 12.2). The epiphyseal plates are flexible during childhood but eventually they are totally ossified.

ACTIVITY 2

Identifying Cartilaginous Joints

Identify the cartilaginous joints on a human skeleton, Table 12.1 on pp. 164 and 165, and on an anatomical chart of joint types. ▮

Synovial Joints

Synovial joints are those in which the articulating bone ends are separated by a joint cavity containing synovial fluid (see Figure 12.1f–h). All synovial joints are diarthroses, or freely movable joints. Their mobility varies, however; some synovial joints can move in only one plane, and others can move in several directions (multiaxial movement). Most joints in the body are synovial joints.

All synovial joints have the following structural characteristics (Figure 12.3):

•   The joint surfaces are enclosed by a two-layered *articular capsule* (a sleeve of connective tissue), creating a joint cavity.

•   The inner layer is a smooth connective tissue membrane, called *synovial membrane,* which produces a lubricating fluid (synovial fluid) that reduces friction. The outer layer, or *fibrous capsule,* is dense irregular connective tissue.

•   *Articular* (hyaline) *cartilage* covers the surfaces of the bones forming the joint.

- The articular capsule is typically reinforced with ligaments and may contain *bursae* (fluid-filled sacs that reduce friction where tendons cross bone).

- Fibrocartilage pads *(articular discs)* may be present within the capsule.

ACTIVITY 3

Examining Synovial Joint Structure

Examine a beef or pig joint to identify the general structural features of diarthrotic joints as listed above.

⚠️ If the joint is freshly obtained from the slaughterhouse and you will be handling it, don disposable gloves before beginning your observations. ■

ACTIVITY 4

Demonstrating the Importance of Friction-Reducing Structures

1. Obtain a small water balloon and clamp. Partially fill the balloon with water (it should still be flaccid), and clamp it closed.

2. Position the balloon atop one of your fists and press down on its top surface with the other fist. Push on the balloon until your two fists touch and move your fists back and forth over one another. Assess the amount of friction generated.

3. Unclamp the balloon and add more water. The goal is to get just enough water in the balloon so that your fists cannot come into contact with one another, but instead remain separated by a thin water layer when pressure is applied to the balloon.

4. Repeat the movements in step 2 to assess the amount of friction generated.

How does the presence of a sac containing fluid influence the amount of friction generated?

_____

_____

What anatomical structure(s) does the water-containing balloon mimic?

_____

_____

What anatomical structures might be represented by your fists?

_____ ■

Types of Synovial Joints

Because there are so many types of synovial joints, they have been divided into the following subcategories on the basis of movements allowed (Figure 12.4):

- Plane (Gliding): Articulating surfaces are flat or slightly curved, allowing sliding movements in one or two planes. Examples are the intercarpal and intertarsal joints and the vertebrocostal joints of ribs 2–7.

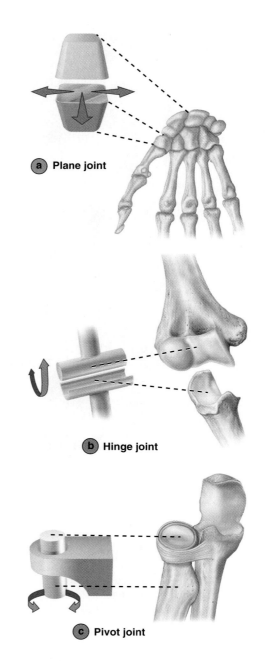

FIGURE 12.4 Types of synovial joints. Dashed lines indicate the articulating bones. **(a)** Plane joint (e.g., intercarpal and intertarsal joints). **(b)** Hinge joint (e.g., elbow joints and interphalangeal joints). **(c)** Pivot joint (e.g., proximal radioulnar joint).

- Hinge: The rounded process of one bone fits into the concave surface of another to allow movement in one plane (uniaxial), usually flexion and extension. Examples are the elbow and interphalangeal joints.

- Pivot: The rounded or conical surface of one bone articulates with a shallow depression or foramen in another bone. Pivot joints allow uniaxial rotation, as in the proximal radioulnar joint and the joint between the atlas and axis (C_1 and C_2).

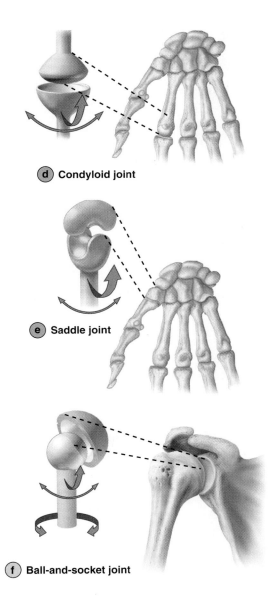

(d) **Condyloid joint**

(e) **Saddle joint**

(f) **Ball-and-socket joint**

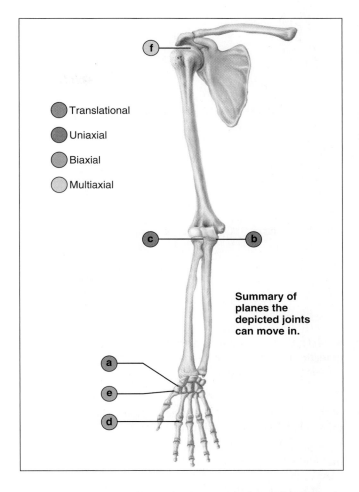

Translational

Uniaxial

Biaxial

Multiaxial

Summary of planes the depicted joints can move in.

FIGURE 12.4 *(continued)* **Types of synovial joints.**
(**d**) Condyloid joint (e.g., metacarpophalangeal joints).
(**e**) Saddle joint (e.g., carpometacarpal joint of the thumb).
(**f**) Ball-and-socket joint (e.g., shoulder joint).

- Condyloid (Ellipsoidal): The oval condyle of one bone fits into an ellipsoidal depression in another bone, allowing biaxial (two-way) movement. The radiocarpal (wrist) joint and the metacarpophalangeal joints (knuckles) are examples.

- Saddle: Articulating surfaces are saddle-shaped; the articulating surface of one bone is convex, and the reciprocal surface is concave. Saddle joints, which are biaxial, include the joint between the thumb metacarpal and the trapezium of the wrist.

- Ball and socket: The ball-shaped head of one bone fits into a cuplike depression of another. These are multiaxial joints, allowing movement in all directions and pivotal rotation. Examples are the shoulder and hip joints.

Movements Allowed by Synovial Joints

Every muscle of the body is attached to bone (or other connective tissue structures) at two points—the **origin** (the stationary, immovable, or less movable attachment) and the **insertion** (the movable attachment). Body movement occurs when muscles contract across diarthrotic synovial joints (Figure 12.5). When the muscle contracts and its fibers shorten, the insertion moves toward the origin. The type of movement depends on the construction of the joint (uniaxial, biaxial, or multiaxial) and on the placement of the muscle relative to the joint. The most common types of body movements are described below and illustrated in Figure 12.6.

ACTIVITY 5

Demonstrating Movements of Synovial Joints

Attempt to demonstrate each movement as you read through the following material:

Flexion (Figure 12.6a and c): A movement, generally in the sagittal plane, that decreases the angle of the joint and reduces the distance between the two bones. Flexion is typical

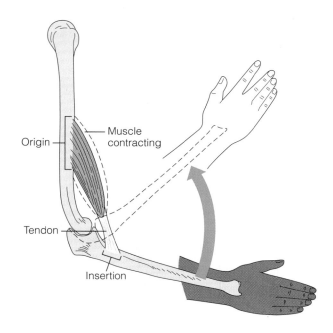

FIGURE 12.5 Muscle attachments (origin and insertion). When a skeletal muscle contracts, its insertion moves toward its origin.

of hinge joints (bending the knee or elbow) but is also common at ball-and-socket joints (bending forward at the hip).

Extension (Figure 12.6a and c): A movement that increases the angle of a joint and the distance between two bones or parts of the body (straightening the knee or elbow); the opposite of flexion. If extension is greater than 180 degrees (bending the trunk backward), it is termed *hyperextension*.

Abduction (Figure 12.6d): Movement of a limb away from the midline or median plane of the body, generally on the frontal plane, or the fanning movement of fingers or toes when they are spread apart.

Adduction (Figure 12.6d): Movement of a limb toward the midline of the body; the opposite of abduction.

Rotation (Figure 12.6b and e): Movement of a bone around its longitudinal axis without lateral or medial displacement. Rotation, a common movement of ball-and-socket joints, also describes the movement of the atlas around the dens of the axis.

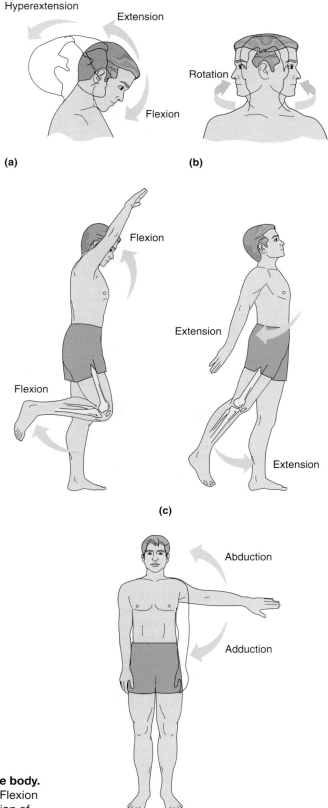

FIGURE 12.6 Movements occurring at synovial joints of the body. (**a**) Flexion and extension of the head. (**b**) Rotation of the head. (**c**) Flexion and extension of the knee and shoulder. (**d**) Abduction and adduction of the arm.

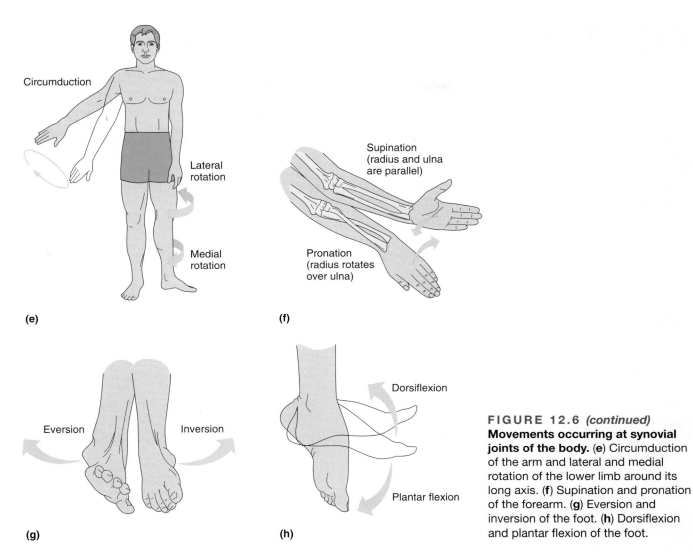

(e) **(f)** **(g)** **(h)**

FIGURE 12.6 *(continued)*
Movements occurring at synovial joints of the body. (**e**) Circumduction of the arm and lateral and medial rotation of the lower limb around its long axis. (**f**) Supination and pronation of the forearm. (**g**) Eversion and inversion of the foot. (**h**) Dorsiflexion and plantar flexion of the foot.

Circumduction (Figure 12.6e): A combination of flexion, extension, abduction, and adduction commonly observed in ball-and-socket joints like the shoulder. The proximal end of the limb remains stationary, and the distal end moves in a circle. The limb as a whole outlines a cone. Condyloid and saddle joints also allow circumduction.

Pronation (Figure 12.6f): Movement of the palm of the hand from an anterior or upward-facing position to a posterior or downward-facing position. The distal end of the radius moves across the ulna.

Supination (Figure 12.6f): Movement of the palm from a posterior position to an anterior position (the anatomical position); the opposite of pronation. During supination, the radius and ulna are parallel.

The last four terms refer to movements of the foot:

Inversion (Figure 12.6g): A movement that results in the medial turning of the sole of the foot.

Eversion (Figure 12.6g): A movement that results in the lateral turning of the sole of the foot; the opposite of inversion.

Dorsiflexion (Figure 12.6h): A movement of the ankle joint in a dorsal direction (standing on one's heels).

Plantar flexion (Figure 12.6h): A movement of the ankle joint in which the foot is flexed downward (standing on one's toes or pointing the toes). ▬

ACTIVITY 6

Demonstrating Uniaxial, Biaxial, and Multiaxial Movements

Using the information gained in the previous activity, perform the following demonstrations and complete the three charts on p. 165. ▬

| TABLE 12.1 | Structural and Functional Characteristics of Body Joints |

Illustration	Joint	Articulating bones	Structural type*	Functional type; movements allowed
	Skull	Cranial and facial bones	Fibrous; suture	Synarthrotic; no movement
	Temporo-mandibular	Temporal bone of skull and mandible	Synovial; modified hinge† (contains articular disc)	Diarthrotic; gliding and uniaxial rotation; slight lateral movement, elevation, depression, protraction, and retraction of mandible
	Atlanto-occipital	Occipital bone of skull and atlas	Synovial; condyloid	Diarthrotic; biaxial; flexion, extension, lateral flexion, circumduction of head on neck
	Atlantoaxial	Atlas (C1) and axis (C2)	Synovial; pivot	Diarthrotic; uniaxial; rotation of the head
	Intervertebral	Between adjacent vertebral bodies	Cartilaginous; symphysis	Amphiarthrotic; slight movement
	Intervertebral	Between articular processes	Synovial; plane	Diarthrotic; gliding
	Vertebrocostal	Vertebrae (transverse processes or bodies) and ribs	Synovial; plane	Diarthrotic; gliding of ribs
	Sternoclavicular	Sternum and clavicle	Synovial; shallow saddle (contains articular disc)	Diarthrotic; multiaxial (allows clavicle to move in all axes)
	Sternocostal (first)	Sternum and rib 1	Cartilaginous; synchondrosis	Synarthrotic; no movement
	Sternocostal	Sternum and ribs 2–7	Synovial; double plane	Diarthrotic; gliding
	Acromio-clavicular	Acromion of scapula and clavicle	Synovial; plane (contains articular disc)	Diarthrotic; gliding and rotation of scapula on clavicle
	Shoulder (glenohumeral)	Scapula and humerus	Synovial; ball and socket	Diarthrotic; multiaxial; flexion, extension, abduction, adduction, circumduction, rotation of humerus
	Elbow	Ulna (and radius) with humerus	Synovial; hinge	Diarthrotic; uniaxial; flexion, extension of forearm
	Radioulnar (proximal)	Radius and ulna	Synovial; pivot	Diarthrotic; uniaxial; rotation of radius around long axis of forearm to allow pronation and supination
	Radioulnar (distal)	Radius and ulna	Synovial; pivot (contains articular disc)	Diarthrotic; uniaxial; rotation (convex head of ulna rotates in ulnar notch of radius)
	Wrist (radiocarpal)	Radius and proximal carpals	Synovial; condyloid	Diarthrotic; biaxial; flexion, extension, abduction, adduction, circumduction of hand
	Intercarpal	Adjacent carpals	Synovial; plane	Diarthrotic; gliding
	Carpometacarpal of digit 1 (thumb)	Carpal (trapezium) and metacarpal 1	Synovial; saddle	Diarthrotic; biaxial; flexion, extension, abduction, adduction, circumduction, opposition of metacarpal 1
	Carpometacarpal of digits 2–5	Carpal(s) and metacarpal(s)	Synovial; plane	Diarthrotic; gliding of metacarpals
	Knuckle (metacarpo-phalangeal)	Metacarpal and proximal phalanx	Synovial; condyloid	Diarthrotic; biaxial; flexion, extension, abduction, adduction, circumduction of fingers
	Finger (interphalangeal)	Adjacent phalanges	Synovial; hinge	Diarthrotic; uniaxial; flexion, extension of fingers

TABLE 12.1	*(continued)*

Illustration	Joint	Articulating bones	Structural type*	Functional type; movements allowed
	Sacroiliac	Sacrum and coxal bone	Synovial; plane	Diarthrotic; little movement, slight gliding possible (more during pregnancy)
	Pubic symphysis	Pubic bones	Cartilaginous; symphysis	Amphiarthrotic; slight movement (enhanced during pregnancy)
	Hip (coxal)	Hip bone and femur	Synovial; ball and socket	Diarthrotic; multiaxial; flexion, extension, abduction, adduction, rotation, circumduction of thigh
	Knee (tibiofemoral)	Femur and tibia	Synovial; modified hinge† (contains articular discs)	Diarthrotic; biaxial; flexion, extension of leg, some rotation allowed
	Knee (femoropatellar)	Femur and patella	Synovial; plane	Diarthrotic; gliding of patella
	Tibiofibular (proximal)	Tibia and fibula (proximally)	Synovial; plane	Diarthrotic; gliding of fibula
	Tibiofibular (distal)	Tibia and fibula (distally)	Fibrous; syndesmosis	Synarthrotic; slight "give" during dorsiflexion
	Ankle	Tibia and fibula with talus	Synovial; hinge	Diarthrotic; uniaxial; dorsiflexion and plantar flexion of foot
	Intertarsal	Adjacent tarsals	Synovial; plane	Diarthrotic; gliding; inversion and eversion of foot
	Tarsometatarsal	Tarsal(s) and metatarsal(s)	Synovial; plane	Diarthrotic; gliding of metatarsals
	Metatarso-phalangeal	Metatarsal and proximal phalanx	Synovial; condyloid	Diarthrotic; biaxial; flexion, extension, abduction, adduction, circumduction of great toe
	Toe (interphalangeal)	Adjacent phalanges	Synovial; hinge	Diarthrotic; uniaxial; flexion, extension of toes

*Fibrous joints indicated by orange circles; cartilaginous joints by blue circles; synovial joints by purple circles.
†These modified hinge joints are structurally bicondylar.

1. Demonstrate movement at two joints that are uniaxial.

Name of joint	Movement allowed

2. Demonstrate movement at two joints that are biaxial.

Name of joint	Movement allowed	Movement allowed

3. Demonstrate movement at two joints that are multiaxial.

Name of joint	Movement allowed	Movement allowed	Movement allowed

Selected Synovial Joints

Now you will have the opportunity to compare and contrast the structure of the hip and knee joints and to investigate the structure and movements of the temporomandibular joint and shoulder joint.

The Hip and Knee Joints

Both of these joints are large weight-bearing joints of the lower limb, but they differ substantially in their security. Read through the brief descriptive material below, and look at the "Selected Synovial Joints" section of the Review Sheet for the questions that pertain to these joints before beginning your comparison.

The Hip Joint The hip joint is a ball-and-socket joint, so movements can occur in all possible planes. However, its movements are definitely limited by its deep socket and strong reinforcing ligaments, the two factors that account for its exceptional stability (Figure 12.7).

The deeply cupped acetabulum that receives the head of the femur is enhanced by a circular rim of fibrocartilage called the *acetabular labrum*. Because the diameter of the labrum is smaller than that of the femur's head, dislocations of the hip are rare. A short ligament, *the ligament of the head of the femur* or *ligamentum teres,* runs from the pitlike *fovea capitis* on the femur head to the acetabulum where it helps to secure the femur. Several strong ligaments, including the *iliofemoral* and *pubofemoral* anteriorly and the *ischiofemoral* that spirals posteriorly (not shown), are arranged so that they "screw" the femur head into the socket when a person stands upright.

ACTIVITY 7

Demonstrating Actions at the Hip Joint

If a functional hip joint model is available, identify the joint parts and manipulate it to demonstrate the following movements: flexion, extension, abduction, and inner and outer rotation that can occur at this joint.

Reread the information on what movements the associated ligaments restrict, and verify that information during your joint manipulations. ▬

The Knee Joint The knee is the largest and most complex joint in the body. Three joints in one (Figure 12.8), it allows extension, flexion, and a little rotation. The *tibiofemoral joint,* actually a duplex joint between the femoral condyles above and the *menisci* (semilunar cartilages) of the tibia below, is functionally a hinge joint, a very unstable one made slightly more secure by the menisci. Some rotation occurs when the knee is partly flexed, but during extension, rotation and side-to-side movements are counteracted by the menisci and ligaments. The other joint is the *femoropatellar joint,* the intermediate joint anteriorly.

The knee is unique in that it is only partly enclosed by an articular capsule. Anteriorly, where the capsule is absent, are three broad ligaments, the *patellar ligament* and the *medial* and *lateral patellar retinacula,* which run from the patella to the tibia below and merge with the capsule on either side.

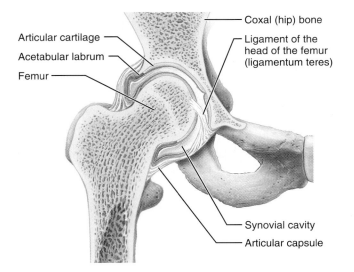

(a)

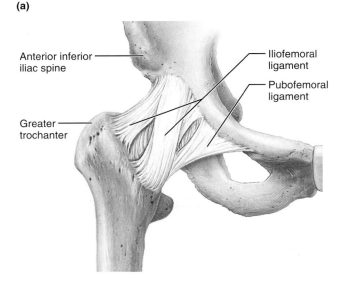

(b)

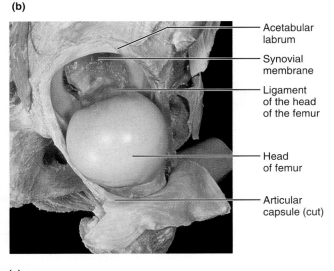

(c)

FIGURE 12.7 Hip joint relationships. (a) Frontal section through the right hip joint. **(b)** Anterior superficial view of the right hip joint. **(c)** Photograph of the interior of the hip joint, lateral view.

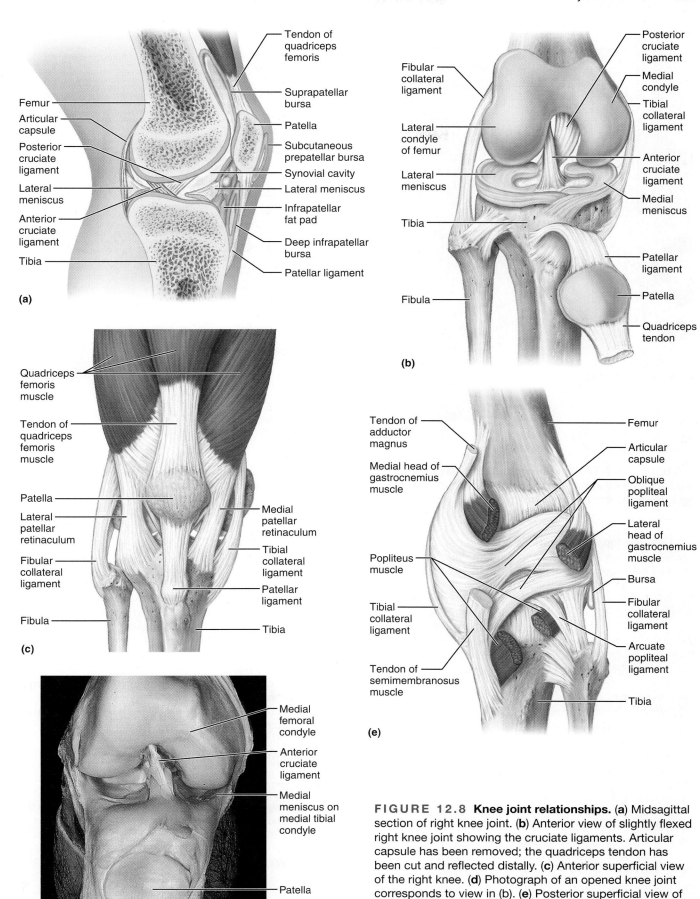

FIGURE 12.8 Knee joint relationships. (a) Midsagittal section of right knee joint. **(b)** Anterior view of slightly flexed right knee joint showing the cruciate ligaments. Articular capsule has been removed; the quadriceps tendon has been cut and reflected distally. **(c)** Anterior superficial view of the right knee. **(d)** Photograph of an opened knee joint corresponds to view in (b). **(e)** Posterior superficial view of the ligaments clothing the knee joint.

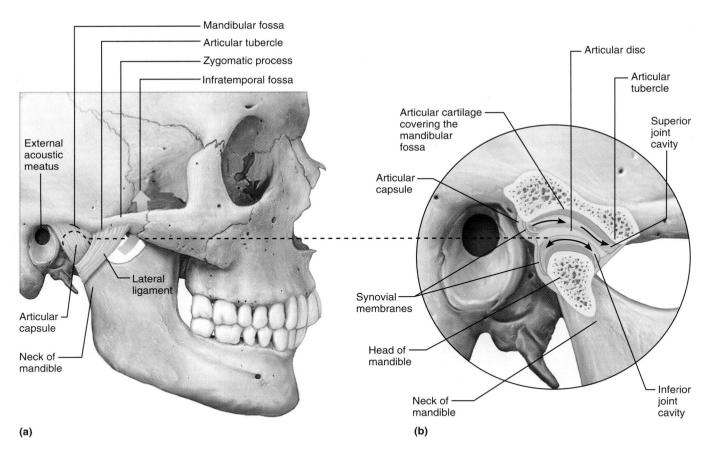

Mandibular fossa
Articular tubercle
Zygomatic process
Infratemporal fossa

External acoustic meatus

Lateral ligament

Articular capsule

Neck of mandible

(a)

Articular disc

Articular tubercle

Superior joint cavity

Articular cartilage covering the mandibular fossa

Articular capsule

Synovial membranes

Head of mandible

Neck of mandible

Inferior joint cavity

(b)

FIGURE 12.9 The temporomandibular (jaw) joint. (a) Location of the joint in the skull. **(b)** Enlargement of a sagittal section through the joint, showing the articular disc, the superior and inferior compartments of the joint cavity, and the two main movements that occur (arrows).

Capsular ligaments including the *fibular* and *tibial collateral ligaments* (which prevent rotation during extension) and the *oblique popliteal* and *arcuate popliteal ligaments* are crucial in reinforcing the knee. The knees have a built-in locking device which must be "unlocked" by the popliteus muscles (Figure 12.8e) before the knees can be flexed again. The *cruciate ligaments* are intracapsular ligaments that cross (*cruci* = cross) in the notch between the femoral condyles. They prevent anterior-posterior displacement of the joint and overflexion and hyperextension of the joint.

ACTIVITY 8

Demonstrating Actions at the Knee Joint

If a functional model of a knee joint is available, identify the joint parts and manipulate it to illustrate the following movements: flexion, extension, and inner and outer rotation.

Reread the information on what movements the various associated ligaments restrict, and verify that information during your joint manipulations. ■

The Temporomandibular Joint

The temporomandibular joint (TMJ) lies just anterior to the ear (Figure 12.9), where the egg-shaped condyle of the mandible articulates with the inferior surface of the squamous region of the temporal bone. The temporal bone joint surface has a complicated shape: posteriorly is the **mandibular fossa** and anteriorly is a bony knob called the **articular tubercle.** The joint's articular capsule, though strengthened laterally by ligament, is slack; an articular disc divides the joint cavity into superior and inferior compartments. Typically, the mandibular condyle–mandibular fossa connection allows the familiar hingelike movements of elevating and depressing the mandible to open and close the mouth. However, when the mouth is opened wide, the mandibular head glides anteriorly and is braced against the dense bone of the articular tubercle so that the mandible is not forced superiorly when we bite hard foods.

ACTIVITY 9

Examining the Action at the TMJ

While placing your fingers over the area just anterior to the ear, open and close your mouth to feel the hinge action at the TMJ. Then, keeping your fingers on the TMJ, yawn to demonstrate the anterior gliding of the mandibular condyle. ■

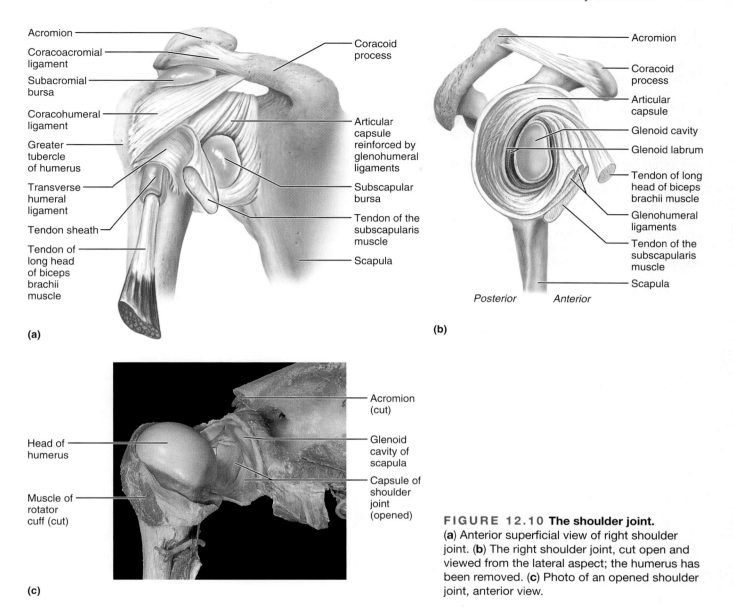

FIGURE 12.10 **The shoulder joint.**
(a) Anterior superficial view of right shoulder joint. (b) The right shoulder joint, cut open and viewed from the lateral aspect; the humerus has been removed. (c) Photo of an opened shoulder joint, anterior view.

The Shoulder Joint

The **shoulder joint** or *glenohumeral joint* is the most freely moving joint of the body. The rounded head of the humerus fits the shallow glenoid cavity of the scapula (Figure 12.10). A rim of fibrocartilage, the **glenoid labrum,** deepens the cavity slightly.

The articular capsule enclosing the joint is thin and loose, contributing to ease of movement. Few ligaments reinforce the shoulder; most are located anteriorly. The *coracohumeral ligament* helps support the weight of the uper limb; three weak *glenohumeral ligaments* strengthen the front of the capsule. Sometimes they are absent. Muscle tendons from the biceps brachii and **rotator cuff** muscles (subscapularis, supraspinatus, infraspinatus, and teres minor) contribute most to shoulder stability.

Demonstrating Actions at the Shoulder Joint

If a functional shoulder joint model is available, identify the joint parts and manipulate it to demonstrate the following movements: flexion, extension, abduction, adduction, circumduction, and inner and outer rotation.

Note where the joint is weakest and verify the most common direction of a dislocated humerus.

Joint Disorders

Most of us don't think about our joints until something goes wrong with them. Joint pains and malfunctions are caused by a variety of things. For example, a hard blow to the knee can cause a painful bursitis, known as "water on the knee," due to damage to, or inflammation of, the patellar bursa. Slippage of a fibrocartilage pad or the tearing of a ligament may result in a painful condition that persists over a long period, since these poorly vascularized structures heal so slowly.

Sprains and dislocations are other types of joint problems. In a **sprain,** the ligaments reinforcing a joint are damaged by excessive stretching or are torn away from the bony attachment. Since both ligaments and tendons are cords of dense connective tissue with a poor blood supply, sprains heal slowly and are quite painful.

Dislocations occur when bones are forced out of their normal position in the joint cavity. They are normally accompanied by torn or stressed ligaments and considerable inflammation. The process of returning the bone to its proper position, called reduction, should be done only by a physician. Attempts by the untrained person to "snap the bone back into its socket" are often more harmful than helpful.

Advancing years also take their toll on joints. Weight-bearing joints in particular eventually begin to degenerate. *Adhesions* (fibrous bands) may form between the surfaces where bones join, and extraneous bone tissue (*spurs*) may grow along the joint edges. Such degenerative changes lead to the complaint so often heard from the elderly: "My joints are getting so stiff. . . ."

• If possible, compare an X ray of an arthritic joint to one of a normal joint. ●

NAME_____

LAB TIME/DATE _____

Articulations and Body Movements

Fibrous, Cartilaginous, and Synovial Joints

1. Use key responses to identify the joint types described below.

   Key: a. cartilaginous   b. fibrous   c. synovial

   _____ 1. typically allows a slight degree of movement

   _____ 2. includes joints between the vertebral bodies and the pubic symphysis

   _____ 3. essentially immovable joints

   _____ 4. sutures are the most remembered examples

   _____ 5. characterized by cartilage connecting the bony portions

   _____ 6. all characterized by a fibrous articular capsule lined with a synovial membrane surrounding a joint cavity

   _____ 7. all are freely movable or diarthrotic

   _____ 8. bone regions are united by fibrous connective tissue

   _____ 9. include the hip, knee, and elbow joints

2. Describe the structure and function of the following structures or tissues in relation to a synovial joint and label the structures indicated by leader lines in the diagram.

   ligament: _____

   _____

   tendon: _____

   _____

   articular cartilage: _____

   _____

   synovial membrane: _____

   _____

   _____

   bursa: _____

3. Match the joint subcategories in column B with their descriptions in column A, and place an asterisk (*) beside all choices that are examples of synovial joints.

Column A	Column B
_____ 1. joint between skull bones	a. ball and socket
_____ 2. joint between the axis and atlas	b. condyloid
_____ 3. hip joint	c. gliding
_____ 4. intervertebral joints (between articular processes)	d. hinge
_____ 5. joint between forearm bones and wrist	e. pivot
_____ 6. elbow	f. saddle
_____ 7. interphalangeal joints	g. suture
_____ 8. intercarpal joints	h. symphysis
_____ 9. joint between tarsus and tibia/fibula	i. synchondrosis
_____ 10. joint between skull and vertebral column	j. syndesmosis
_____ 11. joint between jaw and skull	
_____ 12. joints between proximal phalanges and metacarpal bones	
_____ 13. epiphyseal plate of a child's long bone	
_____ 14. a multiaxial joint	
_____, _____ 15. biaxial joints	
_____, _____ 16. uniaxial joints	

4. Indicate the number of planes in which each of the following joint types can move.

_____ in uniaxial joints, _____ in biaxial joints, _____ in multiaxial joints

5. What characteristics do all joints have in common? _____

_____

Selected Synovial Joints

6. Which joint, the hip or the knee, is more stable? _____

Name two important factors that contribute to the stability of the hip joint.

_____ and _____

Name two important factors that contribute to the stability of the knee.

_____ and _____

7. The diagram shows a frontal section of the hip joint. Identify its major structural elements by using the key letters.

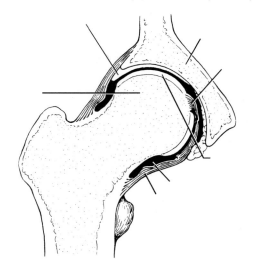

Key:

a.   acetabular labrum

b.   articular capsule

c.   articular cartilage

d.   coxal bone

e.   head of femur

f.   ligamentum teres

g.   synovial cavity

8. The shoulder joint is built for mobility. List four factors that contribute to the large range of motion at the shoulder:

1. _____

2. _____

3. _____

4. _____

9. In which direction does the shoulder usually dislocate? _____

Movements Allowed by Synovial Joints

10. Which letter of the adjacent diagram marks the origin

of the muscle? _____ Which letter marks the

insertion? _____

Insert the words *origin* and *insertion* in to the following sentence:

During muscle contraction, the _____

moves toward the _____.

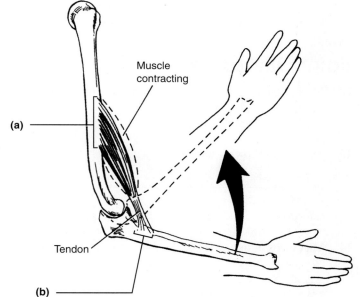

Muscle contracting

(a)

Tendon

(b)

11. Complete the descriptions below the diagrams by inserting the type of movement in each answer blank.

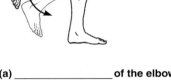

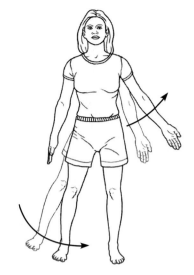

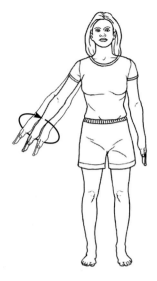

(a) _____ of the elbow

(b) _____ of the knee

(c) _____ of the shoulder

(d) _____ of the hip

(e) _____ of the shoulder

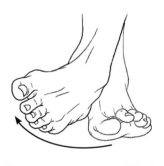

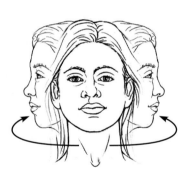

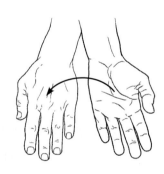

(f) _____ of the foot

(g) _____ of the head

(h) _____ of the hand

Joint Disorders

12. What structural joint changes are common among elderly people? _____

_____

13. Define the following terms.

sprain: _____

dislocation: _____

14. What types of tissue damage might you expect to find in a dislocated joint?

_____

_____

Microscopic Anatomy and Organization of Skeletal Muscle

M A T E R I A L S

- ☐ Three-dimensional model of skeletal muscle cells (if available)
- ☐ Forceps
- ☐ Dissecting needles
- ☐ Clean microscope slides and coverslips
- ☐ 0.9% saline solution in dropper bottles
- ☐ Chicken breast or thigh muscle (freshly obtained from the meat market)
- ☐ Compound microscope
- ☐ Prepared slides of skeletal muscle (l.s. and x.s. views) and skeletal muscle showing neuromuscular junctions
- ☐ Three-dimensional model of skeletal muscle showing neuromuscular junction (if available)

O B J E C T I V E S

1. To describe the structure of skeletal muscle from gross to microscopic levels.

2. To define and explain the role of the following:

actin	myofilament	endomysium
myosin	aponeurosis	perimysium
fiber	tendon	epimysium
myofibril		

3. To describe the structure of a neuromuscular junction and to explain its role in muscle function.

The bulk of the body's muscle is called **skeletal muscle** because it is attached to the skeleton (or associated connective tissue structures). Skeletal muscle influences body contours and shape, allows you to grin and frown, provides a means of locomotion, and enables you to manipulate the environment. The balance of the body's muscle—smooth and cardiac muscle, the major components of the walls of hollow organs and the heart, respectively—is involved with the transport of materials within the body.

Each of the three muscle types has a structure and function uniquely suited to its task in the body. However, because the term *muscular system* applies specifically to skeletal muscle, the primary objective of this unit is to investigate the structure and function of skeletal muscle.

Skeletal muscle is also known as *voluntary muscle* (because it can be consciously controlled) and as *striated muscle* (because it appears to be striped). As you might guess from both of these alternative names, skeletal muscle has some very special characteristics. Thus an investigation of skeletal muscle should begin at the cellular level.

The Cells of Skeletal Muscle

Skeletal muscle is composed of relatively large, long cylindrical cells, sometimes called **fibers,** ranging from 10 to 100 μm in diameter and up to 6 cm in length. However, the cells of large, hard-working muscles like the antigravity muscles of the hip are extremely coarse, ranging up to 25 cm in length, and can be seen with the naked eye.

Skeletal muscle cells (Figure 13.1a) are multinucleate; multiple oval nuclei can be seen just beneath the plasma membrane (called the *sarcolemma* in these cells). The nuclei are pushed peripherally by the longitudinally arranged **myofibrils,** which nearly fill the sarcoplasm. Alternating light (I) and dark (A) bands along the length of the perfectly aligned myofibrils give the muscle fiber as a whole its striped appearance.

Electron microscope studies have revealed that the myo-fibrils are made up of even smaller threadlike structures called **myofilaments** (Figure 13.1b). The myofilaments are composed largely of two varieties of contractile proteins—

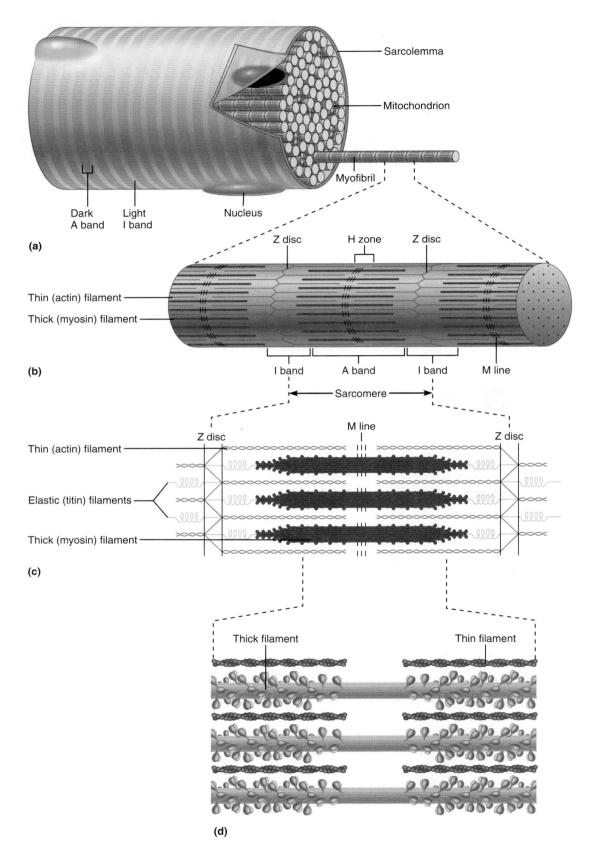

FIGURE 13.1 Anatomy of a skeletal muscle cell (fiber). (**a**) A muscle fiber. One myofibril has been extended. (**b**) Enlarged view of a myofibril showing its banding pattern. (**c**) Enlarged view of one sarcomere (contractile unit) of a myofibril showing its banding pattern. (**d**) Structure of the thick and thin myofilaments found in the sarcomeres.

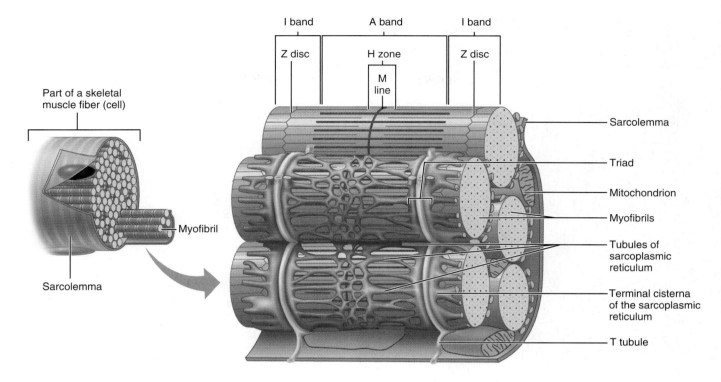

FIGURE 13.2 Relationship of the sarcoplasmic reticulum and T tubules to the myofibrils of skeletal muscle.

actin and **myosin**—which slide past each other during muscle activity to bring about shortening or contraction of the muscle cells. It is the highly specific arrangement of the myofilaments within the myofibrils that is responsible for the banding pattern in skeletal muscle. The actual contractile units of muscle, called **sarcomeres,** extend from the middle of one I band (its Z disc) to the middle of the next along the length of the myofibrils (Figure 13.1c and d).

At each junction of the A and I bands, the sarcolemma indents into the muscle cell, forming a **transverse tubule (T tubule).** These tubules run deep into the muscle cell between cross channels, or **terminal cisternae,** of the elaborate smooth endoplasmic reticulum called the **sarcoplasmic reticulum** (Figure 13.2).

Examining Skeletal Muscle Cell Anatomy

1. Look at the three-dimensional model of skeletal muscle cells, noting the relative shape and size of the cells. Identify the nuclei, myofibrils, and light and dark bands.

2. Obtain forceps, two dissecting needles, slide and coverslip, and a dropper bottle of saline solution. With forceps, remove a very small piece of muscle (about 1 mm diameter) from a fresh chicken breast (or thigh). Place the tissue on a clean microscope slide, and add a drop of the saline solution.

3. Pull the muscle fibers apart (tease them) with the dissecting needles until you have a fluffy-looking mass of tissue. Cover the teased tissue with a coverslip, and observe under

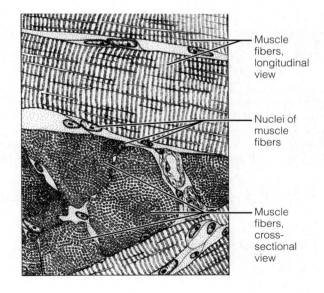

FIGURE 13.3 Muscle fibers, longitudinal and transverse views. (See also Plate 2 in the Histology Atlas.)

the high-power lens of a compound microscope. Look for the banding pattern by examining muscle fibers isolated at the edge of the tissue mass. Regulate the light carefully to obtain the highest possible contrast. Compare what you see in your field to Figure 13.3.

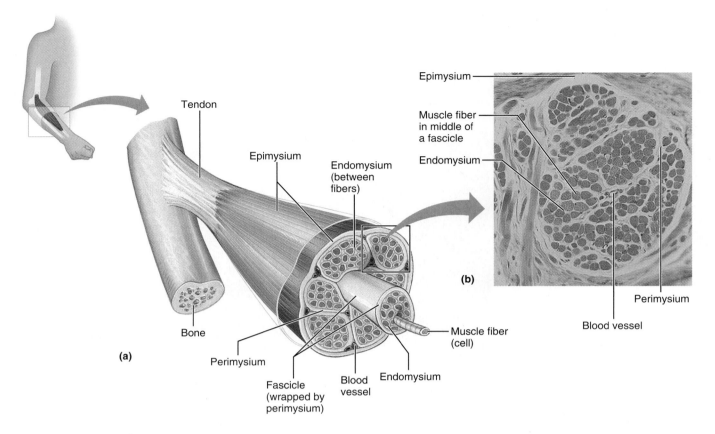

FIGURE 13.4 Connective tissue coverings of skeletal muscle.
(a) Diagrammatic view. (b) Photomicrograph of a cross section of skeletal muscle (73X).

4. Now compare your observations with what can be seen with professionally prepared muscle tissue. Obtain a slide of skeletal muscle (longitudinal section), and view it under high power. From your observations, draw a small section of a muscle fiber in the space provided below. Label the nuclei, sarcolemma, and A and I bands.

What structural details become apparent with the prepared slide?

_____

_____

Organization of Skeletal Muscle Cells into Muscles

Muscle fibers are soft and surprisingly fragile. Thus thousands of muscle fibers are bundled together with connective tissue to form the organs we refer to as skeletal muscles (Figure 13.4). Each muscle fiber is enclosed in a delicate, areolar connective tissue sheath called **endomysium.** Several sheathed muscle fibers are wrapped by a collagenic membrane called **perimysium,** forming a bundle of fibers called a **fascicle,** or **fasciculus.** A large number of fascicles are bound together by a substantially coarser "overcoat" of dense connective tissue called an **epimysium,** which sheathes the entire muscle. These epimysia blend into the **deep fascia,** still coarser sheets of dense connective tissue that bind muscles into functional groups, and into strong cordlike **tendons** or sheetlike **aponeuroses,** which attach muscles to each other or indirectly to bones. As noted in Exercise 12, a muscle's more movable attachment is called its *insertion* whereas its fixed (or immovable) attachment is the *origin.*

Tendons perform several functions, two of the most important being to provide durability and to conserve space. Because tendons are tough collagenic connective tissue, they can span rough bony prominences that would destroy the more delicate muscle tissues. Because of their relatively small size, more tendons than fleshy muscles can pass over a joint.

In addition to supporting and binding the muscle fibers, and providing strength to the muscle as a whole, the connective tissue wrappings provide a route for the entry and exit of nerves and blood vessels that serve the muscle fibers. The larger, more powerful muscles have relatively more connective tissue than muscles involved in fine or delicate movements.

As we age, the mass of the muscle fibers decreases, and the amount of connective tissue increases; thus the skeletal muscles gradually become more sinewy, or "stringier." ●

ACTIVITY 2

Observing the Histological Structure of a Skeletal Muscle

Obtain a slide showing a cross section of skeletal muscle tissue. Using Figure 13.4 as a reference, identify the muscle fibers, their peripherally located nuclei, and their connective tissue wrappings, the endomysium, perimysium, and epimysium (if visible). ▬

The Neuromuscular Junction

The voluntary skeletal muscle cells are always stimulated by motor neurons via nerve impulses. The junction between a nerve fiber (axon) and a muscle cell is called a **neuromuscular,** or **myoneural, junction** (Figure 13.5).

The axon of each motor neuron breaks up into many branches called *axon terminals* as it approaches the muscle, and each of these branches participates in forming a neuromuscular junction with a single muscle cell. Thus a single neuron may stimulate many muscle fibers. Together, a neuron and all the muscle cells it stimulates make up the functional structure called the **motor unit.** Part of a motor unit is shown in Plate 4 of the Histology Atlas. The neuron and muscle fiber membranes, close as they are, do not actually touch. They are separated by a small fluid-filled gap called the **synaptic cleft** (see Figure 13.5).

Within the axon terminals are many mitochondria and vesicles containing a neurotransmitter chemical called acetylcholine (ACh). When a nerve impulse reaches the axon endings, some of these vesicles release their contents into the synaptic cleft. The ACh diffuses across the junction and combines with the receptors on the sarcolemma. If sufficient ACh has been released, a change in the permeability of the sarcolemma occurs. Channels that allow both sodium ions (Na^+) and potassium ions (K^+) to pass open briefly. Because more Na^+ diffuses into the muscle fiber than K^+ diffuses out, depolarization of the sarcolemma and subsequent contraction of the muscle fiber occurs.

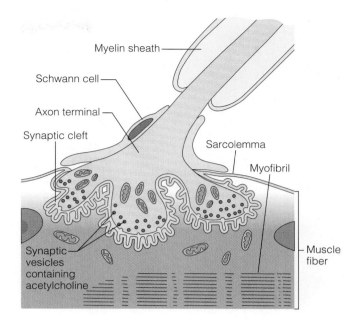

FIGURE 13.5 **The neuromuscular junction.**

ACTIVITY 3

Studying the Structure of a Neuromuscular Junction

1. If possible, examine a three-dimensional model of skeletal muscle cells that illustrates the neuromuscular junction. Identify the structures just described.

2. Obtain a slide of skeletal muscle stained to show a portion of a motor unit. Examine the slide under high power to identify the axon fibers extending leashlike to the muscle cells. Follow one of the axon fibers to its terminus to identify the oval-shaped axon terminal. Compare your observations to Plate 4 of the Histology Atlas. Sketch a small section in the space provided below. Label the motor axon, its terminal branches, and muscle fibers. ▬

Microscopic Anatomy and Organization of Skeletal Muscle

Skeletal Muscle Cells and Their Packaging into Muscles

1. What capability is most highly expressed in muscle tissue? _____

2. Use the items in the key to correctly identify the structures described below.

_____ 1.   connective tissue ensheathing a bundle of muscle cells

_____ 2.   bundle of muscle cells

_____ 3.   contractile unit of muscle

_____ 4.   a muscle cell

_____ 5.   thin reticular connective tissue investing each muscle cell

_____ 6.   plasma membrane of the muscle fiber

_____ 7.   a long filamentous organelle with a banded appearance found within muscle cells

_____ 8.   actin- or myosin-containing structure

_____ 9.   cord of collagen fibers that attaches a muscle to a bone

Key:

a.   endomysium

b.   epimysium

c.   fascicle

d.   fiber

e.   myofibril

f.   myofilament

g.   perimysium

h.   sarcolemma

i.   sarcomere

j.   sarcoplasm

k.   tendon

3. List three reasons the connective tissue wrappings of skeletal muscle are important.

_____

_____

_____

4. Why are there more indirect—that is, tendinous—muscle attachments to bone than there are direct attachments?

_____

_____

_____

5. How does an aponeurosis differ from a tendon structurally? _____

_____

How is an aponeurosis functionally similar to a tendon? ⎯⎯⎯⎯⎯⎯⎯⎯⎯⎯⎯⎯⎯⎯⎯⎯⎯⎯⎯⎯⎯⎯⎯⎯

⎯⎯⎯

6. The diagram illustrates a small portion of a muscle myofibril. Using letters from the key, correctly identify each structure indicated by a leader line or a bracket. Below the diagram make a sketch of how this segment of the myofibril would look if contracted.

Key: a.   A band   d.   myosin filament
     b.   actin filament   e.   sarcomere
     c.   I band   f.   Z disc

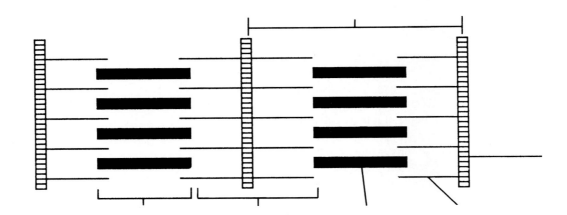

7. On the following figure, label a blood vessel, endomysium, epimysium, a fascicle, a muscle cell, perimysium, and the tendon.

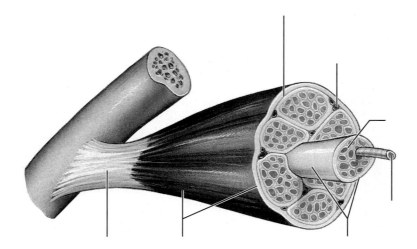

8. The diagram illustrates a small portion of several myofibrils. Using letters from the key, correctly identify each structure indicated by a leader line or a bracket.

Key: a.   A band
        b.   actin filament
        c.   I band

d.   myosin filament
e.   T tubule
f.   terminal cisterna

g.   triad
h.   sarcomere
i.   Z disc

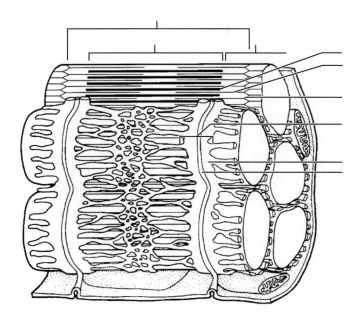

The Neuromuscular Junction

9. Complete the following statements:

The junction between a motor neuron's axon and the muscle cell membrane is called a neuromuscular junction or a __1__ junction. A motor neuron and all of the skeletal muscle cells it stimulates is called a __2__. The actual gap between the axon terminal and the muscle cell is called a __3__. Within the axon terminal are many small vesicles containing a neurotransmitter substance called __4__. When the __5__ reaches the ends of the axon, the neurotransmitter is released and diffuses to the muscle cell membrane to combine with receptors there. The combining of the neurotransmitter with the muscle membrane receptors causes the membrane to become permeable to both sodium and potassium. The greater influx of sodium ions results in __6__ of the membrane. Then contraction of the muscle cell occurs. Before a muscle cell can be stimulated to contract again, __7__ must occur.

1. _____

2. _____

3. _____

4. _____

5. _____

6. _____

7. _____

10. The events that occur at a neuromuscular junction are depicted below. Identify by labeling every structure provided with a leader line.

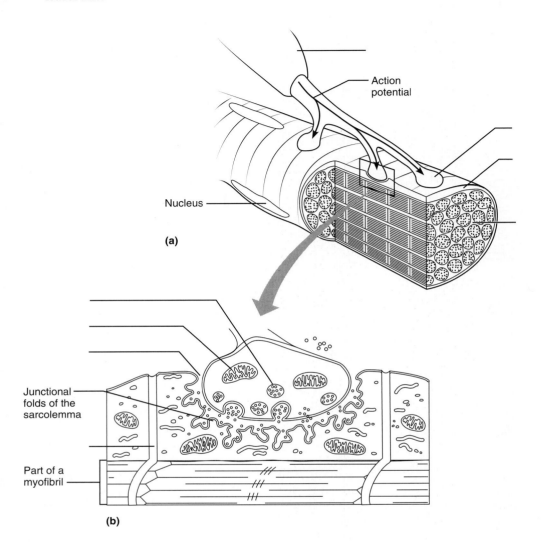

Action potential

Nucleus

(a)

Junctional folds of the sarcolemma

Part of a myofibril

(b)

Key:

a. axon terminal

b. mitochondrion

c. muscle fiber

d. myelinated axon

e. sarcolemma

f. synaptic cleft

g. synaptic vesicle

h. T tubule

Gross Anatomy of the Muscular System

OBJECTIVES

1. To define *agonist* (prime mover), *antagonist, synergist, fixator, origin,* and *insertion.*
2. To cite criteria used in naming skeletal muscles.
3. To name and locate the major muscles of the human body (on a torso model, a human cadaver, a lab chart, or a diagram) and state the action of each.
4. To explain how muscle actions are related to their location.
5. To name muscle origins and insertions as required by the instructor.
6. To identify antagonists of the major prime movers.
7. To name and locate muscles on a dissected cat.
8. To recognize similarities and differences between human and cat musculature.

Classification of Skeletal Muscles

Types of Muscles

Most often, body movements are not a result of the contraction of a single muscle but instead reflect the coordinated action of several muscles acting together. Muscles that are primarily responsible for producing a particular movement are called **prime movers,** or **agonists.**

Muscles that oppose or reverse a movement are called **antagonists.** When a prime mover is active, the fibers of the antagonist are stretched and in the relaxed state. The antagonist can also regulate the prime mover by providing some resistance, to prevent overshoot or to stop its action.

It should be noted that antagonists can be prime movers in their own right. For example, the biceps muscle of the arm (a prime mover of elbow flexion) is antagonized by the triceps (a prime mover of elbow extension).

Synergists aid the action of agonists by reducing undesirable or unnecessary movement. Contraction of a muscle crossing two or more joints would cause movement at all joints spanned if the synergists were not there to stabilize them. For example, you can make a fist without bending your wrist only because synergist muscles stabilize the wrist joint and allow the prime mover to exert its force at the finger joints.

Fixators, or fixation muscles, are specialized synergists. They immobilize the origin of a prime mover so that all the tension is exerted at the insertion. Muscles that help maintain posture are fixators; so too are muscles of the back that stabilize or "fix" the scapula during arm movements.

Naming Skeletal Muscles

Remembering the names of the skeletal muscles is a monumental task, but certain clues help. Muscles are named on the basis of the following criteria:

• **Direction of muscle fibers:** Some muscles are named in reference to some imaginary line, usually the midline of the body or the longitudinal axis of a limb bone. A muscle with fibers (and fascicles) running parallel to that imaginary line

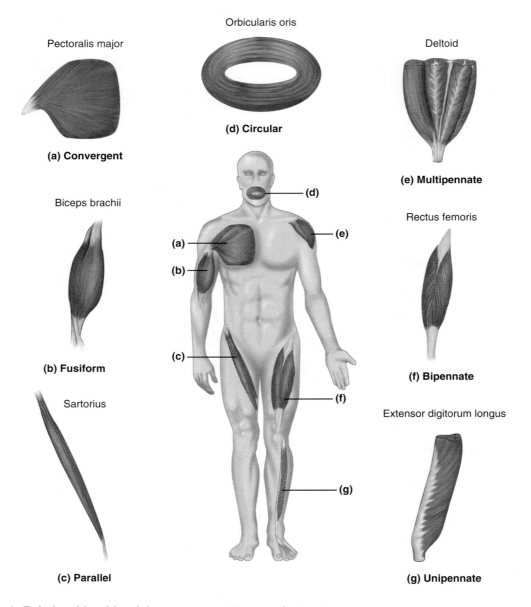

Pectoralis major

(a) Convergent

Orbicularis oris

(d) Circular

Deltoid

(e) Multipennate

Biceps brachii

(b) Fusiform

Rectus femoris

(f) Bipennate

Sartorius

(c) Parallel

Extensor digitorum longus

(g) Unipennate

(a)
(b)
(c)
(d)
(e)
(f)
(g)

FIGURE 14.1 Relationship of fascicle arrangement to muscle structure.

will have the term *rectus* (straight) in its name. For example, the rectus abdominis is the straight muscle of the abdomen. Likewise, the terms *transverse* and *oblique* indicate that the muscle fibers run at right angles and obliquely, respectively, to the imaginary line. Figure 14.1 shows how muscle structure is determined by fascicle arrangement.

- **Relative size of the muscle:** Terms such as *maximus* (largest), *minimus* (smallest), *longus* (long), and *brevis* (short) are often used in naming muscles—as in gluteus maximus and gluteus minimus.

- **Location of the muscle:** Some muscles are named for the bone with which they are associated. For example, the frontalis muscle overlies the frontal bone.

- **Number of origins:** When the term *biceps, triceps,* or *quadriceps* forms part of a muscle name, you can generally assume that the muscle has two, three, or four origins (respectively). For example, the biceps muscle of the arm has two heads, or origins.

- **Location of the muscle's origin and insertion:** For example, the sternocleidomastoid muscle has its origin on the sternum (*sterno*) and clavicle (*cleido*), and inserts on the mastoid process of the temporal bone.

- **Shape of the muscle:** For example, the deltoid muscle is roughly triangular (*deltoid* = triangle), and the trapezius muscle resembles a trapezoid.

- **Action of the muscle:** For example, all the adductor muscles of the anterior thigh bring about its adduction, and all the extensor muscles of the wrist extend the wrist.

Identification of Human Muscles

Muscles of the Head and Neck

The muscles of the head serve many specific functions. For instance, the muscles of facial expression differ from most skeletal muscles because they insert into the skin (or other muscles) rather than into bone. As a result, they move the facial skin, allowing a wide range of emotions to be shown on the face. Other muscles of the head are the muscles of mastication, which manipulate the mandible during chewing, and the six extrinsic eye muscles located within the orbit, which aim the eye. (Orbital muscles are studied in Exercise 18.)

ACTIVITY 1

Identifying Head and Neck Muscles

Neck muscles are primarily concerned with the movement of the head and shoulder girdle. Figures 14.2 and 14.3 are summary figures illustrating the superficial musculature of the body as a whole. Head and neck muscles are discussed in Tables 14.1 and 14.2 and shown in Figures 14.4 and 14.5.

While reading the tables and identifying the head and neck muscles in the figures, try to visualize what happens when the muscle contracts. Then, use a torso model or an anatomical chart to again identify as many of these muscles as possible. (If a human cadaver is available for observation,

specific instructions for muscle examination will be provided by your instructor.) Then carry out the following palpations on yourself:

- To demonstrate the temporalis, place your hands on your temples and clench your teeth. The masseter can also be palpated now at the angle of the jaw. ▪▪▪

Muscles of the Trunk

The trunk musculature includes muscles that move the vertebral column; anterior thorax muscles that act to move ribs, head, and arms; and muscles of the abdominal wall that play a role in the movement of the vertebral column but more importantly form the "natural girdle," or the major portion of the abdominal body wall.

ACTIVITY 2

Identifying Muscles of the Trunk

The trunk muscles are described in Tables 14.3 and 14.4 and shown in Figures 14.6 through 14.9. As before, identify the muscles in the figure as you read the tabular descriptions and then identify them on the torso or laboratory chart. ▪▪▪

ACTIVITY 3

Demonstrating Operation of Trunk Muscles

Now, work with a partner to demonstrate the operation of the following muscles. One of you can demonstrate the movement (the following steps are addressed to this partner). The other can supply resistance and palpate the muscle being tested.

1. Fully abduct the arm and extend the elbow. Now adduct the arm against resistance. You are using the *latissimus dorsi.*

2. To observe the *deltoid,* attempt to abduct your arm against resistance. Now attempt to elevate your shoulder against resistance; you are contracting the upper portion of the *trapezius.*

3. The *pectoralis major* is used when you press your hands together at chest level with your elbows widely abducted. ▪▪▪

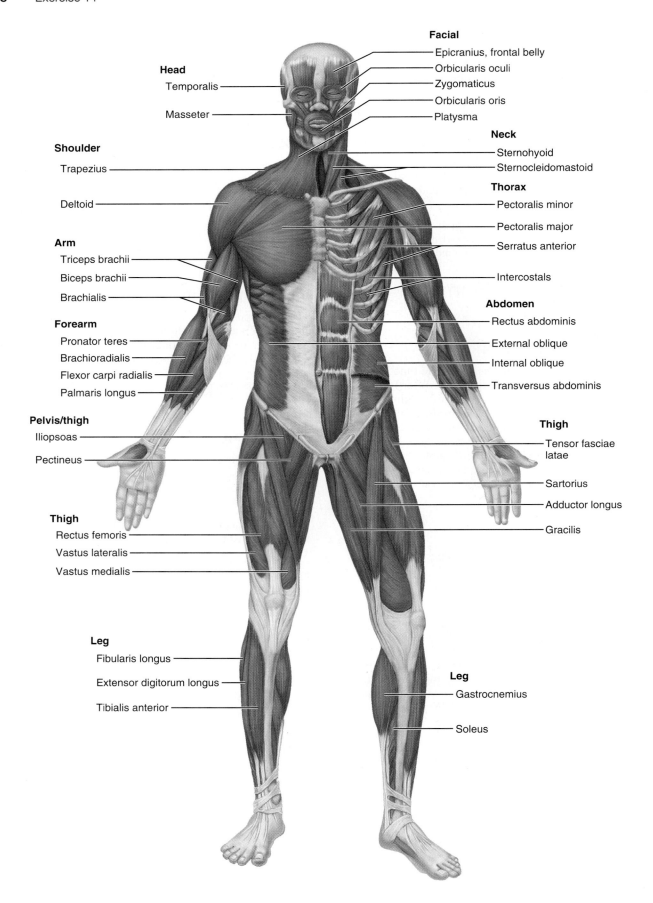

Head
Temporalis
Masseter

Shoulder
Trapezius
Deltoid

Arm
Triceps brachii
Biceps brachii
Brachialis

Forearm
Pronator teres
Brachioradialis
Flexor carpi radialis
Palmaris longus

Pelvis/thigh
Iliopsoas
Pectineus

Thigh
Rectus femoris
Vastus lateralis
Vastus medialis

Leg
Fibularis longus
Extensor digitorum longus
Tibialis anterior

Facial
Epicranius, frontal belly
Orbicularis oculi
Zygomaticus
Orbicularis oris
Platysma

Neck
Sternohyoid
Sternocleidomastoid

Thorax
Pectoralis minor
Pectoralis major
Serratus anterior
Intercostals

Abdomen
Rectus abdominis
External oblique
Internal oblique
Transversus abdominis

Thigh
Tensor fasciae latae
Sartorius
Adductor longus
Gracilis

Leg
Gastrocnemius
Soleus

FIGURE 14.2 Anterior view of superficial muscles of the body. The abdominal surface has been partially dissected on the left side of the body to show somewhat deeper muscles.

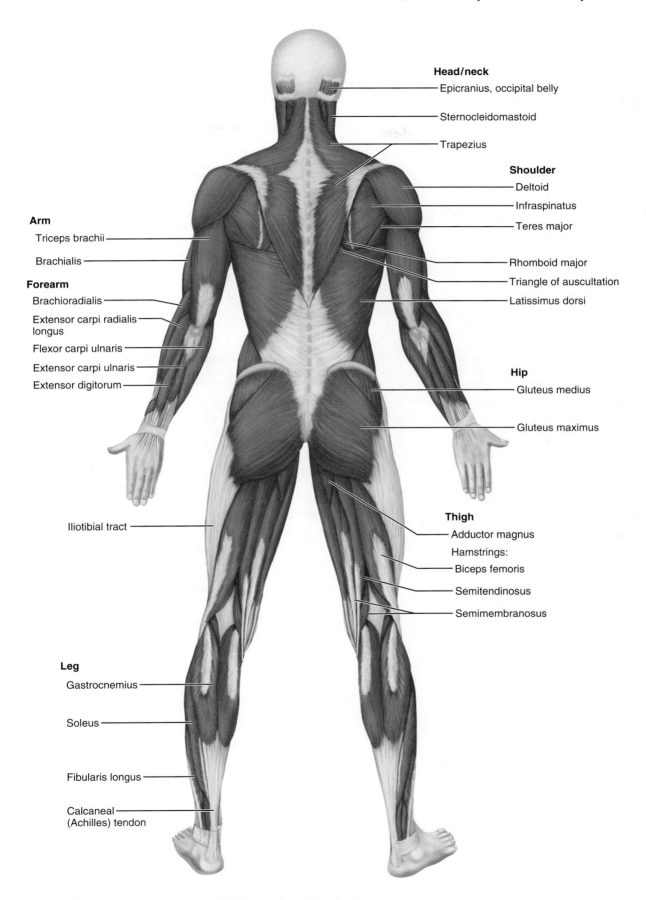

Head/neck
Epicranius, occipital belly

Sternocleidomastoid

Trapezius

Shoulder
Deltoid

Infraspinatus

Teres major

Rhomboid major

Triangle of auscultation

Latissimus dorsi

Arm
Triceps brachii

Brachialis

Forearm
Brachioradialis

Extensor carpi radialis longus

Flexor carpi ulnaris

Extensor carpi ulnaris

Extensor digitorum

Hip
Gluteus medius

Gluteus maximus

Thigh
Adductor magnus

Hamstrings:

Biceps femoris

Semitendinosus

Semimembranosus

Iliotibial tract

Leg
Gastrocnemius

Soleus

Fibularis longus

Calcaneal (Achilles) tendon

FIGURE 14.3 Posterior view of superficial muscles of the body.

TABLE 14.1   Major Muscles of Human Head (see Figure 14.4)

Muscle	Comments	Origin	Insertion	Action
Facial Expression (Figure 14.4)				
Epicranius— frontal and occipital bellies	Bipartite muscle consisting of frontal and occipital parts, which covers dome of skull	Frontal belly—galea aponeurotica (cranial aponeurosis); occipital belly— occipital and temporal bones	Frontal belly— skin of eyebrows and root of nose; occipital belly—galea aponeurotica	With aponeurosis fixed, frontal belly raises eyebrows; occipital belly fixes aponeurosis and pulls scalp posteriorly
Orbicularis oculi	Tripartite sphincter muscle of eyelids	Frontal and maxillary bones and ligaments around orbit	Encircles orbit and inserts in tissue of eyelid	Various parts can be activated individually; closes eyes, produces blinking, squinting, and draws eyebrows inferiorly
Corrugator supercilii	Small muscle; activity associated with that of orbicularis oculi	Arch of frontal bone above nasal bone	Skin of eyebrow	Draws eyebrows medially and inferiorly; wrinkles skin of forehead vertically
Levator labii superioris	Thin muscle between orbicularis oris and inferior eye margin	Zygomatic bone and infraorbital margin of maxilla	Skin and muscle of upper lip and border of nostril	Raises and furrows upper lip; opens lips
Zygomaticus— major and minor	Extends diagonally from corner of mouth to cheekbone	Zygomatic bone	Skin and muscle at corner of mouth	Raises lateral corners of mouth upward (smiling muscle)
Risorius	Slender muscle; runs inferior and lateral to zygomaticus	Fascia of masseter muscle	Skin at angle of mouth	Draws corner of lip laterally; tenses lip; zygomaticus synergist
Depressor labii inferioris	Small muscle from lower lip to mandible	Body of mandible lateral to its midline	Skin and muscle of lower lip	Draws lower lip inferiorly
Depressor anguli oris	Small muscle lateral to depressor labii inferioris	Body of mandible below incisors	Skin and muscle at angle of mouth below insertion of zygomaticus	Zygomaticus antagonist; draws corners of mouth downward and laterally
Orbicularis oris	Multilayered muscle of lips with fibers that run in many different directions; most run circularly	Arises indirectly from maxilla and mandible; fibers blended with fibers of other muscles associated with lips	Encircles mouth; inserts into muscle and skin at angles of mouth	Closes mouth; purses and protrudes lips (kissing and whistling muscle)
Mentalis	One of muscle pair forming V-shaped muscle mass on chin	Mandible below incisors	Skin of chin	Protrudes lower lip; wrinkles chin
Buccinator	Principal muscle of cheek; runs horizontally, deep to the masseter	Molar region of maxilla and mandible	Orbicularis oris	Draws corner of mouth laterally; compresses cheek (as in whistling); holds food between teeth during chewing

(Table continues on p. 192.) ➤

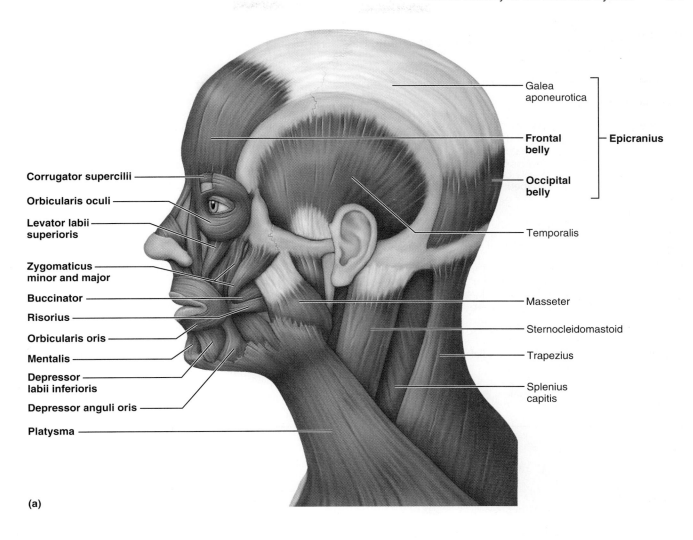

Galea
aponeurotica

**Frontal
belly**   — **Epicranius**

**Occipital
belly**

Corrugator supercilii

Orbicularis oculi

Levator labii
superioris

Zygomaticus
minor and major

Buccinator

Risorius

Orbicularis oris

Mentalis

Depressor
labii inferioris

Depressor anguli oris

Platysma

Temporalis

Masseter

Sternocleidomastoid

Trapezius

Splenius
capitis

(a)

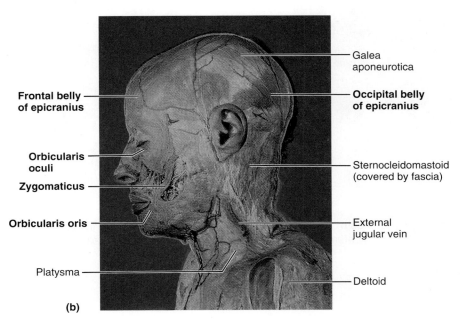

**Frontal belly
of epicranius**

**Orbicularis
oculi**

Zygomaticus

Orbicularis oris

Platysma

Galea
aponeurotica

**Occipital belly
of epicranius**

Sternocleidomastoid
(covered by fascia)

External
jugular vein

Deltoid

(b)

FIGURE 14.4 Muscles of the head (left lateral view). (a) Superficial muscles. **(b)** Photo of superficial
structures of head and neck.

TABLE 14.1	Major Muscles of Human Head (see Figure 14.4) *(continued)*			
Muscle	Comments	Origin	Insertion	Action

Mastication (Figure 14.4c,d)

Muscle	Comments	Origin	Insertion	Action
Masseter	Covers lateral aspect of mandibular ramus; can be palpated on forcible closure of jaws	Zygomatic arch and maxilla	Angle and ramus of mandible	Closes jaw and elevates mandible
Temporalis	Fan-shaped muscle lying over parts of frontal, parietal, and temporal bones	Temporal fossa	Coronoid process of mandible	Closes jaw; elevates and retracts mandible
Buccinator	(See muscles of facial expression.)			
Medial pterygoid	Runs along internal (medial) surface of mandible (thus largely concealed by that bone)	Sphenoid, palatine, and maxillary bones	Medial surface of mandible, near its angle	Synergist of temporalis and masseter; elevates mandible; in conjunction with lateral pterygoid, aids in grinding movements
Lateral pterygoid	Superior to medial pterygoid	Greater wing of sphenoid bone	Mandibular condyle	Protracts jaw (moves it anteriorly); in conjunction with medial pterygoid, aids in grinding movements of teeth

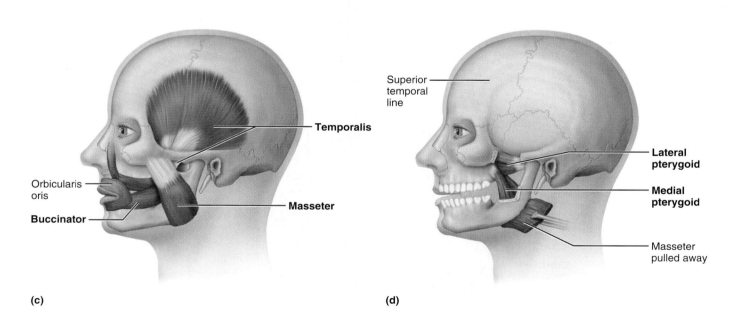

(c)   (d)

FIGURE 14.4 *(continued)* **Muscles of the head: (mastication).** (c) Lateral view of the temporalis, masseter, and buccinator muscles. (d) Lateral view of the deep chewing muscles, the medial and lateral pterygoid muscles.

TABLE 14.2	Anterolateral Muscles of Human Neck (see Figure 14.5)			
Muscle	Comments	Origin	Insertion	Action
Superficial				
Platysma	Unpaired muscle: thin, sheetlike superficial neck muscle, not strictly a head muscle but plays role in facial expression (see also Fig. 14.4a)	Fascia of chest (over pectoral muscles) and deltoid	Lower margin of mandible, skin, and muscle at corner of mouth	Depresses mandible; pulls lower lip back and down (i.e., produces downward sag of the mouth)
Sternocleidomastoid	Two-headed muscle located deep to platysma on anterolateral surface of neck; fleshy parts on either side indicate limits of anterior and posterior triangles of neck	Manubrium of sternum and medial portion of clavicle	Mastoid process of temporal bone and superior nuchal line of occipital bone	Simultaneous contraction of both muscles of pair causes flexion of neck forward, generally against resistance (as when lying on the back); acting independently, rotate head toward shoulder on opposite side
Scalenes—anterior, middle, and posterior	Located more on lateral than anterior neck; deep to platysma and sternocleidomastoid (see Fig. 14.5c)	Transverse processes of cervical vertebrae	Anterolaterally on ribs 1–2	Flex and slightly rotate neck; elevate ribs 1–2 (aid in inspiration)

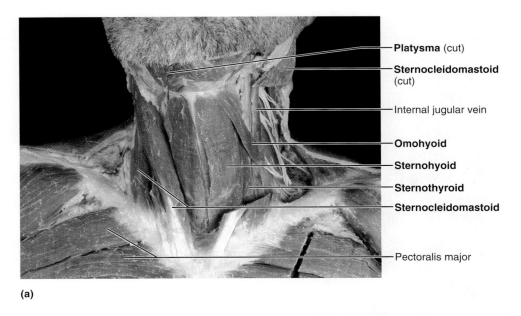

(a)

FIGURE 14.5 Muscles of the anterolateral neck and throat. (a) Photo of the anterior and lateral regions of the neck. The fascia has been partially removed (left side of the photo) to expose the sternocleidomastoid muscle. On the right side of the photo, the sternocleidomastoid muscle is cut to expose the sternohyoid and omohyoid muscles.

TABLE 14.2	Anterolateral Muscles of Human Neck (see Figure 14.5) *(continued)*			
Muscle	Comments	Origin	Insertion	Action
Deep (Figure 14.5a,b)				
Digastric	Consists of two bellies united by an intermediate tendon; assumes a V-shaped configuration under chin	Lower margin of mandible (anterior belly) and mastoid process (posterior belly)	By a connective tissue loop to hyoid bone	Acting in concert, elevate hyoid bone; open mouth and depress mandible
Stylohyoid	Slender muscle parallels posterior border of digastric; below angle of jaw	Styloid process of temporal	Hyoid bone	Elevates and retracts hyoid bone
Mylohyoid	Just deep to digastric; forms floor of mouth	Medial surface of mandible	Hyoid bone and median raphe	Elevates hyoid bone and base of tongue during swallowing
Sternohyoid	Runs most medially along neck; straplike	Manubrium and medial end of clavicle	Lower margin of body of hyoid bone	Acting with sternothyroid and omohyoid (all inferior to hyoid bone), depresses larynx and hyoid bone if mandible is fixed; may also flex skull
Sternothyroid	Lateral and deep to sternohyoid	Posterior surface of manubrium	Thyroid cartilage of larynx	(See Sternohyoid above)
Omohyoid	Straplike with two bellies; lateral to sternohyoid	Superior surface of scapula	Hyoid bone; inferior border	(See Sternohyoid above)
Thyrohyoid	Appears as a superior continuation of sternothyroid muscle	Thyroid cartilage	Hyoid bone	Depresses hyoid bone; elevates larynx if hyoid is fixed

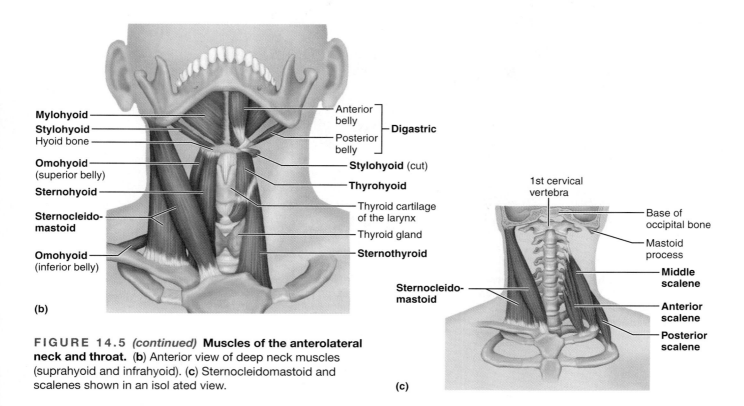

FIGURE 14.5 *(continued)* **Muscles of the anterolateral neck and throat.** **(b)** Anterior view of deep neck muscles (suprahyoid and infrahyoid). **(c)** Sternocleidomastoid and scalenes shown in an isolated view.

TABLE 14.3	Anterior Muscles of Human Thorax, Shoulder, and Abdominal Wall (see Figures 14.6, 14.7, and 14.8)			
Muscle	Comments	Origin	Insertion	Action
Thorax and Shoulder, Superficial (Figure 14.6)				
Pectoralis major	Large fan-shaped muscle covering upper portion of chest	Clavicle, sternum, cartilage of ribs 1–6 (or 7), and aponeurosis of external oblique muscle	Fibers converge to insert by short tendon into intertubercular sulcus of humerus	Prime mover of arm flexion; adducts, medially rotates arm; with arm fixed, pulls chest upward (thus also acts in forced inspiration)
Serratus anterior	Fan-shaped muscle deep to scapula; beneath and inferior to pectoral muscles on lateral rib cage	Lateral aspect of ribs 1–8 (or 9)	Vertebral border of anterior surface of scapula	Moves scapula forward toward chest wall; rotates scapula, causing inferior angle to move laterally and upward; abduction and raising of arm
Deltoid (see also Figure 14.9a)	Fleshy triangular muscle forming shoulder muscle mass; intramuscular injection site	Lateral ⅓ of clavicle; acromion and spine of scapula	Deltoid tuberosity of humerus	Acting as a whole, prime mover of arm abduction; when only specific fibers are active, can aid in flexion, extension, and rotation of humerus
Pectoralis minor	Flat, thin muscle directly beneath and obscured by pectoralis major	Anterior surface of ribs 3–5, near their costal cartilages	Coracoid process of scapula	With ribs fixed, draws scapula forward and inferiorly; with scapula fixed, draws rib cage superiorly

➤

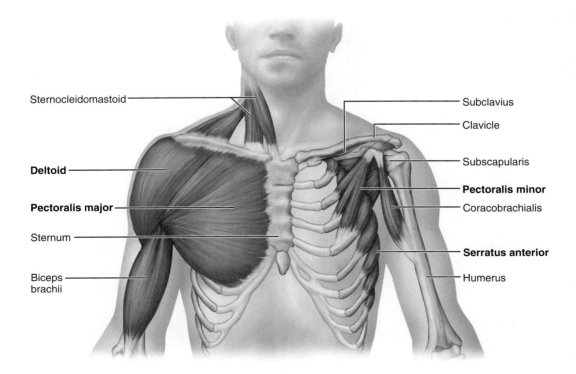

FIGURE 14.6 Superficial muscles of the thorax and shoulder acting on the scapula and arm (anterior view). The superficial muscles, which effect arm movements, are shown on the left. These muscles have been removed on the right side of the figure to show the muscles that stabilize or move the pectoral girdle.

TABLE 14.3	Anterior Muscles of Human Thorax, Shoulder, and Abdominal Wall (see Figures 14.6, 14.7, and 14.8) *(continued)*			
Muscle	Comments	Origin	Insertion	Action

Thorax, Deep: Muscles of Respiration (Figure 14.7)

Muscle	Comments	Origin	Insertion	Action
External intercostals	11 pairs lie between ribs; fibers run obliquely downward and forward toward sternum	Inferior border of rib above (not shown in figure)	Superior border of rib below	Pull ribs toward one another to elevate rib cage; aid in inspiration
Internal intercostals	11 pairs lie between ribs; fibers run deep and at right angles to those of external intercostals	Superior border of rib below	Inferior border of rib above (not shown in figure)	Draw ribs together to depress rib cage; aid in forced expiration; antagonistic to external intercostals
Diaphragm	Broad muscle; forms floor of thoracic cavity; dome-shaped in relaxed state; fibers converge toward a central tendon	Inferior border of rib and sternum, costal cartilages of last six ribs and lumbar vertebrae	Central tendon	Prime mover of inspiration: flattens on contraction, increasing vertical dimensions of thorax; increases intra-abdominal pressure

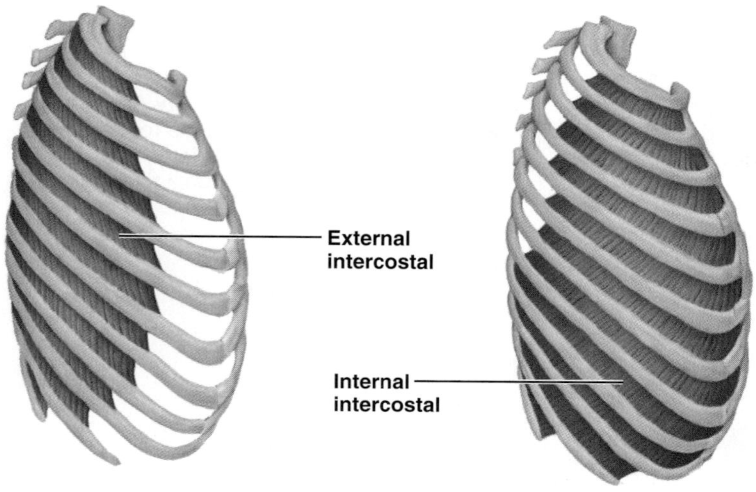

FIGURE 14.7 Deep muscles of the thorax: muscles of respiration.
(a) The external intercostals (inspiratory muscles) (left) and the internal intercostals (expiratory muscles) (right) run obliquely and at right angles to each other. (b) Inferior view of the diaphragm. Notice that its muscle fibers converge toward a central tendon, which causes the diaphragm to flatten and move inferiorly as it contracts.

External intercostal

Internal intercostal

(a)

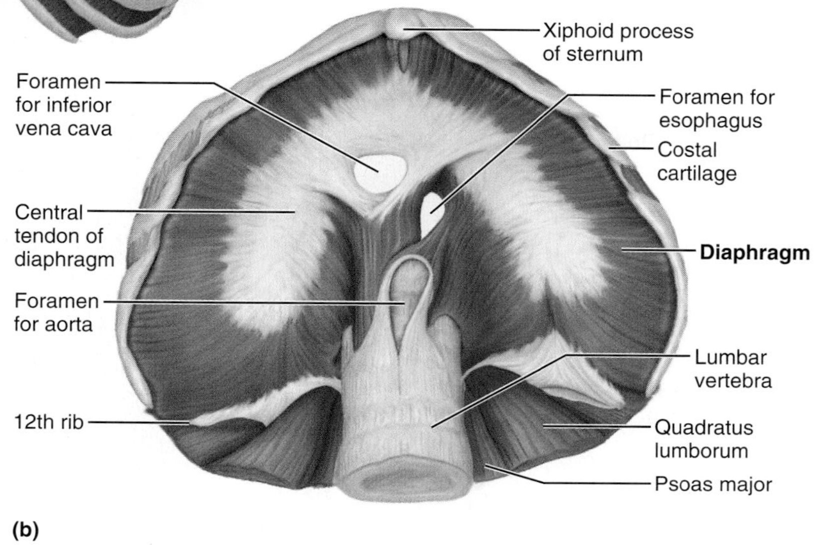

Xiphoid process of sternum

Foramen for inferior vena cava

Foramen for esophagus

Costal cartilage

Central tendon of diaphragm

Diaphragm

Foramen for aorta

Lumbar vertebra

12th rib

Quadratus lumborum

Psoas major

(b)

TABLE 14.3	*(continued)*			
Muscle	Comments	Origin	Insertion	Action

Abdominal Wall (Figure 14.8a and b)

Muscle	Comments	Origin	Insertion	Action
Rectus abdominis	Medial superficial muscle, extends from pubis to rib cage; ensheathed by aponeuroses of oblique muscles; segmented	Pubic crest and symphysis	Xiphoid process and costal cartilages of ribs 5–7	Flexes and rotates vertebral column; increases abdominal pressure; fixes and depresses ribs; stabilizes pelvis during walking; used in sit-ups and curls
External oblique	Most superficial lateral muscle; fibers run downward and medially; ensheathed by an aponeurosis	Anterior surface of last eight ribs	Linea alba,* pubic crest and tubercles, and iliac crest	See rectus abdominis, above; also aids muscles of back in trunk rotation and lateral flexion; used in oblique curls
Internal oblique	Most fibers run at right angles to those of external oblique, which it underlies	Lumbar fascia, iliac crest, and inguinal ligament	Linea alba, pubic crest, and costal cartilages of last three ribs	As for external oblique
Transversus abdominis	Deepest muscle of abdominal wall; fibers run horizontally	Inguinal ligament, iliac crest, cartilages of last five or six ribs, and lumbar fascia	Linea alba and pubic crest	Compresses abdominal contents

*The linea alba (white line) is a narrow, tendinous sheath that runs along the middle of the abdomen from the sternum to the pubic symphysis. It is formed by the fusion of the aponeurosis of the external oblique and transversus muscles.

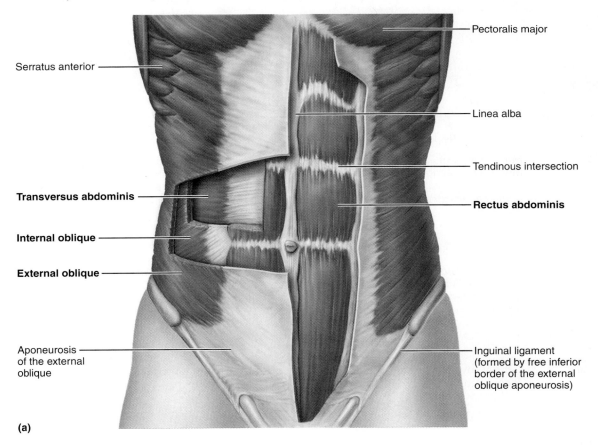

(a)

FIGURE 14.8 Anterior view of the muscles forming the anterolateral abdominal wall. (a) The superficial muscles have been partially cut away on the left side of the diagram to reveal the deeper internal oblique and transversus abdominis muscles.

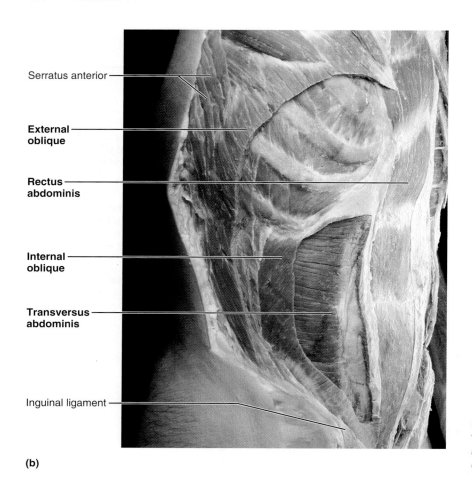

Serratus anterior

External oblique

Rectus abdominis

Internal oblique

Transversus abdominis

Inguinal ligament

(b)

FIGURE 14.8 *(continued)* **Anterior view of the muscles forming the anterolateral abdominal wall. (b)** Photo of the anterolateral abdominal wall.

TABLE 14.4	Posterior Muscles of Human Trunk (see Figure 14.9)			
Muscle	Comments	Origin	Insertion	Action
Muscles of the Neck, Shoulder, and Thorax (Figure 14.9a)				
Trapezius	Most superficial muscle of posterior thorax; very broad origin and insertion	Occipital bone; ligamentum nuchae; spines of C_7 and all thoracic vertebrae	Acromion and spinous process of scapula; lateral third of clavicle	Extends head; raises, rotates, and retracts (adducts) scapula and stabilizes it; superior fibers elevate scapula (as in shrugging the shoulders); inferior fibers depress it
Latissimus dorsi	Broad flat muscle of lower back (lumbar region); extensive superficial origins	Indirect attachment to spinous processes of lower six thoracic vertebrae, lumbar vertebrae, last three to four ribs, and iliac crest	Floor of intertubercular sulcus of humerus	Prime mover of arm extension; adducts and medially rotates arm; depresses scapula; brings arm down in power stroke, as in striking a blow
Infraspinatus	Partially covered by deltoid and trapezius; a rotator cuff muscle	Infraspinous fossa of scapula	Greater tubercle of humerus	Lateral rotation of humerus; helps hold head of humerus in glenoid cavity; stabilizes shoulder
Teres minor	Small muscle inferior to infraspinatus; a rotator cuff muscle	Lateral margin of scapula	Greater tubercle of humerus	As for infraspinatus

TABLE 14.4	*(continued)*			
Muscle	**Comments**	**Origin**	**Insertion**	**Action**
Teres major	Located inferiorly to teres minor	Posterior surface at inferior angle of scapula	Intertubercular sulcus of humerus	Extends, medially rotates, and adducts humerus; synergist of latissimus dorsi
Supraspinatus	Obscured by trapezius; a rotator cuff muscle	Supraspinous fossa of scapula	Greater tubercle of humerus	Assists abduction of humerus; stabilizes shoulder joint
Levator scapulae	Located at back and side of neck, deep to trapezius	Transverse processes of C_1–C_4	Medial border of scapula superior to spine	Elevates and adducts scapula; with fixed scapula, flexes neck to the same side
Rhomboids—major and minor	Beneath trapezius and inferior to levator scapulae; rhomboid minor is the more superior muscle	Spinous processes of C_7 and T_1–T_5	Medial border of scapula	Pulls scapula medially (retraction); stabilizes scapula; rotates glenoid cavity downward

Muscles Associated with the Vertebral Column (Figure 14.9b)

Semispinalis	Deep composite muscle of the back—thoracis, cervicis, and capitis portions	Transverse processes of C_7–T_{12}	Occipital bone and spinous processes of cervical vertebrae and T_1–T_4	Acting together, extend head and vertebral column; independently cause rotation toward opposite side

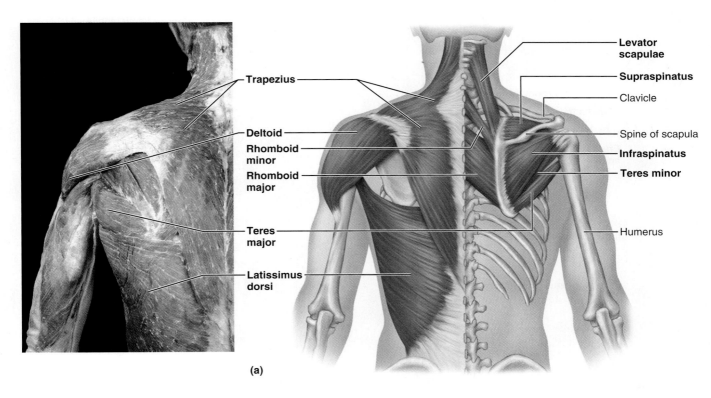

(a)

FIGURE 14.9 Muscles of the neck, shoulder, and thorax (posterior view). (a) The superficial muscles of the back are shown for the left side of the body, with a corresponding photograph. The superficial muscles are removed on the right side of the illustration to reveal the deeper muscles acting on the scapula and the rotator cuff muscles that help to stabilize the shoulder joint.

TABLE 14.4	Posterior Muscles of Human Trunk (see Figure 14.9) *(continued)*			
Muscle	Comments	Origin	Insertion	Action
Erector spinae	A long tripartite muscle composed of iliocostalis (lateral), longissimus, and spinalis (medial) muscle columns; superficial to semispinalis muscles; extends from pelvis to head	Iliac crest, transverse processes of lumbar, thoracic, and cervical vertebrae, and/or ribs 3–6 depending on specific part	Ribs and transverse processes of vertebrae about six segments above origin; longissimus also inserts into mastoid process	Extend and bend the vertebral column laterally; fibers of the longissimus also extend head

(b)

FIGURE 14.9 *(continued)* **Muscles of the neck, shoulder, and thorax (posterior view). (b)** The erector spinae and semispinalis muscles, which respectively form the intermediate and deep muscle layers of the back associated with the vertebral column.

TABLE 14.4	(continued)			
Muscle	**Comments**	**Origin**	**Insertion**	**Action**
Splenius (see Figure 14.9c)	Superficial muscle (capitis and cervicis parts) extending from upper thoracic region to skull	Ligamentum nuchae and spinous processes of C_7–T_6	Mastoid process, occipital bone, and transverse processes of C_2–C_4	As a group, extend or hyperextend head; when only one side is active, head is rotated and bent toward the same side
Quadratus lumborum	Forms greater portion of posterior abdominal wall	Iliac crest and lumbar fascia	Inferior border of rib 12; transverse processes of lumbar vertebrae	Each flexes vertebral column laterally; together extend the lumbar spine and fix rib 12; maintains upright posture

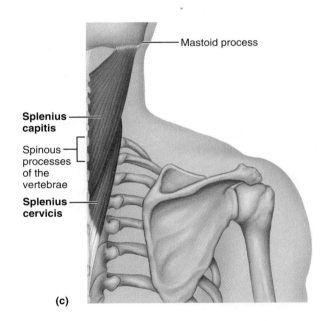

Mastoid process

Splenius capitis

Spinous processes of the vertebrae

Splenius cervicis

(c)

FIGURE 14.9 (*continued*) (c) Deep (splenius) muscles of the posterior neck. Superficial muscles have been removed.

Muscles of the Upper Limb

The muscles that act on the upper limb fall into three groups: those that move the arm, those causing movement at the elbow, and those effecting movements of the wrist and hand.

The muscles that cross the shoulder joint to insert on the humerus and move the arm (subscapularis, supraspinatus and infraspinatus, deltoid, and so on) are primarily trunk muscles that originate on the axial skeleton or shoulder girdle. These muscles are included with the trunk muscles.

The second group of muscles, which cross the elbow joint and move the forearm, consists of muscles forming the musculature of the humerus. These muscles arise primarily from the humerus and insert in forearm bones. They are responsible for flexion, extension, pronation, and supination. The origins, insertions, and actions of these muscles are summarized in Table 14.5 and the muscles are shown in Figure 14.10.

The third group composes the musculature of the forearm. For the most part, these muscles insert on the digits and produce movements at the wrist and fingers. In general, muscles acting on the wrist and hand are more easily identified if their insertion tendons are located first. These muscles are described in Table 14.6 and illustrated in Figure 14.11.

ACTIVITY 4

Identifying Muscles of the Upper Limb

First study the tables and figures, then see if you can identify these muscles on a torso model, anatomical chart, or cadaver. Complete this portion of the exercise with palpation demonstrations as outlined next.

• To observe the *biceps brachii*, attempt to flex your forearm (hand supinated) against resistance. The insertion tendon of this biceps muscle can also be felt in the lateral aspect of the antecubital fossa (where it runs toward the radius to attach).

• If you acutely flex your elbow and then try to extend it against resistance, you can demonstrate the action of your *triceps brachii*.

• Strongly flex your wrist and make a fist. Palpate your contracting wrist flexor muscles (which originate from the medial epicondyle of the humerus) and their insertion tendons, which can be easily felt at the anterior aspect of the wrist.

• Flare your fingers to identify the tendons of the *extensor digitorum* muscle on the dorsum of your hand. ▮

TABLE 14.5		Muscles of Human Humerus That Act on the Forearm (see Figure 14.10)		
Muscle	Comments	Origin	Insertion	Action
Triceps brachii	Sole, large fleshy muscle of posterior humerus; three-headed origin	Long head—inferior margin of glenoid cavity; lateral head—posterior humerus; medial head—distal radial groove on posterior humerus	Olecranon process of ulna	Powerful forearm extensor; antagonist of forearm flexors (brachialis and biceps brachii)
Anconeus (see also Figure 14.11d and e)	Short triangular muscle blended with triceps	Lateral epicondyle of humerus	Lateral aspect of olecranon process of ulna	Abducts ulna during forearm pronation; extends elbow
Biceps brachii	Most familiar muscle of anterior humerus because this two-headed muscle bulges when forearm is flexed	Short head: coracoid process; tendon of long head runs in intertubercular sulcus and within capsule of shoulder joint	Radial tuberosity	Flexion (powerful) of elbow and supination of forearm; "it turns the corkscrew and pulls the cork"; weak arm flexor
Brachioradialis (see also Figure 14.11a)	Superficial muscle of lateral forearm; forms lateral boundary of antecubital fossa	Lateral ridge at distal end of humerus	Base of styloid process of radius	Synergist in forearm flexion
Brachialis	Immediately deep to biceps brachii	Distal portion of anterior humerus	Coronoid process of ulna	A major flexor of forearm

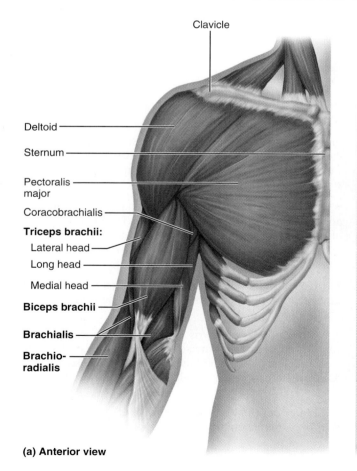

Clavicle

Deltoid

Sternum

Pectoralis major

Coracobrachialis

Triceps brachii:

Lateral head

Long head

Medial head

Biceps brachii

Brachialis

Brachio-radialis

(a) Anterior view

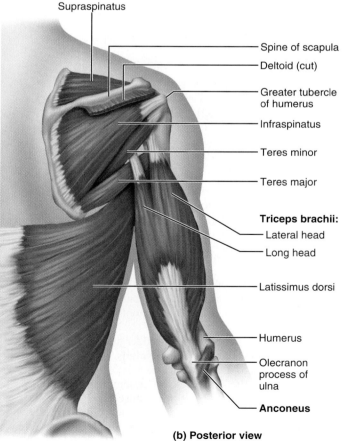

Supraspinatus

Spine of scapula

Deltoid (cut)

Greater tubercle of humerus

Infraspinatus

Teres minor

Teres major

Triceps brachii:

Lateral head

Long head

Latissimus dorsi

Humerus

Olecranon process of ulna

Anconeus

(b) Posterior view

FIGURE 14.10 Muscles causing movements of the forearm. (a) Superficial muscles of the anterior thorax, shoulder, and arm, anterior view. **(b)** Posterior aspect of the arm showing the lateral and long heads of the triceps brachii muscle. The supraspinatus, infraspinatus, teres minor, and subscapularis (Figure 14.6) are rotator cuff muscles.

TABLE 14.6	Muscles of Human Forearm That Act on Hand and Fingers (see Figure 14.11)			
Muscle	**Comments**	**Origin**	**Insertion**	**Action**

Anterior Compartment (Figure 14.11a, b, c)

Superficial

Pronator teres	Seen in a superficial view between proximal margins of brachioradialis and flexor carpi radialis	Medial epicondyle of humerus and coronoid process of ulna	Midshaft of radius	Acts synergistically with pronator quadratus to pronate forearm; weak elbow flexor
Flexor carpi radialis	Superficial; runs diagonally across forearm	Medial epicondyle of humerus	Base of metacarpals 2 and 3	Powerful flexor of wrist; abducts hand
Palmaris longus	Small fleshy muscle with a long tendon; medial to flexor carpi radialis	Medial epicondyle of humerus	Palmar aponeurosis; skin and fascia of palm	Flexes wrist (weak); tenses skin and fascia of palm
Flexor carpi ulnaris	Superficial; medial to palmaris longus	Medial epicondyle of humerus, olecranon process and posterior surface of ulna	Base of metacarpal 5; pisiform and hamate bones	Powerful flexor of wrist; adducts hand

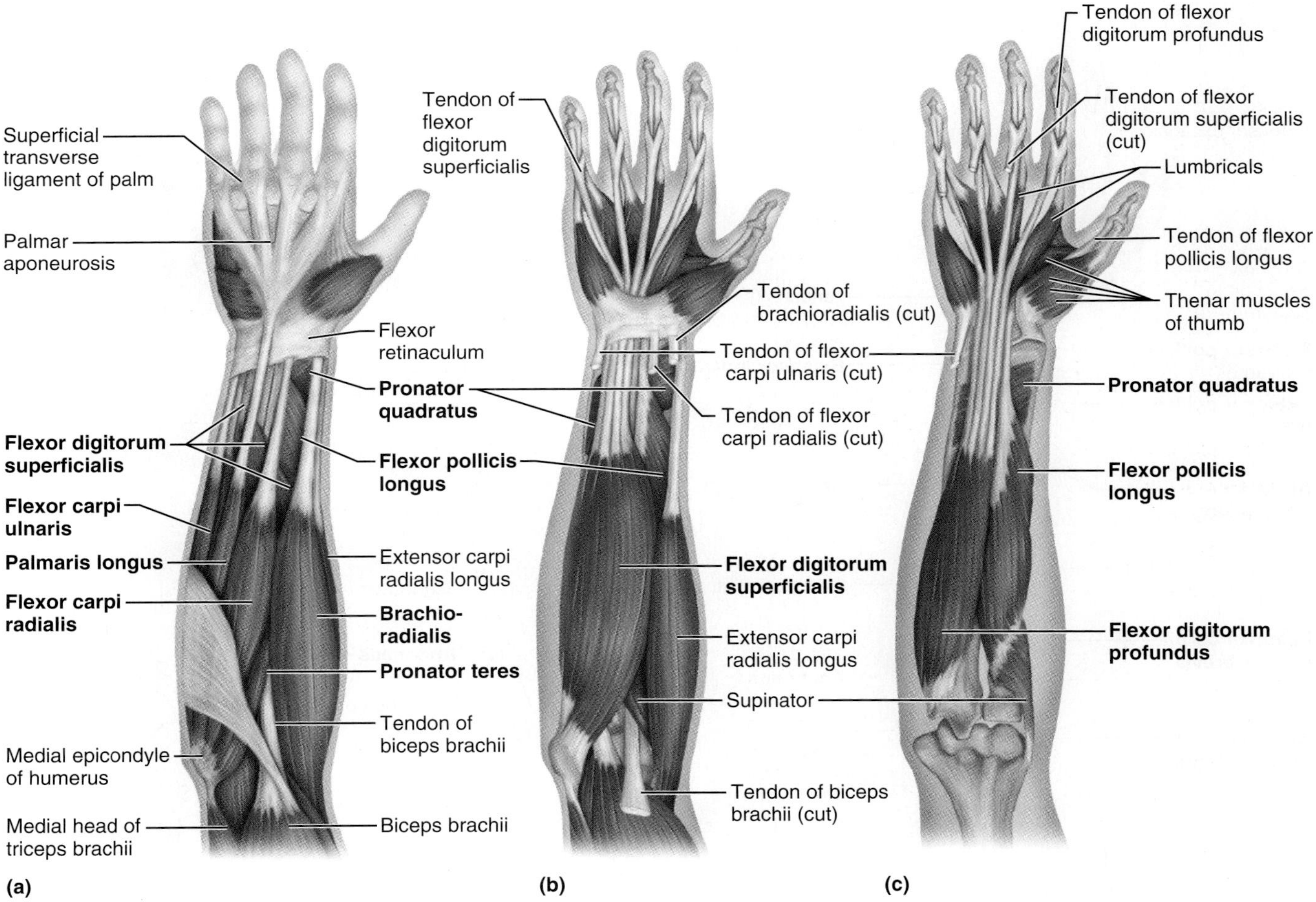

FIGURE 14.11 Muscles of the forearm and wrist. (**a**) Superficial anterior view of right forearm and hand. (**b**) The brachioradialis, flexors carpi radialis and ulnaris, and palmaris longus muscles have been removed to reveal the position of the somewhat deeper flexor digitorum superficialis. (**c**) Deep muscles of the anterior compartment. Superficial muscles have been removed. *Note:* The thenar muscles of the thumb and the lumbricals that help move the fingers are illustrated here but are not described in Table 14.6.

TABLE 14.6	Muscles of Human Forearm That Act on Hand and Fingers (see Figure 14.11) *(continued)*			
Muscle	Comments	Origin	Insertion	Action
Flexor digitorum superficialis	Deeper muscle (deep to muscles named above); visible at distal end of forearm	Medial epicondyle of humerus, coronoid process of ulna, and shaft of radius	Middle phalanges of fingers 2–5	Flexes wrist and middle phalanges of fingers 2–5
Deep				
Flexor pollicis longus	Deep muscle of anterior forearm; distal to and paralleling lower margin of flexor digitorum superficialis	Anterior surface of radius, and interosseous membrane	Distal phalanx of thumb	Flexes thumb (*pollex* is Latin for "thumb")
Flexor digitorum profundus	Deep muscle; overlain entirely by flexor digitorum superficialis	Anteromedial surface of ulna, interosseous membrane, and coronoid process	Distal phalanges of fingers 2–5	Sole muscle that flexes distal phalanges; assists in wrist flexion
Pronator quadratus	Deepest muscle of distal forearm	Distal portion of anterior ulnar surface	Anterior surface of radius, distal end	Pronates forearm

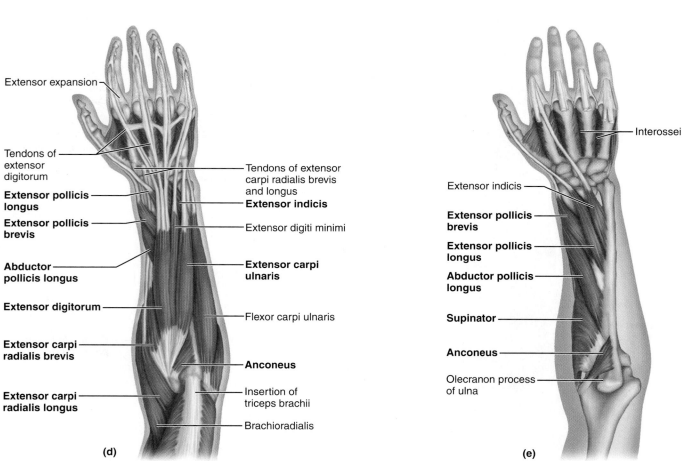

FIGURE 14.11 *(continued)* **Muscles of the forearm and wrist.** (d) Superficial muscles, posterior view. (e) Deep posterior muscles; superficial muscles have been removed. The interossei, the deepest layer of instrinsic hand muscles, are also illustrated.

TABLE 14.6	*(continued)*			
Muscle	**Comments**	**Origin**	**Insertion**	**Action**
Posterior Compartment (Figure 14.11d, e, f)				
Superficial				
Extensor carpi radialis longus	Superficial; parallels brachioradialis on lateral forearm	Lateral supracondylar ridge of humerus	Base of metacarpal 2	Extends and abducts wrist
Extensor carpi radialis brevis	Deep to extensor carpi radialis longus	Lateral epicondyle of humerus	Base of metacarpal 3	Extends and abducts wrist; steadies wrist during finger flexion
Extensor digitorum	Superficial; medial to extensor carpi radialis brevis	Lateral epicondyle of humerus	By four tendons into distal phalanges of fingers 2–5	Prime mover of finger extension; extends wrist; can flare (abduct) fingers
Extensor carpi ulnaris	Superficial; medial posterior forearm	Lateral epicondyle of humerus; posterior border of ulna	Base of metacarpal 5	Extends and adducts wrist
Deep				
Extensor pollicis longus and brevis	Muscle pair with a common origin and action; deep to extensor carpi ulnaris	Dorsal shaft of ulna and radius, interosseous membrane	Base of distal phalanx of thumb (longus) and proximal phalanx of thumb (brevis)	Extends thumb
Abductor pollicis longus	Deep muscle; lateral and parallel to extensor pollicis longus	Posterior surface of radius and ulna; interosseous membrane	Metacarpal 1 and trapezium	Abducts and extends thumb
Supinator	Deep muscle at posterior aspect of elbow	Lateral epicondyle of humerus; proximal ulna	Proximal end of radius	Acts with biceps brachii to supinate forearm; antagonist of pronator muscles

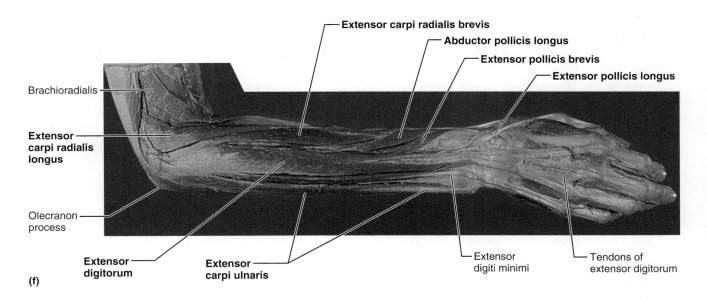

(f)

FIGURE 14.11 *(continued)* **(f)** Photo of deep posterior muscles of the right forearm.

TABLE 14.7	Intrinsic Muscles of the Hand: Fine Movements of the Fingers (see Figure 14.12)			
Muscle	Comments	Origin	Insertion	Action

Thenar Muscles in Ball of Thumb (Figure 14.12a, b)

Abductor pollicis brevis	Lateral muscle of thenar group; superficial	Flexor retinaculum and nearby carpals	Lateral base of thumb's proximal phalanx	Abducts thumb (at carpometacarpal joint)
Flexor pollicis brevis	Medial and deep muscle of thenar group	Flexor retinaculum and trapezium	Lateral side of base of proximal phalanx of thumb	Flexes thumb (at carpometacarpal and metacarpophalangeal joints)
Opponens pollicis	Deep to abductor pollicis brevis, on metacarpal 1	Flexor retinaculum and trapezium	Whole anterior side of metacarpal 1	Opposition: moves thumb to touch tip of little finger
Adductor pollicis	Fan-shaped with horizontal fibers; distal to other thenar muscles; oblique and transverse heads	Capitate bone and bases of metacarpals 2–4 (oblique head); front of metacarpal 3 (transverse head)	Medial side of base of proximal phalanx of thumb	Adducts and helps to oppose thumb

Hypothenar Muscles in Ball of Little Finger (Figure 14.12a, b)

Abductor digiti minimi	Medial muscle of hypothenar group; superficial	Pisiform bone	Medial side of proximal phalanx of little finger	Abducts little finger at metacarpophalangeal joint
Flexor digiti minimi brevis	Lateral deep muscle of hypothenar group	Hamate bone and flexor retinaculum	Same as abductor digiti minimi	Flexes little finger at metacarpophalangeal joint
Opponens digiti minimi	Deep to abductor digiti minimi	Same as flexor digiti minimi brevis	Most of length of medial side of metacarpal 5	Helps in opposition: brings metacarpal 5 toward thumb to cup the hand

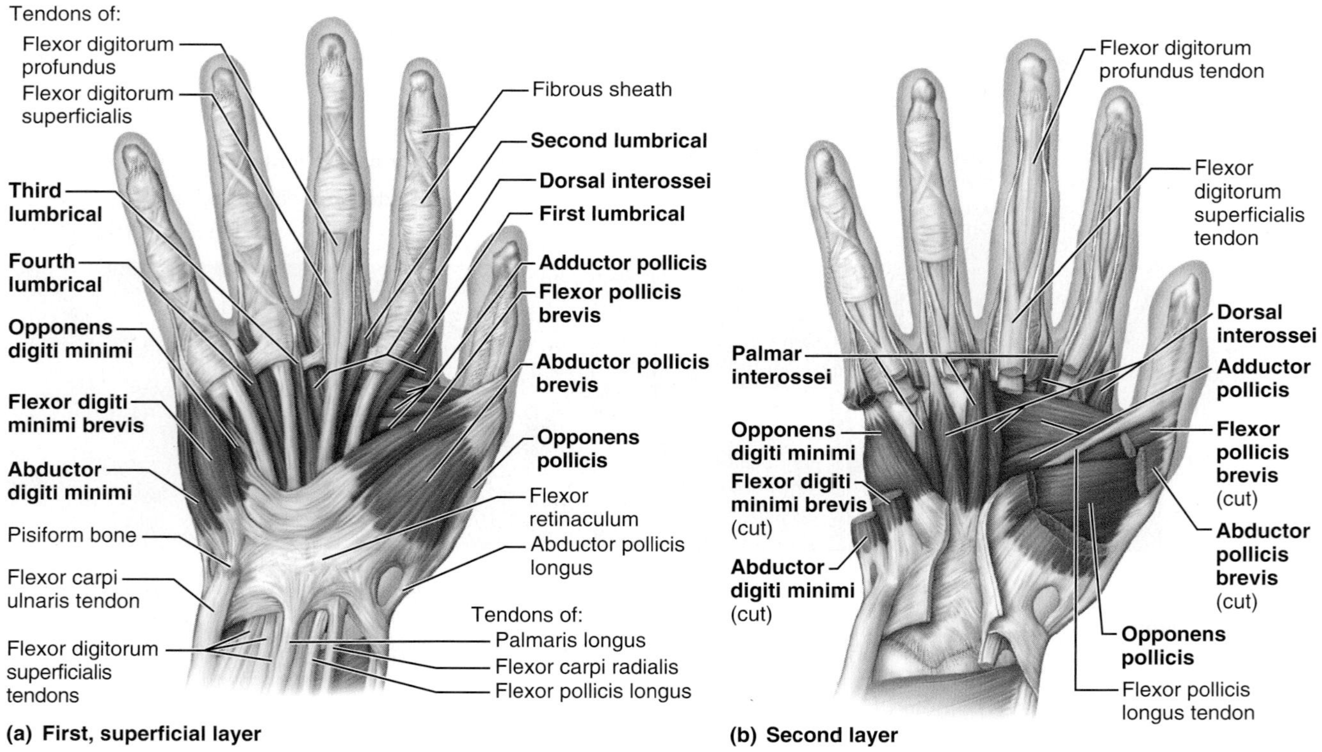

(a) First, superficial layer

(b) Second layer

FIGURE 14.12 Hand muscles, ventral view of right hand.

TABLE 14.7	*(continued)*			
Muscle	**Comments**	**Origin**	**Insertion**	**Action**

Midpalmar Muscles (Figure 14.12a, b, c, d)

Muscle	Comments	Origin	Insertion	Action
Lumbricals	Four worm-shaped muscles in palm, one to each finger (except thumb); odd because they originate from the tendons of another muscle	Lateral side of each tendon of flexor digitorum profundus in palm	Lateral edge of extensor expansion on first phalanx of fingers 2–5	Flex fingers at metacarpophalangeal joints but extend fingers at interphalangeal joints
Palmar interossei	Four long, cone-shaped muscles; lie ventral to the dorsal interossei and between the metacarpals	The side of each metacarpal that faces the midaxis of the hand (metacarpal 3) where it's absent	Extensor expansion on first phalanx of each finger (except finger 3), on side facing midaxis of hand	Adduct fingers; pull fingers in toward third digit; act with lumbricals to extend fingers at interphalangeal joints and flex them at metacarpophalangeal joints
Dorsal interossei	Four bipennate muscles filling spaces between the metacarpals; deepest palm muscles, also visible on dorsal side of hand	Sides of metacarpals	Exterior expansion over first phalanx of fingers 2–4 on side opposite midaxis of hand (finger 3), but on *both* sides of finger 3	Abduct fingers; extend fingers at interphalangeal joints and flex them at metacarpophalangeal joints

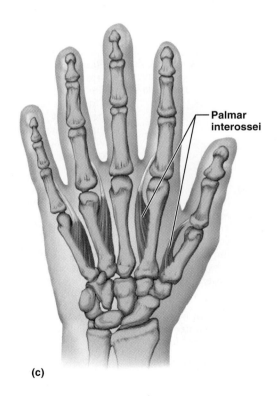

Palmar interossei

(c)

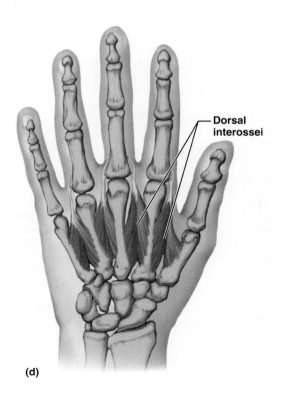

Dorsal interossei

(d)

FIGURE 14.12 *(continued)*

Muscles of the Lower Limb

Muscles that act on the lower limb cause movement at the hip, knee, and foot joints. Since the human pelvic girdle is composed of heavy fused bones that allow very little movement, no special group of muscles is necessary to stabilize it. This is unlike the shoulder girdle, where several muscles (mainly trunk muscles) are needed to stabilize the scapulae.

Muscles acting on the thigh (femur) cause various movements at the multiaxial hip joint (flexion, extension, rotation, abduction, and adduction). These include the iliopsoas, the adductor group, and other muscles summarized in Tables 14.8 and 14.9 and illustrated in Figures 14.13 and 14.14.

Muscles acting on the leg form the major musculature of the thigh. (Anatomically the term *leg* refers only to that portion between the knee and the ankle.) The thigh muscles cross the knee to allow its flexion and extension. They include the hamstrings and the quadriceps and, along with the muscles acting on the thigh, are described in Tables 14.8 and 14.9 and illustrated in Figures 14.13 and 14.14. Since some of these muscles also have attachments on the pelvic girdle, they can cause movement at the hip joint.

The muscles originating on the leg, as well as the intrinsic muscles of the foot, are described in Tables 14.10, 14.11, and 14.12 and shown in Figures 14.15, 14.16, and 14.17.

(Text continues on p. 212.)

TABLE 14.8	Muscles Acting on Human Thigh and Leg, Anterior and Medial Aspects (see Figure 14.13)			
Muscle	**Comments**	**Origin**	**Insertion**	**Action**
Origin on the Pelvis				
Iliopsoas—iliacus and psoas major	Two closely related muscles; fibers pass under inguinal ligament to insert into femur via a common tendon; iliacus is more lateral	Iliacus—iliac fossa and crest, lateral sacrum; psoas major—transverse processes, bodies, and discs of T12 and lumbar vertebrae	On and just below lesser trochanter of femur	Flex trunk on thigh; flex thigh; lateral flexion of vertebral column (psoas)
Sartorius	Straplike superficial muscle running obliquely across anterior surface of thigh to knee	Anterior superior iliac spine	By an aponeurosis into medial aspect of proximal tibia	Flexes, abducts, and laterally rotates thigh; flexes knee; known as "tailor's muscle" because it helps effect cross-legged position in which tailors are often depicted
Medial Compartment				
Adductors—magnus, longus, and brevis	Large muscle mass forming medial aspect of thigh; arise from front of pelvis and insert at various levels on femur	Magnus—ischial and pubic rami and ischial tuberosity; longus—pubis near pubic symphysis; brevis—body and inferior ramus of pubis	Magnus—linea aspera and adductor tubercle of femur; longus and brevis—linea aspera	Adduct and medially rotate and flex thigh; posterior part of magnus is also a synergist in thigh extension
Pectineus	Overlies adductor brevis on proximal thigh	Pectineal line of pubis (and superior ramus)	Inferior from lesser trochanter to linea aspera of femur	Adducts, flexes, and medially rotates thigh
Gracilis	Straplike superficial muscle of medial thigh	Inferior ramus and body of pubis	Medial surface of tibia just inferior to medial condyle	Adducts thigh; flexes and medially rotates leg, especially during walking

(Table continues on p. 210.) ➤

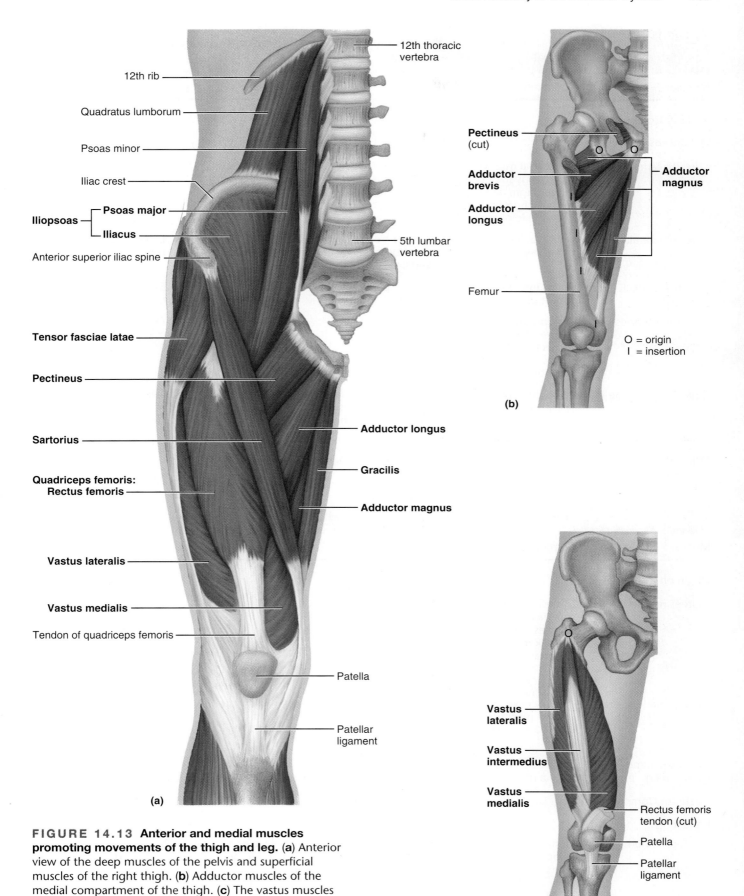

FIGURE 14.13 Anterior and medial muscles promoting movements of the thigh and leg. (**a**) Anterior view of the deep muscles of the pelvis and superficial muscles of the right thigh. (**b**) Adductor muscles of the medial compartment of the thigh. (**c**) The vastus muscles (isolated) of the quadriceps group.

TABLE 14.8	Muscles Acting on Human Thigh and Leg, Anterior and Medial Aspects (see Figure 14.13) *(continued)*			
Muscle	**Comments**	**Origin**	**Insertion**	**Action**
Anterior Compartment				
Quadriceps femoris*				
Rectus femoris	Superficial muscle of thigh; runs straight down thigh; only muscle of group to cross hip joint	Anterior inferior iliac spine and superior margin of acetabulum	Tibial tuberosity and patella	Extends knee and flexes thigh at hip
Vastus lateralis	Forms lateral aspect of thigh	Greater trochanter, intertrochanteric line, and linea aspera	Tibial tuberosity and patella	Extends and stabilizes knee
Vastus medialis	Forms inferomedial aspect of thigh	Linea aspera and intertrochanteric line	Tibial tuberosity and patella	Extends knee; stabilizes patella
Vastus intermedius	Obscured by rectus femoris; lies between vastus lateralis and vastus medialis on anterior thigh	Anterior and lateral surface of femur	Tibial tuberosity and patella	Extends knee
Tensor fasciae latae	Enclosed between fascia layers of thigh	Anterior aspect of iliac crest and anterior superior iliac spine	Iliotibial tract (lateral portion of fascia lata)	Flexes, abducts, and medially rotates thigh; steadies trunk

*The quadriceps form the flesh of the anterior thigh and have a common insertion in the tibial tuberosity via the patellar tendon. They are powerful leg extensors, enabling humans to kick a football, for example.

TABLE 14.9	Muscles Acting on Human Thigh and Leg, Posterior Aspect (see Figure 14.14)			
Muscle	**Comments**	**Origin**	**Insertion**	**Action**
Origin on the Pelvis				
Gluteus maximus	Largest and most superficial of gluteal muscles (which form buttock mass); important injection site	Dorsal ilium, sacrum, and coccyx	Gluteal tuberosity of femur and iliotibial tract*	Complex, powerful thigh extensor (most effective when thigh is flexed, as in climbing stairs—but not as in walking); antagonist of iliopsoas; laterally rotates and abducts thigh
Gluteus medius	Partially covered by gluteus maximus; important injection site	Upper lateral surface of ilium	Greater trochanter of femur	Abducts and medially rotates thigh; steadies pelvis during walking
Gluteus minimus (not shown in figure)	Smallest and deepest gluteal muscle	External inferior surface of ilium	Greater trochanter of femur	Abducts and medially rotates thigh; steadies pelvis
Posterior Compartment				
Hamstrings†				
Biceps femoris	Most lateral muscle of group; arises from two heads	Ischial tuberosity (long head); linea aspera and distal femur (short head)	Tendon passes laterally to insert into head of fibula and lateral condyle of tibia	Extends thigh; laterally rotates leg; flexes knee

TABLE 14.9	(continued)			
Muscle	Comments	Origin	Insertion	Action
Semitendinosus	Medial to biceps femoris	Ischial tuberosity	Medial aspect of upper tibial shaft	Extends thigh; flexes knee; medially rotates leg
Semimembranosus	Deep to semitendi-nosus	Ischial tuberosity	Medial condyle of tibia; lateral condyle of femur	Extends thigh; flexes knee; medially rotates leg

*The iliotibial tract, a thickened lateral portion of the fascia lata, ensheathes all the muscles of the thigh. It extends as a tendinous band from the iliac crest to the knee.

†The hamstrings are the fleshy muscles of the posterior thigh. The name comes from the butchers' practice of using the tendons of these muscles to hang hams for smoking. As a group, they are strong extensors of the hip; they counteract the powerful quadriceps by stabilizing the knee joint when standing.

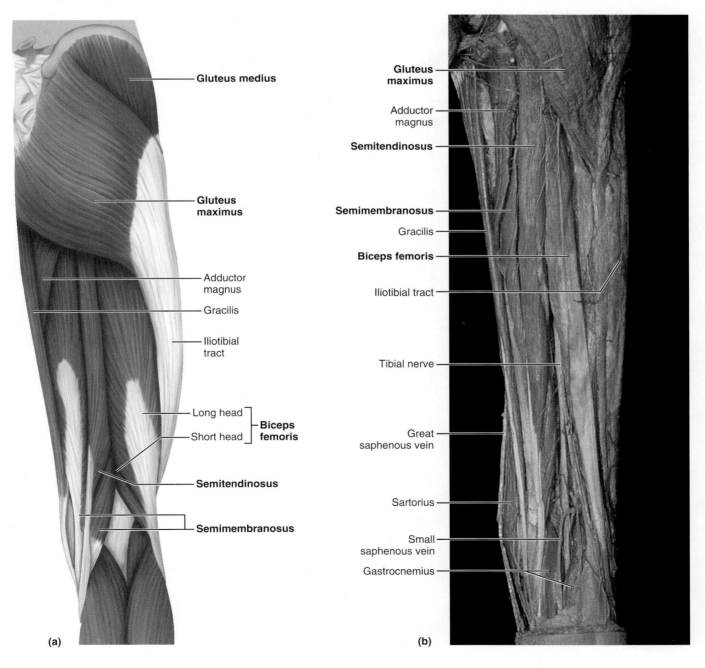

(a)

(b)

FIGURE 14.14 Muscles of the posterior aspect of the right hip and thigh. (a) Superficial view showing the gluteus muscles of the buttock and hamstring muscles of the thigh. **(b)** Photo of muscles of the posterior thigh.

Identifying Muscles
of the Lower Limb

Identify the muscles acting on the thigh, leg, foot, and toes as instructed previously for other muscle groups. ▬

Palpating Muscles of
the Hip and Lower Limb

Complete this exercise by performing the following palpation demonstrations with your lab partner.

• Go into a deep knee bend and palpate your own *gluteus maximus* muscle as you extend your hip to resume the upright posture.

• Demonstrate the contraction of the anterior *quadriceps femoris* by trying to extend your knee against resistance. Do this while seated and note how the patellar tendon reacts. The *biceps femoris* of the posterior thigh comes into play when you flex your knee against resistance.

• Now stand on your toes. Have your partner palpate the lateral and medial heads of the *gastrocnemius* and follow it to its insertion in the calcaneal tendon.

• Dorsiflex and invert your foot while palpating your *tibialis anterior* muscle (which parallels the sharp anterior crest of the tibia laterally). ▬

TABLE 14.10	Muscles Acting on Human Foot and Ankle (see Figures 14.15 and 14.16)			
Muscle	**Comments**	**Origin**	**Insertion**	**Action**
Lateral Compartment (Figure 14.15a, b and Figure 14.16b)				
Fibularis (peroneus) longus	Superficial lateral muscle; overlies fibula	Head and upper portion of fibula	By long tendon under foot to metatarsal 1 and medial cuneiform	Plantar flexes and everts foot; helps keep foot flat on ground
Fibularis (peroneus) brevis	Smaller muscle; deep to fibularis longus	Distal portion of fibula shaft	By tendon running behind lateral malleolus to insert on proximal end of metatarsal 5	Plantar flexes and everts foot, as part of fibular group
Anterior Compartment (Figure 14.15a, b)				
Tibialis anterior	Superficial muscle of anterior leg; parallels sharp anterior margin of tibia	Lateral condyle and upper ⅔ of tibia; interosseous membrane	By tendon into inferior surface of first cuneiform and metatarsal 1	Prime mover of dorsiflexion; inverts foot; supports longitudinal arch of foot
Extensor digitorum longus	Anterolateral surface of leg; lateral to tibialis anterior	Lateral condyle of tibia; proximal ¾ of fibula; interosseous membrane	Tendon divides into four parts; inserts into middle and distal phalanges of toes 2–5	Prime mover of toe extension; dorsiflexes foot
Fibularis (peroneus) tertius	Small muscle; often fused to distal part of extensor digitorum longus	Distal anterior surface of fibula and interosseous membrane	Tendon inserts on dorsum of metatarsal 5	Dorsiflexes and everts foot
Extensor hallucis longus	Deep to extensor digitorum longus and tibialis anterior	Anteromedial shaft of fibula and interosseous membrane	Tendon inserts on distal phalanx of great toe	Extends great toe; dorsiflexes foot

(Table continues on p. 214.) ➤

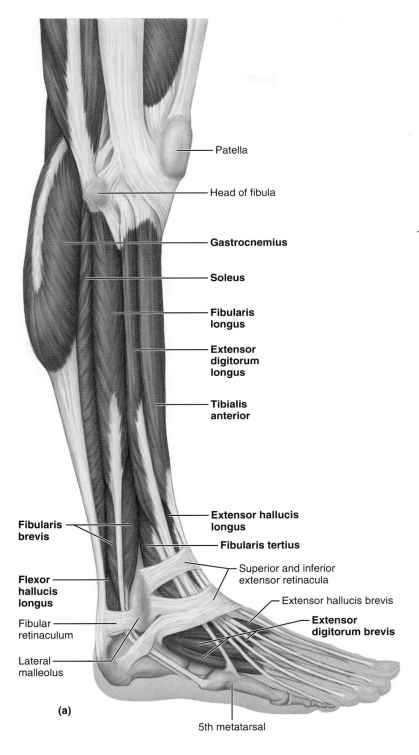

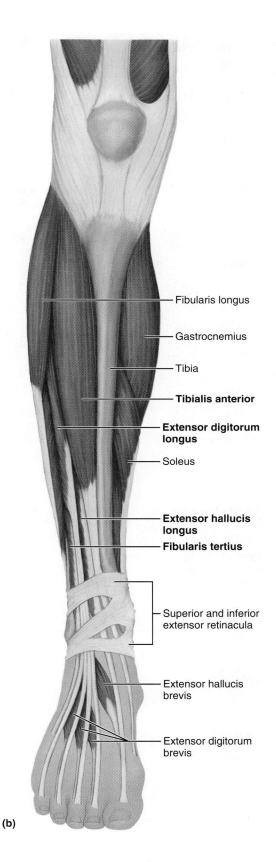

- Patella
- Head of fibula
- **Gastrocnemius**
- **Soleus**
- **Fibularis longus**
- **Extensor digitorum longus**
- **Tibialis anterior**

Fibularis brevis

- **Extensor hallucis longus**
- **Fibularis tertius**

Flexor hallucis longus

- Superior and inferior extensor retinacula
- Extensor hallucis brevis
- **Extensor digitorum brevis**

Fibular retinaculum

Lateral malleolus

(a)

5th metatarsal

- Fibularis longus
- Gastrocnemius
- Tibia
- **Tibialis anterior**
- **Extensor digitorum longus**
- Soleus
- **Extensor hallucis longus**
- **Fibularis tertius**
- Superior and inferior extensor retinacula
- Extensor hallucis brevis
- Extensor digitorum brevis

(b)

FIGURE 14.15 Muscles of the anterolateral aspect of the right leg. (**a**) Superficial view of lateral aspect of the leg, illustrating the positioning of the lateral compartment muscles (fibularis longus and brevis) relative to anterior and posterior leg muscles. (**b**) Superficial view of anterior leg muscles.

TABLE 14.10	Muscles Acting on Human Foot and Ankle (see Figures 14.15 and 14.16) *(continued)*			
Muscle	Comments	Origin	Insertion	Action

Posterior Compartment

Superficial (Figures 14.15 and 14.16)

Triceps surae	Muscle pair that shapes posterior calf		Via common tendon (calcaneal, or Achilles) into heel	Plantar flex foot
Gastrocnemius	Superficial muscle of pair; two prominent bellies	By two heads from medial and lateral condyles of femur	Calcaneus via calcaneal tendon	Plantar flexes foot when knee is extended; crosses knee joint; thus can flex knee (when foot is dorsiflexed)
Soleus	Deep to gastrocnemius	Proximal portion of tibia and fibula; interosseous membrane	Calcaneus via calcaneal tendon	Plantar flexion; is an important muscle for locomotion

Deep (Figure 14.16b)

Popliteus	Thin muscle at posterior aspect of knee	Lateral condyle of femur and lateral meniscus	Proximal tibia	Flexes and rotates leg medially to "unlock" extended knee when knee flexion begins
Tibialis posterior	Thick muscle deep to soleus	Superior portion of tibia and fibula and interosseous membrane	Tendon passes obliquely behind medial malleolus and under arch of foot; inserts into several tarsals and metatarsals 2–4	Prime mover of foot inversion; plantar flexes foot; stabilizes longitudinal arch of foot
Flexor digitorum longus	Runs medial to and partially overlies tibialis posterior	Posterior surface of tibia	Distal phalanges of toes 2–5	Flexes toes; plantar flexes and inverts foot
Flexor hallucis longus (see also Figure 14.15a)	Lies lateral to inferior aspect of tibialis posterior	Middle portion of fibula shaft; interosseous membrane	Tendon runs under foot to distal phalanx of great toe	Flexes great toe (*hallux* = great toe); plantar flexes and inverts foot; the "push-off muscle" during walking

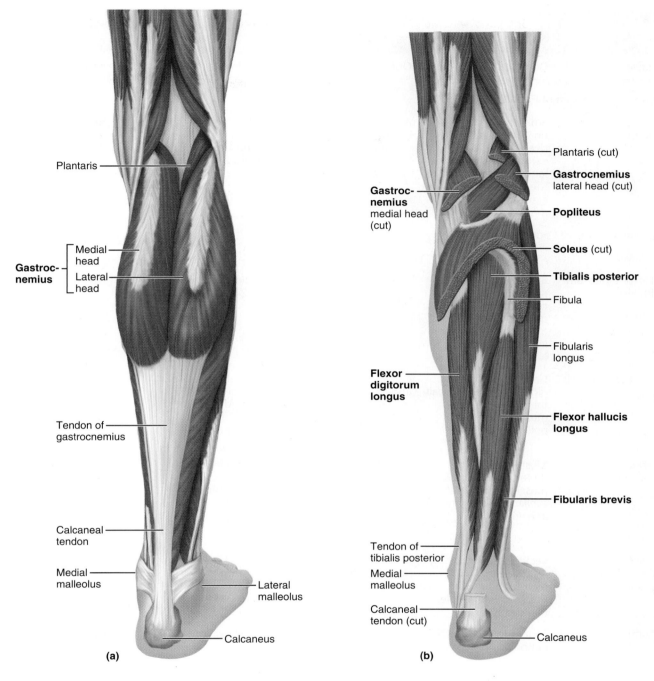

Plantaris

**Gastroc-
nemius**
  Medial
  head
  Lateral
  head

Tendon of
gastrocnemius

Calcaneal
tendon

Medial
malleolus

Lateral
malleolus

Calcaneus

(a)

Plantaris (cut)

Gastrocnemius
lateral head (cut)

**Gastroc-
nemius**
medial head
(cut)

Popliteus

Soleus (cut)

Tibialis posterior

Fibula

Fibularis
longus

**Flexor
digitorum
longus**

**Flexor hallucis
longus**

Fibularis brevis

Tendon of
tibialis posterior

Medial
malleolus

Calcaneal
tendon (cut)

Calcaneus

(b)

FIGURE 14.16 Muscles of the posterior aspect of the right leg. (a) Superficial view of the posterior
leg. **(b)** The triceps surae has been removed to show the deep muscles of the posterior compartment.

TABLE 14.11	Intrinsic Muscles of the Foot: Toe Movement and Foot Support (see Figures 14.15 and 14.17)			
Muscle	Comments	Origin	Insertion	Action

Muscles on Dorsum of Foot (Figure 14.15)

Muscle	Comments	Origin	Insertion	Action
Extensor digitorum brevis	Small, four-part muscle on dorsum of foot; deep to the tendons of extensor digitorum longus; corresponds to the extensor indicis and extensor pollicis muscles of forearm	Anterior part of calcaneus bone; extensor retinaculum	Base of proximal phalanx of big toe; extensor expansions on toes 2–4	Helps extend toes at metatarsophalangeal joints

Muscles on Sole of Foot (Figure 14.17)

First layer

Muscle	Comments	Origin	Insertion	Action
Flexor digitorum brevis	Bandlike muscle in middle of sole; corresponds to flexor digitorum superficialis of forearm and inserts into digits in the same way	Calcaneal tuberosity	Middle phalanx of toes 2–4	Helps flex toes
Abductor hallucis	Lies medial to flexor digitorum brevis; recall the similar thumb muscle, abductor pollicis brevis	Calcaneal tuberosity and flexor retinaculum	Proximal phalanx of great toe, via a sesamoid bone in tendon of flexor hallucis brevis (see below)	Abducts big toe
Abductor digiti minimi	Most lateral of the three superficial sole muscles; recall the similar abductor muscle in palm	Calcaneal tuberosity	Lateral side of base of little toe's proximal phalanx	Abducts and flexes little toe

Second layer

Muscle	Comments	Origin	Insertion	Action
Flexor accessorius (quadratus plantae)	Rectangular muscle just deep to flexor digitorum brevis in posterior half of sole; two heads	Medial and lateral sides of calcaneus	Tendon of flexor digitorum longus in midsole	Straightens out the oblique pull of flexor digitorum longus
Lumbricals	Four little "worms," like lumbricals in hand	From each tendon of flexor digitorum longus	Extensor expansion on proximal phalanx of toes 2–5, medial side	By pulling on extensor expansion, flex toes at metatarsophalangeal joints and extend toes at interphalangeal joints

Third layer

Muscle	Comments	Origin	Insertion	Action
Flexor hallucis brevis	Covers metatarsal 1; splits into two bellies; recall the flexor pollicis brevis of thumb	Mostly from cuboid bone	Via two tendons onto both sides of the base of the proximal phalanx of great toe	Flexes great toe's metatarsophalangeal joint
Adductor hallucis	Oblique and transverse heads; deep to lumbricals; recall adductor pollicis in thumb	From metatarsals 2–4, fibularis longus tendon, and a ligament across metatarsophalangeal joints	Base of proximal phalanx of great toe, lateral side	Helps maintain the transverse arch of foot; weak adductor of great toe

(Table continues on p. 218.) ➤

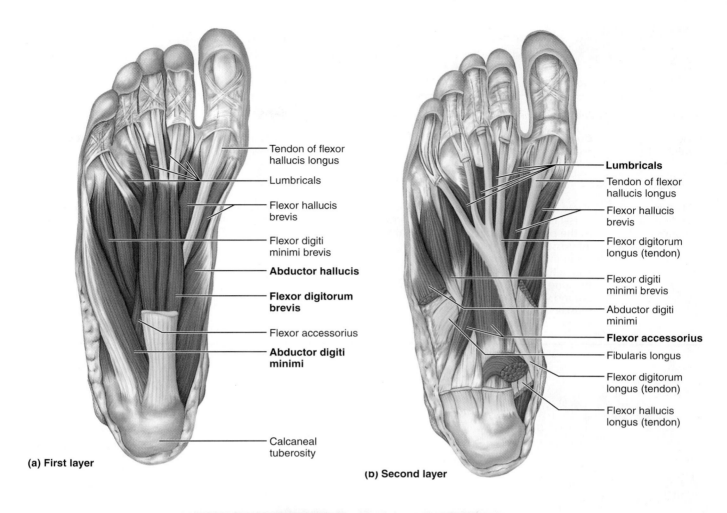

Tendon of flexor
hallucis longus

Lumbricals

Flexor hallucis
brevis

Flexor digiti
minimi brevis

Abductor hallucis

**Flexor digitorum
brevis**

Flexor accessorius

**Abductor digiti
minimi**

Calcaneal
tuberosity

(a) First layer

Lumbricals

Tendon of flexor
hallucis longus

Flexor hallucis
brevis

Flexor digitorum
longus (tendon)

Flexor digiti
minimi brevis

Abductor digiti
minimi

Flexor accessorius

Fibularis longus

Flexor digitorum
longus (tendon)

Flexor hallucis
longus (tendon)

(b) Second layer

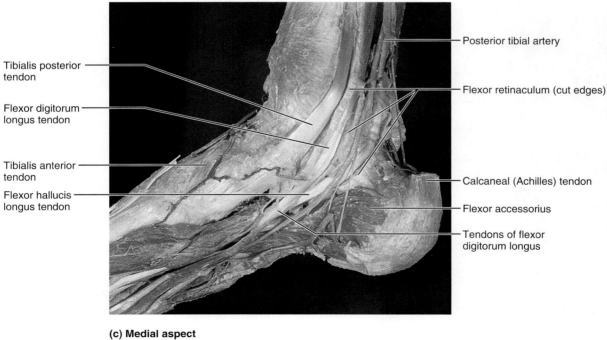

Tibialis posterior
tendon

Flexor digitorum
longus tendon

Tibialis anterior
tendon

Flexor hallucis
longus tendon

Posterior tibial artery

Flexor retinaculum (cut edges)

Calcaneal (Achilles) tendon

Flexor accessorius

Tendons of flexor
digitorum longus

(c) Medial aspect

FIGURE 14.17 Muscles of the right foot, plantar and medial aspects.

TABLE 14.11	Intrinsic Muscles of the Foot: Toe Movement and Foot Support (see Figures 14.15 and 14.17) *(continued)*			
Muscle	**Comments**	**Origin**	**Insertion**	**Action**
Muscles on Sole of Foot *(continued)*				
Flexor digiti minimi brevis	Covers metatarsal 5; recall same-named muscle in hand	Base of metatarsal 5 and tendon of fibularis longus	Base of proximal phalanx of toe 5	Flexes little toe at metatarsophalangeal joint
Fourth layer				
Plantar and dorsal interossei	Three plantar and four dorsal interossei; similar to the palmar and dorsal interossei of hand in locations, attachments, and actions; however, the long axis of foot around which these muscles orient is the second digit, not the third	See palmar and dorsal interossei (Table 14.7)	See palmar and dorsal interossei (Table 14.7)	See palmar and dorsal interossei (Table 14.7)

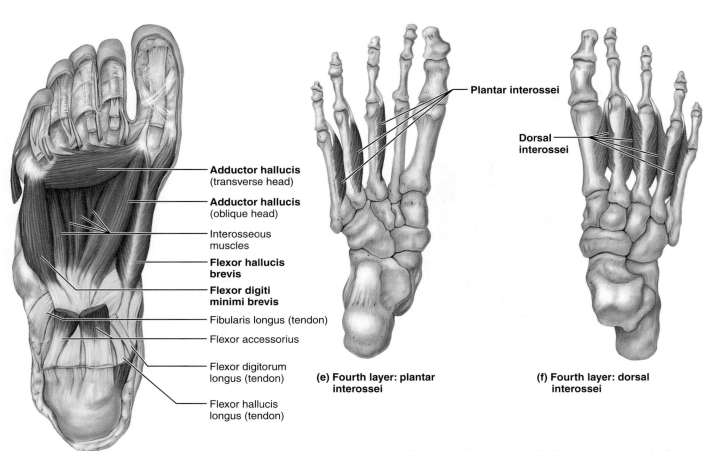

Adductor hallucis (transverse head)

Adductor hallucis (oblique head)

Interosseous muscles

Flexor hallucis brevis

Flexor digiti minimi brevis

Fibularis longus (tendon)

Flexor accessorius

Flexor digitorum longus (tendon)

Flexor hallucis longus (tendon)

(d) Third layer

Plantar interossei

Dorsal interossei

(e) Fourth layer: plantar interossei

(f) Fourth layer: dorsal interossei

FIGURE 14.17 *(continued)* **Muscles of the right foot, plantar and medial aspects.**

Review of Human Musculature

Review the muscles by watching the *Human Musculature* videotape. ■

Making a Muscle Painting

1. Choose a male student to be "muscle painted."

2. Obtain brushes and water-based paints from the supply area while the "volunteer" removes his shirt and rolls up his pant legs (if necessary).

3. Using different colored paints, identify the muscles listed below by painting his skin. If a muscle covers a large body area, you may opt to paint only its borders.

- biceps brachii
- biceps femoris
- deltoid
- extensor carpi radialis longus
- erector spinae
- latissimus dorsi
- pectoralis major
- rectus abdominis
- rectus femoris
- sternocleidomastoid
- tibialis anterior
- trapezius
- triceps brachii
- triceps surae
- vastus lateralis
- vastus medius

4. Check your "human painting" with your instructor before cleaning your bench and leaving the laboratory. ■

 DISSECTION AND IDENTIFICATION

Cat Muscles

The skeletal muscles of all mammals are named in a similar fashion. However, some muscles that are separate in lower animals are fused in humans, and some muscles present in lower animals are lacking in humans. This exercise involves dissection of the cat musculature to enhance your knowledge of the human muscular system. Since the aim is to become familiar with the muscles of the human body, you should pay particular attention to the similarities between cat and human muscles. However, pertinent differences will be pointed out as they are encountered.

Wear a lab coat or apron when dissecting to protect your clothes. ■

Preparing the Cat for Dissection

The preserved laboratory animals purchased for dissection have been embalmed with a solution that prevents deterioration of the tissues. The animals are generally delivered in plastic bags that contain a small amount of the embalming fluid. <u>Do not dispose of this fluid</u> when you remove the cat; the fluid prevents the cat from drying out. It is very important to keep the cat's tissues moist because you will probably use the same cat from now until the end of the course. The embalming fluid

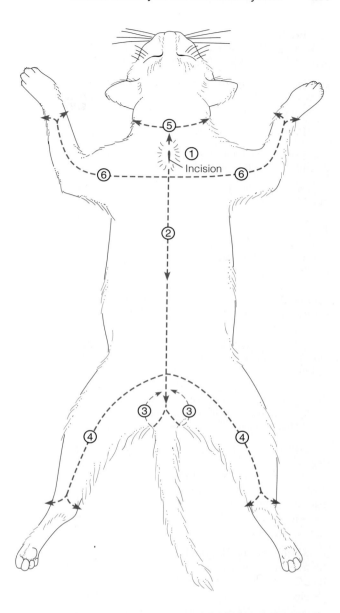

FIGURE 14.18 Incisions to be made in skinning a cat. Numbers indicate sequence.

may cause your eyes to smart and may dry your skin, but these small irritants are preferable to working with a cat that has become hard and odoriferous due to bacterial action.

1. Don disposable gloves and then obtain a cat, dissection tray, dissection instruments, and a name tag. Mark the name tag with the names of the members of your group and set it aside. The name tag will be attached to the plastic bag at the end of the dissection so that you may identify your animal in subsequent laboratories.

2. To begin removing the skin, place the cat ventral side down on the dissecting tray. Cutting away from yourself with a scalpel, make a short, shallow incision in the midline of the neck, just to penetrate the skin. From this point on, use scissors. Continue the cut the length of the back to the sacrolumbar region, stopping at the tail (Figure 14.18).

3. From the dorsal surface of the tail region, continue the incision around the tail, encircling the anus and genital organs. The skin will not be removed from this region.

4. Beginning again at the dorsal tail region, make an incision through the skin down each hind leg nearly to the ankle. Continue the cuts completely around the ankles.

5. Return to the neck. Cut the skin around the neck.

6. Cut down each foreleg to the wrist. Completely cut through the skin around the wrists.

7. Now free the skin from the loose connective tissue (superficial fascia) that binds it to the underlying structures. With one hand, grasp the skin on one side of the midline dorsal incision. Then, using your fingers or a blunt probe, break through the "cottony" connective tissue fibers to release the skin from the muscle beneath. Work toward the ventral surface and then toward the neck. As you pull the skin from the body, you should see small, white, cordlike structures extending from the skin to the muscles at fairly regular intervals. These are the cutaneous nerves that serve the skin. You will also see (particularly as you approach the ventral surface) that a thin layer of muscle fibers remains adhered to the skin. This is the **cutaneous maximus** muscle, which enables the cat to move its skin rather like our facial muscles allow us to express emotion. Where the cutaneous maximus fibers cling to those of the deeper muscles, they should be carefully cut free. Along the ventral surface of the trunk notice the two lines of nipples associated with the mammary glands. These are more prominent in females.

8. You will notice as you start to free the skin in the neck that it is more difficult to remove. Take extra care and time in this area. The large flat **platysma** muscle in the ventral neck region (a skin muscle like the cutaneous maximus) will remain attached to the skin. The skin will not be removed from the head since the cat's muscles are not sufficiently similar to human head muscles to merit study.

9. Complete the skinning process by freeing the skin from the forelimbs, the lower torso, and the hindlimbs in the same manner. The skin is more difficult to remove as you approach the paws so you may need to spend additional time on these areas. Do not discard the skin.

10. Inspect your skinned cat. Notice that it is difficult to see any cleavage lines between the muscles because of the overlying connective tissue, which is white or yellow. If time allows, carefully remove as much of the fat and fascia from the surface of the muscles as possible, using forceps or your fingers. The muscles, when exposed, look grainy or threadlike and are light brown. If this clearing process is done carefully and thoroughly, you will be ready to begin your identification of the superficial muscles.

11. If the muscle dissection exercises are to be done at a later laboratory session, follow the cleanup instructions noted in the following box. *Prepare your cat for storage in this way every time the cat is used.* ▪

Preparing the Dissection Animal for Storage

Before leaving the lab, prepare your animal for storage as follows:

1. To prevent the internal organs from drying out, dampen a layer of folded paper towels with embalming fluid, and wrap them snugly around the animal's torso. (Do not use *water-soaked* paper towels as this will encourage the growth of mold.) Make sure the dissected areas are completely enveloped.

2. Return the animal's skin flaps to their normal position over the ventral cavity body organs.

3. Place the animal in a plastic storage bag. Add more embalming fluid if necessary, press out excess air, and securely close the bag with a rubber band or twine.

4. Make sure your name tag is securely attached, and place the animal in the designated storage container.

5. Clean all dissecting equipment with soapy water, and rinse and dry it for return to the storage area. Wash down the lab bench and properly dispose of organic debris and your gloves before leaving the laboratory.

ACTIVITY 10

Dissecting Trunk and Neck Muscles

The proper dissection of muscles involves careful separation of one muscle from another and transection of superficial muscles in order to study those lying deeper. In general, when directions are given to transect a muscle, it should be completely freed from all adhering connective tissue and then cut through about halfway between its origin and insertion points. *Use caution when working around points of muscle origin or insertion, and do not remove the fascia associated with such attachments.*

As a rule, all the fibers of one muscle are held together by a connective tissue sheath (epimysium) and run in the same general direction. Before you begin dissection, observe your skinned cat. If you look carefully, you can see changes in the direction of the muscle fibers, which will help you to locate the muscle borders. Pulling in slightly different directions on two adjacent muscles will usually allow you to expose the subtle white cleavage line between them. Once cleavage lines have been identified, use a *blunt probe* to break the connective tissue between muscles and to separate them. If the muscles separate as clean, distinct bundles, your procedure is probably correct. If they appear ragged or chewed up, you are probably tearing a muscle apart rather than separating it from adjacent muscles. Only the muscles that are most easily identified and separated out will be identified in this exercise because of time considerations.

Anterior Neck Muscles

1. Using Figure 14.19 as a guide, examine the anterior neck surface of the cat and identify the following superficial neck muscles. (The platysma belongs in this group but was probably removed during the skinning process.) The **sternomastoid** muscle and the more lateral and deeper **cleidomastoid**

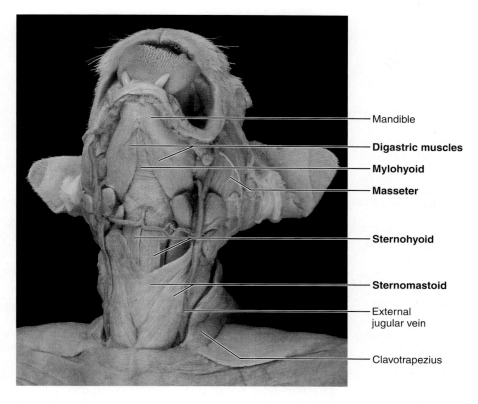

Mandible

Digastric muscles

Mylohyoid

Masseter

Sternohyoid

Sternomastoid

External
jugular vein

Clavotrapezius

FIGURE 14.19 Superficial muscles of the anterior neck of the cat.

muscle (not visible in Figure 14.19) are joined in humans to form the sternocleidomastoid. The large external jugular vein, which drains the head, should be obvious crossing the anterior aspect of these muscles. The **mylohyoid** muscle parallels the bottom aspect of the chin, and the **digastric** muscles form a V over the mylohyoid muscle. Although it is not one of the neck muscles, you can now identify the fleshy **masseter** muscle, which flanks the digastric muscle laterally. Finally, the **sternohyoid** is a narrow muscle between the mylohyoid (superiorly) and the inferior sternomastoid.

2. The deeper muscles of the anterior neck of the cat are small and straplike and hardly worth the effort of dissection. However, one of these deeper muscles can be seen with a minimum of extra effort. Transect the sternomastoid and sternohyoid muscles approximately at midbelly. Reflect the cut ends to reveal the **sternothyroid** muscle (not visible in Figure 14.19), which runs along the anterior surface of the throat just deep and lateral to the sternohyoid muscle. The cleidomastoid muscle, which lies deep to the sternomastoid, is also more easily identified now.

Superficial Chest Muscles

In the cat, the chest or pectoral muscles adduct the arm, just as they do in humans. However, humans have only two pectoral muscles, and cats have four—the pectoralis major, pectoralis minor, xiphihumeralis, and pectoantebrachialis (see Figure 14.20). However, because of their relatively great degree of fusion, the cat's pectoral muscles appear to be a single muscle. The pectoral muscles are rather difficult to dissect and identify, as they do not separate from one another easily.

The **pectoralis major** is 5 to 8 cm (2 to 3 inches) wide and can be seen arising on the manubrium, just inferior to the sternomastoid muscle of the neck, and running to the humerus. Its fibers run at right angles to the longitudinal axis of the cat's body.

The **pectoralis minor** lies beneath the pectoralis major and extends posterior to it on the abdominal surface. It originates on the sternum and inserts on the humerus. Its fibers run obliquely to the long axis of the body, which helps to distinguish it from the pectoralis major. Contrary to what its name implies, the pectoralis minor is a larger and thicker muscle than the pectoralis major.

The **xiphihumeralis** can be distinguished from the posterior edge of the pectoralis minor only by virtue of the fact that its origin is lower—on the xiphoid process of the sternum. Its fibers run parallel to and are fused with those of the pectoralis minor.

The **pectoantebrachialis** is a thin, straplike muscle, about 1.3 cm (½ inch) wide, lying over the pectoralis major. It originates from the manubrium, passes laterally over the pectoralis major, and merges with the muscles of the forelimb approximately halfway down the humerus. It has no homologue in humans.

Identify, free, and trace out the origin and insertion of the cat's chest muscles. Refer to Figure 14.20 as you work.

Muscles of the Abdominal Wall

The superficial trunk muscles include those of the abdominal wall (see Figures 14.20 and 14.21). Cat musculature in this area is quite similar in function to that of humans.

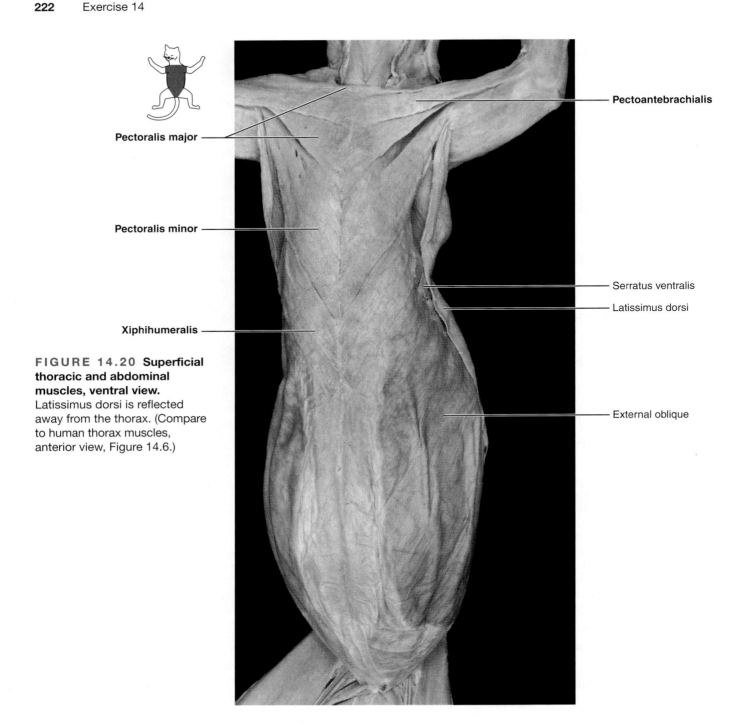

Pectoantebrachialis

Pectoralis major

Pectoralis minor

Serratus ventralis

Latissimus dorsi

Xiphihumeralis

External oblique

FIGURE 14.20 Superficial thoracic and abdominal muscles, ventral view. Latissimus dorsi is reflected away from the thorax. (Compare to human thorax muscles, anterior view, Figure 14.6.)

1. Complete the dissection of the more superficial anterior trunk muscles of the cat by identifying the origins and insertions of the muscles of the abdominal wall. Work carefully here. These muscles are very thin, and it is easy to miss their boundaries. Begin with the **rectus abdominis,** a long band of muscle approximately 2½ cm (1 inch) wide running immediately lateral to the midline of the body on the abdominal surface. Humans have four transverse *tendinous intersections* in the rectus abdominis (see Figure 14.8a), but they are absent or difficult to identify in the cat. Identify the **linea alba,** which separates the rectus abdominis muscles. Note the relationship of the rectus abdominis to the other abdominal muscles and their fascia.

2. The **external oblique** is a sheet of muscle immediately beside the rectus abdominis (see Figure 14.21). Carefully free and then transect the external oblique to reveal the anterior attachment of the rectus abdominis and the deeper **internal oblique.** Reflect the external oblique; observe the deeper muscle. Notice which way the fibers run.

3. Free and then transect the internal oblique muscle to reveal the fibers of the **transversus abdominis,** whose fibers run transversely across the abdomen.

Superficial Muscles of the Shoulder and Dorsal Trunk and Neck

Refer to Figure 14.22 as you dissect the superficial muscles of the dorsal surface of the trunk.

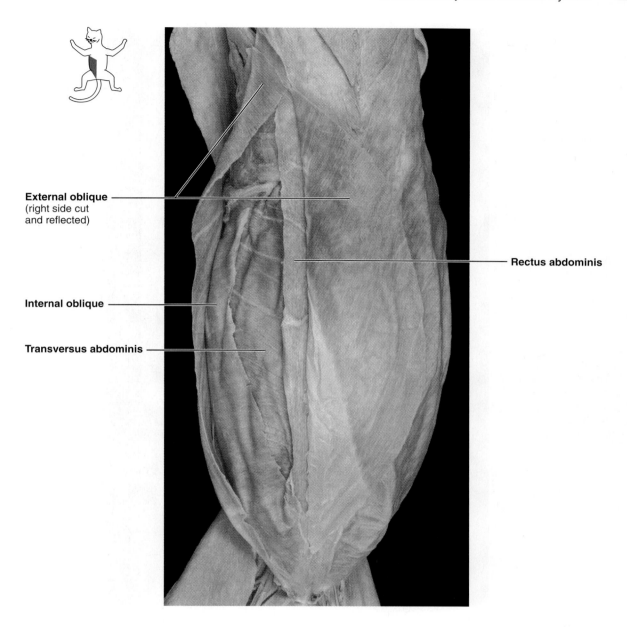

External oblique
(right side cut
and reflected)

Internal oblique

Transversus abdominis

Rectus abdominis

FIGURE 14.21 **Muscles of the abdominal wall of the cat.**

1.   Turn your cat on its ventral surface and start your observations with the **trapezius group.** Humans have a single large trapezius muscle, but the cat has three separate muscles—the clavotrapezius, acromiotrapezius, and spinotrapezius—that together perform a similar function. The prefix (clavo-, acromio-, and spino-) in each case reveals the muscle's site of insertion. The **clavotrapezius,** the most superior muscle of the group, is homologous to that part of the human trapezius that inserts into the clavicle. Slip a probe under this muscle and follow it to its apparent origin.

Where does the clavotrapezius appear to originate?

Is the origin of the clavotrapezius similar to its origin in humans?

The fibers of the clavotrapezius are continuous inferiorly with those of the clavicular part of the cat's deltoid muscle (clavodeltoid), and the two muscles work together to extend the humerus. Release the clavotrapezius muscle from adjoining muscles.

The **acromiotrapezius** is a large, nearly square muscle easily identified by its aponeurosis, which passes over the vertebral border of the scapula. It originates from the cervical and T_1 vertebrae and inserts into the scapular spine. The triangular spinotrapezius runs from the thoracic vertebrae to the scapular spine. This is the most posterior of the trapezius muscles in the cat. Now that you know where they are located, pull on the three trapezius muscles to mimic their action.

Do the trapezius muscles appear to have the same functions in cats as in humans?

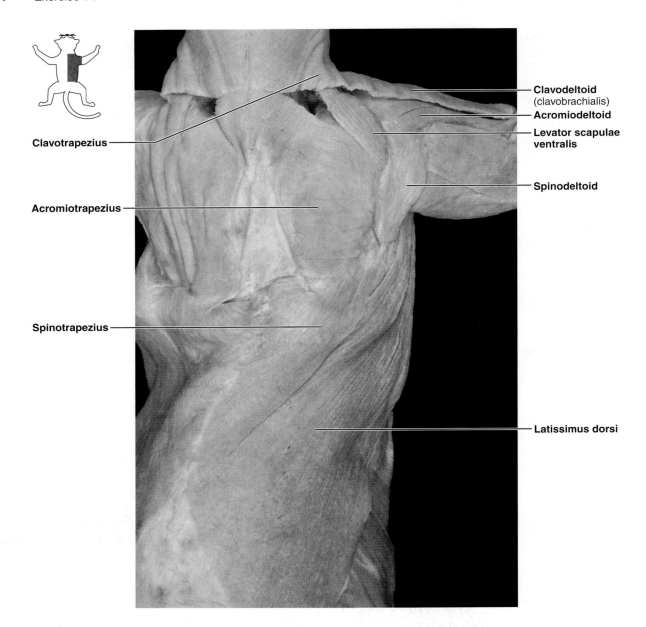

FIGURE 14.22 Superficial muscles of the anterodorsal aspect of the shoulder, trunk, and neck of the cat. (Compare to human thorax muscles, posterior view, Figure 14.9a.)

2. The **levator scapulae ventralis,** a flat, straplike muscle, can be located in the triangle created by the division of the fibers of the clavotrapezius and acromiotrapezius. Its anterior fibers run underneath the clavotrapezius from its origin at the base of the skull (occipital bone), and it inserts on the vertebral border of the scapula. In the cat it helps to hold the upper edges of the scapulae together and draws them toward the head.

What is the function of the levator scapulae in humans?

_____

3. The **deltoid group:** like the trapezius, the human deltoid muscle is represented by three separate muscles in the cat—

the clavodeltoid, acromiodeltoid, and spinodeltoid. The **clavodeltoid** (also called the *clavobrachialis*), the most superficial muscle of the shoulder, is a continuation of the clavotrapezius below the clavicle, which is this muscle's point of origin (see Figure 14.22). Follow its course down the forelimb to the point where it merges along a white line with the pectoantebrachialis. Separate it from the pectoantebrachialis, and then transect it and pull it back.

Where does the clavodeltoid insert?_____

What do you think the function of this muscle is?_____

_____

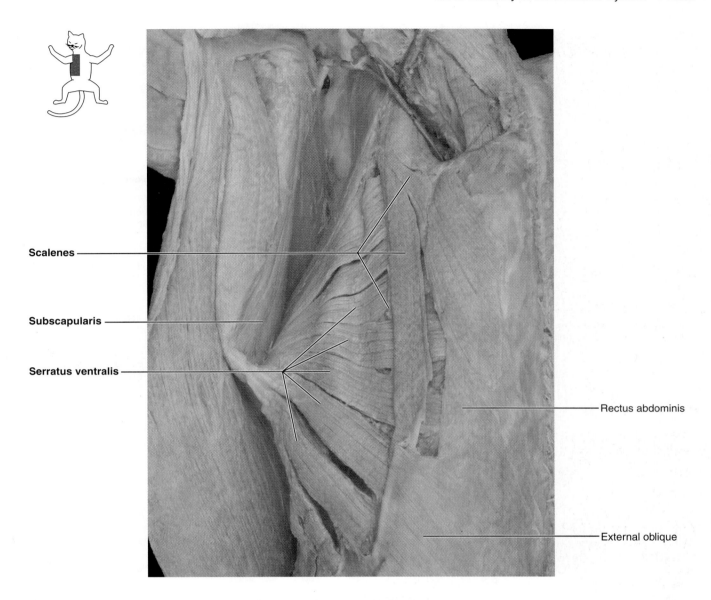

Scalenes

Subscapularis

Serratus ventralis

Rectus abdominis

External oblique

FIGURE 14.23 **Deep muscles of the inferolateral thorax of the cat.**

The **acromiodeltoid** lies posterior to the clavodeltoid and runs over the top of the shoulder. This small triangular muscle originates on the acromion of the scapula. It inserts into the spinodeltoid (a muscle of similar size) posterior to it. The **spinodeltoid** is covered with fascia near the anterior end of the scapula. Its tendon extends under the acromiodeltoid muscle and inserts on the humerus. Notice that its fibers run obliquely to those of the acromiodeltoid. Like the human deltoid muscle, the acromiodeltoid and clavodeltoid muscles in the cat raise and rotate the humerus.

4.   The **latissimus dorsi** is a large flat muscle covering most of the lateral surface of the posterior trunk. Its upper edge is covered by the spinotrapezius. As in humans, it inserts into the humerus. But before inserting, its fibers merge with the fibers of many other muscles, among them the xiphihumeralis of the pectoralis group.

Deep Muscles of the Laterodorsal Trunk and Neck

1.   In preparation, transect the latissimus dorsi, the muscles of the pectoralis group, and the spinotrapezius and reflect them back. Be careful not to damage the large brachial nerve plexus, which lies in the axillary space beneath the pectoralis group.

2.   The **serratus ventralis** represents two separate muscles in humans. The posterior portion, homologous to the serratus anterior of humans, arises deep to the pectoral muscles and covers the lateral surface of the rib cage. It is easily identified by its fingerlike muscular origins, which arise on the first 9 or 10 ribs. It inserts into the scapula. The anterior portion of the serratus ventralis, which arises from the cervical vertebrae, is homologous to the *levator scapulae* in humans. Both portions pull the scapula toward the sternum. Trace this muscle to its insertion. In general, in the cat, this muscle acts to pull the scapula posteriorly and downward. Refer to Figure 14.23.

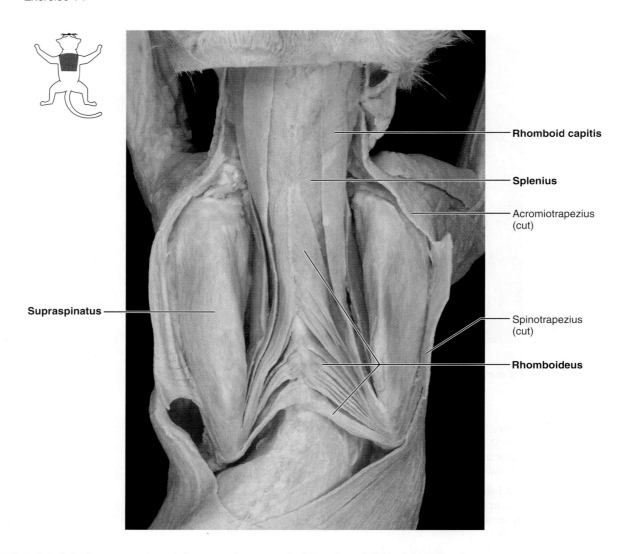

Rhomboid capitis

Splenius

Acromiotrapezius
(cut)

Supraspinatus

Spinotrapezius
(cut)

Rhomboideus

FIGURE 14.24 **Deep muscles of the superior aspect of the dorsal thorax of the cat.**

3. Reflect the upper limb to reveal the **subscapularis,** which occupies most of the ventral surface of the scapula. Humans have a homologous muscle.

4. Locate the anterior, posterior, and middle **scalene** muscles on the lateral surface of the cat's neck and trunk. The most prominent and longest of these muscles is the middle scalene, which lies between the anterior and posterior members. The scalenes originate on the ribs and run cephalad over the serratus ventralis to insert in common on the cervical vertebrae. These muscles draw the ribs anteriorly and bend the neck downward; thus they are homologous to the human scalene muscles, which elevate the ribs and flex the neck. (Notice that the difference is only one of position. Humans walk erect, but cats are quadrupeds.)

5. Reflect the flaps of the transected latissimus dorsi, spinodeltoid, acromiodeltoid, and levator scapulae ventralis. The **splenius** is a large flat muscle occupying most of the side of the neck close to the vertebrae. As in humans, it originates on the ligamentum nuchae at the back of the neck and inserts into the occipital bone. It functions to raise the head. Refer to Figure 14.24.

6. To view the rhomboid muscles, lay the cat on its side and hold its forelegs together to spread the scapulae apart. The rhomboid muscles lie between the scapulae and beneath the acromiotrapezius. All the rhomboid muscles originate on the vertebrae and insert on the scapula. They function to hold the dorsal part of the scapula to the cat's back.

There are three rhomboids in the cat. The ribbonlike **rhomboid capitis,** the most anterolateral muscle of the group, has no counterpart in the human body. The **rhomboid minor,** located posterior to the rhomboid capitis, is much larger. Its fibers run transversely to those of the rhomboid

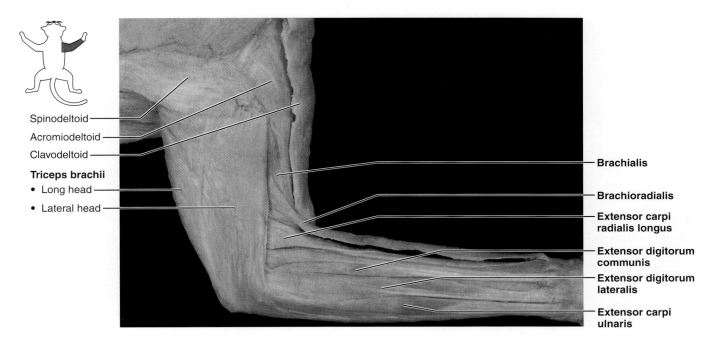

Spinodeltoid
Acromiodeltoid
Clavodeltoid
Triceps brachii
• Long head
• Lateral head

Brachialis
Brachioradialis
Extensor carpi radialis longus
Extensor digitorum communis
Extensor digitorum lateralis
Extensor carpi ulnaris

FIGURE 14.25 Lateral surface of the forelimb of the cat.

capitis. The most posterior muscle of the group, the **rhomboid major,** is so closely fused to the rhomboid minor that many consider them to be one muscle—the **rhomboideus,** which is homologous to human *rhomboid muscles.*

7.   The **supraspinatus** and **infraspinatus** muscles are similar to the same muscles in humans. The supraspinatus can be found under the acromiotrapezius, and the infraspinatus (not visible in Figure 14.24) is deep to the spinotrapezius. Both originate on the lateral scapular surface and insert on the humerus. ▬

ACTIVITY 11

Dissecting Forelimb Muscles

Cat forelimb muscles fall into the same three categories as human upper limb muscles, but in this section the muscles of the entire forelimb are considered together. Refer to Figure 14.25 as you study these muscles.

Muscles of the Lateral Surface

1.   The triceps muscle **(triceps brachii)** of the cat is easily identified if the cat is placed on its side. It is a large, fleshy muscle covering the posterior aspect and much of the side of the humerus. As in humans, this muscle arises from three heads, which originate from the humerus and scapula and insert jointly into the olecranon process of the ulna. Remove the fascia from the superior region of the lateral arm surface to identify the lateral and long heads of the triceps. The long head is approximately twice as long as the lateral head and lies medial to it on the posterior arm surface. The medial head can be exposed by transecting the lateral head and pulling it aside. Now pull on the triceps muscle.

How does the function of the triceps muscle compare in cats and in humans?

_____

Anterior and distal to the medial head of the triceps is the tiny anconeus muscle, sometimes called the fourth head of the triceps muscle. Notice its darker color and the way it wraps the tip of the elbow.

2.   The **brachialis** can be located anterior to the lateral head of the triceps muscle. Identify its origin on the humerus, and trace its course as it crosses the elbow and inserts on the ulna. It flexes the cat's foreleg.

Identification of the forearm muscles is difficult because of the tough fascia sheath that encases them, but give it a try.

3.   Remove as much of the connective tissue as possible and cut through the ligaments that secure the tendons at the wrist (transverse carpal ligaments) so that you will be able to follow the muscles to their insertions. Begin your identification with the muscles at the lateral surface of the forearm. The muscles of this region are very much alike in appearance and are difficult to identify accurately unless a definite order is followed. Thus you will begin with the most anterior muscles and proceed to the posterior aspect. Remember to check carefully the tendons of insertion to verify your muscle identifications.

4.   The ribbonlike muscle on the lateral surface of the humerus is the **brachioradialis.** Observe how it passes down the forearm to insert on the styloid process of the radius. (If your removal of the fascia was not very careful, this muscle may have been removed.)

5.   The **extensor carpi radialis longus** has a broad origin and is larger than the brachioradialis. It extends down the

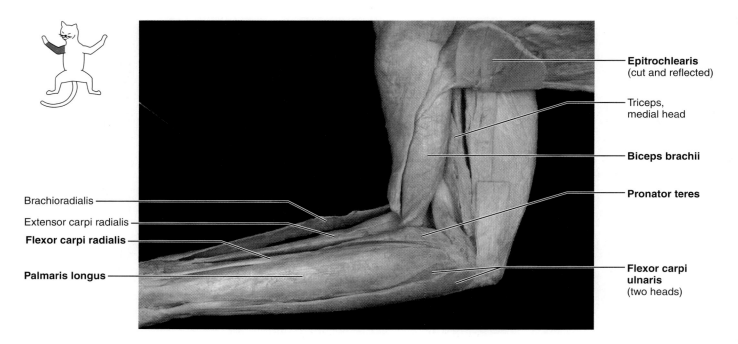

Epitrochlearis
(cut and reflected)

Triceps,
medial head

Biceps brachii

Pronator teres

Brachioradialis

Extensor carpi radialis

Flexor carpi radialis

Palmaris longus

**Flexor carpi
ulnaris**
(two heads)

FIGURE 14.26 Medial surface of the forelimb of the cat.

anterior surface of the radius (see Figure 14.25). Transect this muscle to view the **extensor carpi radialis brevis,** which is partially covered by and sometimes fused with the extensor carpi radialis longus. Both muscles have origins, insertions, and actions similar to their human counterparts.

6. You can see the entire **extensor digitorum communis** along the lateral surface of the forearm. Trace it to its four tendons, which insert on the second to fifth digits. This muscle extends these digits. The **extensor digitorum lateralis** (absent in humans) also extends the digits. This muscle lies immediately posterior to the extensor digitorum communis.

7. Follow the **extensor carpi ulnaris** from the lateral epicondyle of the humerus to the ulnar side of the fifth metacarpal. Often this muscle has a shiny tendon, which helps in its identification.

Muscles of the Medial Surface

1. The **biceps brachii** (refer to Figure 14.26) is a large spindle-shaped muscle medial to the brachialis on the anterior surface of the humerus. Pull back the cut ends of the pectoral muscles to get a good view of the biceps. This muscle is much more prominent in humans, but its origin, insertion, and action are very similar in cats and in humans. Follow the muscle to its origin.

Does the biceps have two heads in the cat? _____

2. The broad, flat, exceedingly thin muscle on the posteromedial surface of the arm is the **epitrochlearis.** Its tendon originates from the fascia of the latissimus dorsi, and the muscle inserts into the olecranon process of the ulna. This muscle extends the forelimb of the cat; it is not found in humans.

3. The **coracobrachialis** of the cat is insignificant (approximately 1.3 cm [½ inch] long) and can be seen as a very small

muscle crossing the ventral aspect of the shoulder joint. It runs beneath the biceps brachii to insert on the humerus and has the same function as the human coracobrachialis.

4. Referring again to Figure 14.26, turn the cat so that the ventral forearm muscles (mostly flexors and pronators) can be observed. As in humans, most of these muscles arise from the medial epicondyle of the humerus. The **pronator teres** runs from the medial epicondyle of the humerus and declines in size as it approaches its insertion on the radius. Do not bother to trace it to its insertion.

5. Like its human counterpart, the **flexor carpi radialis** runs from the medial epicondyle of the humerus to insert into the second and third metacarpals.

6. The large flat muscle in the center of the medial surface is the **palmaris longus.** Its origin on the medial epicondyle of the humerus abuts that of the pronator teres and is shared with the flexor carpi radialis. The palmaris longus extends down the forelimb to terminate in four tendons on the digits. Comparatively speaking, this muscle is much larger in cats than in humans.

The **flexor carpi ulnaris** arises from a two-headed origin (medial epicondyle of the humerus and olecranon of the ulna). Its two bellies (fleshy parts) pass downward to the wrist, where they are united by a single tendon that inserts into the carpals of the wrist. As in humans, this muscle flexes the wrist. ▪

ACTIVITY 12

Dissecting Hindlimb Muscles

Remove the fat and fascia from all thigh surfaces, but do not cut through or remove the **fascia lata** (or iliotibial band), which is a tough white aponeurosis covering the anterolateral surface of the thigh from the hip to the leg. If the cat is a male, the cordlike sperm duct will be embedded in the fat near the pubic symphysis. Carefully clear around, but not in, this region.

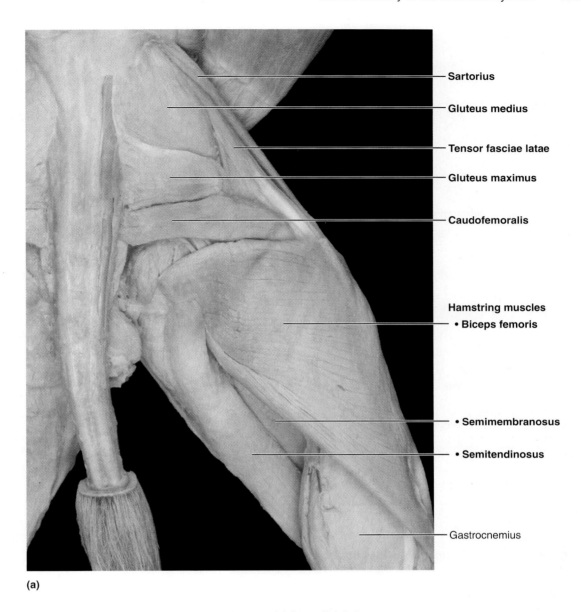

Sartorius

Gluteus medius

Tensor fasciae latae

Gluteus maximus

Caudofemoralis

Hamstring muscles
• Biceps femoris

• Semimembranosus

• Semitendinosus

Gastrocnemius

(a)

FIGURE 14.27 Muscles of the posterolateral thigh in the cat. (a) Superficial view.

Posterolateral Hindlimb Muscles

1.   Turn the cat on its ventral surface and identify the following superficial muscles of the hip and thigh, referring to Figure 14.27. Viewing the lateral aspect of the hindlimb, you will identify these muscles in sequence from the anterior to the posterior aspects of the hip and thigh. Most anterior is the **sartorius.** Approximately 4 cm (1½ inches) wide, it extends around the lateral aspect of the thigh to the anterior surface, where the major portion of it lies (see Figure 14.29a). Free it from the adjacent muscles and pass a blunt probe under it to trace its origin and insertion. Homologous to the sartorius muscle in humans, it adducts and rotates the thigh, but in addition, the cat sartorius acts as a knee extensor. Transect this muscle.

2.   The **tensor fasciae latae** is posterior to the sartorius. It is wide at its superior end, where it originates on the iliac crest, and narrows as it approaches its insertion into the fascia lata,

which runs to the proximal tibial region. Transect its superior end and pull it back to expose the **gluteus medius** lying beneath it. This is the largest of the gluteus muscles in the cat. It originates on the ilium and inserts on the greater trochanter of the femur. The gluteus medius overlays and obscures the gluteus minimus, pyriformis, and gemellus muscles (which will not be identified here).

3.   The **gluteus maximus** is a small triangular hip muscle posterior to the superior end of the tensor fasciae latae and paralleling it. In humans the gluteus maximus is a large fleshy muscle forming most of the buttock mass. In the cat it is only about 1.3 cm (½ inch) wide and 5 cm (2 inches) long, and is smaller than the gluteus medius. The gluteus maximus covers part of the gluteus medius as it extends from the sacral region and the end of the femur. It abducts the thigh.

4.   Posterior to the gluteus maximus, identify the triangular **caudofemoralis,** which originates on the caudal vertebrae

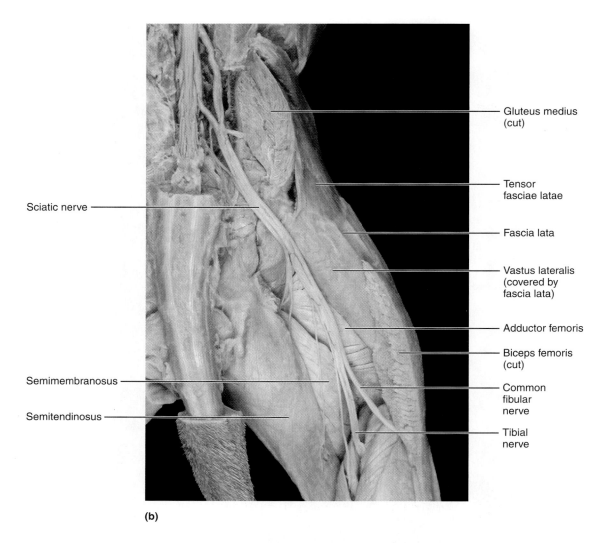

Gluteus medius
(cut)

Tensor
fasciae latae

Fascia lata

Vastus lateralis
(covered by
fascia lata)

Adductor femoris

Biceps femoris
(cut)

Common
fibular
nerve

Tibial
nerve

Sciatic nerve

Semimembranosus

Semitendinosus

(b)

FIGURE 14.27 *(continued)* Muscles of the posterolateral thigh in the cat. (b) Deep muscles.

and inserts into the patella via an aponeurosis. There is no ho-mologue to this muscle in humans; in cats it abducts the thigh and flexes the vertebral column.

5.   The **hamstring muscles** of the hindlimb include the bi-ceps femoris, the semitendinosus, and the semimembranosus muscles. The **biceps femoris** is a large, powerful muscle that covers most of the posterolateral surface of the thigh. It is 4–5 cm (1½ to 2 inches) wide throughout its length. Trace it from its origin on the ischial tuberosity to its insertion on the tibia. Part of the **semitendinosus** can be seen beneath the posterior border of the biceps femoris. Transect and reflect the biceps muscle to reveal the whole length of the semi-tendinosus and the large sciatic nerve positioned under the bi-ceps (Figure 14.27b). Contrary to what its name implies ("half-tendon"), this muscle is muscular and fleshy except at its insertion. It is uniformly about 2 cm (¾ inch) wide as it runs down the thigh from the ischial tuberosity to the medial side

of the ulna. It acts to bend the knee. The **semimembranosus,** a large muscle lying medial to the semitendinosus and largely obscured by it, is best seen in an anterior view of the thigh (see Figure 14.29b). If desired, however, the semitendinosus can be transected to view it from the posterior aspect. The semimembranosus is larger and broader than the semitendi-nosus. Like the other hamstrings, it originates on the ischial tuberosity and inserts on the medial epicondyle of the femur and the medial tibial surface.

How does the semimembranosus compare with its human homologue?

_____

_____

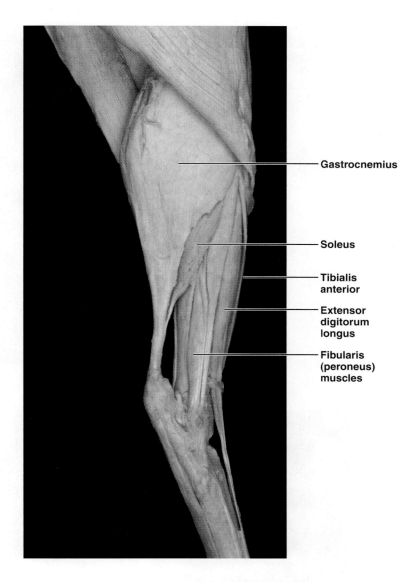

— Gastrocnemius

— Soleus

— Tibialis anterior

— Extensor digitorum longus

— Fibularis (peroneus) muscles

FIGURE 14.28 Superficial muscles of the posterolateral aspect of the shank (leg).

6. Remove the heavy fascia covering the lateral surface of the shank. Moving from the posterior to the anterior aspect, identify the following muscles on the posterolateral shank (leg). (Refer to Figure 14.28.) First reflect the lower portion of the biceps femoris to see the origin of the **triceps surae,** the large composite muscle of the calf. Humans also have a triceps surae. The **gastrocnemius,** part of the triceps surae, is the largest muscle on the shank. As in humans, it has two heads and inserts via the calcaneal (Achilles) tendon into the calcaneus. Run a probe beneath this muscle and then transect it to reveal the **soleus,** which is deep to the gastrocnemius.

7. Another important group of muscles in the leg is the **fibularis (peroneus) muscles** (see Figure 14.28), which col-lectively appear as a slender, evenly shaped superficial mus-cle lying anterior to the triceps surae. Originating on the fibula and inserting on the digits and metatarsals, the fibularis muscles flex the foot.

8. The **extensor digitorum longus** lies anterior to the fibu-laris muscles. Its origin, insertion, and action in cats are sim-ilar to the homologous human muscle. The **tibialis anterior** is anterior to the extensor digitorum longus. The tibialis ante-rior is roughly triangular in cross section and heavier at its proximal end. Locate its origin on the proximal fibula and tibia and its insertion on the first metatarsal. You can see the sharp edge of the tibia at the anterior border of this muscle. As in humans, it is a foot flexor.

FIGURE 14.29 Muscles of the anteromedial thigh. (a) The gracilis and sartorius muscles are intact in this superficial view. (b) The gracilis and sartorius are transected and reflected to show deeper muscles.

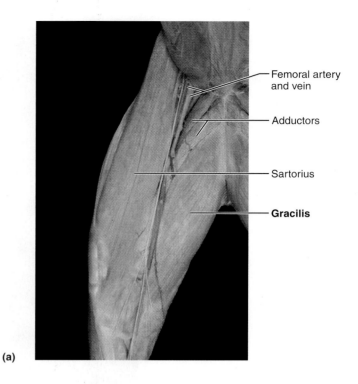

- Femoral artery and vein
- Adductors
- Sartorius
- **Gracilis**

(a)

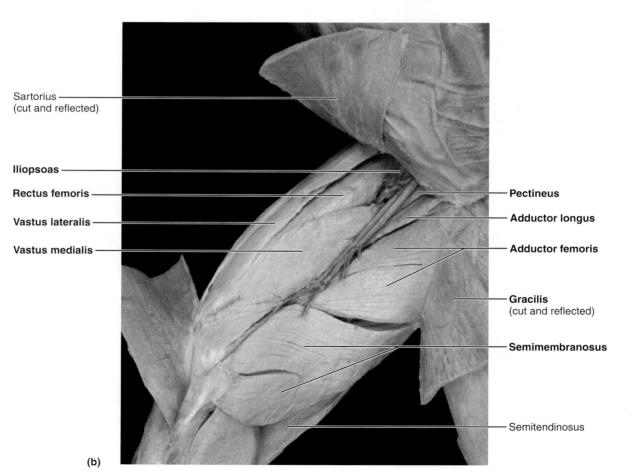

Sartorius (cut and reflected)

Iliopsoas

Rectus femoris

Vastus lateralis

Vastus medialis

Pectineus

Adductor longus

Adductor femoris

Gracilis (cut and reflected)

Semimembranosus

Semitendinosus

(b)

Anteromedial Hindlimb Muscles

1. Turn the cat onto its dorsal surface to identify the muscles of the anteromedial hindlimb (refer to Figure 14.29). Note once again the straplike sartorius at the surface of the thigh, which you have already identified and transected. It originates on the ilium and inserts on the medial region of the tibia.

2. Reflect the cut ends of the sartorius to identify the **quadriceps** muscles. The **vastus medialis** lies just beneath the sartorius. Resting close to the femur, it arises from the ilium and inserts into the patellar ligament. The small cylindrical muscle anterior and lateral to the vastus medialis is the **rectus femoris.** In cats this muscle originates entirely from the femur.

What is the origin of the rectus femoris in humans?

_____

_____

Free the rectus femoris from the most lateral muscle of this group, the large, fleshy **vastus lateralis,** which lies deep to the tensor fasciae latae. The vastus lateralis arises from the lateral femoral surface and inserts, along with the other vasti muscles, into the patellar ligament. Transect this muscle to identify the deep **vastus intermedius,** the smallest of the vasti muscles. It lies medial to the vastus lateralis and merges superiorly with the vastus medialis. (The vastus intermedius is not shown in the figure.)

3. The **gracilis** is a broad muscle that covers the posterior portion of the medial aspect of the thigh (see Figure 14.29). It originates on the pubic symphysis and inserts on the medial proximal tibial surface. In cats the gracilis adducts the leg and draws it posteriorly.

How does this compare with the human gracilis?

_____

_____

4. Free and transect the gracilis to view the adductor muscles deep to it. The **adductor femoris** is a large muscle that lies beneath the gracilis and abuts the semimembranosus medially. Its origin is the pubic ramus and the ischium, and its fibers pass downward to insert on most of the length of the femoral shaft. The adductor femoris is homologous to the human *adductor magnus, brevis,* and *longus.* Its function is to extend the thigh after it has been drawn forward, and to adduct the thigh. A small muscle about 2.5 cm (1 inch) long—the **adductor longus**—touches the superior margin of the adductor femoris. It originates on the pubic bone and inserts on the proximal surface of the femur.

5. Before continuing your dissection, locate the **femoral triangle** (Scarpa's triangle), an important area bordered by the proximal edge of the sartorius and the adductor muscles. It is usually possible to identify the femoral artery (injected with red latex) and the femoral vein (injected with blue latex), which span the triangle (see Figure 14.29). (You will identify these vessels again in your study of the circulatory system.) If your instructor wishes you to identify the pectineus and iliopsoas, remove these vessels and go on to steps 6 and 7.

6. Examine the superolateral margin of the adductor longus to locate the small **pectineus.** It is normally covered by the gracilis (which you have cut and reflected). The pectineus, which originates on the pubis and inserts on the proximal end of the femur, is similar in all ways to its human homologue.

7. Just lateral to the pectineus you can see a small portion of the **iliopsoas,** a long and cylindrical muscle. Its origin is on the transverse processes of T_1 through T_{12} and the lumbar vertebrae, and it passes posteriorly toward the body wall to insert on the medial aspect of the proximal femur. The iliopsoas flexes and laterally rotates the thigh. It corresponds to the human iliopsoas and psoas minor.

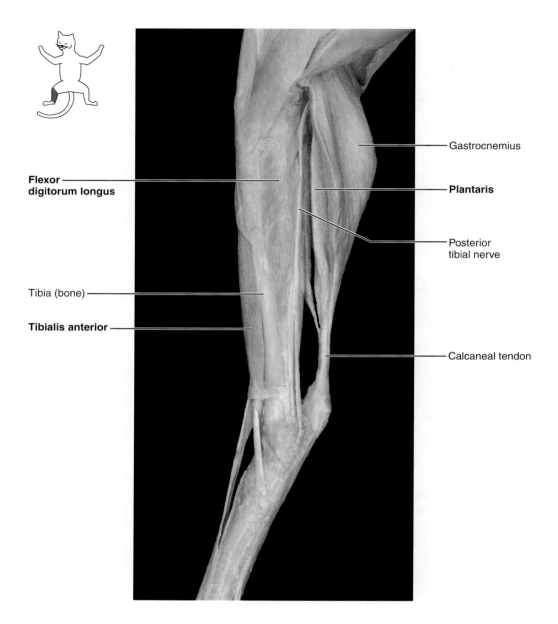

Gastrocnemius

Flexor digitorum longus

Plantaris

Posterior tibial nerve

Tibia (bone)

Tibialis anterior

Calcaneal tendon

FIGURE 14.30 Superficial muscles of the anteromedial shank (leg) of the cat.

8. Reidentify the gastrocnemius of the shank and then the **plantaris,** which is fused with the lateral head of the gastrocnemius. (See Figure 14.30.) It originates from the lateral aspect of the femur and patella, and its tendon passes around the calcaneus to insert on the second phalanx. Working with the triceps surae, it flexes the digits and extends the foot.

9. Anterior to the plantaris is the **flexor digitorum longus,** a long, tapering muscle with two heads. It originates on the lateral surfaces of the proximal fibula and tibia and inserts via four tendons into the terminal phalanges. As in humans, it flexes the toes.

10. The **tibialis posterior** is a long, flat muscle lateral and deep to the flexor digitorum longus. It originates on the medial surface of the head of the fibula and the ventral tibia. It merges with a flat, shiny tendon to insert into the tarsals. It is not shown in the figure.

11. The **flexor hallucis longus** is a long muscle that lies lateral to the tibialis posterior. It originates from the posterior tibia and passes downward to the ankle. It is a uniformly broad muscle in the cat. As in humans, it is a flexor of the great toe. It is not shown in the figure. ▆

NAME_____

LAB TIME/DATE_____

Gross Anatomy of the Muscular System

Classification of Skeletal Muscles

1. Several criteria were given relative to the naming of muscles. For each muscle name, choose from the key all criteria on which the name is based.

Key:

_____ 1. gluteus maximus   a. action of the muscle

_____ 2. adductor magnus   b. shape of the muscle

_____ 3. biceps femoris   c. location of the origin and/or insertion of the muscle

_____ 4. transversus abdominis   d. number of origins

_____ 5. extensor carpi ulnaris   e. location of the muscle relative to a bone or body region

_____ 6. trapezius   f. direction in which the muscle fibers run relative to some imaginary line

_____ 7. rectus femoris   g. relative size of the muscle

_____ 8. external oblique

2. Match the key terms to the muscles and movements described below.

Key: a.   prime mover (agonist)   b.   antagonist   c.   synergist   d.   fixator

_____ 1. term for the biceps brachii during elbow flexion

_____ 2. term that describes the relation of the brachialis to the biceps brachii during elbow flexion

_____ 3. term for the triceps brachii during elbow flexion

_____ 4. term for the iliopsoas during hip extension

_____ 5. term for the gluteus maximus during hip extension when walking up stairs

_____ 6. terms for the rotator cuff muscles and deltoid when the elbow is flexed and the hand grabs a tabletop to lift the table

Muscles of the Head and Neck

3. Using choices from the key at the right, correctly identify muscles provided with leader lines on the diagram.

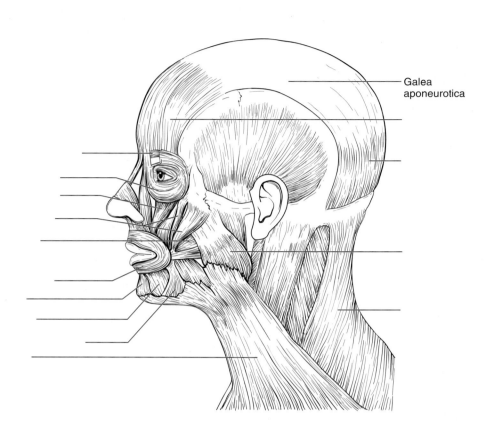

Galea
aponeurotica

Key:

a. buccinator

b. corrugator supercilii

c. depressor anguli oris

d. depressor labii inferioris

e. frontal belly of epicranius

f. levator labii superioris

g. masseter

h. mentalis

i. occipital belly of epicranius

j. orbicularis oculi

k. orbicularis oris

l. platysma

m. trapezius

n. zygomaticus major
and minor

4. Using the key provided in question 3, identify the muscles described next.

_____ 1. used in smiling

_____ 2. used to suck in your cheeks

_____ 3. used in blinking and squinting

_____ 4. used to pout (pulls the corners of the mouth downward)

_____ 5. raises your eyebrows for a questioning expression

_____ 6. used to form the vertical frown crease on the forehead

_____ 7. your "kisser"

_____ 8. prime mover to raise the mandible

_____ 9. tenses skin of the neck during shaving

Muscles of the Trunk

5. Correctly identify both intact and transected (cut) muscles depicted in the diagram, using the key given at the right. (Not all terms will be used in this identification.)

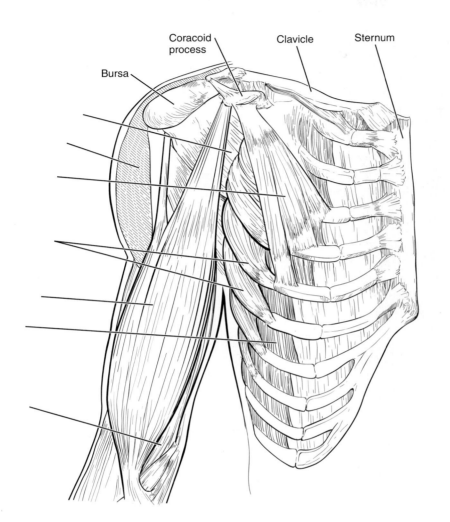

Coracoid process

Clavicle

Sternum

Bursa

Key:

a.   biceps brachii

b.   brachialis

c.   deltoid (cut)

d.   external intercostals

e.   external oblique

f.   internal oblique

g.   latissimus dorsi

h.   pectoralis major (cut)

i.   pectoralis minor

j.   rectus abdominis

k.   rhomboids

l.   serratus anterior

m.   subscapularis

n.   transversus abdominis

o.   trapezius

6. Using the key provided in question 5 above, identify the major muscles described next.

_____ 1.   a major spine flexor

_____ 2.   prime mover for pulling the arm posteriorly

_____ 3.   prime mover for shoulder flexion

_____ 4.   assume major responsibility for forming the abdominal girdle (three pairs of muscles)

_____ 5.   pulls the shoulder backward and downward

_____ 6.   prime mover of shoulder abduction

_____ 7.   important in shoulder adduction; antagonists of the shoulder abductor (two muscles)

_____ 8.   moves the scapula forward and downward

_____ 9.   small, inspiratory muscles between the ribs; elevate the ribs

_____ 10.   extends the head

_____ 11.   pull the scapulae medially

Muscles of the Upper Limb

7. Using terms from the key on the right, correctly identify all muscles provided with leader lines in the diagram. (Note that not all the listed terms will be used in this exercise.)

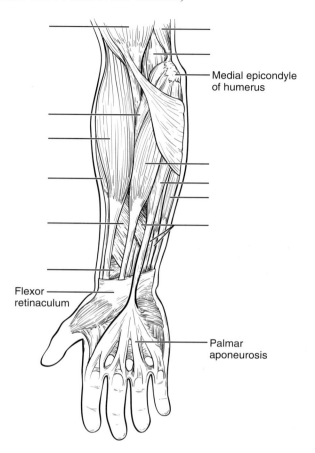

Medial epicondyle of humerus

Flexor retinaculum

Palmar aponeurosis

Key:

a.   biceps brachii

b.   brachialis

c.   brachioradialis

d.   extensor carpi radialis longus

e.   extensor digitorum

f.   flexor carpi radialis

g.   flexor carpi ulnaris

h.   flexor digitorum superficialis

i.   flexor pollicis longus

j.   palmaris longus

k.   pronator quadratus

l.   pronator teres

m.   supinator

n.   triceps brachii

8. Use the key provided in question 7 to identify the muscles described next.

_____ 1. flexes the forearm and supinates the hand

_____ 2. synergist for supinating the hand

_____ 3. forearm flexors; no role in supination (two muscles)

_____ 4. elbow extensor

_____ 5. power wrist flexor and abductor

_____ 6. flexes wrist and middle phalanges

_____ 7. pronate the hand (two muscles)

_____ 8. flexes the thumb

_____ 9. extends and abducts the wrist

_____ 10. extends the wrist and digits

_____ 11. flat muscle that is a weak wrist flexor; tenses skin of palm

Muscles of the Lower Limb

9. Using the terms from the key on the right, correctly identify all muscles provided with leader lines in the diagram below. (Not all listed terms will be used in this exercise.)

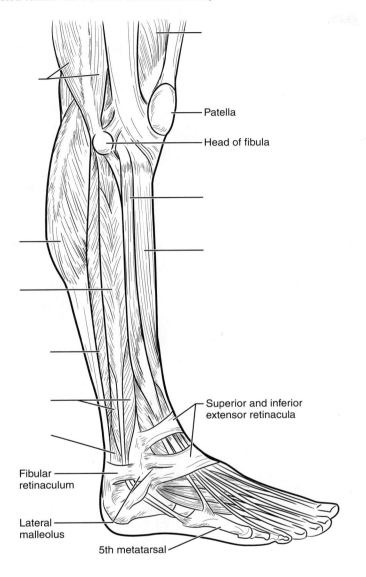

Patella

Head of fibula

Superior and inferior extensor retinacula

Fibular retinaculum

Lateral malleolus

5th metatarsal

Key:

a. adductor group

b. biceps femoris

c. extensor digitorum longus

d. fibularis brevis

e. fibularis longus

f. flexor hallucis longus

g. gastrocnemius

h. gluteus maximus

i. gluteus medius

j. rectus femoris

k. semimembranosus

l. semitendinosus

m. soleus

n. tensor fasciae latae

o. tibialis anterior

p. tibialis posterior

q. vastus lateralis

10. Use the key terms in question 9 to respond to the descriptions below.

_____ 1. flexes the great toe and inverts the ankle

_____ 2. lateral compartment muscles that plantar flex and evert the ankle (two muscles)

_____ 3. abduct the thigh to take the "at ease" stance (two muscles)

_____ 4. used to extend the hip when climbing stairs

_____ 5. prime movers of ankle plantar flexion (two muscles)

_____ 6. major foot inverter

_____ 7. prime mover of dorsiflexion of the foot

_____ 8. adduct the thigh, as when standing at attention

_____ 9. extends the toes

_____ 10. extend thigh and flex knee (three muscles)

_____ 11. extends knee and flexes thigh

General Review: Muscle Recognition

11. Identify the lettered muscles in the diagram of the human anterior superficial musculature by matching the letter with one of the following muscle names:

_____ 1. adductor longus

_____ 2. biceps brachii

_____ 3. brachioradialis

_____ 4. deltoid

_____ 5. extensor digitorum longus

_____ 6. external oblique

_____ 7. fibularis longus

_____ 8. flexor carpi radialis

_____ 9. flexor carpi ulnaris

_____ 10. frontal belly of epicranius

_____ 11. gastrocnemius

_____ 12. gracilis

_____ 13. iliopsoas

_____ 14. internal oblique

_____ 15. latissimus dorsi

_____ 16. masseter

_____ 17. orbicularis oculi

_____ 18. orbicularis oris

_____ 19. palmaris longus

_____ 20. pectineus

_____ 21. pectoralis major

_____ 22. platysma

_____ 23. pronator teres

_____ 24. rectus abdominis

_____ 25. rectus femoris

_____ 26. sartorius

_____ 27. serratus anterior

_____ 28. soleus

_____ 29. sternocleidomastoid

_____ 30. sternohyoid

_____ 31. temporalis

_____ 32. tensor fasciae latae

_____ 33. tibialis anterior

_____ 34. transversus abdominis

_____ 35. trapezius

_____ 36. triceps brachii

_____ 37. vastus lateralis

_____ 38. vastus medialis

_____ 39. zygomaticus

12. Identify each of the lettered muscles in this diagram of the human posterior superficial musculature by matching its letter to one of the following muscle names:

_____ 1. adductor magnus

_____ 2. biceps femoris

_____ 3. brachialis

_____ 4. brachioradialis

_____ 5. deltoid

_____ 6. extensor carpi radialis longus

_____ 7. extensor carpi ulnaris

_____ 8. extensor digitorum

_____ 9. external oblique

_____ 10. flexor carpi ulnaris

_____ 11. gastrocnemius

_____ 12. gluteus maximus

_____ 13. gluteus medius

_____ 14. gracilis

_____ 15. iliotibial tract (tendon)

_____ 16. infraspinatus

_____ 17. latissimus dorsi

_____ 18. occipitalis

_____ 19. semimembranosus

_____ 20. semitendinosus

_____ 21. sternocleidomastoid

_____ 22. teres major

_____ 23. trapezius

_____ 24. triceps brachii

General Review: Muscle Descriptions

13. Identify the muscles described by completing the following statements.

1. The _____, _____, and _____

   are commonly used for intramuscular injections (three muscles).

2. The insertion tendon of the _____ group contains a large sesamoid bone, the patella.

3. The triceps surae insert in common into the _____ tendon.

4. The bulk of the tissue of a muscle tends to lie _____ to the part of the body it causes to move.

5. The extrinsic muscles of the hand originate on the _____.

6. Most flexor muscles are located on the _____ aspect of the body; most

   extensors are located _____. An exception to this generalization is the

   extensor-flexor musculature of the _____.

Dissection and Identification: Cat Muscles

Many human muscles are modified from those of the cat (or any quadruped) as a result of the requirements of an upright posture. The following questions refer to these differences.

14. How does the human trapezius muscle differ from the cat's?

_____

_____

15. How does the deltoid differ?

_____

_____

16. How do the extent and orientation of the human gluteus muscles differ from their relative positions in the cat?

_____

_____

17. Explain these differences in cat and human muscles in terms of differences in function.

_____

_____

18. The human rectus abdominis is definitely divided by four transverse tendons (tendinous intersections). These tendons are absent or difficult to identify in the cat. How do these tendons affect the human upright posture?

_____

_____

19. Match the terms in column B to descriptions in column A.

	Column A	Column B
_____	1. to separate muscles	a. dissect
_____	2. to fold back a muscle	b. embalm
_____	3. to cut through a muscle	c. reflect
_____	4. to preserve tissue	d. transect

Histology of Nervous Tissue

M A T E R I A L S

- ☐ Model of a "typical" neuron (if available)
- ☐ Compound microscope
- ☐ Immersion oil
- ☐ Prepared slides of an ox spinal cord smear and teased myelinated nerve fibers
- ☐ Prepared slides of Purkinje cells (cerebellum), pyramidal cells (cerebrum), and a dorsal root ganglion
- ☐ Prepared slide of a nerve (x.s.)
- ☐ Prepared slides (l.s.) of Pacinian corpuscles, Meissner's corpuscles, Golgi tendon organs, and muscle spindles.

O B J E C T I V E S

1. To differentiate between the functions of neurons and neuroglia.
2. To list six types of neuroglia cells.
3. To identify the important anatomical characteristics of a neuron on an appropriate diagram or projected slide.
4. To state the functions of axons, dendrites, axon terminals, neurofibrils, and myelin sheaths.
5. To explain how a nerve impulse is transmitted from one neuron to another.
6. To explain the role of Schwann cells in the formation of the myelin sheath.
7. To classify neurons according to structure and function.
8. To distinguish between a nerve and a tract and between a ganglion and a nucleus.
9. To describe the structure of a nerve, identifying the connective tissue coverings (endoneurium, perineurium, and epineurium) and citing their functions.
10. To recognize various types of general sensory receptors as studied in the laboratory and to describe the function and location of each type.

The nervous system is the master integrating and coordinating system, continuously monitoring and processing sensory information both from the external environment and from within the body. Every thought, action, and sensation is a reflection of its activity. Like a computer, it processes and integrates new "inputs" with information previously fed into it ("programmed") to produce an appropriate response ("readout"). However, no computer can possibly compare in complexity and scope to the human nervous system.

Despite its complexity, nervous tissue is made up of just two principal cell populations: neurons and supporting cells referred to as **neuroglia** ("nerve glue"), or **glial cells.** The neuroglia in the central nervous system (CNS: brain and spinal cord) include *astrocytes, oligodendrocytes, microglia,* and *ependymal cells* (Figure 15.1). The most important glial cells in the peripheral nervous system (PNS), that is, in the neural structures outside the CNS, are *Schwann cells* and *satellite cells.*

Neuroglia serve the needs of the delicate neurons by bracing and protecting them. In addition, they act as phagocytes (microglia), myelinate the cytoplasmic extensions of the neurons (oligodendrocytes and Schwann cells), play a role in capillary-neuron exchanges, and control the chemical environment around neurons (astrocytes). Although neuroglia resemble neurons in some ways (they have fibrous cellular extensions), they are not capable of generating and transmitting nerve impulses, a capability that is highly developed in neurons. Our focus in this exercise is the highly excitable neurons.

Neuron Anatomy

Neurons are the structural units of nervous tissue. They are highly specialized to transmit messages (nerve impulses) from one part of the body to another. Although neurons differ structurally, they have many identifiable features in common (Figure 15.2a and c). All have a **cell body** from which slender processes or fibers extend. Although neuron cell bodies are typically found in the CNS in clusters called **nuclei,** occasionally they reside in **ganglia** (collections of neuron cell bodies outside

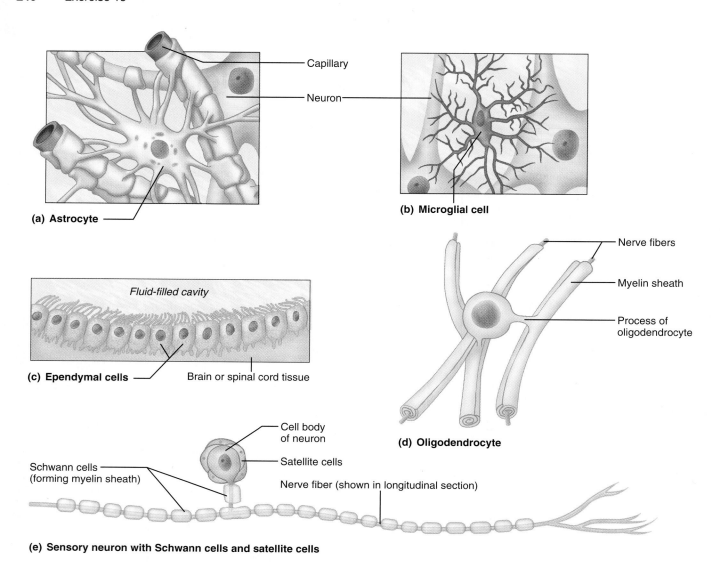

Capillary

Neuron

(a) Astrocyte

(b) Microglial cell

Nerve fibers

Myelin sheath

Process of
oligodendrocyte

Fluid-filled cavity

(c) Ependymal cells — Brain or spinal cord tissue

(d) Oligodendrocyte

Cell body
of neuron

Schwann cells
(forming myelin sheath)

Satellite cells

Nerve fiber (shown in longitudinal section)

(e) Sensory neuron with Schwann cells and satellite cells

FIGURE 15.1 Neuroglia. (a) Astrocyte. **(b)** Microglial cell. **(c)** Ependymal cells. **(d)** Oligodendrocyte. **(e)** Neuron with Schwann cells and satellite cells.

the CNS). They make up the gray matter of the nervous system. Neuron processes running through the CNS form **tracts** of white matter; in the PNS they form the peripheral **nerves.**

The neuron cell body contains a large round nucleus surrounded by cytoplasm *(neuroplasm)*. The cytoplasm is riddled with neurofibrils and with darkly staining structures called Nissl bodies. **Neurofibrils,** the cytoskeletal elements of the neuron, have a support and intracellular transport function. **Nissl** (chromatophilic) **bodies,** an elaborate type of rough endoplasmic reticulum, are involved in the metabolic activities of the cell.

Dendrites are *receptive regions* (they bear receptors for neurotransmitters released by other neurons), whereas **axons** are *nerve impulse generators* and *transmitters*. Neurons have only one axon (which may branch into **collaterals**) but may have many dendrites, depending on the neuron type. Notice that the term *nerve fiber* is a synonym for axon and is thus quite specific.

In general, a neuron is excited by other neurons when their axons release neurotransmitters close to its dendrites or cell body. The electrical current produced travels across

the cell body and (given a threshold stimulus) down the axon. As Figure 15.2a shows, the axon (in motor neurons) begins just distal to a slightly enlarged cell body structure called the **axon hillock.** The point at which the axon hillock narrows to axon diameter is referred to as the *initial segment*. The axon ends in many small structures called **axon terminals,** or synaptic knobs, which form **synapses,** or junctions, with neurons or effector cells. These terminals store the neurotransmitter chemical in tiny vesicles. Each axon terminal is separated from the cell body or dendrites of the next (postsynaptic) neuron by a tiny gap called the **synaptic cleft** (Figure 15.2b). Thus, although they are close, there is no actual physical contact between neurons. When an impulse reaches the axon terminals, some of the *synaptic vesicles* rupture and release neurotransmitter into the synaptic cleft. The neurotransmitter then diffuses across the synaptic cleft to bind to membrane receptors on the next neuron, initiating a synaptic potential. Specialized synapses in skeletal muscle are called neuromuscular junctions. They are discussed in Exercise 13.

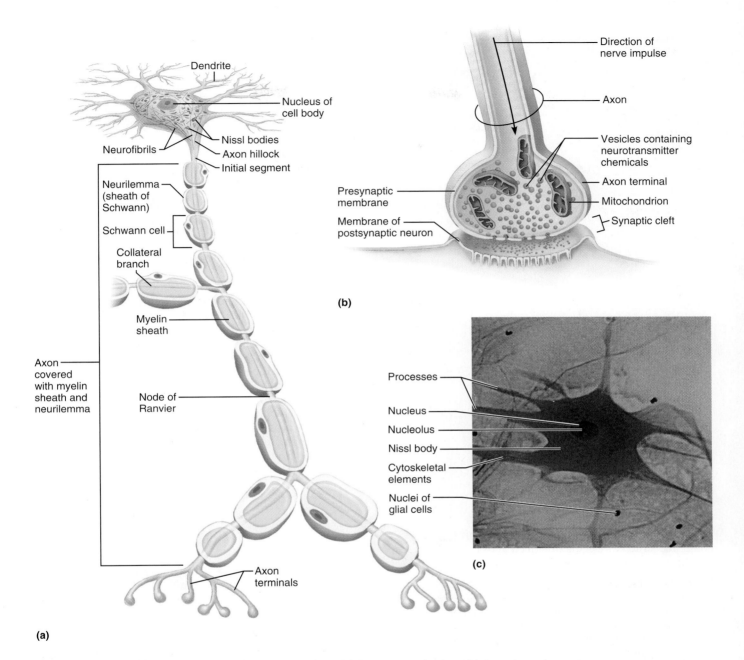

FIGURE 15.2 Structure of a typical motor neuron. (a) Diagrammatic view. **(b)** An enlarged synapse. **(c)** Photomicrograph. (See also Plate 5 in the Histology Atlas.)

Most long nerve fibers are covered with a fatty material called *myelin,* and such fibers are referred to as **myelinated fibers.** Because of its chemical composition, myelin insulates the fibers and greatly increases the speed of neurotransmission by neuron fibers. Axons in the peripheral nervous system are typically heavily myelinated by special supporting cells called **Schwann cells,** which wrap themselves tightly around the axon in jelly-roll fashion (Figure 15.3). During the wrapping process, the cytoplasm is squeezed from between adjacent layers of the Schwann cell membranes, so that when the process is completed a tight core of plasma membrane material (protein-lipoid material) encompasses the axon. This wrapping is the **myelin sheath.** The Schwann cell nucleus

and the bulk of its cytoplasm ends up just beneath the outermost portion of its plasma membrane. This peripheral part of the Schwann cell and its exposed plasma membrane is referred to as the **neurilemma,** or *sheath of Schwann.* Since the myelin sheath is formed by many individual Schwann cells, it is a discontinuous sheath. The gaps or indentations in the sheath are called **nodes of Ranvier,** or **neurofibril nodes** (see Figure 15.2).

Within the CNS, myelination is accomplished by glial cells called **oligodendrocytes** (see Figure 15.1d). These CNS sheaths do not exhibit the neurilemma seen in fibers myelinated by Schwann cells.

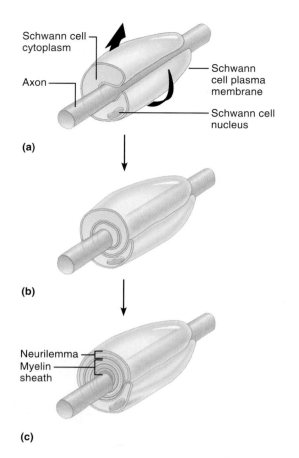

(a)

(b)

(c)

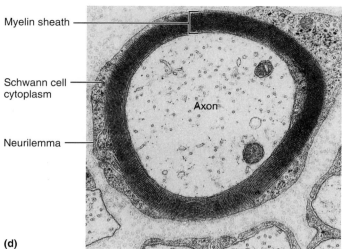

(d)

FIGURE 15.3 **Relationship of Schwann cells to axons on the PNS. (a–c)** Myelination of a nerve fiber (axon). As illustrated, a Schwann cell envelops an axon in a trough. It then rotates around the axon, wrapping it loosely in successive layers of its plasma membrane. Eventually, the Schwann cell cytoplasm is forced from between the membranes and comes to lie peripherally just beneath the exposed portion of the Schwann cell membrane. The tight membrane wrappings surrounding the axon form the myelin sheath. The area of Schwann cell cytoplasm and its exposed membrane is referred to as the neurilemma. **(d)** Electron micrograph of cross section through a myelinated axon (20,000×).

ACTIVITY 1

Identifying Parts of a Neuron

1. Study the typical motor neuron shown in Figure 15.2, noting the structural details described above, and then identify these structures on a neuron model.

2. Obtain a prepared slide of the ox spinal cord smear, which has large, easily identifiable neurons. Study one representative neuron under oil immersion and identify the cell body; the nucleus; the large, prominent "owl's eye" nucleolus; and the granular Nissl bodies. If possible, distinguish the axon from the many dendrites.

Sketch the cell in the space provided below, and label the important anatomical details you have observed. Compare your sketch to Plate 5 of the Histology Atlas. Also reexamine Figure 15.2a, which differentiates the neuronal processes more clearly.

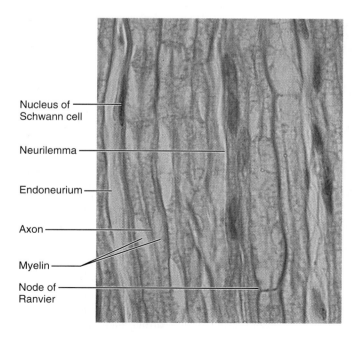

3. Obtain a prepared slide of teased myelinated nerve fibers. Using Figure 15.4 as a guide, identify the following:

FIGURE 15.4 **Photomicrograph of a small portion of a peripheral nerve in longitudinal section (1400×).**

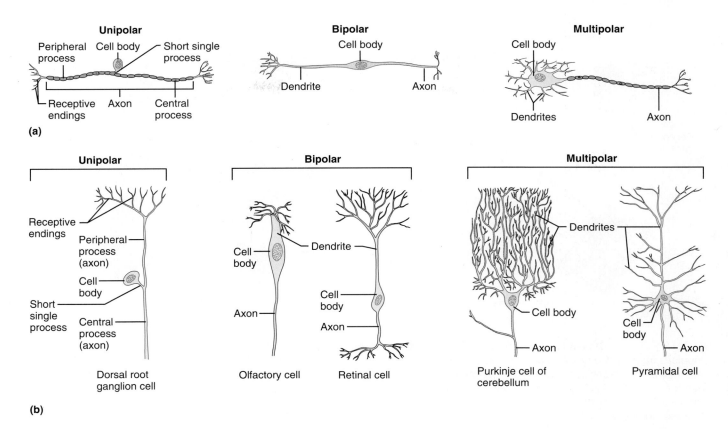

FIGURE 15.5 Classification of neurons according to structure. (a) Classification of neurons based on structure (number of processes extending from the cell body). **(b)** Structural variations within the classes.

nodes of Ranvier, neurilemma, axis cylinder (the axon itself), Schwann cell nuclei, and myelin sheath.

Sketch a portion of a myelinated nerve fiber in the space provided below, illustrating two or three nodes of Ranvier. Label the axon, myelin sheath, nodes, and neurilemma. Compare your sketch to Plate 8 in the Histology Atlas.

Do the nodes seem to occur at consistent intervals, or are they

irregularly distributed? _____

Explain the functional significance of this finding: _____

_____

_____

Neuron Classification

Neurons may be classified on the basis of structure or of function.

Classification by Structure

Structurally, neurons may be differentiated according to the number of processes attached to the cell body (Figure 15.5a). In **unipolar neurons,** one very short process, which divides into *peripheral* and *central processes,* extends from the cell body. Functionally, only the most distal portions of the peripheral process act as receptive endings; the rest acts as an axon along with the central process. Nearly all neurons that conduct impulses toward the CNS are unipolar.

Bipolar neurons have two processes attached to the cell body. This neuron type is quite rare, typically found only as part of the receptor apparatus of the eye, ear, and olfactory mucosa.

Many processes issue from the cell body of **multipolar neurons,** all classified as dendrites except for a single axon. Most neurons in the brain and spinal cord (CNS neurons) and those whose axons carry impulses away from the CNS fall into this last category.

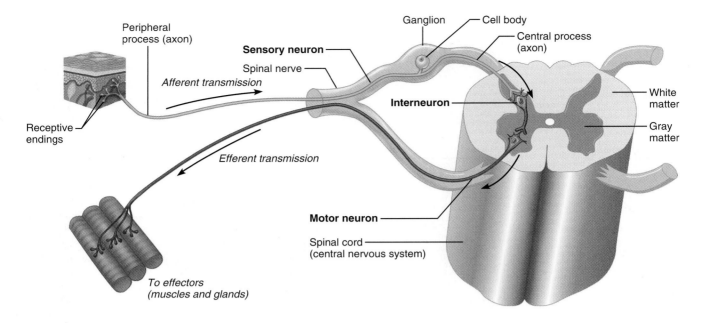

FIGURE 15.6 Classification of neurons on the basis of function. Sensory (afferent) neurons conduct impulses from the body's sensory receptors to the central nervous system; most are unipolar neurons with their nerve cell bodies in ganglia in the peripheral nervous system (PNS). Motor (efferent) neurons transmit impulses from the CNS to effectors such as muscles and glands. Interneurons (association neurons) complete the communication line between sensory and motor neurons. They are typically multipolar and their cell bodies reside in the CNS.

Studying the Microscopic Structure of Selected Neurons

Obtain prepared slides of Purkinje cells of the cerebellar cortex, pyramidal cells of the cerebral cortex, and a dorsal root ganglion. As you observe them under the microscope, try to pick out the anatomical details depicted in Figure 15.5b, and in Plates 6 and 7 of the Histology Atlas. Notice that the neurons of the cerebral and cerebellar tissues (both brain tissues) are extensively branched; in contrast, the neurons of the dorsal root ganglion are more rounded. The many small nuclei visible surrounding the neurons are those of abutting glial cells.

Which of these neuron types would be classified as multipolar neurons?

_____

Which as unipolar? _____ ▬

Classification by Function

In general, neurons carrying impulses from sensory receptors in the internal organs (viscera), the skin, skeletal muscles, joints, or special sensory organs are termed **sensory,** or **afferent, neurons** (see Figure 15.6). The dendritic endings of sensory neurons are often equipped with specialized receptors that are stimulated by specific changes in their immediate environment. The cell bodies of sensory neurons are always found in a ganglion outside the CNS, and these neurons are typically unipolar.

Neurons carrying activating impulses from the CNS to the viscera and/or body muscles and glands are termed **motor,** or **efferent, neurons.** Motor neurons are most often multipolar and their cell bodies are almost always located in the CNS.

The third functional category of neurons is the **interneurons,** or **association neurons,** which are situated between and contribute to pathways that connect sensory and motor neurons. Their cell bodies are always located within the CNS and they are multipolar neurons structurally.

Structure of a Nerve

A nerve is a bundle of neuron fibers or processes wrapped in connective tissue coverings that extends to and/or from the CNS and visceral organs or structures of the body periphery (such as skeletal muscles, glands, and skin).

Like neurons, nerves are classified according to the direction in which they transmit impulses. Nerves carrying both sensory (afferent) and motor (efferent) fibers are called **mixed nerves;** all spinal nerves are mixed nerves. Nerves that carry only sensory processes and conduct impulses only toward the CNS are referred to as **sensory,** or **afferent, nerves.** A few of the cranial nerves are pure sensory nerves, but the majority are mixed nerves. The ventral roots of the spinal cord, which carry only motor fibers, can be considered **motor,** or **efferent, nerves.**

Within a nerve, each fiber is surrounded by a delicate connective tissue sheath called an **endoneurium,** which insulates it from the other neuron processes adjacent to it. The endoneurium is often mistaken for the myelin sheath; it is instead an additional sheath that surrounds the myelin sheath. Groups of fibers are bound by a coarser connective tissue, called the **perineurium,** to form bundles of fibers called **fas-**

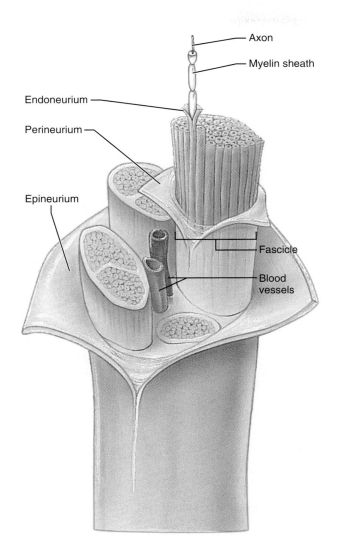

Axon

Myelin sheath

Endoneurium

Perineurium

Epineurium

Fascicle

Blood
vessels

FIGURE 15.7 Three-dimensional view of a portion of a nerve showing connective tissue wrappings.

cicles. Finally, all the fascicles are bound together by a white, fibrous connective tissue sheath called the **epineurium,** forming the cordlike nerve (Figure 15.7). In addition to the connective tissue wrappings, blood vessels and lymphatic vessels serving the fibers also travel within a nerve.

ACTIVITY 3

Examining the Microscopic Structure of a Nerve

Use the compound microscope to examine a prepared cross section of a peripheral nerve. Identify nerve fibers, myelin sheaths, fascicles, and endoneurium, perineurium, and epineurium sheaths. If desired, sketch the nerve in the space below. ▪

Structure of General Sensory Receptors

You cannot become aware of changes in the environment unless your sensory neurons and their receptors are operating properly. Sensory receptors are modified dendritic endings (or specialized cells associated with the dendrites) that are sensitive to certain environmental stimuli. They react to such stimuli by initiating a nerve impulse. Sensory receptors may be classified according to their stimulus source. **Exteroceptors** respond to stimuli in the external environment, and are typically found close to the body surface. **Interoceptors** respond to stimuli arising within the body (including the visceral organs). **Proprioceptors,** a subclass of interoceptors, are found in skeletal muscles, joints, tendons, and ligaments and report on the degree of stretch in these structures.

The receptors of the special sense organs are complex and deserve considerable study. Thus the special senses (vision, hearing, equilibrium, taste, and smell) are covered separately in Exercises 18 through 20. Only the anatomically simpler **general sensory receptors**—cutaneous receptors and proprioceptors—will be studied in this section. Cutaneous receptors reside in the skin (Figure 15.8). Proprioceptors are located in muscles, tendons, and joint capsules where they report on the degree of stretch those structures are subjected to. Although many references link each type of receptor to specific stimuli, there is still considerable controversy about the precise qualitative function of each receptor. It may be that the responses of all these receptors overlap considerably. Certainly, intense stimulation of any of them is always interpreted as pain.

The least specialized of the cutaneous receptors are the **free** or **naked, nerve endings** of sensory neurons (Figure 15.8

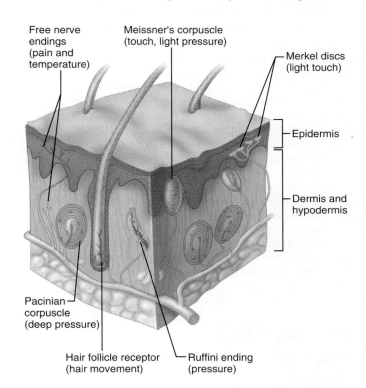

Free nerve endings (pain and temperature)

Meissner's corpuscle (touch, light pressure)

Merkel discs (light touch)

Epidermis

Dermis and hypodermis

Pacinian corpuscle (deep pressure)

Hair follicle receptor (hair movement)

Ruffini ending (pressure)

FIGURE 15.8 Cutaneous receptors. See also Plates 11, 12, and 13 of the Histology Atlas.

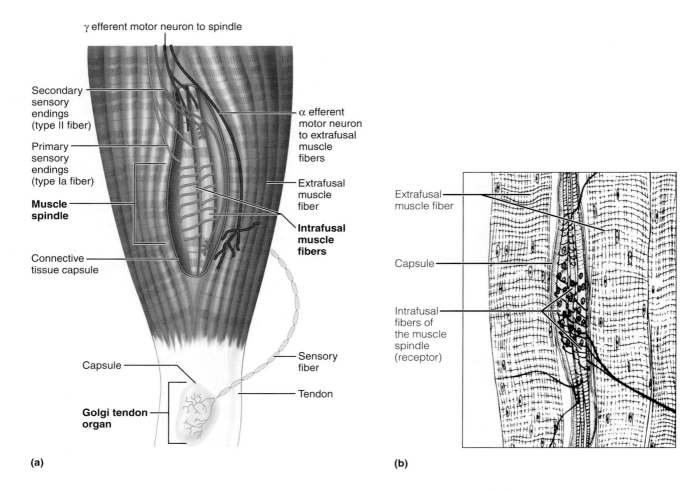

γ efferent motor neuron to spindle

Secondary
sensory
endings
(type II fiber)

Primary
sensory
endings
(type Ia fiber)

Muscle
spindle

Connective
tissue capsule

α efferent
motor neuron
to extrafusal
muscle
fibers

Extrafusal
muscle
fiber

Intrafusal
muscle
fibers

Capsule

Golgi tendon
organ

Sensory
fiber

Tendon

(a)

Extrafusal
muscle fiber

Capsule

Intrafusal
fibers of
the muscle
spindle
(receptor)

(b)

FIGURE 15.9 **Proprioceptors.** **(a)** Diagrammatic view of a muscle spindle and Golgi tendon organ.
(b) Drawing of a photomicrograph of a muscle spindle. See corresponding Plate 14 in the Histology Atlas.

and Plate 12 of the Histology Atlas), which respond chiefly to pain and temperature. (The pain receptors are widespread in the skin and make up a sizable portion of the visceral intero-ceptors.) Certain free nerve endings associate with specific epidermal cells to form **Merkel discs,** or entwine in hair folli-cles to form **hair follicle receptors.** Both Merkel discs and hair follicle receptors function as light touch receptors.

The other cutaneous receptors are a bit more complex, with the nerve endings *encapsulated* by connective tissue cells. **Meissner's corpuscles,** commonly referred to as *tactile recep-tors* because they respond to light touch, are located in the der-mal papillae of hairless skin only. **Ruffini endings** appear to respond to deep pressure and stretch stimuli. As you inspect Figure 15.8, notice that all of the encapsulated receptors are quite similar. However, **Pacinian corpuscles** are anatomically more distinctive and lie deepest in the dermis. These receptors respond only when deep pressure is first applied. They are best suited to monitor high-frequency vibrations.

Studying the Structure of Selected Sensory Receptors

1.   Obtain histologic slides of Pacinian and Meissner's cor-puscles. Locate, under low power, a Meissner's corpuscle in

the dermal layer of the skin. As mentioned above, these are usually found in the dermal papillae. Then switch to the oil immersion lens for a detailed study. Notice that the naked nerve fibers within the capsule are aligned parallel to the skin surface. Compare your observations to Figure 15.8 and Plate 11 of the Histology Atlas.

2.   Next observe a Pacinian corpuscle located much deeper in the dermis. Try to identify the slender naked dendrite end-ing in the center of the receptor and the heavy capsule of con-nective tissue surrounding it (which looks rather like an onion cut lengthwise). Also, notice how much larger the Pacinian corpuscles are than the Meissner's corpuscles. Compare your observations to the views shown in Figure 15.8 and Plate 13 of the Histology Atlas.

3.   Obtain slides of muscle spindles and Golgi tendon or-gans, the two major types of proprioceptors (see Figure 15.9 and Plate 14 of the Histology Atlas). In the slide of **muscle spindles,** note that minute extensions of the dendrites of the sensory neurons coil around specialized slender skeletal mus-cle cells called **intrafusal cells,** or **fibers.** The **Golgi tendon organs** are composed of dendrites that ramify through the tendon tissue close to the muscle tendon attachment. Stretch-ing of muscles or tendons excites these receptors, which then transmit impulses that ultimately reach the cerebellum for in-terpretation. Compare your observations to Figure 15.9. ■

Histology of Nervous Tissue

1. The cellular unit of the nervous system is the neuron. What is the major function of this cell type?

_____

2. Name four types of neuroglia in the CNS, and list at least one function for each type. (You will need to consult your textbook for this.)

Types   **Functions**

a. Most abundant: _____   a. _____

   _____   _____

b. _____   b. _____

c. _____   c. _____

d. _____   d. _____

Name the PNS glial cell that forms myelin. _____

Name the PNS glial cell that surrounds neuron cell bodies in ganglia. _____

3. For each description, choose the appropriate term from the key.

Key: a. afferent neuron   e. interneuron   i. nuclei
       b. central nervous system   f. neuroglia   j. peripheral nervous system
       c. efferent neuron   g. neurotransmitters   k. synapse
       d. ganglion   h. nerve   l. tract

_____ 1. the brain and spinal cord collectively

_____ 2. specialized supporting cells in the CNS

_____ 3. junction or point of close contact between neurons

_____ 4. a bundle of nerve processes inside the CNS

_____ 5. neuron serving as part of the conduction pathway between sensory and motor neurons

_____ 6. ganglia and spinal and cranial nerves

_____ 7. collection of nerve cell bodies found outside the CNS

_____ 8. neuron that conducts impulses away from the CNS to muscles and glands

_____ 9. neuron that conducts impulses toward the CNS from the body periphery

_____ 10. chemicals released by neurons that stimulate or inhibit other neurons or effectors

Neuron Anatomy

4. Match each anatomical term in column B with its description or function in column A.

Column A

Column B

_____ 1.   region of the cell body from which the axon originates

_____ 2.   secretes neurotransmitters

_____ 3.   receptive region of a neuron

_____ 4.   insulates the nerve fibers

_____ 5.   site of the nucleus and is the most important metabolic area

_____ 6.   may be involved in the transport of substances within the neuron

_____ 7.   essentially rough endoplasmic reticulum, important metabolically

_____ 8.   impulse generator and transmitter

a.   axon

b.   axon terminal

c.   axon hillock

d.   dendrite

e.   myelin sheath

f.   neurofibril

g.   neuronal cell body

h.   Nissl bodies

5. Draw a "typical" neuron in the space below. Include and label the following structures on your diagram: cell body, nucleus, nucleolus, Nissl bodies, dendrites, axon, axon collateral branch, myelin sheath, nodes of Ranvier, axon terminals, and neurofibrils.

6. What substance is found in synaptic vesicles? _____

What role does this substance play in neurotransmission? _____

_____

7. What anatomical characteristic determines whether a particular neuron is classified as unipolar, bipolar, or multipolar?

_____

Make a simple line drawing of each type here.

Unipolar neuron   **Bipolar neuron**   **Multipolar neuron**

8. Correctly identify the sensory (afferent) neuron, interneuron (association neuron), and motor (efferent) neuron in the figure below.

Which of these neuron types is/are unipolar? _____

Which is/are most likely multipolar? _____

Receptors (thermal and pain in the skin)

Effector (biceps brachii muscle)

9. Describe how the Schwann cells form the myelin sheath and the neurilemma encasing the nerve processes.

_____

_____

_____

Structure of a Nerve

10. What is a nerve? _____

_____

11. State the location of each of the following connective tissue coverings.

endoneurium: _____

perineurium: _____

epineurium: _____

12. What is the value of the connective tissue wrappings found in a nerve? _____

_____

13. Define *mixed nerve*. _____

_____

14. Identify all indicated parts of the nerve section.

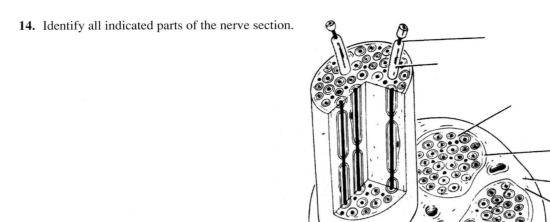

Structure of General Sensory Receptors

15. Differentiate between interoceptors and exteroceptors relative to location and stimulus source:

Interoceptor: _____

Exteroceptor: _____

16. A number of activities and sensations are listed in the chart below. For each, check whether the receptors would be exteroceptors or interoceptors; and then name the specific receptor types. Because interoceptors (visceral receptors) were not described in detail in this exercise, you need only indicate that the receptor is an interoceptor if it falls into that category.

Activity or sensation	Exteroceptor	Interoceptor	Specific receptor type
Backing into a sun-heated iron railing			
Someone steps on your foot			
Reading a book			
Leaning on your elbows			
Doing sit-ups			
The "too full" sensation			
Seasickness			

Gross Anatomy of the Brain and Cranial Nerves

MATERIALS

- ❏ Human brain model (dissectible)
- ❏ Preserved human brain (if available)
- ❏ Three-dimensional model of ventricles
- ❏ Coronally or cross-sectioned human brain slice (if available)
- ❏ Materials as needed for cranial nerve testing (see Table 16.1): aromatic oils (e.g., vanilla and cloves); eye chart; ophthalmoscope; penlight; safety pin; Mall probe (hot and cold); cotton; solutions of sugar, salt, vinegar, and quinine; ammonia; tuning fork, and tongue depressor
- ❏ Preserved sheep brain (meninges and cranial nerves intact)
- ❏ Dissecting instruments and tray
- ❏ Disposable gloves
- ❏ *The Human Nervous System: The Brain and Cranial Nerves* videotape*

AIA See Appendix B, Exercise 16 for links to A.D.A.M.® Interactive Anatomy.

*Available to qualified adopters from Benjamin Cummings.

OBJECTIVES

1. To identify the following brain structures on a dissected specimen, human brain model (or slices), or appropriate diagram, and to state their functions:
   - *Cerebral hemisphere structures:* lobes, important fissures, lateral ventricles, basal ganglia, corpus callosum, fornix, septum pellucidum
   - *Diencephalon structures:* thalamus, intermediate mass, hypothalamus, optic chiasma, pituitary gland, mammillary bodies, pineal body, choroid plexus of the third ventricle, interventricular foramen
   - *Brain stem structures:* corpora quadrigemina, cerebral aqueduct, cerebral peduncles of the midbrain, pons, medulla, fourth ventricle
   - *Cerebellum structures:* cerebellar hemispheres, vermis, arbor vitae
2. To describe the composition of gray and white matter.
3. To locate the well-recognized functional areas of the human cerebral hemispheres.
4. To define *gyri, fissures,* and *sulci*.
5. To identify the three meningeal layers and state their function, and to locate the falx cerebri, falx cerebelli, and tentorium cerebelli.
6. To state the function of the arachnoid villi and dural sinuses.
7. To discuss the formation, circulation, and drainage of cerebrospinal fluid.
8. To identify the cranial nerves by number and name on an appropriate model or diagram, stating the origin and function of each.
9. To identify at least four pertinent anatomical differences between the human brain and that of the sheep (or other mammal).

When viewed alongside all nature's animals, humans are indeed unique, and the key to their uniqueness is found in the brain. Each of us is a composite reflection of our brain's experience. If all past sensory input could mysteriously and suddenly be "erased," we would be unable to walk, talk, or communicate in any manner. Spontaneous movement would occur, as in a fetus, but no voluntary integrated function of any type would be possible. Clearly we would cease to be the same individuals.

Because of the complexity of the nervous system, its anatomical structures are usually considered in terms of two principal divisions: the central nervous system and the peripheral nervous system. The **central nervous system (CNS)** consists of the brain and spinal cord, which primarily interpret incoming sensory information and issue instructions based on past experience. The **peripheral nervous system (PNS)** consists of the cranial and spinal nerves, ganglia, and sensory receptors. These structures serve as communication lines as they carry impulses—from the sensory receptors to the CNS and from the CNS to the appropriate glands or muscles.

The PNS has two major subdivisions: the **sensory portion,** which consists of nerve fibers that conduct impulses toward the CNS, and the **motor portion,** which contains nerve fibers that conduct impulses away from the CNS. The motor arm, in turn, consists of the **somatic division** (sometimes called the *voluntary system*), which controls the skeletal muscles, and the other subdivision, the **autonomic nervous system (ANS),** which controls smooth and cardiac muscles and glands. The ANS is often referred to as the *involuntary nervous system*. Its sympathetic and parasympathetic branches innervate smooth muscle, cardiac

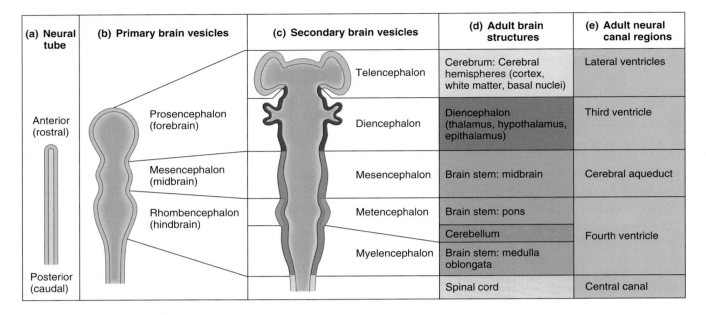

FIGURE 16.1 Embryonic development of the human brain. (a) The neural tube becomes subdivided into **(b)** the primary brain vesicles, which subsequently form **(c)** the secondary brain vesicles, which differentiate into **(d)** the adult brain structures. **(e)** The adult structures derived from the neural canal.

muscle, and glands, and play a major role in maintaining homeostasis.

In this exercise both CNS (brain) and PNS (cranial nerves) structures will be studied because of their close anatomical relationship.

The Human Brain

During embryonic development of all vertebrates, the CNS first makes its appearance as a simple tubelike structure, the **neural tube,** that extends down the dorsal median plane. By the fourth week, the human brain begins to form as an expansion of the anterior or rostral end of the neural tube (the end toward the head). Shortly thereafter, constrictions appear, dividing the developing brain into three major regions— **forebrain, midbrain,** and **hindbrain** (Figure 16.1). The remainder of the neural tube becomes the spinal cord.

During fetal development, two anterior outpocketings extend from the forebrain and grow rapidly to form the cerebral hemispheres. Because of space restrictions imposed by the skull, the cerebral hemispheres are forced to grow posteriorly and inferiorly, and finally end up enveloping and obscuring the rest of the forebrain and most midbrain structures. Somewhat later in development, the dorsal hindbrain also enlarges to produce the cerebellum. The central canal of the neural tube, which remains continuous throughout the brain and cord, enlarges in four regions of the brain, forming chambers called **ventricles** (see Figure 16.8a and b, p. 266).

ACTIVITY 1

Identifying External Brain Structures

Identify external brain structures using the figures cited. Also use a model of the human brain and other learning aids as they are mentioned.

Generally, the brain is studied in terms of four major regions: the cerebral hemispheres, diencephalon, brain stem, and cerebellum. The relationship between these four anatomical regions and the structures of the forebrain, midbrain, and hindbrain is also outlined in Figure 16.1.

Cerebral Hemispheres

The **cerebral hemispheres** are the most superior portion of the brain (Figure 16.2). Their entire surface is thrown into elevated ridges of tissue called **gyri** that are separated by shallow grooves called **sulci** or deeper grooves called **fissures.** Many of the fissures and gyri are important anatomical landmarks.

The cerebral hemispheres are divided by a single deep fissure, the **longitudinal fissure.** The **central sulcus** divides the **frontal lobe** from the **parietal lobe,** and the **lateral sulcus** separates the **temporal lobe** from the parietal lobe. The **parieto-occipital sulcus** on the medial surface of each hemisphere divides the **occipital lobe** from the parietal lobe. It is not visible externally. Notice that the cerebral hemisphere lobes are named for the cranial bones that lie over them.

Some important functional areas of the cerebral hemispheres have also been located (Figure 16.2d). The **primary somatosensory cortex** is located in the **postcentral gyrus** of the parietal lobe. Impulses traveling from the body's sensory receptors (such as those for pressure, pain, and temperature) are localized in this area of the brain. ("This information is from my big toe.") Immediately posterior to the primary somatosensory area is the **somatosensory association area,** in which the meaning of incoming stimuli is analyzed. ("Ouch! I have a *pain* there.") Thus, the somatosensory association area allows you to become aware of pain, coldness, a light touch, and the like.

Impulses from the special sense organs are interpreted in other specific areas also noted in Figure 16.2d. For example,

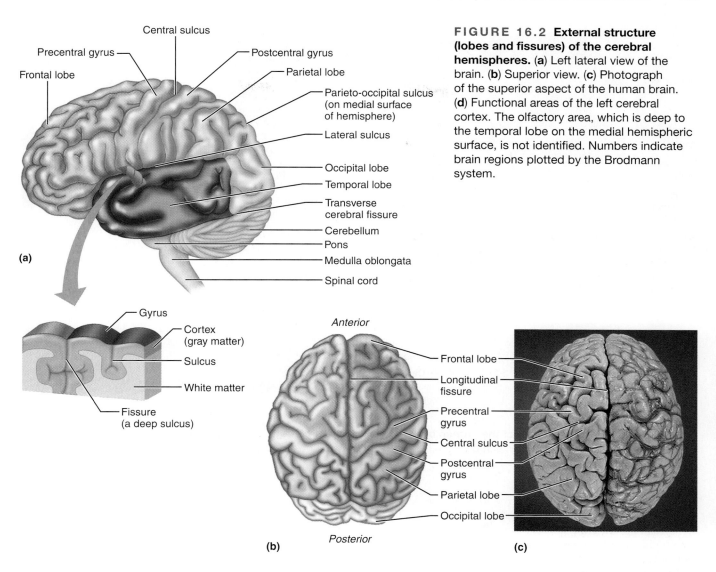

Central sulcus

Precentral gyrus

Frontal lobe

Postcentral gyrus

Parietal lobe

Parieto-occipital sulcus
(on medial surface
of hemisphere)

Lateral sulcus

Occipital lobe

Temporal lobe

Transverse
cerebral fissure

Cerebellum

Pons

Medulla oblongata

Spinal cord

(a)

**FIGURE 16.2 External structure
(lobes and fissures) of the cerebral
hemispheres.** (**a**) Left lateral view of the
brain. (**b**) Superior view. (**c**) Photograph
of the superior aspect of the human brain.
(**d**) Functional areas of the left cerebral
cortex. The olfactory area, which is deep to
the temporal lobe on the medial hemispheric
surface, is not identified. Numbers indicate
brain regions plotted by the Brodmann
system.

Gyrus

Cortex
(gray matter)

Sulcus

White matter

Fissure
(a deep sulcus)

Anterior

Frontal lobe

Longitudinal
fissure

Precentral
gyrus

Central sulcus

Postcentral
gyrus

Parietal lobe

Occipital lobe

Posterior

(b)

(c)

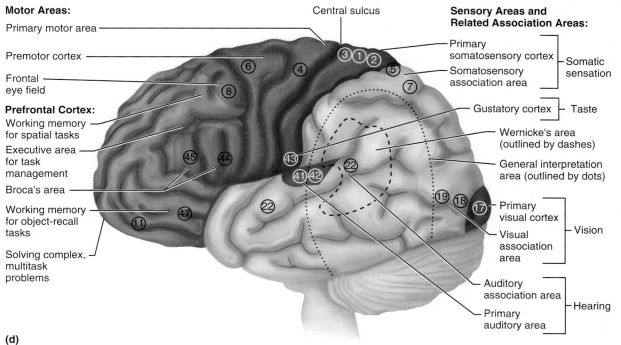

Motor Areas:

Primary motor area

Premotor cortex

Frontal
eye field

Prefrontal Cortex:

Working memory
for spatial tasks

Executive area
for task
management

Broca's area

Working memory
for object-recall
tasks

Solving complex,
multitask
problems

Central sulcus

**Sensory Areas and
Related Association Areas:**

Primary
somatosensory cortex

Somatosensory
association area

Somatic
sensation

Gustatory cortex — Taste

Wernicke's area
(outlined by dashes)

General interpretation
area (outlined by dots)

Primary
visual cortex

Visual
association
area

Vision

Auditory
association area

Primary
auditory area

Hearing

(d)

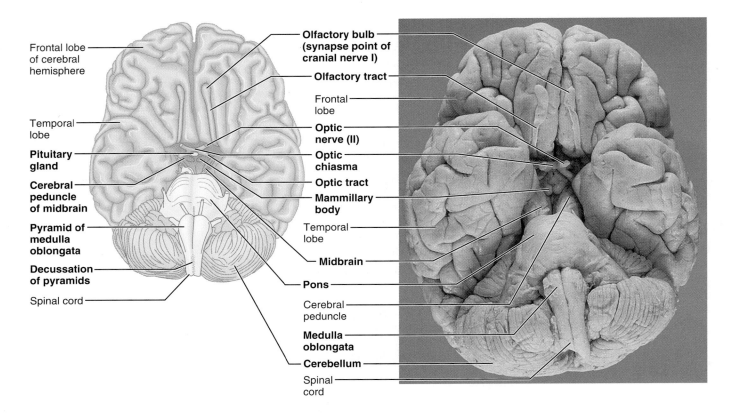

FIGURE 16.3 Ventral aspect of the human brain, showing the three regions of the brain stem. Only a small portion of the midbrain can be seen; the rest is surrounded by other brain regions. (See also Plate E in the Human Anatomy Atlas.)

the visual areas are in the posterior portion of the occipital lobe, and the auditory area is located in the temporal lobe in the gyrus bordering the lateral sulcus. The olfactory area is deep within the temporal lobe along its medial surface, in a region called the **uncus** (see Figure 16.4a).

The **primary motor area,** which is responsible for conscious or voluntary movement of the skeletal muscles, is located in the **precentral gyrus** of the frontal lobe. A specialized motor speech area called **Broca's area** is found at the base of the precentral gyrus just above the lateral sulcus. Damage to this area (which is located only in one cerebral hemisphere, usually the left) reduces or eliminates the ability to articulate words. Areas involved in intellect, complex reasoning, and personality lie in the anterior portions of the frontal lobes, in a region called the **prefrontal cortex.**

A rather poorly defined region at the junction of the parietal and temporal lobes is **Wernicke's area,** an area in which unfamiliar words are sounded out. Like Broca's area, Wernicke's area is located in one cerebral hemisphere only, typically the left.

Although there are many similar functional areas in both cerebral hemispheres, such as motor and sensory areas, each hemisphere is also a "specialist" in certain ways. For example, the left hemisphere is the "language brain" in most of us, because it houses centers associated with language skills and speech. The right hemisphere is more specifically concerned with abstract, conceptual, or spatial processes—skills associated with artistic or creative pursuits.

The cell bodies of cerebral neurons involved in these functions are found only in the outermost gray matter of the

cerebrum, the area called the **cerebral cortex.** Most of the balance of cerebral tissue—the deeper **cerebral white matter**—is composed of fiber tracts carrying impulses to or from the cortex.

Using a model of the human brain (and a preserved human brain, if available), identify the areas and structures of the cerebral hemispheres described above.

Then continue using the model and preserved brain along with the figures as you read about other structures.

Diencephalon

The **diencephalon,** sometimes considered the most superior portion of the brain stem, is embryologically part of the forebrain, along with the cerebral hemispheres.

Turn the brain model so the ventral surface of the brain can be viewed. Using Figure 16.3 as a guide, start superiorly and identify the externally visible structures that mark the position of the floor of the diencephalon. These are the **olfactory bulbs** and **tracts, optic nerves, optic chiasma** (where the fibers of the optic nerves partially cross over), **optic tracts, pituitary gland,** and **mammillary bodies.**

Brain Stem

Continue inferiorly to identify the **brain stem** structures—the **cerebral peduncles** (fiber tracts in the **midbrain** connecting the pons below with the cerebrum above), the pons, and the medulla oblongata. *Pons* means "bridge," and the **pons** consists primarily of motor and sensory fiber tracts connecting the brain with lower CNS centers. The lowest brain stem region, the **medulla oblongata,** is also composed

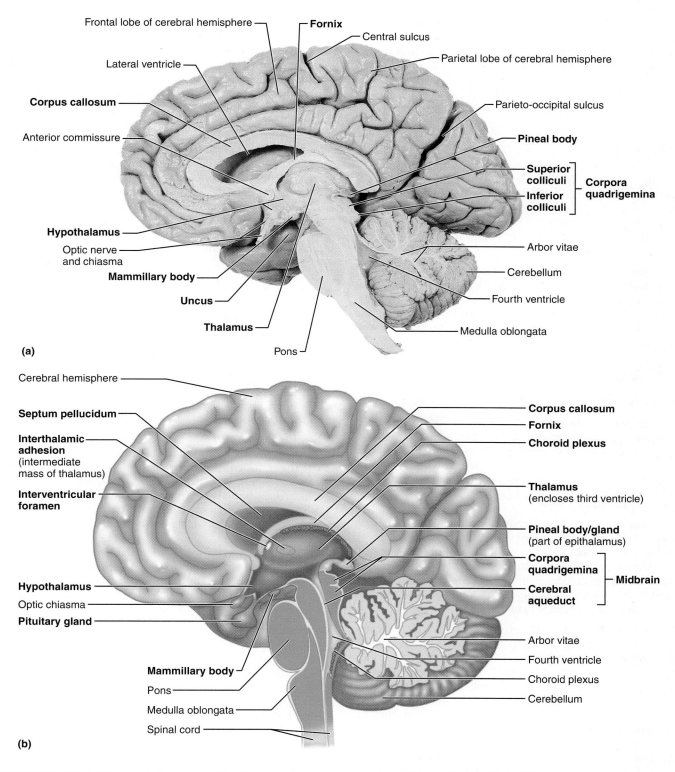

FIGURE 16.4 Diencephalon and brain stem structures as seen in a midsagittal section of the brain. (a) Photograph. **(b)** Diagrammatic view.

primarily of fiber tracts. You can see the **decussation of pyramids,** a crossover point for the major motor tracts (pyramidal tracts) descending from the motor areas of the cerebrum to the cord, on the medulla's anterior surface. The medulla also houses many vital autonomic centers involved in the control of heart rate, respiratory rhythm, and blood pressure as well as involuntary centers involved in vomiting, swallowing, and so on.

Cerebellum

1. Turn the brain model so you can see the dorsal aspect. Identify the large cauliflower-like **cerebellum,** which projects dorsally from under the occipital lobe of the cerebrum. Notice that, like the cerebrum, the cerebellum has two major hemispheres and a convoluted surface (see Figure 16.6). It also has an outer cortex made up of gray matter with an inner region of white matter.

2. Remove the cerebellum to view the **corpora quadrigemina** (Figure 16.4), located on the posterior aspect of the midbrain, a brain stem structure. The two superior prominences are the **superior colliculi** (visual reflex centers); the two smaller inferior prominences are the **inferior colliculi** (auditory reflex centers). ▄▄▄

A C T I V I T Y   2

Identifying Internal Brain Structures

The deeper structures of the brain have also been well mapped. Like the external structures, these can be studied in terms of the four major regions. As the internal brain areas are described, identify them on the figures cited. Also, use the brain model as indicated to help you in this study.

Cerebral Hemispheres

1. Take the brain model apart so you can see a median sagittal view of the internal brain structures (see Figure 16.4). Observe the model closely to see the extent of the outer cortex (gray matter), which contains the cell bodies of cerebral neurons. The pyramidal cells of the cerebral motor cortex (studied in Exercise 15, p. 249) are representative of the neurons seen in the precentral gyrus.

2. Observe the deeper area of white matter, which is composed of fiber tracts. The fiber tracts found in the cerebral hemisphere white matter are called *association tracts* if they connect two portions of the same hemisphere, *projection tracts* if they run between the cerebral cortex and the lower brain or spinal cord, and *commissures* if they run from one hemisphere to another. Observe the large **corpus callosum,** the major commissure connecting the cerebral hemispheres. The corpus callosum arches above the structures of the diencephalon and roofs over the lateral ventricles. Notice also the **fornix,** a bandlike fiber tract concerned with olfaction as well as limbic system functions, and the membranous **septum pellucidum,** which separates the lateral ventricles of the cerebral hemispheres.

3. In addition to the gray matter of the cerebral cortex, there are several "islands" of gray matter (clusters of neuron cell bodies) called **nuclei** buried deep within the white matter of the cerebral hemispheres. One important group of cerebral nuclei, called the **basal ganglia,*** flank the lateral and third ventricles. You can see these nuclei if you have an appropriate dissectible model or a coronally or cross-sectioned human brain slice. Otherwise, Figure 16.5 will suffice.

The basal ganglia, which are important subcortical motor nuclei (and part of the so-called *extrapyramidal system*), are involved in regulating voluntary motor activities. The most important of them are the arching, comma-shaped **caudate nucleus,** and the **lentiform nucleus,** which is composed of the **putamen** and **globus pallidus nuclei.**

The **corona radiata,** a spray of projection fibers coursing down from the precentral (motor) gyrus, combines with sensory fibers traveling to the sensory cortex to form a broad band of fibrous material called the **internal capsule.** The internal capsule passes between the diencephalon and the basal ganglia, and gives these basal ganglia a striped appearance. This is why the caudate nucleus and the lentiform nucleus are sometimes referred to collectively as the **corpus striatum,** or "striped body" (Figure 16.5a).

4. Examine the relationship of the lateral ventricles and corpus callosum to the diencephalon structures; that is, thalamus and third ventricle—from the cross-sectional viewpoint (see Figure 16.5b).

Diencephalon

1. The major internal structures of the diencephalon are the thalamus, hypothalamus, and epithalamus (see Figure 16.4). The **thalamus** consists of two large lobes of gray matter that laterally enclose the shallow third ventricle of the brain. A slender stalk of thalamic tissue, the **interthalamic adhesion,** or **intermediate mass,** connects the two thalamic lobes and bridges the ventricle. The thalamus is a major integrating and relay station for sensory impulses passing upward to the cortical sensory areas for localization and interpretation. Locate also the **interventricular foramen** *(foramen of Monro),* a tiny orifice connecting the third ventricle with the lateral ventricle on the same side.

2. The **hypothalamus** makes up the floor and the inferolateral walls of the third ventricle. It is an important autonomic center involved in regulation of body temperature, water balance, and fat and carbohydrate metabolism as well as in many other activities and drives (sex, hunger, thirst). Locate again the pituitary gland, which hangs from the anterior floor of the hypothalamus by a slender stalk, the **infundibulum.** (The pituitary gland is usually not present in

---

*The historical term for these nuclei, *basal ganglia,* is a misleading term because ganglia are PNS structures. However, the name has been retained to differentiate these nuclei from the basal nuclei of the forebrain in the cerebrum.

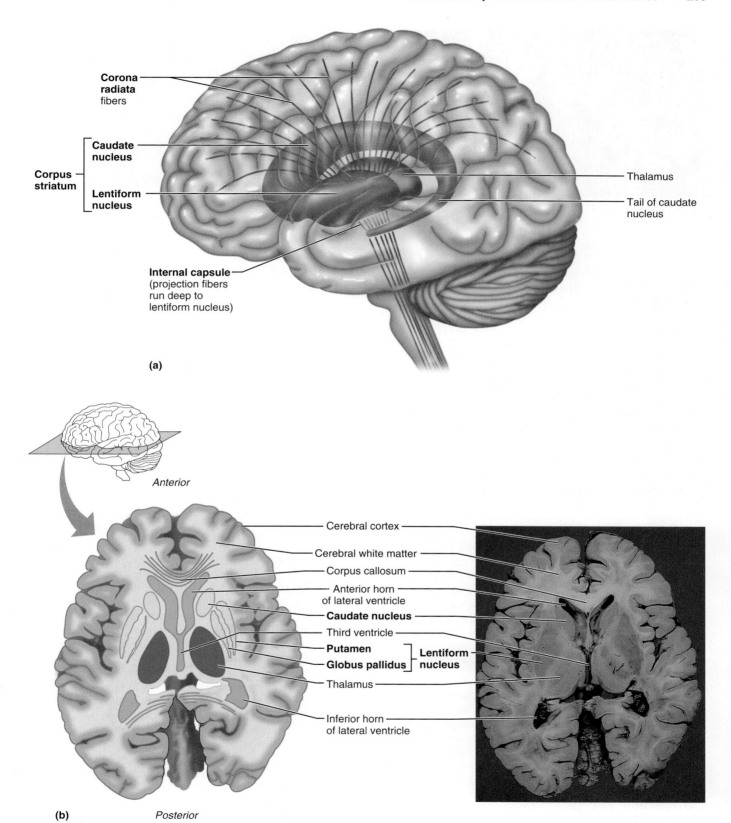

FIGURE 16.5 Basal ganglia. (a) Three-dimensional view of the basal ganglia showing their positions within the cerebrum. **(b)** A transverse section of the cerebrum and diencephalon showing the relationship of the basal ganglia to the thalamus and the lateral and third ventricles. (See also Plate F in the Human Anatomy Atlas.)

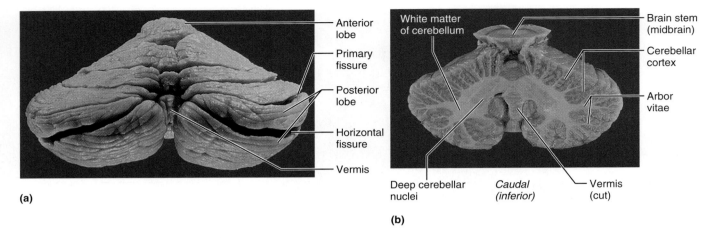

(a)

(b)

FIGURE 16.6 Cerebellum. (a) Posterior (dorsal) view. **(b)** The cerebellum, sectioned to reveal its cortex and medullary regions. (Note that the cerebellum is sectioned frontally and the brain stem is sectioned horizontally in this posterior view.)

preserved brain specimens.) In life, the pituitary rests in the hypophyseal fossa of the sella turcica of the sphenoid bone. Its function is discussed in Exercise 21.

Anterior to the pituitary, identify the optic chiasma portion of the optic pathway to the brain. The **mammillary bodies,** relay stations for olfaction, bulge exteriorly from the floor of the hypothalamus just posterior to the pituitary gland.

3.   The **epithalamus** forms the roof of the third ventricle and is the most dorsal portion of the diencephalon. Important structures in the epithalamus are the **pineal body,** or **gland** (a neuroendocrine structure), and the **choroid plexus** of the third ventricle. The choroid plexuses, knotlike collections of capillaries within each ventricle, form the cerebrospinal fluid.

Brain Stem

1.   Now trace the short midbrain from the mammillary bodies to the rounded pons below. Continue to refer to Figure 16.4. The **cerebral aqueduct** is a slender canal traveling through the midbrain; it connects the third ventricle to the fourth ventricle in the hindbrain below. The cerebral peduncles and the rounded corpora quadrigemina make up the midbrain tissue anterior and posterior (respectively) to the cerebral aqueduct.

2.   Locate the hindbrain structures. Trace the rounded pons to the medulla oblongata below, and identify the fourth ventricle posterior to these structures. Attempt to identify the single median aperture and the two lateral apertures, three orifices found in the walls of the fourth ventricle. These apertures serve as conduits for cerebrospinal fluid to circulate into the subarachnoid space from the fourth ventricle.

Cerebellum

Examine the cerebellum. Notice that it is composed of two lateral hemispheres each with three lobes (*anterior, posterior,*

and a deep *flocculonodular*) connected by a midline lobe called the **vermis** (Figure 16.6). As in the cerebral hemispheres, the cerebellum has an outer cortical area of gray matter and an inner area of white matter. The treelike branching of the cerebellar white matter is referred to as the **arbor vitae,** or "tree of life." The cerebellum is concerned with unconscious coordination of skeletal muscle activity and control of balance and equilibrium. Fibers converge on the cerebellum from the equilibrium apparatus of the internal ear, visual pathways, proprioceptors of tendons and skeletal muscles, and from many other areas. Thus the cerebellum remains constantly aware of the position and state of tension of the various body parts. ▬

Meninges of the Brain

The brain (and spinal cord) are covered and protected by three connective tissue membranes called **meninges** (Figure 16.7). The outermost meninx is the leathery **dura mater,** a double-layered membrane. One of its layers (the *periosteal layer*) is attached to the inner surface of the skull, forming the periosteum. The other (the *meningeal layer*) forms the outermost brain covering and is continuous with the dura mater of the spinal cord.

The dural layers are fused together except in three places where the inner membrane extends inward to form a septum that secures the brain to structures inside the cranial cavity. One such extension, the **falx cerebri,** dips into the longitudinal fissure between the cerebral hemispheres to attach to the crista galli of the ethmoid bone of the skull (Figure 16.7a). The cavity created at this point is the large **superior sagittal sinus,** which collects blood draining from the brain tissue. The **falx cerebelli,** separating the two cerebellar hemispheres, and the **tentorium cerebelli,** separating the cerebrum from the cerebellum below, are two other important inward folds of the inner dural membrane.

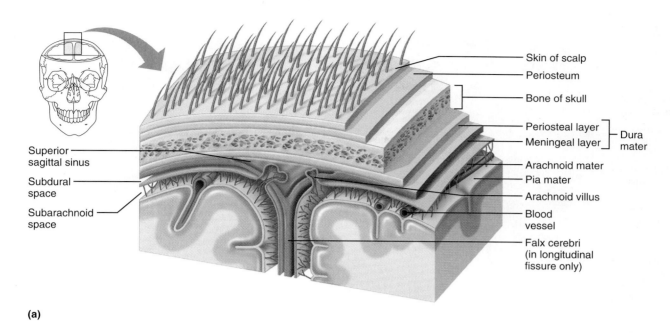

(a)

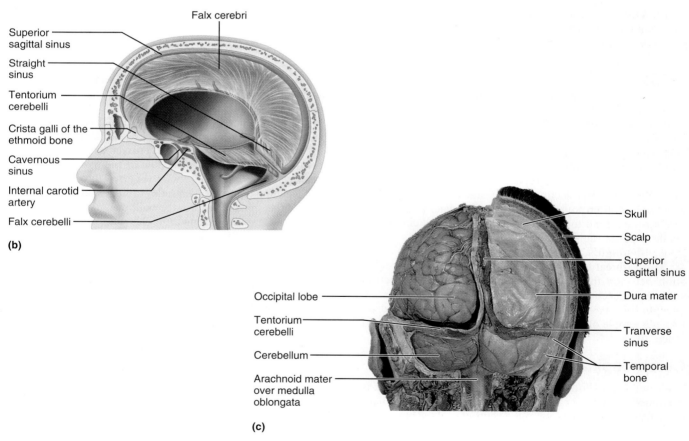

(b)

(c)

FIGURE 16.7 Meninges of the brain. (a) Three-dimensional frontal section showing the relationship of the dura mater, arachnoid mater, and pia mater. The meningeal dura forms the falx cerebri fold, which extends into the longitudinal fissure and attaches the brain to the ethmoid bone of the skull. A dural sinus, the superior sagittal sinus, is enclosed by the dural membranes superiorly. Arachnoid villi, which return cerebrospinal fluid to the dural sinus, are also shown. **(b)** Position of the dural folds, the falx cerebri, tentorium cerebelli, and falx cerebelli. **(c)** Posterior view of the brain in place, surrounded by the dura mater.

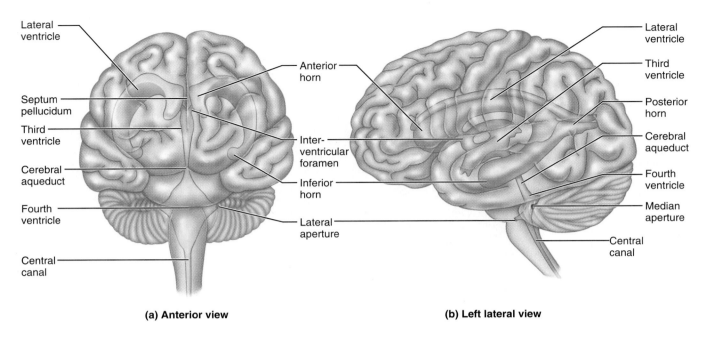

(a) Anterior view   **(b) Left lateral view**

FIGURE 16.8 Location and circulatory pattern of cerebrospinal fluid. (a) Anterior view. **(b)** Lateral view. Note that different regions of the large lateral ventricles are indicated by the terms *anterior horn, posterior horn, and inferior horn.*

The middle meninx, the weblike **arachnoid mater,** underlies the dura mater and is partially separated from it by the **subdural space.** Threadlike projections bridge the **subarachnoid space** to attach the arachnoid to the innermost meninx, the **pia mater.** The delicate pia mater is highly vascular and clings tenaciously to the surface of the brain, following its convolutions.

In life, the subarachnoid space is filled with cerebrospinal fluid. Specialized projections of the arachnoid tissue called **arachnoid villi** protrude through the dura mater to allow the cerebrospinal fluid to drain back into the venous circulation via the superior sagittal sinus and other dural sinuses.

Meningitis, inflammation of the meninges, is a serious threat to the brain because of the intimate association between the brain and meninges. Should infection spread to the neural tissue of the brain itself, life-threatening **encephalitis** may occur. Meningitis is often diagnosed by taking a sample of cerebrospinal fluid from the subarachnoid space. ●

Cerebrospinal Fluid

The cerebrospinal fluid, much like plasma in composition, is continually formed by the **choroid plexuses,** small capillary knots hanging from the roof of the ventricles of the brain. The cerebrospinal fluid in and around the brain forms a watery cushion that protects the delicate brain tissue against blows to the head.

Within the brain, the cerebrospinal fluid circulates from the two lateral ventricles (in the cerebral hemispheres) into the third ventricle via the **interventricular foramina,** and then through the cerebral aqueduct of the midbrain into the fourth ventricle in the hindbrain (Figure 16.8). Some of the fluid reaching the fourth ventricle continues down the central canal of the spinal cord, but the bulk of it circulates into the subarachnoid space, exiting through the three foramina in the walls of the fourth ventricle (the two lateral and the single median apertures). The fluid returns to the blood in the dural sinuses via the arachnoid villi.

Ordinarily, cerebrospinal fluid forms and drains at a constant rate. However, under certain conditions—for example, obstructed drainage or circulation resulting from tumors or anatomical deviations—cerebrospinal fluid accumulates and exerts increasing pressure on the brain which, uncorrected, causes neurological damage in adults. In infants, **hydrocephalus** (literally, "water on the brain") is indicated by a gradually enlarging head. The infant's skull is still flexible and contains fontanelles, so it can expand to accommodate the increasing size of the brain. ●

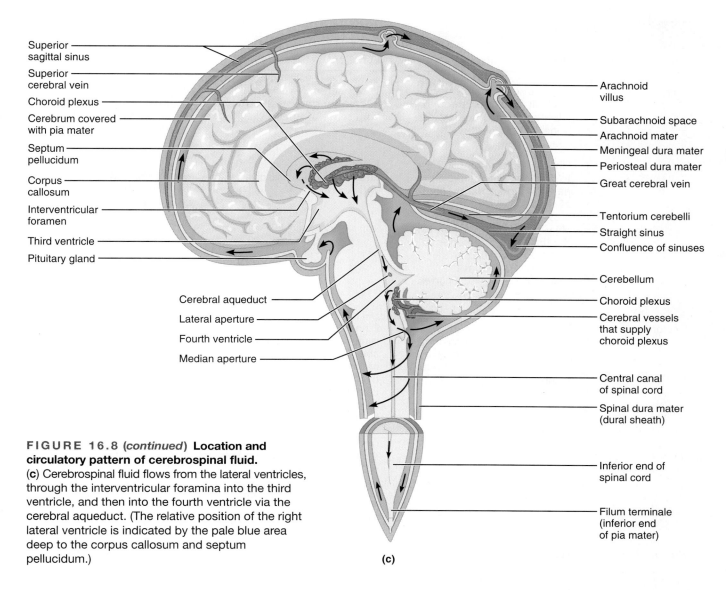

Superior sagittal sinus
Superior cerebral vein
Choroid plexus
Cerebrum covered with pia mater
Septum pellucidum
Corpus callosum
Interventricular foramen
Third ventricle
Pituitary gland

Cerebral aqueduct
Lateral aperture
Fourth ventricle
Median aperture

Arachnoid villus
Subarachnoid space
Arachnoid mater
Meningeal dura mater
Periosteal dura mater
Great cerebral vein
Tentorium cerebelli
Straight sinus
Confluence of sinuses
Cerebellum
Choroid plexus
Cerebral vessels that supply choroid plexus
Central canal of spinal cord
Spinal dura mater (dural sheath)
Inferior end of spinal cord
Filum terminale (inferior end of pia mater)

FIGURE 16.8 (*continued*) **Location and circulatory pattern of cerebrospinal fluid.**
(**c**) Cerebrospinal fluid flows from the lateral ventricles, through the interventricular foramina into the third ventricle, and then into the fourth ventricle via the cerebral aqueduct. (The relative position of the right lateral ventricle is indicated by the pale blue area deep to the corpus callosum and septum pellucidum.)

(**c**)

Cranial Nerves

The **cranial nerves** are part of the peripheral nervous system and not part of the brain proper, but they are most appropriately identified while studying brain anatomy. The 12 pairs of cranial nerves primarily serve the head and neck. Only one pair, the vagus nerves, extends into the thoracic and abdominal cavities. All but the first two pairs (olfactory and optic nerves) arise from the brain stem and pass through foramina in the base of the skull to reach their destination.

The cranial nerves are numbered consecutively, and in most cases their names reflect the major structures they control. The cranial nerves are described by name, number (Roman numeral), origin, course, and function in Table 16.1. This information should be committed to memory. A mnemonic device that might be helpful for remembering

the cranial nerves in order is "**O**n **O**ccasion, **O**ur **T**rusty **T**ruck **A**cts **F**unny—**V**ery **G**ood **V**ehicle **A**ny**H**ow." The first letter of each word and the "a" and "h" of the final word "anyhow" will remind you of the first letter of the cranial nerve name.

Most cranial nerves are mixed nerves (containing both motor and sensory fibers). But close scrutiny of Table 16.1 will reveal that three pairs of cranial nerves (optic, olfactory, and vestibulocochlear) are primarily or exclusively sensory in function.

You may recall that the cell bodies of neurons are always located within the central nervous system (cortex or nuclei) or in specialized collections of cell bodies (ganglia) outside the CNS. Neuron cell bodies of the sensory cranial nerves are located in ganglia; those of the mixed cranial nerves are found both within the brain and in peripheral ganglia.

TABLE 16.1	The Cranial Nerves (see Figure 16.9)		
Number and name	Origin and course	Function*	Testing
I. Olfactory	Fibers arise from olfactory epithelium and run through cribriform plate of ethmoid bone to synapse in olfactory bulbs.	Purely sensory—carries afferent impulses associated with sense of smell.	Person is asked to sniff aromatic substances, such as oil of cloves and vanilla, and to identify each.
II. Optic	Fibers arise from retina of eye to form the optic nerve and pass through optic canal of the orbit. Fibers partially cross over at the optic chiasma and continue on to the thalamus as the optic tracts. Final fibers of this pathway travel from the thalamus to the visual cortex as the optic radiation.	Purely sensory—carries afferent impulses associated with vision.	Vision and visual field are determined with eye chart and by testing the point at which the person first sees an object (finger) moving into the visual field. Fundus of eye viewed with ophthalmoscope to detect papilledema (swelling of optic disc, the point at which optic nerve leaves the eye) and to observe blood vessels.
III. Oculomotor	Fibers emerge from dorsal midbrain and course ventrally to enter the orbit. They exit from skull via superior orbital fissure.	Primarily motor—somatic motor fibers to inferior oblique and superior, inferior, and medial rectus muscles, which direct eyeball, and to levator palpebrae muscles of the superior eyelid; parasympathetic fibers to iris and smooth muscle controlling lens shape (reflex responses to varying light intensity and focusing of eye for near vision).	Pupils are examined for size, shape, and equality. Pupillary reflex is tested with penlight (pupils should constrict when illuminated). Convergence for near vision is tested, as is subject's ability to follow objects with the eyes.
IV. Trochlear	Fibers emerge from midbrain and exit from skull via superior orbital fissure to run to eye.	Primarily motor—provides somatic motor fibers to superior oblique muscle (an extrinsic eye muscle).	Tested in common with cranial nerve III.
V. Trigeminal	Fibers emerge from pons and form three divisions, which exit separately from skull: mandibular division through foramen ovale in sphenoid bone, maxillary division via foramen rotundum in sphenoid bone, and ophthalmic division through superior orbital fissure of eye socket.	Mixed—major sensory nerve of face; conducts sensory impulses from skin of face and anterior scalp, from mucosae of mouth and nose, and from surface of eyes; mandibular division also contains motor fibers that innervate muscles of mastication and muscles of floor of mouth.	Sensations of pain, touch, and temperature are tested with safety pin and hot and cold objects. Corneal reflex tested with wisp of cotton. Motor branch assessed by asking person to clench the teeth, open mouth against resistance, and move jaw side to side.
VI. Abducens	Fibers leave inferior region of pons and exit from skull via superior orbital fissure to run to eye.	Carries motor fibers to lateral rectus muscle of eye.	Tested in common with cranial nerve III.

*Does not include sensory impulses from proprioceptors.

TABLE 16.1 *(continued)*

Number and name	Origin and course	Function*	Testing
VII. Facial	Fibers leave pons and travel through temporal bone via internal acoustic meatus, exiting via stylomastoid foramen to reach the face.	Mixed—supplies somatic motor fibers to muscles of facial expression and parasympathetic motor fibers to lacrimal and salivary glands; carries sensory fibers from taste receptors of anterior portion of tongue.	Anterior two-thirds of tongue is tested for ability to taste sweet (sugar), salty, sour (vinegar), and bitter (quinine) substances. Symmetry of face is checked. Subject is asked to close eyes, smile, whistle, and so on. Tearing is assessed with ammonia fumes.
VIII. Vestibulo-cochlear	Fibers run from internal-ear equilibrium and hearing apparatus, housed in temporal bone, through internal acoustic meatus to enter pons.	Primarily sensory—vestibular branch transmits impulses associated with sense of equilibrium from vestibular apparatus and semicircular canals; cochlear branch transmits impulses associated with hearing from cochlea.	Hearing is checked by air and bone conduction using tuning fork.
IX. Glosso-pharyngeal	Fibers emerge from medulla and leave skull via jugular foramen to run to throat.	Mixed—somatic motor fibers serve pharyngeal muscles, and parasympathetic motor fibers serve salivary glands; sensory fibers carry impulses from pharynx, tonsils, posterior tongue (taste buds), and pressure receptors of carotid artery.	A tongue depressor is used to check the position of the uvula. Gag and swallowing reflexes are checked. Subject is asked to speak and cough. Posterior third of tongue may be tested for taste.
X. Vagus	Fibers emerge from medulla and pass through jugular foramen and descend through neck region into thorax and abdomen.	Mixed—fibers carry somatic motor impulses to pharynx and larynx and sensory fibers from same structures; very large portion is composed of parasympathetic motor fibers, which supply heart and smooth muscles of abdominal visceral organs; transmits sensory impulses from viscera.	As for cranial nerve IX (IX and X are tested in common, since they both innervate muscles of throat and mouth).
XI. Accessory	Fibers arise from medulla and superior aspect of spinal cord and travel through jugular foramen to reach muscles of neck and back.	Mixed (but primarily motor in function)—provides somatic motor fibers to sternocleido-mastoid and trapezius muscles and to muscles of soft palate, pharynx, and larynx (spinal and medullary fibers respectively).	Sternocleidomastoid and trapezius muscles are checked for strength by asking person to rotate head and shoulders against resistance.
XII. Hypoglossal	Fibers arise from medulla and exit from skull via hypoglossal canal to travel to tongue.	Mixed (but primarily motor in function)—carries somatic motor fibers to muscles of tongue.	Person is asked to protrude and retract tongue. Any deviations in position are noted.

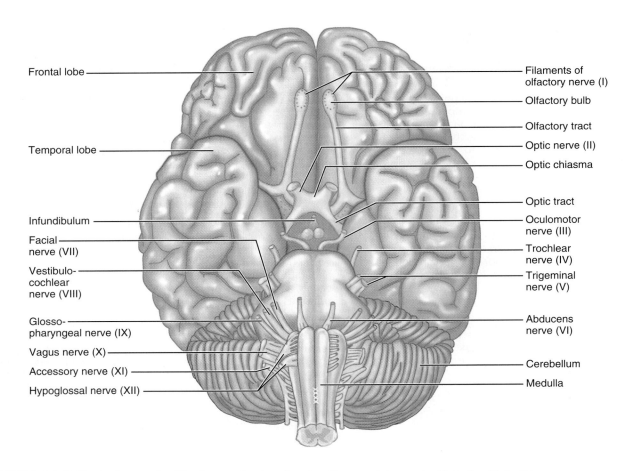

FIGURE 16.9 Ventral aspect of the human brain, showing the cranial nerves. (See also Plate E in the Human Anatomy Atlas.)

Identifying and Testing the Cranial Nerves

1. Observe the anterior surface of the brain model to identify the cranial nerves. Figure 16.9 may also aid you in this study. Notice that the first (olfactory) cranial nerves are not visible on the model because they consist only of short axons that run from the nasal mucosa through the cribriform plate of the ethmoid bone. (However, the synapse points of the first cranial nerves, the *olfactory bulbs, are* visible on the model.)

2. The last column of Table 16.1 describes techniques for testing cranial nerves, which is an important part of any neurological examination. This information may help you understand cranial nerve function, especially as it pertains to some aspects of brain function. Conduct tests of cranial nerve function following directions given in the "testing" column of the table.

3. Several cranial nerve ganglia are named in the accompanying chart. *Using your textbook or an appropriate reference,* fill in the chart by naming the cranial nerve the ganglion is associated with and stating its location. ▇

Cranial nerve ganglion	Cranial nerve	Site of ganglion
Trigeminal		
Geniculate		
Inferior		
Superior		
Spiral		
Vestibular		

DISSECTION: The Sheep Brain

The brain of any mammal is enough like the human brain to warrant comparison. Obtain a sheep brain, disposable gloves, dissecting tray, and instruments, and bring them to your laboratory bench.

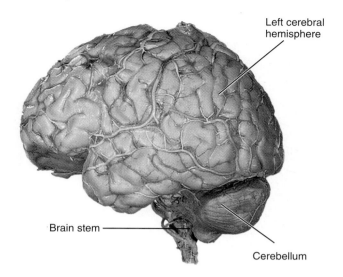

Left cerebral
hemisphere

Brain stem

Cerebellum

FIGURE 16.10 Photo of lateral aspect of the human brain.

1.   Don disposable gloves. Before beginning the dissection, turn your sheep brain so that you are viewing its left lateral aspect. Compare the various areas of the sheep brain (cerebrum, brain stem, cerebellum) to the photo of the human brain in Figure 16.10. Relatively speaking, which of these structures is obviously much larger in the human brain?

2.   Place the intact sheep brain ventral surface down on the dissecting pan, and observe the dura mater. Feel its consistency and note its toughness. Cut through the dura mater along the line of the longitudinal fissure (which separates the cerebral hemispheres) to enter the superior sagittal sinus. Gently force the cerebral hemispheres apart laterally to expose the corpus callosum deep to the longitudinal fissure.

3.   Carefully remove the dura mater and examine the superior surface of the brain. Notice that, like the human brain, its surface is thrown into convolutions (fissures and gyri). Locate the arachnoid mater, which appears on the brain surface as a delicate "cottony" material spanning the fissures. In contrast, the innermost meninx, the pia mater, closely follows the cerebral contours.

Ventral Structures

Figure 16.11a and b shows the important features of the ventral surface of the brain. Turn the brain so that its ventral surface is uppermost.

1.   Look for the clublike olfactory bulbs anteriorly, on the inferior surface of the frontal lobes of the cerebral hemispheres. Axons of olfactory neurons run from the nasal mucosa through the perforated cribriform plate of the ethmoid bone to synapse with the olfactory bulbs.

How does the size of these olfactory bulbs compare with those of humans?

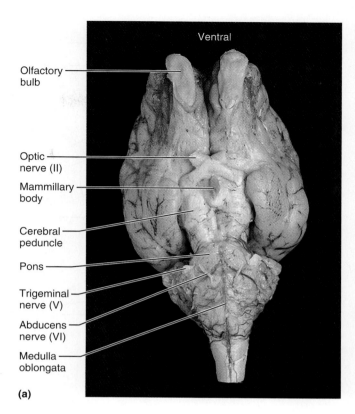

Ventral

Olfactory
bulb

Optic
nerve (II)

Mammillary
body

Cerebral
peduncle

Pons

Trigeminal
nerve (V)

Abducens
nerve (VI)

Medulla
oblongata

(a)

FIGURE 16.11 Intact sheep brain. (a) Photograph of ventral view.

Is the sense of smell more important as a protective and a food-getting sense in sheep or in humans?

2.   The optic nerve (II) carries sensory impulses from the retina of the eye. Thus this cranial nerve is involved in the sense of vision. Identify the optic nerves, optic chiasma, and optic tracts.

3.   Posterior to the optic chiasma, two structures protrude from the ventral aspect of the hypothalamus—the infundibulum (stalk of the pituitary gland) immediately posterior to the optic chiasma and the mammillary body. Notice that the sheep's mammillary body is a single rounded eminence. In humans it is a double structure.

4.   Identify the cerebral peduncles on the ventral aspect of the midbrain, just posterior to the mammillary body of the hypothalamus. The cerebral peduncles are fiber tracts connecting the cerebrum and medulla oblongata. Identify the large oculomotor nerves (III), which arise from the ventral midbrain surface, and the tiny trochlear nerves (IV), which can be seen at the junction of the midbrain and pons. Both of these cranial nerves provide motor fibers to extrinsic muscles of the eyeball.

5.   Move posteriorly from the midbrain to identify first the pons and then the medulla oblongata, both hindbrain structures composed primarily of ascending and descending fiber tracts.

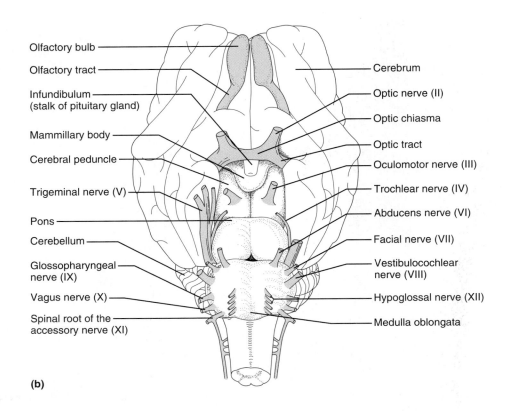

(b)

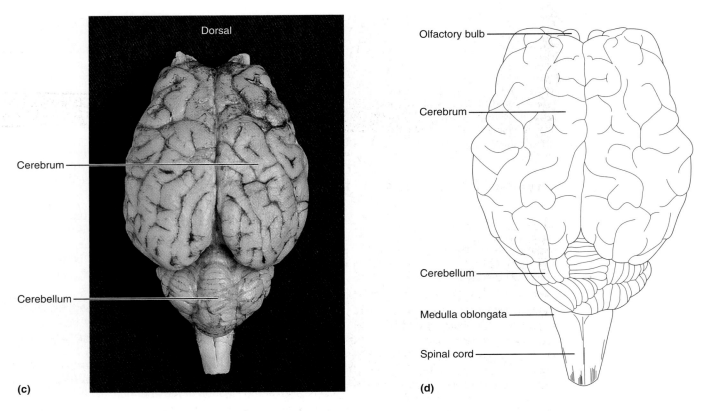

(c)

(d)

FIGURE 16.11 (*continued*) **Intact sheep brain.** (**b**) Diagrammatic ventral view. (**c**) Photograph of dorsal view. (**d**) Diagrammatic dorsal view.

6. Return to the junction of the pons and midbrain, and proceed posteriorly to identify the following cranial nerves, all arising from the pons (Figure 16.11b):

- Trigeminal nerves (V), which are involved in chewing and sensations of the head and face.

- Abducens nerves (VI), which abduct the eye (and thus work in conjunction with cranial nerves III and IV).

- Facial nerves (VII), large nerves involved in taste sensation, gland function (salivary and lacrimal glands), and facial expression.

7. Continue posteriorly to identify:

- Vestibulocochlear nerves (VIII), purely sensory nerves that are involved with hearing and equilibrium.

- Glossopharyngeal nerves (IX), which contain motor fibers innervating throat structures and sensory fibers transmitting taste stimuli (in conjunction with cranial nerve VII).

- Vagus nerves (X), often called "wanderers," which serve many organs of the head, thorax, and abdominal cavity.

- Accessory nerves (XI), which serve muscles of the neck, larynx, and shoulder; notice that the accessory nerves arise from both the medulla and the spinal cord.

- Hypoglossal nerves (XII), which stimulate tongue and neck muscles.

It is likely that some of the cranial nerves will have been broken off during brain removal. If so, observe sheep brains of other students to identify those missing from your specimen.

Dorsal Structures

1. Refer to Figure 16.11c and d as a guide in identifying the following structures. Reidentify the now exposed cerebral hemispheres. How does the depth of the fissures in the sheep's cerebral hemispheres compare to that in the human brain?

_____

2. Examine the cerebellum. Notice that, in contrast to the human cerebellum, it is not divided longitudinally, and that its fissures are oriented differently. What dural falx (falx cerebri or falx cerebelli) is missing that is present in humans?

_____

3. Locate the three pairs of cerebellar peduncles, fiber tracts that connect the cerebellum to other brain structures, by lifting the cerebellum dorsally away from the brain stem. The most posterior pair, the inferior cerebellar peduncles, connect the cerebellum to the medulla. The middle cerebellar peduncles attach the cerebellum to the pons, and the superior cerebellar peduncles run from the cerebellum to the midbrain.

4. To expose the dorsal surface of the midbrain, gently separate the cerebrum and cerebellum, as shown in Figure 16.12. Identify the corpora quadrigemina, which appear as four rounded prominences on the dorsal midbrain surface.

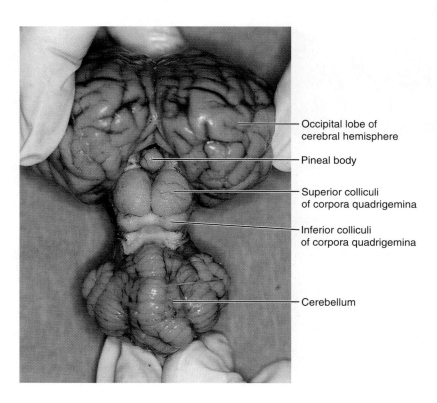

Occipital lobe of cerebral hemisphere

Pineal body

Superior colliculi of corpora quadrigemina

Inferior colliculi of corpora quadrigemina

Cerebellum

FIGURE 16.12 Means of exposing the dorsal midbrain structures of the sheep brain.

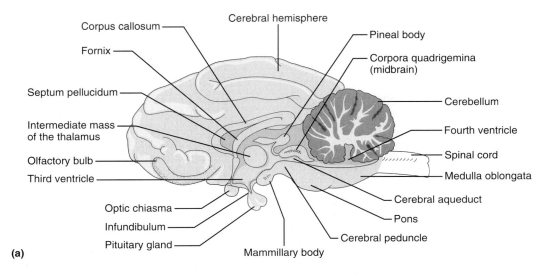

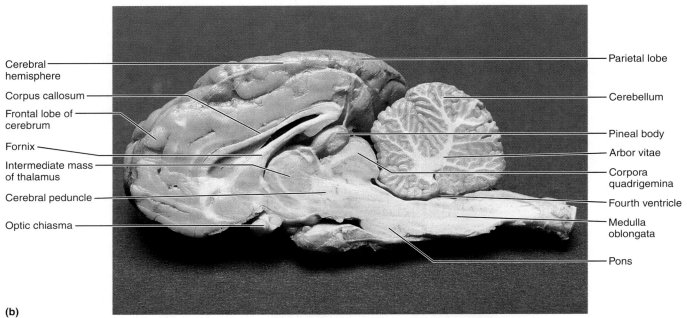

FIGURE 16.13 Sagittal section of the sheep brain showing internal structures. (a) Diagrammatic view. **(b)** Photograph.

What is the function of the corpora quadrigemina?

_____

_____

Also locate the pineal body, which appears as a small oval protrusion in the midline just anterior to the corpora quadrigemina.

Internal Structures

1.   The internal structure of the brain can only be examined after further dissection. Place the brain ventral side down on the dissecting tray and make a cut completely through it in a superior to inferior direction. Cut through the longitudinal

fissure, corpus callosum, and midline of the cerebellum. Refer to Figure 16.13 as you work.

2.   The thin nervous tissue membrane immediately ventral to the corpus callosum that separates the lateral ventricles is the septum pellucidum. Pierce this membrane and probe the lateral ventricle cavity. The fiber tract ventral to the septum pellucidum and anterior to the third ventricle is the fornix.

How does the relative size of the fornix in this brain compare with the human fornix?

_____

_____

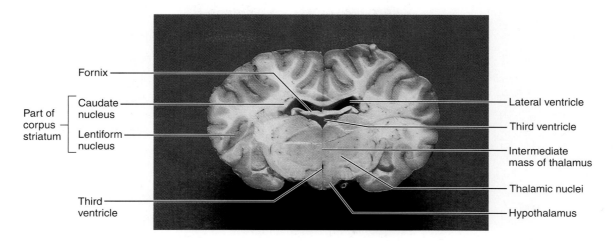

Fornix

Part of corpus striatum
- Caudate nucleus
- Lentiform nucleus

Third ventricle

Lateral ventricle

Third ventricle

Intermediate mass of thalamus

Thalamic nuclei

Hypothalamus

FIGURE 16.14 Frontal section of a sheep brain. Major structures revealed are the location of major basal ganglia in the interior, the thalamus, hypothalamus, and lateral and third ventricles.

Why do you suppose this is so? (Hint: What is the function of this band of fibers?)

_____

_____

3. Identify the thalamus, which forms the walls of the third ventricle and is located posterior and ventral to the fornix. The intermediate mass spanning the ventricular cavity appears as an oval protrusion of the thalamic wall. Anterior to the intermediate mass, locate the interventricular foramen, a canal connecting the lateral ventricle on the same side with the third ventricle.

4. The hypothalamus forms the floor of the third ventricle. Identify the optic chiasma, infundibulum, and mammillary body on its exterior surface. You can see the pineal body at the superoposterior end of the third ventricle, just beneath the junction of the corpus callosum and fornix.

5. Locate the midbrain by identifying the corpora quadrigemina that form its dorsal roof. Follow the cerebral aqueduct (the narrow canal connecting the third and fourth ventricles) through the midbrain tissue to the fourth ventricle. Identify the cerebral peduncles, which form its anterior walls.

6. Identify the pons and medulla oblongata, which lie anterior to the fourth ventricle. The medulla continues into the spinal cord without any obvious anatomical change, but the point at which the fourth ventricle narrows to a small canal is generally accepted as the beginning of the spinal cord.

7. Identify the cerebellum posterior to the fourth ventricle. Notice its internal treelike arrangement of white matter, the arbor vitae.

8. If time allows, obtain another sheep brain and section it along the frontal plane so that the cut passes through the infundibulum. Compare your specimen to the photograph in Figure 16.14, and attempt to identify all the structures shown in the figure.

9. Check with your instructor to determine if cow spinal cord sections (preserved) are available for the spinal cord studies in Exercise 17. If not, save the small portion of the spinal cord from your brain specimen. Otherwise, dispose of all the organic debris in the appropriate laboratory containers and clean the laboratory bench, the dissection instruments, and the tray before leaving the laboratory. ▬

NAME _____

LAB TIME/DATE _____

Gross Anatomy of the Brain and Cranial Nerves

The Human Brain

1. Match the letters on the diagram of the human brain (right lateral view) to the appropriate terms listed at the left.

_____ 1. frontal lobe

_____ 2. parietal lobe

_____ 3. temporal lobe

_____ 4. precentral gyrus

_____ 5. parieto-occipital sulcus

_____ 6. postcentral gyrus

_____ 7. lateral sulcus _____ 10. medulla

_____ 8. central sulcus _____ 11. occipital lobe

_____ 9. cerebellum _____ 12. pons

2. In which of the cerebral lobes would the following functional areas be found?

auditory area: _____ olfactory area: _____

primary motor area: _____ visual area: _____

primary somatosensory area: _____ Broca's area: _____

3. Which of the following structures are not part of the brain stem? (Circle the appropriate response or responses.)

cerebral hemispheres pons midbrain cerebellum medulla diencephalon

4. Complete the following statements by writing the proper word or phrase on the corresponding blanks at the right.

    A(n) __1__ is an elevated ridge of cerebral tissue. The convolutions seen in the cerebrum are important because they increase the __2__. Gray matter is composed of __3__. White matter is composed of __4__. A fiber tract that provides for communication between different parts of the same cerebral hemisphere is called a(n) __5__ tract, whereas one that carries impulses to the cerebrum from, and from the cerebrum to, lower CNS areas is called a(n) __6__ tract. The lentiform nucleus plus the caudate nucleus are collectively called the __7__.

1. _____

2. _____

3. _____

4. _____

5. _____

6. _____

7. _____

5. Identify the structures on the following sagittal view of the human brain by matching the numbered areas to the proper terms in the list.

_____ a.   cerebellum

_____ b.   cerebral aqueduct

_____ c.   cerebral hemisphere

_____ d.   cerebral peduncle

_____ e.   choroid plexus

_____ f.   corpora quadrigemina

_____ g.   corpus callosum

_____ h.   fornix

_____ i.   fourth ventricle

_____ j.   hypothalamus

_____ k.   intermediate mass   _____ n.   optic chiasma   _____ q.   pons

_____ l.   mammillary bodies   _____ o.   pineal body   _____ r.   septum pellucidum

_____ m. medulla oblongata   _____ p.   pituitary gland   _____ s.   thalamus

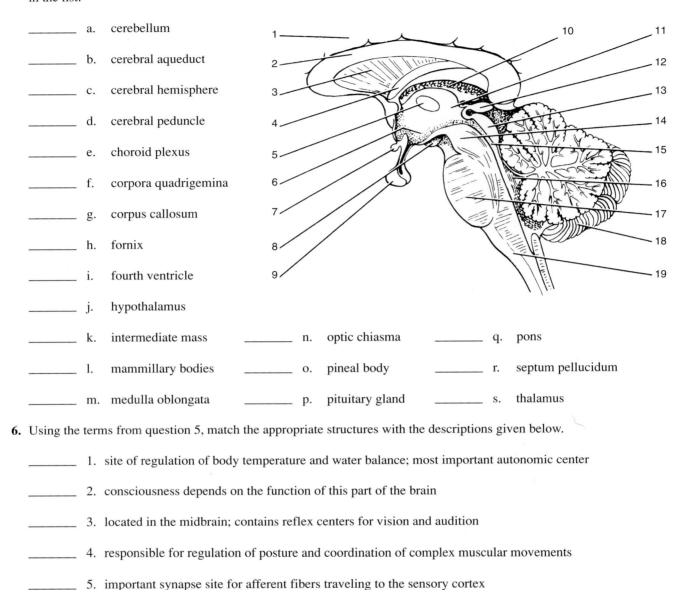

6. Using the terms from question 5, match the appropriate structures with the descriptions given below.

_____ 1.   site of regulation of body temperature and water balance; most important autonomic center

_____ 2.   consciousness depends on the function of this part of the brain

_____ 3.   located in the midbrain; contains reflex centers for vision and audition

_____ 4.   responsible for regulation of posture and coordination of complex muscular movements

_____ 5.   important synapse site for afferent fibers traveling to the sensory cortex

_____ 6.   contains autonomic centers regulating blood pressure, heart rate, and respiratory rhythm, as well as coughing, sneezing, and swallowing centers

_____ 7.   large commissure connecting the cerebral hemispheres

_____ 8.   fiber tract involved with olfaction

_____ 9.   connects the third and fourth ventricles

_____ 10. encloses the third ventricle

7. Embryologically, the brain arises from the rostral end of a tubelike structure that quickly becomes divided into three major regions. Groups of structures that develop from the embryonic brain are listed below. Designate the embryonic origin of each group as the hindbrain, midbrain, or forebrain.

_____ 1.   the diencephalon, including the thalamus, optic chiasma, and hypothalamus

_____ 2.   the medulla, pons, and cerebellum

_____ 3.   the cerebral ganglia

8. What is the function of the basal ganglia? _____

_____

9. What is the corpus striatum, and how is it related to the fibers of the internal capsule? _____

_____

_____

10. A brain hemorrhage within the region of the right internal capsule results in paralysis of the left side of the body.

   Explain why the left side (rather than the right side) is affected. _____

_____

11. Explain why trauma to the base of the brain is often much more dangerous than trauma to the frontal lobes. (Hint: Think about the relative functioning of the cerebral hemispheres and the brain stem structures. Which contain centers more vital to life?)

_____

_____

_____

12. In "split brain" experiments, the main commissure connecting the cerebral hemispheres is cut. Name this commissure.

_____

Meninges of the Brain

13. Identify the meningeal (or associated) structures described below:

_____ 1. outermost meninx covering the brain; composed of tough fibrous connective tissue

_____ 2. innermost meninx covering the brain; delicate and highly vascular

_____ 3. structures instrumental in returning cerebrospinal fluid to the venous blood in the dural sinuses

_____ 4. structure that forms the cerebrospinal fluid

_____ 5. middle meninx; like a cobweb in structure

_____ 6. its outer layer forms the periosteum of the skull

_____ 7. a dural fold that attaches the cerebrum to the crista galli of the skull

_____ 8. a dural fold separating the cerebrum from the cerebellum

Cerebrospinal Fluid

14. Fill in the following flowchart by delineating the circulation of cerebrospinal fluid from its formation site (assume that this is one of the lateral ventricles) to the site of its reabsorption into the venous blood:

Lateral ventricle   ⟶ _____ ⟶ Third ventricle ⟶

_____ ⟶ _____ ⟵ _____

_____ ⟶ _____ ⟶ _____
(surrounding the   (containing
brain and spinal cord)   venous blood)

Now label appropriately the structures involved with circulation of cerebrospinal fluid on the accompanying diagram. (These structures are indicated by leader lines.) Then, add arrows to the figure to indicate the flow of cerebrospinal fluid from its formation in the lateral ventricles to the site of its exit from the fourth ventricle.

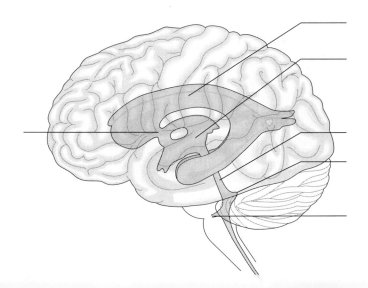

Cranial Nerves

15. Using the terms below, correctly identify all structures indicated by leader lines on the diagram.

a. abducens nerve (VI)

b. accessory nerve (XI)

c. cerebellum

d. cerebral peduncle

e. decussation of the pyramids

f. facial nerve (VII)

g. frontal lobe of cerebral hemisphere

h. glossopharyngeal nerve (IX)

i. hypoglossal nerve (XII)

j. longitudinal fissure

k. mammillary body

l. medulla oblongata

m. oculomotor nerve (III)

n. olfactory bulb

o. olfactory tract

p. optic chiasma

q. optic nerve (II)

r. optic tract

s. pituitary gland

t. pons

u. spinal cord

v. temporal lobe of cerebral hemisphere

w. trigeminal nerve (V)

x. trochlear nerve (IV)

y. vagus nerve (X)

z. vestibulocochlear nerve (VIII)

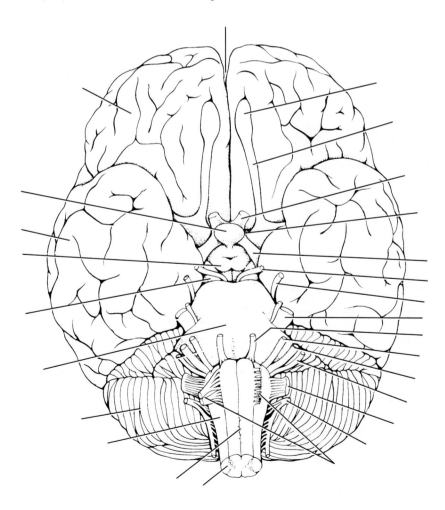

16. Provide the name and number of the cranial nerves involved in each of the following activities, sensations, or disorders.

_____ 1. rotating the head

_____ 2. smelling a flower

_____ 3. raising the eyelids; focusing the lens of the eye for accommodation; and constricting the pupils of the eye

_____ 4. slowing the heart; increasing the motility of the digestive tract

_____ 5. involved in Bell's palsy (facial paralysis)

_____ 6. chewing food

_____ 7. listening to music; seasickness

_____ 8. secreting saliva; tasting well-seasoned food

_____ 9. involved in "rolling" the eyes (three nerves—provide numbers only)

_____ 10. feeling a toothache

_____ 11. reading the newspaper

_____ 12. exclusively or primarily sensory in function (three nerves—provide
numbers only)

Dissection of the Sheep Brain

17. Describe the firmness and texture of the sheep brain tissue as observed when cutting into it.

_____ Because formalin hardens all tissue, what conclusions might you

draw about the firmness and texture of living brain tissue? _____

18. When comparing human and sheep brains, you observe some profound differences between them. Record your observations
in the chart below.

Structure	Human	Sheep
Olfactory bulb		
Pons-medulla relationship		
Location of cranial nerve III		
Mammillary body		
Corpus callosum		
Intermediate mass of thalamus		
Relative size of superior and inferior colliculi		
Pineal gland		

Spinal Cord, Spinal Nerves, and the Autonomic Nervous System

MATERIALS

☐ Spinal cord model (cross section)
☐ Three-dimensional laboratory charts or models of the spinal cord, spinal nerves, and sympathetic chain
☐ Red and blue pencils
☐ Preserved cow spinal cord sections with meninges and nerve roots intact (or spinal cord segment saved from the brain dissection in Exercise 16)
☐ Dissecting instruments and tray
☐ Disposable gloves
☐ Stereomicroscope
☐ Prepared slide of spinal cord (cross section)
☐ Compound microscope
☐ Animal specimen from previous dissections
☐ Embalming fluid
☐ The Human Nervous System: The Spinal Cord and Spinal Nerves videotape*

AIA See Appendix B, Exercise 17 for links to A.D.A.M.® Interactive Anatomy.

*Available to qualified adopters from Benjamin Cummings.

OBJECTIVES

1. To list two major functions of the spinal cord.
2. To define *conus medullaris, cauda equina,* and *filum terminale.*
3. To name the meningeal coverings of the spinal cord, and to state their function.
4. To indicate two major areas where the spinal cord is enlarged, and to explain the reasons for the enlargement.
5. To identify important anatomical areas on a spinal cord model or appropriate diagram of the spinal cord, and to name the neuron type found in these areas (where applicable).
6. To locate on a diagram the fiber tracts in the spinal cord, and to state their functional importance.
7. To describe the origin, fiber composition, and distribution of the spinal nerves, differentiating between roots, the spinal nerve proper, and rami, and to discuss the result of transecting these structures.
8. To discuss the distribution of the dorsal rami and ventral rami of the spinal nerves.
9. To identify the four major nerve plexuses, the major nerves of each, and their distribution.
10. To identify the site of origin and the function of the sympathetic and parasympathetic divisions of the autonomic nervous system, and to state how the autonomic nervous system differs from the somatic nervous system.
11. To identify on a dissected animal the musculocutaneous, radial, median, and ulnar nerves of the upper limb and the femoral, saphenous, sciatic, common peroneal, and tibial nerves of the lower limb.

The cylindrical **spinal cord,** a continuation of the brain stem, is an association and communication center. It plays a major role in spinal reflex activity and provides neural pathways to and from higher nervous centers.

Anatomy of the Spinal Cord

Enclosed within the vertebral canal of the spinal column, the spinal cord extends from the foramen magnum of the skull to the first or second lumbar vertebra, where it terminates in the cone-shaped **conus medullaris** (Figure 17.1). Like the brain, the cord is cushioned and protected by meninges. The dura mater and arachnoid meningeal coverings extend beyond the conus medullaris, approximately to the level of S_2, and the **filum terminale,** a fibrous extension of the pia mater, extends even farther (into the coccygeal canal) to attach to the posterior coccyx. **Denticulate ligaments,** saw-toothed shelves of pia mater, secure the spinal cord to the bony wall of the vertebral column all along its length (see Figure 17.1c).

The fact that the meninges, filled with cerebrospinal fluid, extend well beyond the end of the spinal cord provides an excellent site for removing cerebrospinal fluid for analysis (as when bacterial or viral infections of the spinal

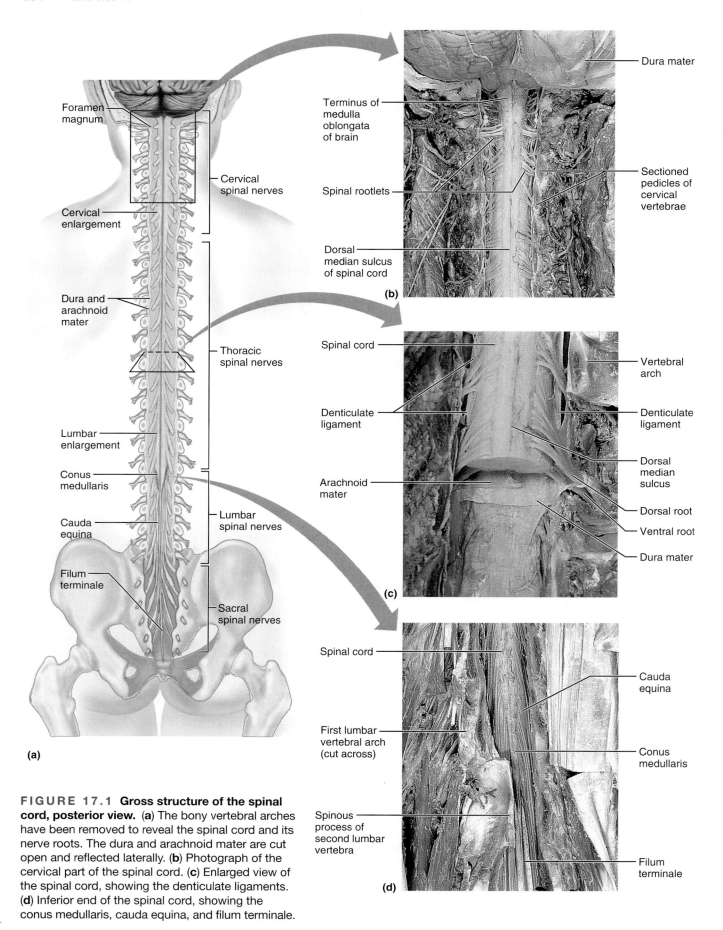

FIGURE 17.1 Gross structure of the spinal cord, posterior view. (a) The bony vertebral arches have been removed to reveal the spinal cord and its nerve roots. The dura and arachnoid mater are cut open and reflected laterally. (b) Photograph of the cervical part of the spinal cord. (c) Enlarged view of the spinal cord, showing the denticulate ligaments. (d) Inferior end of the spinal cord, showing the conus medullaris, cauda equina, and filum terminale.

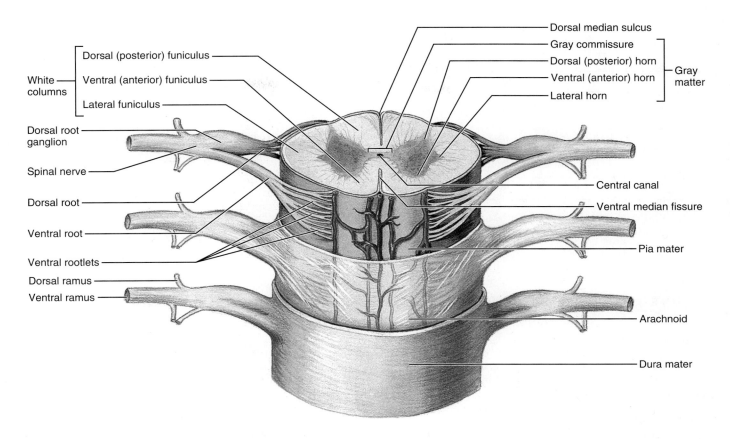

FIGURE 17.2 **Anatomy of the human spinal cord (three-dimensional view).**

cord or the meninges are suspected) without endangering the delicate spinal cord. This procedure, called a *lumbar tap,* is usually performed below L$_3$. Additionally, "saddle block," or caudal anesthesia for childbirth, is normally administered (injected) between L$_3$ and L$_5$.

In humans, 31 pairs of spinal nerves arise from the spinal cord and pass through intervertebral foramina to serve the body area at their approximate level of emergence. The cord is about the size of a finger in circumference for most of its length, but there are obvious enlargements in the cervical and lumbar areas where the nerves serving the upper and lower limbs issue from the cord.

Because the spinal cord does not extend to the end of the vertebral column, the spinal nerves emerging from the inferior end of the cord must travel through the vertebral canal for some distance before exiting at the appropriate intervertebral foramina. This collection of spinal nerves traversing the inferior end of the vertebral canal is called the **cauda equina** (Figure 17.1a and d) because of its similarity to a horse's tail (the literal translation of *cauda equina*).

ACTIVITY 1

Identifying Structures of the Spinal Cord

Obtain a three-dimensional model or laboratory chart of a cross section of a spinal cord and identify its structures as they are described next. ▪

Gray Matter

In cross section, the **gray matter** of the spinal cord looks like a butterfly or the letter H (Figure 17.2). The two posterior projections are called the **dorsal,** or **posterior, horns.** The two anterior projections are the **ventral,** or **anterior, horns.** The tips of the ventral horns are broader and less tapered than those of the dorsal horns. In the thoracic and lumbar regions of the cord, there is also a lateral outpocketing of gray matter on each side referred to as the **lateral horn.** The central area of gray matter connecting the two vertical regions is the **gray commissure.** The gray commissure surrounds the **central canal** of the cord, which contains cerebrospinal fluid.

Neurons with dorsal functions can be localized in the gray matter. The dorsal horns contain interneurons and sensory fibers that enter the cord from the body periphery via the **dorsal root.** The cell bodies of these sensory neurons are found in an enlarged area of the dorsal root called the **dorsal root ganglion.** The ventral horns mainly contain cell bodies of motor neurons of the somatic nervous system (voluntary system), which send their axons out via the **ventral root** of the cord to enter the adjacent spinal nerve. The **spinal nerves** are formed from the fusion of the dorsal and ventral roots. The lateral horns, where present, contain nerve cell bodies of motor neurons of the autonomic nervous system (sympathetic division). Their axons also leave the cord via the ventral roots, along with those of the motor neurons of the ventral horns.

Ascending tracts   **Descending tracts**

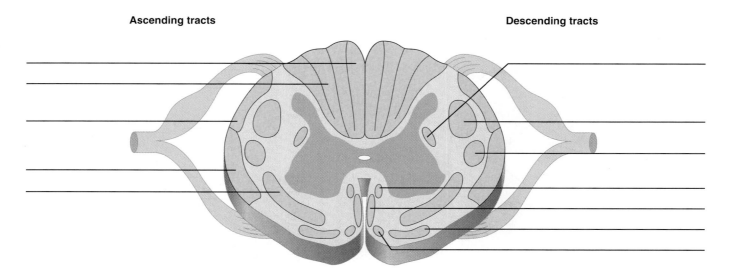

FIGURE 17.3 **Cross section of the spinal cord showing the relative positioning of its major tracts.**

White Matter

The **white matter** of the spinal cord is nearly bisected by fissures (see Figure 17.2). The more open anterior fissure is the **ventral median fissure,** and the shallow posterior one is the **dorsal median sulcus.** The white matter is composed of myelinated fibers—some running to higher centers, some traveling from the brain to the cord, and some conducting impulses from one side of the cord to the other.

Because of the irregular shape of the gray matter, the white matter on each side of the cord can be divided into three primary regions or **white columns:** the **dorsal, lateral,** and **ventral funiculi.** Each funiculus contains a number of fiber **tracts** composed of axons with the same origin, terminus, and function. Tracts conducting sensory impulses to the brain are called *ascending, or sensory, tracts;* those carrying impulses from the brain to the skeletal muscles are *descending, or motor, tracts.*

Because it serves as the transmission pathway between the brain and the body periphery, the spinal cord is an extremely important functional area. Even though it is protected by meninges and cerebrospinal fluid in the vertebral canal, it is highly vulnerable to traumatic injuries, such as might occur in an automobile accident.

When the cord is transected (or severely traumatized), both motor and sensory functions are lost in body areas normally served by that (and lower) regions of the spinal cord. Injury to certain spinal cord areas may even result in a permanent flaccid paralysis of both legs (**paraplegia**) or of all four limbs (**quadriplegia**). ●

ACTIVITY 2

Identifying Spinal Cord Tracts

With the help of your textbook, label Figure 17.3 with the tract names that follow. Each tract is represented on both sides of the cord, but for clarity, label the motor tracts on the right side of the diagram and the sensory tracts on the left side of the diagram. *Color ascending tracts blue and descending tracts red.*

Then fill in the functional importance of each tract beside its name below. As you work, try to be aware of how the naming of the tracts is related to their anatomical distribution.

Fasciculus gracilis _____

Fasciculus cuneatus _____

Dorsal spinocerebellar _____

Ventral spinocerebellar _____

Spinothalamic _____

Lateral corticospinal _____

Ventral corticospinal _____

Rubrospinal _____

Tectospinal _____

Vestibulospinal _____

Medial reticulospinal _____

Lateral reticulospinal _____ ▬

DISSECTION:
Spinal Cord

1.   Obtain a dissecting tray and instruments, disposable gloves, and a segment of preserved spinal cord (from a cow or saved from the brain specimen used in Exercise 16). Identify the tough outer meninx (dura mater) and the weblike arachnoid mater.

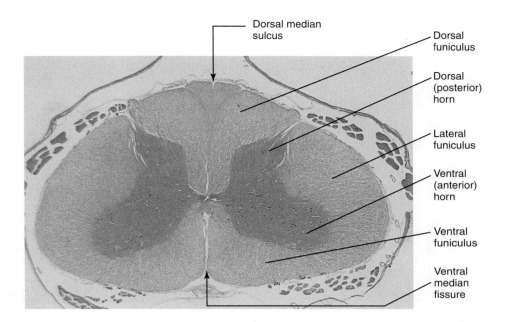

FIGURE 17.4 Cross section of the spinal cord.

What name is given to the third meninx, and where is it found?

_____

_____

Peel back the dura mater and observe the fibers making up the dorsal and ventral roots. If possible, identify a dorsal root ganglion.

2.   Cut a thin cross section of the cord and identify the ventral and dorsal horns of the gray matter with the naked eye or with the aid of a dissecting microscope.

How can you be certain that you are correctly identifying the ventral and dorsal horns?

_____

_____

Also identify the central canal, white matter, ventral median fissure, dorsal median sulcus, and dorsal, ventral, and lateral funiculi.

3.   Obtain a prepared slide of the spinal cord (cross section) and a compound microscope. Refer to Figure 17.4 as you examine the slide carefully under low power. Observe the shape of the central canal.

Is it basically circular or oval? _____

Name the glial cell type that lines this canal. _____

What would you expect to find in this canal in the living

animal? _____

Can any neuron cell bodies be seen? _____

Where? _____

_____

What type of neurons would these most likely be—motor, sensory, or interneurons?

_____ ▬

Spinal Nerves and Nerve Plexuses

The 31 pairs of human spinal nerves arise from the fusions of the ventral and dorsal roots of the spinal cord. Figure 17.5 shows how the nerves are named according to their point of issue. Because the ventral roots contain myelinated axons of motor neurons located in the cord and the dorsal roots carry sensory fibers entering the cord, all spinal nerves are **mixed nerves.** The first pair of spinal nerves leaves the vertebral canal between the base of the occiput and the atlas, but all the rest exit via the intervertebral foramina. The first through seventh pairs of cervical nerves emerge _above_ the vertebra for which they are named; C_8 emerges between C_7 and T_1. (Notice that there are seven cervical vertebrae, but eight pairs of cervical nerves.) The remaining spinal nerve pairs emerge from the spinal cord _below_ the same-numbered vertebra.

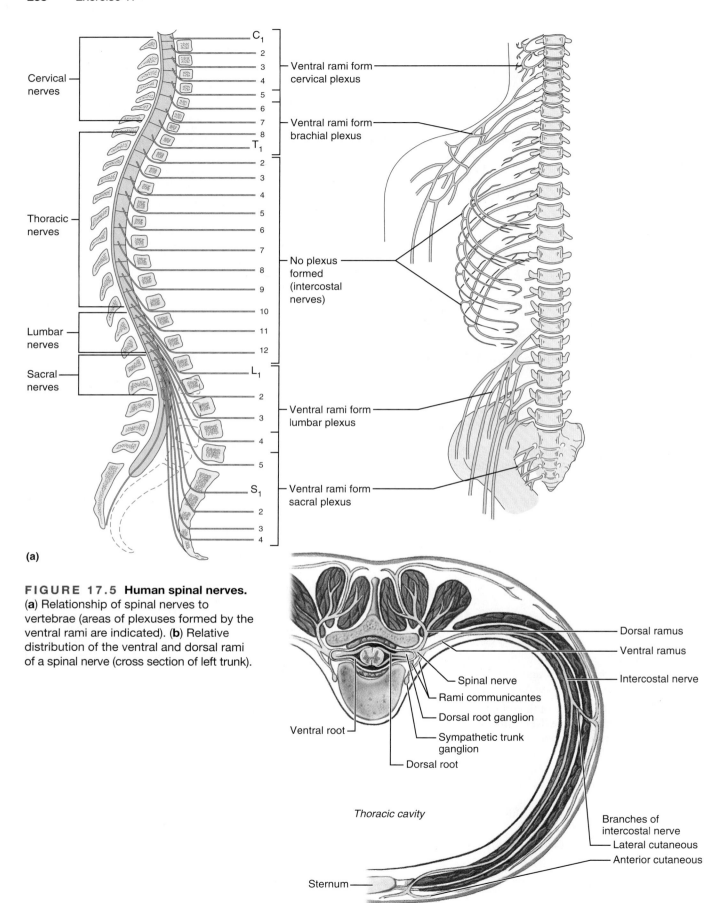

(a)

FIGURE 17.5 Human spinal nerves.
(**a**) Relationship of spinal nerves to vertebrae (areas of plexuses formed by the ventral rami are indicated). (**b**) Relative distribution of the ventral and dorsal rami of a spinal nerve (cross section of left trunk).

Cervical nerves

Thoracic nerves

Lumbar nerves

Sacral nerves

C_1
2
3
4
5
6
7
8
T_1
2
3
4
5
6
7
8
9
10
11
12
L_1
2
3
4
5
S_1
2
3
4

Ventral rami form cervical plexus

Ventral rami form brachial plexus

No plexus formed (intercostal nerves)

Ventral rami form lumbar plexus

Ventral rami form sacral plexus

Dorsal ramus
Ventral ramus
Intercostal nerve
Spinal nerve
Rami communicantes
Dorsal root ganglion
Sympathetic trunk ganglion
Ventral root
Dorsal root

Thoracic cavity

Branches of intercostal nerve
Lateral cutaneous
Anterior cutaneous

Sternum

(b)

TABLE 17.1	Branches of the Cervical Plexus (See Figure 17.6)	
Nerves	**Spinal roots (ventral rami)**	**Structures served**
Cutaneous Branches (Superficial)		
Lesser occipital	C_2 (C_3)	Skin on posterolateral aspect of neck
Greater auricular	C_2, C_3	Skin of ear, skin over parotid gland
Transverse cutaneous (cervical)	C_2, C_3	Skin on anterior and lateral aspect of neck
Supraclavicular (medial, intermediate, and lateral)	C_3, C_4	Skin of shoulder and anterior aspect of chest
Motor Branches (Deep)		
Ansa cervicalis (superior and inferior roots)	C_1–C_3	Infrahyoid muscles of neck (omohyoid, sternohyoid, and sternothyroid)
Segmental and other muscular branches	C_1–C_5	Deep muscles of neck (geniohyoid and thyrohyoid) and portions of scalenes, levator scapulae, trapezius, and sternocleidomastoid muscles
Phrenic	C_3–C_5	Diaphragm (sole motor nerve supply)

Almost immediately after emerging, each nerve divides into **dorsal** and **ventral rami.** (Thus each spinal nerve is only about 1 or 2 cm long.) The rami, like the spinal nerves, contain both motor and sensory fibers. The smaller dorsal rami serve the skin and musculature of the posterior body trunk at their approximate level of emergence. The ventral rami of spinal nerves T_2 through T_{12} pass anteriorly as the **intercostal nerves** to supply the muscles of intercostal spaces, and the skin and muscles of the anterior and lateral trunk. The ventral rami of all other spinal nerves form complex networks of nerves called **plexuses.** These plexuses serve the motor and sensory needs of the muscles and skin of the limbs. The fibers of the ventral rami unite in the plexuses (with a few rami supplying fibers to more than one plexus). From the plexuses the fibers diverge again to form peripheral nerves, each of which contains fibers from more than one spinal nerve. The four major nerve plexuses and their chief peripheral nerves are described in Tables 17.1–17.4 and illustrated in Figures 17.6–17.9. Their names and sites of origin should be committed to memory.

Cervical Plexus and the Neck

The **cervical plexus** (Figure 17.6 and Table 17.1) arises from the ventral rami of C_1 through C_5 to supply muscles of the shoulder and neck. The major motor branch of this plexus is the **phrenic nerve,** which arises from C_3 through C_4 (plus some fibers from C_5) and passes into the thoracic cavity in front of the first rib to innervate the diaphragm. The primary danger of a broken neck is that the phrenic nerve may be severed, leading to paralysis of the diaphragm and cessation of breathing. A jingle to help you remember the rami (roots) forming the phrenic nerves is "C_3, C_4, C_5 keep the diaphragm alive."

Brachial Plexus and the Upper Limb

The **brachial plexus** is large and complex, arising from the ventral rami of C_5 through C_8 and T_1 (Table 17.2). The plexus, after being rearranged consecutively into *trunks, divisions,* and *cords,* finally becomes subdivided into five major *peripheral nerves* (Figure 17.7 and Plate I of the Human Anatomy Atlas).

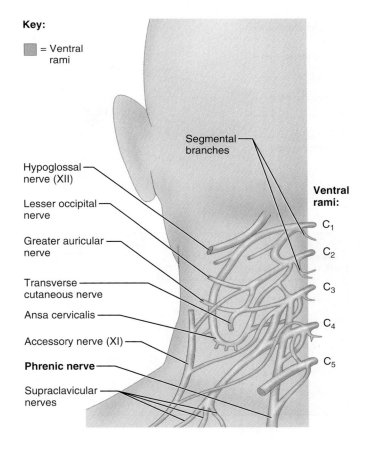

Key:

■ = Ventral rami

Hypoglossal nerve (XII)

Lesser occipital nerve

Greater auricular nerve

Transverse cutaneous nerve

Ansa cervicalis

Accessory nerve (XI)

Phrenic nerve

Supraclavicular nerves

Segmental branches

Ventral rami:

C_1
C_2
C_3
C_4
C_5

FIGURE 17.6 The cervical plexus. The nerves colored gray connect to the plexus but do not belong to it. (See Table 17.1.)

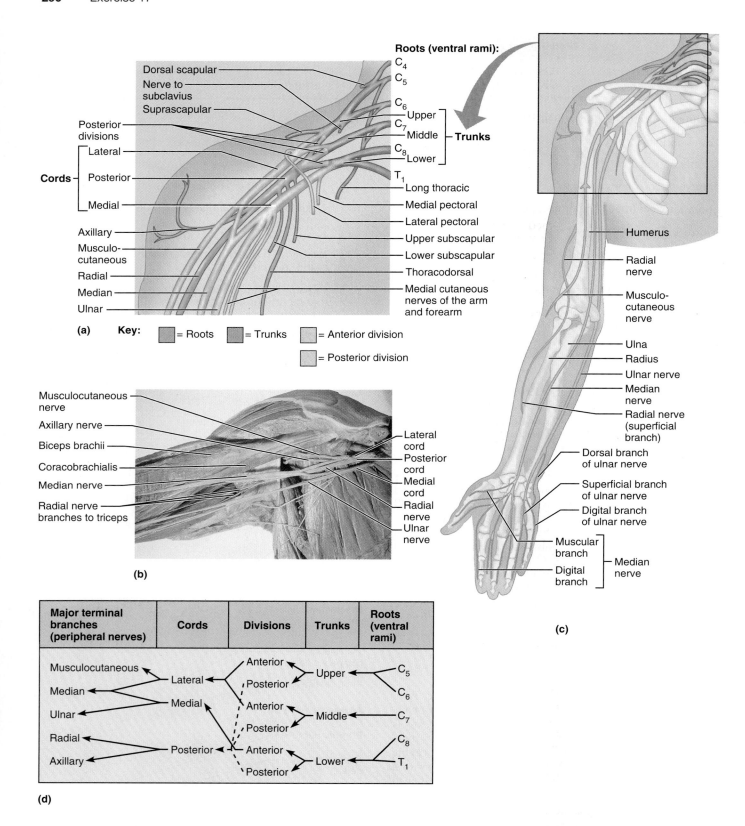

Key: ▨ = Roots ▨ = Trunks ▢ = Anterior division ▢ = Posterior division

Major terminal branches (peripheral nerves)	Cords	Divisions	Trunks	Roots (ventral rami)

FIGURE 17.7 The brachial plexus. (a and c) Distribution of the major peripheral nerves of the upper limb. **(b)** Photograph of the brachial plexus from a cadaver, anterior view. **(d)** Flowchart of consecutive branches in the brachial plexus from the major nerves formed from the cords to the spinal roots (ventral rami). (See Table 17.2. See also Plate I in the Human Anatomy Atlas.)

TABLE 17.2	Branches of the Brachial Plexus (See Figure 17.7)	
Nerves	**Cord and spinal roots (ventral rami)**	**Structures served**
Axillary	Posterior cord (C5, C6)	Muscular branches: deltoid and teres minor muscles Cutaneous branches: some skin of shoulder region
Musculocutaneous	Lateral cord (C5–C7)	Muscular branches: flexor muscles in anterior arm (biceps brachii, brachialis, coracobrachialis) Cutaneous branches: skin on anterolateral forearm (extremely variable)
Median	By two branches, one from medial cord (C8, T1) and one from the lateral cord (C5–C7)	Muscular branches to flexor group of anterior forearm (palmaris longus, flexor carpi radialis, flexor digitorum superficialis, flexor pollicis longus, lateral half of flexor digitorum profundus, and pronator muscles); intrinsic muscles of lateral palm and digital branches to the fingers Cutaneous branches: skin of lateral two-thirds of hand, palm side and dorsum of fingers 2 and 3
Ulnar	Medial cord (C8, T1)	Muscular branches: flexor muscles in anterior forearm (flexor carpi ulnaris and medial half of flexor digitorum profundus); most intrinsic muscles of hand Cutaneous branches: skin of medial third of hand, both anterior and posterior aspects
Radial	Posterior cord (C5–C8, T1)	Muscular branches: posterior muscles of arm, forearm, and hand (triceps brachii, anconeus, supinator, brachioradialis, extensors carpi radialis longus and brevis, extensor carpi ulnaris, and several muscles that extend the fingers) Cutaneous branches: skin of posterolateral surface of entire limb (except dorsum of fingers 2 and 3)
Dorsal scapular	Branches of C5 rami	Rhomboid muscles and levator scapulae
Long thoracic	Branches of C5–C7 rami	Serratus anterior muscle
Subscapular	Posterior cord; branches of C5 and C6 rami	Teres major and subscapular muscles
Suprascapular	Upper trunk (C5, C6)	Shoulder joint; supraspinatus and infraspinatus muscles
Pectoral (lateral and medial)	Branches of lateral and medial cords (C5–T1)	Pectoralis major and minor muscles

The **axillary nerve,** which serves the muscles and skin of the shoulder, has the most limited distribution. The large **radial nerve** passes down the posterolateral surface of the arm and forearm, supplying all the extensor muscles of the arm, forearm, and hand and the skin along its course. The radial nerve is often injured in the axillary region by the pressure of a crutch or by hanging one's arm over the back of a chair. The **median nerve** passes down the anteromedial surface of the arm to supply most of the flexor muscles in the forearm and several muscles in the hand (plus the skin of the lateral surface of the palm of the hand).

• Hyperextend your wrist to identify the long, obvious tendon of your palmaris longus muscle, which crosses the exact midline of the anterior wrist. Your median nerve lies immediately deep to that tendon, and the radial nerve lies just *lateral* to it.

The **musculocutaneous nerve** supplies the arm muscles that flex the forearm and the skin of the lateral surface of the

forearm. The **ulnar nerve** travels down the posteromedial surface of the arm. It courses around the medial epicondyle of the humerus to supply the flexor carpi ulnaris, the ulnar head of the flexor digitorum profundus of the forearm, and all intrinsic muscles of the hand not served by the median nerve. It supplies the skin of the medial third of the hand, both the anterior and posterior surfaces. Trauma to the ulnar nerve, which often occurs when the elbow is hit, produces a smarting sensation commonly referred to as "hitting the funny bone."

Severe injuries to the brachial plexus cause weakness or paralysis of the entire upper limb. Such injuries may occur when the upper limb is pulled hard and the plexus is stretched (as when a football tackler yanks the arm of the halfback), and by blows to the shoulder that force the humerus inferiorly (as when a cyclist is pitched headfirst off his motorcycle and grinds his shoulder into the pavement). ●

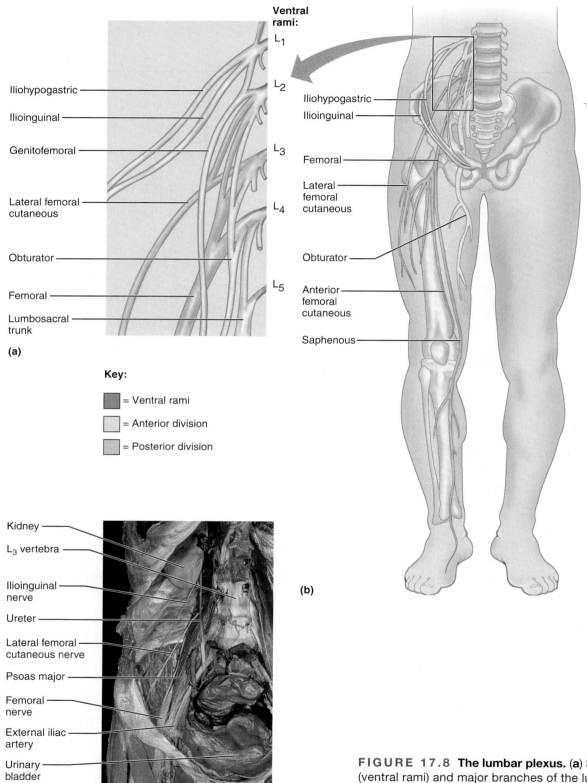

Ventral rami:

L₁

L₂

L₃

L₄

L₅

Iliohypogastric

Ilioinguinal

Genitofemoral

Lateral femoral cutaneous

Obturator

Femoral

Lumbosacral trunk

(a)

Key:

= Ventral rami

= Anterior division

= Posterior division

Iliohypogastric

Ilioinguinal

Femoral

Lateral femoral cutaneous

Obturator

Anterior femoral cutaneous

Saphenous

(b)

Kidney

L₃ vertebra

Ilioinguinal nerve

Ureter

Lateral femoral cutaneous nerve

Psoas major

Femoral nerve

External iliac artery

Urinary bladder

Femoral artery

(c)

FIGURE 17.8 The lumbar plexus. (a) Spinal roots (ventral rami) and major branches of the lumbar plexus. **(b)** Distribution of the major peripheral nerves of the lumbar plexus in the lower limb. (See Table 17.3. See also Plate K in the Human Anatomy Atlas.) **(c)** Photograph of the lumbar plexus from a cadaver, anterior view.

the axons of the somatic motor neurons), enter the spinal nerve, and then travel briefly in the ventral ramus (Figure 17.11). From the ventral ramus, they pass through a small branch called the **white ramus communicans** to enter a **sympathetic trunk ganglion** in the **sympathetic trunk,** or **chain.** These trunks lie alongside the vertebral column, so the ganglia are also called *paravertebral ganglia.*

Having reached the ganglion, a preganglionic axon may take one of three main courses (see Figure 17.11). First, it may synapse with a ganglionic neuron in the sympathetic trunk at that level. Second, the axon may travel upward or downward through the sympathetic chain to synapse with a ganglionic neuron in a sympathetic trunk ganglion at another level. In either of these two instances, the postganglionic axons then reenter the spinal nerve via a **gray ramus communicans** and travel in branches of a dorsal or ventral ramus to innervate skin structures (sweat glands, arrector pili muscles attached to hair follicles, and the smooth muscles of blood vessel walls). Third, the axon may pass through the ganglion without synapsing and form part of the **splanchnic nerves,** which travel to the viscera to synapse with a ganglionic neuron in a **collateral,** or **prevertebral, ganglion.** The major collateral ganglia—the *celiac, superior mesenteric, inferior mesenteric,* and *inferior hypogastric ganglia*—supply the abdominal and pelvic visceral organs. The postganglionic axon then leaves the ganglion and travels to a nearby visceral organ which it innervates.

> **ACTIVITY 4**
>
> ## Locating the Sympathetic Chain
>
> Locate the sympathetic chain on the spinal nerve chart. ▬

Autonomic Functioning

As noted earlier, most body organs served by the autonomic nervous system receive fibers from both the sympathetic and parasympathetic divisions. The only exceptions are the structures of the skin (sweat glands and arrector pili muscles attached to the hair follicles), the adrenal medulla, and essentially all blood vessels except those of the external genitalia, all of which receive sympathetic innervation only. When both divisions serve an organ, they have antagonistic effects. This is because their postganglionic axons release different neurotransmitters. The parasympathetic fibers, called **cholinergic fibers,** release acetylcholine; the sympathetic postganglionic fibers, called **adrenergic fibers,** release norepinephrine. (However, there are isolated examples of postganglionic sympathetic fibers, such as those serving blood vessels in the skeletal muscles, that release acetylcholine.) The preganglionic fibers of both divisions release acetylcholine.

The parasympathetic division is often referred to as the housekeeping, or "rest-and-digest," system because it maintains the visceral organs in a state most suitable for normal functions and internal homeostasis; that is, it promotes normal digestion and elimination. In contrast, activation of the sympathetic division is referred to as the "fight-or-flight" response because it readies the body to cope with situations that threaten homeostasis. Under such emergency conditions, the sympathetic nervous system induces an increase in heart rate and blood pressure, dilates the bronchioles of the lungs, increases blood sugar levels, and promotes many other effects that help the individual cope with a stressor.

As we grow older, our sympathetic nervous system gradually becomes less and less efficient, particularly in causing vasoconstriction of blood vessels. When elderly people stand up quickly after sitting or lying down, they often become light-headed or faint. This is because the sympathetic nervous system is not able to react quickly enough to counteract the pull of gravity by activating the vasoconstrictor fibers. So, blood pools in the feet. This condition, **orthostatic hypotension,** is a type of low blood pressure resulting from changes in body position as described. Orthostatic hypotension can be prevented to some degree if *slow* changes in position are made. This gives the sympathetic nervous system a little more time to react and adjust. ●

Organ or function	Parasympathetic effect	Sympathetic effect
Heart		
Bronchioles of lungs		
Digestive tract activity		
Urinary bladder		
Iris of the eye		
Blood vessels (most)		
Penis/clitoris		
Sweat glands		
Adrenal medulla		
Pancreas		

ACTIVITY 5

Comparing Sympathetic and Parasympathetic Effects

Several body organs are listed in the chart above. Using your textbook as a reference, list the effect of the sympathetic and parasympathetic divisions on each. ■■

 **DISSECTION AND IDENTIFICATION:**

Cat Spinal Nerves

The cat has 38 or 39 pairs of spinal nerves (as compared to 31 in humans). Of these, 8 are cervical, 13 thoracic, 7 lumbar, 3 sacral, and 7 or 8 caudal.

A complete dissection of the cat's spinal nerves would be extraordinarily time-consuming and exacting, and is not warranted in a basic anatomy course. However, it is desirable for you to have some dissection work to complement your study of the anatomical charts. Thus at this point you will carry out a partial dissection of the brachial plexus and lumbosacral plexus and identify some of the major nerves. ■■

ACTIVITY 6

Dissecting Nerves of the Brachial Plexus

1.   Don disposable gloves. Place your cat specimen on the dissecting tray, dorsal side down. Reflect the cut ends of the left pectoralis muscles to expose the large brachial plexus in the axillary region (Figure 17.12). Carefully clean the exposed nerves as far back toward their points of origin as possible.

2.   The **musculocutaneous nerve** is the most superior nerve of this group. It splits into two subdivisions that run under the margins of the coracobrachialis and biceps brachii muscles. Trace its fibers into the ventral muscles of the arm it serves.

3.   Locate the large **radial nerve** inferior to the musculocutaneous nerve. The radial nerve serves the dorsal muscles of the arm and forearm. Follow it into the three heads of the triceps brachii muscle.

4.   In the cat, the **median nerve** is closely associated with the brachial artery and vein. It courses through the arm to supply the ventral muscles of the forearm (with the exception of the flexor carpi ulnaris and the ulnar head of the flexor digitorum profundus). It also innervates some of the intrinsic hand muscles, as in humans.

5.   The **ulnar nerve** is the most posterior of the large brachial plexus nerves. Follow it as it travels down the forelimb, passing over the medial epicondyle of the humerus, to supply the flexor carpi ulnaris and the ulnar head of the flexor digitorum profundus (and the hand muscles). ■■

ACTIVITY 7

Dissecting Nerves of the Lumbosacral Plexus

1.   To locate the **femoral nerve** arising from the lumbar plexus, first identify the right *femoral triangle*, which is bordered by the sartorius and adductor muscles of the anterior

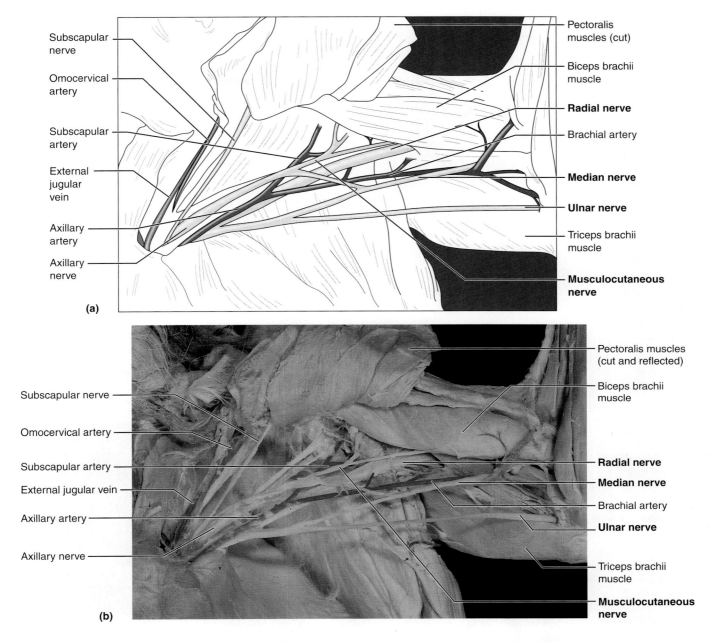

Subscapular nerve

Omocervical artery

Subscapular artery

External jugular vein

Axillary artery

Axillary nerve

(a)

Pectoralis muscles (cut)

Biceps brachii muscle

Radial nerve

Brachial artery

Median nerve

Ulnar nerve

Triceps brachii muscle

Musculocutaneous nerve

Subscapular nerve

Omocervical artery

Subscapular artery

External jugular vein

Axillary artery

Axillary nerve

(b)

Pectoralis muscles (cut and reflected)

Biceps brachii muscle

Radial nerve

Median nerve

Brachial artery

Ulnar nerve

Triceps brachii muscle

Musculocutaneous nerve

FIGURE 17.12 Brachial plexus and major blood vessels of the left forelimb of the cat, ventral aspect. (a) Diagrammatic view. **(b)** Photograph.

thigh (Figure 17.13). The large femoral nerve travels through this region after emerging from the psoas major muscle in close association with the femoral artery and vein. Follow the nerve into the muscles and skin of the anterior thigh, which it supplies. Notice also its cutaneous branch in the cat, the **saphenous nerve,** which continues down the anterior medial surface of the thigh (with the great saphenous artery and vein) to supply the skin of the anterior shank and foot.

2.   Turn the cat ventral side down so you can view the posterior aspect of the lower limb (Figure 17.14). Reflect the ends of the transected biceps femoris muscle to view the large cord-like sciatic nerve. The **sciatic nerve** arises from the sacral

plexus and serves the dorsal thigh muscles and all the muscles of the leg and foot. Follow the nerve as it travels down the posterior thigh lateral to the semimembranosus muscle. Note that just superior to the gastrocnemius muscle of the calf, it divides into its two major branches, which serve the leg.

3.   Identify the **tibial nerve** medially and the **common fibular (peroneal) nerve,** which curves over the lateral surface of the gastrocnemius.

4.   When you have finished making your observations, wrap the cat for storage and clean all dissecting tools and equipment according to the boxed instruction on p. 220 before leaving the laboratory.

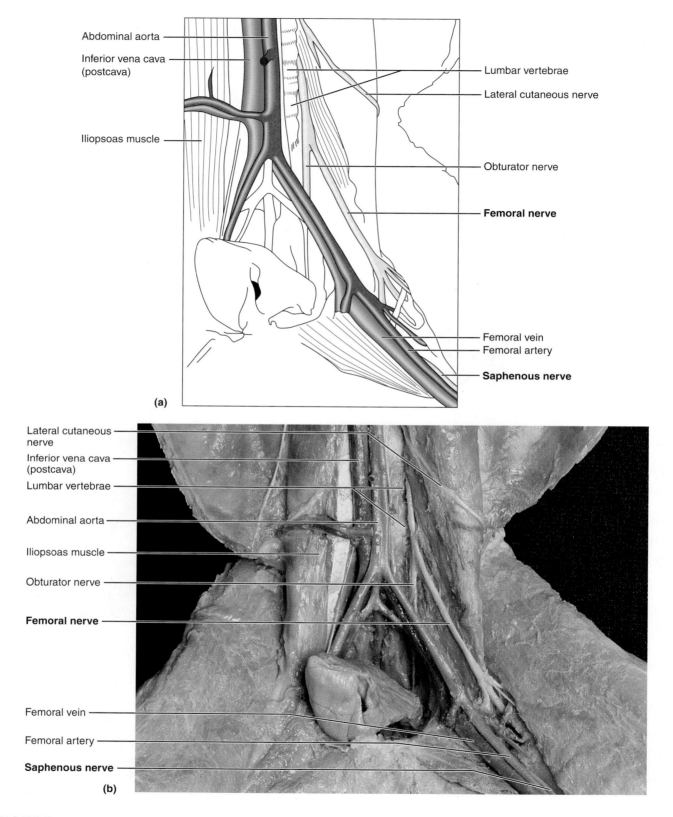

Abdominal aorta

Inferior vena cava
(postcava)

Iliopsoas muscle

Lumbar vertebrae

Lateral cutaneous nerve

Obturator nerve

Femoral nerve

Femoral vein
Femoral artery
Saphenous nerve

(a)

Lateral cutaneous
nerve

Inferior vena cava
(postcava)

Lumbar vertebrae

Abdominal aorta

Iliopsoas muscle

Obturator nerve

Femoral nerve

Femoral vein

Femoral artery

Saphenous nerve

(b)

FIGURE 17.13 Lumbar plexus of the cat, ventral aspect. (a) Diagrammatic view. **(b)** Photograph.

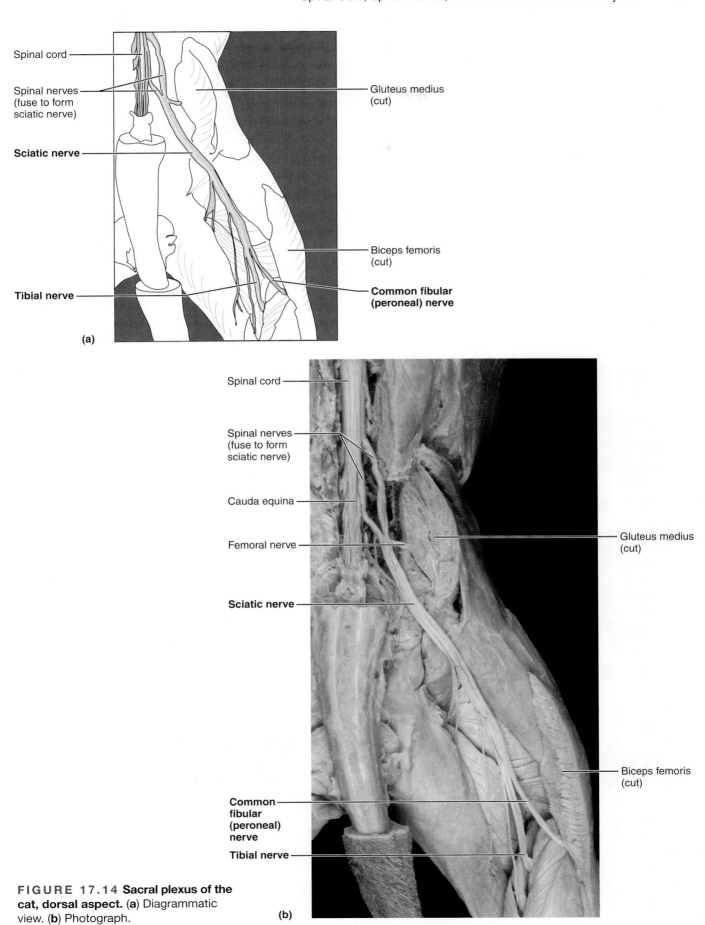

FIGURE 17.14 Sacral plexus of the cat, dorsal aspect. (a) Diagrammatic view. **(b)** Photograph.

Spinal Cord, Spinal Nerves, and the Autonomic Nervous System

Anatomy of the Spinal Cord

1. Match each description with the proper anatomical term from the key.

Key: a.   cauda equina   b.   conus medullaris   c.   filum terminale   d.   foramen magnum

_____ 1.   most superior boundary of the spinal cord

_____ 2.   meningeal extension beyond the spinal cord terminus

_____ 3.   spinal cord terminus

_____ 4.   collection of spinal nerves traveling in the vertebral canal below the terminus of the spinal cord

2. Match the letters on the diagram with the following terms.

_____ 1. arachnoid mater   _____ 6. dorsal root of spinal nerve   _____ 11. spinal nerve

_____ 2. central canal   _____ 7. dura mater   _____ 12. ventral horn

_____ 3. dorsal horn   _____ 8. gray commissure   _____ 13. ventral ramus of spinal nerve

_____ 4. dorsal ramus of spinal nerve   _____ 9. lateral horn   _____ 14. ventral root of spinal nerve

_____ 5. dorsal root ganglion   _____ 10. pia mater   _____ 15. white matter

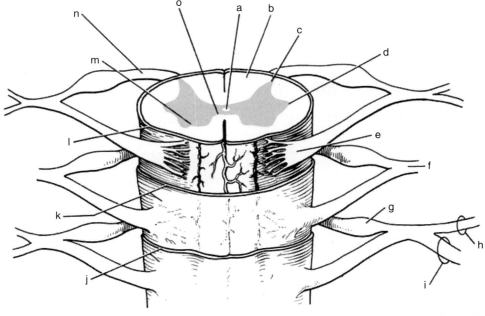

3. Choose the proper answer from the key to respond to the descriptions relating to spinal cord anatomy.

Key: a.   sensory   b.   motor   c.   both sensory and motor   d.   interneurons

_____ 1.   neuron type found in dorsal horn   _____ 4.   fiber type in ventral root

_____ 2.   neuron type found in ventral horn   _____ 5.   fiber type in dorsal root

_____ 3.   neuron type in dorsal root ganglion   _____ 6.   fiber type in spinal nerve

4. Where in the vertebral column is a lumbar puncture generally done? _____

Why is this the site of choice? _____

_____

5. The spinal cord is enlarged in two regions, the _____ and the _____ regions.

What is the significance of these enlargements? _____

_____

6. How does the position of the gray and white matter differ in the spinal cord and the cerebral hemispheres?

_____

_____

7. From the key to the right, choose the name of the tract that might be damaged when the following conditions are observed. (More than one choice may apply.)

_____ 1.   uncoordinated movement

_____ 2.   lack of voluntary movement

_____ 3.   tremors, jerky movements

_____ 4.   diminished pain perception

_____ 5.   diminished sense of touch

Key: a.   fasciculus cuneatus
b.   fasciculus gracilis
c.   lateral corticospinal tract
d.   ventral corticospinal tract
e.   tectospinal tract
f.   rubrospinal tract
g.   vestibulospinal tract
h.   lateral spinothalamic tract
i.   anterior spinothalamic tract
j.   dorsal spinocerebellar tract
k.   vental spinocerebellar tract

Dissection of the Spinal Cord

8. Compare and contrast the meninges of the spinal cord and the brain. _____

_____

9. How can you distinguish between the ventral and dorsal horns? _____

_____

Spinal Nerves and Nerve Plexuses

10. In the human, there are 31 pairs of spinal nerves, named according to the region of the vertebral column from which they issue. The spinal nerves are named below. Indicate how they are numbered.

cervical nerves _____   sacral nerves _____

lumbar nerves _____   ventral nerves _____

11. The ventral rami of spinal nerves C_1 through T_1 and T_{12} through S_4 take part in forming _____,

which serve the _____ of the body. The ventral rami of T_2 through T_{12} run

between the ribs to serve the _____. The dorsal rami of the spinal nerves

serve _____.

12. What would happen if the following structures were damaged or transected? (Use the key choices for responses.)

Key: a.   loss of motor function   b.   loss of sensory function   c.   loss of both motor and sensory function

_____ 1.   dorsal root of a spinal nerve   _____ 3.   ventral ramus of a spinal nerve

_____ 2.   ventral root of a spinal nerve

13. Define *plexus.* _____

_____

14. Name the major nerves that serve the following body areas.

_____ 1.   head, neck, shoulders (name plexus only)

_____ 2.   diaphragm

_____ 3.   posterior thigh

_____ 4.   leg and foot (name two)

_____ 5.   anterior forearm muscles (name two)

_____ 6.   arm muscles (name two)

_____ 7.   abdominal wall (name plexus only)

_____ 8.   anterior thigh

_____ 9.   medial side of the hand

The Autonomic Nervous System

15. For the most part, sympathetic and parasympathetic fibers serve the same organs and structures. How can they exert antagonistic effects? (After all, nerve impulses are nerve impulses—aren't they?)

_____

16. Name three structures that receive sympathetic but not parasympathetic innervation.

_____

17. A pelvic splanchnic nerve contains (circle one):

a. preganglionic sympathetic fibers   c. preganglionic parasympathetic fibers

b. postganglionic sympathetic fibers   d. postganglionic parasympathetic fibers

18. The following chart states a number of conditions. Use a check mark to show which division of the autonomic nervous system is involved in each.

Sympathetic division	Condition	Parasympathetic division
	Secretes norepinephrine; adrenergic fibers	
	Secretes acetylcholine; cholinergic fibers	
	Long preganglionic axon; short postganglionic axon	
	Short preganglionic axon; long postganglionic axon	
	Arises from cranial and sacral nerves	
	Arises from spinal nerves T_1 through L_3	
	Normally in control	
	"Fight-or-flight" system	
	Has more specific control (Look it up!)	

Dissection and Identification: Cat Spinal Nerves

19. From anterior to posterior, put the nerves issuing from the brachial plexus in their proper order (i.e., the median, musculocutaneous, radial, and ulnar nerves).

_____

20. Which of the nerves named above serves the cat's forearm extensor muscles? _____

Which serves the forearm flexors? _____

21. Just superior to the gastrocnemius muscle, the sciatic nerve divides into its two main branches, the _____

and _____ nerves.

22. What name is given to the cutaneous nerve of the cat's thigh? _____

Special Senses: Vision

MATERIALS

☐ Chart of eye anatomy
☐ Dissectible eye model
☐ Prepared slide of longitudinal section of an eye showing retinal layers
☐ Compound microscope
☐ Preserved cow or sheep eye
☐ Dissecting instruments and tray
☐ Disposable gloves
☐ Metric ruler; meter stick
☐ Common straight pins
☐ Snellen eye chart (floor marked with chalk to indicate 20-ft. distance from posted Snellen chart)
☐ Ishihara's color plates
☐ Two pencils
☐ Test tubes
☐ Ophthalmoscope (if available)

AIA See Appendix B, Exercise 18 for links to A.D.A.M.® Interactive Anatomy.

OBJECTIVES

1. To describe the structure and function of the accessory visual structures.
2. To identify the structural components of the eye when provided with a model, an appropriate diagram, or a preserved sheep or cow eye, and to list the function(s) of each.
3. To describe the cellular makeup of the retina.
4. To trace the visual pathway to the visual cortex, and to indicate the effects of damage to various parts of this pathway.
5. To discuss the mechanism of image formation on the retina.
6. To define the following terms:

conjunctivitis	emmetropia
cataract	myopia
glaucoma	hyperopia
refraction	astigmatism
accommodation	

7. To explain the difference between rods and cones with respect to visual perception and retinal localization.
8. To state the importance of an ophthalmoscopic examination.

Anatomy of the Eye

External Anatomy and Accessory Structures

The adult human eye is a sphere measuring about 2.5 cm (1 inch) in diameter. Only about one-sixth of the eye's anterior surface is observable (Figure 18.1); the remainder is enclosed and protected by a cushion of fat and the walls of the bony orbit.

The **lacrimal apparatus** consists of the lacrimal gland, lacrimal canaliculi, lacrimal sac, and the nasolacrimal duct. The **lacrimal glands** are situated superior to the lateral aspect of each eye. They continually liberate a dilute salt solution (tears) that flows onto the anterior surface of the eyeball through several small ducts. The tears flush across the eyeball and through the **lacrimal puncta,** the tiny openings of the **lacrimal canaliculi** medially, then into the **lacrimal sac,** and finally into the **nasolacrimal duct,** which empties into the nasal cavity. The lacrimal secretion also contains **lysozyme,** an antibacterial enzyme. Because it constantly flushes the eyeball, the lacrimal fluid cleanses and protects the eye surface as it moistens and lubricates it. As we age, our eyes tend to become dry due to decreased lacrimation, and thus are more vulnerable to bacterial invasion and irritation.

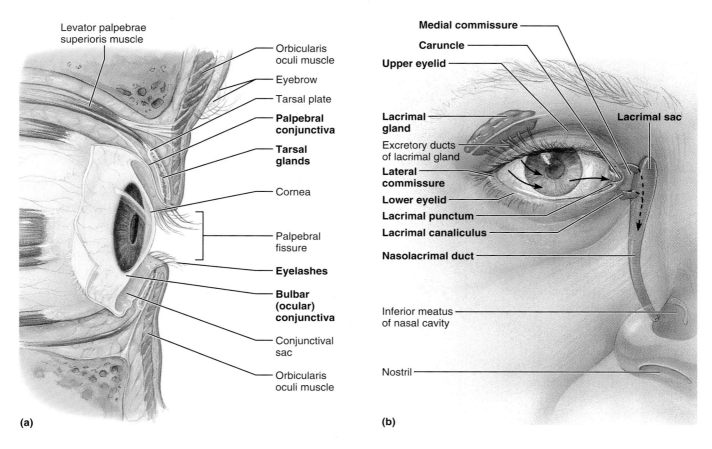

Levator palpebrae
superioris muscle

Orbicularis
oculi muscle

Eyebrow

Tarsal plate

**Palpebral
conjunctiva**

**Tarsal
glands**

Cornea

Palpebral
fissure

Eyelashes

**Bulbar
(ocular)
conjunctiva**

Conjunctival
sac

Orbicularis
oculi muscle

(a)

Medial commissure

Caruncle

Upper eyelid

Lacrimal
gland

Excretory ducts
of lacrimal gland

**Lateral
commissure**

Lower eyelid

Lacrimal punctum

Lacrimal canaliculus

Nasolacrimal duct

Inferior meatus
of nasal cavity

Nostril

Lacrimal sac

(b)

FIGURE 18.1 External anatomy of the eye and accessory structures. (a) Sagittal section.
(b) Anterior view.

The anterior surface of each eye is protected by the **eye-lids,** or **palpebrae.** (See Figure 18.1.) The medial and lateral junctions of the upper and lower eyelids are referred to as the **medial** and **lateral commissures** *(canthi),* respectively. The **caruncle,** a fleshy elevation at the medial commissure, produces a whitish oily secretion. A mucous membrane, the **conjunctiva,** lines the internal surface of the eyelids (as the *palpebral conjunctiva*) and continues over the anterior surface of the eyeball to its junction with the corneal epithelium (as the *bulbar* or *ocular conjunctiva*). The conjunctiva secretes mucus, which aids in lubricating the eyeball. Inflammation of the conjunctiva, often accompanied by redness of the eye, is called **conjunctivitis.**

Projecting from the border of each eyelid is a row of short hairs, the **eyelashes.** The **ciliary glands,** modified sweat glands, lie between the eyelash hair follicles and help lubricate the eyeball. Small sebaceous glands associated with the hair follicles and the larger **tarsal** *(Meibomian)* **glands,** located posterior to the eyelashes, secrete an oily substance. An inflammation of one of the ciliary glands or a small oil gland is called a **sty.**

Six **extrinsic eye muscles** attached to the exterior surface of each eyeball control eye movement and make it possible for the eye to follow a moving object. The names and positioning of these extrinsic muscles are noted in Figure 18.2. Their actions are given in the chart accompanying that figure.

ACTIVITY 1

Identifying Accessory Eye Structures

Using Figure 18.1 or a chart of eye anatomy, observe the eyes of another student, and identify as many of the accessory structures as possible. Ask the student to look to the left. What extrinsic eye muscles are responsible for this action?

Right eye: _____

Left eye: _____

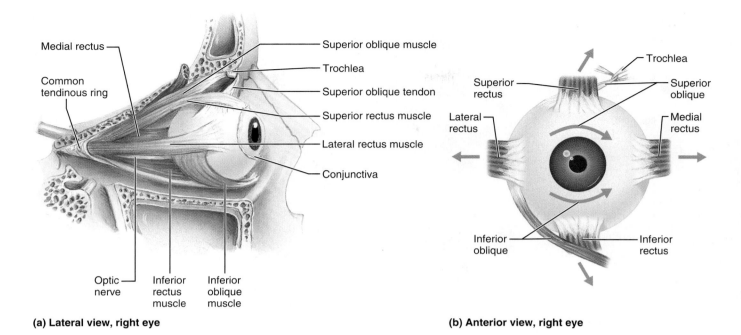

(a) Lateral view, right eye

(b) Anterior view, right eye

Name	Action	Controlling cranial nerve
Lateral rectus	Moves eye laterally	VI (abducens)
Medial rectus	Moves eye medially	III (oculomotor)
Superior rectus	Elevates eye and turns it medially	III (oculomotor)
Inferior rectus	Depresses eye and turns it medially	III (oculomotor)
Inferior oblique	Elevates eye and turns it laterally	III (oculomotor)
Superior oblique	Depresses eye and turns it laterally	IV (trochlear)

(c)

FIGURE 18.2 Extrinsic muscles of the eye. (a) Lateral view of the right eye. **(b)** Superior view of the right eye. **(c)** Summary of actions of the extrinsic eye muscles and cranial nerves that control them.

Internal Anatomy of the Eye

Anatomically, the wall of the eye is constructed of three layers (Figure 18.3). The outermost **fibrous layer** is a protective layer composed of dense avascular connective tissue. It has two obviously different regions: The opaque white **sclera** forms the bulk of the fibrous layer and is observable anteriorly as the "white of the eye." Its anteriormost portion is modified structurally to form the transparent **cornea,** through which light enters the eye.

The middle layer, called the **uvea,** is the **vascular layer.** Its posteriormost part, the **choroid,** is a blood-rich nutritive layer containing a dark pigment that prevents light scattering within the eye. Anteriorly, the choroid is modified to form the **ciliary body,** which is chiefly composed of *ciliary muscles,* important in controlling lens shape, and **ciliary processes.** The ciliary processes secrete aqueous humor. The most anterior part of the uvea is the pigmented **iris.** The iris is incomplete, resulting in a rounded opening, the **pupil,** through which light passes.

The iris is composed of circularly and radially arranged smooth muscle fibers and acts as a reflexively activated diaphragm to regulate the amount of light entering the eye. In close vision and bright light, the circular muscles of the iris contract, and the pupil constricts. In distant vision and in dim light, the radial fibers contract, enlarging (dilating) the pupil and allowing more light to enter the eye.

The innermost **sensory layer** of the eye is the delicate, two-layered **retina** (Figures 18.3 and 18.4). The outer **pigmented epithelium** abuts the choroid and extends anteriorly to cover the ciliary body and the posterior side of the iris. The transparent inner **neural layer** extends anteriorly only to the ciliary body. It contains the photoreceptors, *rods* and *cones,* which begin the chain of electrical events that ultimately result in the transduction of light energy into nerve impulses that are transmitted to the optic cortex of the brain. Vision is the result. The photoreceptor cells are distributed over the entire neural retina, except where the optic nerve leaves the eyeball. This site is called the **optic disc,** or *blind spot.* Lateral to each blind spot, and directly posterior to the lens, is an area called the **macula lutea,** "yellow

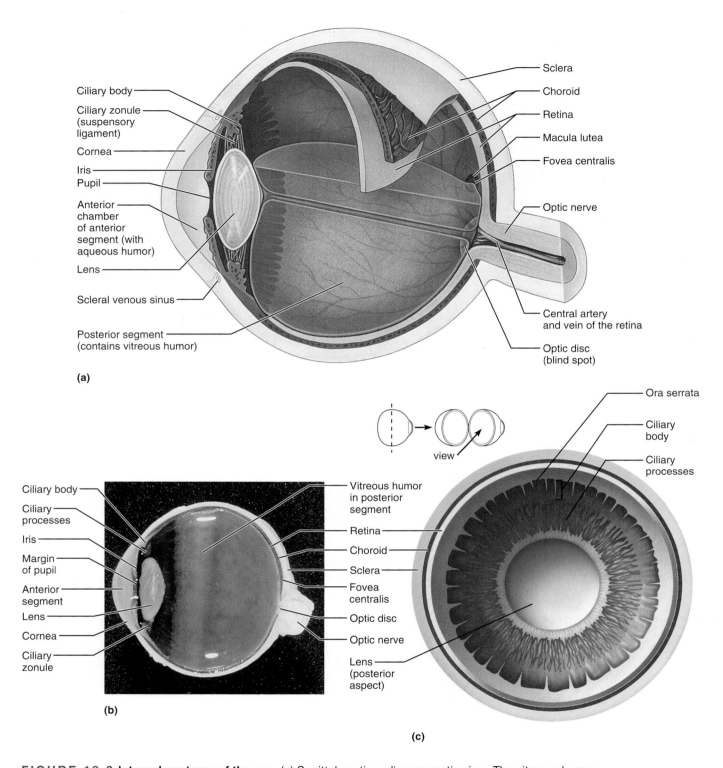

FIGURE 18.3 Internal anatomy of the eye. (a) Sagittal section, diagrammatic view. The vitreous humor is illustrated only in the bottom half of the eyeball. (b) Photograph of a sagittal section of the human eye. (c) Posterior view of anterior half of the eye.

spot," an area of high cone density. In its center is the **fovea centralis,** a minute pit about 0.4 mm in diameter, which contains mostly cones and is the area of greatest visual acuity. Focusing for discriminative vision occurs in the fovea centralis.

Light entering the eye is focused on the retina by the **lens,** a flexible crystalline structure held vertically in the eye's interior by the **suspensory ligament,** more specifically called the **ciliary zonule,** attached to the ciliary body. Activity of the ciliary muscle, which accounts for the bulk of ciliary body tissue, changes lens thickness to allow light to be properly focused on the retina.

In the elderly the lens becomes increasingly hard and opaque. **Cataracts,** which often result from this process, cause vision to become hazy or entirely obstructed. ●

The lens divides the eye into two segments: the **anterior segment** anterior to the lens, which contains a clear watery fluid called the **aqueous humor,** and the **posterior segment** behind the lens, filled with a gel-like substance, the **vitreous humor,** or **vitreous body.** The anterior segment is further divided into **anterior** and **posterior chambers,** located before and after the iris, respectively. The aqueous humor is continually formed by the capillaries of the **ciliary processes** of the ciliary body. It helps to maintain the intraocular pressure of the eye and provides nutrients for the avascular lens and cornea. The aqueous humor is reabsorbed into the **scleral venous sinus.** The vitreous humor provides the major internal reinforcement of the posterior part of the eyeball, and helps to keep the retina pressed firmly against the wall of the eyeball. It is formed *only* before birth.

Anything that interferes with drainage of the aqueous fluid increases intraocular pressure. When intraocular pressure reaches dangerously high levels, the retina and optic nerve are compressed, resulting in pain and possible blindness, a condition called **glaucoma.** ●

ACTIVITY 2

Identifying Internal Structures of the Eye

Obtain a dissectible eye model and identify its internal structures described above. As you work, also refer to Figure 18.3. ▩

Microscopic Anatomy of the Retina

As described above, the retina consists of two main types of cells: a *pigmented epithelium,* which abuts the choroid, and an inner cell layer composed of *neurons,* which is in contact with the vitreous humor (see Figure 18.4). The inner nervous layer is composed of three major neuronal populations. These are, from outer to inner aspect, the **photoreceptors** (rods and cones), the **bipolar cells,** and the **ganglion cells.**

The **rods** are the specialized receptors for dim light. Visual interpretation of their activity is in gray tones. The **cones** are color receptors that permit high levels of visual acuity, but they function only under conditions of high light intensity; thus, for example, no color vision is possible in moonlight. Mostly cones are found in the fovea centralis, and their number decreases as the retinal periphery is approached. By contrast, rods are most numerous in the periphery, and their density decreases as the macula is approached.

Light must pass through the ganglion cell layer and the bipolar neuron layer to reach and excite the rods and cones. As a result of a light stimulus, the photoreceptors undergo changes in their membrane potential that influence the bipolar neurons. These in turn stimulate the ganglion cells, whose axons leave the retina in the tight bundle of fibers known as the **optic nerve** (Figure 18.3). The retinal layer is thickest where the optic nerve attaches to the eyeball because an increasing number of ganglion cell axons converge at this point. It thins as it approaches the ciliary body. In addition to these three major cell types, the retina also contains horizontal cells and amacrine cells, which play a role in visual processing.

ACTIVITY 3

Studying the Microscopic Anatomy of the Retina

Use a compound microscope to examine a histologic slide of a longitudinal section of the eye. Identify the retinal layers by comparing your view to Figure 18.4. ▩

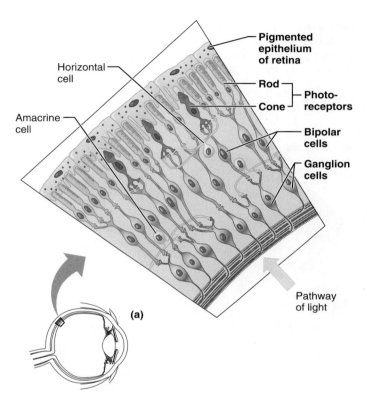

(a)

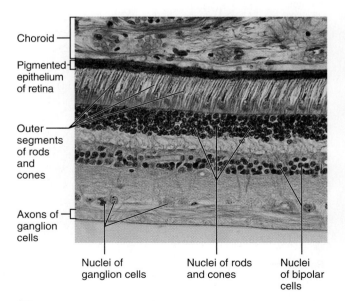

(b)

FIGURE 18.4 Microscopic anatomy of the cellular layers of the retina. (a) Diagrammatic view. **(b)** Photomicrograph of the retina (500×). (See also Plate 15 of the Histology Atlas.)

Visual Pathways to the Brain

The axons of the ganglion cells of the retina converge at the posterior aspect of the eyeball and exit from the eye as the optic nerve. At the **optic chiasma,** the fibers from the medial side of each eye cross over to the opposite side (Figure 18.5). The fiber tracts thus formed are called the **optic tracts.** Each optic tract contains fibers from the lateral side of the eye on the same side and from the medial side of the opposite eye.

The optic tract fibers synapse with neurons in the **lateral geniculate nucleus** of the thalamus, whose axons form the **optic radiation,** terminating in the **primary visual cortex** in the occipital lobe of the brain. Here they synapse with the cortical cells, and visual interpretation occurs.

ACTIVITY 4

Predicting the Effects of Visual Pathway Lesions

After examining Figure 18.5, determine what effects lesions in the following areas would have on vision:

In the right optic nerve: _____

_____

Through the optic chiasma: _____

_____

In the left optic tract: _____

_____

In the right cerebral cortex (visual area): _____

_____

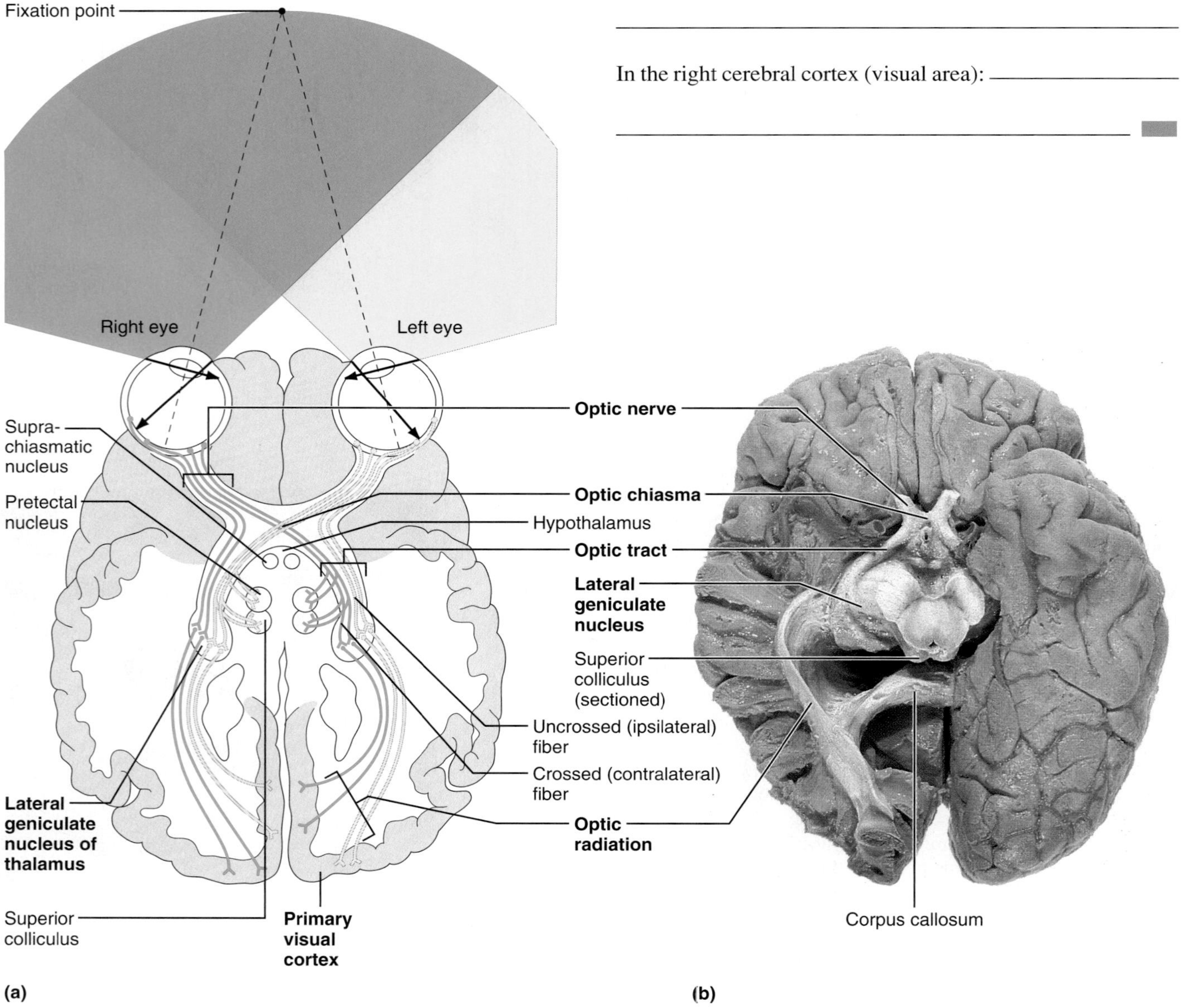

(a)

(b)

FIGURE 18.5 Inferior views of the visual pathway to the brain. (a) Diagram. (Note that fibers from the lateral portion of each retinal field do not cross at the optic chiasma.) (b) Photograph.

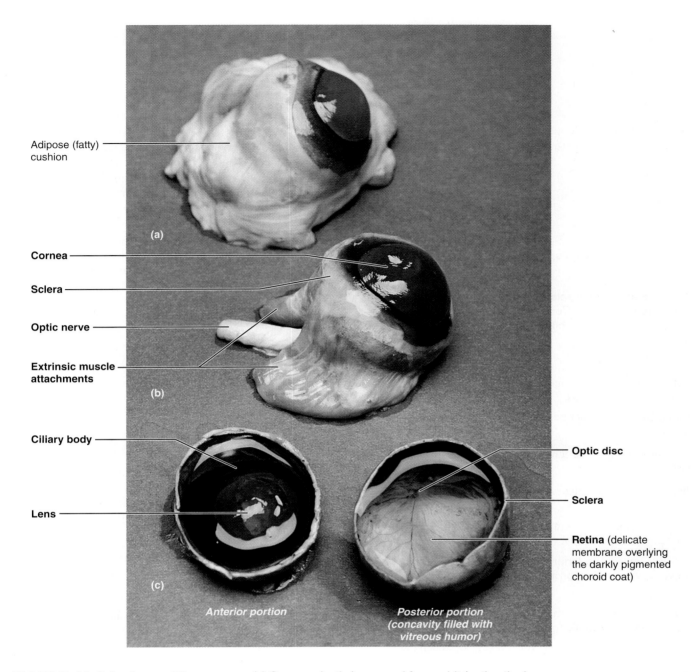

FIGURE 18.6 Anatomy of the cow eye. (a) Cow eye (entire) removed from orbit (notice the large amount of fat cushioning the eyeball). **(b)** Cow eye (entire) with fat removed to show the extrinsic muscle attachments and optic nerve. **(c)** Cow eye cut along the frontal plane to reveal internal structures.

DISSECTION:
The Cow (Sheep) Eye

1.   Obtain a preserved cow or sheep eye, dissecting instruments, and a dissecting tray. Don disposable gloves.

2.   Examine the external surface of the eye, noting the thick cushion of adipose tissue. Identify the optic nerve (cranial nerve II) as it leaves the eyeball, the remnants of the extrinsic eye muscles, the conjunctiva, the sclera, and the cornea. The normally transparent cornea is opalescent or opaque if the eye has been preserved. Refer to Figure 18.6 as you work.

3.   Trim away most of the fat and connective tissue, but leave the optic nerve intact. Holding the eye with the cornea facing downward, carefully make an incision with a sharp scalpel into the sclera about 6 mm (¼ inch) above the cornea. (The sclera of the preserved eyeball is very tough so you will have to apply substantial pressure to penetrate it.) Using scissors, complete the incision around the circumference of the eyeball paralleling the corneal edge.

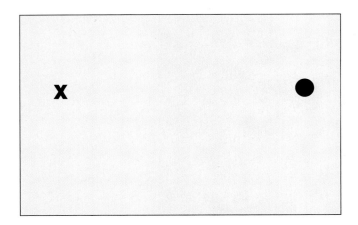

FIGURE 18.7 Blind spot test figure.

4. Carefully lift the anterior part of the eyeball away from the posterior portion. Conditions being proper, the vitreous body should remain with the posterior part of the eyeball.

5. Examine the anterior part of the eye, and identify the following structures:

Ciliary body: Black pigmented body that appears to be a halo encircling the lens.

Lens: Biconvex structure that is opaque in preserved specimens.

Carefully remove the lens and identify the adjacent structures:

Iris: Anterior continuation of the ciliary body penetrated by the pupil.

Cornea: More convex anteriormost portion of the sclera; normally transparent but cloudy in preserved specimens.

6. Examine the posterior portion of the eyeball. Carefully remove the vitreous humor, and identify the following structures:

Retina: The neural layer of the retina appears as a delicate tan, probably crumpled membrane that separates easily from the pigmented choroid.

Note its point of attachment. What is this point called?

_____

Pigmented choroid coat: Appears iridescent in the cow or sheep eye owing to a special reflecting surface called the **tapetum lucidum.** This specialized surface reflects the light within the eye and is found in the eyes of animals that live under conditions of low-intensity light. It is not found in humans. ■

Visual Tests and Experiments
The Blind Spot

ACTIVITY 5

Demonstrating the Blind Spot

1. Hold Figure 18.7 about 46 cm (18 inches) from your eyes. Close your left eye, and focus your right eye on the X, which should be positioned so that it is directly in line with your right eye. Move the figure slowly toward your face, keeping your right eye focused on the X. When the dot focuses on the blind spot, which lacks photoreceptors, it will disappear.

2. Have your laboratory partner obtain a metric ruler and record in metric units the distance at which this occurs. The dot will reappear as the figure is moved closer. Distance at which the dot disappears:

Right eye _____

Repeat the test for the left eye, this time closing the right eye and focusing the left eye on the dot. Record the distance at which the X disappears:

Left eye _____ ■

Refraction, Visual Acuity, and Astigmatism

When light rays pass from one medium to another, their velocity, or speed of transmission, changes, and the rays are bent, or **refracted.** Thus the light rays in the visual field are refracted as they encounter the cornea, lens, and aqueous and vitreous humor of the eye.

The refractive index (bending power) of the cornea and humors are constant. But the lens's refractive index can be varied by changing the lens's shape—that is, by making it more or less convex so that the light is properly converged and focused on the retina. The greater the lens convexity, or bulge, the more the light will be bent and the stronger the lens. Conversely, the less the lens convexity (the flatter it is), the less it bends the light.

In general, light from a distant source (over 6 m, or 20 feet) approaches the eye as parallel rays, and no change in lens convexity is necessary for it to focus properly on the retina. However, light from a close source tends to diverge, and the convexity of the lens must increase to make close vision possible. To achieve this, the ciliary muscle contracts, decreasing the tension on the suspensory ligament attached to the lens and allowing the elastic lens to "round up." Thus, a lens capable of bringing a *close* object into sharp focus is stronger (more convex) than a lens focusing on a more distant object. The ability of the eye to focus differentially for objects of near vision (less than 6 m, or 20 feet) is called **accommodation.** It should be noted that the image formed on the retina as a result of the refractory activity of the lens (Figure 18.8) is a **real image** (reversed from left to right, inverted, and smaller than the object).

The normal, or **emmetropic, eye** is able to accommodate properly (Figure 18.9a). However, visual problems may result from (1) lenses that are too strong or too "lazy" (over-converging and underconverging, respectively), (2) from structural problems such as an eyeball that is too long or too short to provide for proper focusing by the lens, or (3) a cornea or lens with improper curvatures.

Individuals in whom the image normally focuses in front of the retina are said to have **myopia,** or nearsightedness (Figure 18.9b); they can see close objects without difficulty, but distant objects are blurred or seen indistinctly. Correction requires a concave lens, which causes the light reaching the eye to diverge.

If the image focuses behind the retina, the individual is said to have **hyperopia,** or farsightedness. Such persons have no problems with distant vision but need glasses with convex lenses to augment the converging power of the lens for close vision (Figure 18.9c).

Irregularities in the curvatures of the lens and/or the cornea lead to a blurred vision problem called **astigmatism.**

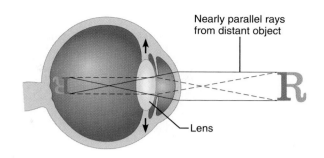

FIGURE 18.8 Refraction and real images. The refraction of light in the eye produces a real image (reversed, inverted, and reduced) on the retina.

Cylindrically ground lenses, which compensate for inequalities in the curvatures of the refracting surfaces, are prescribed to correct the condition. ●

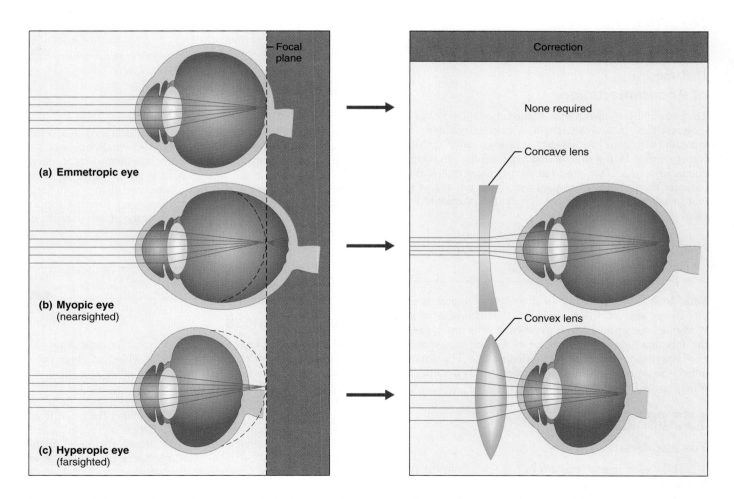

FIGURE 18.9 Problems of refraction. (a) In the emmetropic (normal) eye, light from both near and far objects is focused properly on the retina. **(b)** In a myopic eye, light from distant objects is brought to a focal point before reaching the retina. It then diverges. **(c)** In the hyperopic eye, light from a near object is brought to a focal point behind (past) the retina. (Refractory effect of cornea is ignored.)

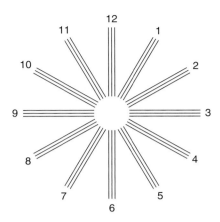

FIGURE 18.10 Astigmatism testing chart.

Near-Point Accommodation The elasticity of the lens decreases dramatically with age, resulting in difficulty in focusing for near or close vision. This condition is called **presbyopia**—literally, "old vision." Lens elasticity can be tested by measuring the **near point of accommodation.** The near point of vision is about 10 cm from the eye in young adults. It is closer in children and farther in elderly people.

ACTIVITY 6

Determining Near Point of Accommodation

To determine your near point of accommodation, hold a common straight pin at arm's length in front of one eye. (If desired, the text in the lab manual can be used rather than a pin.) Slowly move the pin toward that eye until the pin image becomes distorted. Have your lab partner use a metric ruler to measure the distance from your eye to the pin at this point, and record the distance below. Repeat the procedure for the other eye.

Near point for right eye: _____

Near point for left eye: _____ ▆

Visual Acuity **Visual acuity,** or sharpness of vision, is generally tested with a Snellen eye chart, which consists of letters of various sizes printed on a white card. This test is based on the fact that letters of a certain size can be seen clearly by eyes with normal vision at a specific distance. The distance at which the normal, or emmetropic, eye can read a line of letters is printed at the end of that line.

ACTIVITY 7

Testing Visual Acuity

1. Have your partner stand 6 m (20 feet) from the posted Snellen eye chart and cover one eye with a card or hand. As your partner reads each consecutive line aloud, check for

accuracy. If this individual wears glasses, give the test twice—first with glasses off and then with glasses on. *Do not remove contact lenses, but note that they were in place during the test.*

2. Record the number of the line with the smallest-sized letters read. If it is 20/20, the person's vision for that eye is normal. If it is 20/40, or any ratio with a value less than one, he or she has less than the normal visual acuity. (Such an individual is myopic.) If the visual acuity is 20/15, vision is better than normal, because this person can stand at 6 m (20 feet) from the chart and read letters that are only discernible by the normal eye at 4.5 m (15 feet). Give your partner the number of the line corresponding to the smallest letters read, to record in step 4.

3. Repeat the process for the other eye.

4. Have your partner test and record your visual acuity. If you wear glasses, the test results *without* glasses should be recorded first.

Visual acuity, right eye without glasses: _____

Visual acuity, right eye with glasses: _____

Visual acuity, left eye without glasses: _____

Visual acuity, left eye with glasses: _____ ▆

ACTIVITY 8

Testing for Astigmatism

The astigmatism chart (Figure 18.10) is designed to test for defects in the refracting surface of the lens and/or cornea.

View the chart first with one eye and then with the other, focusing on the center of the chart. If all the radiating lines appear equally dark and distinct, there is no distortion of your refracting surfaces. If some of the lines are blurred or appear less dark than others, at least some degree of astigmatism is present.

Is astigmatism present in your left eye? _____

Right eye? _____ ▆

Color Blindness

Ishihara's color plates are designed to test for deficiencies in the cones or color photoreceptor cells. There are three cone types, each containing a different light-absorbing pigment. One type primarily absorbs the red wavelengths of the visible light spectrum, another the blue wavelengths, and a third the green wavelengths. Nerve impulses reaching the brain from these different photoreceptor types are then interpreted (seen) as red, blue, and green, respectively. Interpretation of the intermediate colors of the visible light spectrum is a result of overlapping input from more than one cone type.

Testing for Color Blindness

1.   Find the interpretation table that accompanies the Ishihara color plates, and prepare a sheet to record data for the test. Note which plates are patterns rather than numbers.

2.   View the color plates in bright light or sunlight while holding them about 0.8 m (30 inches) away and at right angles to your line of vision. Report to your laboratory partner what you see in each plate. Take no more than 3 seconds for each decision.

3.   Your partner should record your responses and then check their accuracy with the correct answers provided in the color plate book. Is there any indication that you have some

degree of color blindness?_____

If so, what type? _____

_____

Repeat the procedure to test your partner's color vision. ■■

Binocular Vision

Humans, cats, predatory birds, and most primates are endowed with **binocular** (two-eyed) **vision.** Although both eyes look in approximately the same direction, they see slightly different views. Their visual fields, each about 170 degrees, overlap to a considerable extent; thus there is two-eyed vision at the overlap area (see Figures 18.5 and 18.11).

In contrast, the eyes of many animals (rabbits, pigeons, and others) are more on the sides of their head. Such animals see in two different directions and thus have a panoramic field of view and **panoramic vision.** A mnemonic device to keep these straight is "Eyes in the front—likes to hunt. Eyes on the side—likes to hide."

Although both types of vision have their good points, binocular vision provides three-dimensional vision and an accurate means of locating objects in space. The slight differences between the views seen by the two eyes are fused by the higher centers of the visual cortex to give us *depth perception.* Because of the manner in which the visual cortex resolves these two different views into a single image, it is sometimes referred to as the "cyclopean eye of the binocular animal."

Testing for Binocular Vision

1.   To demonstrate that a slightly different view is seen by each eye, perform the following simple experiment.

Close your left eye. Hold a pencil at arm's length directly in front of your right eye. Position another pencil directly beneath it and then move the lower pencil about half the distance toward you. As you move the lower pencil, make sure it remains in the *same plane* as the stationary pencil, so that the two pencils continually form a straight line. Then, without moving the pencils, close your right eye and open your left eye. Notice that with only the right eye open, the moving pencil stays in the same plane as the fixed pencil, but that when viewed with the left eye, the moving pencil is displaced laterally away from the plane of the fixed pencil.

2.   To demonstrate the importance of two-eyed binocular vision for depth perception, perform this second simple experiment.

Have your laboratory partner hold a test tube erect about arm's length in front of you. With both eyes open, quickly insert a pencil into the test tube. Remove the pencil, bring it back close to your body, close one eye, and quickly and without hesitation insert the pencil into the test tube. *(Do not feel for the test tube with the pencil!)* Repeat with the other eye closed.

Was it as easy to dunk the pencil with one eye closed as with both eyes open?

_____ ■■

Ophthalmoscopic Examination of the Eye (Optional)

The ophthalmoscope is an instrument used to examine the *fundus,* or eyeball interior, to determine visually the condition of the retina, optic disc, and internal blood vessels. Certain pathologic conditions such as diabetes mellitus, arteriosclerosis, and degenerative changes of the optic nerve and retina can be detected by such an examination. The ophthalmoscope consists of a set of lenses mounted on a rotating disc (the **lens selection disc**), a light source regulated by a **rheostat control,** and a mirror that reflects the light so that the eye interior can be illuminated.

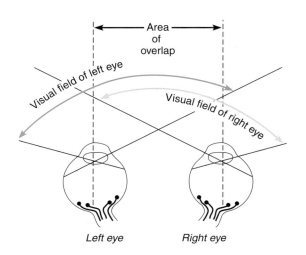

FIGURE 18.11 Overlapping of the visual fields.

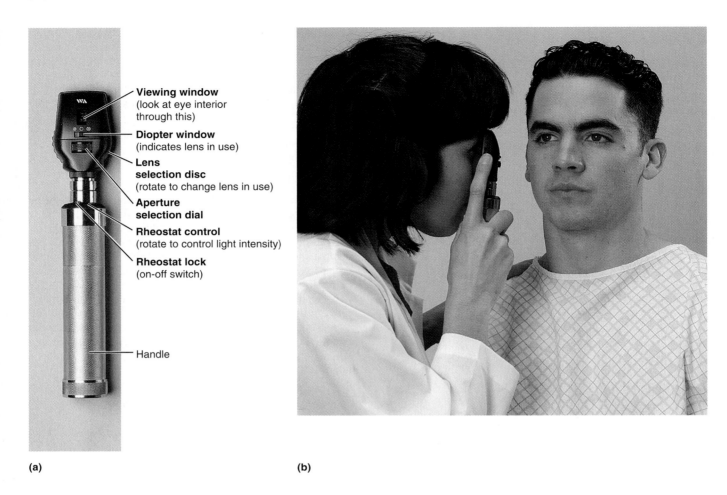

(a)   **(b)**

FIGURE 18.12 Structure and use of an ophthalmoscope. (a) Photograph of an ophthalmoscope.
(b) Proper position for beginning to examine the right eye with an ophthalmoscope.

The lens selection disc is positioned in a small slit in the mirror, and the examiner views the eye interior through this slit, appropriately called the **viewing window** (Figure 18.12a). The focal length of each lens is indicated in diopters preceded by a plus (+) sign if the lens is convex and by a negative (−) sign if the lens is concave. When the zero (0) is seen in the **diopter window,** there is no lens positioned in the slit. The depth of focus for viewing the eye interior is changed by changing the lens.

The light is turned on by depressing the red **rheostat lock button** and then rotating the rheostat control in the clockwise direction. The **aperture selection dial** on the front of the instrument allows the nature of the light beam to be altered. Generally, green light allows for clearest viewing of the blood vessels in the eye interior and is most comfortable for the subject.

Once you have examined the ophthalmoscope and have become familiar with it, you are ready to conduct an eye examination.

Conducting an Ophthalmoscopic Examination

1. Conduct the examination in a dimly lit or darkened room with the subject comfortably seated and gazing straight ahead. To examine the right eye, sit face-to-face with the subject, hold the instrument in your right hand, and use your right eye to view the eye interior (Figure 18.12b). You may want to steady yourself by resting your left hand on the subject's shoulder. To view the left eye, use your left eye, hold the instrument in your left hand, and steady yourself with your right hand.

2. Begin the examination with the 0 (no lens) in position. Grasp the instrument so that the lens disc may be rotated with the index finger. Holding the ophthalmoscope about 15 cm (6 inches) from the subject's eye, direct the light into the pupil at a slight angle—through the pupil edge rather than directly through its center. You will see a red circular area that is the illuminated eye interior.

3. Move in as close as possible to the subject's cornea (to within 5 cm, or 2 inches) as you continue to observe the area. Steady your instrument-holding hand on the subject's cheek if necessary. If both your eye and that of the subject are normal,

Central artery and vein
emerging from the optic disc

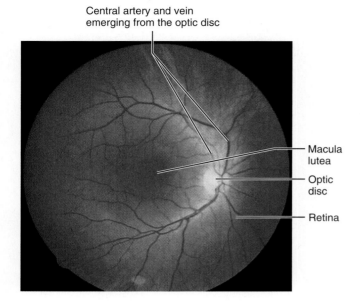

Macula
lutea

Optic
disc

Retina

FIGURE 18.13 Posterior portion of right retina.

the fundus can be viewed clearly without further adjustment of the ophthalmoscope. If the fundus cannot be focused, slowly rotate the lens disc counterclockwise until the fundus can be clearly seen. When the ophthalmoscope is correctly set, the fundus of the right eye should appear as shown in Figure 18.13. (**Note:** If a positive [convex] lens is required and your eyes are normal, the subject has hyperopia. If a negative [concave] lens is necessary to view the fundus and your eyes are normal, the subject is myopic.)

When the examination is proceeding correctly, the subject can often see images of retinal vessels in his own eye that appear rather like cracked glass. If you are unable to achieve a sharp focus or to see the optic disc, move medially or laterally and begin again.

4. Examine the optic disc for color, elevation, and sharpness of outline, and observe the blood vessels radiating from near its center. Locate the macula, lateral to the optic disc. It is a darker area in which blood vessels are absent, and the fovea appears to be a slightly lighter area in its center. The macula is most easily seen when the subject looks directly into the light of the ophthalmoscope.

! Do not examine the macula for longer than 1 second at a time.

5. When you have finished examining your partner's retina, shut off the ophthalmoscope. Change places with your partner (become the subject) and repeat steps 1–4. ▪

Special Senses: Vision

Anatomy of the Eye

1. Name five accessory eye structures that contribute to the formation of tears and/or aid in lubrication of the eyeball, and then name the major secretory product of each. Indicate which has antibacterial properties by circling the correct secretory product.

Accessory structures	Product

2. The eyeball is wrapped in adipose tissue within the orbit. What is the function of the adipose tissue?

_____

3. Why does one often have to blow one's nose after crying? _____

_____

4. Identify the extrinsic eye muscle predominantly responsible for the actions described below.

_____ 1.   turns the eye laterally

_____ 2.   turns the eye medially

_____ 3.   turns the eye up and laterally

_____ 4.   turns the eye inferiorly and medially

_____ 5.   turns the eye superiorly and medially

_____ 6.   turns the eye down and laterally

5. What is a sty? _____

_____

Conjunctivitis? _____

6. Using the terms in the key on the right, correctly identify all structures provided with leader lines in the diagram.

Key:

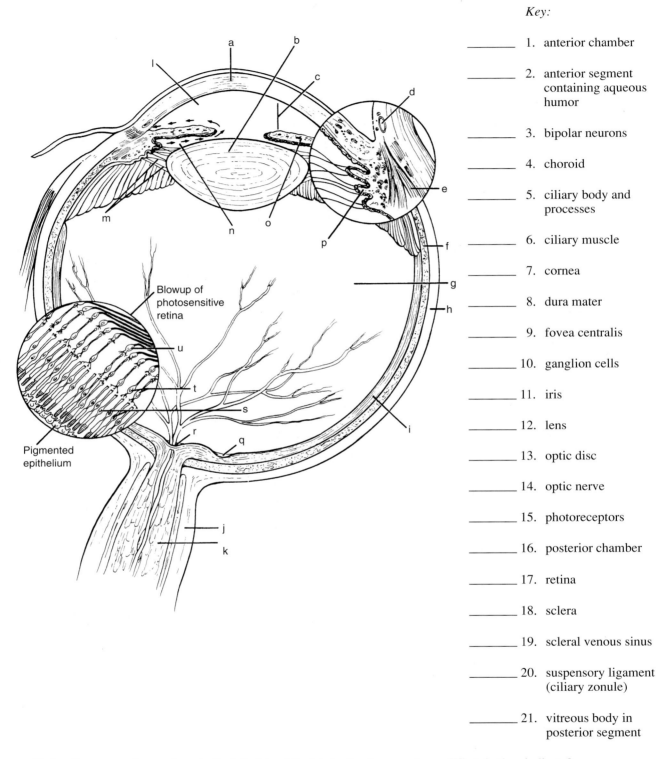

Blowup of
photosensitive
retina

Pigmented
epithelium

_____ 1. anterior chamber

_____ 2. anterior segment
containing aqueous
humor

_____ 3. bipolar neurons

_____ 4. choroid

_____ 5. ciliary body and
processes

_____ 6. ciliary muscle

_____ 7. cornea

_____ 8. dura mater

_____ 9. fovea centralis

_____ 10. ganglion cells

_____ 11. iris

_____ 12. lens

_____ 13. optic disc

_____ 14. optic nerve

_____ 15. photoreceptors

_____ 16. posterior chamber

_____ 17. retina

_____ 18. sclera

_____ 19. scleral venous sinus

_____ 20. suspensory ligament
(ciliary zonule)

_____ 21. vitreous body in
posterior segment

Notice the arrows drawn close to the left side of the iris in the diagram above. What do they indicate?

_____

_____

7. The iris is composed primarily of two smooth muscle layers, one arranged radially and the other circularly.

Which of these dilates the pupil? _____

8. Match the key responses with the descriptive statements that follow.

Key: a.   aqueous humor   e.   cornea   j.   retina
      b.   choroid   f.   fovea centralis   k.   sclera
      c.   ciliary body   g.   iris   l.   scleral venous sinus
      d.   ciliary processes of   h.   lens   m.   vitreous humor
          the ciliary body   i.   optic disc

_____ 1.   fluid filling the anterior segment of the eye

_____ 2.   the "white" of the eye

_____ 3.   part of the retina that lacks photoreceptors

_____ 4.   modification of the choroid that controls the shape of the crystalline lens and contains the ciliary muscle

_____ 5.   drains the aqueous humor from the eye

_____ 6.   layer containing the rods and cones

_____ 7.   substance occupying the posterior segment of the eyeball

_____ 8.   forms the bulk of the heavily pigmented vascular layer

_____ , and _____ 9. smooth muscle structures (2)

_____ 10.   area of critical focusing and discriminatory vision

_____ 11.   form (by filtration) the aqueous humor

_____ , and _____, _____,

_____ 12.   light-bending media of the eye (4)

_____ 13.   anterior continuation of the sclera—your "window on the world"

_____ 14.   composed of tough, white, opaque, fibrous connective tissue

9. You would expect the pupil to be dilated in which of the following circumstances? Circle the correct response(s).

a.   in brightly lit surroundings   c.   during focusing for near vision

b.   in dimly lit surroundings   d.   in observing distant objects

10. The intrinsic eye muscles are under the control of which of the following? (Circle the correct response.)

autonomic nervous system   somatic nervous system

Microscopic Anatomy of the Retina

11. The two major layers of the retina are the epithelial and nervous layers. In the nervous layer, the neuron populations are arranged as follows from the epithelial layer to the vitreous humor. (Circle the proper response.)

bipolar cells, ganglion cells, photoreceptors   photoreceptors, ganglion cells, bipolar cells

ganglion cells, bipolar cells, photoreceptors   photoreceptors, bipolar cells, ganglion cells

12. The axons of the _____ cells form the optic nerve, which exits from the eyeball.

13. Complete the following statements by writing either *rods* or *cones* on each blank.

The dim light receptors are the _____. Only _____ are found in the fovea centralis, whereas mostly _____ are

found in the periphery of the retina. _____ are the photoreceptors that operate best in bright light and allow for color vision.

Visual Pathways to the Brain

14. The visual pathway to the occipital lobe of the brain consists most simply of a chain of five neurons. Beginning with the photoreceptor cell of the retina, name them and note their location in the pathway.

1. _____   4. _____

2. _____   5. _____

3. _____

15. Visual field tests are done to reveal destruction along the visual pathway from the retina to the optic region of the brain. Note where the lesion is likely to be in the following cases.

Normal vision in left eye visual field; absence of vision in right eye visual field: _____

Normal vision in both eyes for right half of the visual field; absence of vision in both eyes for left half of the visual

field: _____

16. How is the right optic *tract* anatomically different from the right optic *nerve*? _____

_____

_____

Dissection of the Cow (Sheep) Eye

17. What modification of the choroid that is not present in humans is found in the cow eye? _____

_____ What is its function? _____

18. What does the retina look like? _____

_____

At what point is it attached to the posterior aspect of the eyeball? _____

Visual Tests and Experiments

19. Match the terms in column B with the descriptions in column A.

Column A

_____ 1. light bending

_____ 2. ability to focus for close (less than 20 feet) vision

_____ 3. normal vision

_____ 4. inability to focus well on close objects (farsightedness)

_____ 5. nearsightedness

_____ 6. blurred vision due to unequal curvatures of the lens or cornea

_____ 7. medial movement of the eyes during focusing on close objects

Column B

a. accommodation

b. astigmatism

c. convergence

d. emmetropia

e. hyperopia

f. myopia

g. refraction

20. Complete the following statements:

In farsightedness, the light is focused ___1___ the retina. The lens required to treat myopia is a ___2___ lens. The "near point" increases with age because the ___3___ of the lens decreases as we get older. A convex lens, like that of the eye, produces an image that is upside down and reversed from left to right. Such an image is called a ___4___ image.

1. _____

2. _____

3. _____

4. _____

21. Use terms from the key to complete the statements concerning near and distance vision.

Key: a. contracted   b. decreased   c. increased   d. relaxed   e. taut

During distance vision, the ciliary muscle is _____, the suspensory ligament is _____, the convexity of the lens

is _____, and light refraction is _____. During close vision, the ciliary muscle is _____, the suspensory ligament is

_____, lens convexity is _____, and light refraction is _____.

22. Explain why vision is lost when light hits the blind spot. _____

_____

23. Using your Snellen eye test results, answer the following questions.

Is your visual acuity normal, less than normal, or better than normal? _____

Explain your answer. _____

_____

Explain why each eye is tested separately when using the Snellen eye chart. _____

_____

Explain what "20/40 vision" means. _____

_____

Explain what "20/10 vision" means. _____

_____

24. Define *astigmatism*. _____

_____

How can it be corrected? _____

25. Record the distance of your near point of accommodation as tested in the laboratory:

right eye: _____ left eye: _____

Is your near point within the normal range for your age? _____

26. Define *presbyopia*. _____

_____

What causes it? _____

27. To which wavelengths of light do the three cone types of the retina respond maximally?

_____, _____, and _____

28. How can you explain the fact that we see a great range of colors even though only three cone types exist?

_____

_____

29. Explain the difference between binocular and panoramic vision. _____

_____

What is the advantage of binocular vision? _____

_____

30. What is the usual cause of color blindness? _____

_____

31. Why is the ophthalmoscopic examination an important diagnostic tool? _____

_____

32. Many college students struggling through mountainous reading assignments are told that they need glasses for "eyestrain." Why is it more of a strain on the extrinsic and intrinsic eye muscles to look at close objects than at far objects?

_____

_____

Special Senses: Hearing and Equilibrium

MATERIALS

- ☐ Three-dimensional dissectible ear model and/or chart of ear anatomy
- ☐ Otoscope (if available)
- ☐ Disposable otoscope tips (if available) and autoclave bag
- ☐ Alcohol swabs
- ☐ Compound microscope
- ☐ Prepared slides of the cochlea of the ear
- ☐ Absorbent cotton
- ☐ Pocket watch or clock that ticks
- ☐ Metric ruler
- ☐ Tuning forks (range of frequencies)
- ☐ Rubber mallet
- ☐ Demonstration: Microscope focused on a slide of a crista ampullaris receptor of a semicircular canal
- ☐ Blackboard and chalk

OBJECTIVES

1. To identify, by appropriately labeling a diagram, the anatomical structures of the external, middle, and internal ear, and to explain their functions.
2. To describe the anatomy of the organ of hearing (spiral organ of Corti in the cochlea), and to explain its function in sound reception.
3. To describe the anatomy of the equilibrium organs of the internal ear (cristae ampullares and maculae), and to explain their relative function in maintaining equilibrium.
4. To explain how one is able to localize the source of sounds.
5. To define or explain sensorineural *deafness, conduction deafness,* and *nystagmus.*
6. To state the purpose of the Weber, Rinne, balance, and Romberg tests.
7. To describe the effects of acceleration on the semicircular canals.
8. To explain the role of vision in maintaining equilibrium.

Anatomy of the Ear

Gross Anatomy

The ear is a complex structure containing sensory receptors for hearing and equilibrium. The ear is divided into three major areas: the *external ear,* the *middle ear,* and the *internal ear* (Figure 19.1). The external and middle ear structures serve the needs of the sense of hearing *only,* while internal ear structures function both in equilibrium and hearing reception.

ACTIVITY 1

Identifying Structures of the Ear

Obtain a dissectible ear model or chart of ear anatomy and identify the structures described below. Refer to Figure 19.1 as you work. ■■■

The **external,** or **outer, ear** is composed primarily of the pinna and the external auditory canal. The **auricle,** or **pinna,** is the skin-covered cartilaginous structure encircling the auditory canal opening. In many animals, it collects and directs sound waves into the external acoustic meatus. In humans this function of the auricle is largely lost. The portion of the auricle lying inferior to the external acoustic meatus is the **lobule.**

The **external acoustic meatus** (or external **auditory canal**) is a short, narrow (about 2.5 cm long by 0.6 cm wide) chamber carved into the temporal bone. In its skin-lined walls are wax-secreting glands called **ceruminous glands.** Sound waves that enter the external auditory canal eventually encounter the **tympanic membrane,** or **eardrum,** which vibrates at exactly the same frequency as the sound wave(s) hitting it. The membranous eardrum separates the outer from the middle ear.

The **middle ear** is essentially a small chamber—the **tympanic cavity**—found within the temporal bone. The cavity is spanned by three small bones, collectively called the **auditory ossicles (malleus, incus,** and **stapes),** which articulate to form a lever system that amplifies and transmits the vibratory motion of the eardrum to the fluids of the inner ear via the **oval window.** The ossicles are often referred to by their common names, that is, hammer, anvil, and stirrup, respectively.

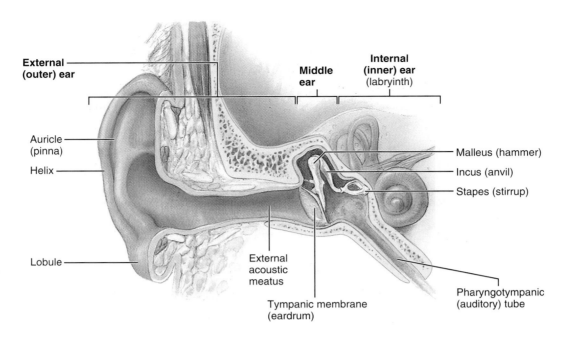

FIGURE 19.1 Anatomy of the ear.

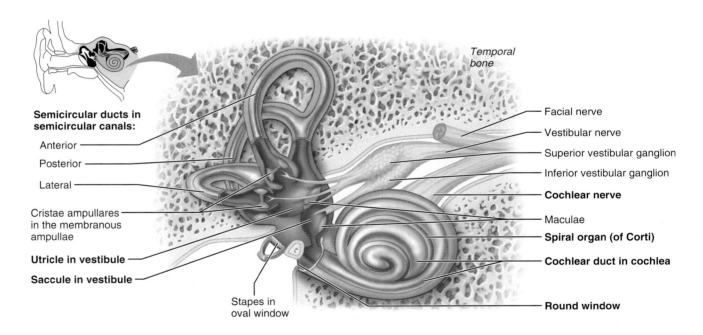

FIGURE 19.2 Internal ear. Right membranous labyrinth shown within the bony labyrinth.

Connecting the middle ear chamber with the nasopharynx is the **pharyngotympanic,** or **auditory, tube** (formerly known as the eustachian tube). Normally this tube is flattened and closed, but swallowing or yawning can cause it to open temporarily to equalize the pressure of the middle ear cavity with external air pressure. This is an important function. The eardrum does not vibrate properly unless the pressure on both of its surfaces is the same.

Because the mucosal membranes of the middle ear cavity and nasopharynx are continuous through the pharyngotympanic tube, **otitis media,** or inflammation of the middle ear, is a fairly common condition, especially among youngsters prone to sore throats. In cases where large amounts of fluid or pus accumulate in the middle ear cavity, an emergency myringotomy (lancing of the eardrum) may be necessary to relieve the pressure. Frequently, tiny ventilating tubes are put in during the procedure. ●

The **internal,** or **inner, ear** consists of a system of bony and rather tortuous chambers called the **osseous,** or **bony, labyrinth,** which is filled with an aqueous fluid called **perilymph** (Figure 19.2). Suspended in the perilymph is the **membranous labyrinth,** a system that mostly follows the contours

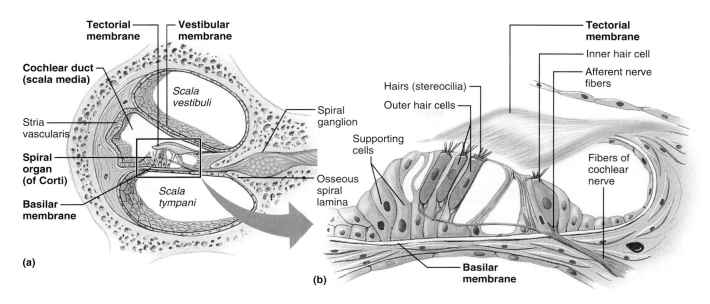

FIGURE 19.3 Anatomy of the cochlea. (a) Magnified cross-sectional view of one turn of the cochlea, showing the relationship of the three scalae. The scalae vestibuli and tympani contain perilymph; the cochlear duct (scala media) contains endolymph. **(b)** Detailed structure of the spiral organ of Corti.

of the osseous labyrinth. The membranous labyrinth is filled with a more viscous fluid called **endolymph.** The three subdivisions of the bony labyrinth are the cochlea, the vestibule, and the semicircular canals, with the vestibule situated between the cochlea and semicircular canals. The **vestibule** and the **semicircular canals** are involved with equilibrium.

The snail-like **cochlea** (see Figures 19.2 and 19.3) contains the sensory receptors for hearing. The cochlear membranous labyrinth, the **cochlear duct,** is a soft wormlike tube about 3.8 cm long. It winds through the full two and three-quarter turns of the cochlea and separates the perilymph-containing cochlear cavity into upper and lower chambers, the **scala vestibuli** and **scala tympani** (the vestibular and tympanic ducts), respectively. The scala vestibuli terminates at the oval window, which "seats" the foot plate of the stirrup located laterally in the tympanic cavity. The scala tympani is bounded by a membranous area called the **round window.** The cochlear duct, itself filled with endolymph, supports the **spiral organ of Corti,** which contains the receptors for hearing—the sensory hair cells and nerve endings of the **cochlear nerve,** a division of the vestibulocochlear nerve (VIII).

ACTIVITY 2

Examining the Ear with an Otoscope (Optional)

1. Obtain an otoscope and two alcohol swabs. Inspect your partner's ear canal and then select the largest-*diameter* (not length!) speculum that will fit comfortably into his or her ear to permit full visibility. Clean the speculum thoroughly with an alcohol swab, and then attach the speculum to the battery-containing otoscope handle. Before beginning, check that the otoscope light beam is strong. (If not, obtain another otoscope or new batteries.) Some otoscopes come with disposable tips. Be sure to use a new tip for each ear examined. Dispose of these tips in an autoclave bag after use.

2. When you are ready to begin the examination, hold the lighted otoscope securely between your thumb and forefinger (like a pencil), and rest the little finger of the otoscope-holding hand against your partner's head. This maneuver forms a brace that allows the speculum to move as your partner moves and prevents the speculum from penetrating too deeply into the ear canal during unexpected movements.

3. Grasp the ear auricle firmly and pull it up, back, and slightly laterally. If your partner experiences pain or discomfort when the auricle is manipulated, an inflammation or infection of the external ear may be present. If this occurs, do not attempt to examine the ear canal.

4. Carefully insert the speculum of the otoscope into the external acoustic meatus in a downward and forward direction only far enough to permit examination of the tympanic membrane or eardrum. Note its shape, color, and vascular network. The healthy tympanic membrane is pearly white. During the examination, notice if there is any discharge or redness in the canal and identify earwax.

5. After the examination, thoroughly clean the speculum with the second alcohol swab before returning the otoscope to the supply area. ■

Microscopic Anatomy of the Organ of Corti and the Mechanism of Hearing

The anatomical details of the spiral organ of Corti are shown in Figure 19.3. The hair (auditory receptor) cells rest on the **basilar membrane,** which forms the floor of the cochlear duct, and their "hairs" (stereocilia) project into a gelatinous membrane, the **tectorial membrane,** that overlies them. The roof of the cochlear duct is called the **vestibular membrane.** The endolymph-filled chamber of the cochlear duct is the **scala media.**

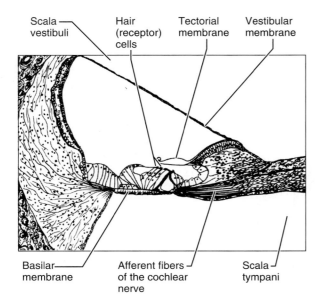

FIGURE 19.4 Microscopic view of the spiral organ of Corti. (See also Plate 16 in the Histology Atlas.)

ACTIVITY 3

Examining the Microscopic Structure of the Cochlea

Obtain a compound microscope and a prepared microscope slide of the cochlea and identify the areas shown in Figure 19.4. (See Plate 16 in the Histology Atlas.) ▮

The mechanism of hearing begins as sound waves pass through the external acoustic meatus and through the middle ear into the internal ear, where the vibration eventually reaches the spiral organ of Corti, which contains the receptors for hearing.

The popular "traveling wave" hypothesis of von Békésy suggests that vibration of the stirrup at the oval window initiates traveling waves that cause maximal displacements of the basilar membrane where they peak and stimulate the hair cells of the spiral organ of Corti in that region. Since the area at which the traveling waves peak is a high-pressure area, the vestibular membrane is compressed at this point and, in turn, compresses the endolymph and the basilar membrane of the cochlear duct. The resulting pressure on the perilymph in the scala tympani causes the membrane of the round window to bulge outward into the middle ear chamber, thus acting as a relief valve for the compressional wave. Georg von Békésy found that high-frequency waves (high-pitched sounds) peaked close to the oval window and that low-frequency waves (low-pitched sounds) peaked farther up the basilar membrane near the apex of the cochlea. Although the mechanism of sound reception by the spiral organ of Corti is not completely understood, we do know that hair cells on the basilar membrane are uniquely stimulated by sounds of various frequencies and amplitude and that once stimulated they depolarize and begin the chain of nervous impulses via the cochlear nerve to the auditory centers of the temporal lobe cortex. This series of events results in the phenomenon we call hearing (Figure 19.5).

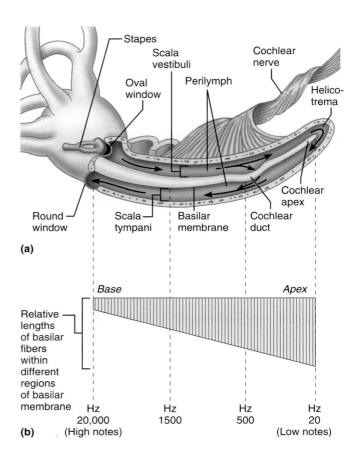

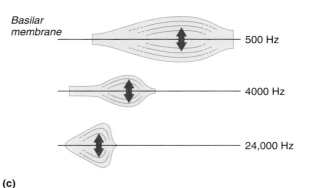

FIGURE 19.5 Resonance of the basilar membrane. (a) Fluid movement in the cochlea following the stirrup thrust at the oval window. The compressional wave thus created causes the round window to bulge into the middle ear. Pressure waves set up vibrations in the basilar membrane. (b) Fibers span the basilar membrane. The length of the fibers "tunes" specific regions to vibrate at specific frequencies. (c) Different frequencies of pressure waves in the cochlea stimulate particular hair cells and neurons.

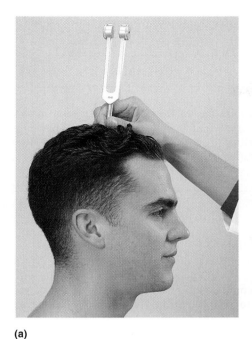
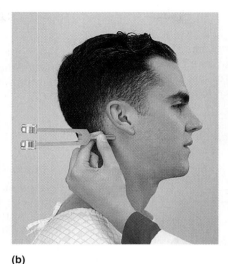
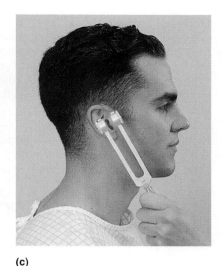

(a)   **(b)**   **(c)**

FIGURE 19.6 The Weber and Rinne tuning fork tests. (a) The Weber test to evaluate whether the sound remains centralized (normal) or lateralizes to one side or the other (indicative of some degree of conductive or sensorineural deafness). **(b, c)** The Rinne test to compare bone conduction and air conduction.

By the time most people are in their 60s, a gradual deterioration and atrophy of the spiral organ of Corti begins, and leads to a loss in the ability to hear high tones and speech sounds. This condition, **presbycusis,** is a type of sensorineural deafness. Because many elderly people refuse to accept their hearing loss and resist using hearing aids, they begin to rely more and more on their vision for clues as to what is going on around them and may be accused of ignoring people.

Although presbycusis is considered to be a disability of old age, it is becoming much more common in younger people as our world grows noisier. The damage (breakage of the "hairs" of the hair cells) caused by excessively loud sounds is progressive and cumulative. Each assault causes a bit more damage. Music played and listened to at deafening levels definitely contributes to the deterioration of hearing receptors. ●

ACTIVITY 4

Conducting Laboratory Tests of Hearing

Perform the following hearing tests in a quiet area.

Weber Test to Determine Conductive and Sensorineural Deafness

Strike a tuning fork on the heel of your hand or with a rubber mallet, and place the handle of the tuning fork medially on your partner's head (see Figure 19.6a). Is the tone equally loud in both ears, or is it louder in one ear?

If it is equally loud in both ears, you have equal hearing or equal loss of hearing in both ears. If **sensorineural deafness** is present in one ear, the tone will be heard in the unaffected ear, but not in the ear with sensorineural deafness. If **conduction deafness** is present, the sound will be heard more strongly in the ear in which there is a hearing loss due to sound conduction by the bone of the skull. Conduction deafness can be simulated by plugging one ear with cotton to interfere with the conduction of sound to the inner ear.

Rinne Test for Comparing Bone- and Air-Conduction Hearing

1.   Strike the tuning fork, and place its handle on your partner's mastoid process (Figure 19.6b).

2.   When your partner indicates that the sound is no longer audible, hold the still-vibrating prongs close to his or her acoustic meatus (Figure 19.6c). If your partner hears the fork again (by air conduction) when it is moved to that position, hearing is not impaired and the test result is to be recorded as positive (+). Record in step 5 below.

3.   Repeat the test, but this time test air-conduction hearing first.

4.   After the tone is no longer heard by air conduction, hold the handle of the tuning fork on the bony mastoid process. If the subject hears the tone again by bone conduction after hearing by air conduction is lost, there is some conductive deafness and the result is recorded as negative (−).

5.   Repeat the sequence for the opposite ear.

Right ear: _____ Left ear: _____

Does the subject hear better by bone or by air conduction?

_____

Acuity Test

Have your lab partner pack one ear with cotton and sit quietly with eyes closed. Obtain a ticking clock or pocket watch and hold it very close to his or her *unpacked* ear. Then slowly move it away from the ear until your partner signals that the ticking is no longer audible. Record the distance in centimeters at which ticking is inaudible and then remove the cotton from the packed ear.

Right ear: _____ Left ear: _____

Is the threshold of audibility sharp or indefinite?

_____

Sound Localization

Ask your partner to close both eyes. Hold the pocket watch at an audible distance (about 15 cm) from his or her ear, and move it to various locations (front, back, sides, and above his or her head). Have your partner locate the position by pointing in each instance. Can the sound be localized equally well

at all positions? _____

If not, at what position(s) was the sound less easily located?

_____

_____

The ability to localize the source of a sound depends on two factors—the difference in the loudness of the sound reaching each ear and the time of arrival of the sound at each ear. How does this information help to explain your findings?

_____

_____

Frequency Range of Hearing

Obtain three tuning forks: one with a low frequency (75 to 100 hertz [Hz; 1 Hz = 1 cycle per second, or cps]), one with a frequency of approximately 1000 Hz, and one with a frequency of 4000 to 5000 Hz. Strike the lowest-frequency fork and hold it close to your partner's ear. Repeat with the other two forks.

Which fork was heard most clearly and comfortably?

_____ Hz

Which was heard least well? _____ Hz

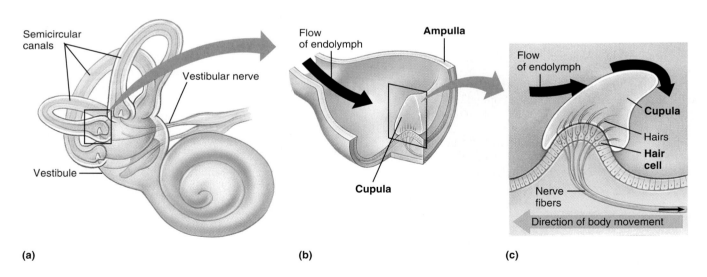

(a)　　　　　　　　　　　　　**(b)**　　　　　　　　　　　　　**(c)**

FIGURE 19.7 Structure and function of the crista ampullaris. (a) Arranged in the three spatial planes, the semicircular ducts in the semicircular canals each have a swelling called an ampulla at their base. **(b)** Each ampulla contains a crista ampullaris, a receptor that is essentially a cluster of hair cells with hairs projecting into a gelatinous cap called the cupula. **(c)** When the rate of rotation changes, inertia prevents the endolymph in the semicircular canals from moving with the head, so the fluid presses against the cupula, bending the hair cells in the opposite direction. The bending increases the frequency of action potentials in the sensory neurons in direct proportion to the amount of rotational acceleration. The mechanism adjusts quickly if rotation continues at a constant speed.

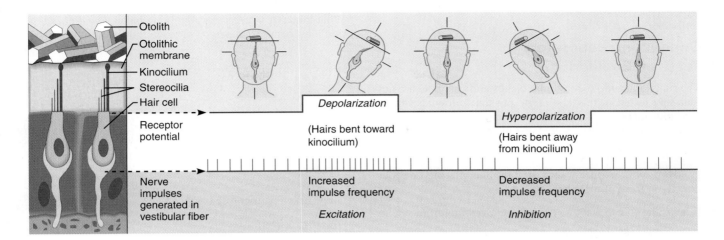

FIGURE 19.8 The effect of gravitational pull on a macula receptor in the utricle. When movement of the otolithic membrane bends the hair cells in the direction of the kinocilium, the vestibular fibers depolarize and generate action potentials more rapidly. When the hairs are bent in the direction away from the kinocilium, the hair cells become hyperpolarized, and the nerve fibers send impulses at a reduced rate (i.e., below the resting rate of discharge).

Microscopic Anatomy of the Equilibrium Apparatus and Mechanisms of Equilibrium

The equilibrium apparatus of the inner ear, the **vestibular apparatus,** is in the vestibule and semicircular canals of the bony labyrinth. Their chambers are filled with perilymph, in which membranous labyrinth structures are suspended. The vestibule contains the saclike **utricle** and **saccule,** and the semicircular chambers contain **membranous semicircular ducts** (see Figure 19.2). Like the cochlear duct, these membranes are filled with endolymph and contain receptor cells that are activated by the bending of their cilia.

The semicircular canals are centrally involved in the **mechanism of dynamic equilibrium.** They are 1.2 cm in circumference and are oriented in three planes—horizontal, frontal, and sagittal. At the base of each semicircular duct is an enlarged region, the **ampulla,** which communicates with the utricle of the vestibule. Within each ampulla is a receptor region called a **crista ampullaris,** which consists of a tuft of hair cells covered with a gelatinous cap, or **cupula** (Figure 19.7). When your head position changes in an angular direction, as when twirling on the dance floor or when taking a rough boat ride, the endolymph in the canal lags behind, pushing the cupula—like a swinging door—in a direction opposite to that of the angular motion (Figure 19.7c). This movement depolarizes the hair cells, resulting in enhanced impulse transmission up the vestibular division of the eighth cranial nerve to the brain. Likewise, when the angular motion stops suddenly, the inertia of the endolymph causes it to continue to move, pushing the cupula in the same direction as the previous body motion. This movement again initiates electrical changes in the hair cells (in this case, it hyperpolarizes them). (This phenomenon accounts for the reversed motion

sensation you feel when you stop suddenly after twirling.) When you move at a constant rate of motion, the endolymph eventually comes to rest and the cupula gradually returns to its original position. The hair cells, no longer bent, send no new signals, and you lose the sensation of spinning. Thus the response of these dynamic equilibrium receptors is a reaction to *changes* in angular motion rather than to motion itself.

ACTIVITY 5

Examining the Microscopic Structure of the Crista Ampullaris

Go to the demonstration area and examine the slide of a crista ampullaris. Identify the areas depicted in Figure 19.7b and c. ▨

Maculae in the vestibule contain the **hair cells,** receptors that are essential to the **mechanism of static equilibrium.** The maculae respond to gravitational pull, thus providing information on which way is up or down, and to linear or straightforward changes in speed. They are located on the walls of the saccule and utricle. The hair cells in each macula are embedded in the **otolithic membrane,** a gelatinous material containing small grains of calcium carbonate (**otoliths).** When the head moves, the otoliths move in response to variations in gravitational pull. As they deflect different hair cells, they trigger hyperpolarization or depolarization of the hair cells and modify the rate of impulse transmission along the vestibular nerve (Figure 19.8).

Although the receptors of the semicircular canals and the vestibule are responsible for dynamic and static equilibrium respectively, they rarely act independently. Complex interaction of many of the receptors is the rule. Processing is also complex and involves the brain stem and cerebellum as well as input from proprioceptors and the eyes.

Conducting Laboratory Tests on Equilibrium

The function of the semicircular canals and vestibule are not routinely tested in the laboratory, but the following simple tests illustrate normal equilibrium apparatus function as well as some of the complex processing interactions.

Balance Tests

1. Have your partner walk a straight line, placing one foot directly in front of the other.

Is he or she able to walk without undue wobbling from side to

side ? _____

Did he or she experience any dizziness? _____

The ability to walk with balance and without dizziness, unless subject to rotational forces, indicates normal function of the equilibrium apparatus.

Was nystagmus* present? _____

2. Place three coins of different sizes on the floor. Ask your lab partner to pick up the coins, and carefully observe his or her muscle activity and coordination.

Did your lab partner have any difficulty locating and picking

up the coins? _____

Describe your observations and your lab partner's observations during the test.

_____

_____

_____

_____

*Nystagmus is the involuntary rolling of the eyes in any direction or the trailing of the eyes slowly in one direction, followed by their rapid movement in the opposite direction. It is normal after rotation; abnormal otherwise. The direction of nystagmus is that of its quick phase on acceleration.

What kinds of interactions involving balance and coordination must occur for a person to move fluidly during this test?

_____

_____

3. If a person has a depressed nervous system, mental concentration may result in a loss of balance. Ask your lab partner to stand up and count backward from ten as rapidly as possible.

Did your lab partner lose balance? _____

Romberg Test

The Romberg test determines the integrity of the dorsal white column of the spinal cord, which transmits impulses to the brain from the proprioceptors involved with posture.

1. Have your partner stand with his or her back to the blackboard.

2. Draw one line parallel to each side of your partner's body. He or she should stand erect, with eyes open and staring straight ahead for 2 minutes while you observe any movements. Did you see any gross swaying movements?

_____

_____

3. Repeat the test. This time the subject's eyes should be closed. Note and record the degree of side-to-side movement.

_____

_____

4. Repeat the test with the subject's eyes first open and then closed. This time, however, the subject should be positioned with his or her left shoulder toward, but not touching, the board so that you may observe and record the degree of front-to-back swaying.

_____

_____

_____

Do you think the equilibrium apparatus of the inner ear was operating equally well in all these tests?

_____

The proprioceptors? _____

Why was the observed degree of swaying greater when the eyes were closed?

_____

_____

What conclusions can you draw regarding the factors necessary for maintaining body equilibrium and balance?

_____

_____

_____

_____

Role of Vision in Maintaining Equilibrium

To further demonstrate the role of vision in maintaining equilibrium, perform the following experiment. (Ask your lab partner to record observations and act as a "spotter.") Stand erect, with your eyes open. Raise your left foot approximately 30 cm off the floor, and hold it there for 1 minute.

Record the observations: _____

_____

_____

Rest for 1 or 2 minutes; and then repeat the experiment with the same foot raised but with your eyes closed. Record the observations:

_____

_____

Special Senses: Hearing and Equilibrium

Anatomy of the Ear

1. Select the terms from column B that apply to the column A descriptions. Some terms are used more than once.

Column A

_____, _____, _____ 1. structures composing the outer or external ear (3)

_____, _____, _____ 2. structures composing the internal ear (3)

_____, _____, _____ 3. collectively called the auditory ossicles (3)

_____ 4. involved in equalizing the pressure in the middle ear with atmospheric pressure

_____ 5. vibrates at the same frequency as sound waves hitting it; transmits the vibrations to the auditory ossicles

_____ 6. transmits the vibratory motion of the stirrup to the fluid in the scala vestibuli of the internal ear

_____ 7. acts as a pressure relief valve for the increased fluid pressure in the scala tympani; bulges into the tympanic cavity

_____ 8. passage between the throat and the tympanic cavity

_____ 9. fluid contained within the membranous labyrinth

_____ 10. fluid contained within the osseous labyrinth and bathing the membranous labyrinth

Column B

a. cochlea

b. endolymph

c. external acoustic meatus

d. incus (anvil)

e. malleus (hammer)

f. oval window

g. perilymph

h. pharyngotympanic (auditory) tube

i. pinna (auricle)

j. round window

k. semicircular canals

l. stapes (stirrup)

m. tympanic membrane

n. vestibule

2. Identify all indicated structures and ear regions in the following diagram.

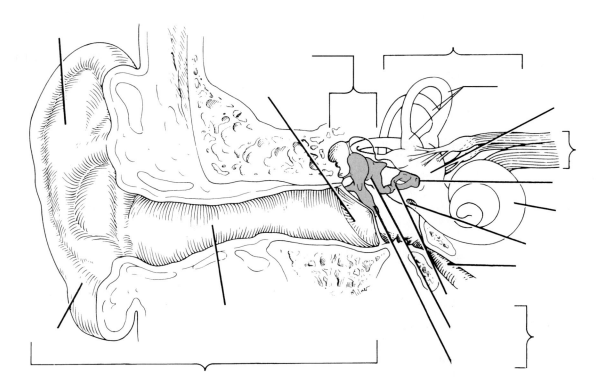

3. Match the membranous labyrinth structures listed in column B with the descriptive statements in column A:

Column A

_____, _____ 1. sacs found within the vestibule

_____ 2. contains the spiral organ of Corti

_____, _____ 3. sites of the maculae

_____ 4. positioned in all spatial planes

_____ 5. hair cells of spiral organ of Corti rest on this membrane

_____ 6. gelatinous membrane overlying the hair cells of the spiral organ of Corti

_____ 7. contains the crista ampullaris

_____, _____, _____, _____ 8. function in static equilibrium

_____, _____, _____, _____ 9. function in dynamic equilibrium

_____ 10. carries auditory information to the brain

_____ 11. gelatinous cap overlying hair cells of the crista ampullaris

_____ 12. grains of calcium carbonate in the maculae

Column B

a. ampulla

b. basilar membrane

c. cochlear duct

d. cochlear nerve

e. cupula

f. otoliths

g. saccule

h. semicircular ducts

i. tectorial membrane

j. utricle

k. vestibular nerve

4. Sound waves hitting the eardrum initiate its vibratory motion. Trace the pathway through which vibrations and fluid currents are transmitted to finally stimulate the hair cells in the spiral organ of Corti. (Name the appropriate ear structures in their correct sequence.)

Tympanic membrane _____

_____

_____

5. Describe how sounds of different frequency (pitch) are differentiated in the cochlea. _____

_____

_____

_____

6. Explain the role of the endolymph of the semicircular canals in activating the receptors during angular motion.

_____

_____

_____

7. Explain the role of the otoliths in perception of static equilibrium (head position). _____

_____

_____

_____

Laboratory Tests

8. Was the auditory acuity measurement made during the experiment on p. 332 the same or different for both ears?

_____ What factors might account for a difference in the acuity of the two ears?

_____

_____

9. During the sound localization experiment on p. 332, in which position(s) was the sound least easily located?

_____

How can this phenomenon be explained? _____

_____

10. In the frequency experiment on p. 332, which tuning fork was the most difficult to hear? _____ Hz

What conclusion can you draw? _____

_____

11. When the tuning fork handle was pressed to your forehead during the Weber test, where did the sound seem to originate?

_____

Where did it seem to originate when one ear was plugged with cotton? _____

How do sound waves reach the cochlea when conduction deafness is present? _____

_____

12. Indicate whether the following conditions relate to conduction deafness (C) or sensorineural deafness (S).

_____ 1. can result from the fusion of the ossicles

_____ 2. can result from a lesion on the cochlear nerve

_____ 3. sound heard in one ear but not in the other during bone and air conduction

_____ 4. can result from otitis media

_____ 5. can result from impacted cerumen or a perforated eardrum

_____ 6. can result from a blood clot in the auditory cortex

13. The Rinne test evaluates an individual's ability to hear sounds conducted by air or bone. Which is more indicative of normal

hearing? _____

14. Define _nystagmus._ _____

_____

Define _vertigo._ _____

_____

15. What is the usual reason for conducting the Romberg test? _____

_____

Was the degree of sway greater with the eyes open or closed? Why? _____

_____

16. Normal balance, or equilibrium, depends on input from a number of sensory receptors. Name them.

_____

Special Senses: Olfaction and Taste

MATERIALS

- ☐ Prepared slides: the tongue showing taste buds; nasal olfactory epithelium (l.s.)
- ☐ Compound microscope
- ☐ Small mirror
- ☐ Paper towels
- ☐ Packets of granulated sugar
- ☐ Disposable autoclave bag
- ☐ Cotton-tipped swabs
- ☐ Prepared vials of oil of cloves, oil of peppermint, and oil of wintergreen, or corresponding flavors found in the condiment section of a supermarket
- ☐ Nose clips
- ☐ Paper cups
- ☐ Flask of distilled or tap water
- ☐ Absorbent cotton
- ☐ Paper plates
- ☐ Foil-lined egg carton containing equal-size food cubes of cheese, apple, raw potato, dried prunes, banana, raw carrot, and hard-cooked egg white
- ☐ Toothpicks
- ☐ Disposable gloves
- ☐ Chipped ice

OBJECTIVES

1. To describe the location and cellular composition of the olfactory epithelium.
2. To describe the structure and function of the taste receptors.
3. To name the five basic qualities of taste sensation, and to list the chemical substances that elicit them.
4. To explain the interdependence between the senses of smell and taste.
5. To define *olfactory adaptation*.
6. To name two factors other than olfaction that influence taste appreciation of foods.

The receptors for olfaction and taste are classified as **chemoreceptors** because they respond to chemicals in solution. Although five relatively specific types of taste receptors have been identified, the olfactory receptors are considered sensitive to a much wider range of chemical sensations. The sense of smell is the least understood of the special senses.

Localization and Anatomy of the Olfactory Receptors

The **olfactory epithelium** (organ of smell) occupies an area of about 5 cm^2 in the roof of the nasal cavity (Figure 20.1a). Because the air entering the human nasal cavity must make a hairpin turn to enter the respiratory passages below, the nasal epithelium is in a rather poor position for performing its function. This is why sniffing, which brings more air into contact with the receptors, intensifies the sense of smell.

The specialized receptor cells in the olfactory epithelium are surrounded by **supporting cells,** non-sensory epithelial cells (Figure 20.1b, c). The **olfactory receptor cells** are bipolar neurons whose **olfactory cilia** extend outward from the epithelium. Axonal nerve filaments emerging from their basal ends penetrate the cribriform plate of the ethmoid bone and proceed as the *olfactory nerves* to synapse in the olfactory bulbs lying on either side of the crista galli of the ethmoid bone. Impulses from neurons of the olfactory bulbs are then conveyed to the olfactory portion of the cortex (uncus) without synapsing in the thalamus.

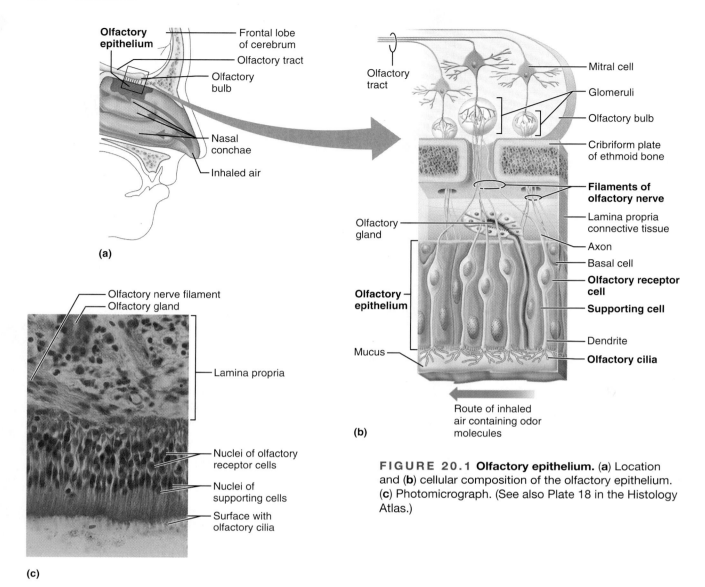

FIGURE 20.1 Olfactory epithelium. (a) Location and **(b)** cellular composition of the olfactory epithelium. **(c)** Photomicrograph. (See also Plate 18 in the Histology Atlas.)

Microscopic Examination of the Olfactory Epithelium

Obtain a longitudinal section of olfactory epithelium. Examine it closely using a compound microscope, comparing it to Figure 20.1c and Plate 18 in the Histology Atlas. ▪

Localization and Anatomy of Taste Buds

The **taste buds,** specific receptors for the sense of taste, are widely but not uniformly distributed in the oral cavity. Most are located in **papillae,** peglike projections of the mucosa, on the dorsal surface of the tongue (as described next). A few are found on the soft palate, epiglottis, pharynx, and inner surface of the cheeks.

The taste buds are located primarily on the sides of the large, round **circumvallate papillae** (arranged in a V formation on the posterior surface of the tongue); in the side walls of the **foliate papillae;** and on the tops of the more numerous **fungiform papillae.** The latter look rather like minute mushrooms and are widely distributed on the tongue. (See Figure 20.2.)

• Use a mirror to examine your tongue. Which of the various papillae types can you pick out?

_____

_____

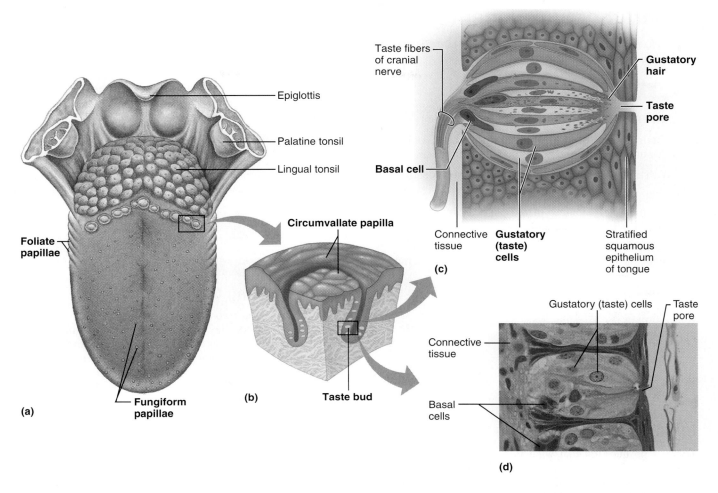

FIGURE 20.2 Location and structure of taste buds. (**a**) Taste buds on the tongue are associated with papillae, projections of the tongue mucosa. (**b**) A sectioned circumvallate papilla shows the position of the taste buds in its lateral walls. (**c**) An enlarged view of a taste bud. (**d**) Photomicrograph of a taste bud. See also Plate 17 in the Histology Atlas.

Each taste bud consists largely of a globular arrangement of two types of modified epithelial cells: the **gustatory,** or **taste cells,** which are the actual receptor cells, and **basal cells.** Several nerve fibers enter each taste bud and supply sensory nerve endings to each of the taste cells. The long microvilli of the receptor cells penetrate the epithelial surface through an opening called the **taste pore.** When these microvilli, called **gustatory hairs,** contact specific chemicals in the solution, the taste cells depolarize. The afferent fibers from the taste buds to the sensory cortex in the postcentral gyrus of the brain are carried in three cranial nerves: the *facial nerve (VII)* serves the anterior two-thirds of the tongue; the *glossopharyngeal nerve (IX)* serves the posterior third of the tongue; and the *vagus nerve (X)* carries a few fibers from the pharyngeal region.

Microscopic Examination of Taste Buds

Obtain a microscope and a prepared slide of a tongue cross section. Use Figure 20.2b as a guide to aid you in locating the taste buds on the tongue papillae. Make a detailed study of one taste bud. Identify the taste pore and gustatory hairs if observed. Compare your observations to Figure 20d and Plate 17 in the Histology Atlas. ▪

When taste is tested with pure chemical compounds, most taste sensations can be grouped into one of five basic qualities—sweet, sour, bitter, salty, or umami (u-mam′e; "delicious"). Although all taste buds are believed to respond in some degree to all five classes of chemical stimuli, each type responds optimally to only one.

Laboratory Experiments

! *Notify instructor of any food or scent allergies before beginning experiments.*

ACTIVITY 3

Stimulating Taste Buds

1. Obtain several paper towels, a sugar packet, and a disposable autoclave bag and bring them to your bench.

2. With a paper towel, dry the dorsal surface of your tongue.

! Immediately dispose of the paper towel in the autoclave bag.

3. Tear off a corner of the sugar packet and shake a few sugar crystals on your dried tongue. Do *not* close your mouth.

Time how long it takes to taste the sugar. _____ sec

Why couldn't you taste the sugar immediately?

_____ ▬

ACTIVITY 4

Examining the Effect of Olfactory Stimulation

There is no question that what is commonly referred to as taste depends heavily on stimulation of the olfactory receptors, particularly in the case of strongly odoriferous substances. The following experiment should illustrate this fact.

1. Obtain vials of oil of wintergreen, peppermint, and cloves, a paper cup, flask of water, paper towels, and some fresh cotton-tipped swabs. Ask the subject to sit so that he or she cannot see which vial is being used, and to dry the tongue and close the nostrils.

2. Use a cotton swab to apply a drop of one of the oils to the subject's tongue. Can he or she distinguish the flavor?

_____

! Put the used swab in the autoclave bag. *Do not redip the swab into the oil.*

3. Have the subject open the nostrils, and record the change in sensation he or she reports.

_____

4. Have the subject rinse the mouth well and dry the tongue.

5. Prepare two swabs, each with one of the two remaining oils.

6. Hold one swab under the subject's open nostrils, while touching the second swab to the tongue.

Record the reported sensations. _____

_____

_____

_____

7. Dispose of the used swabs and paper towels in the autoclave bag before continuing.

Which sense, taste or smell, appears to be more important in the proper identification of a strongly flavored volatile substance?

_____ ▬

ACTIVITY 5

Demonstrating Olfactory Adaption

When olfactory receptors are subjected to the same odor for a prolonged period, they eventually stop responding to that stimulus, a phenomenon called **olfactory adaptation.** This activity allows you to demonstrate olfactory adaptation.

Obtain some absorbent cotton and two of the following oils (oil of wintergreen, peppermint, or cloves). Place several drops of one oil on the absorbent cotton. Press one nostril shut. Hold the cotton under the open nostril and exhale through the mouth. Record the time required for the odor to disappear (for olfactory adaption to occur).

_____ sec

Repeat the procedure with the other nostril.

_____ sec

Immediately test another oil with the nostril that has just experienced olfactory adaptation. What are the results?

_____

What conclusions can you draw? _____

_____ ▬

ACTIVITY 6

Examining the Combined Effects of Smell, Texture, and Temperature on Taste

Effects of Smell and Texture

1. Ask the subject to sit with eyes closed and to pinch his or her nostrils shut.

2. Using a paper plate, obtain samples of the food items provided by your laboratory instructor. At no time should the subject be allowed to see the foods being tested. Wear plastic gloves and use toothpicks to handle food.

Identification by Texture and Smell

Food tested	Texture only	Chewing with nostrils pinched	Chewing with nostrils open	Identification not made

3. For each test, place a cube of food in the subject's mouth and ask him or her to identify the food by using the following sequence of activities:

- First, manipulate the food with the tongue.
- Second, chew the food.
- Third, if a positive identification is not made with the first two techniques and the taste sense, ask the subject to release the pinched nostrils and to continue chewing with the nostrils open to determine if a positive identification can be made.

In the chart above, record the type of food, and then put a check mark in the appropriate column for the result.

Was the sense of smell equally important in all cases?

_____

Where did it seem to be important and why?

_____

_____

Discard gloves in autoclave bag.

Effect of Temperature

In addition to the effect that olfaction and food texture play in determining our taste sensations, the temperature of foods also helps determine if the food is appreciated or even tasted. To illustrate this, have your partner hold some chipped ice on the tongue for approximately a minute and then close his or her eyes. Immediately place any of the foods previously identified in his or her mouth and ask for an identification.

_____

Results? _____

_____

_____

Special Senses: Olfaction and Taste

Localization and Anatomy of the Olfactory Receptors

1. Describe the cellular composition and the location of the olfactory epithelium. _____

_____

_____

2. How and why does sniffing improve your sense of smell? _____

_____

Localization and Anatomy of Taste Buds

3. Name five sites where receptors for taste are found, and circle the predominant site.

_____ , _____ , _____ ,

_____ , and _____

4. Describe the cellular makeup and arrangement of a taste bud._____

_____

Laboratory Experiments

5. Taste and smell receptors are both classified as _____, because they both

respond to _____

6. Why is it impossible to taste substances with a dry tongue? _____

_____

7. Name the five basic taste sensations.

1._____   4._____

2._____   5._____

3._____

8. Name three factors that influence our appreciation of foods. Substantiate each choice with an example from the lab experience.

1. _____   Substantiation _____

_____

2. _____   Substantiation _____

_____

3. _____   Substantiation _____

_____

Expand on your choices by explaining why a cold greasy hamburger is unappetizing to most people. _____

_____

9. How palatable is food when you have a cold? _____

Explain your answer. _____

_____

10. In your opinion, is olfactory adaptation desirable? _____

Explain your answer. _____

_____

Functional Anatomy of the Endocrine Glands

M A T E R I A L S

- ☐ Human torso model
- ☐ Anatomical chart of the human endocrine system
- ☐ Compound microscope
- ☐ Prepared slides of the anterior pituitary,* posterior pituitary, thyroid gland, parathyroid glands, adrenal gland, and pancreas*
- ☐ Dissection animal, tray, and instruments
- ☐ Bone cutters
- ☐ Embalming fluid
- ☐ Disposable gloves

 See Appendix B, Exercise 21 for links to A.D.A.M.® Interactive Anatomy.

*With differential staining if possible

O B J E C T I V E S

1. To identify and name the major endocrine glands and tissues of the body when provided with an appropriate diagram.
2. To list the hormones produced by the endocrine glands and discuss the general function of each.
3. To indicate the means by which hormones contribute to body homeostasis by giving appropriate examples of hormonal actions.
4. To cite mechanisms by which the endocrine glands are stimulated to release their hormones.
5. To describe the structural and functional relationship between the hypothalamus and the pituitary.
6. To describe a major pathological consequence of hypersecretion and hyposecretion of several of the hormones considered.
7. To correctly identify the histologic structure of the thyroid, parathyroid, pancreas, anterior and posterior pituitary, adrenal cortex and medulla, ovary, and testis by microscopic inspection or when presented with an appropriate photomicrograph or diagram.
8. To name and point out the specialized hormone-secreting cells in the above tissues as studied in the laboratory.
9. To identify and name the major endocrine organs on a dissected cat.

The **endocrine system** is the second major controlling system of the body. Acting with the nervous system, it helps coordinate and integrate the activity of the body's cells. However, the nervous system employs electrochemical impulses to bring about rapid control, while the more slowly acting endocrine system employs chemical "messengers," or **hormones,** which are released into the blood to be transported throughout the body.

The term *hormone* comes from a Greek word meaning "to arouse." The body's hormones, which are steroids or amino acid–based molecules, arouse the body's tissues and cells by stimulating changes in their metabolic activity. These changes lead to growth and development and to the physiological homeostasis of many body systems. Although all hormones are bloodborne, a given hormone affects the biochemical activity of only a specific organ or organs. Organs that respond to a particular hormone are referred to as the **target organs** of that hormone. The ability of the target tissue to respond seems to depend on the ability of the hormone to bind with specific receptors (proteins) occurring on the cells' plasma membrane or within the cells.

Although the function of some hormone-producing glands (the anterior pituitary, thyroid, adrenals, parathyroids) is purely endocrine, the function of others (the pancreas and gonads) is mixed—both endocrine and exocrine. Both types of glands are derived from epithelium, but the endocrine, or ductless, glands release their product (always hormonal) directly into the blood or lymph. The exocrine glands release their products at the body's surface or outside an epithelial membrane via ducts. In addition, there are varied numbers of hormone-producing cells within the intestine, stomach, kidney, and placenta, organs whose functions are primarily nonendocrine. Only the major endocrine organs are considered here.

Gross Anatomy and Basic Function of the Endocrine Glands

Pituitary Gland (Hypophysis)

The *pituitary gland,* or *hypophysis,* is located in the concavity of the sella turcica of the sphenoid bone. It consists largely of two functional lobes, the **adenohypophysis,** or **anterior pituitary,** and the **neurohypophysis,** consisting mainly of the **posterior pituitary** (Figure 21.1). The pituitary gland is attached to the hypothalamus by a stalk called the **infundibulum.**

Anterior Pituitary Hormones   The anterior pituitary, or adenohypophysis, secretes a number of hormones. Four of these are **tropic hormones.** A tropic hormone stimulates its target organ, which is also an endocrine gland, to secrete its hormones. Target organ hormones then exert their effects on other body organs and tissues. The anterior pituitary tropic hormones include:

- **Gonadotropins—follicle-stimulating hormone (FSH)** and **luteinizing hormone (LH)**—regulate gamete production and hormonal activity of the gonads (ovaries and testes).

- **Adrenocorticotropic hormone (ACTH)** regulates the endocrine activity of the cortex portion of the adrenal gland.

- **Thyroid-stimulating hormone (TSH),** or **thyrotropin,** influences the growth and activity of the thyroid gland.

The two other important hormones produced by the anterior pituitary are not directly involved in the regulation of other endocrine glands of the body.

- **Growth hormone (GH)** is a general metabolic hormone that plays an important role in determining body size. It affects many tissues of the body; however, it mainly affects the growth of muscle and the long bones of the body. Hyposecretion results in pituitary dwarfism in children. Hypersecretion causes gigantism in children and **acromegaly** (overgrowth of bones in hands, feet, and face) in adults. ●

- **Prolactin (PRL)** stimulates breast development and promotes and maintains lactation by the mammary glands after childbirth. It may stimulate testosterone production in males.

Less important secretory products of the anterior pituitary are MSH (melanocyte-stimulating hormone), endorphins, and lipotropin.

The anterior pituitary controls the activity of so many other endocrine glands that it has often been called the *master endocrine gland.* However, the anterior pituitary is not autonomous in its control because release of anterior pituitary hormones is controlled by neurosecretions, *releasing* or

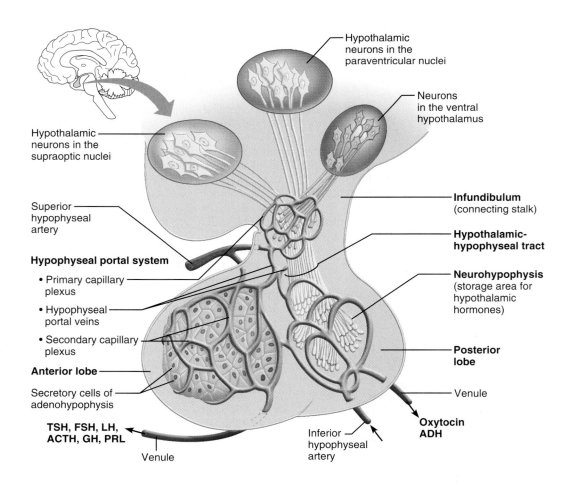

FIGURE 21.1 Hypothalamus and pituitary gland. Neural and vascular relationships between the hypothalamus and the anterior and posterior lobes of the pituitary are depicted.

inhibiting hormones, produced by neurons of the ventral hypothalamus. These hypothalamic hormones are liberated into the **hypophyseal portal system,** which serves the circulatory needs of the anterior pituitary (Figure 21.1).

Posterior Pituitary Hormones The posterior pituitary is not an endocrine gland in a strict sense because it does not synthesize the hormones it releases. (This relationship is also indicated in Figure 21.1.) Instead, it acts as a storage area for two hormones transported to it via the axons of neurons in the paraventricular and supraoptic nuclei of the hypothalamus. These axons form the hypothalamic-hypophyseal tract. The hormones are released in response to nerve impulses in these neurons. The first of these hormones is **oxytocin,** which stimulates powerful uterine contractions during birth and coitus and also causes milk ejection in the lactating mother. The second, **antidiuretic hormone (ADH),** causes the distal and collecting tubules of the kidneys to resorb more water from the urinary filtrate, thereby reducing urine output and conserving body water. It also plays a minor role in increasing blood pressure because of its vasoconstrictor effect on the arterioles.

Hyposecretion of ADH results in dehydration from excessive urine output, a condition called **diabetes insipidus.** Individuals with this condition experience an insatiable thirst. Hypersecretion results in edema, headache, and disorientation. ●

Thyroid Gland

The *thyroid gland* is composed of two lobes joined by a central mass, or isthmus. It is located in the throat, just inferior to the larynx. It produces two major hormones, thyroid hormone and calcitonin.

Thyroid hormone (TH) is actually two physiologically active hormones known as T_4 **(thyroxine)** and T_3 **(triiodothyronine).** Because its primary function is to control the rate of body metabolism and cellular oxidation, TH affects virtually every cell in the body.

Hyposecretion of thyroxine leads to a condition of mental and physical sluggishness, which is called **myxedema** in the adult. Hypersecretion causes elevated metabolic rate, nervousness, weight loss, sweating, and irregular heartbeat. ●

Calcitonin decreases blood calcium levels by stimulating calcium salt deposit in the bones. It acts antagonistically to parathyroid hormone, the hormonal product of the parathyroid glands.

● Try to palpate your thyroid gland. Place your fingers against your windpipe. As you swallow, the thyroid gland will move up and down on the sides and front of the windpipe.

Parathyroid Glands

The *parathyroid glands* are found embedded in the posterior surface of the thyroid gland. Typically, there are two small oval glands on each lobe, but there may be more and some may be located in other regions of the neck. They secrete **parathyroid hormone (PTH),** the most important regulator of calcium balance of the blood. When blood calcium levels decrease below a certain critical level, the parathyroids release PTH, which causes release of calcium from bone matrix and prods the kidney to resorb more calcium and less phosphate from the filtrate. PTH also stimulates the kidneys to activate vitamin D.

Hyposecretion increases neural excitability and may lead to **tetany,** prolonged muscle spasms that can result in respiratory paralysis and death. Hypersecretion of PTH results in loss of calcium from bones, causing deformation, softening, and spontaneous fractures. ●

Adrenal Glands

The two bean-shaped *adrenal,* or *suprarenal, glands* are located atop or close to the kidneys. Anatomically, the **adrenal medulla** develops from neural crest tissue, and it is directly controlled by sympathetic nervous system neurons. The medullary cells respond to this stimulation by releasing **epinephrine** (80%) or **norepinephrine** (20%), which act in conjunction with the sympathetic nervous system to elicit the fight-or-flight response to stressors.

The **adrenal cortex** produces three major groups of steroid hormones, collectively called **corticosteroids.** The **mineralocorticoids,** chiefly **aldosterone,** regulate water and electrolyte balance in the extracellular fluids, mainly by regulating sodium ion resorption by kidney tubules. The **glucocorticoids** (cortisone, hydrocortisone, and corticosterone) enable the body to resist long-term stressors, primarily by increasing blood glucose levels. The **gonadocorticoids,** or **sex hormones,** produced by the adrenal cortex are chiefly androgens (male sex hormones), but some estrogens (female sex hormones) are formed.

The gonadocorticoids are produced throughout life in relatively insignificant amounts; however, hypersecretion of these hormones produces abnormal hairiness **(hirsutism),** and masculinization occurs. ●

Pancreas

The *pancreas,* located partially behind the stomach in the abdomen, functions as both an endocrine and exocrine gland. It produces digestive enzymes as well as insulin and glucagon, important hormones concerned with the regulation of blood sugar levels.

Elevated blood glucose levels stimulate release of **insulin,** which decreases blood sugar levels, primarily by accelerating the transport of glucose into the body cells, where it is oxidized for energy or converted to glycogen or fat for storage.

Hyposecretion of insulin or some deficiency in the insulin receptors leads to **diabetes mellitus,** which is characterized by the inability of body cells to utilize glucose and the subsequent loss of glucose in the urine. Alterations of protein and fat metabolism also occur secondary to derangements in carbohydrate metabolism. Hypersecretion causes low blood sugar, or **hypoglycemia.** Symptoms include anxiety, nervousness, tremors, and weakness. ●

Glucagon acts antagonistically to insulin. Its release is stimulated by low blood glucose levels, and its action is basically hyperglycemic. It stimulates the liver, its primary target organ, to break down its glycogen stores to glucose and subsequently to release the glucose to the blood.

The Gonads

The *female gonads,* or *ovaries,* are paired, almond-sized organs located in the pelvic cavity. In addition to producing the female sex cells (ova), the ovaries produce two steroid hormone groups, the estrogens and progesterone. The endocrine and exocrine functions of the ovaries do not begin until the

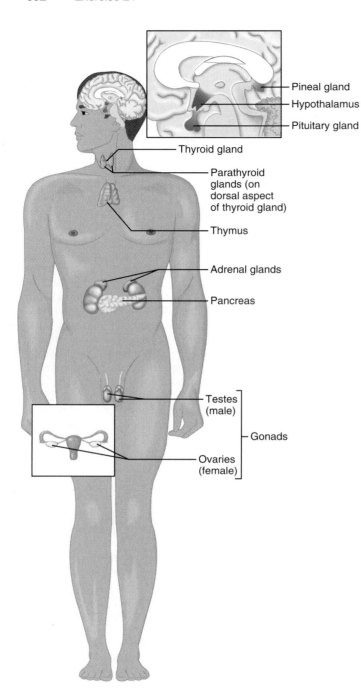

FIGURE 21.2 Human endocrine organs.

onset of puberty, when the anterior pituitary gonadotropic hormones prod the ovary into action that produces rhythmic ovarian cycles in which ova develop and hormonal levels rise and fall. The **estrogens** are responsible for the development of the secondary sex characteristics of the female at puberty (primarily maturation of the reproductive organs and development of the breasts) and act with progesterone to bring about cyclic changes of the uterine lining that occur during the menstrual cycle. The estrogens also help prepare the mammary glands for lactation.

Progesterone, as already noted, acts with estrogen to bring about the menstrual cycle. During pregnancy it maintains the uterine musculature in a quiescent state and helps to prepare the breast tissue for lactation.

The paired oval *testes* of the male are suspended in a pouchlike sac, the scrotum, outside the pelvic cavity. In addition to the male sex cells, sperm, the testes produce the male sex hormone, **testosterone.** Testosterone promotes the maturation of the reproductive system accessory structures, brings about the development of the male secondary sex characteristics, and is responsible for sexual drive, or libido. Both the endocrine and exocrine functions of the testes begin at puberty under the influence of the anterior pituitary gonadotropins.

Two glands not mentioned earlier as major endocrine glands should also be briefly considered here, the thymus and the pineal gland.

Thymus

The *thymus* is a bilobed gland situated in the superior thorax, posterior to the sternum and anterior to the heart and lungs. Conspicuous in the infant, it begins to atrophy at puberty, and by old age it is relatively inconspicuous. The thymus produces hormones called **thymosin** and **thymopoietin,** which help direct the maturation and specialization of a unique population of white blood cells called T lymphocytes, or T cells. T lymphocytes are responsible for the cellular immunity aspect of body defense; that is, rejection of foreign grafts, tumors, or virus-infected cells.

Pineal Gland

The *pineal gland,* or *epiphysis cerebri,* is a small cone-shaped gland located in the roof of the third ventricle of the brain. Its major endocrine product is **melatonin.**

The endocrine role of the pineal body in humans is still controversial, but it is known to play a role in the biological rhythms (particularly mating and migratory behavior) of other animals. In humans, melatonin appears to exert some inhibitory effect on the reproductive system that prevents precocious sexual maturation.

ACTIVITY 1

Identifying the Endocrine Organs

Locate the endocrine organs on Figure 21.2. Also locate these organs on the anatomical charts or torso. ▆

DISSECTION AND IDENTIFICATION:

Selected Endocrine Organs of the Cat

If you have not previously opened the ventral body cavity, follow the directions from the beginning of this section. Otherwise, begin with Activity 3, "Identifying Organs." ▆

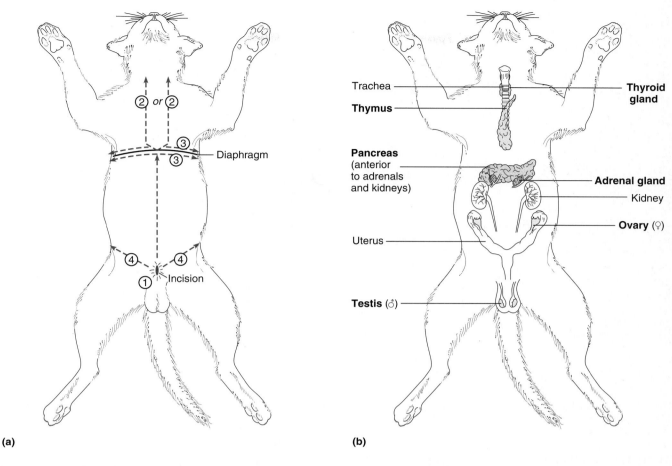

FIGURE 21.3 Endocrine organs of the cat. (a) Incisions to be made in opening the ventral body cavity of a cat. Numbers indicate sequence. (b) Location of the cat's endocrine organs.

Opening the Ventral Body Cavity

1. Don gloves and then obtain your dissection animal. Place the animal on the dissecting tray, ventral side up. Using scissors, make a longitudinal median incision through the ventral body wall. Begin your cut just superior to the midline of the pubic bone and continue it anteriorly to the rib cage. Check the incision guide provided in Figure 21.3a as you work.

2. Angle the scissors slightly (1.3 cm or ½ in.) to the right or left of the sternum, and continue the cut through the rib cartilages, just lateral to the body midline, to the base of the throat.

3. Make two lateral cuts on both sides of the ventral body surface, anterior and posterior to the diaphragm, which separates the thoracic and abdominal parts of the ventral body cavity. *Leave the diaphragm intact*. Spread the thoracic walls laterally to expose the thoracic organs.

4. Make an angled lateral cut on each side of the median incision line just superior to the pubic bone, and spread the flaps to expose the abdominal cavity organs. ▪▪▪

Identifying Organs

A helpful adjunct to identifying selected endocrine organs of the cat is a general overview of ventral body cavity organs as shown in Figure 21.4. Since you will study the organ systems housed in the ventral body cavity in later units, the objective here is simply to identify the most important organs and those that will help you to locate the desired endocrine organs (marked * in the following lists). A schematic showing the relative positioning of several of the animal's endocrine organs is provided in Figure 21.3b.

Neck and Thoracic Cavity Organs

Trachea: The windpipe; runs down the midline of the throat and then divides just anterior to the lungs to form the bronchi, which plunge into the lungs on either side.

*Thyroid: Its dark lobes straddle the trachea. This endocrine organ's hormones are the main hormones regulating the body's metabolic rate.

*Thymus: Glandular structure superior to and partly covering the heart. The thymus is intimately involved (via its hormones) in programming the immune system. If you have a

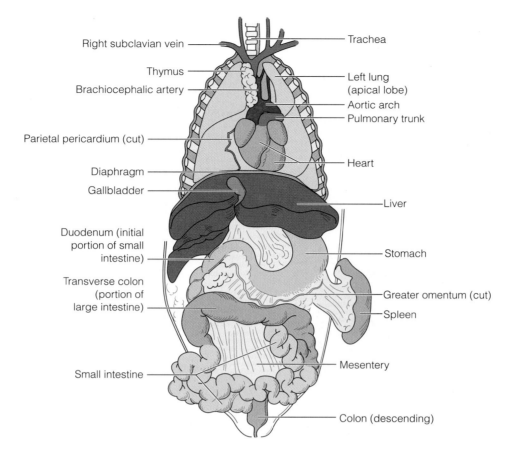

FIGURE 21.4 Ventral body cavity organs of the cat. Superficial view with greater omentum removed. (Also see Figure 27.18, p. 473.)

young cat, the thymus will be quite large. In old cats, most of this organ has been replaced by fat.

Heart: In the mediastinum enclosed by the pericardium.

Lungs: Paired organs flanking the heart.

Abdominal Cavity Organs

Liver: Large multilobed organ lying under the umbrella of the diaphragm.

Lift the drapelike, fat-infiltrated greater omentum covering the abdominal organs to expose the following organs:

Stomach: Dorsally located sac to the left side of the liver.

Spleen: Flattened brown organ curving around the lateral aspect of the stomach.

Small intestine: Tubelike organ continuing posteriorly from the stomach.

*Pancreas: Diffuse gland lying deep to and between the small intestine and stomach. Lift the first section of the small intestine with your forceps; you should see the pancreas situated in the delicate mesentery behind the stomach. This gland is extremely important in regulating blood sugar levels.

Large intestine: Taking a U-shaped course around the small intestine to terminate in the rectum.

Push the intestines to one side with a probe to reveal the deeper organs in the abdominal cavity.

Kidneys: Bean-shaped organs located toward the dorsal body wall surface and behind the peritoneum.

*Adrenal glands: Seen above and medial to each kidney, these small glands produce corticosteroids important in preventing stress and abnormalities of water and electrolyte balance in the body.

*Gonads (ovaries or testes): Sex organs producing sex hormones. The location of the gonads is illustrated in Figure 21.3b, but their identification is deferred until the reproductive system organs are considered (Exercise 29).

Before leaving the lab, prepare your animal for storage as instructed on p. 220. Then clean and dry all dissecting equipment, wash down your lab bench, and properly dispose of your gloves. ■

Microscopic Anatomy of Selected Endocrine Glands

Examining the Microscopic Structure of Endocrine Glands

To prepare for the histologic study of the endocrine glands, obtain a microscope and one of each slide on the materials list. We will study only organs in which it is possible to identify the endocrine-producing cells. Compare your observations with the histology images in Figure 21.5a–f.

Thyroid Gland

1. Scan the thyroid under low power, noting the **follicles,** spherical sacs containing a pink-stained material (*colloid*). Stored T_3 and T_4 are attached to the protein colloidal material stored in the follicles as **thyroglobulin** and are released gradually to the blood. Compare the tissue viewed to Figure 21.5a.

2. Observe the tissue under high power. Notice that the walls of the follicles are formed by simple cuboidal or squamous epithelial cells that synthesize the follicular products. The **parafollicular,** or **C, cells** you see between the follicles are responsible for calcitonin production.

When the thyroid gland is actively secreting, the follicles appear small, and the colloidal material has a ruffled border. When the thyroid is hypoactive or inactive, the follicles are large and plump and the follicular epithelium appears to be squamouslike. What is the physiological state of the tissue

you have been viewing? _____

Parathyroid Glands

Observe the parathyroid tissue under low power to view its two major cell types, the chief cells and the oxyphil cells. Compare your observations to Figure 21.5b. The **chief cells,** which synthesize parathyroid hormone (PTH), are small and abundant, and arranged in thick branching cords. The function of the scattered, much larger **oxyphil cells** is unknown.

Pancreas

1. Observe pancreas tissue under low power to identify the roughly circular **pancreatic islets (islets of Langerhans),** the endocrine portions of the pancreas. The islets are scattered amid the more numerous acinar cells and stain differently (usually lighter), which makes their identification possible. (See Figure 27.16.) The acinar cells produce the enzymatic exocrine product of the pancreas that is released to the duodenum via the pancreatic duct. Alkaline fluid produced by the duct cells accompanies the hydrolytic enzymes.

2. Focus on islet cells under high power. Notice that they are densely packed and have no definite arrangement. In contrast, the cuboidal acinar cells are arranged around secretory ducts. If special stains are used, it will be possible to distinguish the **alpha cells,** which tend to cluster at the periphery of the islets and produce glucagon, from the **beta cells,** which synthesize insulin. With these specific stains, the beta cells are larger and stain gray-blue, and the alpha cells are smaller and appear bright pink, as hinted at in Figure 21.5c.

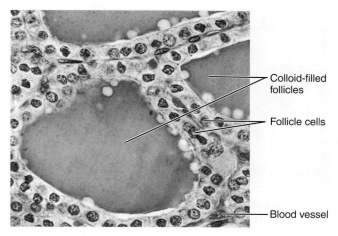

(a) Thyroid gland (630×)

Colloid-filled follicles
Follicle cells
Blood vessel

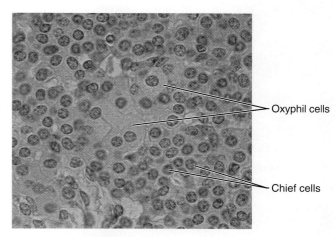

(b) Parathyroid gland (560×)

Oxyphil cells
Chief cells

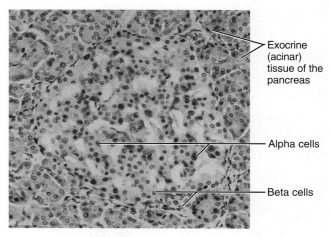

(c) Pancreatic islet (200×)

Exocrine (acinar) tissue of the pancreas
Alpha cells
Beta cells

FIGURE 21.5 Microscopic anatomy of selected endocrine organs.

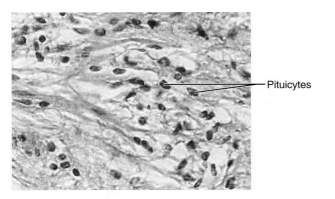

(d) Anterior pituitary (600×)

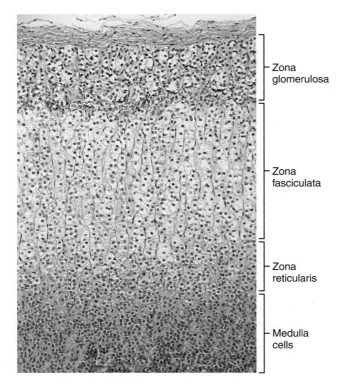

(e) Posterior pituitary (400×)

(f) Adrenal gland (250×)

FIGURE 21.5 (*continued*) Microscopic anatomy of selected endocrine organs.

Pituitary Gland

1. Observe the general structure of the pituitary gland under low power to differentiate between the glandular anterior pituitary and the neural posterior pituitary. Figure 21.5d and e should help you get started.

2. Using the high-power lens, focus on the nests of cells of the anterior pituitary. It is possible to identify the specialized cell types that secrete the specific hormones when differential stains are used. Using the photomicrograph in Figure 21.5d as a guide, locate the reddish brown–stained **acidophil cells,** which produce growth hormone and prolactin, and the **basophil cells,** whose deep-blue granules are responsible for the production of the tropic hormones (TSH, ACTH, FSH, and LH). **Chromophobes,** the third cellular population, do not take up the stain and appear rather dull and colorless. The role of the chromophobes is controversial, but they apparently are not involved in hormone production.

3. Switch your focus to the posterior pituitary. Observe the nerve fibers (axons of hypophyseal neurons) that compose most of this portion of the pituitary. Also note the **pituicytes,** glial cells which are randomly distributed among the nerve fibers. Refer to Figure 21.5e as you scan the slide.

What two hormones are stored here?

_____ and _____

What is their source? _____

Adrenal Gland

1. Hold the slide of the adrenal gland up to the light to distinguish the outer cortex and inner medulla areas. Then scan the cortex under low power to distinguish the differences in cell appearance and arrangement in the three cortical areas. Refer to Figure 21.5f and the following descriptions to identify the cortical areas:

• Connective tissue capsule of the adrenal gland.

• The outermost **zona glomerulosa,** where most mineralocorticoid production occurs and where the tightly packed cells are arranged in spherical clusters.

• The deeper intermediate **zona fasciculata,** which produces glucocorticoids. This is the thickest part of the cortex. Its cells are arranged in parallel cords.

• The innermost cortical zone, the **zona reticularis** abutting the medulla, which produces sex hormones and some glucocorticoids. The cells here stain intensely and form a branching network.

2. Switch focus to view the large, lightly stained cells of the adrenal medulla under high power. Notice their clumped arrangement.

What hormones are produced by the medulla?

_____ and _____

Ovary and Testis

The histology of the ovary and testis is considered with the reproductive system in Exercise 29. ▪

Functional Anatomy of the Endocrine Glands

Gross Anatomy and Basic Function of the Endocrine Glands

1. Both the endocrine and nervous systems are major regulating systems of the body; however, the nervous system has been compared to an airmail delivery system and the endocrine system to the pony express. Briefly explain this comparison.

_____

_____

_____

2. Define *hormone*. _____

_____

3. Chemically, hormones belong chiefly to two molecular groups: _____ and _____ .

4. What do all hormones have in common? _____

_____

5. Define *target organ*. _____

_____

6. If hormones travel in the bloodstream, why don't all tissues respond to all hormones? _____

_____

7. Identify the endocrine organ described by each of the following statements.

_____ 1. located in the throat; bilobed gland connected by an isthmus

_____ 2. found close to the kidney

_____ 3. a mixed gland, located close to the stomach and small intestine

_____ 4. paired glands suspended in the scrotum

_____ 5. ride "horseback" on the thyroid gland

_____ 6. found in the pelvic cavity of the female, concerned with ova and female hormone production

_____ 7. found in the upper thorax overlying the heart; large during youth

_____ 8. found in the roof of the third ventricle

8. For each statement describing hormonal effects, identify the hormone(s) involved by choosing a number from key A, and note the hormone's site of production with a letter from key B. More than one hormone may be involved in some cases.

Key A:

1. ACTH	13. progesterone	
2. ADH	14. prolactin	
3. aldosterone	15. PTH	
4. calcitonin	16. T_4 / T_3	
5. cortisone	17. testosterone	
6. epinephrine	18. thymosin	
7. estrogens	19. TSH	
8. FSH		
9. glucagon		
10. insulin		
11. LH		
12. oxytocin		

Key B:

a. adrenal cortex
b. adrenal medulla
c. anterior pituitary
d. hypothalamus
e. ovaries
f. pancreas
g. parathyroid glands
h. pineal gland
i. posterior pituitary
j. testes
k. thymus
l. thyroid gland

_____, _____ 1. programming of T lymphocytes

_____, _____ and _____, _____ 2. regulate blood calcium levels

_____, _____ and _____, _____ 3. released in response to stressors

_____, _____ and _____, _____ 4. drive development of secondary sexual characteristics

_____, _____; _____, _____; _____, _____; and

_____, _____ 5. regulate the function of another endocrine gland

_____, _____ 6. mimics the sympathetic nervous system

_____, _____ and _____, _____ 7. regulate blood glucose levels; produced by the same "mixed" gland

_____, _____ and _____, _____ 8. directly responsible for regulation of the menstrual cycle

_____, _____ and _____, _____ 9. maintenance of salt and water balance in the extracellular fluid

_____, _____ and _____, _____ 10. directly involved in milk production and ejection

9. Although the pituitary gland is often referred to as the master gland of the body, the hypothalamus exerts some control over the pituitary gland. How does the hypothalamus control both anterior and posterior pituitary functioning?

_____

_____

_____

10. Name the hormone(s) produced in *inadequate* amounts that directly result in the following conditions. (Use your textbook as necessary.)

_____ 1.   tetany

_____ 2.   excessive diuresis without high blood glucose levels

_____ 3.   loss of glucose in urine

_____ 4.   abnormally small stature, normal proportions

_____ 5.   lethargy, hair loss, low metabolic rate, mental and physical sluggishness

11. Name the hormone(s) produced in *excessive* amounts that directly result in the following conditions. (Use your textbook as necessary.)

_____ 1.   large facial bones, hands, and feet in the adult

_____ 2.   bulging eyeballs, nervousness, increased pulse rate, sweating

_____ 3.   demineralization of bones, spontaneous fractures

Microscopic Anatomy of Selected Endocrine Glands

12. Choose a response from the key below to name the hormone(s) produced by the cell types listed.

Key: a. calcitonin   d. glucocorticoids   g. PTH
       b. GH, prolactin   e. insulin   h. T_4 / T_3
       c. glucagon   f. mineralocorticoids   i. TSH, ACTH, FSH, LH

_____ 1.   parafollicular cells of the thyroid

_____ 2.   follicular epithelial cells of the thyroid

_____ 3.   beta cells of the pancreatic islets (islets of Langerhans)

_____ 4.   alpha cells of the pancreatic islets (islets of Langerhans)

_____ 5.   basophil cells of the anterior pituitary

_____ 6.   zona fasciculata cells

_____ 7.   zona glomerulosa cells

_____ 8.   chief cells

_____ 9.   acidophil cells of the anterior pituitary

13. Six diagrams of the microscopic structures of the endocrine glands are presented here. Identify each and name all structures indicated by a leader line or bracket.

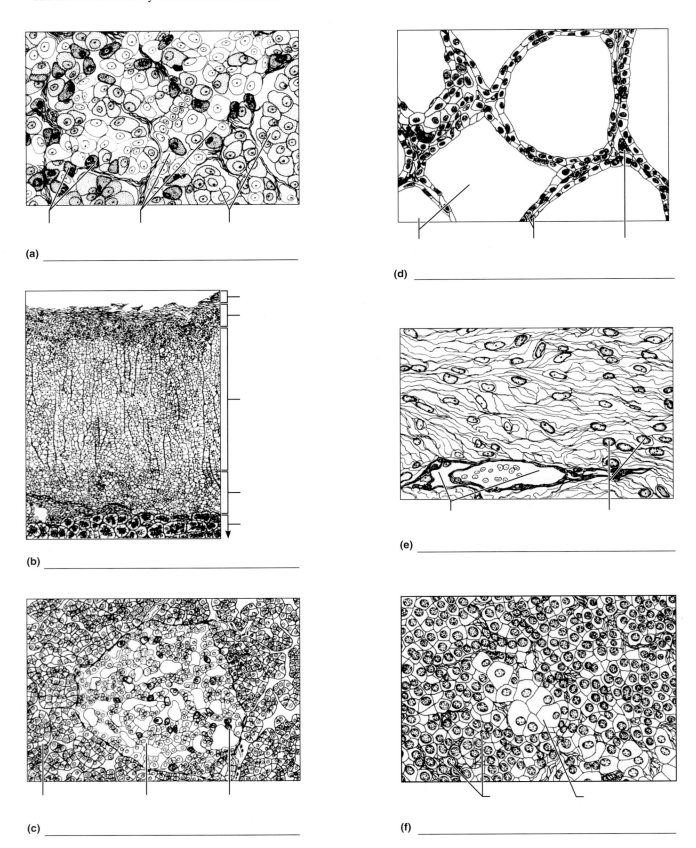

(a) _____

(b) _____

(c) _____

(d) _____

(e) _____

(f) _____

Dissection and Identification: Selected Endocrine Organs of the Cat

14. How do the locations of the endocrine organs in the cat compare with those in the human?

_____

15. Name two endocrine organs located in the neck region: _____ and _____

16. Name three endocrine organs located in the abdominal cavity.

_____

17. Given the assumption (not necessarily true) that human beings have more stress than cats, which endocrine organs would you expect to be relatively larger in humans?

_____

18. Cats are smaller animals than humans. Which would you expect to have a (relatively speaking) more active thyroid gland—

cats or humans? _____ Why? (We know we are asking a lot with this one, but give it a whirl.)

_____

_____

Blood

MATERIALS

General Supply Area*

☐ Disposable gloves

☐ Safety glasses (student-provided)

☐ Bucket or large beaker containing 10% household bleach solution for slide and glassware disposal

☐ Spray bottles containing 10% bleach solution

☐ Autoclave bag

☐ Designated lancet (sharps) disposal container

☐ Plasma (obtained from an animal hospital or prepared by centrifuging animal blood [for example, cattle or sheep blood] obtained from a biological supply house)

☐ Test tubes and test tube racks

☐ Wide-range pH paper

☐ Stained smears of human blood from a biological supply house or, if desired by the instructor, heparinized animal blood obtained from a biological supply house or an animal hospital (for example, dog blood), or EDTA-treated red cells (reference cells[†]) with blood type labels obscured (available from Immunocor, Inc.)

☐ Clean microscope slides

☐ Glass stirring rods

☐ Wright's stain in a dropper bottle

☐ Distilled water in a dropper bottle

☐ Sterile lancets

*Note to the Instructor:** See directions for handling of soiled glassware and disposable items on p. 27.

[†]The blood in these kits (each containing four blood cell types—A1, A2, B, and O—individually supplied in 10-ml vials) is used to calibrate cell counters and other automated clinical laboratory equipment. This blood has been carefully screened and can be safely used by students for blood typing and determining hematocrits. It is not usable for hemoglobin determinations or coagulation studies.

Text continues on next page

OBJECTIVES

1. To name the two major components of blood, and to state their average percentages in whole blood.
2. To describe the composition and functional importance of plasma.
3. To define *formed elements* and list the cell types composing them, cite their relative percentages, and describe their major functions.
4. To identify red blood cells, basophils, eosinophils, monocytes, lymphocytes, and neutrophils when provided with a microscopic preparation or appropriate diagram.
5. To provide the normal values for a total white blood cell count and a total red blood cell count, and to state the importance of these tests.
6. To conduct the following blood test determinations in the laboratory, and to state their norms and the importance of each.

   differential white blood cell count
   hematocrit
   hemoglobin determination
   clotting time
   ABO and Rh blood typing
   plasma cholesterol concentration

7. To discuss the reason for transfusion reactions resulting from the administration of mismatched blood.
8. To define *anemia, polycythemia, leukopenia, leukocytosis,* and *leukemia* and to cite a possible reason for each condition.

In this exercise you will study plasma and formed elements of blood and conduct various hematologic tests. These tests are useful diagnostic tools for the physician because blood composition (number and types of blood cells, and chemical composition) reflects the status of many body functions and malfunctions.

ALERT: Special precautions when handling blood. This exercise provides information on blood from several sources: human, animal, human treated, and artificial blood. The decision to use animal blood for testing or to have students test their own blood will be made by the instructor in accordance with the educational goals of the student group. For example, for students in the nursing or laboratory technician curricula, learning how to safely handle human blood or other human wastes is essential. Whenever blood is being handled, special attention must be paid to safety precautions. These precautions should be used regardless of the source of the blood. This will both teach good technique and ensure the safety of the students.

Follow exactly the safety precautions listed below.

1. Wear safety gloves at all times. Discard appropriately.

2. Wear safety glasses throughout the exercise.

3. Handle only your own, freshly let (human) blood.

4. Be sure you understand the instructions and have all supplies on hand before you begin any part of the exercise.

5. Do not reuse supplies and equipment once they have been exposed to blood.

☐ Absorbent cotton balls

☐ Alcohol swabs (wipes)

☐ Paper towels

☐ Compound microscope

☐ Immersion oil

☐ Three-dimensional models (if available) and charts of blood cells

☐ Assorted slides of white blood count pathologies labeled "Unknown Sample ____"

☐ Timer

Because many blood tests are to be conducted in this exercise, it is advisable to set up a number of appropriately labeled supply areas for the various tests, as designated below. Some needed supplies are located in the general supply area.

Note: Artificial blood prepared by Ward's Natural Science can be used for differential counts, hematocrit, and blood typing.

Activity 4: Hematocrit

☐ Heparinized capillary tubes

☐ Microhematocrit centrifuge and reading gauge (if the reading gauge is not available, a millimeter ruler may be used)

☐ Capillary tube sealer or modeling clay

Activity 5: Hemoglobin Determination

☐ Hemoglobinometer, hemolysis applicator, and lens paper, or Tallquist hemoglobin scale and test paper

Activity 6: Coagulation Time

☐ Capillary tubes (nonheparinized)

☐ Fine triangular file

Activity 7: Blood Typing

☐ Blood typing sera (anti-A, anti-B, and anti-Rh [anti-D])

☐ Rh typing box

☐ Wax marking pencil

☐ Toothpicks

☐ Blood test cards or microscope slides

☐ Medicine dropper

Activity 8: Demonstration

☐ Microscopes set up with prepared slides demonstrating the following bone (or bone marrow) conditions: macrocytic hypochromic anemia, microcytic hypochromic anemia, sickle cell disease, lymphocytic leukemia (chronic), and eosinophilia

Activity 9: Cholesterol Measurement

☐ Cholesterol test cards and color scale

6.   Keep the lab area clean. Do not let anything that has come in contact with blood touch surfaces or other individuals in the lab. Pay attention to the location of any supplies and equipment that come into contact with blood.

7.   Dispose of lancets immediately after use in a designated disposal container. Do not put them down on the lab bench, even temporarily.

8.   Dispose of all used cotton balls, alcohol swabs, blotting paper, and so forth in autoclave bags and place all soiled glassware in containers of 10% bleach solution.

9.   Wipe down the lab bench with 10% bleach solution when you are finished.

Composition of Blood

Circulating blood is a rather viscous substance that varies from bright scarlet to a dull brick red, depending on the amount of oxygen it is carrying. The average volume of blood in the body is about 5–6 liters in adult males and 4–5 liters in adult females.

Blood is classified as a type of connective tissue because it consists of a nonliving fluid matrix (the **plasma**) in which living cells (**formed elements**) are suspended. The fibers typical of a connective tissue matrix become visible in blood only when clotting occurs. They then appear as fibrin threads, which form the structural basis for clot formation.

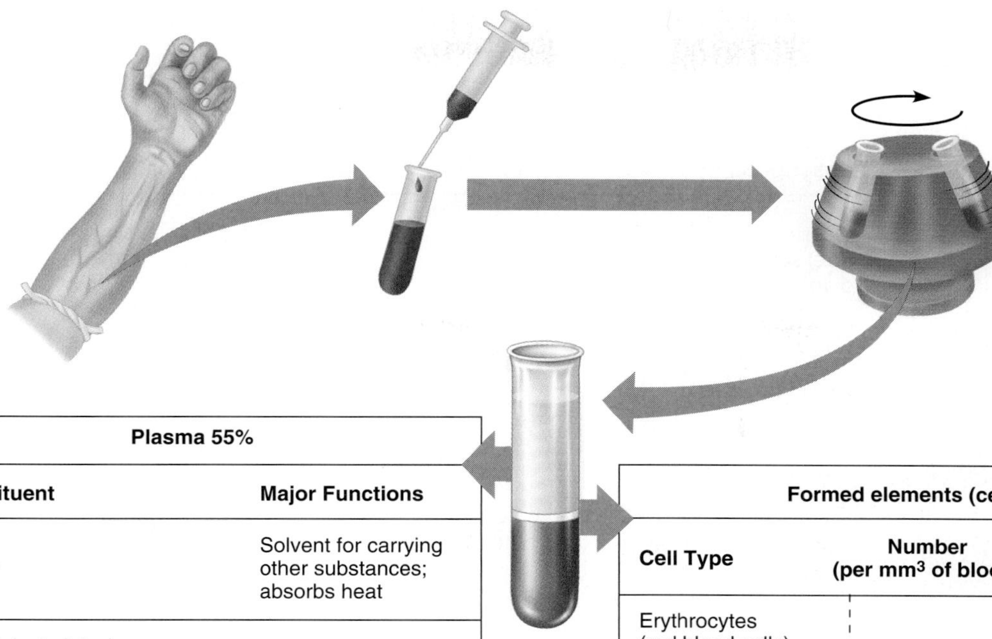

Plasma 55%	
Constituent	**Major Functions**
Water	Solvent for carrying other substances; absorbs heat
Salts (electrolytes) Sodium Potassium Calcium Magnesium Chloride Bicarbonate	Osmotic balance, pH buffering, regulation of membrane permeability
Plasma proteins Albumin Fibrinogen Globulins	Osmotic balance, pH buffering Clotting of blood Defense (antibodies) and lipid transport
Substances transported by blood Nutrients (glucose, fatty acids, amino acids, vitamins) Waste products of metabolism (urea, uric acid) Respiratory gases (O_2 and CO_2) Hormones	

Formed elements (cells) 45%		
Cell Type	**Number (per mm^3 of blood)**	**Functions**
Erythrocytes (red blood cells)	4 – 6 million	Transport oxygen and help transport carbon dioxide
Leukocytes (white blood cells)	4000 – 11,000	Defense and immunity
Basophil		Lymphocyte
Eosinophil		
Neutrophil		Monocyte
Platelets	250,000 – 500,000	Blood clotting

FIGURE 22.1 The composition of blood.

More than 100 different substances are dissolved or suspended in plasma (Figure 22.1), which is over 90% water. These include nutrients, gases, hormones, various wastes and metabolites, many types of proteins, and electrolytes. The composition of plasma varies continuously as cells remove or add substances to the blood.

Three types of formed elements are present in blood (Table 22.1). Most numerous are **erythrocytes,** or **red blood cells (RBCs),** which are literally sacs of hemoglobin molecules that transport the bulk of the oxygen carried in the blood (and a small percentage of the carbon dioxide). **Leukocytes,** or **white blood cells (WBCs),** are part of the body's nonspecific defenses and the immune system, and **platelets** function in hemostasis (blood clot formation). Formed elements normally constitute 45% of whole blood; plasma accounts for the remaining 55%.

ACTIVITY 1

Determining the Physical Characteristics of Plasma

Go to the general supply area and carefully pour a few milliliters of plasma into a test tube. Also obtain some wide-range pH paper, and then return to your laboratory bench to make the following simple observations.

pH of Plasma

Test the pH of the plasma with wide-range pH paper. Record

the pH observed. _____

| TABLE 22.1 | Summary of Formed Elements of the Blood |

Cell type	Illustration	Description*	Number of cells/mm^3 (μl) of blood	Duration of development (D) and life span (LS)	Function
Erythrocytes (red blood cells, RBCs)		Biconcave, anucleate disc; salmon-colored; diameter 7–8 μm	4–6 million	D: about 15 days LS: 100–120 days	Transport oxygen and carbon dioxide
Leukocytes (white blood cells, WBCs)		Spherical, nucleated cells	4,800–10,800		
Granulocytes Neutrophil		Nucleus multilobed; inconspicuous cytoplasmic granules; diameter 10–12 μm	3,000–7,000	D: about 14 days LS: 6 hours to a few days	Phagocytize bacteria
Eosinophil		Nucleus bilobed; red cytoplasmic granules; diameter 10–14 μm	100–400	D: about 14 days LS: 8–12 days	Kill parasitic worms; destroy antigen-antibody complexes; inactivate some inflammatory chemicals of allergy
Basophil		Nucleus lobed; large blue-purple cytoplasmic granules; diameter 10–14 μm	20–50	D: 3–7 days LS: ? (a few hours to a few days)	Release histamine and other mediators of inflammation; contain heparin, an anticoagulant
Agranulocytes Lymphocyte		Nucleus spherical or indented; pale blue cytoplasm; diameter 5–17 μm	1,500–3,000	D: days to weeks LS: hours to years	Mount immune response by direct cell attack or via antibodies
Monocyte		Nucleus U- or kidney-shaped; gray-blue cytoplasm; diameter 14–24 μm	100–700	D: 2–3 days LS: months	Phagocytosis; develop into macrophages in tissues
Platelets		Discoid cytoplasmic fragments containing granules; stain deep purple; diameter 2–4 μm	150,000–400,000	D: 4–5 days LS: 5–10 days	Seal small tears in blood vessels; instrumental in blood clotting

*Appearance when stained with Wright's stain.

Color and Clarity of Plasma

Hold the test tube up to a source of natural light. Note and record its color and degree of transparency. Is it clear, translucent, or opaque?

Color_____

Degree of transparency_____

Consistency

Dip your finger and thumb into plasma and then press them firmly together for a few seconds. Gently pull them apart. How would you describe the consistency of plasma (slippery, watery, sticky, granular)? Record your observations.

_____

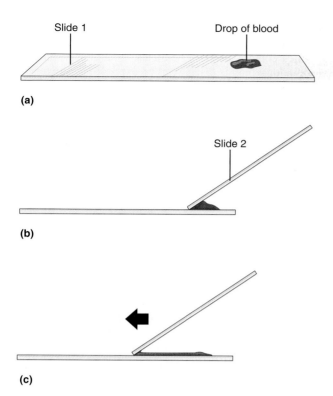

(a)

Slide 1   Drop of blood

(b)

Slide 2

(c)

FIGURE 22.2 Procedure for making a blood smear.
(a) Place a drop of blood on slide 1 approximately ½ inch
from one end. **(b)** Hold slide 2 at a 30° to 40° angle to
slide 1 (it should touch the drop of blood) and allow blood
to spread along entire bottom edge of angled slide.
(c) Smoothly advance slide 2 to end of slide 1 (blood
should run out before reaching the end of slide 1). Then lift
slide 2 away from slide 1 and place it on a paper towel.

ACTIVITY 2

Examining the Formed Elements of Blood Microscopically

In this section, you will observe blood cells on an already
prepared (purchased) blood slide or on a slide prepared from
your own blood or blood provided by your instructor.

• Those using the purchased blood slide are to obtain a
slide and begin their observations at step 6.

• Those testing blood provided by a biological supply
source or an animal hospital are to obtain a tube of the supplied blood, disposable gloves, and the supplies listed in
step 1, except for the lancets and alcohol swabs. After
donning gloves, those students will go to step 3b to begin
their observations.

• If you are examining your own blood, you will perform
all the steps described below *except* step 3b.

1. Obtain two glass slides, a glass stirring rod, dropper bottles of Wright's stain and distilled water, two or three lancets,

cotton balls, and alcohol swabs. Bring this equipment to the
laboratory bench. Clean the slides thoroughly and dry them.

2. Open the alcohol swab packet and scrub your third or
fourth finger with the swab. (Because the pricked finger
may be a little sore later, it is better to prepare a finger on the
hand used less often.) Circumduct your hand (swing it in a
cone-shaped path) for 10 to 15 seconds. This will dry the alcohol and cause your fingers to become engorged with
blood. Then, open the lancet packet and grasp the lancet by
its blunt end. Quickly jab the pointed end into the prepared
finger to produce a free flow of blood. It is *not* a good idea
to squeeze or "milk" the finger, as this forces out tissue fluid
as well as blood. If the blood is not flowing freely, another
puncture should be made.

⚠ *Under no circumstances is a lancet to be used for
more than one puncture*. Dispose of the lancets in the
designated disposal container immediately after use.

3a. With a cotton ball, wipe away the first drop of blood;
then allow another large drop of blood to form. Touch the
blood to one of the cleaned slides approximately 1.3 cm, or
½ inch, from the end. Then quickly (to prevent clotting) use the
second slide to form a blood smear as shown in Figure 22.2.
When properly prepared, the blood smear is uniformly thin.
If the blood smear appears streaked, the blood probably be-
gan to clot or coagulate before the smear was made, and another slide should be prepared. Continue at step 4.

3b. Dip a glass rod in the blood provided, and transfer a gen-
erous drop of blood to the end of a cleaned microscope slide.
For the time being, lay the glass rod on a paper towel on the
bench. Then, as described in step 3a and Figure 22.2, use the
second slide to make your blood smear.

4. Dry the slide by waving it in the air. When it is completely dry, it will look dull. Place it on a paper towel, and
flood it with Wright's stain. Count the number of drops of stain
used. Allow the stain to remain on the slide for 3 to 4 minutes,
and then flood the slide with an equal number of drops of distilled water. Allow the water and Wright's stain mixture to
remain on the slide for 4 or 5 minutes or until a metallic green
film or scum is apparent on the fluid surface. Blow on the
slide gently every minute or so to keep the water and stain
mixed during this interval.

5. Rinse the slide with a stream of distilled water. Then
flood it with distilled water, and allow it to lie flat until the
slide becomes translucent and takes on a pink cast. Then
stand the slide on its long edge on the paper towel, and allow
it to dry completely. Once the slide is dry, you can begin your
observations.

6. Obtain a microscope and scan the slide under low power to
find the area where the blood smear is the thinnest. After scanning the slide in low power to find the areas with the largest
numbers of nucleated WBCs, read the following descriptions of
cell types, and find each one on Figure 22.1 and Table 22.1.
(The formed elements are also shown in Plates 50 through 55 in
the Histology Atlas.) Then, switch to the oil immersion lens,
and observe the slide carefully to identify each cell type.

7. Set your prepared slide aside for use in Activity 3.

Erythrocytes

Erythrocytes, or red blood cells, which average 7.5 μm in diameter, vary in color from a salmon red color to pale pink, depending on the effectiveness of the stain. They have a distinctive biconcave disk shape and appear paler in the center than at the edge (see Plate 51 in the Histology Atlas).

As you observe the slide, notice that the red blood cells are by far the most numerous blood cells seen in the field. Their number averages 4.5 million to 5.5 million cells per cubic millimeter of blood (for women and men, respectively).

Red blood cells differ from the other blood cells because they are anucleate when mature and circulating in the blood. As a result, they are unable to reproduce or repair damage and have a limited life span of 100 to 120 days, after which they begin to fragment and are destroyed in the spleen and other reticuloendothelial tissues of the body.

In various anemias, the red blood cells may appear pale (an indication of decreased hemoglobin content) or may be nucleated (an indication that the bone marrow is turning out cells prematurely). ●

Leukocytes

Leukocytes, or white blood cells, are nucleated cells that are formed in the bone marrow from the same blood stem cells (*hematopoietic stem cells*) as red blood cells. They are much less numerous than the red blood cells, averaging from 4,800 to 10,800 cells per cubic millimeter. Basically, white blood cells are protective, pathogen-destroying cells that are transported to all parts of the body in the blood or lymph. Important to their protective function is their ability to move in and out of blood vessels, a process called **diapedesis,** and to wander through body tissues by **amoeboid motion** to reach sites of inflammation or tissue destruction. They are classified into two major groups, depending on whether or not they contain conspicuous granules in their cytoplasm.

Granulocytes make up the first group. The granules in their cytoplasm stain differentially with Wright's stain, and they have peculiarly lobed nuclei, which often consist of expanded nuclear regions connected by thin strands of nucleoplasm. There are three types of granulocytes:

Neutrophil: The most abundant of the white blood cells (40% to 70% of the leukocyte population); nucleus consists of 3 to 7 lobes and the pale lilac cytoplasm contains fine cytoplasmic granules, which are generally indistinguishable and take up both the acidic (red) and basic (blue) dyes (*neutrophil* = neutral loving); functions as an active phagocyte. The number of neutrophils increases exponentially during acute infections. (See Plates 50 and 51 in the Histology Atlas.)

Eosinophil: Represents 2% to 4% of the leukocyte population; nucleus is generally figure-8 or bilobed in shape; contains large cytoplasmic granules (elaborate lysosomes) that stain redorange with the acid dyes in Wright's stain (see Plate 54 in the Histology Atlas). Eosinophils are about the size of neutrophils and play a role in counterattacking parasitic worms. They also lessen allergy attacks by phagocytizing antigen-antibody complexes and inactivating some inflammatory chemicals.

Basophil: Least abundant leukocyte type representing less than 1% of the population; large U- or S-shaped nucleus with two or more indentations. Cytoplasm contains coarse, sparse granules that are stained deep purple by the basic dyes in Wright's stain (see Plate 55 in the Histology Atlas). The granules contain several chemicals, including histamine, a vasodilator which is discharged on exposure to antigens and helps mediate the inflammatory response. Basophils are about the size of neutrophils.

The second group, **agranulocytes,** or **agranular leukocytes,** contains no *visible* cytoplasmic granules. Although found in the bloodstream, they are much more abundant in lymphoid tissues. Their nuclei tend to be closer to the norm, that is, spherical, oval, or kidney-shaped. Specific characteristics of the two types of agranulocytes are listed below.

Lymphocyte: The smallest of the leukocytes, approximately the size of a red blood cell (see Plates 50 and 52 in the Histology Atlas). The nucleus stains dark blue to purple, is generally spherical or slightly indented, and accounts for most of the cell mass. Sparse cytoplasm appears as a thin blue rim around the nucleus. Concerned with immunologic responses in the body; one population, the *B lymphocytes,* oversees the production of antibodies that are released to blood. The second population, *T lymphocytes,* plays a regulatory role and destroys grafts, tumors, and virus-infected cells. Represents 25% or more of the WBC population.

Monocyte: The largest of the leukocytes; approximately twice the size of red blood cells (see Plate 61 in the Histology Atlas). Represents 3 to 8% of the leukocyte population. Dark blue nucleus is generally kidney-shaped; abundant cytoplasm stains gray-blue. Once in the tissues, monocytes convert to macrophages, active phagocytes (the "long-term cleanup team"), increasing dramatically in number during chronic infections such as tuberculosis.

Students are often asked to list the leukocytes in order from the most abundant to the least abundant. The following silly phrase may help you with this task: *N*ever *l*et *m*onkeys *e*at *b*ananas (neutrophils, lymphocytes, monocytes, eosinophils, basophils).

Platelets

Platelets are cell fragments of large multinucleate cells (**megakaryocytes**) formed in the bone marrow. They appear as darkly staining, irregularly shaped bodies interspersed among the blood cells (see Plate 50 in the Histology Atlas). The normal platelet count in blood ranges from 150,000 to 400,000 per cubic millimeter. Platelets are instrumental in the clotting process that occurs in plasma when blood vessels are ruptured.

After you have identified these cell types on your slide, observe charts and three-dimensional models of blood cells if these are available. Do not dispose of your slide, as it will be used later for the differential white blood cell count. ■

Hematologic Tests

When someone enters a hospital as a patient, several hematologic tests are routinely done to determine general level of health as well as the presence of pathologic conditions. You will be conducting the most common of these tests in this exercise.

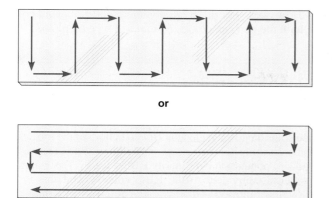

FIGURE 22.3 Alternative methods of moving the slide for a differential WBC count.

⚠ Materials such as cotton balls, lancets, and alcohol swabs are used in nearly all of the following diagnostic tests. These supplies are at the general supply area and should be properly disposed of (glassware to the bleach bucket, lancets in a designated disposal container, and disposable items to the autoclave bag) immediately after use.

Other necessary supplies and equipment are at specific supply areas marked according to the test with which they are used. Since nearly all of the tests require a finger stab, if you will be using your own blood it might be wise to quickly read through the tests to determine in which instances more than one preparation can be done from the same finger stab. For example, the hematocrit capillary tubes and sedimentation rate samples might be prepared at the same time. A little planning will save you the discomfort of a multiple-punctured finger.

An alternative to using blood obtained from the finger stab technique is using heparinized blood samples supplied by your instructor. The purpose of using heparinized tubes is to prevent the blood from clotting. Thus blood collected and stored in such tubes will be suitable for all tests except coagulation time testing.

Total White and Red Blood Cell Counts

A **total WBC count** or **total RBC count** determines the total number of that cell type per unit volume of blood. Total WBC and RBC counts are a routine part of any physical exam. Most clinical agencies use computers to conduct these counts. Since the hand counting technique typically done in college labs is rather outdated, total RBC and WBC counts will not be done here, but the importance of such counts (both normal and abnormal values) is briefly described below.

Total White Blood Cell Count   Since white blood cells are an important part of the body's defense system, it is essential to note any abnormalities in them.

◤ **Leukocytosis,** an abnormally high WBC count, may indicate bacterial or viral infection, metabolic disease, hemorrhage, or poisoning by drugs or chemicals. A decrease in the white cell number below 4000/mm^3 (**leukopenia**) may indicate typhoid fever, measles, infectious hepatitis or

cirrhosis, tuberculosis, or excessive antibiotic or X-ray therapy. A person with leukopenia lacks the usual protective mechanisms. **Leukemia,** a malignant disorder of the lymphoid tissues characterized by uncontrolled proliferation of abnormal WBCs accompanied by a reduction in the number of RBCs and platelets, is detectable not only by a total WBC count but also by a differential WBC count. ●

Total Red Blood Cell Count   Since RBCs are absolutely necessary for oxygen transport, a doctor typically investigates any excessive change in their number immediately.

◤ An increase in the number of RBCs (**polycythemia**) may result from bone marrow cancer or from living at high altitudes where less oxygen is available. A decrease in the number of RBCs results in anemia. (The term **anemia** simply indicates a decreased oxygen-carrying capacity of blood that may result from a decrease in RBC number or size or a decreased hemoglobin content of the RBCs.) A decrease in RBCs may result suddenly from hemorrhage or more gradually from conditions that destroy RBCs or hinder RBC production. ●

Differential White Blood Cell Count

To make a **differential white blood cell count,** 100 WBCs are counted and classified according to type. Such a count is routine in a physical examination and in diagnosing illness, since any abnormality or significant elevation in percentages of WBC types may indicate a problem or the source of pathology.

ACTIVITY 3

Conducting a Differential WBC Count

1. Use the slide prepared for the identification of the blood cells in Activity 2. Begin at the edge of the smear and move the slide in a systematic manner on the microscope stage—either up and down or from side to side as indicated in Figure 22.3.

2. Record each type of white blood cell you observe by making a count on the chart at the top of p. 370 (for example, ‖‖ ‖ = 7 cells) until you have observed and recorded a total of 100 WBCs. Using the following equation, compute the percentage of each WBC type counted, and record the percentages on the Hematologic Test Data Sheet on p. 370.

$$\text{Percent (\%)} = \frac{\text{\# observed}}{\text{Total \# counted (100)}} \times 100$$

3. Select a slide marked "Unknown sample," record the slide number, and again use the count chart on p. 370 to conduct a differential count. Record the percentages on the data sheet at the bottom of p. 370.

How does the differential count from the unknown sample slide compare to a normal count?

_____

_____

Count of 100 WBCs

	Number observed	
Cell type	Student smear	Unknown sample #____
Neutrophils		
Eosinophils		
Basophils		
Lymphocytes		
Monocytes		

Using the text and other references, try to determine the blood pathology on the unknown slide. Defend your answer.

_____

_____

_____

_____

4. How does your differential white blood cell count correlate with the percentages given for each type on p. 368?

_____

Hematocrit

The **hematocrit,** or **packed cell volume (PCV),** is routinely determined when anemia is suspected. Centrifuging whole blood spins the formed elements to the bottom of the tube, with plasma forming the top layer (see Figure 22.1). Since the blood cell population is primarily RBCs, the PCV is generally considered equivalent to the RBC volume, and this is the only value reported. However, the relative percentage of WBCs can be differentiated, and both WBC and plasma volume will be reported here. Normal hematocrit values for the male and female, respectively, are 47.0 ± 7 and 42.0 ± 5.

ACTIVITY 4

Determining the Hematocrit

The hematocrit is determined by the micromethod, so only a drop of blood is needed. If possible (and the centrifuge allows), all members of the class should prepare their capillary tubes at the same time so the centrifuge can be run only once.

1. Obtain two heparinized capillary tubes, capillary tube sealer or modeling clay, a lancet, alcohol swabs, and some cotton balls.

2. If you are using your own blood, cleanse a finger, and allow the blood to flow freely. Wipe away the first few drops and, holding the red-line-marked end of the capillary tube to

Hematologic Test Data Sheet

Differential WBC count:

WBC	Student smear	Unknown sample #____
% neutrophils	_____	_____
% eosinophils	_____	_____
% basophils	_____	_____
% monocytes	_____	_____
% lymphocytes	_____	_____

Hematocrit (PCV):

RBC _____ % of blood volume

WBC _____ % of blood volume } not generally reported

Plasma _____ % of blood

Hemoglobin (Hb) content:

Hemoglobinometer (type: _____)

_____ g/100 ml of blood; _____ % Hb

Tallquist method _____ g/100 ml of blood; ____ % Hb

Ratio (PCV to grams of Hb per 100 ml of blood): _____

Coagulation time _____

Blood typing:

ABO group _____   Rh factor _____

Cholesterol concentration _____ mg/dl of blood

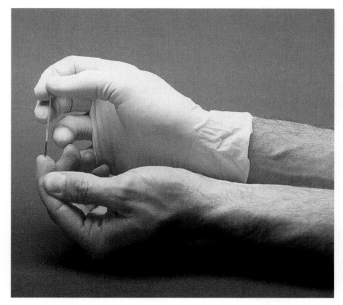

(a)

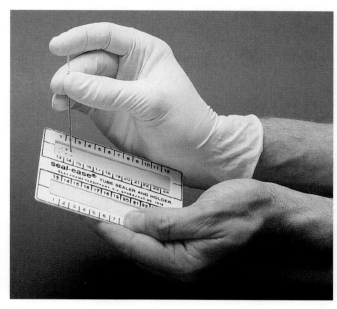

(b)

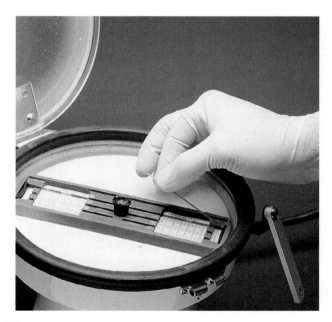

(c)

FIGURE 22.4 Steps in a hematocrit determination.
(**a**) Load a heparinized capillary tube with blood. (**b**) Plug the blood-containing end of the tube with clay. (**c**) Place the tube in a microhematocrit centrifuge. (Centrifuge must be balanced.)

the blood drop, allow the tube to fill at least three-fourths full by capillary action (Figure 22.4a). If the blood is not flowing freely, the end of the capillary tube will not be completely submerged in the blood during filling, air will enter, and you will have to prepare another sample.

If you are using instructor-provided blood, simply immerse the red-marked end of the capillary tube in the blood sample and fill it three-quarters full as just described.

3. Plug the blood-containing end by pressing it into the capillary tube sealer or clay (Figure 22.4b). Prepare a second tube in the same manner.

4. Place the prepared tubes opposite one another in the radial grooves of the microhematocrit centrifuge with the sealed ends abutting the rubber gasket at the centrifuge periphery (Figure 22.4c). This loading procedure balances the centrifuge and prevents blood from spraying everywhere by centrifugal force. *Make a note of the numbers of the grooves your tubes are in.* When all the tubes have been loaded, make sure the centrifuge is properly balanced, and secure the centrifuge cover. Turn the centrifuge on, and set the timer for 4 or 5 minutes.

5. Determine the percentage of RBCs, WBCs, and plasma by using the microhematocrit reader. The RBCs are the bottom layer, the plasma is the top layer, and the WBCs are the buff-colored layer between the two. If the reader is not available, use a millimeter ruler to measure the length of the filled capillary tube occupied by each element, and compute its percentage by using the following formula:

$$\frac{\text{Height of the column composed of the element (mm)}}{\text{Height of the original column of whole blood (mm)}} \times 100$$

Record your calculations below and on the data sheet on p. 370.

% RBC _____ % WBC _____% plasma _____

Usually WBCs constitute 1% of the total blood volume. How do your blood values compare to this figure and to the normal percentages for RBCs and plasma? (See p. 365.)

_____

As a rule, a hematocrit is considered a more accurate test than the total RBC count for determining the RBC composition of the blood. A hematocrit within the normal range generally indicates a normal RBC number, whereas an abnormally high or low hematocrit is cause for concern. ▉

Hemoglobin Concentration

As noted earlier, a person can be anemic even with a normal RBC count. Since hemoglobin (Hb) is the RBC protein responsible for oxygen transport, perhaps the most accurate way of measuring the oxygen-carrying capacity of the blood is to determine its hemoglobin content. Oxygen, which combines reversibly with the heme (iron-containing portion) of the hemoglobin molecule, is picked up by the blood cells in the lungs and unloaded in the tissues. Thus, the more hemoglobin molecules the RBCs contain, the more oxygen they will be able to transport. Normal blood contains 12 to 18 g of hemoglobin per 100 ml of blood. Hemoglobin content in men is slightly higher (13 to 18 g) than in women (12 to 16 g).

ACTIVITY 5

Determining Hemoglobin Concentration

Several techniques have been developed to estimate the hemoglobin content of blood, ranging from the old, rather inaccurate Tallquist method to expensive colorimeters, which are precisely calibrated and yield highly accurate results. Directions for both the Tallquist method and a hemoglobinometer are provided here.

Tallquist Method

1. Obtain a Tallquist hemoglobin scale, test paper, lancets, alcohol swabs, and cotton balls.

2. Use instructor-provided blood or prepare the finger as previously described. (For best results, make sure the alcohol evaporates before puncturing your finger.) Place one good-sized drop of blood on the special absorbent paper provided with the color scale. The blood stain should be larger than the holes on the color scale.

3. As soon as the blood has dried and loses its glossy appearance, match its color, under natural light, with the color standards by moving the specimen under the comparison scale so that the blood stain appears at all the various apertures. (The blood should not be allowed to dry to a brown color, as this will result in an inaccurate reading.) Because the colors on the scale represent 1% variations in hemoglobin content, it may be necessary to estimate the percentage if the color of your blood sample is intermediate between two color standards.

4. On the data sheet, record your results as the percentage of hemoglobin concentration and as grams per 100 ml of blood.

Hemoglobinometer Determination

1. Obtain a hemoglobinometer, hemolysis applicator, alcohol swab, and lens paper, and bring them to your bench. Test the hemoglobinometer light source to make sure it is working; if not, request new batteries before proceeding and test it again.

2. Remove the blood chamber from the slot in the side of the hemoglobinometer and disassemble the blood chamber by separating the glass plates from the metal clip. Notice as you do this that the larger glass plate has an H-shaped depression cut into it that acts as a moat to hold the blood, whereas the smaller glass piece is flat and serves as a coverslip.

3. Clean the glass plates with an alcohol swab, and then wipe them dry with lens paper. Hold the plates by their sides to prevent smearing during the wiping process.

4. Reassemble the blood chamber (remember: larger glass piece on the bottom with the moat up), but leave the moat plate about halfway out to provide adequate exposed surface to charge it with blood.

5. Obtain a drop of blood (from the provided sample or from your fingertip as before), and place it on the depressed area of the moat plate that is closest to you (Figure 22.5a).

6. Using the wooden hemolysis applicator, stir or agitate the blood to rupture (lyse) the RBCs (Figure 22.5b). This usually takes 35 to 45 seconds. Hemolysis is complete when the blood appears transparent rather than cloudy.

7. Push the blood-containing glass plate all the way into the metal clip and then firmly insert the charged blood chamber back into the slot on the side of the instrument (Figure 22.5c).

8. Hold the hemoglobinometer in your left hand with your left thumb resting on the light switch located on the underside of the instrument. Look into the eyepiece and notice that there is a green area divided into two halves (a split field).

9. With the index finger of your right hand, slowly move the slide on the right side of the hemoglobinometer back and forth until the two halves of the green field match (Figure 22.5d).

10. Note and record on the data sheet on p. 370 the grams of Hb (hemoglobin)/100 ml of blood indicated on the uppermost scale by the index mark on the slide. Also record % Hb, indicated by one of the lower scales.

11. Disassemble the blood chamber once again, and carefully place its parts (glass plates and clip) into a bleach-containing beaker.

Generally speaking, the relationship between the PCV and grams of hemoglobin per 100 ml of blood is 3:1—for example, a PCV of 35 with 12 g of Hb per 100 ml of blood is a ratio of 3:1. How do your values compare?

Record on the data sheet the value obtained from your data. ▉

Bleeding Time

Normally a sharp prick of the finger or earlobe results in bleeding that lasts from 2 to 7 minutes (Ivy method) or 0 to 5 minutes (Duke method), although other factors such as altitude affect the time. How long the bleeding lasts is referred to as **bleeding time** and tests the ability of platelets to stop bleeding in capillaries and small vessels. Absence of some clotting factors may affect bleeding time, but prolonged bleeding time is most often associated with deficient or abnormal platelets.

Coagulation Time

Blood clotting, or **coagulation,** is a protective mechanism that minimizes blood loss when blood vessels are ruptured. This process requires the interaction of many substances

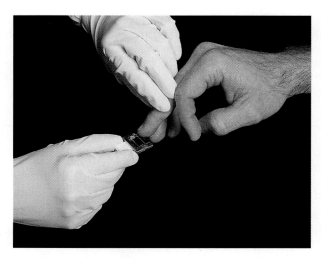

(a) A drop of blood is added to the moat plate of the blood chamber. The blood must flow freely.

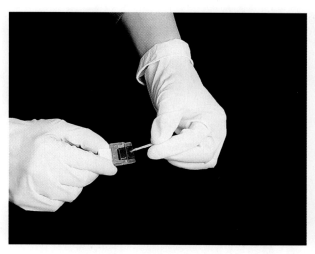

(b) The blood sample is hemolyzed with a wooden hemolysis applicator. Complete hemolysis requires 35 to 45 seconds.

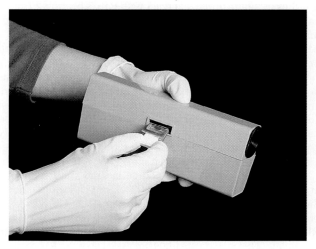

(c) The charged blood chamber is inserted into the slot on the side of the hemoglobinometer.

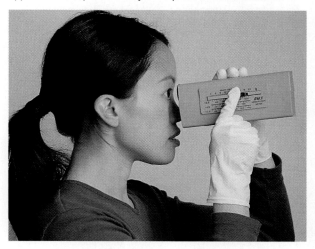

(d) The colors of the green split screen are found by moving the slide with the right index finger. When the two colors match in density, the grams/100 ml and %Hb are read on the scale.

FIGURE 22.5 Hemoglobin determination using a hemoglobinometer.

normally present in the plasma (clotting factors, or procoagulants) as well as some released by platelets and injured tissues. Basically hemostasis proceeds as follows (Figure 22.6a): The injured tissues and platelets release **tissue factor (TF)** and **PF₃** respectively, which trigger the clotting mechanism, or cascade. Tissue factor and PF₃ interact with other blood protein clotting factors and calcium ions to form **prothrombin activator,** which in turn converts **prothrombin** (present in plasma) to **thrombin.** Thrombin then acts enzymatically to polymerize the soluble **fibrinogen** proteins (present in plasma) into insoluble **fibrin,** which forms a meshwork of strands that traps the RBCs and forms the basis of the clot (Figure 22.6b). Normally, blood removed from the body clots within 2 to 6 minutes.

Determining Coagulation Time

1. Obtain a *nonheparinized* capillary tube, a timer (or watch), a lancet, cotton balls, a triangular file, and alcohol swabs.

2. Clean and prick the finger to produce a free flow of blood. Discard the lancet in the disposal container.

3. Place one end of the capillary tube in the blood drop, and hold the opposite end at a lower level to collect the sample.

4. Lay the capillary tube on a paper towel.

Record the time. _____

Injury to lining of vessel exposes collagen fibers; platelets adhere

Platelet plug forms

Fibrin clot with trapped red blood cells

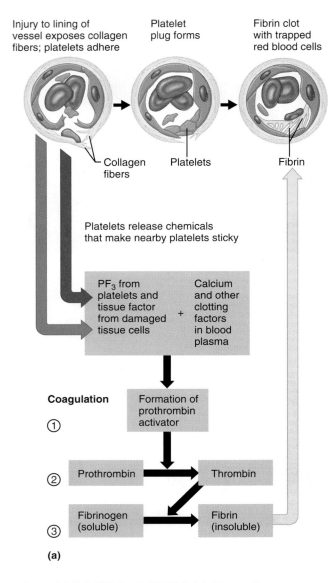

Collagen fibers

Platelets

Fibrin

Platelets release chemicals that make nearby platelets sticky

PF₃ from platelets and tissue factor from damaged tissue cells

$+$

Calcium and other clotting factors in blood plasma

Coagulation

① → Formation of prothrombin activator

② Prothrombin → Thrombin

③ Fibrinogen (soluble) → Fibrin (insoluble)

(a)

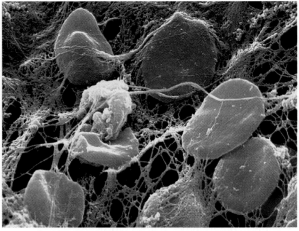

(b)

FIGURE 22.6 Events of hemostasis and blood clotting. (a) Simple schematic of events. Steps numbered 1–3 represent the major events of coagulation. (b) Photomicrograph of RBCs trapped in a fibrin mesh (3000×).

5. At 30-second intervals, make a small nick on the tube close to one end with the triangular file, and then carefully break the tube. Slowly separate the ends to see if a gel-like thread of fibrin spans the gap. When this occurs, record below and on the data sheet on p. 370 the time for coagulation to occur. Are your results within the normal time range?

6. Put used supplies in the autoclave bag and broken capillary tubes into the sharps container. ▭

Blood Typing

Blood typing is a system of blood classification based on the presence of specific glycoproteins on the outer surface of the RBC plasma membrane. Such proteins are called **antigens,** or **agglutinogens,** and are genetically determined. In many cases, these antigens are accompanied by plasma proteins, **antibodies** or **agglutinins,** that react with RBCs bearing different antigens, causing them to be clumped, agglutinated, and eventually hemolyzed. It is because of this phenomenon that a person's blood must be carefully typed before a whole blood or packed cell transfusion.

Several blood typing systems exist, based on the various possible antigens, but the factors routinely typed for are antigens of the ABO and Rh blood groups which are most commonly involved in transfusion reactions. Other blood factors, such as Kell, Lewis, M, and N, are not routinely typed for unless the individual will require multiple transfusions. The basis of the ABO typing is shown in Table 22.2.

Individuals whose red blood cells carry the Rh antigen are Rh positive (approximately 85% of the U.S. population); those lacking the antigen are Rh negative. Unlike ABO blood groups, neither the blood of the Rh-positive (Rh⁺) nor Rh-negative (Rh⁻) individuals carries preformed anti-Rh antibodies. This is understandable in the case of the Rh-positive individual. However, Rh-negative persons who receive transfusions of Rh-positive blood become sensitized by the Rh antigens of the donor RBCs, and their systems begin to produce anti-Rh antibodies. On subsequent exposures to Rh-positive blood, typical transfusion reactions occur, resulting in the clumping and hemolysis of the donor blood cells.

Although the blood of dogs and other mammals does react with some of the human agglutinins (present in the antisera), the reaction is not as pronounced and varies with the animal blood used. Hence, the most accurate and predictable blood typing results are obtained with human blood. The artificial blood kit does not use any body fluids and produces results similar to but not identical to results for human blood.

ACTIVITY 7

Typing for ABO and Rh Blood Groups

Blood may be typed on glass slides or using blood test cards. Both methods are described next.

Typing Blood Using Glass Slides

1. Obtain two clean microscope slides, a wax marking pencil, anti-A, anti-B, and anti-Rh typing sera, toothpicks, lancets, alcohol swabs, medicine dropper, and the Rh typing box.

TABLE 22.2	ABO Blood Typing		% of U.S. population		
ABO blood type	Antigens present on RBC membranes	Antibodies present in plasma	White	Black	Asian
A	A	Anti-B	40	27	28
B	B	Anti-A	11	20	27
AB	A and B	None	4	4	5
O	Neither	Anti-A and anti-B	45	49	40

2. Divide slide 1 into halves with the wax marking pencil. Label the lower left-hand corner "anti-A" and the lower right-hand corner "anti-B." Mark the bottom of slide 2 "anti-Rh."

3. Place one drop of anti-A serum on the *left* side of slide 1. Place one drop of anti-B serum on the *right* side of slide 1. Place one drop of anti-Rh serum in the center of slide 2.

4. If you are using your own blood, cleanse your finger with an alcohol swab, pierce the finger with a lancet, and wipe away the first drop of blood. Obtain 3 drops of freely flowing blood, placing one drop on each side of slide 1 and a drop on slide 2. Immediately dispose of the lancet in a designated disposal container.

If using instructor-provided animal blood or EDTA-treated red cells, use a medicine dropper to place one drop of blood on each side of slide 1 and a drop of blood on slide 2.

Blood Typing

Result	Observed (+)	Not observed (−)
Presence of clumping with anti-A		
Presence of clumping with anti-B		
Presence of clumping with anti-Rh		

5. Quickly mix each blood-antiserum sample with a *fresh* toothpick. Then dispose of the toothpicks and used alcohol swab in the autoclave bag.

6. Place slide 2 on the Rh typing box and rock gently back and forth. (A slightly higher temperature is required for precise Rh typing than for ABO typing.)

7. After 2 minutes, observe all three blood samples for evidence of clumping. The agglutination that occurs in the positive test for the Rh factor is very fine and difficult to perceive; thus if there is any question, observe the slide under the microscope. Record your observations in the chart titled "Blood Typing."

8. Interpret your ABO results in light of the information in Figure 22.7. If clumping was observed on slide 2, you are Rh positive. If not, you are Rh negative.

9. Record your blood type in the data sheet at the bottom of p. 370.

10. Put the used slides in the bleach-containing bucket at the general supply area; put disposable supplies in the autoclave bag.

Using Blood Typing Cards

1. Obtain a blood typing card marked A, B, and Rh, dropper bottles of anti-A serum, anti-B serum, and anti-Rh serum, toothpicks, lancets, and alcohol swabs.

2. Place a drop of anti-A serum in the spot marked anti-A, place a drop of anti-B serum on the spot marked anti-B, and place a drop of anti-Rh serum on the spot marked anti-Rh (or anti-D).

3. Carefully add a drop of blood to each of the spots marked "Blood" on the card. If you are using your own blood, refer to step 4 in the alternative instructions above, "Typing Blood Using Glass Slides." Immediately discard the lancet in the designated disposal container.

4. Using a new toothpick for each test, mix the blood sample with the antibody. Dispose of the toothpicks appropriately.

5. Gently rock the card to allow the blood and antibodies to mix.

6. After 2 minutes, observe the card for evidence of clumping. The Rh clumping is very fine and may be difficult to observe. Record your observations in the chart on the left. Use Figure 22.7 to interpret your results.

7. Record your blood type in the data sheet at the bottom of p. 370, and discard the card in an autoclave bag.

Observing Demonstration Slides

Before continuing on to the cholesterol determination, take the time to look at the slides of *macrocytic hypochromic anemia, microcytic hypochromic anemia, sickle cell disease, lymphocytic leukemia* (chronic), and *eosinophilia* that have been put on demonstration by your instructor. Record your observations in the appropriate section of the Review Sheet

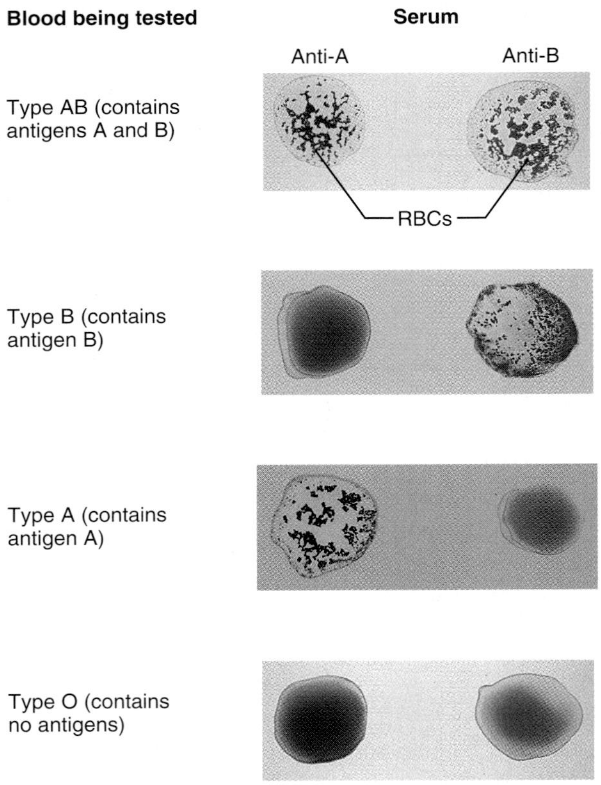

Blood being tested

Serum

Anti-A   Anti-B

Type AB (contains antigens A and B)

RBCs

Type B (contains antigen B)

Type A (contains antigen A)

Type O (contains no antigens)

FIGURE 22.7 Blood typing of ABO blood types.
When serum containing anti-A or anti-B antibodies (agglutinins) is added to a blood sample, agglutination will occur between the antibody and the corresponding antigen (agglutinogen A or B). As illustrated, agglutination occurs with both sera in blood group AB, with anti-B serum in blood group B, with anti-A serum in blood group A, and with neither serum in blood group O.

for this exercise. You can refer to your notes, the text, and other references later to respond to questions about the blood pathologies represented on the slides. ▬

Cholesterol Concentration in Plasma

Atherosclerosis is the disease process in which the body's blood vessels become increasingly occluded by plaques. Because the plaques narrow the arteries, they can contribute to hypertensive heart disease. They also serve as focal points for the formation of blood clots (thrombi), which may break away and block smaller vessels farther downstream in the circulatory pathway and cause heart attacks or strokes.

Ever since medical clinicians discovered that cholesterol is a major component of the smooth muscle plaques formed during atherosclerosis, it has had a bad press. Today, virtually no physical examination of an adult is considered complete until cholesterol levels are assessed along with other lifestyle risk factors. A normal value for plasma cholesterol in adults ranges from 130 to 200 mg per 100 ml of plasma; you will use blood to make such a determination.

Although the total plasma cholesterol concentration is valuable information, it may be misleading, particularly if a person's high-density lipoprotein (HDL) level is high and low-density lipoprotein (LDL) level is relatively low. Cholesterol, being water insoluble, is transported in the blood complexed to lipoproteins. In general, cholesterol bound into HDLs is destined to be degraded by the liver and then eliminated from the body, whereas that forming part of the LDLs is "traveling" to the body's tissue cells. When LDL levels are excessive, cholesterol is deposited in the blood vessel walls; hence, LDLs are considered to carry the "bad" cholesterol.

ACTIVITY 9

Measuring Plasma Cholesterol Concentration

1. Go to the appropriate supply area, and obtain a cholesterol test card and color scale, lancet, and alcohol swab.

2. Clean your fingertip with the alcohol swab, allow it to dry, then prick it with a lancet. Place a drop of blood on the test area of the card. Put the lancet in the designated disposal container.

3. After 3 minutes, remove the blood sample strip from the card and discard in the autoclave bag.

4. Analyze the underlying test spot, using the included color scale. Record the cholesterol level below and on the data sheet on p. 370.

Cholesterol level _____ mg/dl

⚠ 5. Before leaving the laboratory, use the spray bottle of bleach solution and saturate a paper towel to thoroughly wash down your laboratory bench. ▬

Blood

Composition of Blood

1. What is the blood volume of an average-size adult male? _____ liters   An average adult female? _____ liters

2. What determines whether blood is bright red or a dull brick-red? _____

_____

3. Use the key to identify the cell type(s) or blood elements that fit the following descriptive statements.

Key: a. red blood cell   d. basophil   g. lymphocyte
      b. megakaryocyte   e. monocyte   h. formed elements
      c. eosinophil   f. neutrophil   i. plasma

_____ 1. most numerous leukocyte

_____, _____, and_____ 2. granulocytes

_____ 3. also called an erythrocyte; anucleate formed element

_____, _____ 4. actively phagocytic leukocytes

_____, _____ 5. agranulocytes

_____ 6. ancestral cell of platelets

_____ 7. (a) through (g) are all examples of these

_____ 8. number rises during parasite infections

_____ 9. releases histamine; promotes inflammation

_____ 10. many formed in lymphoid tissue

_____ 11. transports oxygen

_____ 12. primarily water, noncellular; the fluid matrix of blood

_____ 13. increases in number during prolonged infections

_____, _____, _____,

_____, _____ 14. also called white blood cells

4. List four classes of nutrients normally found in plasma. _____,

_____, _____, and _____

Name two gases. _____ and _____

Name three ions. _____, _____, and _____

5. Describe the consistency and color of the plasma you observed in the laboratory. _____

_____

6. What is the average life span of a red blood cell? How does its anucleate condition affect this life span?

_____

_____

7. From memory, describe the structural characteristics of each of the following blood cell types as accurately as possible, and note the percentage of each in the total white blood cell population.

eosinophils: _____

_____

neutrophils: _____

_____

lymphocytes: _____

_____

basophils: _____

_____

monocytes: _____

_____

8. Correctly identify the blood pathologies described in column A by matching them with selections from column B:

Column A		Column B	
_____ 1.	abnormal increase in the number of WBCs	a.	anemia
_____ 2.	abnormal increase in the number of RBCs	b.	leukocytosis
_____ 3.	condition of too few RBCs or of RBCs with hemoglobin deficiencies	c.	leukopenia
_____ 4.	abnormal decrease in the number of WBCs	d.	polycythemia

Hematologic Tests

9. Broadly speaking, why are hematologic studies of blood so important in the diagnosis of disease?

_____

_____

10. In the chart below, record information from the blood tests you read about or conducted. Complete the chart by recording values for healthy male adults and indicating the significance of high or low values for each test.

Test	Student test results	Normal values (healthy male adults)	Significance	
			High values	Low values
Total WBC count	No data			
Total RBC count	No data			
Hematocrit				
Hemoglobin determination				
Bleeding time	No data			
Coagulation time				

11. Why is a differential WBC count more valuable than a total WBC count when trying to pin down the specific source of

pathology? _____

_____

12. Define *hematocrit*. _____

13. If you had a high hematocrit, would you expect your hemoglobin determination to be high or low? _____

Why? _____

_____

14. What is an anticoagulant? _____

Name two anticoagulants used in conducting the hematologic tests. _____

and _____

What is the body's natural anticoagulant? _____

15. If your blood clumped with both anti-A and anti-B sera, your ABO blood type would be _____

To what ABO blood groups could you give blood? _____

From which ABO donor types could you receive blood? _____

Which ABO blood type is most common? _____ Least common? _____

16. Assume the blood of two patients has been typed for ABO blood type.

Typing results
Mr. Adams:

Typing results
Mr. Calhoon:

Blood drop
and anti-A serum

Blood drop
and anti-B serum

Blood drop
and anti-A serum

Blood drop
and anti-B serum

On the basis of these results, Mr. Adams has type _____ blood, and Mr. Calhoon has type _____ blood.

17. Record your observations of the five demonstration slides viewed.

a. Macrocytic hypochromic anemia: _____

b. Microcytic hypochromic anemia: _____

_____

c. Sickle cell disease: _____

d. Lymphocytic leukemia (chronic): _____

_____

e. Eosinophilia: _____

Which of the slides (a through e) above corresponds with the following conditions?

_____ 1. iron-deficient diet

_____ 4. lack of vitamin B_{12}

_____ 2. a type of bone marrow cancer

_____ 5. a tapeworm infestation in the body

_____ 3. genetic defect that causes hemoglobin
to become sharp/spiky

_____ 6. a bleeding ulcer

18. Provide the normal, or at least "desirable," range for plasma cholesterol concentration.

_____ mg/100 ml

19. Describe the relationship between high blood cholesterol levels and cardiovascular diseases such as hypertension, heart attacks, and strokes.

_____

_____

_____

_____

Anatomy of the Heart

MATERIALS

- ☐ X ray of the human thorax for observation of the position of the heart in situ; X-ray viewing box
- ☐ Three-dimensional heart model and torso model or laboratory chart showing heart anatomy
- ☐ Red and blue pencils
- ☐ Three-dimensional models of cardiac and skeletal muscle
- ☐ Compound microscope
- ☐ Prepared slides of cardiac muscle (l.s.)
- ☐ Preserved sheep heart, pericardial sacs intact (if possible)
- ☐ Dissecting instruments and tray
- ☐ Pointed glass rods for probes (or Mall probes)
- ☐ Disposable gloves
- ☐ Plastic ruler
- ☐ Container for disposal of organic debris
- ☐ Laboratory detergent
- ☐ Spray bottle with 10% household bleach solution
- ☐ *Human Cardiovascular System: The Heart* videotape*

AIA See Appendix B, Exercise 23 for links to A.D.A.M.® Interactive Anatomy.

*Available to qualified adopters from Benjamin Cummings.

OBJECTIVES

1. To describe the location of the heart.
2. To name and locate the major anatomical areas and structures of the heart when provided with an appropriate model, diagram, or dissected sheep heart, and to explain the function of each.
3. To trace the pathway of blood through the heart.
4. To explain why the heart is called a double pump, and to compare the pulmonary and systemic circuits.
5. To explain the operation of the atrioventricular and semilunar valves.
6. To name and follow the functional blood supply of the heart.
7. To describe the histology of cardiac muscle, and to note the importance of its intercalated discs and the spiral arrangement of its cells.

The major function of the **cardiovascular system** is transportation. Using blood as the transport vehicle, the system carries oxygen, digested foods, cell wastes, electrolytes, and many other substances vital to the body's homeostasis to and from the body cells. The system's propulsive force is the contracting heart, which can be compared to a muscular pump equipped with one-way valves. As the heart contracts, it forces blood into a closed system of large and small plumbing tubes (blood vessels) within which the blood is confined and circulated. This exercise deals with the structure of the heart, or circulatory pump. The anatomy of the blood vessels is considered separately in Exercise 24.

Gross Anatomy of the Human Heart

The **heart,** a cone-shaped organ approximately the size of a fist, is located within the mediastinum, or medial cavity, of the thorax. It is flanked laterally by the lungs, posteriorly by the vertebral column, and anteriorly by the sternum (Figure 23.1). Its more pointed **apex** extends slightly to the left and rests on the diaphragm, approximately at the level of the fifth intercostal space. Its broader **base,** from which the great vessels emerge, lies beneath the second rib and points toward the right shoulder. In situ, the right ventricle of the heart forms most of its anterior surface.

- If an X ray of a human thorax is available, verify the relationships described above; otherwise, Figure 23.1 should suffice.

The heart is enclosed within a double-walled fibroserous sac called the pericardium. The thin **visceral pericardium,** or **epicardium,** is closely applied to the heart muscle. It reflects downward at the base of the heart to form its companion serous membrane, the outer, loosely applied **parietal pericardium,** which is attached at the heart apex to the diaphragm. Serous fluid produced by these membranes allows the heart to beat in a relatively frictionless environment. The serous parietal pericardium, in turn, lines the loosely fitting superficial **fibrous pericardium** composed of dense connective tissue.

Inflammation of the pericardium, **pericarditis,** causes painful adhesions between the serous pericardial layers. These adhesions interfere with heart movements. ●

Midsternal line
2nd rib
Sternum
Diaphragm
Point of maximal intensity (PMI)

FIGURE 23.1 Location of the heart in the thorax.

The walls of the heart are composed primarily of cardiac muscle—the **myocardium**—which is reinforced internally by a dense fibrous connective tissue network. This network—the *fibrous skeleton of the heart*—is more elaborate and thicker in certain areas, for example, around the valves and at the base of the great vessels leaving the heart.

Figure 23.2 shows three views of the heart—an external anterior view and two frontal sections. As its anatomical areas are described in the text, consult the figure.

Heart Chambers

The heart is divided into four chambers: two superior **atria** (singular, *atrium*) and two inferior **ventricles,** each lined by thin serous endothelium called the **endocardium.** The septum that divides the heart longitudinally is referred to as the **interatrial** or **interventricular septum,** depending on which chambers it partitions. Functionally, the atria are receiving chambers and are relatively ineffective as pumps. Blood flows into the atria under low pressure from the veins of the body. The right atrium receives relatively oxygen-poor blood from the body via the **superior** and **inferior venae cavae** and the coronary sinus. Four **pulmonary veins** deliver oxygen-rich blood from the lungs to the left atrium.

The inferior thick-walled ventricles, which form the bulk of the heart, are the discharging chambers. They force blood out of the heart into the large arteries that emerge from its base. The right ventricle pumps blood into the **pulmonary trunk,** which routes blood to the lungs to be oxygenated. The left ventricle discharges blood into the **aorta,** from which all systemic arteries of the body diverge to supply the body tissues. Discussions of the heart's pumping action usually refer to ventricular activity.

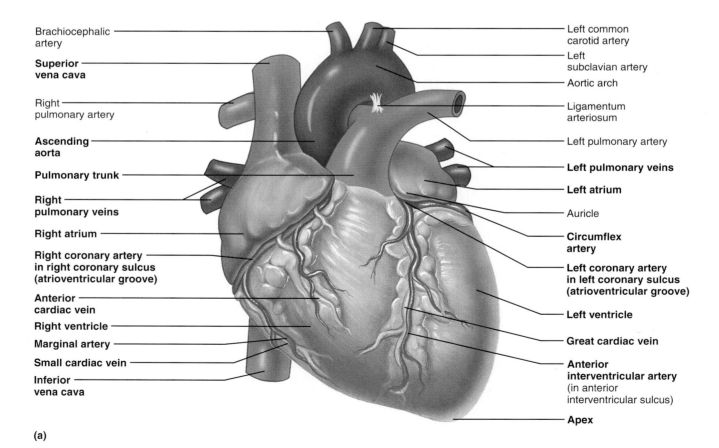

Brachiocephalic artery
Superior vena cava
Right pulmonary artery
Ascending aorta
Pulmonary trunk
Right pulmonary veins
Right atrium
Right coronary artery in right coronary sulcus (atrioventricular groove)
Anterior cardiac vein
Right ventricle
Marginal artery
Small cardiac vein
Inferior vena cava

Left common carotid artery
Left subclavian artery
Aortic arch
Ligamentum arteriosum
Left pulmonary artery
Left pulmonary veins
Left atrium
Auricle
Circumflex artery
Left coronary artery in left coronary sulcus (atrioventricular groove)
Left ventricle
Great cardiac vein
Anterior interventricular artery (in anterior interventricular sulcus)
Apex

(a)

FIGURE 23.2 Anatomy of the human heart. (a) External anterior view.

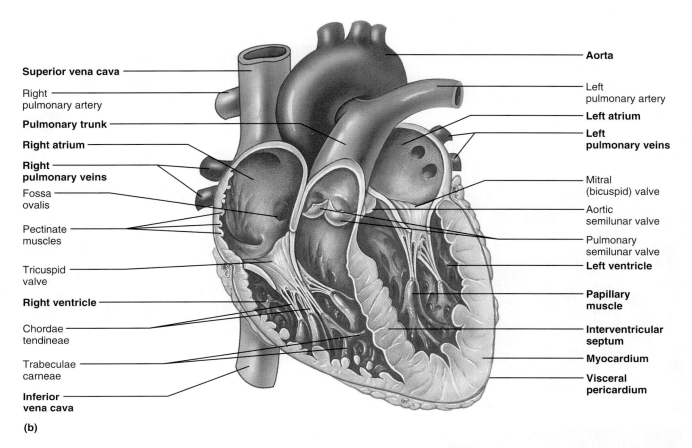

Superior vena cava

Right
pulmonary artery

Pulmonary trunk

Right atrium

**Right
pulmonary veins**

Fossa
ovalis

Pectinate
muscles

Tricuspid
valve

Right ventricle

Chordae
tendineae

Trabeculae
carneae

**Inferior
vena cava**

Aorta

Left
pulmonary artery

Left atrium

**Left
pulmonary veins**

Mitral
(bicuspid) valve

Aortic
semilunar valve

Pulmonary
semilunar valve

Left ventricle

**Papillary
muscle**

**Interventricular
septum**

Myocardium

**Visceral
pericardium**

(b)

FIGURE 23.2 (*continued*) **Anatomy
of the human heart.** (**b**) Frontal section,
diagrammatic view. (**c**) Frontal section,
photograph.

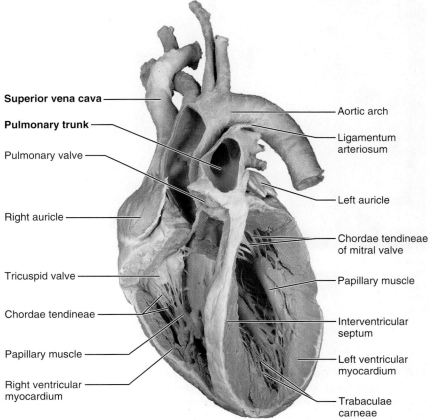

Superior vena cava

Pulmonary trunk

Pulmonary valve

Right auricle

Tricuspid valve

Chordae tendineae

Papillary muscle

Right ventricular
myocardium

Aortic arch

Ligamentum
arteriosum

Left auricle

Chordae tendineae
of mitral valve

Papillary muscle

Interventricular
septum

Left ventricular
myocardium

Trabaculae
carneae

(c)

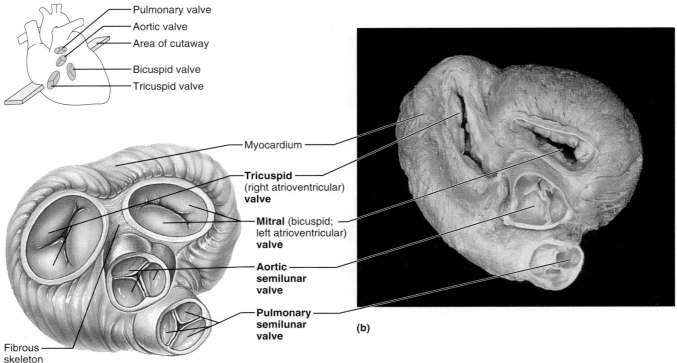

(a)

(b)

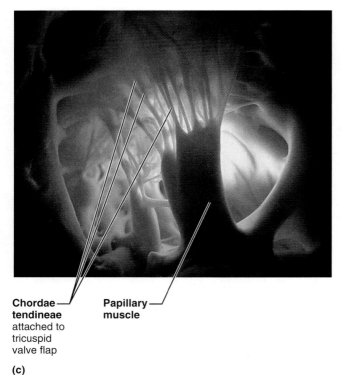

Chordae tendineae attached to tricuspid valve flap

Papillary muscle

(c)

FIGURE 23.3 Heart valves. (a) Superior view of the two sets of heart valves (atria removed). **(b)** Photograph of the heart valves, superior view. **(c)** Photograph of the right AV valve. View begins in the right ventricle, looking toward the right atrium.

Heart Valves

Four valves enforce a one-way blood flow through the heart chambers. The **atrioventricular (AV) valves,** located between the atrial and ventricular chambers on each side, prevent backflow into the atria when the ventricles are contracting. The left atrioventricular valve, also called the **mitral** or **bicuspid valve,** consists of two cusps, or flaps, of endocardium. The right atrioventricular valve, the **tricuspid valve,** has three cusps (Figure 23.3). Tiny white collagenic cords called the **chordae tendineae** (literally, "heart strings") anchor the cusps to the ventricular walls. The chordae tendineae originate from small bundles of cardiac muscle, called **papillary muscles,** that project from the myocardial wall (see Figure 23.2b).

When blood is flowing passively into the atria and then into the ventricles during **diastole** (the period of ventricular filling), the AV valve flaps hang limply into the ventricular chambers and then are carried passively toward the atria by the accumulating blood. When the ventricles contract (**systole**) and compress the blood in their chambers, the intraventricular blood pressure rises, causing the valve flaps to be reflected superiorly, which closes the AV valves. The chordae tendineae, pulled taut by the contracting papillary muscles, anchor the flaps in a closed position that prevents backflow into the atria during ventricular contraction. If unanchored, the flaps would blow upward into the atria rather like an umbrella being turned inside out by a strong wind.

The second set of valves, the **pulmonary** and **aortic semilunar valves,** each composed of three pocketlike cusps, guards the bases of the two large arteries leaving the ventricular chambers. The valve cusps are forced open and flatten against the walls of the artery as the ventricles discharge their blood into the large arteries during systole. However, when the ventricles relax, blood flows backward toward the heart and the cusps fill with blood, closing the semilunar valves and preventing arterial blood from reentering the heart.

Using the Heart Model to Study Heart Anatomy

When you have located in Figure 23.2 all the structures described above, observe the human heart model and laboratory charts and reidentify the same structures without referring to the figure. ▬▬

Pulmonary, Systemic, and Cardiac Circulations

Pulmonary and Systemic Circulations

The heart functions as a double pump. The right side serves as the **pulmonary circulation** pump, shunting the carbon dioxide–rich blood entering its chambers to the lungs to unload carbon dioxide and pick up oxygen, and then back to the left side of the heart (Figure 23.4). The function of this circuit is strictly to provide for gas exchange. The second circuit, which carries oxygen-rich blood from the left heart through the body tissues and back to the right heart, is called the **systemic circulation.** It provides the functional blood supply to all body tissues.

Tracing the Path of Blood Through the Heart

Use colored pencils to trace the pathway of a red blood cell through the heart by adding arrows to the frontal section diagram (Figure 23.2b). Use red arrows for the oxygen-rich blood and blue arrows for the less oxygen-rich blood. ▬▬

Cardiac Circulation

Even though the heart chambers are almost continually bathed with blood, this contained blood does not nourish the myocardium. The functional blood supply of the heart is provided by the right and left coronary arteries (see Figures 23.2a and 23.5). The **coronary arteries** issue from the base of the aorta just above the aortic semilunar valve and encircle the heart in the **coronary sulcus (atrioventricular groove)** at the junction of the atria and ventricles. They then ramify over the heart's surface, the right coronary artery supplying the posterior surface of the ventricles and the lateral aspect of the right side of the heart, largely through its **posterior interventricular** and **marginal artery** branches. The left coronary artery supplies the anterior ventricular walls and the laterodorsal part of the left side of the heart via its two major branches, the **anterior interventricular artery** and the **circumflex artery.** The coronary arteries and their branches are compressed during systole and fill when the heart is relaxed.

The myocardium is largely drained by the **great, middle,** and **small cardiac veins,** which empty into the **coronary sinus.** The coronary sinus, in turn, empties into the right atrium. In addition, several **anterior cardiac veins** empty directly into the right atrium (Figure 23.5).

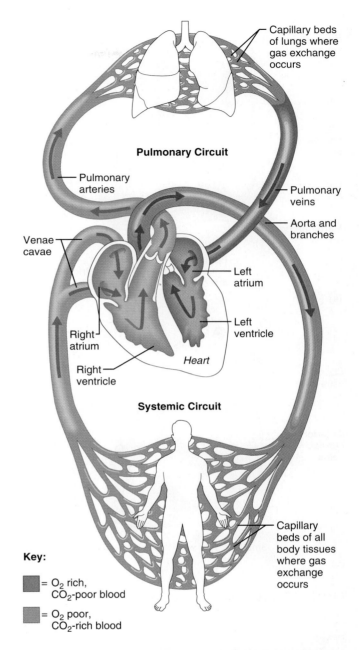

Key:

■ = O₂ rich, CO₂-poor blood

▨ = O₂ poor, CO₂-rich blood

FIGURE 23.4 The systemic and pulmonary circuits. The heart is a double pump that serves two circulations. The right side of the heart pumps blood through the pulmonary circuit to the lungs and back to the left heart. (For simplicity, the actual number of two pulmonary arteries and four pulmonary veins has been reduced to one each.) The left heart pumps blood via the systemic circuit to all body tissues and back to the right heart. Notice that blood flowing through the pulmonary circuit gains oxygen (O_2) and loses carbon dioxide (CO_2) as depicted by the color change from blue to red. Blood flowing through the systemic circuit loses oxygen and picks up carbon dioxide (red to blue color change).

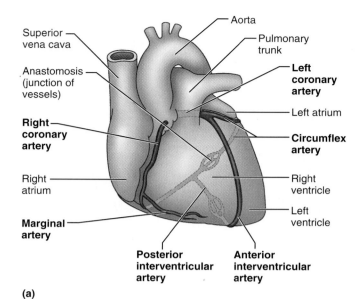

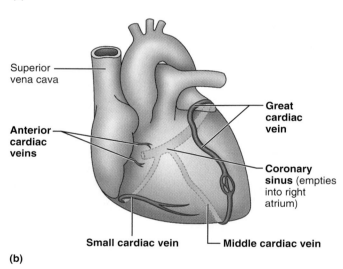

FIGURE 23.5 Cardiac circulation.

ACTIVITY 3

Using the Heart Model to Study Cardiac Circulation

On a model of the heart, locate all the cardiac blood vessels shown in Figure 23.5. Use your finger to trace the pathway of blood from the right coronary artery to the lateral aspect of the right side of the heart and back to the right atrium. Name the arteries and veins along the pathway. Trace the pathway of blood from the left coronary artery to the anterior ventricular walls and back to the right atrium. Name the arteries and veins along the pathway. Note that there are multiple different pathways to distribute blood to these parts of the heart. ■

DISSECTION:

The Sheep Heart

Dissection of a sheep heart is valuable because it is similar in size and structure to the human heart. Also, a dissection experience allows you to view structures in a way not possible with models and diagrams. Refer to Figure 23.6 as you proceed with the dissection.

1. Obtain a preserved sheep heart, a dissecting tray, dissecting instruments, a glass probe, a plastic ruler, and gloves. Rinse the sheep heart in cold water to remove excessive preservatives and to flush out any trapped blood clots. Now you are ready to make your observations.

2. Observe the texture of the pericardium. Also, note its point of attachment to the heart. Where is it attached?

_____

3. If the serous pericardial sac is still intact, slit open the parietal pericardium and cut it from its attachments. Observe the visceral pericardium (epicardium). Using a sharp scalpel, carefully pull a little of this serous membrane away from the myocardium. How do its position, thickness, and apposition to the heart differ from those of the parietal pericardium?

_____

_____

_____

4. Examine the external surface of the heart. Notice the accumulation of adipose tissue, which in many cases marks the separation of the chambers and the location of the coronary arteries that nourish the myocardium. Carefully scrape away some of the fat with a scalpel to expose the coronary blood vessels.

5. Identify the base and apex of the heart, and then identify the two wrinkled **auricles,** earlike flaps of tissue projecting from the atrial chambers. The balance of the heart muscle is ventricular tissue. To identify the left ventricle, compress the ventricular chambers on each side of the longitudinal fissures carrying the coronary blood vessels. The side that feels thicker and more solid is the left ventricle. The right ventricle is much thinner and feels somewhat flabby when compressed. This difference reflects the greater demand placed on the left ventricle, which must pump blood through the much longer systemic circulation, a pathway with much higher resistance than the pulmonary circulation served by the right ventricle. Hold the heart in its anatomical position (Figure 23.6a), with the anterior surface uppermost. In this position the left ventricle composes the entire apex and the left side of the heart.

6. Identify the pulmonary trunk and the aorta extending from the superior aspect of the heart. The pulmonary trunk is more anterior, and you may see its division into the right and left pulmonary arteries if it has not been cut too closely to the heart. The thicker-walled aorta, which branches almost immediately, is located just beneath the pulmonary trunk. The first

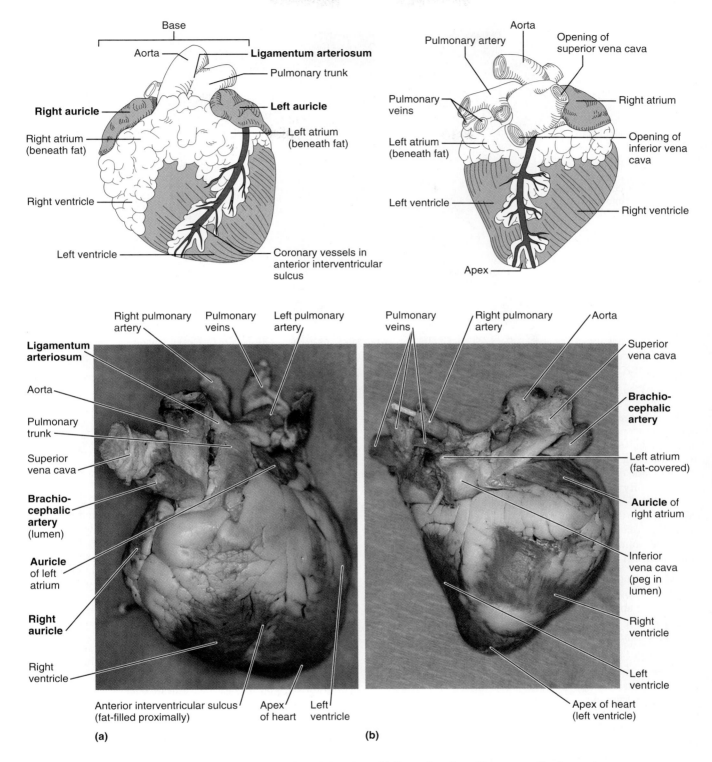

FIGURE 23.6 Anatomy of the sheep heart. (a) Anterior view. **(b)** Posterior view. Diagrammatic views at top; photographs at bottom.

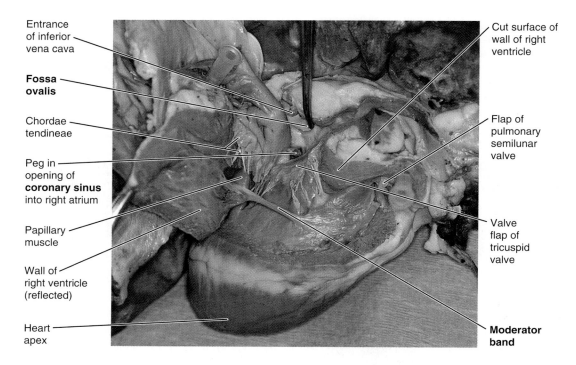

Entrance of inferior vena cava

Fossa ovalis

Chordae tendineae

Peg in opening of **coronary sinus** into right atrium

Papillary muscle

Wall of right ventricle (reflected)

Heart apex

Cut surface of wall of right ventricle

Flap of pulmonary semilunar valve

Valve flap of tricuspid valve

Moderator band

FIGURE 23.7 Right side of the sheep heart opened and reflected to reveal internal structures.

observable branch of the sheep aorta, the **brachiocephalic artery,** is identifiable unless the aorta has been cut immediately as it leaves the heart. The brachiocephalic artery splits to form the right carotid and subclavian arteries, which supply the right side of the head and right forelimb, respectively.

Carefully clear away some of the fat between the pulmonary trunk and the aorta to expose the **ligamentum arteriosum,** a cordlike remnant of the **ductus arteriosus.** (In the fetus, the ductus arteriosus allows blood to pass directly from the pulmonary trunk to the aorta, thus bypassing the nonfunctional fetal lungs.)

7. Cut through the wall of the aorta until you see the aortic semilunar valve. Identify the two openings to the coronary arteries just above the valve. Insert a probe into one of these holes to see if you can follow the course of a coronary artery across the heart.

8. Turn the heart to view its posterior surface. The heart will appear as shown in Figure 23.6b. Notice that the right and left ventricles appear equal-sized in this view. Try to identify the four thin-walled pulmonary veins entering the left atrium. Identify the superior and inferior venae cavae entering the right atrium. Due to the way the heart is trimmed, the pulmonary veins and superior vena cava may be very short or missing. If possible, compare the approximate diameter of the superior vena cava with the diameter of the aorta.

Which is larger? _____

Which has thicker walls?_____

Why do you suppose these differences exist?

_____

_____

_____

9. Insert a probe into the superior vena cava, through the right atrium, and out the inferior vena cava. Use scissors to cut along the probe so that you can view the interior of the right atrium. Observe the right atrioventricular valve.

How many flaps does it have?_____

Pour some water into the right atrium and allow it to flow into the ventricle. *Slowly and gently* squeeze the right ventricle to watch the closing action of this valve. (If you squeeze too vigorously, you'll get a face full of water!) Drain the water from the heart before continuing.

10. Return to the pulmonary trunk and cut through its anterior wall until you can see the pulmonary semilunar valve (Figure 23.7). Pour some water into the base of the pulmonary trunk to observe the closing action of this valve. How does its action differ from that of the atrioventricular valve?

_____

_____

_____

After observing semilunar valve action, drain the heart once again. Extend the cut through the pulmonary trunk into the right ventricle. Cut down, around, and up through the atrioventricular valve to make the cut continuous with the cut across the right atrium (see Figure 23.7).

11. Reflect the cut edges of the superior vena cava, right atrium, and right ventricle to obtain the view seen in Figure 23.7. Observe the comblike ridges of muscle throughout most of the right atrium. This is called **pectinate muscle** (*pectin* means "comb"). Identify, on the ventral atrial wall, the large opening of the inferior vena cava and follow it to its external opening with a probe. Notice that the atrial walls in the vicinity of the venae cavae are smooth and lack the roughened appearance (pectinate musculature) of the other regions of the atrial walls. Just below the inferior vena caval opening, identify the opening of the **coronary sinus,** which returns venous blood of the coronary circulation to the right atrium. Nearby, locate an oval depression, the **fossa ovalis,** in the interatrial septum. This depression marks the site of an opening in the fetal heart, the **foramen ovale,** which allows blood to pass from the right to the left atrium, thus bypassing the fetal lungs.

12. Identify the papillary muscles in the right ventricle, and follow their attached chordae tendineae to the flaps of the tricuspid valve. Notice the pitted and ridged appearance (**trabeculae carneae**) of the inner ventricular muscle.

13. Identify the **moderator band** (septomarginal band), a bundle of cardiac muscle fibers connecting the interventricular septum to anterior papillary muscles. It contains a branch of the atrioventricular bundle and helps coordinate contraction of the ventricle.

14. Make a longitudinal incision through the left atrium and continue it into the left ventricle. Notice how much thicker the myocardium of the left ventricle is than that of the right ventricle. Measure the thickness of the right and left

ventricular walls and record the numbers: left _____,

right _____

Compare the *shape* of the left ventricular cavity to the shape of the right ventricular cavity. (See Figure 23.8.)

_____

_____

_____

Are the papillary muscles and chordae tendineae observed in

the right ventricle also present in the left ventricle?_____

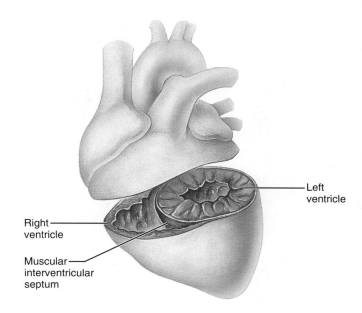

FIGURE 23.8 Anatomical differences in the right and left ventricles. The left ventricle has thicker walls, and its cavity is basically circular; by contrast, the right ventricle cavity is crescent-shaped and wraps around the left ventricle.

Count the number of cusps in the left atrioventricular valve. How does this compare with the number seen in the right atrioventricular valve?

_____

_____

How do the sheep valves compare with their counterparts in humans?

_____

15. Reflect the cut edges of the atrial wall, and attempt to locate the entry points of the pulmonary veins into the left atrium. Follow the pulmonary veins, if present, to the heart exterior with a probe. Notice how thin-walled these vessels are.

16. Dispose of the organic debris in the designated container, clean the dissecting tray and instruments with detergent and water, and wash the lab bench with bleach solution before continuing on to Activity 4. ■■

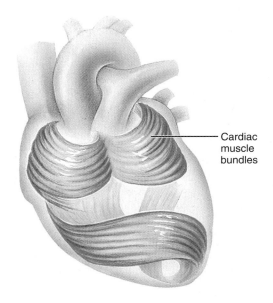

FIGURE 23.9 Longitudinal view of the heart chambers showing the spiral arrangement of the cardiac muscle fibers.

Microscopic Anatomy of Cardiac Muscle

Cardiac muscle is found in only one place—the heart. The heart acts as a vascular pump, propelling blood to all tissues of the body; cardiac muscle is thus very important to life. Cardiac muscle is involuntary, ensuring a constant blood supply.

The cardiac cells, only sparingly invested in connective tissue, are arranged in spiral or figure-8-shaped bundles (Figure 23.9). When the heart contracts, its internal chambers become smaller (or are temporarily obliterated), forcing the blood into the large arteries leaving the heart.

ACTIVITY 4

Examining Cardiac Muscle Tissue Anatomy

1. Observe the three-dimensional model of cardiac muscle, examining its branching cells and the areas where the cells

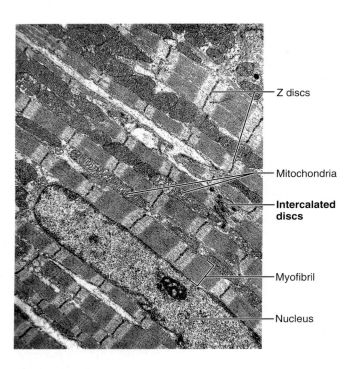

FIGURE 23.10 Photomicrograph of cardiac muscle.

interdigitate, the **intercalated discs.** These two structural features provide a continuity to cardiac muscle not seen in other muscle tissues and allow close coordination of heart activity.

2. Compare the model of cardiac muscle to the model of skeletal muscle. Note the similarities and differences between the two kinds of muscle tissue.

3. Obtain and observe a longitudinal section of cardiac muscle under high power. Identify the nucleus, striations, intercalated discs, and sarcolemma of the individual cells and then compare your observations to the view seen in Figure 23.10. ▪

NAME_____

LAB TIME/DATE_____

Anatomy of the Heart

Gross Anatomy of the Human Heart

1. An anterior view of the heart is shown here. Match each structure listed on the left with the correct letter in the figure.

_____ 1. right atrium

_____ 2. right ventricle

_____ 3. left atrium

_____ 4. left ventricle

_____ 5. superior vena cava

_____ 6. inferior vena cava

_____ 7. ascending aorta

_____ 8. aortic arch

_____ 9. brachiocephalic artery

_____ 10. left common carotid artery

_____ 11. left subclavian artery

_____ 12. pulmonary trunk

_____ 13. right pulmonary artery

_____ 14. left pulmonary artery

_____ 15. ligamentum arteriosum

_____ 16. right pulmonary veins

_____ 17. left pulmonary veins

_____ 18. right coronary artery

_____ 19. anterior cardiac vein

_____ 20. left coronary artery

_____ 21. circumflex artery

_____ 22. anterior interventricular artery

_____ 23. apex of heart

_____ 24. great cardiac vein

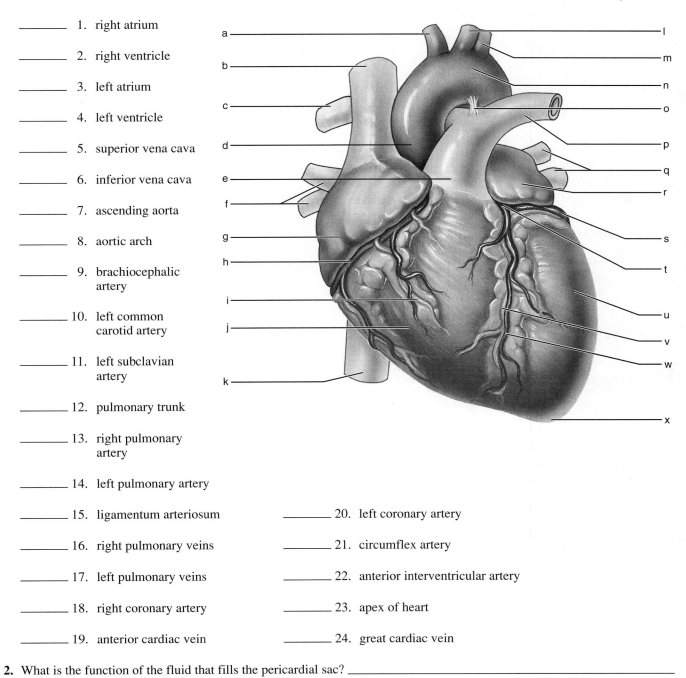

2. What is the function of the fluid that fills the pericardial sac? _____

_____

3. Match the terms in the key to the descriptions provided below.

                                                               Key:

_____ 1. location of the heart in the thorax   a.   atria

_____ 2. superior heart chambers   b.   coronary arteries

_____ 3. inferior heart chambers   c.   coronary sinus

_____ 4. visceral pericardium   d.   endocardium

_____ 5. "anterooms" of the heart   e.   epicardium

_____ 6. equals cardiac muscle   f.   mediastinum

_____ 7. provide nutrient blood to the heart muscle   g.   myocardium

_____ 8. lining of the heart chambers   h.   ventricles

_____ 9. actual "pumps" of the heart

_____ 10. drains blood into the right atrium

4. What is the function of the valves found in the heart? _____

_____

Can the heart function with leaky valves? (Think! Can a water pump function with leaky valves?) _____

5. What is the role of the chordae tendineae? _____

_____

Pulmonary, Systemic, and Cardiac Circulations

6. A simple schematic of a so-called general circulation is shown below. What part of the circulation is missing from this diagram?

_____ Add to the diagram as best you can to make it depict a complete systemic/

pulmonary circulation, and label each circuit.

7. Differentiate clearly between the roles of the pulmonary and systemic circulations. _____

_____

_____

8. Complete the following scheme of circulation of a red blood cell in the human body.

   Right atrium through the tricuspid valve to the _____, through the _____

   _____ valve to the pulmonary trunk, to the _____, to the capillary

   beds of the lungs, to the _____, to the _____ of the heart, through

   the _____ valve to the _____, through the _____

   valve to the _____, to the systemic arteries, to the _____ of the

   tissues, to the systemic veins, to the _____, _____, and

   _____ entering the right atrium of the heart.

9. If the mitral valve does not close properly, which circulation is affected? _____

10. Why might a thrombus (blood clot) in the anterior descending branch of the left coronary artery cause sudden death?

   _____

   _____

Dissection of the Sheep Heart

11. During the sheep heart dissection, you were asked initially to identify the right and left ventricles without cutting into the heart. During this procedure, what differences did you observe between the two chambers?

   _____

   _____

   Knowing that structure and function are related, how would you say this structural difference reflects the relative functions

   of these two heart chambers? _____

   _____

12. Semilunar valves prevent backflow into the _____; AV valves prevent backflow into the

   _____. Using your own observations, explain how the operation of the semilunar valves

   differs from that of the AV valves. _____

   _____

   _____

   _____

13. Compare and contrast the structure of the right and left atrioventricular valves. _____

   _____

14. Two remnants of fetal structures are observable in the heart—the ligamentum arteriosum and the fossa ovalis. What were they called in the fetal heart, where was each located, and what common purpose did they serve as functioning fetal structures?

_____

_____

_____

Microscopic Anatomy of Cardiac Muscle

15. How would you distinguish the structure of cardiac muscle from the structure of skeletal muscle? _____

_____

_____

_____

_____

16. Add the following terms to the photograph of cardiac muscle at the right.

   a.   intercalated disc

   b.   nucleus of cardiac fiber

   c.   striations

   d.   cardiac muscle fiber

17. What role does the unique structure of cardiac muscle play in its function? (Note: Before attempting a response, _describe_ the

unique anatomy.) _____

_____

_____

_____

Anatomy of Blood Vessels

MATERIALS

- ☐ Compound microscope
- ☐ Prepared microscope slides showing cross sections of an artery and a vein
- ☐ Anatomical charts of human arteries and veins (or a three-dimensional model of the human circulatory system)
- ☐ Anatomical charts of the following specialized circulations: pulmonary circulation, hepatic portal circulation, fetal circulation, arterial supply and cerebral arterial circle of the brain (or a brain model showing this circulation)
- ☐ *Human Cardiovascular System: The Blood Vessels* videotape*
- ☐ Dissection animal, tray, and instruments
- ☐ Bone cutters
- ☐ Scissors
- ☐ Disposable gloves or protective skin cream
- ☐ Embalming fluid

AIA See Appendix B, Exercise 24 for links to A.D.A.M.® Interactive Anatomy.

*Available qualified adopters from Benjamin Cummings.

OBJECTIVES

1. To describe the tunics of blood vessel walls, and to state the function of each layer.
2. To correlate differences in artery, vein, and capillary structure with the functions of these vessels.
3. To recognize a cross-sectional view of an artery and vein when provided with a microscopic view or appropriate diagram.
4. To list and/or identify the major arteries arising from the aorta, and to indicate the body region supplied by each.
5. To list and/or identify the major veins draining into the superior and inferior venae cavae, and to indicate the body regions drained.
6. To point out and/or discuss the unique features of special circulations (hepatic portal system, cerebral arterial circle, pulmonary circulation, fetal circulation) in the body.
7. To identify several of the most important blood vessels of the cat.
8. To point out anatomical differences between the vascular system of the human and the laboratory dissection specimen.

The blood vessels constitute a closed transport system. As the heart contracts, blood is propelled into the large arteries leaving the heart. It moves into successively smaller arteries and then to the arterioles, which feed the capillary beds in the tissues. Capillary beds are drained by the venules, which in turn empty into veins that ultimately converge on the great veins entering the heart.

Arteries, carrying blood away from the heart, and veins, which drain the tissues and return blood to the heart, function simply as conducting vessels or conduits. Only the tiny capillaries that connect the arterioles and venules and ramify throughout the tissues directly serve the needs of the body's cells. It is through the capillary walls that exchanges are made between tissue cells and blood. Respiratory gases, nutrients, and wastes move along diffusion gradients. Thus, oxygen and nutrients diffuse from the blood to the tissue cells, and carbon dioxide and metabolic wastes move from the cells to the blood.

In this exercise you will examine the microscopic structure of blood vessels and identify the major arteries and veins of the systemic circulation and other special circulations.

Microscopic Structure of the Blood Vessels

Except for the microscopic capillaries, the walls of blood vessels are constructed of three coats, or *tunics* (Figure 24.1). The **tunica intima,** or **interna,** which lines the lumen of a vessel, is a single thin layer of *endothelium* (squamous cells underlain by a scant basal lamina) that is continuous with the endocardium of the heart. Its cells fit closely together, forming an extremely smooth blood vessel lining that helps decrease resistance to blood flow.

The **tunica media** is the more bulky middle coat and is composed primarily of smooth muscle and elastin. The smooth muscle, under the control of the sympathetic nervous system, plays an active role in regulating the diameter of blood vessels, which in turn alters peripheral resistance and blood pressure.

FIGURE 24.1 Generalized structure of arteries, veins, and capillaries. (a) Light photomicrograph of a muscular artery and the corresponding vein in cross section (100×). (b) The walls of the arteries and veins have three layers, the tunica intima, tunica media, and tunica externa. Capillaries have only endothelium and a sparse basal lamina.

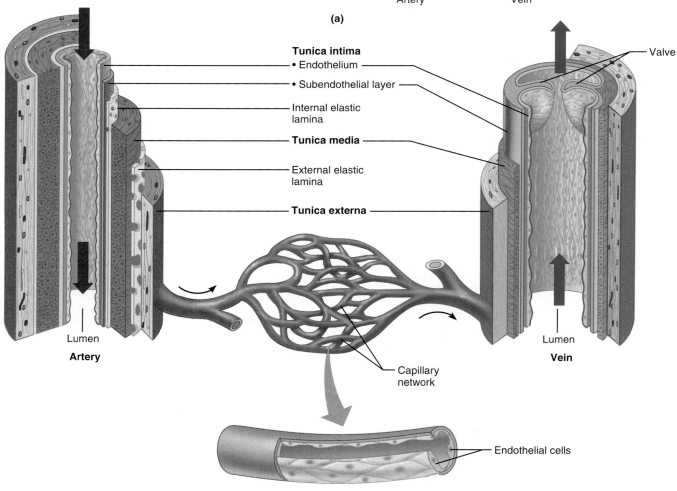

Artery   Vein

(a)

Tunica intima
• Endothelium
• Subendothelial layer
Internal elastic lamina
Tunica media
External elastic lamina
Tunica externa

Valve

Lumen

Artery

Lumen

Vein

Capillary network

Endothelial cells

Capillary

(b)

The **tunica externa,** or **adventitia,** the outermost tunic, is composed of areolar or fibrous connective tissue. Its function is basically supportive and protective.

In general, the walls of arteries are thicker than those of veins. The tunica media in particular tends to be much heavier and contains substantially more smooth muscle and elastic tissue. This anatomical difference reflects a functional difference in the two types of vessels. Arteries, which are closer to the pumping action of the heart, must be able to expand as an increased volume of blood is propelled into them and then recoil passively as the blood flows off into the circulation during diastole. Their walls must be sufficiently strong and

resilient to withstand such pressure fluctuations. Since these larger arteries have such large amounts of elastic tissue in their media, they are often referred to as *elastic arteries.* Smaller arteries, further along in the circulatory pathway, are exposed to less extreme pressure fluctuations. They have less elastic tissue but still have substantial amounts of smooth muscle in their media. For this reason, they are called *muscular arteries.* A schematic of the systemic arteries is provided in Figure 24.2.

By contrast, veins, which are far removed from the heart in the circulatory pathway, are not subjected to such pressure fluctuations and are essentially low-pressure vessels. Thus,

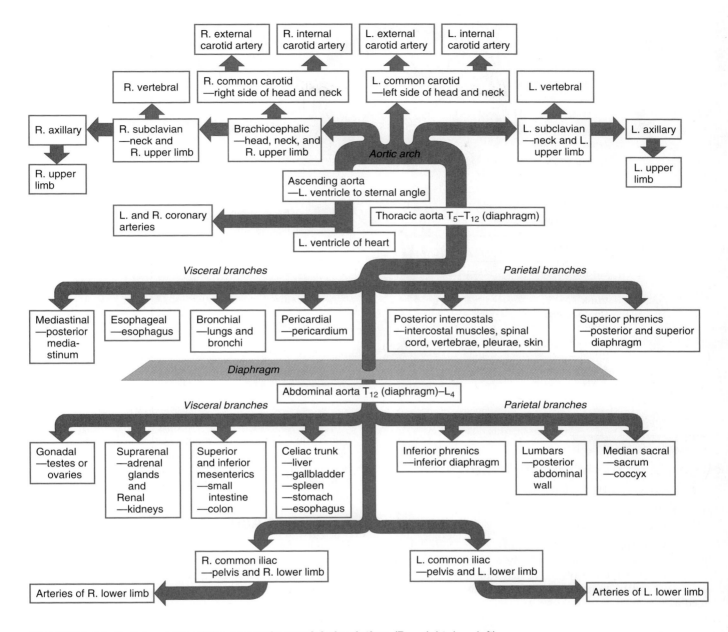

FIGURE 24.2 Schematic of the systemic arterial circulation. (R. = right, L. = left)

veins may be thinner-walled without jeopardy. However, the low-pressure condition itself and the fact that blood returning to the heart often flows against gravity require structural modifications to ensure that venous return equals cardiac output. Thus, the lumens of veins tend to be substantially larger than those of corresponding arteries, and valves in larger veins act to prevent backflow of blood in much the same manner as the semilunar valves of the heart. The skeletal muscle "pump" also promotes venous return; as the skeletal muscles surrounding the veins contract and relax, the blood is milked through the veins toward the heart. (Anyone who has been standing relatively still for an extended time will be happy to show you their swollen ankles, caused by blood pooling in their feet during the period of muscle inactivity!) Pressure changes that occur in the thorax during breathing also aid the return of blood to the heart.

• To demonstrate how efficiently venous valves prevent backflow of blood, perform the following simple experiment. Allow one hand to hang by your side until the blood vessels on the dorsal aspect become distended. Place two fingertips against one of the distended veins and, pressing firmly, move the superior finger proximally along the vein and then release this finger. The vein will remain flattened and collapsed despite gravity. Then remove the distal fingertip and observe the rapid filling of the vein.

The transparent walls of the tiny capillaries are only one cell layer thick, consisting of just the endothelium underlain by a basal lamina, that is, the tunica intima. Because of this exceptional thinness, exchanges are easily made between the blood and tissue cells.

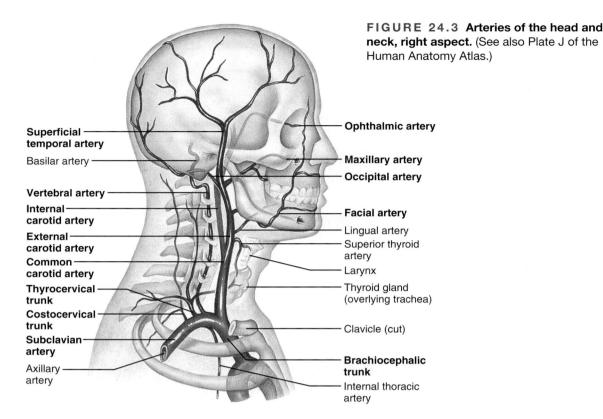

FIGURE 24.3 Arteries of the head and neck, right aspect. (See also Plate J of the Human Anatomy Atlas.)

Labels on figure:
- Superficial temporal artery
- Basilar artery
- Vertebral artery
- Internal carotid artery
- External carotid artery
- Common carotid artery
- Thyrocervical trunk
- Costocervical trunk
- Subclavian artery
- Axillary artery
- Ophthalmic artery
- Maxillary artery
- Occipital artery
- Facial artery
- Lingual artery
- Superior thyroid artery
- Larynx
- Thyroid gland (overlying trachea)
- Clavicle (cut)
- Brachiocephalic trunk
- Internal thoracic artery

ACTIVITY 1

Examining the Microscopic Structure of Arteries and Veins

1. Obtain a slide showing a cross-sectional view of blood vessels and a microscope.

2. Using Figure 24.1 and Plate 21 in the Histology Atlas as a guide, scan the section to identify a thick-walled artery. Very often, but not always, its lumen will appear scalloped due to the constriction of its walls by the elastic tissue of the media.

3. Identify a vein. Its lumen may be elongated or irregularly shaped and collapsed, and its walls will be considerably thinner. Notice the difference in the relative amount of elastic fibers in the media of the two vessels. Also, note the thinness of the intima layer, which is composed of flat squamous-type cells. ▪

Major Systemic Arteries of the Body

The **aorta** is the largest artery of the body. Extending upward as the *ascending aorta* from the left ventricle, it arches posteriorly and to the left *(aortic arch)* and then courses downward as the *descending aorta* through the thoracic cavity. It penetrates the diaphragm to enter the abdominal cavity just anterior to the vertebral column.

Figure 24.2 depicts the relationship of the aorta and its major branches. As you locate the arteries on the figure and other anatomical charts and models, be aware of ways in

which you can make your memorization task easier. In many cases the name of the artery reflects the body region traversed (axillary, subclavian, brachial, popliteal), the organ served (renal, hepatic), or the bone followed (tibial, femoral, radial, ulnar).

Ascending Aorta

The only branches of the ascending aorta are the **right** and the **left coronary arteries,** which supply the myocardium. The coronary arteries are described in Exercise 23 in conjunction with heart anatomy.

Aortic Arch and Thoracic Aorta

The **brachiocephalic** (literally, "arm-head") **trunk** is the first branch of the aortic arch (Figure 24.3). The other two major arteries branching off the aortic arch are the **left common carotid artery** and the **left subclavian artery.** The brachiocephalic artery persists briefly before dividing into the **right common carotid artery** and the **right subclavian artery.**

Arteries Serving the Head and Neck The common carotid artery on each side divides to form an **internal carotid artery,** which serves the brain and branches forming the **ophthalmic artery** that supplies orbital structures, and an external carotid artery. The **external carotid artery** supplies the extracranial tissues of the neck and head, largely via its **superficial temporal, maxillary, facial,** and **occipital** arterial branches. (Notice that several arteries are shown in the figure that are not described here. Ask your instructor which arteries you are required to identify.)

The right and left subclavian arteries each give off several branches to the head and neck. The first of these is the **vertebral artery,** which runs up the posterior neck to supply the cerebellum, part of the brain stem, and the posterior cerebral

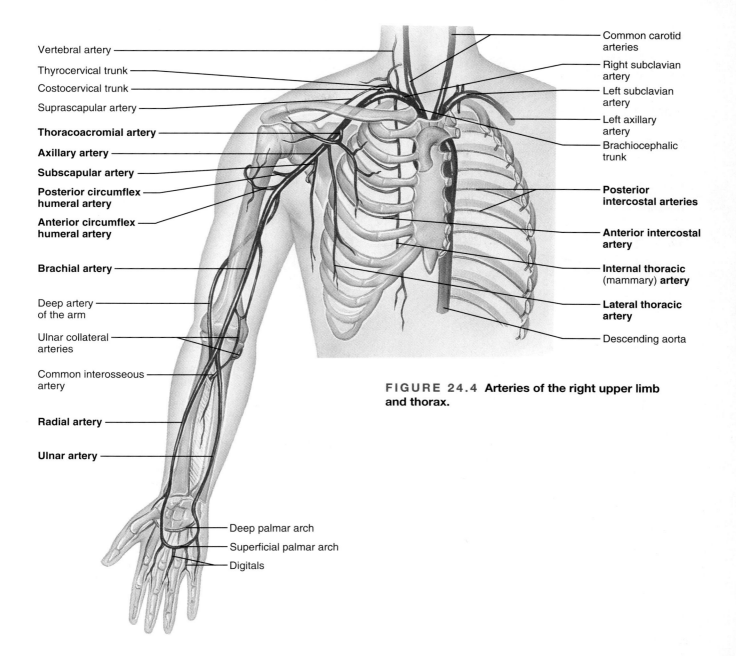

Vertebral artery

Thyrocervical trunk

Costocervical trunk

Suprascapular artery

Thoracoacromial artery

Axillary artery

Subscapular artery

Posterior circumflex humeral artery

Anterior circumflex humeral artery

Brachial artery

Deep artery of the arm

Ulnar collateral arteries

Common interosseous artery

Radial artery

Ulnar artery

Common carotid arteries

Right subclavian artery

Left subclavian artery

Left axillary artery

Brachiocephalic trunk

Posterior intercostal arteries

Anterior intercostal artery

Internal thoracic (mammary) artery

Lateral thoracic artery

Descending aorta

Deep palmar arch

Superficial palmar arch

Digitals

FIGURE 24.4 Arteries of the right upper limb and thorax.

hemispheres. Issuing just lateral to the vertebral artery are the **thyrocervical trunk,** which mainly serves the thyroid gland and some scapular muscles, and the **costocervical trunk,** which supplies deep neck muscles and some of the upper intercostal muscles. In the armpit, the subclavian artery becomes the axillary artery, which serves the upper limb.

Arteries Serving the Thorax and Upper Limbs   As the **axillary artery** runs through the axilla, it gives off several branches to the chest wall and shoulder girdle (Figure 24.4). These include the **thoracoacromial artery** (to shoulder and pectoral region), the **lateral thoracic artery** (lateral chest wall), the **subscapular artery** (to scapula and dorsal thorax), and the **anterior** and **posterior circumflex humeral arteries** (to the shoulder and the deltoid muscle). At the inferior edge of the teres major muscle, the axillary artery becomes the **brachial artery** as it enters the arm. The brachial artery gives off a deep branch, the *deep artery of the arm,* and as it nears

the elbow it gives off several small branches, the *ulnar collateral arteries,* that anastomose with other vessels in the region. At the elbow, the brachial artery divides into the **radial** and **ulnar arteries,** which follow the same-named bones to supply the forearm and hand.

The **internal thoracic (mammary) arteries** that arise from the subclavian arteries supply the mammary glands, most of the thorax wall, and anterior intercostal structures via their **anterior intercostal artery** branches. The first two pairs of **posterior intercostal arteries** arise from the costocervical trunk, noted above. (The more inferior pairs arise from the thoracic aorta.) Not shown in Figure 24.4 are the small arteries that serve the diaphragm *(phrenic arteries),* esophagus *(esophageal arteries),* bronchi *(bronchial arteries),* and other structures of the mediastinum (mediastinal and pericardial arteries).

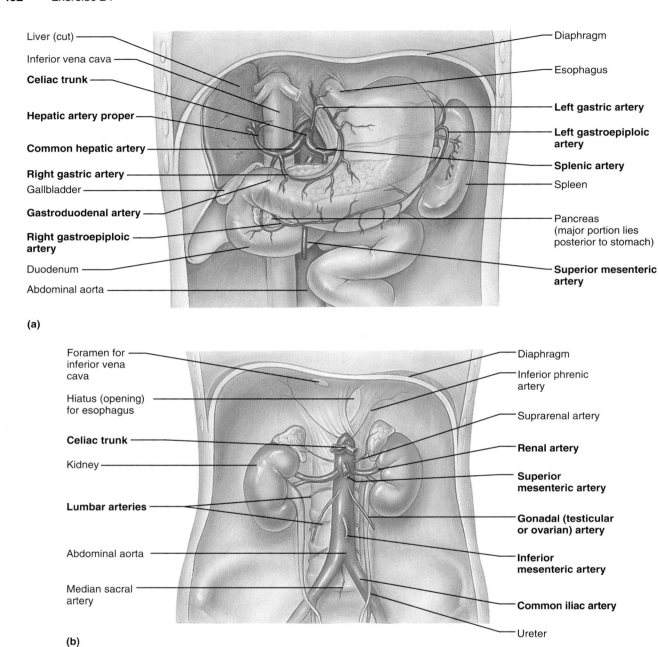

Liver (cut)
Inferior vena cava
Celiac trunk
Hepatic artery proper
Common hepatic artery
Right gastric artery
Gallbladder
Gastroduodenal artery
Right gastroepiploic artery
Duodenum
Abdominal aorta

Diaphragm
Esophagus
Left gastric artery
Left gastroepiploic artery
Splenic artery
Spleen
Pancreas (major portion lies posterior to stomach)
Superior mesenteric artery

(a)

Foramen for inferior vena cava
Hiatus (opening) for esophagus
Celiac trunk
Kidney
Lumbar arteries
Abdominal aorta
Median sacral artery

Diaphragm
Inferior phrenic artery
Suprarenal artery
Renal artery
Superior mesenteric artery
Gonadal (testicular or ovarian) artery
Inferior mesenteric artery
Common iliac artery
Ureter

(b)

FIGURE 24.5 Arteries of the abdomen. (a) The celiac trunk and its major branches. **(b)** Major branches of the abdominal aorta. (See also Plate O in the Human Anatomy Atlas.)

Abdominal Aorta

Although several small branches of the descending aorta serve the thorax (see text above), the more major branches of the descending aorta are those serving the abdominal organs and ultimately the lower limbs (Figure 24.5).

Arteries Serving Abdominal Organs   The **celiac trunk** is an unpaired artery that subdivides almost immediately into three branches: the **left gastric artery** supplying the stomach, the **splenic artery** supplying the spleen, and the **common hepatic artery,** which runs superiorly and gives off branches to the stomach (**right gastric artery**), duodenum, and pancreas.

Where the **gastroduodenal artery** branches off, the common hepatic artery becomes the **hepatic artery proper,** which serves the liver. The **right** and **left gastroepiploic arteries,** branches of the gastroduodenal and splenic arteries respectively, serve the left (greater) curvature of the stomach.

The largest branch of the abdominal aorta, the **superior mesenteric artery,** supplies most of the small intestine (via the *intestinal arteries*) and the first half of the large intestine (via the *ileocolic* and *colic arteries*). (These are not shown in Figure 24.5.) Flanking the superior mesenteric artery on the left and right are the tiny **suprarenal arteries** that serve the adrenal glands, which sit atop the kidneys.

The paired **renal arteries** supply the kidneys, and the **gonadal arteries,** arising from the ventral aortic surface just below the renal arteries, run inferiorly to serve the gonads. They are called **ovarian arteries** in the female and **testicular arteries** in the male. Since these vessels must travel through the inguinal canal to supply the testes, they are considerably longer in the male than the female.

The final major branch of the abdominal aorta is the **inferior mesenteric artery,** which supplies the distal half of the large intestine via several branches. Just below this, four pairs of **lumbar arteries** arise from the posterolateral surface of the aorta to supply the posterior abdominal wall (lumbar region).

In the pelvic region, the descending aorta divides into the two large **common iliac arteries,** which serve the pelvis, lower abdominal wall, and the lower limbs.

Arteries Serving the Lower Limbs   Each of the common iliac arteries extends for about 5 cm (2 inches) into the pelvis before it divides into the internal and external iliac arteries (Figure 24.6). The **internal iliac artery** supplies the gluteal muscles via the **superior** and **inferior gluteal arteries** and the adductor muscles of the medial thigh via the **obturator artery,** as well as the external genitalia and perineum (via the *internal pudendal artery,* not illustrated).

The **external iliac artery** supplies the anterior abdominal wall and the lower limb. As it continues into the thigh, its name changes to **femoral artery.** Proximal branches of the femoral artery, the **circumflex femoral arteries,** supply the head and neck of the femur and the hamstring muscles. Slightly lower, the femoral artery gives off a deep branch, the **deep artery of the thigh,** which supplies the posterior thigh (knee flexor muscles). In the knee region, the femoral artery briefly becomes the **popliteal artery;** its subdivisions—the **anterior** and **posterior tibial arteries**—supply the leg, ankle, and foot. The posterior tibial, which supplies flexor muscles, gives off one main branch, the **fibular artery,** that serves the lateral calf (fibular muscles), and then divides into the **lateral** and **medial plantar arteries** that supply blood to the sole of the foot. The anterior tibial artery supplies the extensor muscles and terminates with the **dorsalis pedis artery.** The dorsalis pedis supplies the dorsum of the foot and continues on as the **arcuate artery** which issues the **metatarsal arteries** to the metatarsus of the foot. The dorsalis pedis is often palpated in patients with circulation problems of the leg to determine the circulatory efficiency to the limb as a whole.

- Palpate your own dorsalis pedis artery.

Locating Arteries on an Anatomical Chart or Model

Now that you have identified the arteries on Figures 24.2–24.6, attempt to locate and name them (without a reference) on a large anatomical chart or three-dimensional model of the vascular system. ■

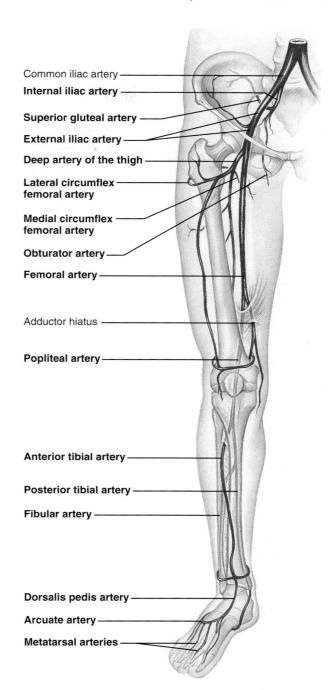

Common iliac artery
Internal iliac artery
Superior gluteal artery
External iliac artery
Deep artery of the thigh
Lateral circumflex femoral artery
Medial circumflex femoral artery
Obturator artery
Femoral artery
Adductor hiatus
Popliteal artery
Anterior tibial artery
Posterior tibial artery
Fibular artery
Dorsalis pedis artery
Arcuate artery
Metatarsal arteries

FIGURE 24.6 Arteries of the right pelvis and lower limb.

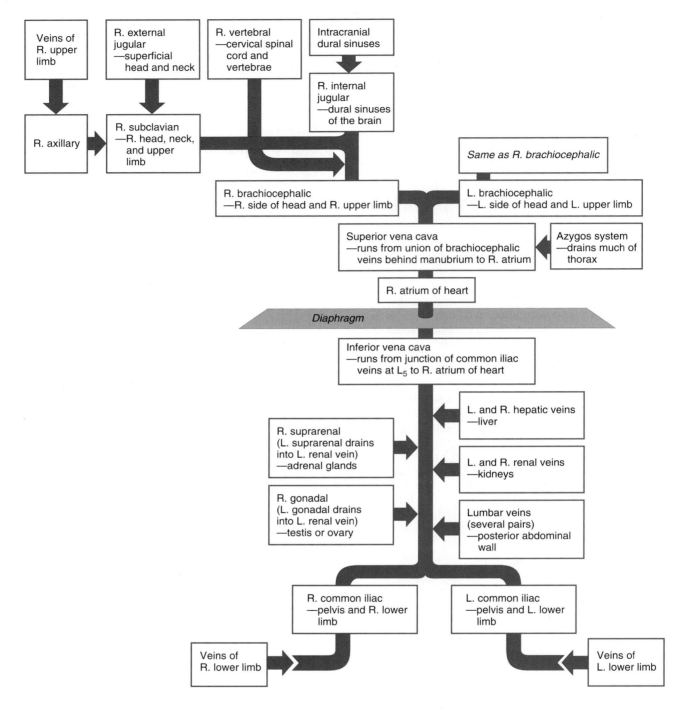

FIGURE 24.7 Schematic of systemic venous circulation.

Major Systemic Veins of the Body

Arteries are generally located in deep, well-protected body areas. However, many veins follow a more superficial course and are often easily seen and palpated on the body surface. Most deep veins parallel the course of the major arteries, and in many cases the naming of the veins and arteries is identical except for the designation of the vessels as veins. Whereas the major systemic arteries branch off the aorta, the veins tend to converge on the venae cavae, which enter the right atrium of the heart. Veins draining the head and upper extremities empty into the **superior vena cava,** and those draining the lower body empty into the **inferior vena cava.** Figure 24.7 is a schematic of the systemic veins and their relationship to the venae cavae to get you started.

Veins Draining into the Inferior Vena Cava

The inferior vena cava, a much longer vessel than the superior vena cava, returns blood to the heart from all body regions below the diaphragm (see Figure 24.7). It begins in the lower abdominal region with the union of the paired **common iliac veins,** which drain venous blood from the legs and pelvis.

Veins of the Lower Limbs Each common iliac vein is formed by the union of the **internal iliac vein,** draining the pelvis, and the **external iliac vein,** which receives venous blood from the lower limb (Figure 24.8). Veins of the leg include the **anterior** and **posterior tibial veins,** which serve the calf and foot. The anterior tibial vein is a superior continuation of the **dorsalis pedis vein** of the foot. The posterior tibial vein is formed by the union of the **medial** and **lateral plantar veins,** and ascends deep in the calf muscles. It receives the **fibular (peroneal) vein** in the calf and then joins with the anterior tibial vein at the knee to produce the **popliteal vein,** which crosses the back of the knee. The popliteal vein becomes the **femoral vein** in the thigh; the femoral vein in turn becomes the external iliac vein in the inguinal region.

The **great saphenous vein,** a superficial vein, is the longest vein in the body. Beginning in common with the **small saphenous vein** from the **dorsal venous arch,** it extends up the medial side of the leg, knee, and thigh to empty into the femoral vein. The small saphenous vein runs along the lateral aspect of the foot and through the calf muscle, which it drains, and then empties into the popliteal vein at the knee (Figure 24.8b).

Veins of the Abdomen Moving superiorly in the abdominal cavity (Figure 24.9), the inferior vena cava receives blood from the posterior abdominal wall via several pairs of lumbar veins, and from the right ovary or testis via the right gonadal vein. (The left gonadal [ovarian or testicular] vein drains into the left renal vein superiorly.) The paired renal veins drain the kidneys. Just above the right renal vein, the right suprarenal vein (receiving blood from the adrenal gland on the same side) drains into the inferior vena cava, but its partner, the left suprarenal vein, empties into the left renal vein inferiorly. The right and left hepatic veins drain the liver. The unpaired veins draining the digestive tract organs empty into a special vessel, the hepatic portal vein, which carries blood to the liver to be processed before it enters the systemic venous system. (The hepatic portal system is discussed separately on p. 409.)

Veins Draining into the Superior Vena Cava

Veins draining into the superior vena cava are named from the superior vena cava distally, *but remember that the flow of blood is in the opposite direction.*

Veins of the Head and Neck The **right** and **left brachiocephalic veins** drain the head, neck, and upper extremities and unite to form the superior vena cava (Figure 24.10). Notice that although there is only one brachiocephalic artery, there are two brachiocephalic veins.

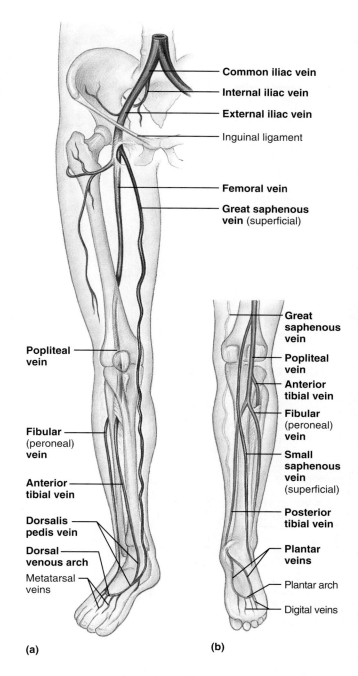

FIGURE 24.8 Veins of the right lower limb.
(**a**) Anterior view. (**b**) Posterior view.

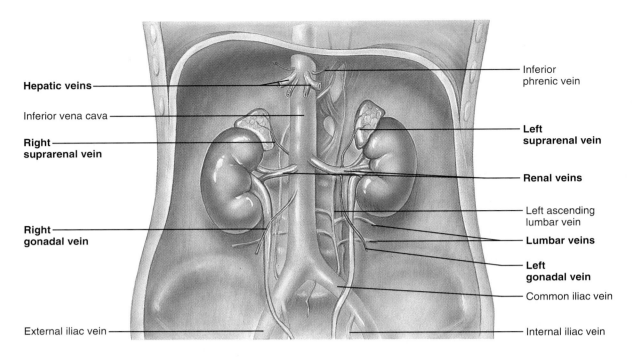

FIGURE 24.9 Venous drainage of abdominal organs not drained by the hepatic portal vein.

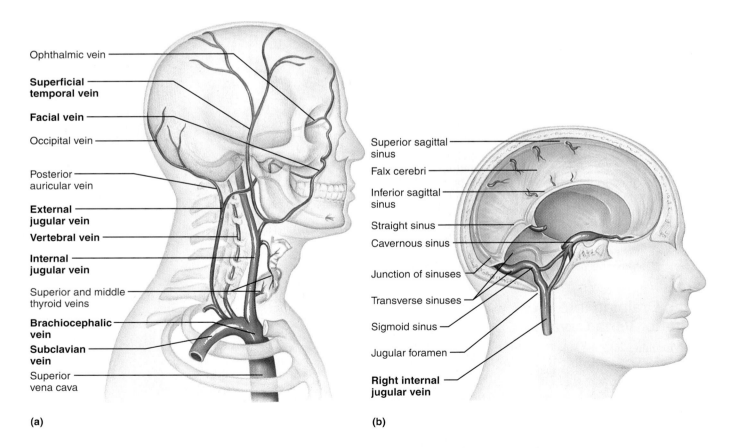

(a)

(b)

FIGURE 24.10 Venous drainage of the head, neck, and brain. (a) Veins of the head and neck, right superficial aspect. (b) Dural sinuses of the brain, right aspect. (See also Plate J of the Human Anatomy Atlas.)

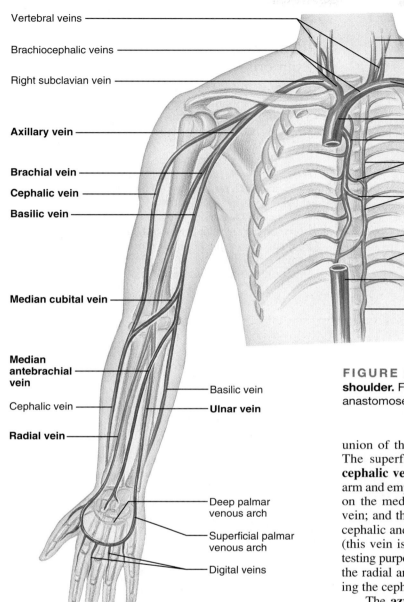

Vertebral veins

Brachiocephalic veins

Right subclavian vein

Axillary vein

Brachial vein

Cephalic vein

Basilic vein

Median cubital vein

Median antebrachial vein

Cephalic vein

Radial vein

Internal jugular vein

External jugular vein

Left subclavian vein

Superior vena cava

Azygos vein

Accessory hemiazygos vein

Hemiazygos vein

Posterior intercostals

Inferior vena cava

Ascending lumbar vein

Basilic vein

Ulnar vein

Deep palmar venous arch

Superficial palmar venous arch

Digital veins

FIGURE 24.11 Veins of the right upper limb and shoulder. For clarity, the abundant branching and anastomoses of these vessels are not shown.

Branches of the brachiocephalic veins include the internal jugular, vertebral, and subclavian veins. The **internal jugular veins** are large veins that drain the superior sagittal sinus and other **dural sinuses** of the brain. As they move inferiorly, they receive blood from the head and neck via the **superficial temporal** and **facial veins.** The **vertebral veins** drain the posterior aspect of the head including the cervical vertebrae and spinal cord. The **subclavian veins** receive venous blood from the upper extremity. The **external jugular vein** joins the subclavian vein near its origin to return the venous drainage of the extra-cranial (superficial) tissues of the head and neck.

Veins of the Upper Limb and Thorax   As the subclavian vein traverses the axilla, it becomes the **axillary vein** and then the **brachial vein** as it courses along the posterior aspect of the humerus (Figure 24.11). The brachial vein is formed by the

union of the deep **radial** and **ulnar veins** of the forearm. The superficial venous drainage of the arm includes the **cephalic vein,** which courses along the lateral aspect of the arm and empties into the axillary vein; the **basilic vein,** found on the medial aspect of the arm and entering the brachial vein; and the **median cubital vein,** which runs between the cephalic and basilic veins in the anterior aspect of the elbow (this vein is often the site of choice for removing blood for testing purposes). The **median antebrachial vein** lies between the radial and ulnar veins, and terminates variably by entering the cephalic or basilic vein at the elbow.

The **azygos system** (Figure 24.11) drains the intercostal muscles of the thorax and provides an accessory venous system to drain the abdominal wall. The **azygos vein,** which drains the right side of the thorax, enters the dorsal aspect of the superior vena cava immediately before that vessel enters the right atrium. Also part of the azygos system are the **hemiazygos** (a continuation of the **left ascending lumbar vein** of the abdomen) and the **accessory hemiazygos veins,** which together drain the left side of the thorax and empty into the azygos vein.

ACTIVITY 3

Identifying the Systemic Veins

Identify the important veins of the systemic circulation on the large anatomical chart or model without referring to the figures. ■

Special Circulations

Pulmonary Circulation

The pulmonary circulation (discussed previously in relation to heart anatomy on p. 387) differs in many ways from systemic circulation because it does not serve the metabolic needs of the body tissues with which it is associated (in this case, lung tissue). It functions instead to bring the blood into close contact with the alveoli of the lungs to permit gas exchanges that rid the blood of excess carbon dioxide and replenish its supply of vital oxygen. The arteries of the pulmonary circulation are structurally much like veins, and they create a low-pressure bed in the lungs. (If the arterial pressure in the systemic circulation is 120/80, the pressure in the pulmonary artery is likely to be approximately 24/8.) The functional blood supply of the lungs is provided by the **bronchial arteries,** which diverge from the thoracic portion of the descending aorta.

ACTIVITY 4

Identifying Vessels of the Pulmonary Circulation

As you read the descriptions below find the vessels of the pulmonary circulation on an anatomical chart (if one is available). Then, using the terms provided in Figure 24.12, label all structures provided with leader lines. ▬

Pulmonary circulation begins with the large **pulmonary trunk,** which leaves the right ventricle and divides into the **right** and **left pulmonary arteries** about 5 cm (2 inches) above its origin. The right and left pulmonary arteries plunge into the lungs, where they subdivide into **lobar arteries** (three on the right and two on the left). The lobar arteries accompany the main bronchi into the lobes of the lungs and branch extensively within the lungs to form arterioles, which finally terminate in the capillary networks surrounding the

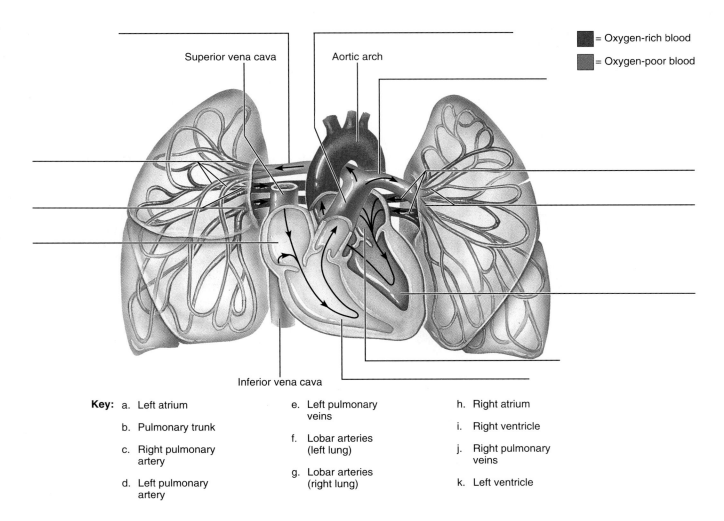

■ = Oxygen-rich blood

■ = Oxygen-poor blood

Superior vena cava

Aortic arch

Inferior vena cava

Key:
a. Left atrium
b. Pulmonary trunk
c. Right pulmonary artery
d. Left pulmonary artery
e. Left pulmonary veins
f. Lobar arteries (left lung)
g. Lobar arteries (right lung)
h. Right atrium
i. Right ventricle
j. Right pulmonary veins
k. Left ventricle

FIGURE 24.12 The pulmonary circulation.

alveolar sacs of the lungs. Diffusion of the respiratory gases occurs across the walls of the alveoli and **pulmonary capillaries.** The pulmonary capillary beds are drained by venules, which converge to form sequentially larger veins and finally the four **pulmonary veins** (two leaving each lung), which return the blood to the left atrium of the heart.

ACTIVITY 5

Tracing the Hepatic Portal Circulation

Locate on Figure 24.13, and on an anatomical chart of the hepatic portal circulation (if available), the vessels named below.

Hepatic Portal Circulation

Blood vessels of the hepatic portal circulation drain the digestive viscera, spleen, and pancreas and deliver this blood to the liver for processing via the **hepatic portal vein.** If a meal has recently been eaten, the hepatic portal blood will be nutrient-rich. The liver is the key body organ involved in maintaining proper sugar, fatty acid, and amino acid concentrations in the blood, and this system ensures that these substances pass through the liver before entering the systemic circulation. As blood percolates through the liver sinusoids, some of the nutrients are removed to be stored or processed in various ways for release to the general circulation. At the same time, the hepatocytes are detoxifying alcohol and other possibly harmful chemicals present in the blood, and the liver's macrophages are removing bacteria and other debris from the passing blood. The liver in turn is drained by the hepatic veins that enter the inferior vena cava.

The **inferior mesenteric vein,** draining the distal portions of the large intestine, joins the **splenic vein,** which drains the spleen and part of the pancreas and stomach. The splenic vein and the **superior mesenteric vein,** which receives blood from the small intestine and the ascending and transverse colon, unite to form the hepatic portal vein. The **left gastric vein,** which drains the lesser curvature of the stomach, drains directly into the hepatic portal vein.

Fetal Circulation

In a developing fetus, the lungs and digestive system are not yet functional, and all nutrient, excretory, and gaseous exchanges occur through the placenta (see Figure 24.14a). Nutrients and oxygen move across placental barriers from the mother's blood into fetal blood, and carbon dioxide and other metabolic wastes move from the fetal blood supply to the mother's blood.

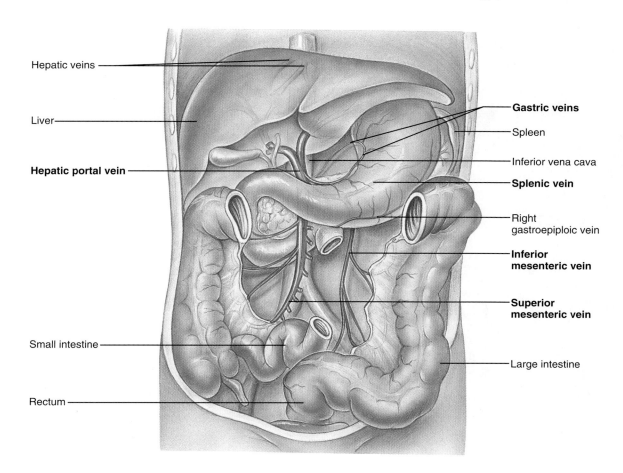

FIGURE 24.13 Hepatic portal circulation.

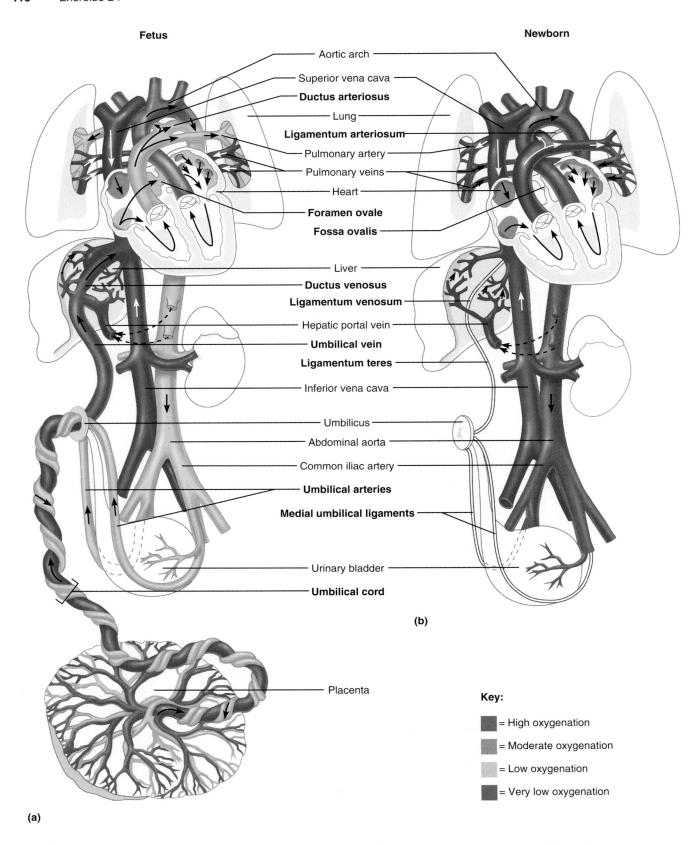

Fetus

Newborn

Aortic arch
Superior vena cava
Ductus arteriosus
Lung
Ligamentum arteriosum
Pulmonary artery
Pulmonary veins
Heart
Foramen ovale
Fossa ovalis
Liver
Ductus venosus
Ligamentum venosum
Hepatic portal vein
Umbilical vein
Ligamentum teres
Inferior vena cava
Umbilicus
Abdominal aorta
Common iliac artery
Umbilical arteries
Medial umbilical ligaments
Urinary bladder
Umbilical cord

(b)

Placenta

Key:

= High oxygenation

= Moderate oxygenation

= Low oxygenation

= Very low oxygenation

(a)

FIGURE 24.14 **Circulation in fetus and newborn.** Arrows indicate direction of blood flow. (**a**) Special adaptations for embryonic and fetal life. The umbilical vein carries oxygen- and nutrient-rich blood from the placenta to the fetus. The umbilical arteries carry waste-laden blood from the fetus to the placenta; the ductus arteriosus and foramen ovale bypass the nonfunctional lungs; and the ductus venosus allows blood to partially bypass the liver. (**b**) Changes in the cardiovascular system at birth. The umbilical vessels are occluded, as are the liver and lung bypasses (ductus venosus and arteriosus, and the foramen ovale).

Fetal blood travels through the umbilical cord, which contains three blood vessels: two smaller umbilical arteries and one large umbilical vein. The **umbilical vein** carries blood rich in nutrients and oxygen to the fetus; the **umbilical arteries** carry carbon dioxide and waste-laden blood from the fetus to the placenta. The umbilical arteries, which transport blood away from the fetal heart, meet the umbilical vein at the *umbilicus* (navel, or belly button) and wrap around the vein within the cord en route to their placental attachments. Newly oxygenated blood flows in the umbilical vein superiorly toward the fetal heart. Some of this blood perfuses the liver, but the larger proportion is ducted through the relatively nonfunctional liver to the inferior vena cava via a shunt vessel called the **ductus venosus,** which carries the blood to the right atrium of the heart.

Because fetal lungs are nonfunctional and collapsed, two shunting mechanisms ensure that blood almost entirely bypasses the lungs. Much of the blood entering the right atrium is shunted into the left atrium through the **foramen ovale,** a flaplike opening in the interatrial septum. The left ventricle then pumps the blood out the aorta to the systemic circulation. Blood that does enter the right ventricle and is pumped out of the pulmonary trunk encounters a second shunt, the **ductus arteriosus,** a short vessel connecting the pulmonary trunk and the aorta. Because the collapsed lungs present an extremely high-resistance pathway, blood more readily enters the systemic circulation through the ductus arteriosus.

The aorta carries blood to the tissues of the body; this blood ultimately finds its way back to the placenta via the umbilical arteries. The only fetal vessel that carries highly oxygenated blood is the umbilical vein. All other vessels contain varying degrees of oxygenated and deoxygenated blood.

At birth, or shortly after, the foramen ovale closes and becomes the **fossa ovalis,** and the ductus arteriosus collapses and is converted to the fibrous **ligamentum arteriosum** (Figure 24.14b). Lack of blood flow through the umbilical vessels leads to their eventual obliteration, and the circulatory pattern becomes that of the adult. Remnants of the umbilical arteries persist as the **medial umbilical ligaments** on the inner surface of the anterior abdominal wall, of the umbilical vein as the **ligamentum teres** (or **round ligament**) of the liver, and of the ductus venosus as a fibrous band called the **ligamentum venosum** on the inferior surface of the liver.

ACTIVITY 6

Tracing the Pathway of Fetal Blood Flow

The pathway of fetal blood flow is indicated with arrows on Figure 24.14a. Follow the flow of blood from the placenta to the fetal heart and back, noting the names of all specialized fetal circulatory structures. ▆▆

Arterial Supply of the Brain and the Cerebral Arterial Circle

A continuous blood supply to the brain is crucial because oxygen deprivation for even a few minutes causes irreparable damage to the delicate brain tissue. The brain is supplied by two pairs of arteries arising from the region of the aortic arch—the *internal carotid arteries* and the *vertebral arteries.* Figure 24.15a is a diagram of the brain's arterial supply.

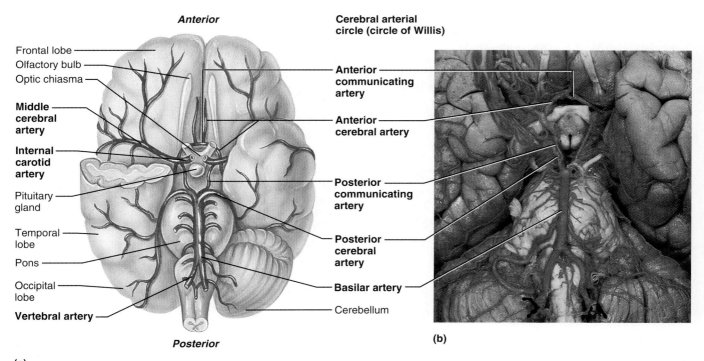

(a)

(b)

FIGURE 24.15 Arterial supply of the brain. (a) Drawing of cerebral arteries. Cerebellum is not shown on the left side of the figure. **(b)** Cerebral arterial circle (circle of Willis) in a human brain.

A C T I V I T Y   7

Tracing the Arterial Supply of the Brain

As you read the description of the blood supply below, locate the vessels in Figure 24.15. Also consult an anatomical chart or brain model showing the *cerebral arterial circle (circle of Willis)* and cerebral arteries. ▆▆

The **internal carotid arteries,** branches of the common carotid arteries, follow a deep course through the neck and along the pharynx, entering the skull through the carotid canals of the temporal bone. Within the cranium, each divides into **anterior** and **middle cerebral arteries,** which supply the bulk of the cerebrum. The internal carotid arteries also contribute to the formation of the **cerebral arterial circle (circle of Willis),** an arterial anastomosis at the base of the brain surrounding the pituitary gland and the optic chiasma, by contributing to a **posterior communicating artery** on each side. The circle is completed by the **anterior communicating artery,** a short shunt connecting the right and left anterior cerebral arteries.

The paired **vertebral arteries** diverge from the subclavian arteries and pass superiorly through the foramina of the transverse process of the cervical vertebrae to enter the skull through the foramen magnum. Within the skull, the vertebral arteries unite to form a single **basilar artery,** which continues superiorly along the ventral aspect of the brain stem, giving off branches to the pons, cerebellum, and inner ear. At the base of the cerebrum, the basilar artery divides to form the **posterior cerebral arteries.** These supply portions of the temporal and occipital lobes of the cerebrum and also become part of the cerebral arterial circle by joining with the posterior communicating arteries.

The uniting of the blood supply of the internal carotid arteries and the vertebral arteries via the cerebral arterial circle is a protective device that theoretically provides an alternate set of pathways for blood to reach the brain tissue in the case of arterial occlusion or impaired blood flow anywhere in the system. In actuality, the communicating arteries are tiny, and in many cases the communicating system is defective.

D I S S E C T I O N   A N D   I D E N T I F I C A T I O N :
The Blood Vessels of the Cat

If you have already opened your animal's ventral body cavity and identified many of its organs, begin this exercise with Activity 9. ▆▆

A C T I V I T Y   8

Opening the Ventral Body Cavity and Preliminary Organ Identification

If the ventral body cavity has not yet been opened, do so by following instructions in Exercise 21, p. 353.

A helpful prelude to identifying and tracing the blood supply of the various organs of the cat is a preliminary identification of ventral body cavity organs shown in Figure 24.16. Since you will study the organ systems contained in the ventral cavity in later units, the objective here is simply

to identify the most important organs. Using Figure 24.16 as a guide, identify the following body cavity organs:

Thoracic Cavity Organs

Heart: In the mediastinum enclosed by the pericardium.

Lungs: Flanking the heart.

Thymus: Superior to and partially covering the heart (see Figure 21.3b, p. 355). The thymus is quite large in young cats but is largely replaced by fat as cats age.

Abdominal Cavity Organs

Liver: Posterior to the diaphragm.

• Lift the large, drapelike, fat-infiltrated greater omentum covering the abdominal organs to expose the following:

Stomach: Dorsally located and to the left side of the liver.

Spleen: A flattened, brown organ curving around the lateral aspect of the stomach.

Small intestine: Continuing posteriorly from the stomach.

Large intestine: Taking a U-shaped course around the small intestine and terminating in the rectum. ▆▆

A C T I V I T Y   9

Identifying the Blood Vessels

1.   Carefully clear away any thymus tissue or fat obscuring the heart and the large vessels associated with the heart. Before identifying the blood vessels, try to locate the *phrenic nerve* (from the cervical plexus), which innervates the diaphragm. The phrenic nerves lie ventral to the root of the lung on each side, as they pass to the diaphragm. Also attempt to locate the *vagus nerve* (cranial nerve X) passing laterally along the trachea and dorsal to the root of the lung.

2.   Slit the parietal pericardium and reflect it superiorly. Then, cut it away from its heart attachments. Review the structures of the heart. Notice its pointed inferior end (apex) and its broader superior portion. Identify the two *atria,* which appear darker than the inferior *ventricles.*

3.   Identify the **aorta,** the largest artery in the body, issuing from the left ventricle. Also identify the *coronary arteries* in the sulcus on the ventral surface of the heart; these should be injected with red latex. (As an aid to blood vessel identification, the arteries of laboratory dissection specimens are injected with red latex; the veins are injected with blue latex. Exceptions to this will be noted as they are encountered.)

4.   Identify the two large venae cavae—the **superior** and **inferior venae cavae**—entering the right atrium. The superior vena cava is the largest dark-colored vessel entering the base of the heart. These vessels are called the **precava** and **postcava**, respectively, in the cat. The caval veins drain the same relative body areas as in humans. Also identify the **pulmonary trunk** (usually injected with blue latex) extending anteriorly from the right ventricle and the right and left pulmonary arteries. Trace the **pulmonary arteries** until they enter the lungs. Locate the **pulmonary veins** entering the left atrium and the ascending aorta arising from the left ventricle and running dorsally to the precava and to the left of the body midline.

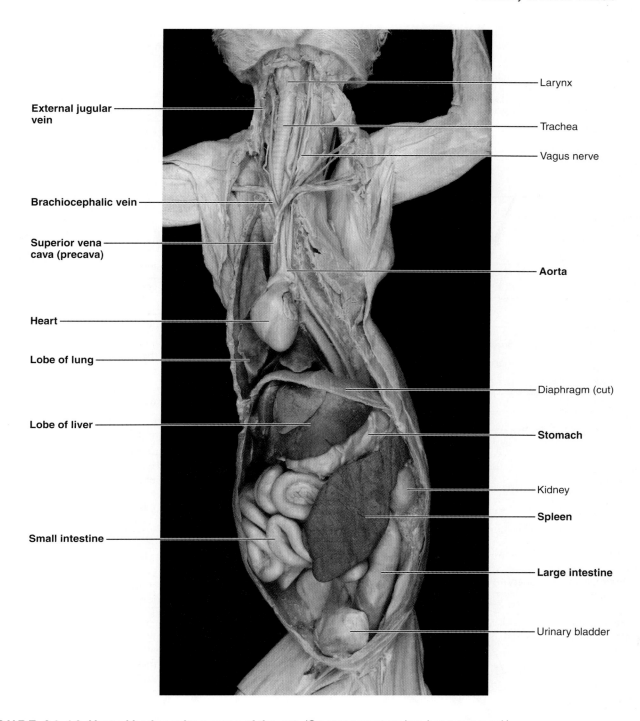

External jugular vein

Brachiocephalic vein

Superior vena cava (precava)

Heart

Lobe of lung

Lobe of liver

Small intestine

Larynx

Trachea

Vagus nerve

Aorta

Diaphragm (cut)

Stomach

Kidney

Spleen

Large intestine

Urinary bladder

FIGURE 24.16 Ventral body cavity organs of the cat. (Greater omentum has been removed.)

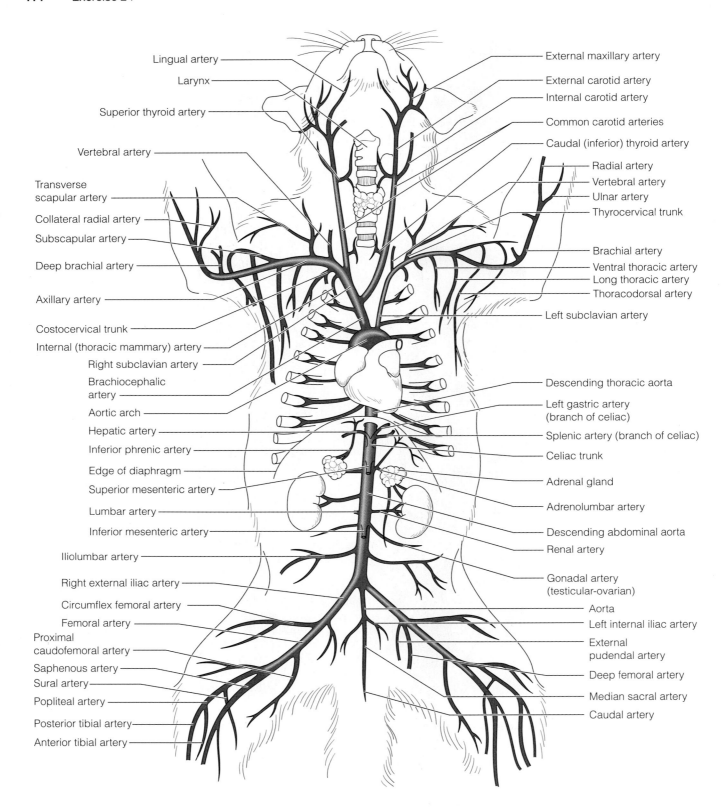

FIGURE 24.17 Arterial system of the cat. (See also Figure 24.20 on p. 420.)

Arteries of the Cat

Refer to Figure 24.17 and to the summary photo in Figure 24.20 on p. 420 as you study the arterial system of the cat.

1.   Reidentify the aorta as it emerges from the left ventricle. As you observed in the dissection of the sheep heart, the first branches of the aorta are the **coronary arteries,** which supply the myocardium. The coronary arteries emerge from the base of the aorta and can be seen on the surface of the heart. Follow the aorta as it arches (aortic arch), and identify its major branches. In the cat, the aortic arch gives off two large vessels, the **brachiocephalic artery** and the **left subclavian artery.** The brachiocephalic artery has three major branches, the right subclavian artery and the right and left common carotid arteries. (Note that in humans, the left common carotid artery is a direct branch off the aortic arch.)

2.   Follow the **right common carotid artery** along the right side of the trachea as it moves anteriorly, giving off branches to the neck muscles, thyroid gland, and trachea. At the level of the larynx, it branches to form the **external** and **internal carotid arteries.** The internal carotid is quite small in the cat and it may be difficult to locate. It may even be absent. The distribution of the carotid arteries parallels that in humans.

3.   Follow the **right subclavian artery** laterally. It gives off four branches, the first being the tiny **vertebral artery,** which along with the internal carotid artery provides the arterial circulation of the brain. Other branches of the subclavian artery include the **costocervical trunk** (to the costal and cervical regions), the **thyrocervical trunk** (to the shoulder), and the **internal thoracic (mammary) artery** (serving the ventral thoracic wall). As the subclavian passes in front of the first rib it becomes the **axillary artery.** Its branches, which supply the trunk and shoulder muscles, are the **ventral thoracic artery** (the pectoral muscles), the **long thoracic artery** (pectoral muscles and latissimus dorsi), and the **subscapular artery** (the trunk muscles). As the axillary artery enters the arm, it is called the **brachial artery,** and it travels with the median nerve down the length of the humerus. At the elbow, the brachial artery branches to produce the two major arteries serving the forearm and hand, the **radial** and **ulnar arteries.**

4.   Return to the thorax, lift the left lung, and follow the course of the **descending aorta** through the thoracic cavity. The esophagus overlies it along its course. Notice the paired intercostal arteries that branch laterally from the aorta in the thoracic region.

5.   Follow the aorta through the diaphragm into the abdominal cavity. Carefully pull the peritoneum away from its ventral surface and identify the following vessels:

Celiac trunk: The first branch diverging from the aorta immediately as it enters the abdominal cavity; supplies the stomach, liver, gallbladder, pancreas, and spleen. (Trace as many of its branches to these organs as possible.)

Superior mesenteric artery: Immediately posterior to the celiac trunk; supplies the small intestine and most of the large intestine. (Spread the mesentery of the small intestine to observe the branches of this artery as they run to supply the small intestine.)

Adrenolumbar arteries: Paired arteries diverging from the aorta slightly posterior to the superior mesenteric artery; supply the muscles of the body wall and adrenal glands.

Renal arteries: Paired arteries supplying the kidneys.

Gonadal arteries (testicular or ovarian): Paired arteries supplying the gonads.

Inferior mesenteric artery: An unpaired thin vessel arising from the ventral surface of the aorta posterior to the genital arteries; supplies the second half of the large intestine.

Iliolumbar arteries: Paired, rather large arteries that supply the body musculature in the iliolumbar region.

External iliac arteries: Paired arteries which continue through the body wall and pass under the inguinal ligament to the hindlimb.

6.   After giving off the external iliac arteries, the aorta persists briefly and then divides into three arteries: the two **internal iliac arteries** which supply the pelvic viscera, and the **median sacral artery.** As the median sacral artery enters the tail, it comes to be called the **caudal artery.** (Note that there is no common iliac artery in the cat.

7.   Trace the external iliac artery into the thigh, where it becomes the **femoral artery.** The femoral artery is most easily identified in the **femoral triangle** at the medial surface of the upper thigh. Follow the femoral artery as it courses through the thigh (along with the femoral vein and nerve) and gives off branches to the thigh muscles. (These various branches are indicated on Figure 24.17.) As you approach the knee, the **saphenous artery** branches off the femoral artery to supply the medial portion of the leg. The femoral artery then descends deep to the knee to become the **popliteal artery** in the popliteal region. The popliteal artery in turn gives off two main branches, the **sural artery** and the **posterior tibial artery,** and continues as the **anterior tibial artery.** These branches supply the leg and foot.

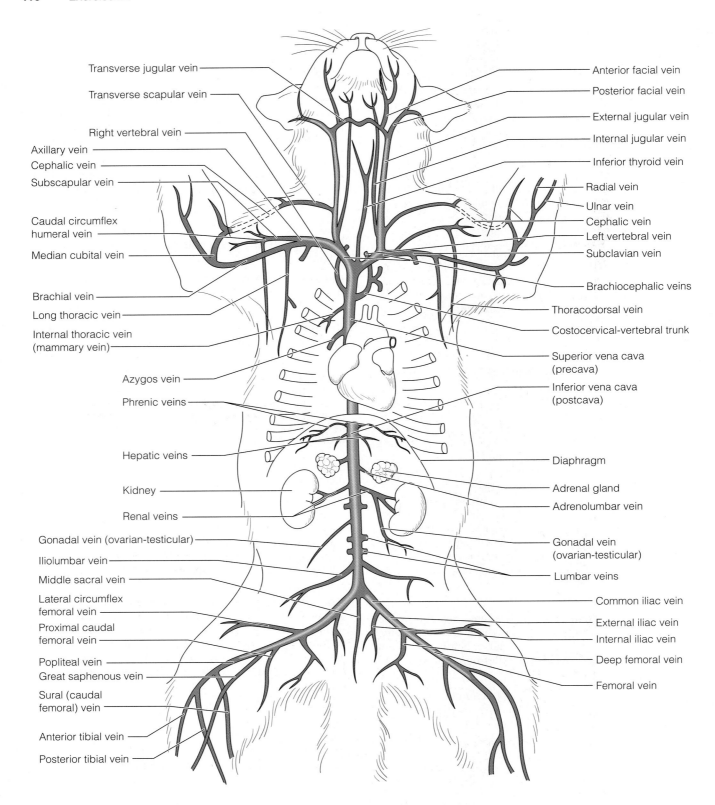

Transverse jugular vein

Transverse scapular vein

Right vertebral vein

Axillary vein

Cephalic vein

Subscapular vein

Caudal circumflex humeral vein

Median cubital vein

Brachial vein

Long thoracic vein

Internal thoracic vein (mammary vein)

Azygos vein

Phrenic veins

Hepatic veins

Kidney

Renal veins

Gonadal vein (ovarian-testicular)

Iliolumbar vein

Middle sacral vein

Lateral circumflex femoral vein

Proximal caudal femoral vein

Popliteal vein

Great saphenous vein

Sural (caudal femoral) vein

Anterior tibial vein

Posterior tibial vein

Anterior facial vein

Posterior facial vein

External jugular vein

Internal jugular vein

Inferior thyroid vein

Radial vein

Ulnar vein

Cephalic vein

Left vertebral vein

Subclavian vein

Brachiocephalic veins

Thoracodorsal vein

Costocervical-vertebral trunk

Superior vena cava (precava)

Inferior vena cava (postcava)

Diaphragm

Adrenal gland

Adrenolumbar vein

Gonadal vein (ovarian-testicular)

Lumbar veins

Common iliac vein

External iliac vein

Internal iliac vein

Deep femoral vein

Femoral vein

FIGURE 24.18 Venous system of the cat. (See also Figure 24.20 on p. 420.)

Veins of the Cat

Refer to Figure 24.18 and to summary Figure 24.20 on p. 420 as you study the venous system of the cat. Keep in mind that the vessels are named for the region drained, not for the point of union with other veins. (As you continue with the dissection, notice that not all vessels shown on Figure 24.20 are discussed.)

1.   Reidentify the inferior vena cava (precava) as it enters the right atrium. Trace it anteriorly to identify veins that enter it:

Azygos vein: Passing directly into its dorsal surface; drains the thoracic intercostal muscles.

Internal thoracic (mammary) veins: Drain the chest and abdominal walls.

Right vertebral vein: Drains the spinal cord and brain; usually enters right side of precava approximately at the level of the internal mammary veins but may enter the brachiocephalic vein in your specimen.

Right and left brachiocephalic veins: Form the precava by their union.

2.   Reflect the pectoral muscles, and trace the brachiocephalic vein laterally. Identify the two large veins that unite to form it—the external jugular vein and the subclavian vein. Notice that this differs from what is seen in humans, where the brachiocephalic veins are formed by the union of the internal jugular and subclavian veins.

3.   Follow the **external jugular vein** as it courses anteriorly along the side of the neck to the point where it is joined on its medial surface by the **internal jugular vein.** The internal jugular veins are small and may be difficult to identify in the cat. Notice the difference in cat and human jugular veins. The internal jugular is considerably larger in humans and drains into the subclavian vein. In the cat, the external jugular is larger, and the interior jugular vein drains into it. Identify the *common carotid artery,* since it accompanies the internal jugular vein in this region. Also attempt to find the *sympathetic trunk,* which is located in the same area running lateral to the trachea. Several other vessels drain into the external jugular vein (transverse scapular vein, facial veins, and others). These are not discussed here but are shown on the figure and may be traced if time allows.

4.   Return to the shoulder region and follow the course of the **subclavian vein** as it moves laterally toward the forelimb. It becomes the **axillary vein** as it passes in front of the first rib and runs through the brachial plexus, giving off several branches, the first of which is the **subscapular vein.** The subscapular vein drains the proximal part of the arm and shoulder. The four other branches that receive drainage from the shoulder, pectoral, and latissimus dorsi muscles are shown in the figure but need not be identified in this dissection.

5.   Follow the axillary vein into the arm, where it becomes the **brachial vein.** You can locate this vein on the medial side of the arm accompanying the brachial artery and nerve. Trace it to the point where it receives the **radial** and **ulnar veins** (which drain the forelimb) at the inner bend of the elbow. Also locate the superficial **cephalic vein** on the dorsal side of the arm. It communicates with the brachial vein via the median cubital vein in the elbow region and then enters the transverse scapular vein in the shoulder.

6.   Reidentify the posterior vena cava (postcaval vein), and trace it to its passage through the diaphragm. Notice again as you follow its course that the **intercostal veins** drain into a much smaller vein lying dorsal to the postcava, the **azygos vein.**

7.   Attempt to identify the **hepatic veins** entering the postcava from the liver. These may be seen if some of the anterior liver tissue is scraped away where the postcava enters the liver.

8.   Displace the intestines to the left side of the body cavity, and proceed posteriorly to identify the following veins in order. All of these veins empty into the postcava and drain the organs served by the same-named arteries. In the cat, variations in the connections of the veins to be located are common, and in some cases the postcaval vein may be double below the level of the renal veins. If you observe deviations, call them to the attention of your instructor.

Adrenolumbar veins: From the adrenal glands and body wall.

Renal veins: From the kidneys (it is common to find two renal veins on the right side).

Gonadal veins (testicular or ovarian veins): The left vein of this venous pair enters the left renal vein anteriorly.

Iliolumbar veins: Drain muscles of the back.

Common iliac veins: Unite to form the postcava.

The common iliac veins are formed in turn by the union of the **internal iliac** and **external iliac veins.** The more medial internal iliac veins receive branches from the pelvic organs and gluteal region whereas the external iliac vein receives venous drainage from the lower extremity. As the external iliac vein enters the thigh by running beneath the inguinal ligament, it receives the **deep femoral vein,** which drains the thigh and the external genital region. Just inferior to that point, the external iliac vein becomes the **femoral vein,** which receives blood from the thigh, leg, and foot. Follow the femoral vein down the thigh to identify the **great saphenous vein,** a superficial vein that courses up the inner aspect of the calf and across the inferior portion of the gracilis muscle (accompanied by the great saphenous artery and nerve) to enter the femoral vein. The femoral vein is formed by the union of this vein and the popliteal vein. The **popliteal vein** is located deep in the thigh beneath the semimembranosus and semitendinosus muscles in the popliteal space accompanying the popliteal artery. Trace the popliteal vein to its point of division into the **posterior** and **anterior tibial veins,** which drain the leg.

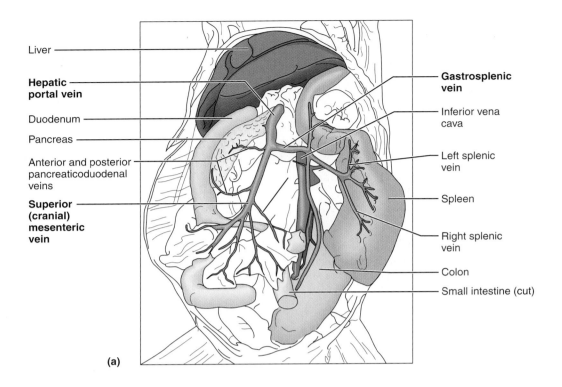

(a)

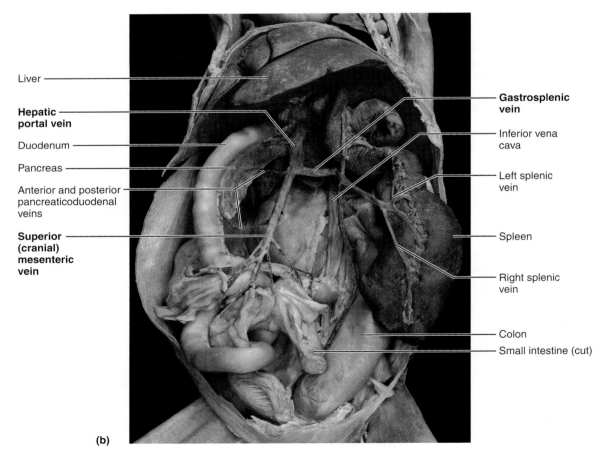

(b)

FIGURE 24.19 Hepatic portal circulation of the cat. (a) Diagrammatic view. (b) Photograph of hepatic portal system of the cat. Intestines have been pulled inferiorly. The mesentery of the small intestine has been partially dissected to show the veins of the portal system.

9.   In your specimen, trace the hepatic portal drainage depicted in Figure 24.19. Locate the **hepatic portal vein** by removing the peritoneum between the first portion of the small intestine and the liver. It appears brown due to coagulated blood, and it is unlikely that it or any of the vessels of this circulation contain latex. In the cat, the hepatic portal vein is formed by the union of the **gastrosplenic** and **superior mesenteric veins.** (In the human, the hepatic portal vein is formed by the union of the splenic and superior mesenteric veins.) If possible, locate the following vessels, which empty into the hepatic portal vein:

Gastrosplenic vein: Carries blood from the spleen and stomach; located dorsal to the stomach.

Superior cranial mesenteric vein: A large vein draining the small and large intestines and the pancreas.

Inferior caudal mesenteric vein: Parallels the course of the inferior mesenteric artery and empties into the superior mesenteric vein. In humans, this vessel merges with the splenic vein.

Coronary vein: Drains the lesser curvature of the stomach.

Pancreaticoduodenal veins (anterior and posterior): The anterior branch empties into the hepatic portal vein; the posterior branch empties into the superior mesenteric vein. (In humans, both of these are branches of the superior mesenteric vein.)

If the structures of the lymphatic system of the cat are to be studied during this laboratory session, turn to the dissection in Exercise 25 for instructions to conduct the study. Otherwise, properly clean your dissecting instruments and dissecting pan, and wrap and tag your cat for storage as described in the box on p. 220. ▪

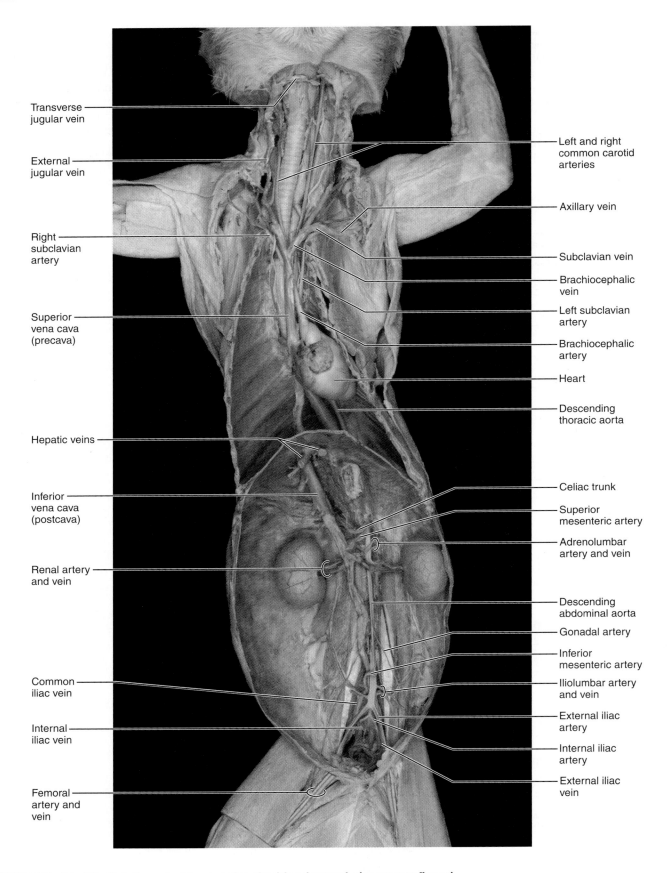

Transverse jugular vein

External jugular vein

Right subclavian artery

Superior vena cava (precava)

Hepatic veins

Inferior vena cava (postcava)

Renal artery and vein

Common iliac vein

Internal iliac vein

Femoral artery and vein

Left and right common carotid arteries

Axillary vein

Subclavian vein

Brachiocephalic vein

Left subclavian artery

Brachiocephalic artery

Heart

Descending thoracic aorta

Celiac trunk

Superior mesenteric artery

Adrenolumbar artery and vein

Descending abdominal aorta

Gonadal artery

Inferior mesenteric artery

Iliolumbar artery and vein

External iliac artery

Internal iliac artery

External iliac vein

FIGURE 24.20 Cat dissected to reveal major blood vessels (summary figure).

Anatomy of Blood Vessels

Microscopic Structure of the Blood Vessels

1. Use the key choices to identify the blood vessel tunics described.

Key: a.   tunica intima   b.   tunica media   c.   tunica externa

_____ 1.   innermost tunic

_____ 2.   bulky middle tunic; contains smooth muscle and elastin

_____ 3.   its smooth surface decreases resistance to blood flow

_____ 4.   tunic(s) of capillaries

_____, _____, _____ 5.   tunic(s) of arteries and veins

_____ 6.   is especially thick in elastic arteries

_____ 7.   most superficial tunic

2. Servicing the capillaries is the essential function of the organs of the circulatory system. Explain this statement.

_____

_____

_____

3. Cross-sectional views of an artery and of a vein are shown here. Identify each; and on the lines to the sides, note the structural details that enabled you to make these identifications:

(vessel type)   (vessel type)

_____   _____

(a)   (a)

_____   _____

(b)   (b)

4. Why are valves present in veins but not in arteries? _____

_____

_____

5. Name two events *occurring within the body* that aid in venous return.

_____ and _____

421

6. Why are the walls of arteries proportionately thicker than those of the corresponding veins? _____

_____

_____

Major Systemic Arteries and Veins of the Body

7. Use the key on the right to identify the arteries or veins described on the left.

_____ 1. the arterial system has one of these; the venous system has two

_____ 2. these arteries supply the myocardium

_____ , _____ 3. two paired arteries serving the brain

_____ 4. longest vein in the lower limb

_____ 5. artery on the dorsum of the foot checked after leg surgery

_____ 6. serves the posterior thigh

_____ 7. supplies the diaphragm

_____ 8. formed by the union of the radial and ulnar veins

_____ , _____ 9. two superficial veins of the arm

_____ 10. artery serving the kidney

_____ 11. veins draining the liver

_____ 12. artery that supplies the distal half of the large intestine

_____ 13. drains the pelvic organs

_____ 14. what the external iliac artery becomes on entry into the thigh

_____ 15. major artery serving the arm

_____ 16. supplies most of the small intestine

_____ 17. join to form the inferior vena cava

_____ 18. an arterial trunk that has three major branches, which run to the liver, spleen, and stomach

_____ 19. major artery serving the tissues external to the skull

_____ , _____ , _____ 20. three veins serving the leg

_____ 21. artery generally used to take the pulse at the wrist

Key:
a. anterior tibial
b. basilic
c. brachial
d. brachiocephalic
e. celiac trunk
f. cephalic
g. common carotid
h. common iliac
i. coronary
j. deep femoral
k. dorsalis pedis
l. external carotid
m. femoral
n. fibular
o. great saphenous
p. hepatic
q. inferior mesenteric
r. internal carotid
s. internal iliac
t. phrenic
u. posterior tibial
v. radial
w. renal
x. subclavian
y. superior mesenteric
z. vertebral

8. The human arterial and venous systems are diagrammed on this page and the next. Identify all indicated blood vessels.

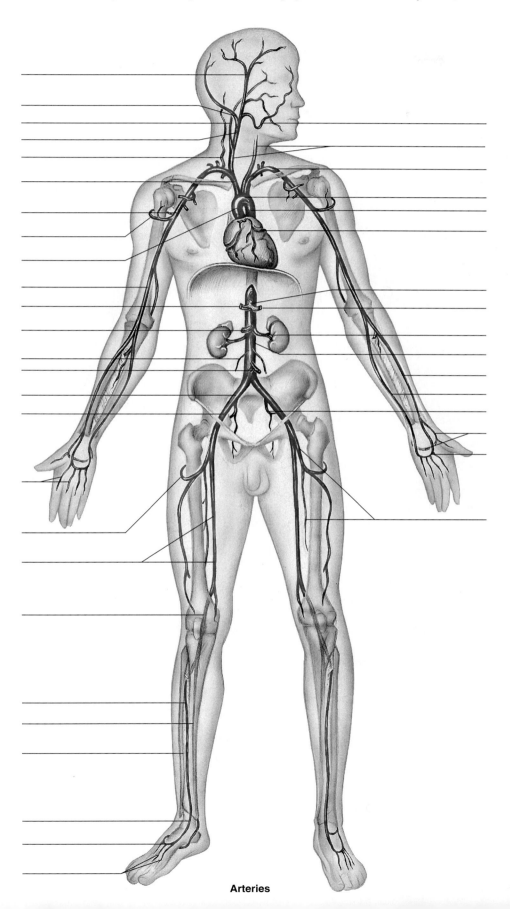

Arteries

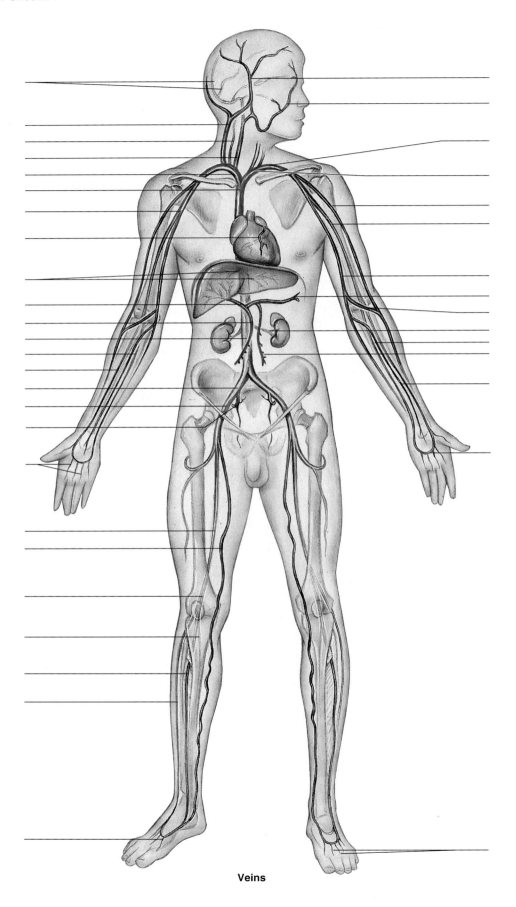

Veins

9. Trace the blood flow for each of the following situations.

   a. from the capillary beds of the left thumb to the capillary beds of the right thumb: _____

_____

_____

_____

_____

_____

   b. from the mitral valve to the tricuspid valve by way of the great toe: _____

_____

_____

_____

_____

   c. from the pulmonary vein to the pulmonary artery by way of the right side of the brain: _____

_____

_____

_____

_____

_____

_____

Pulmonary Circulation

10. Trace the pathway of a carbon dioxide gas molecule in the blood from the inferior vena cava until it leaves the bloodstream. Name all structures (vessels, heart chambers, and others) passed through en route.

_____

_____

_____

11. Trace the pathway of an oxygen gas molecule from an alveolus of the lung to the right atrium of the heart. Name all structures through which it passes. Circle the areas of gas exchange. _____

_____

_____

12. Most arteries of the adult body carry oxygen-rich blood, and the veins carry oxygen-depleted, carbon dioxide–rich blood. How does this differ in the pulmonary arteries and veins? _____

_____

_____

13. How do the arteries of the pulmonary circulation differ structurally from the systemic arteries? What condition is indicated by this anatomical difference? _____

_____

_____

Hepatic Portal Circulation

14. What is the source of blood in the hepatic portal system? _____

_____

15. Why is this blood carried to the liver before it enters the systemic circulation? _____

_____

_____

16. The hepatic portal vein is formed by the union of (a) _____, which drains the

_____, _____, _____,

and (b) _____, which drains the _____ and _____

_____. The _____ vein, which drains the lesser curvature of the

stomach, empties directly into the hepatic portal vein.

17. Trace the flow of a drop of blood from the small intestine to the right atrium of the heart, noting all structures encountered or passed through on the way. _____

_____

_____

Fetal Circulation

18. The failure of two of the fetal bypass structures to become obliterated after birth can cause congenital heart disease, in which the youngster would have improperly oxygenated blood. Which two structures are these?

_____ and _____

19. For each of the following structures, first indicate its function in the fetus; and then note its fate (what happens to it or what it is converted to after birth). Circle the blood vessel that carries the most oxygen-rich blood.

Structure	Function in fetus	Fate
Umbilical artery		
Umbilical vein		
Ductus venosus		
Ductus arteriosus		
Foramen ovale		

20. What organ serves as a respiratory/digestive/excretory organ for the fetus? _____

Arterial Supply of the Brain and the Cerebral Arterial Circle

21. What two paired arteries enter the skull to supply the brain?

_____ and _____

22. Branches of the paired arteries just named cooperate to form a ring of blood vessels encircling the pituitary gland, at the base

of the brain. What name is given to this communication network? _____

What is its function? _____

_____

23. What portion of the brain is served by the anterior and middle cerebral arteries? _____

_____

Both the anterior and middle cerebral arteries arise from the _____ arteries.

24. Trace the pathway of a drop of blood from the aorta to the left occipital lobe of the brain, noting all structures through which

it flows. _____

_____

Dissection and Identification: The Blood Vessels of the Cat

25. What differences did you observe between the origin of the left common carotid arteries in the cat and in the human?

_____

_____

Between the origin of the internal and external iliac arteries? _____

_____

_____

26. How do the relative sizes of the external and internal jugular veins differ in the human and the cat? _____

_____

_____

27. In the cat the inferior vena cava is called the _____ ,

and the superior vena cava is referred to as the _____ .

28. Define the following terms.

ascending aorta: _____

aortic arch: _____

descending thoracic aorta: _____

descending abdominal aorta: _____

The Lymphatic System and Immune Response

MATERIALS

- ☐ Large anatomical chart of the human lymphatic system
- ☐ Prepared slides of lymph node, spleen, and tonsil
- ☐ Compound microscope
- ☐ Dissection tray and instruments
- ☐ Animal specimen from previous dissections
- ☐ Embalming fluid
- ☐ Disposable gloves

AIA See Appendix B, Exercise 25 for links to A.D.A.M.® Interactive Anatomy.

OBJECTIVES

1. To name the components of the lymphatic system.
2. To relate the function of the lymphatic system to that of the blood vascular system.
3. To describe the formation and composition of lymph, and to describe how it is transported through the lymphatic vessels.
4. To relate immune function to immunological memory, specificity, and differentiation of self from nonself.
5. To differentiate between the roles of B cells and T cells in the immune response.
6. To describe the structure and function of lymph nodes, and to indicate the localization of T cells, B cells, and macrophages in a typical lymph node.
7. To compare and contrast lymphatic structures of the cat to those of a human.

The overall function of the lymphatic system is twofold: (1) It transports tissue fluid (lymph) to the blood vessels, and (2) it protects the body by removing foreign material such as bacteria from the lymphatic stream and by serving as a site for lymphocyte "policing" of body fluids and lymphocyte multiplication.

The Lymphatic System

The **lymphatic system** consists of a network of lymphatic vessels (lymphatics), lymphatic tissue, lymph nodes, and a number of other lymphoid organs, such as the tonsils, thymus, and spleen. We will focus on the lymphatic vessels and lymph nodes in this section. The white blood cells, which are the central actors in body immunity, are described later in this exercise.

Distribution and Function of Lymphatic Vessels and Lymph Nodes

As blood circulates through the body, the hydrostatic and osmotic pressures operating at the capillary beds result in fluid outflow at the arterial end of the bed and in its return at the venous end. However, not all of the lost fluid is returned to the bloodstream by this mechanism, and the fluid that lags behind in the tissue spaces must eventually return to the blood if the vascular system is to operate properly. (If it does not, fluid accumulates in the tissues, producing a condition called *edema*.) It is the microscopic, blind-ended **lymphatic capillaries** (Figure 25.1a), which ramify through nearly all the tissues of the body, that pick up this leaked fluid (primarily water and a small amount of dissolved proteins) and carry it through successively larger vessels—**lymphatic collecting vessels** to **lymphatic trunks**—until the lymph finally returns to the blood vascular system through one of the two large ducts in the thoracic region (Figure 25.1b). The **right lymphatic duct,** present in some but not all individuals, drains lymph from the right upper extremity, head, and thorax delivered by the jugular, subclavian, and broncho-mediastinal trunks. In individuals without a right lymphatic duct, those trunks open directly into veins of the neck. The large **thoracic duct** receives lymph

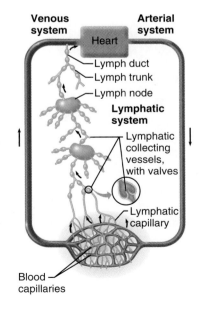

FIGURE 25.1 Lymphatic system.
(a) Simplified scheme of the relationship of lymphatic vessels to blood vessels of the cardiovascular system.

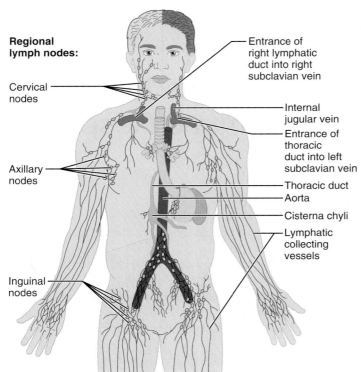

Regional lymph nodes:

Cervical nodes

Axillary nodes

Inguinal nodes

Entrance of right lymphatic duct into right subclavian vein

Internal jugular vein

Entrance of thoracic duct into left subclavian vein

Thoracic duct

Aorta

Cisterna chyli

Lymphatic collecting vessels

(b)

FIGURE 25.1 (*continued*) **Lymphatic system** (**b**) Distribution of lymphatic vessels and lymph nodes. The green-shaded area represents body area drained by the right lymphatic duct. (**c**) Relationship of the major lymphatic trunks to the thoracic and right lymphatic ducts, and the entry points of the ducts into the subclavian veins. (**d**) Photograph showing the course of the thoracic duct.

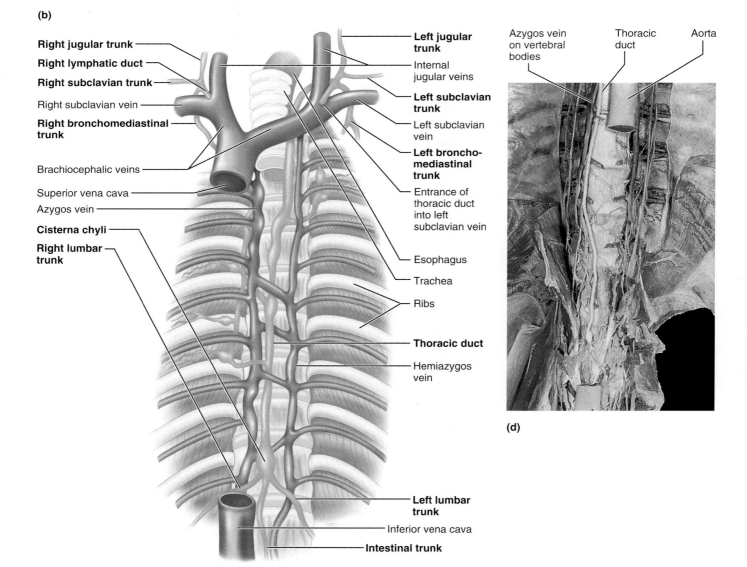

Right jugular trunk

Right lymphatic duct

Right subclavian trunk

Right subclavian vein

Right bronchomediastinal trunk

Brachiocephalic veins

Superior vena cava

Azygos vein

Cisterna chyli

Right lumbar trunk

Left jugular trunk

Internal jugular veins

Left subclavian trunk

Left subclavian vein

Left broncho-mediastinal trunk

Entrance of thoracic duct into left subclavian vein

Esophagus

Trachea

Ribs

Thoracic duct

Hemiazygos vein

Left lumbar trunk

Inferior vena cava

Intestinal trunk

(c)

Azygos vein on vertebral bodies

Thoracic duct

Aorta

(d)

from the rest of the body (see Figure 25.1c). In humans, both ducts empty the lymph into the venous circulation at the junction of the internal jugular vein and the subclavian vein, on their respective sides of the body. Notice that the lymphatic system, lacking both a contractile "heart" and arteries, is a one-way system; it carries lymph only toward the heart.

Like veins of the blood vascular system, the lymphatic collecting vessels have three tunics and are equipped with valves (see Plate 23 in the Histology Atlas). However, lymphatics tend to be thinner-walled, to have *more* valves, and to anastomose (form branching networks) more than veins. Since the lymphatic system is a pumpless system, lymph transport depends largely on the milking action of the skeletal muscles and on pressure changes within the thorax that occur during breathing.

As lymph is transported, it filters through bean-shaped **lymph nodes,** which cluster along the lymphatic vessels of the body. There are thousands of lymph nodes, but because they are usually embedded in connective tissue, they are not ordinarily seen. Within the lymph nodes are **macrophages,** phagocytes that destroy bacteria, cancer cells, and other foreign matter in the lymphatic stream, thus rendering many harmful substances or cells harmless before the lymph enters the bloodstream. Particularly large collections of lymph nodes are found in the inguinal, axillary, and cervical regions of the body. Although we are not usually aware of the filtering and protective nature of the lymph nodes, most of us have experienced "swollen glands" during an active infection. This swelling is a manifestation of the trapping function of the nodes.

Other lymphoid organs—the tonsils, thymus, and spleen (Figure 25.2)—resemble the lymph nodes histologically, and house similar cell populations (lymphocytes and macrophages).

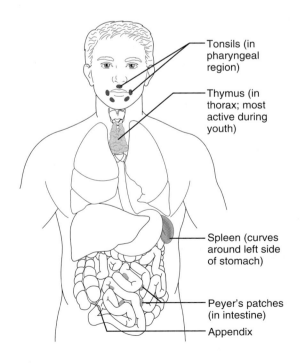

FIGURE 25.2 Body location of the tonsils, thymus, spleen, appendix, and Peyer's patches.

Tonsils (in pharyngeal region)

Thymus (in thorax; most active during youth)

Spleen (curves around left side of stomach)

Peyer's patches (in intestine)

Appendix

Identifying the Organs of the Lymphatic System

Study the large anatomical chart to observe the general plan of the lymphatic system. Notice the distribution of lymph nodes, various lymphatics, the lymphatic trunks, and the location of the right lymphatic duct and the thoracic duct. Also identify the **cisterna chyli,** the enlarged terminus of the thoracic duct that receives lymph from the digestive viscera. ▮

The Immune Response

The **adaptive immune system** is a functional system that recognizes something as foreign and acts to destroy or neutralize it. This response is known as the **immune response.** It is a systemic response and is not restricted to the initial infection site. When operating effectively, the immune response protects us from bacterial and viral infections, bacterial toxins, and cancer. When it fails or malfunctions, the body is quickly devastated by pathogens or its own assaults.

Major Characteristics of the Immune Response

The most important characteristics of the immune response are its (1) **memory,** (2) **specificity,** and (3) **ability to differentiate self from nonself.** Not only does the immune system have a "memory" for previously encountered foreign antigens (the chicken pox virus for example), but this memory is also remarkably accurate and highly specific.

An almost limitless variety of macromolecules is *antigenic*—that is, capable of provoking an immune response and reacting with its products. Nearly all foreign proteins, many polysaccharides, and many small molecules (haptens), when linked to our own body proteins, exhibit this capability. The cells that recognize antigens and initiate the immune response are lymphocytes, the second most numerous members of the leukocyte, or white blood cell (WBC), population. Each immunocompetent lymphocyte is virtually monospecific; that is, it has receptors on its surface allowing it to bind with only one or a few very similar antigens.

As a rule, our own proteins are tolerated, a fact that reflects the ability of the immune system to distinguish our own tissues (self) from foreign antigens (nonself). Nevertheless, an inability to recognize self can and does occasionally happen and our own tissues are attacked by the immune system. This phenomenon is called *autoimmunity.* Autoimmune diseases include multiple sclerosis (MS), myasthenia gravis, Graves' disease, glomerulonephritis, rheumatoid arthritis (RA), and insulin-dependent diabetes mellitus (IDDM), which is also called type 1 or juvenile diabetes.

Organs, Cells, and Cell Interactions of the Immune Response

The immune system utilizes as part of its arsenal the **lymphoid organs,** including the thymus, lymph nodes, spleen, tonsils, appendix, and bone marrow. Of these, the thymus and bone marrow are considered to be the *primary lymphoid organs*. The others are *secondary lymphoid areas*.

The stem cells that give rise to the immune system arise in the bone marrow. Their subsequent differentiation into one of

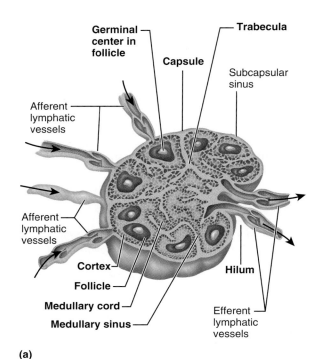

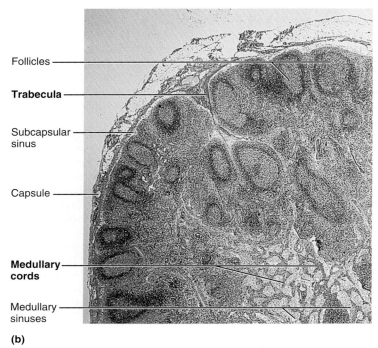

Follicles

Trabecula

Subcapsular
sinus

Capsule

**Medullary
cords**

Medullary
sinuses

(b)

(a)

FIGURE 25.3 Structure of lymph node.
(**a**) Longitudinal section of a lymph node, diagrammatic
view. Notice that the afferent vessels outnumber the
efferent vessels, which slows the rate of lymph flow.
The arrows indicate the direction of the lymph flow.
(**b**) Photomicrograph of a part of a lymph node
(60×). (See also Plate 22 in the Histology Atlas.)

the two populations of immunocompetent lymphocytes occurs
in the primary lymphoid organs. The **B cells** (B lymphocytes)
differentiate in bone marrow, and the **T cells** (T lymphocytes)
differentiate in the thymus. While in their "programming
organs" the lymphocytes become *immunocompetent,* an event
indicated by the appearance of specific cell-surface proteins
that enable the lymphocytes to respond (by binding) to a
particular antigen.

After differentiation, the B and T cells leave the bone marrow and thymus, respectively; enter the bloodstream; and travel
to peripheral (secondary) lymphoid organs, where clonal selection occurs. **Clonal selection** is triggered when an antigen
binds to the specific cell-surface receptors of a T or B cell. This
event causes the lymphocyte to proliferate rapidly, forming a
clone of like cells, all bearing the same antigen-specific receptors. Then, in the presence of certain regulatory signals, the
members of the clone specialize, or differentiate—some forming memory cells and others becoming effector cells. Upon
subsequent meetings with the same antigen, the immune response proceeds considerably faster because the troops are already mobilized and awaiting further orders, so to speak.

In the case of B cell clones, some become **memory
B cells;** the others form antibody-producing **plasma cells.**
Because the B cells act indirectly through the antibodies that
their progeny release into the bloodstream (or other body fluids), they are said to provide **humoral immunity.** T cell
clones are more diverse. Although all T cell clones also contain memory cells, some clones contain *cytotoxic T cells*
(effector cells that directly attack virus-infected tissue cells).

Others contain regulatory cells such as the *helper cells* (that
help activate the B cells and cytotoxic T cells) and still others
contain *suppressor cells* that can inhibit the immune response.
Because certain T cells act directly to destroy cells infected
with viruses, certain bacteria or parasites, and cancer cells,
and to reject foreign grafts, T cells are said to mediate **cellular immunity.**

Absence or failure of thymic differentiation of
T lymphocytes results in a marked depression of both
antibody and cell-mediated immune functions. Additionally,
the observation that the thymus naturally involutes with age
has been correlated with the relatively immune-deficient status of elderly individuals. ●

All lymphoid tissues except the thymus and bone marrow contain both T and B cell–dependent regions.

ACTIVITY 2

Studying the Microscopic Anatomy
of a Lymph Node, the Spleen,
and a Tonsil

1. Obtain a compound microscope and prepared slides of a
lymph node, spleen, and a tonsil. As you examine the lymph
node slide, notice the following anatomical features, depicted
in Figure 25.3 and Plate 22 in the Histology Atlas. The node
is enclosed within a fibrous **capsule,** from which connective
tissue septa (**trabeculae**) extend inward to divide the node

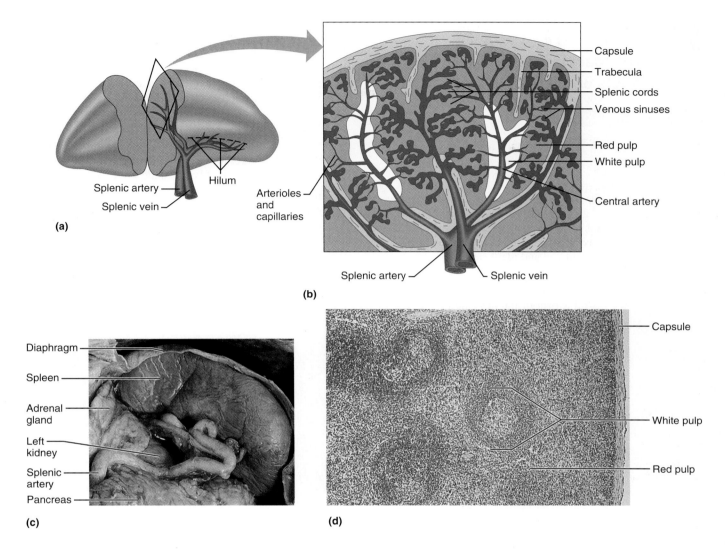

(a)

Splenic artery
Splenic vein
Hilum

Arterioles
and
capillaries

Capsule
Trabecula
Splenic cords
Venous sinuses
Red pulp
White pulp
Central artery

Splenic artery
Splenic vein

(b)

Diaphragm
Spleen
Adrenal
gland
Left
kidney
Splenic
artery
Pancreas

(c)

Capsule

White pulp

Red pulp

(d)

FIGURE 25.4 The spleen. (a) Gross structure. (b) Diagram of the histological structure. (c) Photograph of the spleen in its normal position in the abdominal cavity, anterior view. (d) Photomicrograph of spleen tissue showing white and red pulp regions (30×).

into several compartments. Very fine strands of reticular connective tissue issue from the trabeculae, forming the stroma of the gland within which cells are found.

In the outer region of the node, the **cortex,** some of the cells are arranged in globular masses, referred to as germinal centers. The **germinal centers** contain rapidly dividing B cells. The rest of the cortical cells are primarily T cells that circulate continuously, moving from the blood into the node and then exiting from the node in the lymphatic stream.

In the internal portion of the node, the **medulla,** the cells are arranged in cordlike fashion. Most of the medullary cells are macrophages. Macrophages are important not only for their phagocytic function but also because they play an essential role in "presenting" the antigens to the T cells.

Lymph enters the node through a number of *afferent vessels,* circulates through *lymph sinuses* within the node, and leaves the node through *efferent vessels* at the **hilum.** Since each node has fewer efferent than afferent vessels, the lymph flow stagnates somewhat within the node. This allows time for the generation of an immune response and for the macrophages to remove debris from the lymph before it reenters the blood vascular system.

2. As you observe the slide of the spleen, look for the areas of lymphocytes suspended in reticular fibers, the **white pulp,** clustered around central arteries (Figure 25.4). The remaining tissue in the spleen is the **red pulp,** which is composed of venous sinuses and areas of reticular tissue and macrophages called the **splenic cords.** The white pulp, composed primarily of lymphocytes, is responsible for the immune functions of the spleen. Macrophages remove worn-out red blood cells, debris, bacteria, viruses, and toxins from blood flowing through the sinuses of the red pulp. (See Plate 24 in the Histology Atlas.)

3. As you examine the tonsil slide, notice the **follicles** containing **germinal centers** surrounded by scattered lymphocytes. The characteristic **crypts** (invaginations of the mucosal epithelium) of the tonsils trap bacteria and other foreign material. Eventually the bacteria work their way into the lymphoid tissue and are destroyed. (See Plate 25 in the Histology Atlas.)

4. Compare and contrast the structure of the lymph node, spleen, and tonsils.

DISSECTION AND
IDENTIFICATION:

The Main Lymphatic
Ducts of the Cat

ACTIVITY 3

Identifying the Main Lymphatic
Ducts of the Cat

1.   Don disposable gloves. Obtain your cat and a dissecting tray and instruments. Because lymphatic vessels are extremely thin-walled, it is difficult to locate them in a dissection unless the animal has been triply injected (with yellow or green latex for the lymphatic system). However, the large thoracic duct can be localized and identified.

2.   Move the thoracic organs to the side to locate the **thoracic duct.** Typically it lies just to the left of the mid-dorsal line, abutting the dorsal aspect of the descending aorta. It is usually about the size of pencil lead and red-brown with a segmented or beaded appearance caused by the valves within it. Trace it anteriorly to the site where it passes behind the left brachiocephalic vein and then bends and enters the venous system at the junction of the left subclavian and external jugular veins. If the veins are well injected, some of the blue latex may have slipped past the valves and entered the first portion of the thoracic duct.

3.   While in this region, also attempt to identify the short **right lymphatic duct** draining into the right subclavian vein, and notice the collection of lymph nodes in the axillary region.

4.   If the cat is triply injected, trace the thoracic duct posteriorly to identify the cisterna chyli, the saclike enlargement of its distal end. This structure, which receives fat-rich lymph from the intestine, begins at the level of the diaphragm and can be localized posterior to the left kidney.

5.   When you finish identifying these lymphatic structures, clean the dissecting instruments and tray, and properly wrap and return the cat to storage. ▰

The Lymphatic System and Immune Response

The Lymphatic System

1. Match the terms below with the correct letters on the diagram.

_____ 1. axillary lymph nodes

_____ 2. bone marrow

_____ 3. cervical lymph nodes

_____ 4. cisterna chyli

_____ 5. inguinal lymph nodes

_____ 6. lymphatic vessels

_____ 7. Peyer's patches (in intestine)

_____ 8. right lymphatic duct

_____ 9. spleen

_____ 10. thoracic duct

_____ 11. thymus gland

_____ 12. tonsils

2. Explain why the lymphatic system is a one-way system, whereas the blood vascular system is a two-way system.

_____

_____

3. How do lymphatic vessels resemble veins? _____

How do lymphatic capillaries differ from blood capillaries? _____

_____

4. What is the function of the lymphatic vessels? _____

_____

5. What is lymph? _____

6. What factors are involved in the flow of lymphatic fluid? _____

_____

7. What name is given to the terminal duct draining most of the body? _____

8. What is the cisterna chyli? _____

_____

How does the composition of lymph in the cisterna chyli differ from that in the general lymphatic stream?

_____

9. Which portion of the body is drained by the right lymphatic duct? _____

10. Note three areas where lymph nodes are densely clustered: _____,

_____, and _____

11. What are the two major functions of the lymph nodes? _____

and _____

12. The radical mastectomy is an operation in which a cancerous breast, surrounding tissues, and the underlying muscles of the anterior thoracic wall, plus the axillary lymph nodes, are removed. After such an operation, the arm usually swells, or becomes edematous, and is very uncomfortable—sometimes for months. Why?

_____

The Immune Response

13. What is the function of B cells in the immune response? _____

_____

14. What is the role of T cells? _____

_____

_____

Studying the Microscopic Anatomy of a Lymph Node, the Spleen, and a Tonsil

15. In the space below, make a rough drawing of the structure of a lymph node. Identify the cortex area, germinal centers, and medulla. For each identified area, note the cell type (T cell, B cell, or macrophage) most likely to be found there.

16. What structural characteristic ensures a *slow* flow of lymph through a lymph node? _____

_____

Why is this desirable? _____

_____

17. What similarities in structure and function are found in the lymph nodes, spleen, and tonsils? _____

_____

_____

Dissection and Identification: Main Lymphatic Ducts of the Cat

18. How does the cat's lymphatic drainage pattern compare to that of humans? _____

_____

19. What is the role of the following?

a. thoracic duct: _____

_____

b. right lymphatic duct: _____

_____

Anatomy of the Respiratory System

MATERIALS

- ☐ Resin cast of the respiratory tree (if available)
- ☐ Human torso model
- ☐ Respiratory organ system model and/or chart of the respiratory system
- ☐ Larynx model (if available)
- ☐ Preserved inflatable lung preparation (obtained from a biological supply house) or sheep pluck fresh from the slaughterhouse
- ☐ Source of compressed air
- ☐ 0.6 m (2-foot) length of laboratory rubber tubing
- ☐ Dissecting tray and instruments
- ☐ Disposable gloves
- ☐ Disposable autoclave bag
- ☐ Animal specimen from previous dissections
- ☐ Prepared slides of the following (if available): trachea (cross section), lung tissue, both normal and pathological specimens (for example, sections taken from lung tissues exhibiting bronchitis, pneumonia, emphysema, or lung cancer)
- ☐ Compound and stereomicroscopes

AIA See Appendix B, Exercise 26 for links to A.D.A.M.® Interactive Anatomy.

OBJECTIVES

1. To define the following terms: *respiratory system, pulmonary ventilation, external respiration,* and *internal respiration*.
2. To label the major respiratory system structures on a diagram (or identify them on a model), and to describe the function of each.
3. To recognize the histologic structure of the trachea (cross section) and lung tissue on prepared slides, and to describe the functions the observed structural modifications serve.
4. To identify the major respiratory system organs in a dissected animal.

Body cells require an abundant and continuous supply of oxygen. As the cells use oxygen, they release carbon dioxide, a waste product that the body must get rid of. These oxygen-using cellular processes, collectively referred to as *cellular respiration,* are more appropriately described in conjunction with the topic of cellular metabolism. The major role of the **respiratory system,** our focus in this exercise, is to supply the body with oxygen and dispose of carbon dioxide. To fulfill this role, at least four distinct processes, collectively referred to as **respiration,** must occur:

Pulmonary ventilation: The tidelike movement of air into and out of the lungs so that the gases in the alveoli are continuously changed and refreshed. Also more simply called *ventilation,* or *breathing*.

External respiration: The gas exchange between the blood and the air-filled chambers of the lungs (oxygen loading/carbon dioxide unloading).

Transport of respiratory gases: The transport of respiratory gases between the lungs and tissue cells of the body accomplished by the cardiovascular system, using blood as the transport vehicle.

Internal respiration: Exchange of gases between systemic blood and tissue cells (oxygen unloading and carbon dioxide loading).

Only the first two processes are the exclusive province of the respiratory system, but all four must occur for the respiratory system to "do its job." Hence, the respiratory and circulatory systems are irreversibly linked. If either system fails, cells begin to die from oxygen starvation and accumulation of carbon dioxide. Uncorrected, this situation soon causes death of the entire organism.

Upper Respiratory System Structures

The upper respiratory system structures—the nose, pharynx, and larynx—are shown in Figure 26.1 and described below. As you read through the descriptions, identify each structure in the figure.

Air generally passes into the respiratory tract through the external **nares (nostrils),** and enters the **nasal cavity** (divided by the **nasal septum**). It then flows posteriorly over three pairs of lobelike structures, the **inferior, superior, and middle nasal conchae,** which increase the air turbulence. As the air passes through the nasal cavity, it is also warmed, moistened, and filtered by the nasal mucosa. The air that flows directly beneath the superior part of the nasal cavity may chemically stimulate the olfactory receptors located in the mucosa of that region.

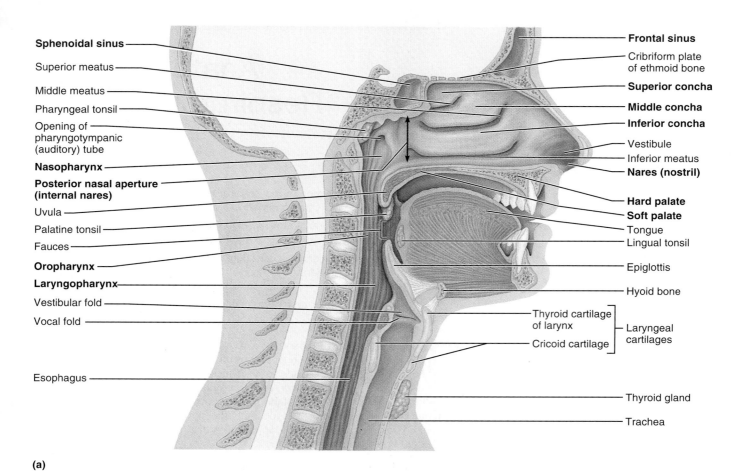

Sphenoidal sinus

Superior meatus

Middle meatus

Pharyngeal tonsil

Opening of pharyngotympanic (auditory) tube

Nasopharynx

Posterior nasal aperture (internal nares)

Uvula

Palatine tonsil

Fauces

Oropharynx

Laryngopharynx

Vestibular fold

Vocal fold

Esophagus

Frontal sinus

Cribriform plate of ethmoid bone

Superior concha

Middle concha

Inferior concha

Vestibule

Inferior meatus

Nares (nostril)

Hard palate

Soft palate

Tongue

Lingual tonsil

Epiglottis

Hyoid bone

Thyroid cartilage of larynx

Cricoid cartilage

Laryngeal cartilages

Thyroid gland

Trachea

(a)

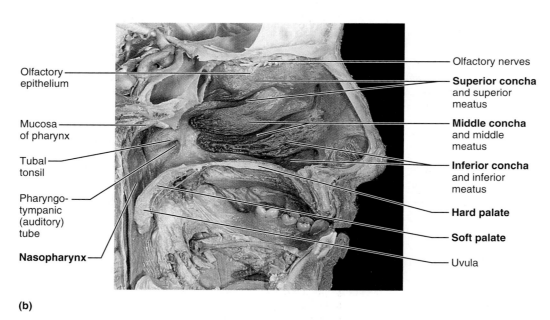

Olfactory epithelium

Mucosa of pharynx

Tubal tonsil

Pharyngo-tympanic (auditory) tube

Nasopharynx

Olfactory nerves

Superior concha and superior meatus

Middle concha and middle meatus

Inferior concha and inferior meatus

Hard palate

Soft palate

Uvula

(b)

FIGURE 26.1 Structures of the upper respiratory tract (sagittal section). (a) Diagrammatic view. **(b)** Photograph.

The nasal cavity is surrounded by the **paranasal sinuses** in the frontal, sphenoid, ethmoid, and maxillary bones. These sinuses, named for the bones in which they are located, act as resonance chambers in speech and their mucosae, like that of the nasal cavity, warm and moisten the incoming air.

The nasal passages are separated from the oral cavity below by a partition composed anteriorly of the **hard palate** and posteriorly by the **soft palate.**

The genetic defect called **cleft palate** (failure of the palatine bones and/or the palatine processes of the maxillary bones to fuse medially) causes difficulty in breathing and oral cavity functions such as sucking and, later, mastication and speech. ●

Of course, air may also enter the body via the mouth. From there it passes through the oral cavity to move into the pharynx posteriorly, where the oral and nasal cavities are joined temporarily.

Commonly called the *throat,* the funnel-shaped **pharynx** connects the nasal and oral cavities to the larynx and esophagus inferiorly. It has three named parts (Figure 26.1):

1.   The **nasopharynx** lies posterior to the nasal cavity and is continuous with it via the **posterior nasal aperture,** also called the **internal nares.** It lies above the soft palate; hence, it serves only as an air passage. High on its posterior wall is the *pharyngeal tonsil,* masses of lymphoid tissue that help to protect the respiratory passages from invading pathogens. The *pharyngotympanic (auditory) tubes,* which allow middle ear pressure to become equalized to atmospheric pressure, drain into the lateral aspects of the nasopharynx. The *tubal tonsils* surround the openings of these tubes into the nasopharynx (Figure 26.1b).

Because of the continuity of the middle ear and nasopharyngeal mucosae, nasal infections may invade the middle ear cavity and cause **otitis media,** which is difficult to treat. ●

2.   The **oropharynx** is continuous posteriorly with the oral cavity. Since it extends from the soft palate to the epiglottis of the larynx inferiorly, it serves as a common conduit for food and air. In its lateral walls are the *palatine tonsils.* The *lingual tonsil* covers the base of the tongue.

3.   The **laryngopharynx,** like the oropharynx, accommodates both ingested food and air. It lies directly posterior to the upright epiglottis and extends to the larynx, where the common pathway divides into the respiratory and digestive channels. From the laryngopharynx, air enters the lower respiratory passageways by passing through the larynx (voice box) and into the trachea below.

The **larynx** (Figure 26.2) consists of nine cartilages. The two most prominent are the large shield-shaped **thyroid cartilage,** whose anterior medial laryngeal prominence is commonly referred to as *Adam's apple,* and the inferiorly located, ring-shaped **cricoid cartilage,** whose widest dimension faces posteriorly. All the laryngeal cartilages are composed of hyaline cartilage except the flaplike **epiglottis,** a flexible elastic cartilage located superior to the opening of the larynx. The epiglottis, sometimes referred to as the "guardian of the airways," forms a lid over the larynx when we swallow. This closes off the respiratory passageways to incoming food or drink, which is routed into the posterior esophagus, or food chute.

●   Palpate your larynx by placing your hand on the anterior neck surface approximately halfway down its length. Swallow. Can you feel the cartilaginous larynx rising?

If anything other than air enters the larynx, a cough reflex attempts to expel the substance. Note that this reflex operates only when a person is conscious. Therefore, you should never try to feed or pour liquids down the throat of an unconscious person.

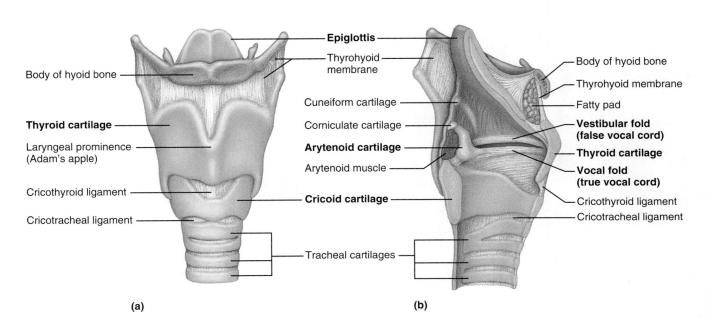

(a)   (b)

FIGURE 26.2 Structure of the larynx. (a) Anterior view. **(b)** Sagittal section.

The mucous membrane of the larynx is thrown into two pairs of folds—the upper **vestibular folds,** also called the **false vocal cords,** and the lower **vocal folds,** or **true vocal cords,** which vibrate with expelled air for speech. The vocal cords are attached posterolaterally to the small triangular **arytenoid cartilages** by the *vocal ligaments.* The slitlike passageway between the folds is called the *glottis.*

Lower Respiratory System Structures

Air entering the **trachea,** or windpipe, from the larynx travels down its length (about 11.0 cm or 4 inches) to the level of the *sternal angle* (or the disc between the fourth and fifth thoracic vertebrae). There the passageway divides into the right and left **main** *(primary)* **bronchi** (Figure 26.3), which plunge into their respective lungs at an indented area called the **hilum** (see Figure 26.5c). The right main bronchus is wider, shorter, and more vertical than the left, and foreign objects that enter the respiratory passageways are more likely to become lodged in it.

The trachea is lined with a ciliated mucus-secreting, pseudostratified columnar epithelium, as are many of the other respiratory system passageways. The cilia propel mucus (produced by goblet cells) laden with dust particles, bacteria, and other debris away from the lungs and toward the throat, where it can be expectorated or swallowed. The walls of the trachea are reinforced with C-shaped cartilaginous rings, the incomplete portion located posteriorly. These C-shaped cartilages serve a double function: The incomplete

parts allow the esophagus to expand anteriorly when a large food bolus is swallowed. The solid portions reinforce the trachea walls to maintain its open passageway regardless of the pressure changes that occur during breathing.

The main bronchi further divide into smaller and smaller branches—the lobar (secondary), segmental (tertiary), and on down—finally becoming the **bronchioles,** which have terminal branches called **respiratory bronchioles** (Figure 26.3b). All but the most minute branches have cartilaginous reinforcements in their walls, usually in the form of small plates of hyaline cartilage rather than cartilaginous rings. As the respiratory tubes get smaller and smaller, the relative amount of smooth muscle in their walls increases as the amount of cartilage declines and finally disappears. The complete layer of smooth muscle present in the bronchioles enables them to provide considerable resistance to airflow under certain conditions (asthma, hay fever, etc.). The continuous branching of the respiratory passageways in the lungs is often referred to as the **respiratory tree.** The comparison becomes much more meaningful if you observe a resin cast of the respiratory passages.

• Observe a resin cast of respiratory passages if one is available for observation in the laboratory.

The respiratory bronchioles in turn subdivide into several **alveolar ducts,** which terminate in alveolar sacs that rather resemble clusters of grapes. **Alveoli,** tiny balloonlike expansions along the alveolar sacs and occasionally found protruding from alveolar ducts and respiratory bronchioles, are composed of a single thin layer of squamous epithelium overlying a wispy basal lamina. The external surfaces of the alveoli

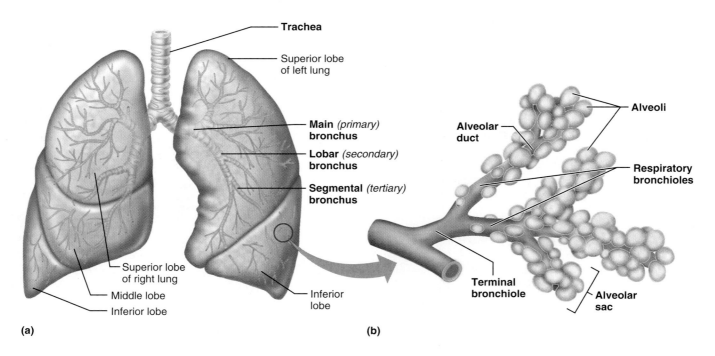

(a)

(b)

FIGURE 26.3 Structures of the lower respiratory tract. (a) Diagrammatic view.
(b) Enlarged view of alveoli.

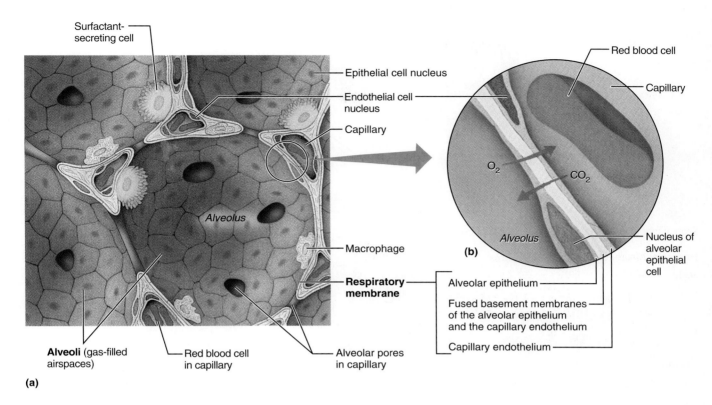

FIGURE 26.4 Relationship between the alveoli and pulmonary capillaries involved in gas exchange. Diagrammatic views. **(a)** One alveolus surrounded by capillaries. **(b)** Enlargement of the respiratory membrane.

are densely spiderwebbed with a network of pulmonary capillaries (Figure 26.4). Together, the alveolar and capillary walls and their fused basement membranes form the **respiratory membrane,** also called the **air-blood barrier.**

Because gas exchanges occur by simple diffusion across the respiratory membrane—oxygen passing from the alveolar air to the capillary blood and carbon dioxide leaving the capillary blood to enter the alveolar air—the alveolar sacs, alveolar ducts, and respiratory bronchioles are referred to collectively as **respiratory zone structures.** All other respiratory passageways (from the nasal cavity to the terminal bronchioles) simply serve as access or exit routes to and from these gas exchange chambers and are called **conducting zone structures.** Because the conducting zone structures have no exchange function, they are also referred to as *anatomical dead space.*

The Lungs and Their Pleural Coverings

The paired lungs are soft, spongy organs that occupy the entire thoracic cavity except for the *mediastinum,* which houses the heart, bronchi, esophagus, and other organs (Figure 26.5). Each lung is connected to the mediastinum by a *root* containing its vascular and bronchial attachments. The structures of the root enter (or leave) the lung via a medial indentation called the *hilum.* All structures distal to the main bronchi are found within the lung substance. A lung's *apex,* the narrower superior aspect, lies just deep to the clavicle, and its *base,* the inferior concave surface, rests on the diaphragm. Anterior, lateral, and posterior lung surfaces are in close contact with

the ribs and, hence, are collectively called the *costal surface.* The medial surface of the left lung exhibits a concavity called the *cardiac impression,* which accommodates the heart where it extends left from the body midline. Fissures divide the lungs into a number of *lobes*—two in the left lung and three in the right. Other than the respiratory passageways and air spaces that make up the bulk of their volume, the lungs are mostly elastic connective tissue, which allows them to recoil passively during expiration.

Each lung is enclosed in a double-layered sac of serous membrane called the **pleura.** The outer layer, the **parietal pleura,** is attached to the thoracic walls and the **diaphragm;** the inner layer, covering the lung tissue, is the **visceral pleura.** The two pleural layers are separated by the *pleural cavity,* which is more of a potential space than an actual one. The pleural layers produce lubricating serous fluid that causes them to adhere closely to one another, holding the lungs to the thoracic wall and allowing them to move easily against one another during the movements of breathing.

ACTIVITY 1

Identifying Respiratory System Organs

Before proceeding, be sure to locate on Figure 26.5, the torso model, respiratory organ system model, larynx model, or an anatomical chart all the respiratory structures described— both upper and lower respiratory system organs. ▪

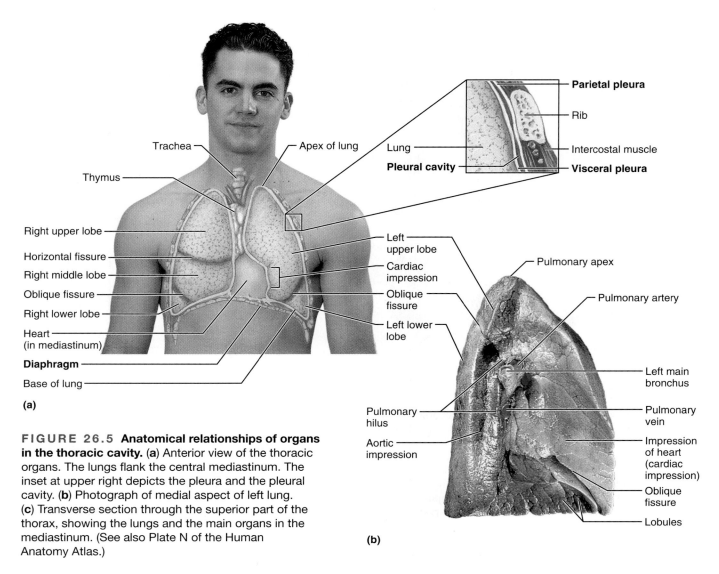

Trachea — — Apex of lung

Thymus —

Lung —
Pleural cavity —

Parietal pleura
— Rib
— Intercostal muscle
— **Visceral pleura**

Right upper lobe —

Horizontal fissure —

Right middle lobe —

Oblique fissure —

Right lower lobe —

Heart (in mediastinum) —

Diaphragm —

Base of lung —

— Left upper lobe
— Cardiac impression
— Oblique fissure
— Left lower lobe

(a)

FIGURE 26.5 Anatomical relationships of organs in the thoracic cavity. (a) Anterior view of the thoracic organs. The lungs flank the central mediastinum. The inset at upper right depicts the pleura and the pleural cavity. **(b)** Photograph of medial aspect of left lung. **(c)** Transverse section through the superior part of the thorax, showing the lungs and the main organs in the mediastinum. (See also Plate N of the Human Anatomy Atlas.)

— Pulmonary apex

— Pulmonary artery

Pulmonary hilus —

Aortic impression —

— Left main bronchus
— Pulmonary vein
— Impression of heart (cardiac impression)
— Oblique fissure
— Lobules

(b)

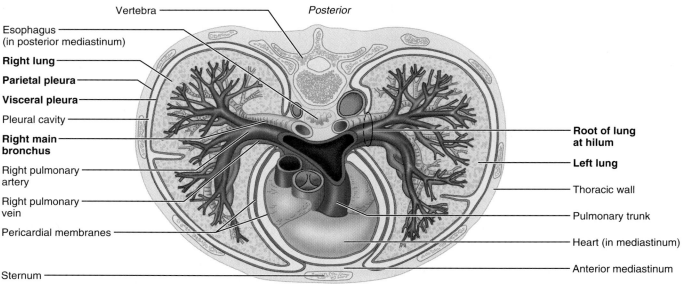

Vertebra — — *Posterior*

Esophagus (in posterior mediastinum) —

Right lung —

Parietal pleura —

Visceral pleura —

Pleural cavity —

Right main bronchus —

Right pulmonary artery —

Right pulmonary vein —

Pericardial membranes —

Sternum —

— **Root of lung at hilum**
— **Left lung**
— Thoracic wall
— Pulmonary trunk
— Heart (in mediastinum)
— Anterior mediastinum

Anterior

(c)

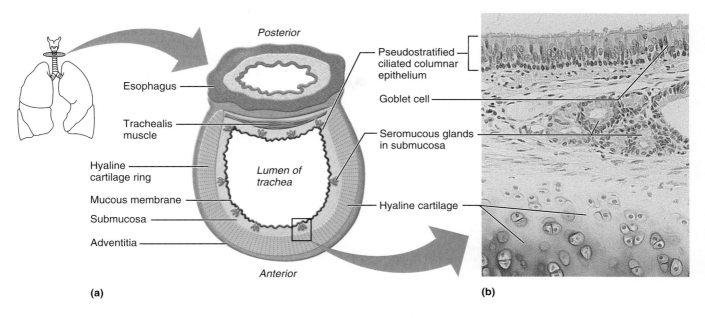

FIGURE 26.6 Microscopic structure of the trachea. (a) Cross-sectional view of the trachea.
(b) Photomicrograph of a portion of the tracheal wall (225×).

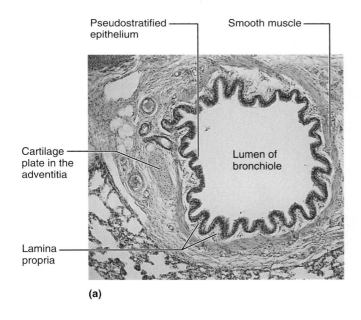

(a)

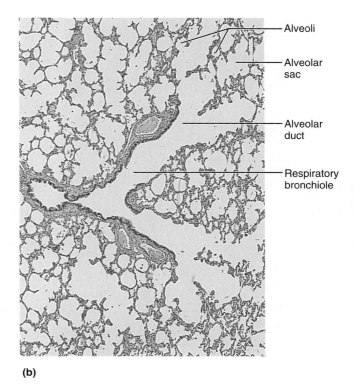

(b)

**FIGURE 26.7 Microscopic structure of a bronchiole
and alveoli. (a)** Photomicrograph of a section of a
bronchiole. **(b)** Photomicrograph of alveoli (40×).

ACTIVITY 2

Examining Prepared Slides
of Trachea and Lung Tissue

1.   Obtain a compound microscope and a slide of a cross section of the tracheal wall. Identify the smooth muscle layer, the
hyaline cartilage supporting rings, and the pseudostratified ciliated epithelium. Using Figure 26.6 as a guide, also try to identify a few goblet cells in the epithelium.

2.   Obtain a slide of lung tissue for examination. The alveolus is the main structural and functional unit of the lung
and is the actual site of gas exchange. Identify a bronchiole
(Figure 26.7a) and the thin squamous epithelium of the
alveolar walls (Figure 26.7b).

3.   Examine slides of pathological lung tissues, and compare them to the normal lung specimens. Record your observations in the Exercise 26 Review Sheet.

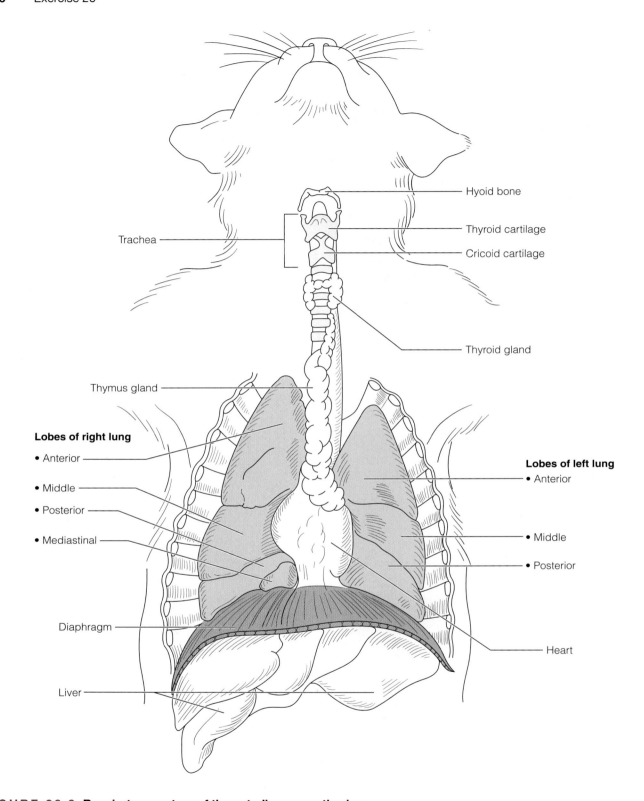

Hyoid bone

Thyroid cartilage

Cricoid cartilage

Trachea

Thyroid gland

Thymus gland

Lobes of right lung

• Anterior

• Middle

• Posterior

• Mediastinal

Lobes of left lung

• Anterior

• Middle

• Posterior

Diaphragm

Heart

Liver

FIGURE 26.8 Respiratory system of the cat, diagrammatic view.

Demonstrating Lung Inflation in a Sheep Pluck

A *sheep pluck* includes the larynx, trachea with attached lungs, the heart and pericardium, and portions of the major blood vessels found in the mediastinum (aorta, pulmonary artery and vein, venae cavae). If a sheep pluck is not available, a good substitute is a preserved inflatable pig lung.

 Don disposable gloves, obtain a dissecting tray and a fresh sheep pluck (or a preserved pluck of another animal), and identify the lower respiratory system organs. Once you have completed your observations, insert a hose from an air compressor (vacuum pump) into the trachea and alternately allow air to flow in and out of the lungs. Notice how the lungs inflate. This observation is educational in a preserved pluck but it is a spectacular sight in a fresh one. Another advantage of using a fresh pluck is that the lung pluck changes color (becomes redder) as hemoglobin in trapped RBCs becomes loaded with oxygen.

If air compressors are not available, the same effect may be obtained by using a length of laboratory rubber tubing to blow into the trachea. Obtain a cardboard mouthpiece and fit it into the cut end of the laboratory tubing before attempting to inflate the lungs.

 Dispose of the mouthpiece and gloves in the autoclave bag immediately after use. ▬

 DISSECTION AND IDENTIFICATION:

The Respiratory System of the Cat

In this dissection exercise, you will be examining both the gross and fine structure of respiratory system organs. Don disposable gloves and then obtain your dissection animal, and dissecting tray and instruments. ▬

Identifying Organs of the Respiratory System of the Cat

1. Examine the external nares, oral cavity, and oral pharynx. Use a probe to demonstrate the continuity between the oral pharynx and the nasal pharynx above.

2. After securing the animal to the dissecting tray, dorsal surface down, expose the more distal respiratory structures by retracting the cut muscle and rib cage. Do not sever nerves and blood vessels located on either side of the trachea if these have not been studied. If you have not previously opened the thoracic cavity, make a medial longitudinal incision through the neck muscles and thoracic musculature to expose and view the thoracic organs (see Figure 21.3, p. 353).

3. Using the orientation diagram in Figure 26.8 and the photos in Figures 26.9 and 26.10 as guides, identify the structures named in items 3 through 5. Examine the **trachea,** and determine by finger examination whether the cartilage rings are complete or incomplete posteriorly. Locate the *thyroid gland* inferior to the larynx on the trachea. Free the **larynx** from the attached muscle tissue for ease of examination. Identify the **thyroid** and **cricoid cartilages** and the flaplike **epiglottis.** Find the *hyoid bone,* located anterior to the larynx. Make a longitudinal incision through the ventral wall of the larynx and locate the *true vocal cords* (Figure 26.9) and *false vocal cords* on the inner wall.

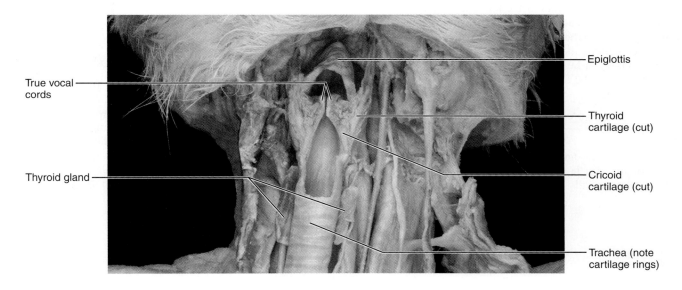

FIGURE 26.9 **Anterior view of larynx (opened) and trachea.**

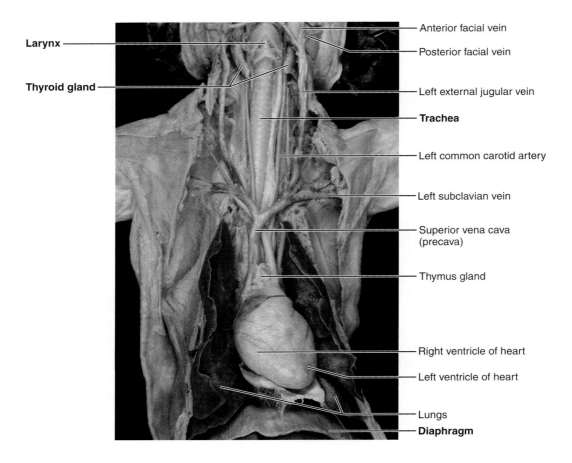

Larynx

Thyroid gland

Anterior facial vein

Posterior facial vein

Left external jugular vein

Trachea

Left common carotid artery

Left subclavian vein

Superior vena cava (precava)

Thymus gland

Right ventricle of heart

Left ventricle of heart

Lungs

Diaphragm

FIGURE 26.10 Photograph of the respiratory system of the cat.

4. Locate the large *right* and *left common carotid arteries* (Figure 26.10) and the *internal jugular veins* on either side of the trachea. Also locate a conspicuous white band, the *vagus nerve,* which lies alongside the trachea, adjacent to the common carotid artery.

5. Examine the contents of the thoracic cavity. Follow the trachea as it bifurcates into two **main primary bronchi,** which plunge into the lungs. Note that there are two *pleural cavities* containing the lungs and that each lung is composed of many lobes. In humans there are three lobes in the right lung and two in the left. How does this compare to what is seen in the cat?

_____

Identify the pericardial sac containing the heart located in the mediastinum (if it is still present). Examine the pleura, and note its exceptionally smooth texture.

6. Locate the **diaphragm** and the **phrenic nerve.** The phrenic nerve, clearly visible as a white "thread" running along the pericardium to the diaphragm, controls the activity of the diaphragm in breathing. Lift one lung and find the esophagus beneath the parietal pleura. Follow it through the diaphragm to the stomach. ▧

ACTIVITY 5

Observing Lung Tissue Microscopically

Make a longitudinal incision in the outer tissue of one lung lobe beginning at a main bronchus. Attempt to follow part of the respiratory tree from this point down into the smaller subdivisions. Carefully observe the cut lung tissue (under a dissection scope, if one is available), noting the richness of the vascular supply and the irregular or spongy texture of the lung. Prepare your cat for storage and clean the area as instructed on p. 220 before leaving the lab. ▧

NAME_____

LAB TIME/DATE_____

Anatomy of the Respiratory System

Upper and Lower Respiratory System Structures

1. Complete the labeling of the diagram of the upper respiratory structures (sagittal section).

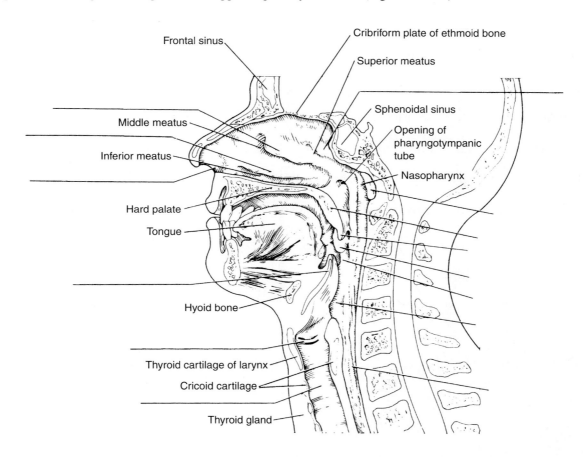

Frontal sinus

Cribriform plate of ethmoid bone

Superior meatus

Middle meatus

Inferior meatus

Sphenoidal sinus

Opening of pharyngotympanic tube

Nasopharynx

Hard palate

Tongue

Hyoid bone

Thyroid cartilage of larynx

Cricoid cartilage

Thyroid gland

2. Two pairs of vocal folds are found in the larynx. Which pair are the true vocal cords (superior or inferior)?

_____

3. Name the specific cartilages in the larynx that correspond to the following descriptions.

forms the Adam's apple: _____   shaped like a signet ring: _____

a "lid" for the larynx: _____   vocal cord attachment: _____

4. What is the significance of the fact that the human trachea is reinforced with cartilaginous rings?

_____

Of the fact that the rings are incomplete posteriorly? _____

_____

5. What is the function of the pleural membranes? _____

_____

_____

6. Name two functions of the nasal cavity mucosa. _____

and _____

7. The following questions refer to the main bronchi.

Which is longer?_____   Larger in diameter?_____   More horizontal? _____

Which is more likely to trap a foreign object that has entered the respiratory passageways? _____

8. Appropriately label all structures provided with leader lines on the diagrams below.

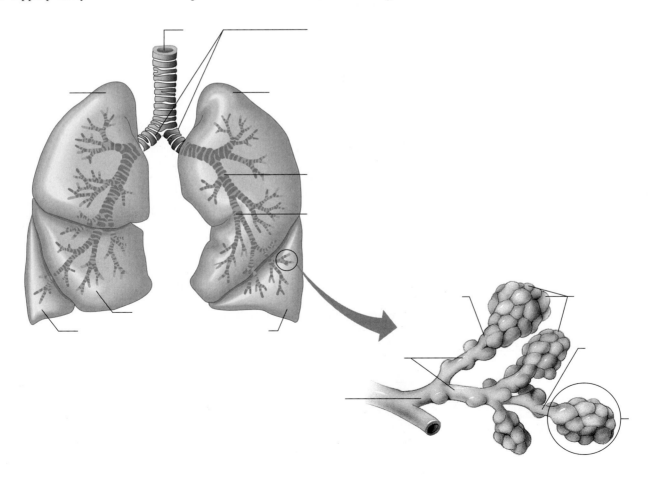

9. Trace a molecule of oxygen from the external nares to the pulmonary capillaries of the lungs: External nares →

_____

_____

_____

10. Match the terms in column B to the descriptions in column A.

Column A

_____ 1. connects the larynx to the primary bronchi

_____ 2. site of tonsils

_____ 3. food passageway posterior to the trachea

_____ 4. covers the glottis during swallowing of food

_____ 5. contains the vocal cords

_____ 6. nerve that activates the diaphragm during inspiration

_____ 7. pleural layer lining the walls of the thorax

_____ 8. site from which oxygen enters the pulmonary blood

_____ 9. connects the middle ear to the nasopharynx

_____ 10. opening between the vocal folds

_____ 11. increases air turbulence in the nasal cavity

_____ 12. separates the oral cavity from the nasal cavity

Column B

a. alveolus

b. bronchiole

c. concha

d. epiglottis

e. esophagus

f. glottis

g. larynx

h. main bronchi

i. opening of pharyngotympanic tube

j. palate

k. parietal pleura

l. pharynx

m. phrenic nerve

n. trachea

o. vagus nerve

p. visceral pleura

11. What portions of the respiratory system are referred to as anatomical dead space? _____

_____

_____

Why? _____

12. Define the following terms.

external respiration: _____

_____

internal respiration: _____

_____

13. On the diagram below identify alveolar epithelium, capillary endothelium, alveoli, and red blood cells. Bracket the respiratory membrane.

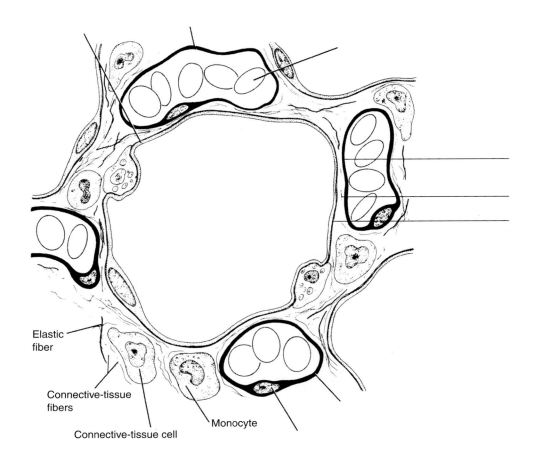

Elastic fiber

Connective-tissue fibers

Connective-tissue cell

Monocyte

Examining Prepared Slides of Lung and Tracheal Tissue

14. The tracheal epithelium is ciliated and has goblet cells. What is the function of each of these modifications?

Cilia: _____

Goblet cells: _____

15. The tracheal epithelium is said to be pseudostratified. Why? _____

_____

_____

16. What structural characteristics of the alveoli make them an ideal site for the diffusion of gases?

_____

Why does oxygen move from the alveoli into the pulmonary capillary blood? _____

_____

_____

17. If you observed pathological lung sections, record your observations. Also record how the tissue differed from normal lung tissue. Complete the table below using your answers.

Slide type	Observations	Comparison to normal lung tissue

Demonstrating Lung Inflation in a Sheep Pluck

18. Does the lung inflate part by part or as a whole, like a balloon? _____

19. What happened when the pressure was released? _____

20. What type of tissue ensures this phenomenon? _____

Dissection and Identification:
The Respiratory System of the Cat

21. Are the cartilaginous rings in the cat trachea complete or incomplete? _____

22. How does the number of lung lobes in the cat compare with the number in humans? _____

_____

23. Describe the appearance of the bronchial tree in the cat lung. _____

_____

24. Describe the appearance of lung tissue under the dissection microscope. _____

_____

_____

Anatomy of the Digestive System

MATERIALS

- ☐ Dissectible torso model
- ☐ Anatomical chart of the human digestive system
- ☐ Prepared slides of the liver, pancreas, and mixed salivary glands; of longitudinal sections of the gastroesophageal junction and a tooth; and of cross sections of the stomach, duodenum, and ileum
- ☐ Compound microscope
- ☐ Three-dimensional model of a villus (if available)
- ☐ Jaw model or human skull
- ☐ Three-dimensional model of liver lobules (if available)
- ☐ *Human Digestive System videotape**
- ☐ Dissection animal, tray, and instruments
- ☐ Bone cutters
- ☐ Disposable gloves
- ☐ Embalming fluid
- ☐ Hand lens

AIA See Appendix B, Exercise 27 for links to A.D.A.M.® Interactive Anatomy.

*Available to qualified adopters from Benjamin Cummings.

OBJECTIVES

1. To state the overall function of the digestive system.
2. To identify on an appropriate diagram or torso model the organs comprising the alimentary canal, and to name their subdivisions if any.
3. To name and/or identify the accessory digestive organs.
4. To describe the general functions of the digestive system organs or structures.
5. To describe the general histologic structure of the alimentary canal wall and/or label a cross-sectional diagram of the wall with the following terms: mucosa, submucosa, muscularis externa, and serosa or adventitia.
6. To list and explain the specializations in the structure of the stomach and small intestine that contribute to their functional roles.
7. To list the major enzymes or enzyme groups produced by the salivary glands, stomach, small intestine, and pancreas.
8. To name human deciduous and permanent teeth, and to describe the anatomy of the generalized tooth.
9. To recognize (by microscopic inspection or by viewing an appropriate diagram or photomicrograph) the histologic structure of the following organs:

small intestine	pancreas	stomach
salivary glands	tooth	liver

10. To identify on a dissected animal the organs composing the alimentary canal, and to name their subdivisions if any.
11 To identify the accessory organs of digestion in the dissection animal.

The **digestive system** provides the body with the nutrients, water, and electrolytes essential for health. The organs of this system ingest, digest, and absorb food and eliminate the undigested remains as feces.

The digestive system consists of a hollow tube extending from the mouth to the anus, into which various accessory organs or glands empty their secretions (Figure 27.1). Food material within this tube, the **alimentary canal,** is technically outside the body because it has contact only with the cells lining the tract. For ingested food to become available to the body cells, it must first be broken down *physically* (by chewing or churning) and *chemically* (by enzymatic hydrolysis) into its smaller diffusible molecules—a process called **digestion.** The digested end products can then pass through the epithelial cells lining the tract into the blood for distribution to the body cells—a process called **absorption.** In one sense, the digestive tract can be viewed as a disassembly line, in which food is carried from one stage of its digestive processing to the next by muscular activity, and its nutrients are made available to the cells of the body en route.

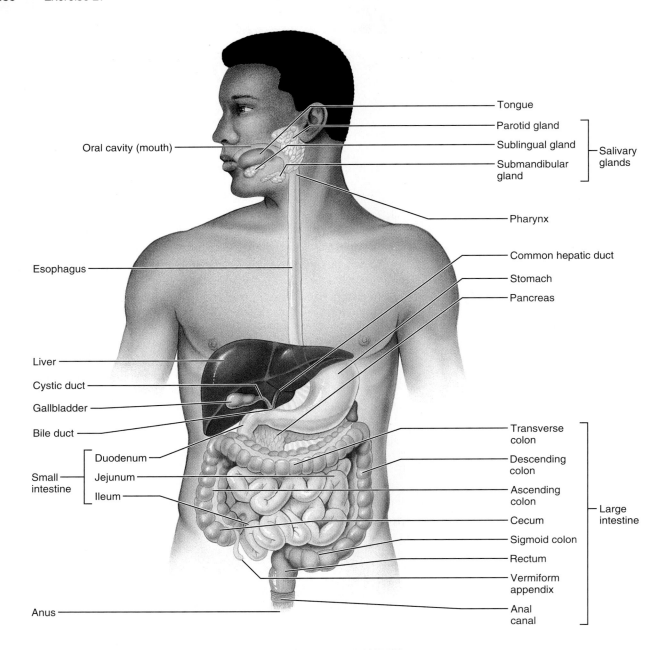

FIGURE 27.1 The human digestive system: alimentary tube and accessory organs. (Liver and gallbladder are reflected superiorly and to the right.)

The organs of the digestive system are traditionally separated into two major groups: the **alimentary canal,** or **gastrointestinal (GI) tract,** and the **accessory digestive organs.** The alimentary canal is approximately 9 meters long in a cadaver but is considerably shorter in a living person due to muscle tone. It consists of the mouth, pharynx, esophagus, stomach, and small and large intestines. The accessory structures include the teeth, which physically break down foods, and the salivary glands, gallbladder, liver, and pancreas, which secrete their products into the alimentary canal. These individual organs are described shortly.

General Histological Plan of the Alimentary Canal

Because the alimentary canal has a shared basic structural plan (particularly from the esophagus to the anus), it makes sense to review that structure as we begin studying this group of organs. Then, as the individual organs are described, we can focus on their specializations for unique functions in the digestive process.

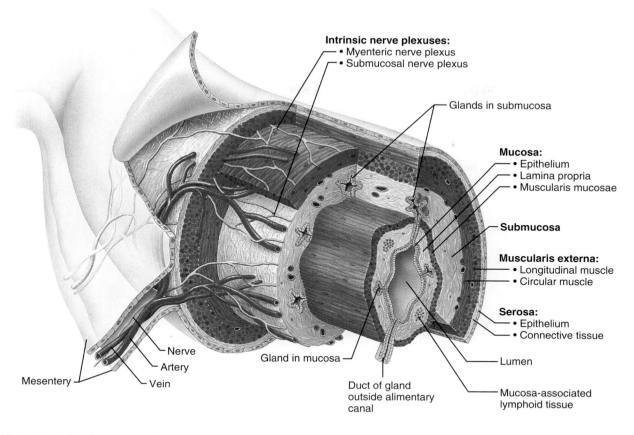

Intrinsic nerve plexuses:
• Myenteric nerve plexus
• Submucosal nerve plexus

Glands in submucosa

Mucosa:
• Epithelium
• Lamina propria
• Muscularis mucosae

Submucosa

Muscularis externa:
• Longitudinal muscle
• Circular muscle

Serosa:
• Epithelium
• Connective tissue

Lumen

Mucosa-associated
lymphoid tissue

Nerve

Artery

Vein

Mesentery

Gland in mucosa

Duct of gland
outside alimentary
canal

FIGURE 27.2 Basic structural pattern of the alimentary canal wall. (See also Plate 31 in the Histology Atlas.)

Essentially the alimentary canal walls have four basic **tunics** (layers). From the lumen outward, these are the *mucosa,* the *submucosa,* the *muscularis externa,* and either a *serosa or adventitia* (Figure 27.2). Each of these tunics has a predominant tissue type and a specific function in the digestive process.

Mucosa (mucous membrane): The mucosa is the wet epithelial membrane abutting the alimentary canal lumen. It consists of a surface *epithelium* (in most cases, a simple columnar), a *lamina propria* (areolar connective tissue on which the epithelial layer rests), and a *muscularis mucosae* (a scant layer of smooth muscle fibers that enable local movements of the mucosa). The major functions of the mucosa are secretion (of enzymes, mucus, hormones, etc.), absorption of digested foodstuffs, and protection (against bacterial invasion). A particular mucosal region may be involved in one or all three functions.

Submucosa: Superficial to the mucosa, the submucosa is moderately dense connective tissue containing blood and lymphatic vessels, scattered lymph nodules, and nerve fibers. Its intrinsic nerve supply is called the *submucosal plexus.* Its major functions are nutrition and protection.

Muscularis externa: The muscularis externa, also simply called the *muscularis,* typically is a bilayer of smooth muscle, with the deeper layer running circularly and the superficial layer running longitudinally. Another important intrinsic

nerve plexus, the *myenteric plexus,* is associated with this tunic. By controlling the smooth muscle of the muscularis, this plexus is the major regulator of GI motility.

Serosa: The outermost serosa is the *visceral peritoneum.* It consists of mesothelium associated with a thin layer of areolar connective tissue. In areas *outside* the abdominopelvic cavity, the serosa is replaced by an **adventitia,** a layer of coarse fibrous connective tissue that binds the organ to surrounding tissues. (This is the case with the esophagus.) The serosa reduces friction as the mobile digestive system organs work and slide across one another and the cavity walls. The adventitia anchors and protects the surrounded organ.

Organs of the Alimentary Canal

ACTIVITY 1

Identifying Alimentary Canal Organs

The sequential pathway and fate of food as it passes through the alimentary canal organs are described in the next sections. Identify each structure in Figure 27.1 and on the torso model or anatomical chart of the digestive system as you work. ■

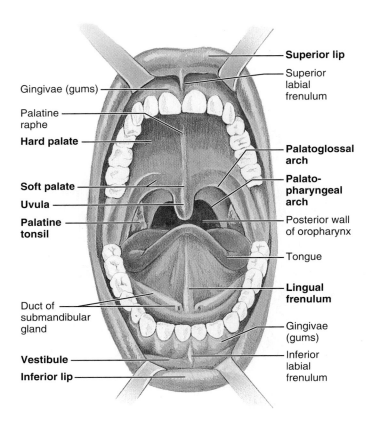

Gingivae (gums)
Palatine raphe
Hard palate
Soft palate
Uvula
Palatine tonsil
Duct of submandibular gland
Vestibule
Inferior lip

Superior lip
Superior labial frenulum
Palatoglossal arch
Palato-pharyngeal arch
Posterior wall of oropharynx
Tongue
Lingual frenulum
Gingivae (gums)
Inferior labial frenulum

FIGURE 27.3 Anterior view of the oral cavity.

Oral Cavity or Mouth

Food enters the digestive tract through the **oral cavity,** or **mouth** (Figure 27.3). Within this mucous membrane–lined cavity are the gums, teeth, tongue, and openings of the ducts of the salivary glands. The **lips (labia)** protect the opening of the chamber anteriorly, the **cheeks** form its lateral walls, and the **palate,** its roof. The anterior portion of the palate is referred to as the **hard palate** because bone (the palatine processes of the maxillae and the palatine bones) underlies it. The posterior **soft palate** is a fibromuscular structure that is unsupported by bone. The **uvula,** a fingerlike projection of the soft palate, extends inferiorly from its posterior margin. The soft palate rises to close off the oral cavity from the nasal and pharyngeal passages during swallowing. The floor of the oral cavity is occupied by the muscular **tongue** (Figure 27.4), which is largely supported by the *mylohyoid muscle* and attaches to the hyoid bone, mandible, styloid processes, and pharynx. A membrane called the **lingual frenulum** secures the inferior midline of the tongue to the floor of the mouth. The space between the lips and cheeks and the teeth is the **vestibule;** the area that lies within the teeth and gums (gingivae) is the *oral cavity* proper. (The teeth and gums are discussed in more detail on p. 466.)

On each side of the mouth at its posterior end are masses of lymphoid tissue, the **palatine tonsils** (see Figure 27.3). Each lies in a concave area bounded anteriorly and posteriorly by membranes, the **palatoglossal arch** (anterior membrane) and the **palatopharyngeal arch** (posterior membrane). Another mass of lymphoid tissue, the **lingual tonsil**

(see Figure 27.4), covers the base of the tongue, posterior to the oral cavity proper. The tonsils, in common with other lymphoid tissues, are part of the body's defense system.

Very often in young children, the palatine tonsils become inflamed and enlarge, partially blocking the entrance to the pharynx posteriorly and making swallowing difficult and painful. This condition is called **tonsillitis.** ●

Three pairs of salivary glands duct their secretion, saliva, into the oral cavity. One component of saliva, salivary amylase, begins the digestion of starchy foods within the oral cavity. (The salivary glands are discussed in more detail on p. 467.)

As food enters the mouth, it is mixed with saliva and masticated (chewed). The cheeks and lips help hold the food between the teeth during mastication, and the highly mobile tongue manipulates the food during chewing and initiates swallowing. Thus the mechanical and chemical breakdown of food begins before the food has left the oral cavity. As noted in Exercise 20, the surface of the tongue is covered with papillae, many of which contain taste buds, receptors for taste sensation. So, in addition to its manipulative function, the tongue permits the enjoyment and appreciation of the food ingested.

Pharynx

When the tongue initiates swallowing, the food passes posteriorly into the pharynx, a common passageway for food, fluid, and air (see Figure 27.4). The pharynx is subdivided anatomically into three parts—the **nasopharynx** (behind the nasal cavity), the oropharynx (behind the oral cavity extending from the soft palate to the epiglottis overlying the

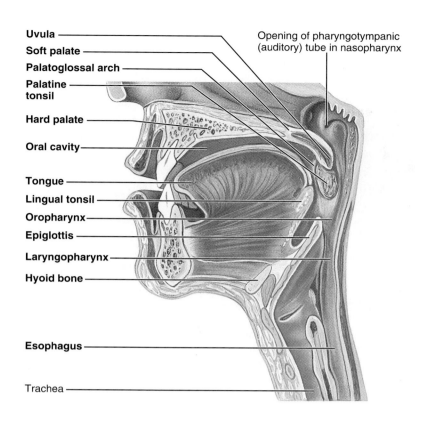

Uvula
Soft palate
Palatoglossal arch
Palatine tonsil
Hard palate
Oral cavity
Tongue
Lingual tonsil
Oropharynx
Epiglottis
Laryngopharynx
Hyoid bone
Esophagus
Trachea

Opening of pharyngotympanic (auditory) tube in nasopharynx

FIGURE 27.4 Sagittal view of the head showing oral, nasal, and pharyngeal cavities.

larynx), and the **laryngopharynx** (extending from the epiglottis to the base of the larynx), which is continuous with the esophagus.

The walls of the pharynx consist largely of two layers of skeletal muscles: an inner layer of longitudinal muscle (the levator muscles) and an outer layer of circular constrictor muscles, which initiate wavelike contractions that propel the food inferiorly into the esophagus. Its mucosa, like that of the oral cavity, contains a friction-resistant stratified squamous epithelium.

Esophagus

The **esophagus,** or gullet, extends from the pharynx through the diaphragm to the gastroesophageal sphincter in the superior aspect of the stomach. Approximately 25 cm long in humans, it is essentially a food passageway that conducts food to the stomach in a wavelike peristaltic motion. The esophagus has no digestive or absorptive function. The walls at its superior end contain skeletal muscle, which is replaced by smooth muscle in the area nearing the stomach. The **gastroesophageal sphincter,** a slight thickening of the smooth muscle layer at the esophagus-stomach junction, controls food passage into the stomach (see Figure 27.5). Since the esophagus is located in the thoracic rather than the abdominal cavity, its outermost layer is an *adventitia* in place of a serosa.

Stomach

The **stomach** (Figures 27.1 and 27.5) is on the left side of the abdominal cavity and is hidden by the liver and diaphragm. Different regions of the saclike stomach are the **cardiac region** (the area surrounding the cardiac orifice through which food

enters the stomach from the esophagus), the fundus (the expanded portion of the stomach, superolateral to the cardiac region), the **body** (midportion of the stomach, inferior to the fundus), and the funnel-shaped **pyloric region** (consisting of the superiormost *pyloric antrum,* the more narrow *pyloric canal,* and the terminal *pylorus,* which is continuous with the small intestine through the **pyloric sphincter**).

The concave medial surface of the stomach is called the lesser **curvature;** its convex lateral surface is the **greater curvature.** Extending from these curvatures are two mesenteries, called *omenta.* The lesser omentum extends from the liver to the **lesser curvature** of the stomach. The **greater omentum,** a saclike mesentery, extends from the greater curvature of the stomach, reflects downward over the abdominal contents to cover them in an apronlike fashion, and then blends with the **mesocolon** attaching the transverse colon to the posterior body wall. Figure 27.6 illustrates the omenta as well as the other peritoneal attachments of the abdominal organs.

The stomach is a temporary storage region for food as well as a site for mechanical and chemical breakdown of food. It contains a third (innermost) *obliquely* oriented layer of smooth muscle in its muscularis externa that allows it to churn, mix, and pummel the food, physically reducing it to smaller fragments. **Gastric glands** of the mucosa secrete hydrochloric acid (HCl) and hydrolytic enzymes (primarily pepsinogen, the inactive form of *pepsin,* a protein-digesting enzyme), which begin the enzymatic, or chemical, breakdown of protein foods. The *mucosal glands* also secrete a viscous mucus that helps prevent the stomach itself from being digested by the proteolytic enzymes. Most digestive activity occurs in the pyloric region of the stomach. After the food is processed in the stomach, it resembles a creamy mass **(chyme),** which enters the small intestine through the pyloric sphincter.

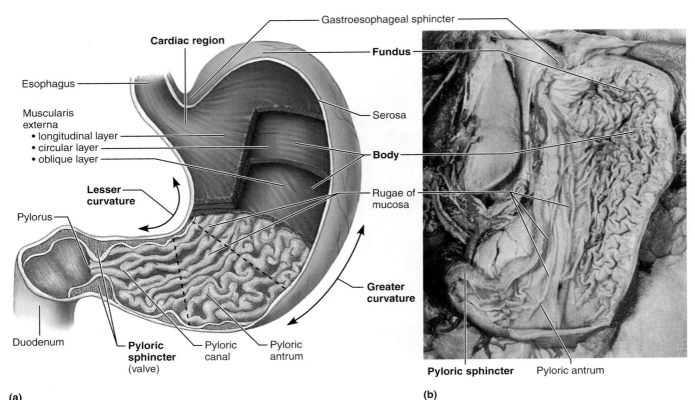

(a)

(b)

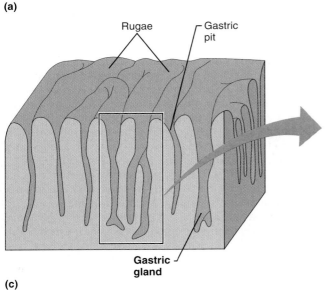

(c)

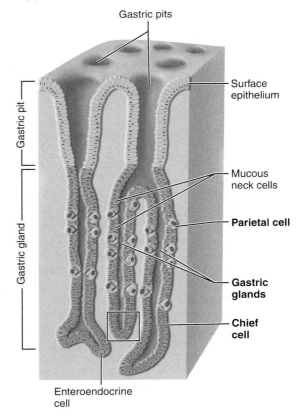

(d)

FIGURE 27.5 Anatomy of the stomach.
(**a**) Gross internal and external anatomy. (**b**) Photograph of internal aspect of stomach. (**c**) Section of the stomach wall showing rugae and gastric pits. (**d**) Detailed structure of the gastric pits and glands.

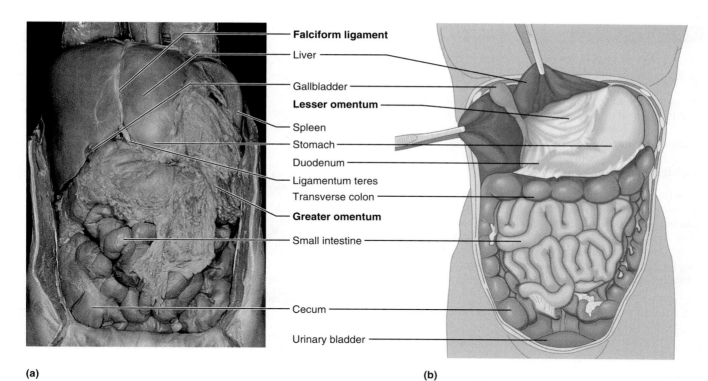

(a)

(b)

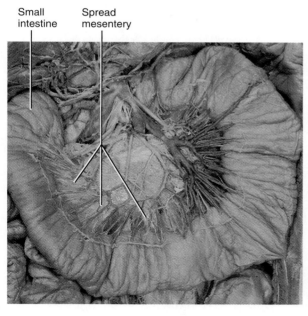

Small intestine

Spread mesentery

(c)

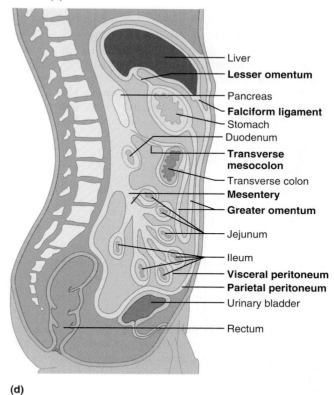

(d)

FIGURE 27.6 Peritoneal attachments of the abdominal organs. Superficial anterior views of the abdominal cavity. (**a**) Photograph with the greater omentum in place. (**b**) Diagram showing greater omentum removed and liver and gallbladder reflected superiorly. (**c**) Mesentery of the small intestine. (**d**) Sagittal view of a male torso.

Studying the Histological Structure of Selected Digestive System Organs

To prepare for the histologic studies you will be conducting now and later in the lab, obtain a microscope and the following slides: salivary glands (submandibular or sublingual); pancreas; liver; cross sections of the duodenum, ileum, and stomach; and longitudinal sections of a tooth and the gastroesophageal junction.

1.   **Stomach:** The stomach slide will be viewed first. Refer to Figure 27.7a and Plate 31 of the Histology Atlas as you scan the tissue under low power to locate the muscularis externa; then move to high power to more closely examine this layer. Try to pick out the three smooth muscle layers. How does the extra (oblique) layer of smooth muscle found in the stomach correlate with the stomach's churning movements?

_____

_____

_____

Identify the gastric glands and the gastric pits (see Figures 27.5 and 27.7b and Plate 32 of the Histology Atlas). If the section is taken from the stomach fundus and is appropriately stained, you can identify, in the gastric glands, the blue-staining **chief (or zymogenic) cells,** which produce pepsinogen, and the red-staining **parietal cells,** which secrete HCl. The enteroendocrine cells that release hormones are indistinguishable. Draw a small section of the stomach wall, and label it appropriately.

2.   **Gastroesophageal junction:** Scan the slide under low power to locate the mucosal junction between the end of the esophagus and the beginning of the stomach, the gastroesophageal junction. Compare your observations to Figure 27.7c and Plate 30 of the Histology Atlas. What is the functional importance of the epithelial differences seen in the two organs?

_____

_____

_____

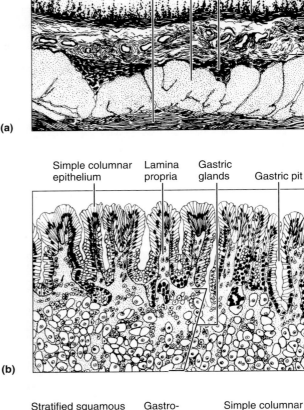

(a)

(b)

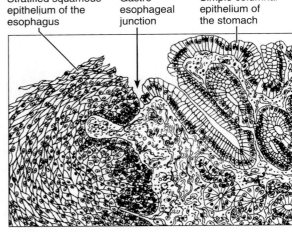

(c)

FIGURE 27.7 Histology of selected regions of the stomach and gastroesophageal junction. (a) Stomach wall. **(b)** Gastric pits and glands. **(c)** Gastroesophageal junction, longitudinal section.

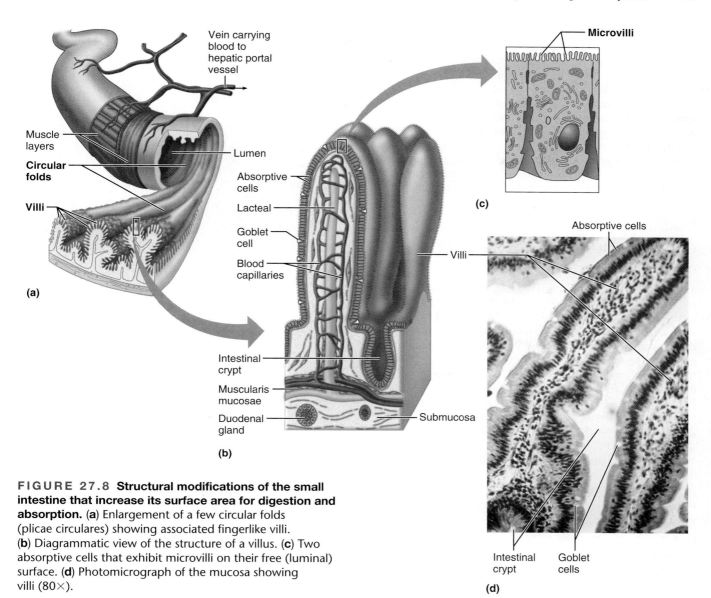

Vein carrying blood to hepatic portal vessel

Muscle layers

Circular folds

Villi

Lumen

(a)

Absorptive cells

Lacteal

Goblet cell

Blood capillaries

Intestinal crypt

Muscularis mucosae

Duodenal gland

Submucosa

Villi

(b)

Microvilli

(c)

Absorptive cells

Villi

Intestinal crypt

Goblet cells

(d)

FIGURE 27.8 Structural modifications of the small intestine that increase its surface area for digestion and absorption. (a) Enlargement of a few circular folds (plicae circulares) showing associated fingerlike villi. (b) Diagrammatic view of the structure of a villus. (c) Two absorptive cells that exhibit microvilli on their free (luminal) surface. (d) Photomicrograph of the mucosa showing villi (80×).

Small Intestine

The **small intestine** is a convoluted tube, 6 to 7 meters (about 20 feet) long in a cadaver but only about 2 m (6 feet) long during life because of its muscle tone. It extends from the pyloric sphincter to the ileocecal valve. The small intestine is suspended by a double layer of peritoneum, the fan-shaped **mesentery,** from the posterior abdominal wall (see Figure 27.6), and it lies, framed laterally and superiorly by the large intestine, in the abdominal cavity. The small intestine has three subdivisions (see Figure 27.1): (1) the **duodenum** extends from the pyloric sphincter for about 25 cm (10 inches) and curves around the head of the pancreas; most of the duodenum lies in a retroperitoneal position. (2) The **jejunum,** continuous with the duodenum, extends for 2.5 m (about 8 feet). Most of the jejunum occupies the umbilical region of the abdominal cavity. (3) The ileum, the terminal portion of the small intestine, is about 3.6 m (12 feet) long and joins the large intestine at the **ileocecal valve.** It is located inferiorly and somewhat to the right in the abdominal cavity, but its major portion lies in the hypogastric region.

Brush border enzymes, hydrolytic enzymes bound to the microvilli of the columnar epithelial cells, and, more importantly, enzymes produced by the pancreas and ducted into the duodenum via the **pancreatic duct** complete the enzymatic digestion process in the small intestine. Bile (formed in the liver) also enters the duodenum via the **bile duct** in the same area. At the duodenum, the ducts join to form the bulblike **hepatopancreatic ampulla** and empty their products into the duodenal lumen through the **major duodenal papilla,** an orifice controlled by a muscular valve called the **hepatopancreatic sphincter (sphincter of Oddi).**

Nearly all nutrient absorption occurs in the small intestine, where three structural modifications that increase the mucosa absorptive area appear—the microvilli, villi, and circular folds (Figure 27.8). **Microvilli** are minute projections of the surface plasma membrane of the columnar epithelial lining cells of the mucosa. **Villi** are the fingerlike projections of the mucosa tunic that give it a velvety appearance and texture. The **circular folds (plicae circulares)** are deep folds of the mucosa and submucosa layers that force chyme to spiral through the intestine, mixing it and slowing its progress. These structural modifications, which increase the surface area, decrease in frequency and elaboration toward the end of the small intestine. Any residue remaining undigested and unabsorbed at the terminus of the small intestine enters the large intestine through the ileocecal valve. In contrast, the amount of lymphoid tissue in the submucosa of the small intestine (especially the aggregated lymphoid nodules called **Peyer's patches,** Figure 27.9b) increases along the length of the small intestine and is very apparent in the ileum. This reflects the fact that the remaining undigested food residue contains large numbers of bacteria that must be prevented from entering the bloodstream.

ACTIVITY 3

Observing the Histological Structure of the Small Intestine

1. **Duodenum:** Secure the slide of the duodenum (cross section) to the microscope stage. Observe the tissue under low power to identify the four basic tunics of the intestinal wall—that is, the **mucosa** (the lining and its three sublayers), the **submucosa** (areolar connective tissue layer deep to the mucosa), the **muscularis externa** (composed of circular and longitudinal smooth muscle layers), and the **serosa** (the outermost layer, also called the *visceral peritoneum*). Consult Figure 27.9a and Plates 33 and 34 in the Histology Atlas to help you identify the scattered mucus-producing **duodenal glands** (Brunner's glands) in the submucosa.

What type of epithelium do you see here? _____

_____

Examine the large leaflike *villi,* which increase the surface area for absorption. Notice the scattered mucus-producing goblet cells in the epithelium of the villi. Note also the **intestinal crypts** (crypts of Lieberkühn, see also Figure 27.8), invaginated areas of the mucosa between the villi containing the cells that produce intestinal juice, a watery mucus-containing mixture that serves as a carrier fluid for absorption of nutrients from the chyme.

2. **Ileum:** The structure of the ileum resembles that of the duodenum, except that the villi are less elaborate (most of the absorption has occurred by the time the ileum is reached). Secure a slide of the ileum to the microscope stage for viewing. Observe the villi, and identify the four layers of the wall and the large, generally spherical Peyer's patches (Figure 27.9b and Plate 35 in the Histology Atlas). What tissue composes Peyer's patches?

_____

3. If a villus model is available, identify the following cells or regions before continuing: absorptive epithelium, goblet cells, lamina propria, slips of the muscularis mucosae, capillary bed, and lacteal. If possible, also identify the intestinal crypts that lie between the villi. ▪

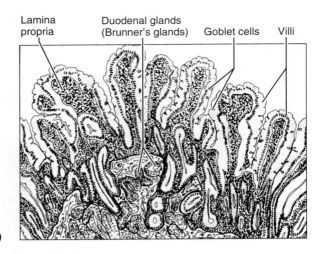

(a)

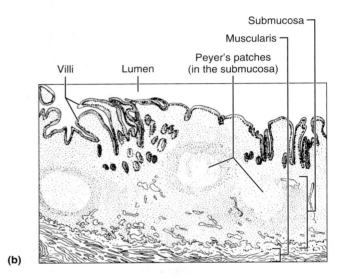

(b)

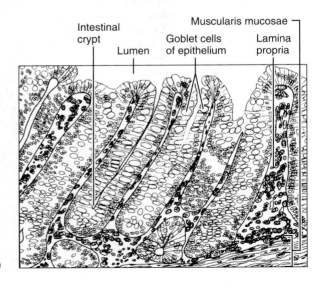

(c)

FIGURE 27.9 Histology of selected regions of the small and large intestines. Cross-sectional views. **(a)** Duodenum of the small intestine. **(b)** Ileum of the small intestine. **(c)** Large intestine.

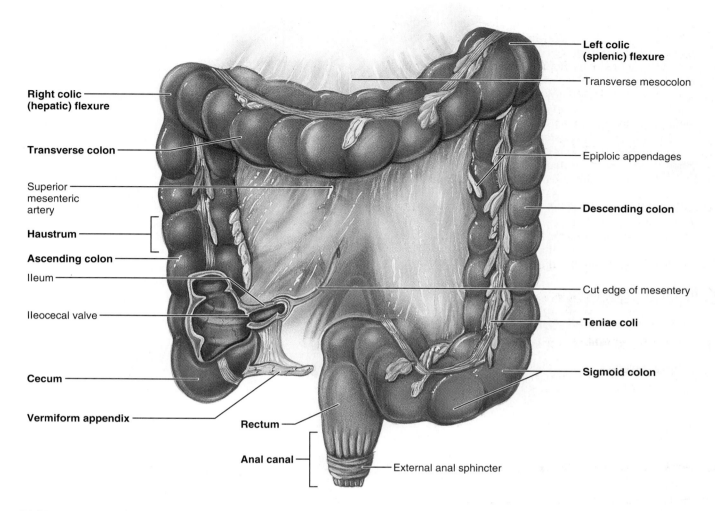

Right colic (hepatic) flexure

Transverse colon

Superior mesenteric artery

Haustrum

Ascending colon

Ileum

Ileocecal valve

Cecum

Vermiform appendix

Rectum

Anal canal

Left colic (splenic) flexure

Transverse mesocolon

Epiploic appendages

Descending colon

Cut edge of mesentery

Teniae coli

Sigmoid colon

External anal sphincter

FIGURE 27.10 The large intestine. (Section of the cecum removed to show the ileocecal valve.)

Large Intestine

The **large intestine** (Figure 27.10) is about 1.5 m (5 feet) long and extends from the ileocecal valve to the anus. It encircles the small intestine on three sides and consists of the following subdivisions: **cecum, vermiform appendix, colon, rectum,** and **anal canal.**

The blind tubelike appendix, which hangs from the cecum, is a trouble spot in the large intestine. Since it is generally twisted, it provides an ideal location for bacteria to accumulate and multiply. Inflammation of the appendix, or appendicitis, is the result. ●

The colon is divided into several distinct regions. The **ascending colon** travels up the right side of the abdominal cavity and makes a right-angle turn at the **right colic (hepatic) flexure** to cross the abdominal cavity as the **transverse colon.** It then turns at the **left colic (splenic) flexure** and continues down the left side of the abdominal cavity as the **descending colon,** where it takes an S-shaped course as the **sigmoid colon.** The sigmoid colon, rectum, and the anal canal lie in the pelvis anterior to the sacrum and thus are not considered abdominal cavity structures. Except for the transverse and sigmoid colons, which are secured to the dorsal body wall by mesocolons (see Figure 27.6), the colon is retroperitoneal.

The anal canal terminates in the **anus,** the opening to the exterior of the body. The anus, which has an external sphincter of skeletal muscle (the voluntary sphincter) and an internal sphincter of smooth muscle (the involuntary sphincter), is normally closed except during defecation when the undigested remains of the food and bacteria are eliminated from the body as feces.

In the large intestine, the longitudinal muscle layer of the muscularis externa is reduced to three longitudinal muscle bands called the **teniae coli.** Since these bands are shorter than the rest of the wall of the large intestine, they cause the wall to pucker into small pocketlike sacs called **haustra.** Fat-filled pouches of visceral peritoneum, called *epiploic appendages,* hang from the colon's surface.

The major function of the large intestine is to consolidate and propel the unusable fecal matter toward the anus and eliminate it from the body. While it does that chore, it (1) provides a site for the manufacture, by intestinal bacteria, of some vitamins (B and K), which it then absorbs into the bloodstream; and (2) reclaims most of the remaining water from undigested food, thus conserving body water.

Watery stools, or **diarrhea,** result from any condition that rushes undigested food residue through the large intestine before it has had sufficient time to absorb the water (as in irritation of the colon by bacteria). Conversely, when food residue remains in the large intestine for extended periods (as with atonic colon or failure of the defecation reflex), excessive water is absorbed and the stool becomes hard and difficult to pass (**constipation**). ●

ACTIVITY 4

Examining the Histological Structure of the Large Intestine

Examine Figure 27.9c and Plate 36 in the Histology Atlas to compare the histology of the large intestine to that of the small intestine just studied. ■

Accessory Digestive Organs

Teeth

By the age of 21, two sets of teeth have developed (Figure 27.11). The initial set, called the **deciduous** (or **milk**) **teeth,** normally appears between the ages of 6 months and 2½ years. The first of these to erupt are the lower central incisors. The child begins to shed the deciduous teeth around the age of 6, and a second set of teeth, the **permanent teeth,** gradually replaces them. As the deeper permanent teeth progressively enlarge and develop, the roots of the deciduous teeth are resorbed, leading to their final shedding. During years 6 to 12, the child has mixed dentition—both permanent and deciduous teeth. Generally, by the age of 12, all of the deciduous teeth have been shed, or exfoliated.

Teeth are classified as **incisors, canines** (*eyeteeth*), **premolars** (*bicuspids*), and **molars.** Teeth names reflect differences in relative structure and function. The incisors are chisel-shaped and exert a shearing action used in biting. Canines are cone-shaped or fanglike, the latter description being much more applicable to the canines of animals whose teeth are used for the tearing of food. Incisors, canines, and premolars typically have single roots, though the first upper premolars may have two. The lower molars have two roots but the upper molars usually have three. The premolars have two *cusps* (grinding surfaces); the molars have broad crowns with rounded cusps specialized for the fine grinding of food.

Dentition is described by means of a **dental formula,** which designates the numbers, types, and position of the

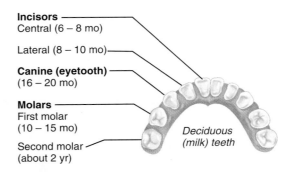

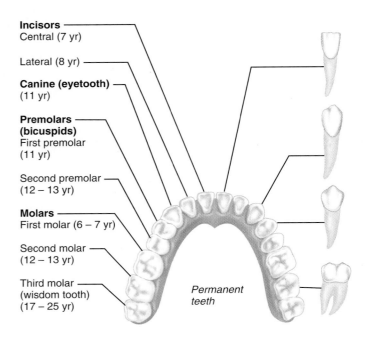

FIGURE 27.11 Human deciduous teeth and permanent teeth. (Approximate time of teeth eruption shown in parentheses.)

teeth in one side of the jaw. (Because tooth arrangement is bilaterally symmetrical, it is only necessary to designate one side of the jaw.) The complete dental formula for the deciduous teeth from the medial aspect of each jaw and proceeding posteriorly is as follows:

$$\frac{\text{Upper teeth: 2 incisors, 1 canine, 0 premolars, 2 molars}}{\text{Lower teeth: 2 incisors, 1 canine, 0 premolars, 2 molars}} \times 2$$

This formula is generally abbreviated to read as follows:

$$\frac{2,1,0,2}{2,1,0,2} \times 2 = 20 \text{ (number of deciduous teeth)}$$

The 32 permanent teeth are then described by the following dental formula:

$$\frac{2,1,2,3}{2,1,2,3} \times 2 = 32 \text{ (number of permanent teeth)}$$

Although 32 is designated as the normal number of permanent teeth, not everyone develops a full complement. In many people, the third molars, commonly called *wisdom teeth,* never erupt.

A C T I V I T Y   5

Identifying Types of Teeth

Identify the four types of teeth (incisors, canines, premolars, and molars) on the jaw model or human skull. ▮▮

A tooth consists of two major regions, the *crown* and the *root.* A longitudinal section made through a tooth shows the following basic anatomical plan (Figure 27.12). The **crown** is the superior portion of the tooth. The portion of the crown visible above the **gingiva,** or **gum,** is referred to as the *clinical crown.* The entire area covered by **enamel** is called the *anatomical crown.* Enamel is the hardest substance in the body and is fairly brittle. It consists of 95% to 97% inorganic calcium salts (chiefly $CaPO_4$) and thus is heavily mineralized. The crevice between the end of the anatomical crown and the upper margin of the gingiva is referred to as the *gingival sulcus* and its apical border is the *gingival margin.*

That portion of the tooth embedded in the alveolar portion of the jaw is the **root,** and the root and crown are connected by a slight constriction, the **neck.** The outermost surface of the root is covered by **cementum,** which is similar to bone in composition and less brittle than enamel. The cementum attaches the tooth to the **periodontal ligament,** which holds the tooth in the alveolar socket and exerts a cushioning effect. **Dentin,** which composes the bulk of the tooth, is the bonelike material medial to the enamel and cementum.

The **pulp cavity** occupies the central portion of the tooth. **Pulp,** connective tissue liberally supplied with blood vessels, nerves, and lymphatics, occupies this cavity and provides for tooth sensation and supplies nutrients to the tooth tissues. **Odontoblasts,** specialized cells that reside in the outer margins of the pulp cavity, produce the dentin. The pulp cavity extends into distal portions of the root and becomes the **root canal.** An opening at the root apex, the **apical foramen,** provides a route of entry into the tooth for blood vessels, nerves, and other structures from the tissues beneath.

A C T I V I T Y   6

Studying Microscopic Tooth Anatomy

Observe a slide of a longitudinal section of a tooth, and compare your observations with the structures detailed in Figure 27.12. Identify as many of these structures as possible. ▮▮

Salivary Glands

Three pairs of major **salivary glands** (Figure 27.13) empty their secretions into the oral cavity.

Parotid glands: Large glands located anterior to the ear and ducting into the mouth over the second upper molar through the parotid duct.

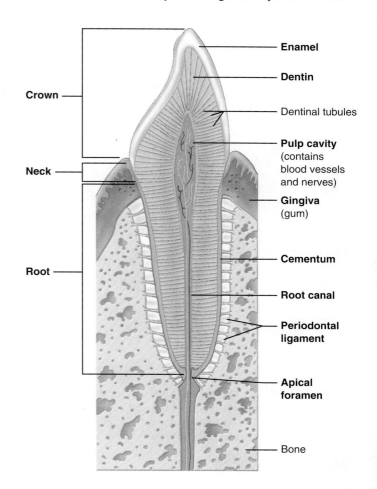

FIGURE 27.12 Longitudinal section of human canine tooth within its bony alveolus.

Submandibular glands: Located along the medial aspect of the mandibular body in the floor of the mouth, and ducting under the tongue to the base of the lingual frenulum.

Sublingual glands: Small glands located most anteriorly in the floor of the mouth and emptying under the tongue via several small ducts.

Food in the mouth and mechanical pressure (even chewing rubber bands or wax) stimulate the salivary glands to secrete saliva. Saliva consists primarily of *mucin* (a viscous glycoprotein), which moistens the food and helps to bind it together into a mass called a **bolus,** and a clear serous fluid containing the enzyme *salivary amylase.* Salivary amylase begins the digestion of starch (a large polysaccharide), breaking it down into disaccharides, or double sugars, and glucose. Parotid gland secretion is mainly serous, whereas the submandibular is a mixed gland that produces both mucin and serous components. The sublingual gland produces mostly mucin.

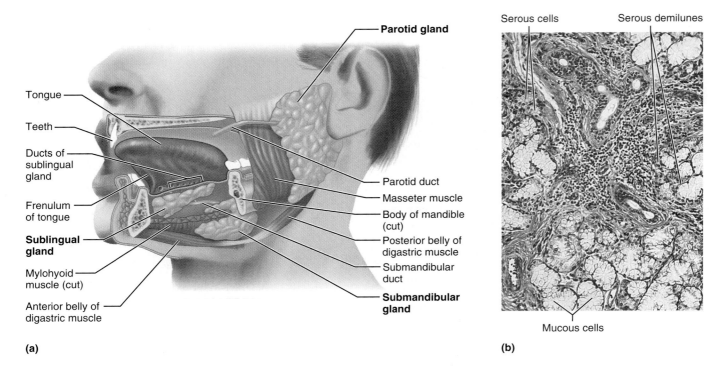

(a)

(b)

FIGURE 27.13 **The salivary glands.** (a) The parotid, submandibular, and sublingual salivary glands associated with the left aspect of the oral cavity. (b) Photomicrograph of the sublingual salivary gland (40×), which is a mixed salivary gland. Mucus-producing cells stain light blue and serous-secreting units stain purple. The serous cells sometimes form demilunes (caps) around the bases of the mucous cells.

ACTIVITY 7

Examining Salivary Gland Tissue

Examine salivary gland tissue under low power and then high power to become familiar with the appearance of a glandular tissue. Notice the clustered arrangement of the cells around their ducts. The cells are basically triangular, with their pointed ends facing the duct orifice. If possible, differentiate between mucus-producing cells, which look hollow or have a clear cytoplasm, and serous cells, which produce the clear, enzyme-containing fluid and have granules in their cytoplasm. The serous cells often form *demilunes* (caps) around the more central mucous cells. Figure 27.13b and Plate 37 in the Histology Atlas may be helpful in this task.

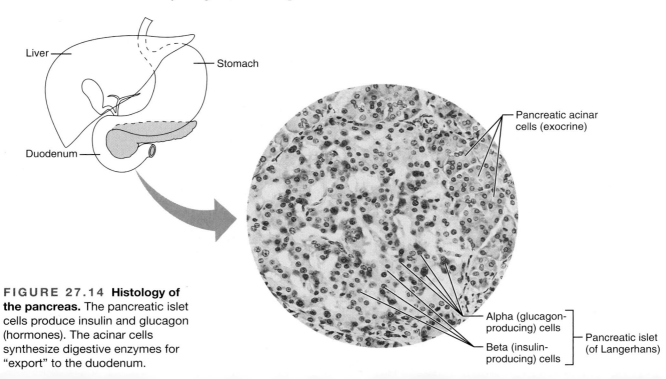

FIGURE 27.14 **Histology of the pancreas.** The pancreatic islet cells produce insulin and glucagon (hormones). The acinar cells synthesize digestive enzymes for "export" to the duodenum.

Pancreas

The **pancreas** is a soft, triangular gland that extends horizontally across the posterior abdominal wall from the spleen to the duodenum (Figure 27.14). Like the duodenum, it is a retroperitoneal organ (see Figure 27.6). As noted in Exercise 21, the pancreas has both an endocrine function (it produces the hormones insulin and glucagon) and an exocrine (enzyme-producing) function. It produces a whole spectrum of hydrolytic enzymes, which it secretes in an alkaline fluid into the duodenum through the pancreatic duct. Pancreatic juice is very alkaline. Its high concentration of bicarbonate ion (HCO_3^-) neutralizes the acidic chyme entering the duodenum from the stomach, enabling the pancreatic and intestinal enzymes to operate at their optimal pH. (Optimal pH for digestive activity to occur in the stomach is very acidic and results from the presence of HCl; that for the small intestine is slightly alkaline.)

ACTIVITY 8

Examining the Histology of the Pancreas

Observe pancreatic tissue under low power and then high power to distinguish between the lighter-staining, endocrine-producing clusters of cells (**pancreatic islets** or islets of Langerhans) and the deeper-staining **acinar cells,** which produce the hydrolytic enzymes and form the major portion of the pancreatic tissue (Figure 27.14 and Plate 38 in the Histology Atlas). Notice the arrangement of the exocrine cells around their central ducts. If the tissue is differentially stained, you will also be able to identify specifically the lavender blue–stained insulin-secreting beta cells and the red–stained glucagon-secreting alpha cells of the pancreas. ■

Liver and Gallbladder

The **liver** (see Figure 27.1), the largest gland in the body, is located inferior to the diaphragm, more to the right than the left side of the body. As noted earlier, it hides the stomach from view in a superficial observation of abdominal contents. The human liver has four lobes and is suspended from the diaphragm and anterior abdominal wall by the **falciform ligament** (see Figures 27.6a and 27.15).

The liver is one of the body's most important organs, and it performs many metabolic roles. However, its digestive function is to produce bile, which leaves the liver through the **common hepatic duct** and then enters the duodenum through the **bile duct.** Bile has no enzymatic action but emulsifies fats (breaks up large fat particles into smaller ones), thus creating a larger surface area for more efficient lipase activity. Without bile, very little fat digestion or absorption occurs.

When digestive activity is not occurring in the digestive tract, bile backs up into the **cystic duct** and enters the **gallbladder,** a small, green sac on the inferior surface of the liver. It is stored there until needed for the digestive process. While in the gallbladder, bile is concentrated by the removal of water and some ions. When fat-rich food enters the duodenum, a hormonal stimulus causes the gallbladder to contract, releasing the stored bile and making it available to the duodenum.

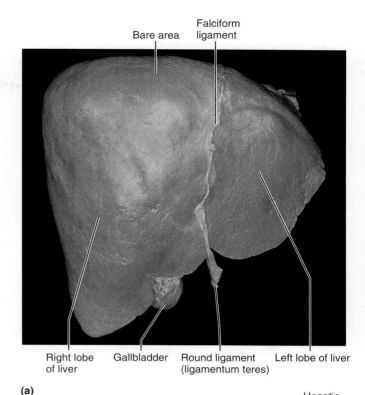

Falciform
ligament
Bare area

Right lobe   Gallbladder   Round ligament   Left lobe of liver
of liver   (ligamentum teres)

(a)

Hepatic
vein (cut)

Left lobe of liver   Caudate   Sulcus for inferior   Bare area
                      lobe of liver   vena cava

Porta hepatis   Ligamentum   Quadrate   Bile duct
containing hepatic   teres   lobe of liver   (cut)
artery (left) and   Right lobe
hepatic portal vein   Gallbladder   of liver
(right)

(b)

FIGURE 27.15 Gross anatomy of the human liver.
(**a**) Anterior view. (**b**) Posteroinferior aspect. The four liver lobes are separated by a group of fissures in this view.

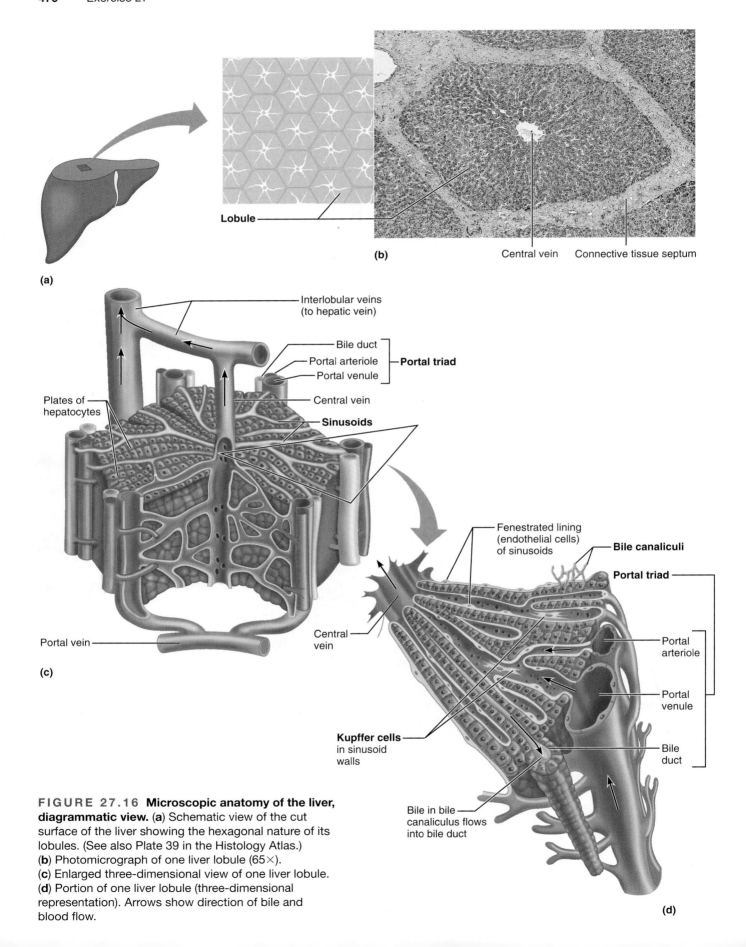

(a)

(b)

Lobule

Central vein   Connective tissue septum

Interlobular veins
(to hepatic vein)

Bile duct
Portal arteriole **Portal triad**
Portal venule

Plates of
hepatocytes

Central vein

Sinusoids

Portal vein

(c)

Fenestrated lining
(endothelial cells)
of sinusoids

Bile canaliculi

Portal triad

Central
vein

Portal
arteriole

Portal
venule

Kupffer cells
in sinusoid
walls

Bile
duct

Bile in bile
canaliculus flows
into bile duct

(d)

**FIGURE 27.16 Microscopic anatomy of the liver,
diagrammatic view.** (a) Schematic view of the cut
surface of the liver showing the hexagonal nature of its
lobules. (See also Plate 39 in the Histology Atlas.)
(**b**) Photomicrograph of one liver lobule (65×).
(**c**) Enlarged three-dimensional view of one liver lobule.
(**d**) Portion of one liver lobule (three-dimensional
representation). Arrows show direction of bile and
blood flow.

If the common hepatic or bile duct is blocked (for example, by wedged gallstones), bile is prevented from entering the small intestine, accumulates, and eventually backs up into the liver. This exerts pressure on the liver cells, and bile begins to enter the bloodstream. As the bile circulates through the body, the tissues become yellow, or jaundiced.

Blockage of the ducts is just one cause of jaundice. More often it results from actual liver problems such as **hepatitis** (an inflammation of the liver) or **cirrhosis,** a condition in which the liver is severely damaged and becomes hard and fibrous. Cirrhosis is almost guaranteed in those who drink excessive alcohol for many years. ●

As demonstrated by its highly organized anatomy, the liver (Figure 27.16) is very important in the initial processing of the nutrient-rich blood draining the digestive organs. Its structural and functional units are called **lobules.** Each lobule is a basically cylindrical structure consisting of cordlike arrays of *hepatocytes,* which radiate outward from a central vein running upward in the longitudinal axis of the lobule. At each of the six corners of the lobule is a **portal triad** (portal tract), so named because three basic structures are always present there: a *portal arteriole* (a branch of the *hepatic artery,* the functional blood supply of the liver), a *portal venule* (a branch of the *hepatic portal vein* carrying nutrient-rich blood from the digestive viscera), and a *bile duct.* Between the hepatocytes are blood-filled spaces, or **sinusoids,** through which blood from the hepatic portal vein and hepatic artery percolates. Special phagocytic cells, **Kupffer cells,** line the sinusoids and remove debris such as bacteria from the blood as it flows past, while the hepatocytes pick up oxygen and nutrients. Much of the glucose transported to the liver from the digestive system is stored as glycogen in the liver for later use, and amino acids are taken from the blood by the liver cells and utilized to make plasma proteins. The sinusoids empty into the central vein, and the blood ultimately drains from the liver via the *hepatic vein.*

Bile is continuously being made by the hepatocytes. It flows through tiny canals, the **bile canaliculi,** which run between adjacent hepatocytes toward the bile duct branches in the triad regions, where the bile eventually leaves the liver. Notice that the directions of blood and bile flow in the liver lobule are exactly opposite.

ACTIVITY 9

Examining the Histology of the Liver

Examine a slide of liver tissue and identify as many as possible of the structural features illustrated in Figure 27.16 and Plates 39 and 40 in the Histology Atlas. Also examine a three-dimensional model of liver lobules if this is available. ▪

DISSECTION AND IDENTIFICATION:

The Digestive System of the Cat

Don gloves and obtain your cat and secure it to the dissecting tray, dorsal surface down. Obtain all necessary dissecting instruments. If you have completed the dissection of the circulatory and respiratory systems, the abdominal cavity is already exposed and many of the digestive system structures have been previously identified. However, duplication of effort generally provides a good learning experience, so all of the digestive system structures will be traced and identified in this exercise.

If the abdominal cavity has not been previously opened, do so by following instructions in Exercise 21, p. 353.

Observe the shiny membrane lining the inner surface of the abdominal wall, which is the **parietal peritoneum.** We will return to identify digestive organs in the abdominal cavity shortly. But first we will expose and identify the salivary glands. ▪

ACTIVITY 10

Exposing and Viewing the Salivary Glands and Oral Cavity Structures

1. To expose and identify the **salivary glands,** which secrete saliva into the mouth, remove the skin from one side of the head and clear the connective tissue away from the angle of the jaw, below the ear, and superior to the masseter muscle. Many dark, kidney-shaped lymph nodes are in this area and you should remove them if they obscure the salivary glands, which are light tan and lobular in structure. The cat possesses five pairs of salivary glands, but only those glands described in humans are easily localized and identified (Figure 27.17). Locate the **parotid gland** on the cheek just inferior to the ear. Follow its duct over the surface of the masseter muscle to the angle of the mouth. The **submandibular gland** is posterior to the parotid, near the angle of the jaw, and the **sublingual gland** is just anterior to the submandibular gland within the lower jaw. The ducts of the submandibular and sublingual glands run deep and parallel to each other and empty on the side of the frenulum of the tongue. These need not be identified on the cat.

2. To expose and identify the structures of the oral cavity, cut through the mandible with bone cutters just anterior to the angle to free the lower jaw from the maxilla.

Identify the **hard** and **soft palates,** and use a probe to trace the hard palate to its posterior limits. Note the transverse ridges, or *rugae,* on the hard palate, which play a role in holding food in place while chewing.

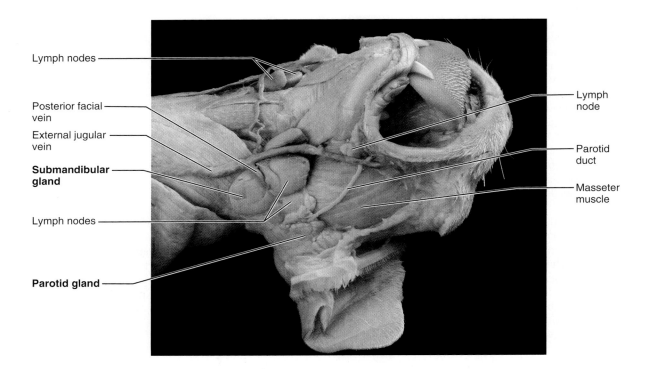

FIGURE 27.17 Photograph of salivary glands of the cat.

Do these appear in humans? _____

Does the cat have a uvula? _____

    Identify the **oropharynx** at the rear of the oral cavity and the palatine tonsils on the posterior walls at the junction between the oral cavity and oropharynx. Identify the **tongue** and rub your finger across its surface to feel the papillae. Some of the papillae, especially at the anterior end of the tongue, should feel sharp and bristly. These are the filiform papillae, which are much more numerous in the cat than in humans. What do you think their function is?

_____

    Locate the **lingual frenulum** attaching the tongue to the floor of the mouth. Trace the tongue posteriorly until you locate the **epiglottis**, the flap of tissue that covers the entrance to the respiratory passageway when swallowing occurs. Identify the **esophageal opening** posterior to the epiglottis.

    Observe the **teeth** of the cat. The dental formula for the adult cat is as follows:

$$\frac{3,1,3,1}{3,1,2,1} \times 2 = 30$$

ACTIVITY 11

Identifying Alimentary Canal Organs

1.   Using Figure 27.18, locate the abdominal alimentary canal structures.

2.   Identify the large reddish brown **liver** just beneath the diaphragm and the greater omentum covering the abdominal contents. The greater omentum assists in regulating body temperature and its phagocytic cells help to protect the body. Notice that the greater omentum is riddled with fat deposits. Lift the greater omentum, noting its two-layered structure and attachments, and lay it to the side or remove it to make subsequent organ identifications easier. Does the liver of the cat have the same number of lobes as the human liver?

_____

3.   Lift the liver and examine its inferior surface to locate the **gallbladder,** a dark greenish sac embedded in the liver's ventral surface. Identify the **falciform ligament,** a delicate layer of mesentery separating the main lobes of the liver (right and left median lobes) and attaching the liver superiorly to the abdominal wall. Also identify the thickened area along the posterior edge of the falciform ligament, the *round ligament,* or *ligamentum teres,* a remnant of the umbilical vein of the embryo.

4.   Displace the left lobes of the liver to expose the **stomach.** Identify the cardiac, fundic, body, and pyloric regions of the stomach. What is the general shape of the stomach?

_____

Locate the **lesser omentum,** the serous membrane attaching the lesser curvature of the stomach to the liver. Make an incision through the stomach wall to expose its inner surface. Can you see the **rugae**? (When the stomach is empty, its mucosa is thrown into large folds called rugae. As the stomach fills, the rugae gradually disappear and are no longer visible.) Identify the pyloric sphincter at the distal end of the stomach.

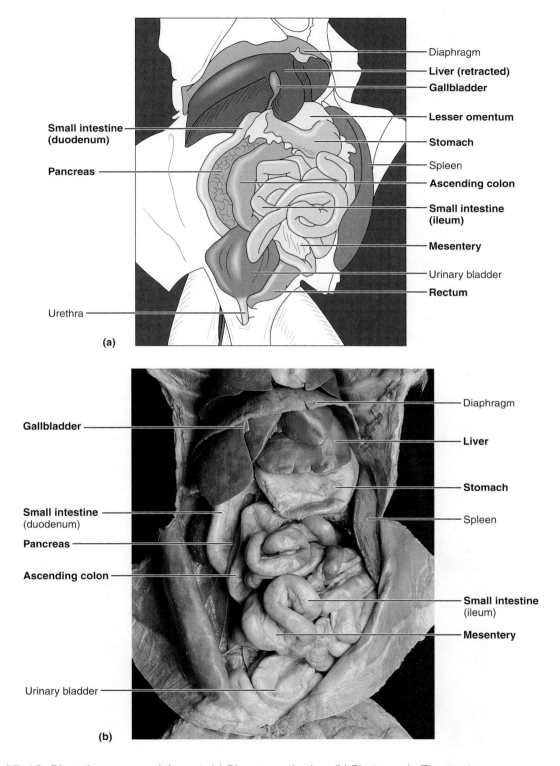

FIGURE 27.18 Digestive organs of the cat. (a) Diagrammatic view. **(b)** Photograph. The greater omentum has been cut from its attachment to the stomach.

5.   Lift the stomach and locate the **pancreas,** which appears as a grayish or brownish diffuse glandular mass in the mesentery. It extends from the vicinity of the spleen and greater curvature of the stomach and wraps around the duodenum. Attempt to find the **pancreatic duct** as it empties into the duodenum at a swollen area referred to as the **hepatopancre-**

atic ampulla. Close to the pancreatic duct, locate the **bile duct** and trace its course superiorly to the point where it diverges into the **cystic duct** (gallbladder duct) and the **common hepatic duct** (duct from the liver). Notice that the duodenum assumes a looped position.

6. Lift the **small intestine** to investigate how it is attached to the posterior body wall by the **mesentery.** Observe the mesentery closely. What types of structures do you see in this double peritoneal fold?

_____

Other than providing support for the intestine, what other functions does the mesentery have?

_____

_____

Trace the course of the small intestine from its proximal, (duodenal) end to its distal (ileal) end. Can you see any obvious differences in the external anatomy of the small intestine from one end to the other?

_____

With a scalpel, slice open the distal portion of the ileum and flush out the inner surface with water. Feel the inner surface with your fingertip. How does it feel?

_____

Use a hand lens to see if you can see any **villi** and to locate the areas of lymphatic tissue called **Peyer's patches,** which appear as scattered white patches on the inner intestinal surface. See also Plate 35 the Histology Atlas.

Return to the duodenal end of the small intestine. Make an incision into the duodenum. As before, flush the surface with water, and feel the inner surface. Does it feel any different than the ileal mucosa?

_____ If so, describe the difference. _____

_____

Use the hand lens to observe the villi. What differences do you see in the villi in the two areas of the small intestine?

_____

_____

7. Make an incision into the junction between the ileum and cecum to locate the **ileocecal valve** (Figure 27.19). Observe the **cecum,** the initial expanded part of the large intestine. (Lymph nodes may have to be removed from this area to observe it clearly.) Does the cat have an appendix?

_____

8. Identify the short ascending, transverse, and descending portions of the **colon** and the **mesocolon,** a membrane that attaches the colon to the posterior body wall. Trace the descending colon to the **rectum,** which penetrates the body wall, and identify the **anus.**

Identify the two portions of the peritoneum, the parietal peritoneum lining the abdominal wall (identified previously) and the visceral peritoneum, which is the outermost layer of the wall of the abdominal organs (serosa).

9. Prepare your cat for storage as instructed on p. 220, wash the dissecting tray and instruments, and discard your gloves before continuing or leaving the laboratory. ▪

FIGURE 27.19 Ileocecal valve.

Anatomy of the Digestive System

General Histological Plan of the Alimentary Canal

1. The general anatomical features of the alimentary canal are listed below. Fill in the table to complete the information.

Wall layer	Subdivisions of the layer (if applicable)	Major functions
mucosa		
submucosa		
muscularis externa		
serosa or adventitia		

Organs of the Alimentary Canal

2. The tubelike digestive system canal that extends from the mouth to the anus is known as the _____ canal or the _____ tract.

3. How is the muscularis externa of the stomach modified? _____

_____

How does this modification relate to the function of the stomach? _____

_____

4. What transition in epithelial type exists at the gastroesophageal junction? _____

_____

How do the epithelia of these two organs relate to their specific functions? _____

_____

5. Differentiate between the colon and the large intestine. _____

_____

6. Match the items in column B with the descriptive statements in column A.

Column A

_____ 1. structure that suspends the small intestine from the posterior body wall

_____ 2. fingerlike extensions of the intestinal mucosa that increase the surface area for absorption

_____ 3. large collections of lymphoid tissue found in the submucosa of the small intestine

_____ 4. deep folds of the mucosa and submucosa that extend completely or partially around the circumference of the small intestine

_____, _____ 5. regions that break down foodstuffs mechanically

_____ 6. mobile organ that manipulates food in the mouth and initiates swallowing

_____ 7. conduit for both air and food

_____, _____, _____ 8. three structures continuous with and representing modifications of the peritoneum

_____ 9. the "gullet"; no digestive or absorptive function

_____ 10. folds of the gastric mucosa

_____ 11. sacculations of the large intestine

_____ 12. projections of the plasma membrane of a mucosal epithelial cell

_____ 13. valve at the junction of the small and large intestines

_____ 14. primary region of food and water absorption

_____ 15. membrane securing the tongue to the floor of the mouth

_____ 16. absorbs water and forms feces

_____ 17. area between the teeth and lips/cheeks

_____ 18. wormlike sac that outpockets from the cecum

_____ 19. initiates protein digestion

_____ 20. structure attached to the lesser curvature of the stomach

_____ 21. organ distal to the stomach

_____ 22. valve controlling food movement from the stomach into the duodenum

_____ 23. posterosuperior boundary of the oral cavity

_____ 24. location of the hepatopancreatic sphincter through which pancreatic secretions and bile pass

_____ 25. serous lining of the abdominal cavity wall

_____ 26. principal site for the synthesis of vitamin K by microorganisms

_____ 27. region containing two sphincters through which feces are expelled from the body

_____ 28. bone-supported anterosuperior boundary of the oral cavity

Column B

a. anus

b. appendix

c. circular folds

d. esophagus

e. frenulum

f. greater omentum

g. hard palate

h. haustra

i. ileocecal valve

j. large intestine

k. lesser omentum

l. mesentery

m. microvilli

n. oral cavity

o. parietal peritoneum

p. Peyer's patches

q. pharynx

r. pyloric valve

s. rugae

t. small intestine

u. soft palate

v. stomach

w. tongue

x. vestibule

y. villi

z. visceral peritoneum

7. Correctly identify all organs depicted in the diagram below.

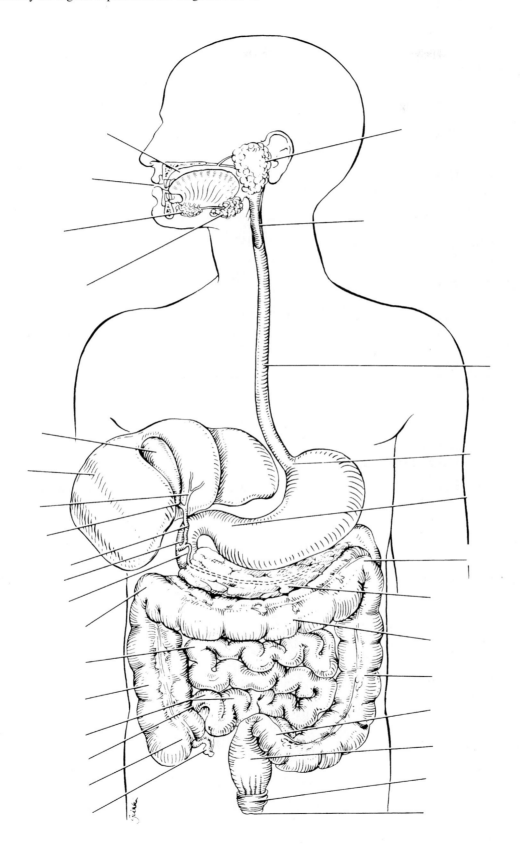

8. You have studied the histological structure of a number of organs in this laboratory. Three of these are diagrammed below. Identify and correctly label each.

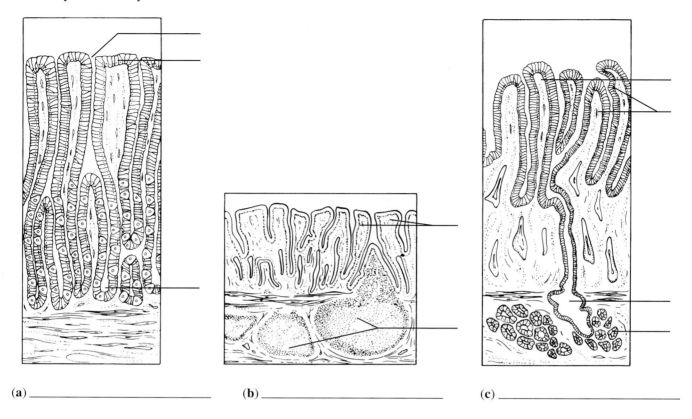

(a) _____   (b) _____   (c) _____

Accessory Digestive Organs

9. Correctly label all structures provided with leader lines in the diagram of a molar below. (Note: Some of the terms in the key for question 10 may be helpful in this task.)

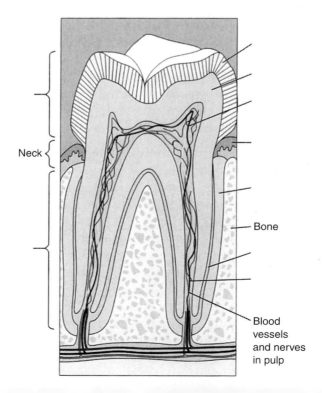

Neck

Bone

Blood vessels and nerves in pulp

10. Use the key to identify each tooth area described below.

_____ 1. visible portion of the tooth in situ

_____ 2. material covering the tooth root

_____ 3. hardest substance in the body

_____ 4. attaches the tooth to bone and surrounding alveolar structures

_____ 5. portion of the tooth embedded in bone

_____ 6. forms the major portion of tooth structure; similar to bone

_____ 7. produces the dentin

_____ 8. site of blood vessels, nerves, and lymphatics

_____ 9. entire portion of the tooth covered with enamel

Key: a. anatomical crown

b. cementum

c. clinical crown

d. dentin

e. enamel

f. gingiva

g. odontoblast

h. periodontal ligament

i. pulp

j. root

11. In the human, the number of deciduous teeth is _____; the number of permanent

teeth is _____.

12. The dental formula for permanent teeth is $\frac{2,1,2,3}{2,1,2,3} \times 2$. Explain what this means. _____

_____

_____

What is the dental formula for the deciduous teeth? _____ $\times$ _____ = _____

13. What teeth are the "wisdom teeth"? _____

_____

14. Various types of glands form a part of the alimentary tube wall or duct their secretions into it. Match the glands listed in column B with the function/locations described in column A.

Column A

_____ 1. produce(s) mucus; found in the submucosa of the small intestine

_____ 2. produce(s) a product containing amylase that begins starch breakdown in the mouth

_____ 3. produce(s) a whole spectrum of enzymes and an alkaline fluid that is secreted into the duodenum

_____ 4. produce(s) bile that it secretes into the duodenum via the bile duct

_____ 5. produce(s) HCl and pepsinogen

_____ 6. found in the mucosa of the small intestine; produce(s) intestinal juice

Column B

a. duodenal glands

b. gastric glands

c. intestinal crypts

d. liver

e. pancreas

f. salivary glands

15. Which of the salivary glands produces a secretion that is mainly serous? _____

16. What is the role of the gallbladder? _____

17. Name three structures always found in the portal triad regions of the liver. _____,

   _____ and _____

18. Where would you expect to find the Kupffer cells of the liver? _____

   What is their function? _____

19. Why is the liver so dark red in the living animal? _____

   _____

20. The pancreas has two major populations of secretory cells—those in the islets and the acinar cells. Which population serves

   the digestive process? _____

Dissection and Identification: The Digestive System of the Cat

21. Several differences between cat and human digestive anatomy should have become apparent during the dissection. Note the pertinent differences between the human and the cat relative to the following structures:

Structure	Cat	Human
tongue papillae		
number of liver lobes		
appendix		

Anatomy of the Urinary System

M A T E R I A L S

☐ Human dissectible torso model, three-dimensional model of the urinary system, and/or anatomical chart of the human urinary system

☐ Dissecting instruments and tray

☐ Pig or sheep kidney, doubly or triply injected

☐ Disposable gloves

☐ Animal specimen from previous dissections

☐ Embalming fluid

☐ Three-dimensional models of the cut kidney and of a nephron (if available)

☐ Compound microscope

☐ Prepared slides of section of kidney (l.s.) and of bladder (x.s.)

AIA See Appendix B, Exercise 28 for links to A.D.A.M.® Interactive Anatomy.

O B J E C T I V E S

1. To describe the function of the urinary system.
2. To identify, on an appropriate diagram or torso model, the urinary system organs and to describe the general function of each.
3. To compare the course and length of the urethra in males and females.
4. To identify these regions of the dissected kidney (longitudinal section): hilum, cortex, medulla, renal pyramids, major and minor calyces, pelvis, renal columns, and fibrous and perirenal fat capsules.
5. To trace the blood supply of the kidney from the renal artery to the renal vein.
6. To define the nephron as the physiological unit of the kidney, and to describe its anatomy.
7. To define *glomerular filtration, tubular resorption,* and *tubular secretion,* and to indicate the nephron areas involved in these processes.
8. To define *micturition,* and to explain pertinent differences in the control of the two bladder sphincters (internal and external).
9. To recognize microscopic or diagrammatic views of the histologic structure of the kidney and bladder.
10. To identify on a dissection specimen the urinary system organs and to describe the general function of each.

Metabolism of nutrients by the body produces wastes (carbon dioxide, nitrogenous wastes, ammonia, and so on) that must be eliminated from the body if normal function is to continue. Although excretory processes involve several organ systems (the lungs excrete carbon dioxide and skin glands excrete salts and water), it is the **urinary system** that is primarily concerned with the removal of nitrogenous wastes from the body. In addition to this purely excretory function, the kidney maintains the electrolyte, acid-base, and fluid balances of the blood and is thus a major, if not *the* major, homeostatic organ of the body.

To perform its functions, the kidney acts first as a blood filter, and then as a blood processor. It allows toxins, metabolic wastes, and excess ions to leave the body in the urine, while simultaneously retaining needed substances and returning them to the blood. Malfunction of the urinary system, particularly of the kidneys, leads to a failure in homeostasis which, unless corrected, is fatal.

Gross Anatomy of the Human Urinary System

The urinary system (Figure 28.1) consists of the paired kidneys and ureters and the single urinary bladder and urethra. The **kidneys** perform the functions described above and manufacture urine in the process. The remaining organs of the system provide temporary storage reservoirs or transportation channels for urine.

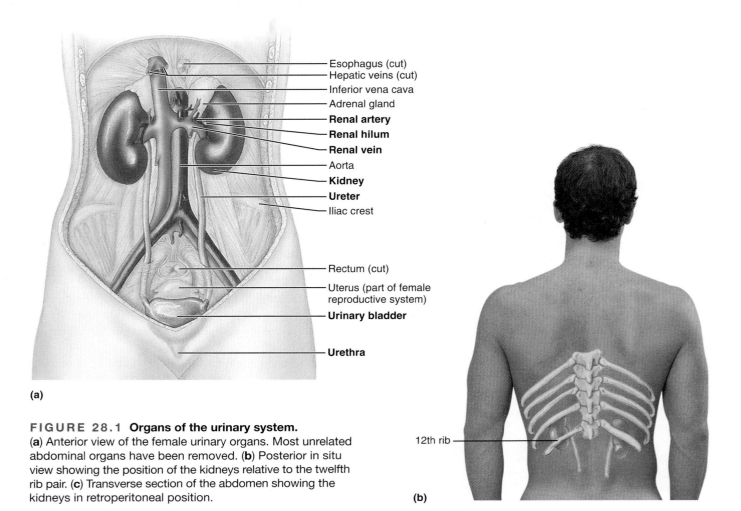

(a)

FIGURE 28.1 Organs of the urinary system.
(a) Anterior view of the female urinary organs. Most unrelated abdominal organs have been removed. **(b)** Posterior in situ view showing the position of the kidneys relative to the twelfth rib pair. **(c)** Transverse section of the abdomen showing the kidneys in retroperitoneal position.

(b)

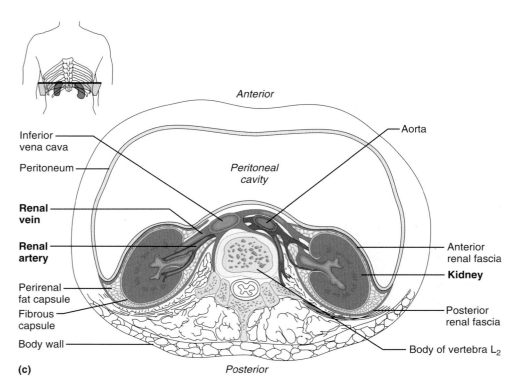

(c)

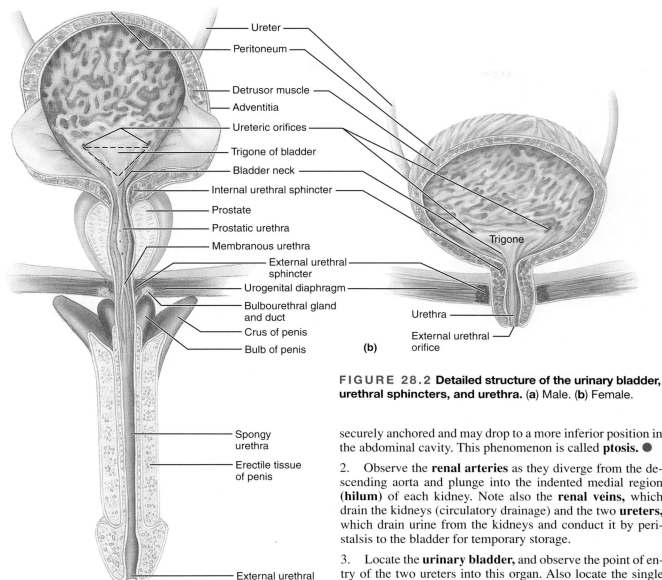

(a)

Labels for figure (a):
- Ureter
- Peritoneum
- Detrusor muscle
- Adventitia
- Ureteric orifices
- Trigone of bladder
- Bladder neck
- Internal urethral sphincter
- Prostate
- Prostatic urethra
- Membranous urethra
- External urethral sphincter
- Urogenital diaphragm
- Bulbourethral gland and duct
- Crus of penis
- Bulb of penis
- Spongy urethra
- Erectile tissue of penis
- External urethral orifice

Labels for figure (b):
- Trigone
- Urethra
- External urethral orifice

(b)

FIGURE 28.2 Detailed structure of the urinary bladder, urethral sphincters, and urethra. (a) Male. **(b)** Female.

securely anchored and may drop to a more inferior position in the abdominal cavity. This phenomenon is called **ptosis.** ●

2. Observe the **renal arteries** as they diverge from the descending aorta and plunge into the indented medial region (**hilum**) of each kidney. Note also the **renal veins,** which drain the kidneys (circulatory drainage) and the two **ureters,** which drain urine from the kidneys and conduct it by peristalsis to the bladder for temporary storage.

3. Locate the **urinary bladder,** and observe the point of entry of the two ureters into this organ. Also locate the single **urethra,** which drains the bladder. The triangular region of the bladder that is delineated by these three openings (two ureteral and one urethral orifice) is referred to as the **trigone** (Figure 28.2).

4. Follow the course of the urethra to the body exterior. In the male, it is approximately 20 cm (8 inches) long, travels the length of the **penis,** and opens at its tip. Its three named regions—the *prostatic, membranous,* and *spongy urethrae*— are described in more detail in Exercise 29 and illustrated in Figure 29.1 (p. 501). The male urethra has a dual function: It is a urine conduit to the body exterior, and it provides a passageway for semen ejaculation. Thus, in the male, the urethra is part of both the urinary and reproductive systems. In females, the urethra is very short, approximately 4 cm (1½ inches) long (see Figure 28.2). There are no common urinary-reproductive pathways in the female, and the female's urethra serves only to transport urine to the body exterior. Its external opening, the **external urethral orifice,** lies anterior to the vaginal opening. ■

A C T I V I T Y   1

Identifying Urinary System Organs

Examine the human torso model, a large anatomical chart, or a three-dimensional model of the urinary system to locate and study the anatomy and relationships of the urinary organs.

1. Locate the paired kidneys on the dorsal body wall in the superior lumbar region. Notice that they are not positioned at exactly the same level. Because it is crowded by the liver, the right kidney is slightly lower than the left kidney. In a living person, transparent membranes (the *fibrous capsules*), fat deposits (the *perirenal fat capsules*), and the fibrous renal fascia surround and hold the kidneys in place in a retroperitoneal position.

When the fatty material surrounding the kidneys is reduced or too meager in amount (in cases of rapid weight loss or in very thin individuals), the kidneys are less

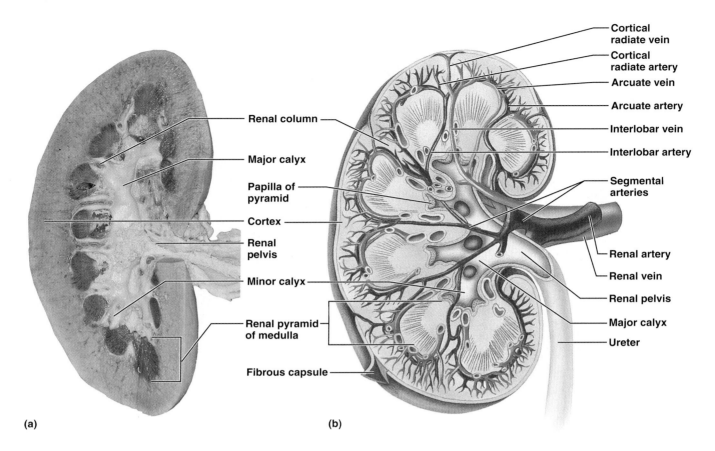

FIGURE 28.3 Frontal section of a kidney. (a) Photograph of a triple-injected pig kidney. Arteries and veins injected with red and blue latex respectively; pelvis and ureter injected with yellow latex. **(b)** Diagrammatic view showing the larger arteries supplying the kidney tissue.

DISSECTION:
Gross Internal Anatomy
of the Pig or Sheep Kidney

1. In preparation for dissection, don gloves. Obtain a preserved sheep or pig kidney, dissecting tray, and instruments. Observe the kidney to identify the **fibrous capsule,** a smooth transparent membrane that adheres tightly to the external aspect of the kidney.

2. Find the ureter, renal vein, and renal artery at the hilum (indented) region. The renal vein has the thinnest wall and will be collapsed. The ureter is the largest of these structures and has the thickest wall.

3. Make a cut through the longitudinal axis (frontal section) of the kidney and locate the anatomical areas described below and depicted in Figure 28.3.

Kidney cortex: The superficial kidney region, which is lighter in color. If the kidney is doubly injected with latex, you will see a predominance of red and blue latex specks in this region indicating its rich vascular supply.

Medullary region: Deep to the cortex; a darker, reddish-brown color. The medulla is segregated into triangular regions that have a striped, or striated, appearance—the **renal pyramids.** The base of each pyramid faces toward the cortex.

Its more pointed **papilla,** or **apex,** points to the innermost kidney region.

Renal columns: Areas of tissue, more like the cortex in appearance, which segregate and dip inward between the pyramids.

Renal pelvis: Lateral to the hilum; a relatively flat, basinlike cavity that is continuous with the **ureter,** which exits from the hilum region. Fingerlike extensions of the pelvis should be visible. The larger, or primary, extensions are called the **major calyces** (singular, *calyx*); subdivisions of the major calyces are the **minor calyces.** Notice that the minor calyces terminate in cuplike areas that enclose the apexes of the medullary pyramids and collect urine draining from the pyramidal tips into the pelvis.

4. If the preserved kidney is doubly or triply injected, follow the renal blood supply from the renal artery to the *glomeruli.* The glomeruli appear as little red and blue specks in the cortex region. (See Figures 28.3 and 28.4.)

Approximately a fourth of the total blood flow of the body is delivered to the kidneys each minute by the large **renal arteries.** As a renal artery approaches the kidney, it breaks up into branches called **segmental arteries,** which enter the hilum. Each segmental artery, in turn, divides into several **interlobar arteries,** which ascend toward the cortex in

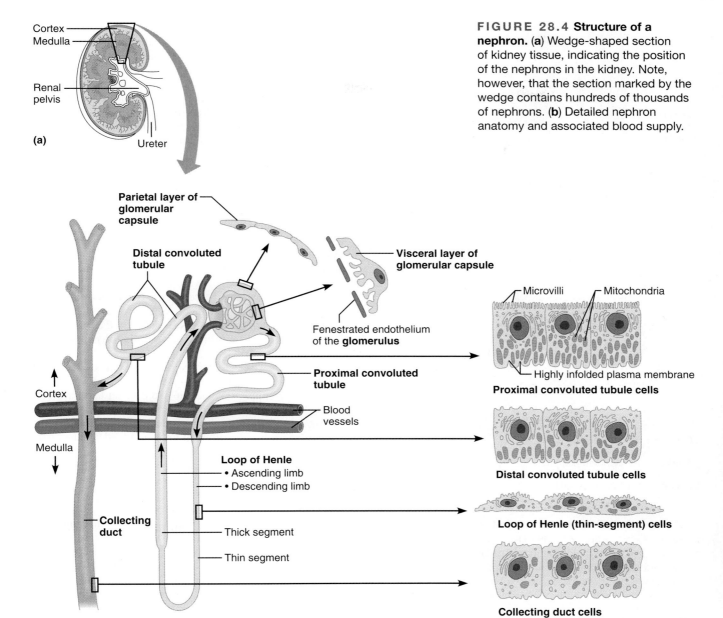

FIGURE 28.4 Structure of a nephron. (a) Wedge-shaped section of kidney tissue, indicating the position of the nephrons in the kidney. Note, however, that the section marked by the wedge contains hundreds of thousands of nephrons. **(b)** Detailed nephron anatomy and associated blood supply.

the renal column areas. At the top of the medullary region, these arteries give off arching branches, the **arcuate arteries,** which curve over the bases of the medullary pyramids. Small **cortical radiate arteries** branch off the arcuate arteries and ascend into the cortex, giving off the individual **afferent arterioles** (see Figure 28.5), which provide the capillary networks (glomeruli and peritubular capillary beds) that supply the nephrons, or functional units, of the kidney. Blood draining from the nephron capillary networks in the cortex enters the **cortical radiate veins** and then drains through the **arcuate veins** and the **interlobar veins** to finally enter the **renal vein** in the pelvis region. (There are no segmental veins.)

Dispose of the kidney specimen as your instructor specifies. ▨

Functional Microscopic Anatomy of the Kidney and Bladder

Kidney

Each kidney contains over a million **nephrons,** which are the anatomical units responsible for forming urine. Figure 28.4 depicts the detailed structure and the relative positioning of the nephrons in the kidney.

Each nephron consists of two major structures: a **glomerulus** (a capillary knot) and a renal tubule. During

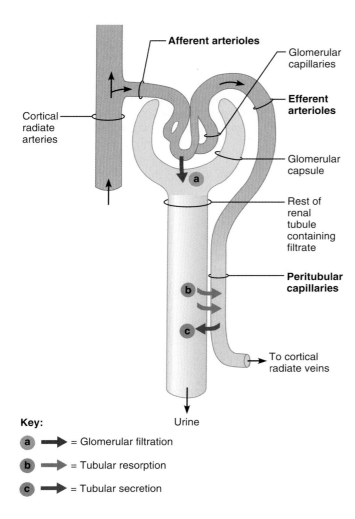

Cortical radiate arteries

Afferent arterioles

Glomerular capillaries

Efferent arterioles

Glomerular capsule

Rest of renal tubule containing filtrate

Peritubular capillaries

To cortical radiate veins

Urine

Key:

a ➡ = Glomerular filtration

b ➡ = Tubular resorption

c ➡ = Tubular secretion

FIGURE 28.5 The kidney depicted as a single, large nephron. A kidney actually has millions of nephrons acting in parallel. The three major mechanisms by which the kidneys adjust the composition of plasma are (**a**) glomerular filtration, (**b**) tubular resorption, and (**c**) tubular secretion. Black arrows show the path of blood flow through the renal microcirculation.

entering a collecting duct. In order from the glomerular capsule, the anatomical areas of the renal tubule are: the **proximal convoluted tubule, loop of Henle** (descending and ascending limbs), and the **distal convoluted tubule.** The wall of the renal tubule is composed almost entirely of cuboidal epithelial cells, with the exception of part of the descending limb (and sometimes part of the ascending limb) of the loop of Henle, which is simple squamous epithelium. The lumen surfaces of the cuboidal cells in the proximal convoluted tubule have dense microvilli (a cellular modification that greatly increases the surface area exposed to the lumen contents, or filtrate). Microvilli also occur on cells of the distal convoluted tubule but in greatly reduced numbers, revealing its less significant role in reclaiming filtrate contents.

Most nephrons, called **cortical nephrons,** are located entirely within the cortex. However, parts of the loops of Henle of the **juxtamedullary nephrons** (located close to the cortex-medulla junction) penetrate well into the medulla. The **collecting ducts,** each of which receives urine from many nephrons, run downward through the renal pyramids, giving them their striped appearance. As the collecting ducts approach the renal pelvis, they fuse together and empty the final urinary product into the minor calyces via the papillae of the pyramids.

The function of the nephron depends on several unique features of the renal circulation (see Figure 28.5). The capillary vascular supply consists of two distinct capillary beds, the *glomerulus* and the *peritubular capillary bed.* Vessels leading to and from the glomerulus, the first capillary bed, are both arterioles: the **afferent arteriole** feeds the bed while the **efferent arteriole** drains it. The glomerular capillary bed has no parallel elsewhere in the body. It is a high-pressure bed along its entire length. Its high pressure is a result of two major factors: (1) The bed is *fed and drained* by arterioles (arterioles are high-resistance vessels as opposed to venules, which are low-resistance vessels), and (2) the afferent feeder arteriole is larger in diameter than the efferent arteriole draining the bed. The high hydrostatic pressure created by these two anatomical features forces out fluid and blood components smaller than proteins from the glomerulus into the glomerular capsule. That is, it forms the filtrate which is processed by the nephron tubule.

The **peritubular capillary bed** arises from the efferent arteriole draining the glomerulus. This set of capillaries clings intimately to the renal tubule and empties into the cortical radiate veins that leave the cortex. The peritubular capillaries are *low-pressure* porous capillaries adapted for absorption rather than filtration and readily take up the solutes and water resorbed from the filtrate by the tubule cells. The juxtamedullary nephrons have additional looping vessels, called the **vasa recta** (straight vessels), that parallel the long loops of Henle in the medulla. Hence, the two capillary beds of the nephron have very different, but complementary, roles: The glomerulus produces the filtrate and the peritubular capillaries reclaim most of that filtrate.

Additionally, each nephron has a region called a **juxtaglomerular apparatus (JGA),** which plays an important role in forming concentrated urine. The JGA consists of (1) *granular* or *juxtaglomerular (JG) cells,* blood pressure

embryologic development, each **renal tubule** begins as a blind-ended tubule that gradually encloses an adjacent capillary cluster, or glomerulus. The enlarged end of the tubule encasing the glomerulus is the **glomerular (Bowman's) capsule,** and its inner, or visceral, wall consists of highly specialized cells called **podocytes.** Podocytes have long, branching processes *(foot processes)* that interdigitate with those of other podocytes and cling to the endothelial wall of the glomerular capillaries, thus forming a very porous epithelial membrane surrounding the glomerulus. The glomerulus-capsule complex is sometimes called the **renal corpuscle.**

The rest of the tubule is approximately 3 cm (1.25 inches) long. As it emerges from the glomerular capsule, it becomes highly coiled and convoluted, drops down into a long hairpin loop, and then again coils and twists before

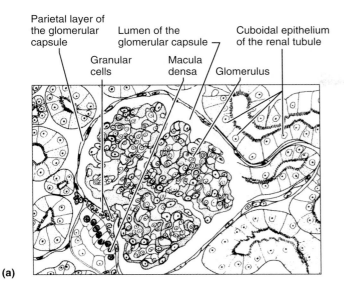

(a)

Parietal layer of the glomerular capsule
Granular cells
Lumen of the glomerular capsule
Macula densa
Glomerulus
Cuboidal epithelium of the renal tubule

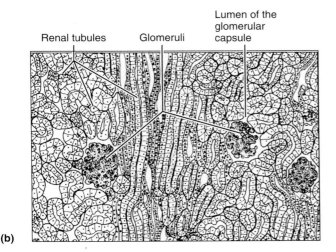

(b)

Renal tubules
Glomeruli
Lumen of the glomerular capsule

FIGURE 28.6 Microscopic structure of kidney tissue.
(a) Detailed structure of the glomerulus. (b) Low-power view of the renal cortex. (See also Plates 41 and 42 in the Histology Atlas.)

sensors in the walls of the arterioles near the glomerulus, and (2) a *macula densa,* a specialized group of columnar chemoreceptor cells in the distal convoluted tubule abutting the granular cells (Figure 28.6a and Plate 42 in the Histology Atlas).

Urine formation is a result of three processes: *filtration, resorption,* and *secretion* (see Figure 28.5). **Filtration,** the role of the glomerulus, is largely a passive process in which a portion of the blood passes from the glomerular bed into the glomerular capsule. This filtrate then enters the proximal convoluted tubule, where tubular resorption and secretion begin. During **tubular resorption,** many of the filtrate components move through the tubule cells and return to the blood in the peritubular capillaries. Some of this resorption is passive, such as that of water which passes by osmosis, but the resorption of most substances depends on active transport processes and is highly selective. Which substances are resorbed at a particular time depends on the composition of the blood and the needs of the body at that time. Substances that

are almost entirely resorbed from the filtrate include water, glucose, and amino acids. Various ions are selectively resorbed or allowed to go out in the urine according to what is required to maintain appropriate blood pH and electrolyte composition. Waste products (urea, creatinine, uric acid, and drug metabolites) are resorbed to a much lesser degree or not at all. Most (75% to 80%) of tubular resorption occurs in the proximal convoluted tubule. The balance occurs in other areas, especially the distal convoluted tubules and collecting ducts.

Tubular secretion is essentially the reverse process of tubular resorption. Substances such as hydrogen and potassium ions and creatinine move either from the blood of the peritubular capillaries through the tubular cells or from the tubular cells into the filtrate to be disposed of in the urine. This process is particularly important for the disposal of substances not already in the filtrate (such as drug metabolites), and as a device for controlling blood pH.

ACTIVITY 2

Studying Nephron Structure

1. Begin your study of nephron structure by identifying the glomerular capsule, proximal and distal convoluted tubule regions, and the loop of Henle on a model of the nephron. Then, obtain a compound microscope and a prepared slide of kidney tissue to continue with the microscope study of the kidney.

2. Hold the longitudinal section of the kidney up to the light to identify cortical and medullary areas. Then secure the slide on the microscope stage, and scan the slide under low power.

3. Move the slide so that you can see the cortical area. Identify a glomerulus, which appears as a ball of tightly packed material containing many small nuclei (Figures 28.6b and 28.7, and Plate 41 in the Histology Atlas). It is usually

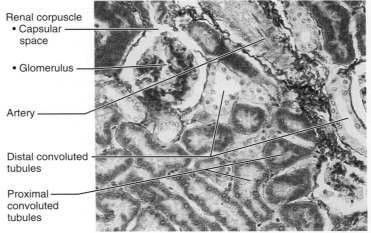

Renal corpuscle
• Capsular space
• Glomerulus
Artery
Distal convoluted tubules
Proximal convoluted tubules

FIGURE 28.7 Photomicrograph of renal cortical tissue. Notice the renal corpuscles and the sections through the various tubules. In the proximal convoluted tubules, the lumens appear "fuzzy" because they are filled with the long microvilli of the epithelial cells that form the tubule walls. In the distal tubules, by contrast, the lumens are clear (200×).

delineated by a vacant-appearing region (the *capsular space*) between the visceral and parietal layers of the glomerular capsule that surrounds it.

4. Notice that the renal tubules are cut at various angles. Try to differentiate between the fuzzy cuboidal epithelium of the proximal convoluted tubule, which has dense microvilli, and that of the distal convoluted tubule with sparse microvilli (Figure 28.7). Also identify the thin-walled loop of Henle. ▬

Bladder

Although urine production by the kidney is a continuous process, urine is usually removed from the body when voiding is convenient. In the meantime the **urinary bladder,** which receives urine via the ureters and discharges it via the urethra, stores it temporarily.

Voiding, or **micturition,** is the process in which urine empties from the bladder. Two sphincter muscles or valves (see Figure 28.2), the **internal urethral sphincter** (more superiorly located) and the **external urethral sphincter** (more inferiorly located) control the outflow of urine from the bladder. Ordinarily, the bladder continues to collect urine until about 200 ml have accumulated, at which time the stretching of the bladder wall activates stretch receptors. Impulses transmitted to the central nervous system subsequently produce reflex contractions of the bladder wall through parasympathetic nervous system pathways (in other words, via the pelvic splanchnic nerves). As contractions increase in force and frequency, stored urine is forced past the internal sphincter, which is a smooth muscle involuntary sphincter, into the superior part of the urethra. It is then that a person feels the urge to void. The inferior external sphincter consists of skeletal muscle and is voluntarily controlled. If it is not convenient to void, the opening of this sphincter can be inhibited. Conversely, if the time is convenient, the sphincter may be relaxed and the stored urine flushed from the body. If voiding is inhibited, the reflex contractions of the bladder cease temporarily and urine continues to accumulate in the bladder. After another 200 to 300 ml of urine have been collected, the *micturition reflex* will again be initiated.

Lack of voluntary control over the external sphincter is referred to as **incontinence.** Incontinence is normal in children 2 years old or younger, as they have not yet gained control over the voluntary sphincter. In adults and older children, incontinence is generally a result of spinal cord injury, emotional problems, bladder irritability, or some other pathology of the urinary tract. ●

ACTIVITY 3

Studying Bladder Structure

1. Return the kidney slide to the supply area, and obtain a slide of bladder tissue. Scan the bladder tissue. Identify its three layers: mucosa, muscular layer, and fibrous adventitia.

2. Study the mucosa with its highly specialized transitional epithelium. The plump, transitional epithelial cells have the ability to slide over one another, thus decreasing the thickness of the mucosa layer as the bladder fills and stretches to accommodate the increased urine volume. Depending on the degree of stretching of the bladder, the mucosa may be three

to eight cell layers thick. Compare the transitional epithelium of the mucosa to that shown in Figure 5.3h (p. 59).

3. Examine the heavy muscular wall (detrusor muscle), which consists of three irregularly arranged muscular layers. The innermost and outermost muscle layers are arranged longitudinally; the middle layer is arranged circularly. Attempt to differentiate the three muscle layers.

4. Compare the structure of the bladder wall you are observing to the structure of the ureter wall shown in Plate 43 in the Histology Atlas. How are the two organs similar histologically?

_____

_____

What is/are the most obvious differences?

_____

_____ ▬

DISSECTION AND IDENTIFICATION:
The Urinary System of the Cat

The structures of the reproductive and urinary systems are often considered together as the *urogenital system,* since they have common embryologic origins. However, the emphasis in this dissection is on identifying the structures of the urinary tract (Figures 28.8 and 28.9) with only a few references to contiguous reproductive structures. The anatomy of the reproductive system is studied in the cat dissection section of Exercise 29. ▬

ACTIVITY 4

Identifying Organs of the Urinary System

1. Don gloves. Obtain your dissection specimen, and place it ventral side up on the dissection tray. Reflect the abdominal viscera (most importantly the small intestine) to locate the kidneys high on the dorsal body wall. Note that the **kidneys** in the cat, as well as in the human, are retroperitoneal (behind the peritoneum).

2. Carefully remove the peritoneum, and clear away the bed of fat that invests the kidneys. Then locate the adrenal (suprarenal) glands that lie superiorly and medial to the kidneys.

3. Identify the **renal artery** (red latex injected), the **renal vein** (blue latex injected), and the ureter at the hilum region of the kidney. (You may find two renal veins leaving one kidney in the cat but not in humans.)

4. To observe the gross internal anatomy of the kidney, slit the connective tissue *fibrous capsule* encasing a kidney and peel it back. Make a midfrontal cut through the kidney and examine one cut surface with a hand lens to identify the granular *cortex* and the central darker *medulla,* which will appear striated. Notice that the cat's renal medulla consists of

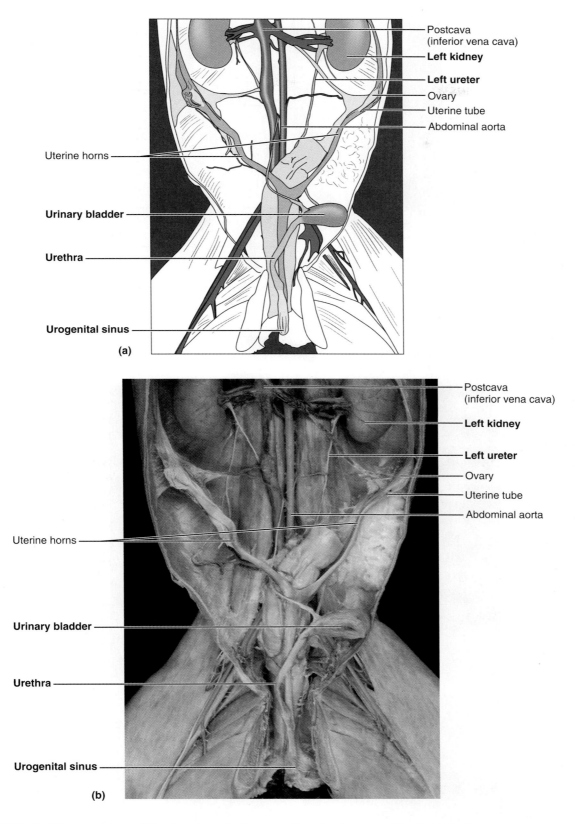

FIGURE 28.8 Urinary system of the female cat. (Reproductive structures are also indicated.)
(**a**) Diagrammatic view. (**b**) Photograph of female urogenital system.

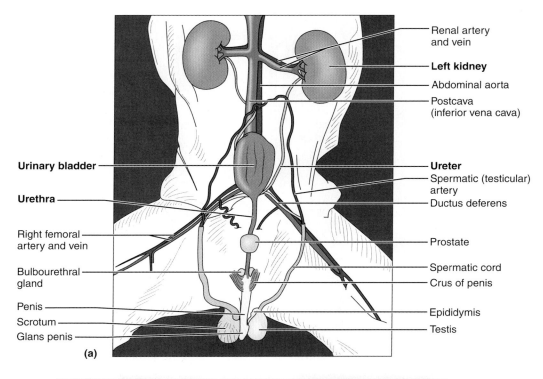

- Renal artery and vein
- **Left kidney**
- Abdominal aorta
- Postcava (inferior vena cava)

Urinary bladder —

Urethra —

- **Ureter**
- Spermatic (testicular) artery
- Ductus deferens

Right femoral artery and vein —

Bulbourethral gland —

Penis —
Scrotum —
Glans penis —

- Prostate
- Spermatic cord
- Crus of penis
- Epididymis
- Testis

(a)

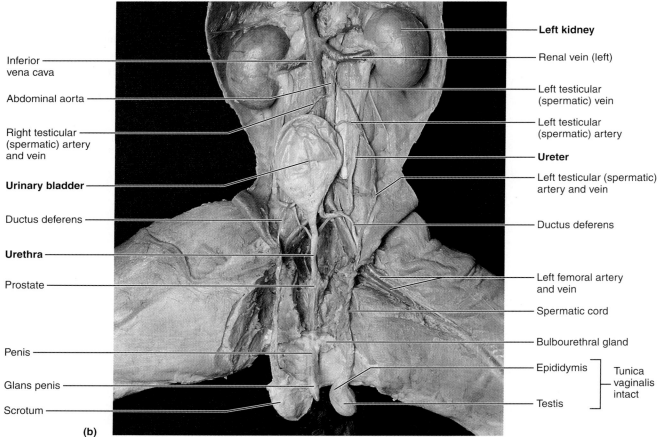

Inferior vena cava —

Abdominal aorta —

Right testicular (spermatic) artery and vein —

Urinary bladder —

Ductus deferens —

Urethra —

Prostate —

Penis —

Glans penis —

Scrotum —

- **Left kidney**
- Renal vein (left)
- Left testicular (spermatic) vein
- Left testicular (spermatic) artery
- **Ureter**
- Left testicular (spermatic) artery and vein
- Ductus deferens
- Left femoral artery and vein
- Spermatic cord
- Bulbourethral gland
- Epididymis   ⎫ Tunica
- Testis   ⎬ vaginalis intact

(b)

FIGURE 28.9 Urinary system of the male cat. (Reproductive structures are also indicated.)
(a) Diagrammatic view. **(b)** Photograph of male urogenital system.

just one pyramid as compared to the multipyramidal human kidney.

5.   Trace the **ureters** to the **urinary bladder,** a smooth muscular sac located superiorly to the small intestine. If your cat is a female, be careful not to confuse the ureters with the uterine tubes, which lie superior to the bladder in the same general region. (See Figure 28.8.) Observe the sites where the ureters enter the bladder. How would you describe the entrance point anatomically?

_____

_____

6.   Cut through the bladder wall, and examine the region where the **urethra** exits to see if you can discern any evidence of the *internal sphincter.*

7.   If your cat is a male, identify the prostate (part of the male reproductive system), which encircles the urethra distal to the neck of the bladder (Figure 28.9). Notice that the urinary bladder is somewhat fixed in position by ligaments.

8.   Using a probe, trace the urethra as it exits the bladder. In the male it goes through the prostate and enters the penis. In the female cat the urethra terminates in the **urogenital sinus,** a common chamber into which both the vagina and the urethra empty. In the human female, the vagina and the urethra have separate external openings. Dissection to expose the urethra along its entire length should not be done at this time because of possible damage to the reproductive structures, which you will study in Exercise 29.

9.   Before cleaning up the dissection materials, observe a cat of the opposite sex. Prepare your cat for storage as described in the box on p. 220. ▰

NAME_____

LAB TIME/DATE_____

Anatomy of the Urinary System

Gross Anatomy of the Human Urinary System

1. Complete the following statements.

The kidney is referred to as an excretory organ because it excretes __1__ wastes. It is also a major homeostatic organ because it maintains the electrolyte, __2__ , and __3__ balance of the blood.

Urine is continuously formed by the __4__ and is routed down the __5__ by the mechanism of __6__ to a storage organ called the __7__ . Eventually, the urine is conducted to the body __8__ by the urethra. In the male, the urethra is __9__ centimeters long and transports both urine and __10__ . The female urethra is __11__ centimeters long and transports only urine.

Voiding or emptying the bladder is called __12__ . Voiding has both voluntary and involuntary components. The voluntary sphincter is the __13__ sphincter. An inability to control this sphincter is referred to as __14__ .

1. _____

2. _____

3. _____

4. _____

5. _____

6. _____

7. _____

8. _____

9. _____

10. _____

11. _____

12. _____

13. _____

14. _____

2. What is the function of the fat cushion that surrounds the kidneys in life? _____

_____

3. Define *ptosis.* _____

_____

4. Why is incontinence a normal phenomenon in the child under 1½ to 2 years old? _____

_____

What events may lead to its occurrence in the adult? _____

_____

_____

5. Complete the labeling of the diagram to correctly identify the urinary system organs.

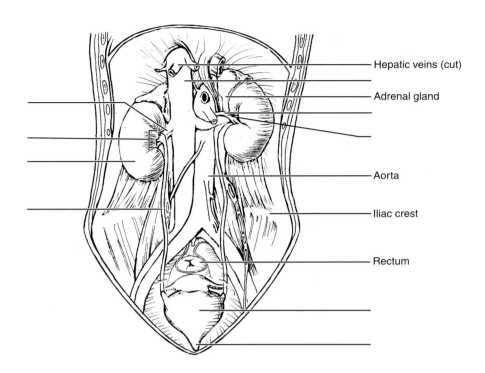

Hepatic veins (cut)

Adrenal gland

Aorta

Iliac crest

Rectum

Gross Internal Anatomy of the Pig or Sheep Kidney

6. Match the appropriate structure in column B to its description in column A.

Column A

Column B

_____ 1. smooth membrane, tightly adherent to the kidney surface

a. cortex

_____ 2. portion of the kidney containing mostly collecting ducts

b. fibrous capsule

_____ 3. portion of the kidney containing the bulk of the nephron structures

c. medulla

_____ 4. superficial region of kidney tissue

d. minor calyx

_____ 5. basinlike area of the kidney, continuous with the ureter

e. renal column

_____ 6. a cup-shaped extension of the pelvis that encircles the apex of a pyramid

f. renal pelvis

_____ 7. area of cortical tissue running between the medullary pyramids

Functional Microscopic Anatomy of the Kidney and Bladder

7. Match each lettered structure in the diagram of the nephron (and associated renal blood supply) with the correct name in the numbered list.

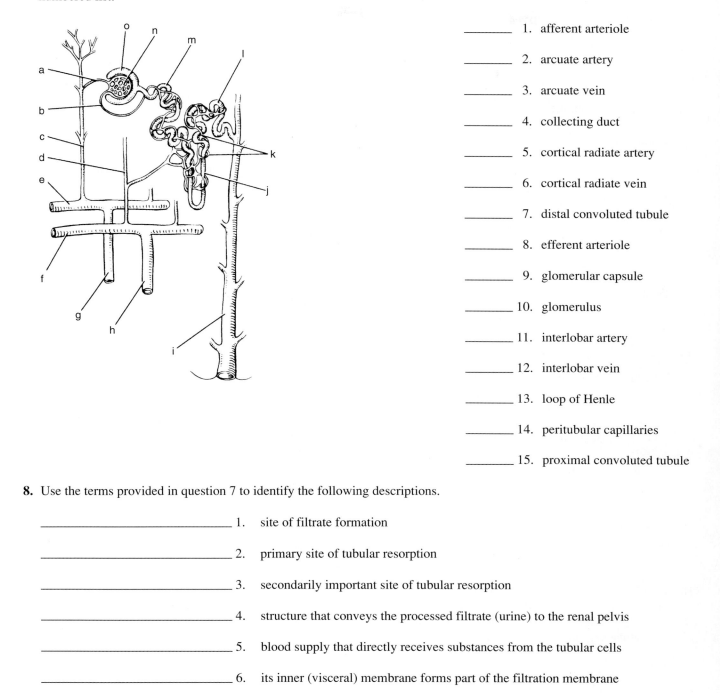

_____ 1. afferent arteriole

_____ 2. arcuate artery

_____ 3. arcuate vein

_____ 4. collecting duct

_____ 5. cortical radiate artery

_____ 6. cortical radiate vein

_____ 7. distal convoluted tubule

_____ 8. efferent arteriole

_____ 9. glomerular capsule

_____ 10. glomerulus

_____ 11. interlobar artery

_____ 12. interlobar vein

_____ 13. loop of Henle

_____ 14. peritubular capillaries

_____ 15. proximal convoluted tubule

8. Use the terms provided in question 7 to identify the following descriptions.

_____ 1. site of filtrate formation

_____ 2. primary site of tubular resorption

_____ 3. secondarily important site of tubular resorption

_____ 4. structure that conveys the processed filtrate (urine) to the renal pelvis

_____ 5. blood supply that directly receives substances from the tubular cells

_____ 6. its inner (visceral) membrane forms part of the filtration membrane

9. Explain _why_ the glomerulus is such a high-pressure capillary bed. _____

_____

How does its high-pressure condition aid its function of filtrate formation? _____

_____

10. What structural modification of certain tubule cells enhances their ability to resorb substances from the filtrate?

_____

11. Explain the mechanism of tubular secretion, and explain its importance in the urine formation process. _____

_____

_____

12. Compare and contrast the composition of blood plasma and glomerular filtrate. _____

_____

13. Trace a drop of blood from the time it enters the kidney in the renal artery until it leaves the kidney through the renal vein.

Renal artery → _____ ⎯⎯

_____

_____ → renal vein

14. Define _juxtaglomerular apparatus._ _____

_____

15. Label the figure using the key letters of the correct terms.

Key: a.   granular cells

      b.   cuboidal epithelium

      c.   macula densa

      d.   glomerular capsule (parietal layer)

      e.   distal convoluted tubule

16. Trace the anatomical pathway of a molecule of creatinine (metabolic waste) from the glomerular capsule to the urethra. Note each microscopic and/or gross structure it passes through in its travels. Name the subdivisions of the renal tubule.

Glomerular capsule → _____

_____

_____ → urethra

17. What is important functionally about the specialized epithelium (transitional epithelium) in the bladder?

_____

Dissection and Identification: The Urinary System of the Cat

18. How does the position of the kidneys in the cat differ from their position in humans? _____

_____

_____

_____

_____

19. How does the site of urethral emptying in the female cat differ from its termination point in the human female?

_____

_____

_____

20. What gland encircles the neck of the bladder in the male? _____ Is this part of the urinary system?

_____ What is its function? _____

_____

_____

Anatomy of the Reproductive System

M A T E R I A L S

☐ Three-dimensional models or large laboratory charts of the male and female reproductive tracts

☐ Prepared slides of sperm and of cross sections of the testis, penis, epididymis, seminal vesicles, uterine tube, uterus showing endometrium (proliferative phase), and ovary

☐ Compound microscope

☐ Immersion oil

☐ Dissection animal, tray, and instruments

☐ Disposable gloves

☐ Embalming fluid

☐ Bone cutters

☐ Small metric rulers

AIA See Appendix B, Exercise 29 for links to A.D.A.M.® Interactive Anatomy.

O B J E C T I V E S

1. To discuss the general function of the reproductive system.
2. To identify and name the structures of the male and female reproductive systems when provided with an appropriate model or diagram, and to discuss the general function of each.
3. To define *semen,* discuss its composition, and name the organs involved in its production.
4. To trace the pathway followed by a sperm from its site of formation to the external environment.
5. To name the exocrine and endocrine products of the testes and ovaries, indicating the cell types or structures responsible for the production of each.
6. To identify homologous structures of the male and female systems.
7. To discuss the microscopic structure of the penis, epididymis, uterine (fallopian) tube, and uterus, and to relate structure to function.
8. To define *gonad, ejaculation,* and *erection.*
9. To discuss the function of the fimbriae and ciliated epithelium of the uterine tubes.
10. To identify the fundus, body, and cervical regions of the uterus.
11. To define *endometrium, myometrium,* and *ovulation.*
12. To identify the major reproductive structures of the male and female dissection animal, and to recognize and discuss pertinent differences between the reproductive structures of humans and the dissection animal.

O ther organ systems of the body function primarily to sustain the existing individual, but the reproductive system is unique. Most simply stated, the biological function of the **reproductive system** is to perpetuate the species.

The essential organs of reproduction are the **gonads,** the testes and the ovaries, which produce the germ cells. The reproductive role of the male is to manufacture sperm and to deliver them to the female reproductive tract. The female, in turn, produces eggs. If the time is suitable, the combination of sperm and egg produces a fertilized egg, which is the first cell of a new individual. Once fertilization has occurred, the female uterus provides a nurturing, protective environment in which the embryo, later called the fetus, develops until birth.

Gross Anatomy of the Human Male Reproductive System

The primary reproductive organs of the male are the **testes,** the male gonads, which have both an exocrine (sperm production) and an endocrine (testosterone production) function. All other reproductive structures are conduits or sources of secretions, which aid in the safe delivery of the sperm to the body exterior or female reproductive tract.

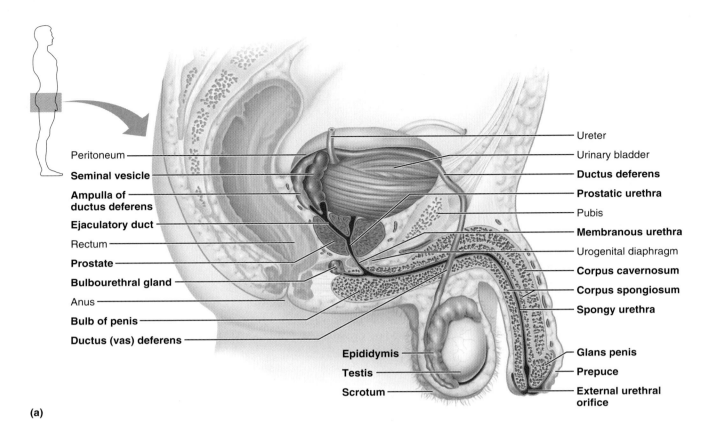

(a)

FIGURE 29.1 Reproductive system of the human male. (a) Midsagittal section.

Identifying Male Reproductive Organs

As the following organs and structures are described, locate them on Figure 29.1, and then identify them on a three-dimensional model of the male reproductive system or on a large laboratory chart.

The paired oval testes lie in the **scrotum** outside the abdominopelvic cavity. The temperature there (approximately 94°F, or 34°C) is slightly lower than body temperature, a requirement for producing viable sperm.

The accessory structures forming the *duct system* are the epididymis, the ductus deferens, the ejaculatory duct, and the urethra. The **epididymis** is an elongated structure running up the posterolateral aspect of the testis and capping its superior aspect. The epididymis forms the first portion of the duct system and provides a site for immature sperm entering it from the testis to complete their maturation process. The **ductus deferens,** or **vas deferens** (sperm duct), arches superiorly from the epididymis, passes through the inguinal canal into the pelvic cavity, and courses over the superior aspect of the urinary bladder. In life, the ductus deferens is enclosed along with blood vessels and nerves in a connective tissue sheath called the **spermatic cord** (see Figure 29.2). The terminus of the ductus deferens enlarges to form the region called the **ampulla,** which empties into the **ejaculatory duct.** During **ejaculation,** contraction of the ejaculatory duct propels the sperm through the prostate to the **prostatic urethra,** which in turn empties into the **membranous urethra** and then into the

spongy urethra, which runs through the length of the penis to the body exterior.

The spermatic cord is easily palpated through the skin of the scrotum. When a *vasectomy* is performed, a small incision is made in each side of the scrotum, and each ductus deferens is cut through or cauterized. Although sperm are still produced, they can no longer reach the body exterior; thus a man is sterile after this procedure (and 12 to 15 ejaculations to clear the conducting tubules).

The *accessory glands* include the prostate, the paired seminal vesicles, and the bulbourethral glands. These glands produce **seminal fluid,** the liquid medium in which sperm leave the body. The **seminal vesicles,** which produce about 60% of seminal fluid, lie at the posterior wall of the urinary bladder close to the terminus of the ductus deferens. They produce a viscous alkaline secretion containing fructose (a simple sugar) and other substances that nourish the sperm passing through the tract or that promote the fertilizing capability of sperm in some way. The duct of each seminal vesicle merges with a ductus deferens to form the ejaculatory duct (mentioned above); thus sperm and seminal fluid enter the urethra together.

The **prostate** encircles the urethra just inferior to the bladder. It secretes a milky fluid into the urethra, which plays a role in activating the sperm.

Hypertrophy of the prostate, a troublesome condition commonly seen in elderly men, constricts the urethra so that urination is difficult. ●

The **bulbourethral glands** are tiny, pea-shaped glands inferior to the prostate. They produce a thick, clear, alkaline mucus that drains into the membranous urethra. This secretion acts to wash residual urine out of the urethra when ejaculation

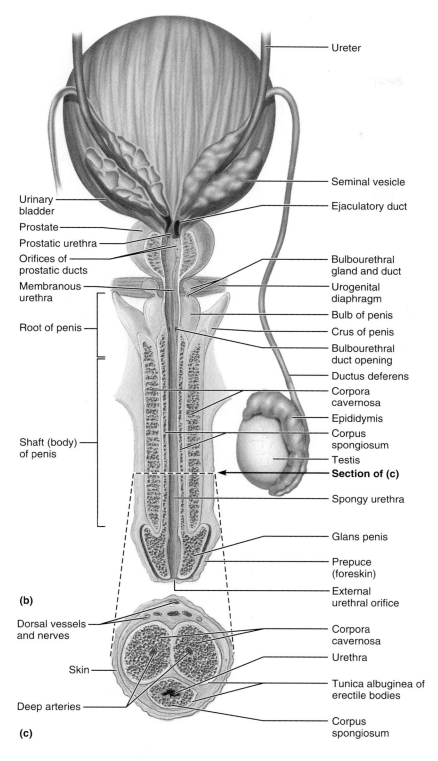

Ureter

Seminal vesicle

Ejaculatory duct

Urinary bladder

Prostate

Prostatic urethra

Orifices of prostatic ducts

Membranous urethra

Root of penis

Shaft (body) of penis

Bulbourethral gland and duct

Urogenital diaphragm

Bulb of penis

Crus of penis

Bulbourethral duct opening

Ductus deferens

Corpora cavernosa

Epididymis

Corpus spongiosum

Testis

Section of (c)

Spongy urethra

Glans penis

Prepuce (foreskin)

External urethral orifice

(b)

Dorsal vessels and nerves

Skin

Deep arteries

Corpora cavernosa

Urethra

Tunica albuginea of erectile bodies

Corpus spongiosum

(c)

FIGURE 29.1 (continued) (**b**) Longitudinal section of the penis. (**c**) Transverse section of the penis.

of **semen** (sperm plus seminal fluid) occurs. The relative alkalinity of seminal fluid also buffers the sperm against the acidity of the female reproductive tract.

The **penis,** part of the external genitalia of the male along with the scrotal sac, is the copulatory organ of the male. Designed to deliver sperm into the female reproductive tract, it consists of a shaft, which terminates in an enlarged tip,

the **glans penis** (see Figure 29.1a and b). The skin covering the penis is loosely applied, and it reflects downward to form a circular fold of skin, the **prepuce,** or **foreskin,** around the proximal end of the glans. (The foreskin is removed in the surgical procedure called *circumcision.*) Internally, the penis consists primarily of three elongated cylinders of erectile tissue, which engorge with blood during sexual excitement.

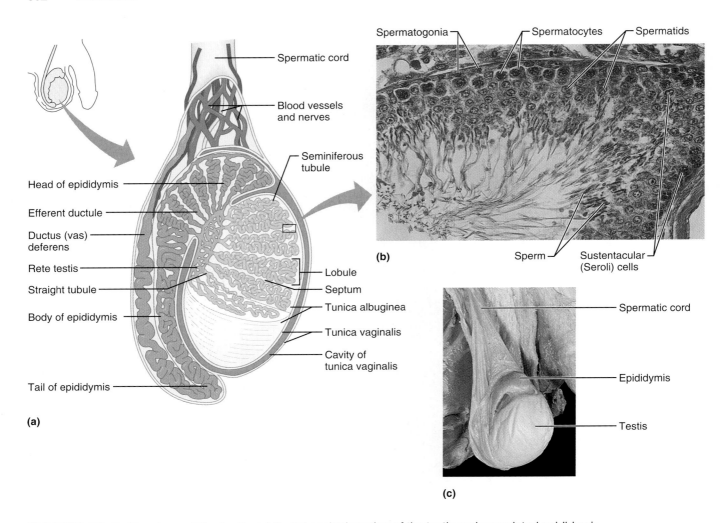

FIGURE 29.2 Structure of the testis. (a) Partial sagittal section of the testis and associated epididymis. **(b)** Micrograph of an active seminiferous tubule. **(c)** External view of a testis from a cadaver; same orientation as in (a).

This causes the penis to become rigid and enlarged so that it may more adequately serve as a penetrating device. This event is called **erection.** The paired dorsal cylinders are the **corpora cavernosa.** The single ventral **corpus spongiosum** surrounds the spongy urethra (see Figure 29.1c).

Conducting a Microscopic Study of Selected Male Reproductive Organs

Testis

Each testis is covered by a dense connective tissue capsule called the **tunica albuginea** (literally, "white tunic"). Extensions of this sheath enter the testis, dividing it into a number of lobes, each of which houses one to four highly coiled **seminiferous tubules,** the sperm-forming factories (Figure 29.2). The seminiferous tubules of each lobe converge to empty the sperm into a straight tubule which in turn delivers its contents into another set of tubules, the **rete testis,** at the mediastinum of the testis. Sperm traveling through the rete testis then enter the epididymis, located on the exterior aspect of the testis, as previously described. Lying between the

seminiferous tubules and softly padded with connective tissue are the **interstitial cells,** which produce testosterone, the hormonal product of the testis.

1. Obtain a slide of the testis and a microscope. Examine the slide under low power to identify the cross-sectional views of the cut seminiferous tubules. Then rotate the high-power lens into position and observe the wall of one of the cut tubules. As you work, refer to Figure 29.2b and Plate 46 in the Histology Atlas to make the following identifications.

2. Scrutinize the cells at the periphery of the tubule. The cells in this area are the **spermatogonia,** which undergo frequent mitoses to increase their number and maintain their population. About half of the spermatogonia's "offspring" become **spermatocytes,** spermatogenic cells that undergo meiosis, which leads to the formation of spermatids having half the usual genetic composition. The remaining daughter cells resulting from mitotic divisions of spermatogonia remain at the tubule periphery to maintain the germ cell line.

3. Observe the cells in the middle of the tubule wall. There you should see a large number of spermatocytes that are obviously undergoing a nuclear division process. Look for coarse clumps of chromatin or threadlike chromosomes

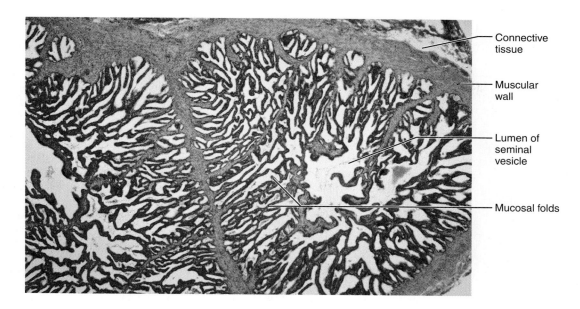

FIGURE 29.3 Histology of a seminal vesicle. Cross-sectional view showing the elaborate network of mucosal folds (40×). The vesicular secretion is seen in the lumen.

(visible only during nuclear division) which have the appearance of coiled springs.

4. Examine the cells at the tubule lumen. Identify the small round-nucleated spermatids, many of which may appear lopsided and look as though they are starting to lose their cytoplasm. See if you can find a spermatid embedded in a elongated cell type, a **sustentacular** or **Sertoli cell,** which extends inward from the periphery of the tubule. The sustentacular cells nourish the spermatids as they begin their transformation into sperm. Also in the adluminal area, locate sperm, which can be identified by their tails. The sperm develop directly from the spermatids by the loss of extraneous cytoplasm and the development of a propulsive tail.

5. Identify the testosterone-producing **interstitial cells** lying external to and between the seminiferous tubules. The interstitial cells produce testosterone, which stimulates sperm production.

6. Obtain a prepared slide of human sperm and view it with the oil immersion lens. Compare it to the photograph of sperm in Plate 47 in the Histology Atlas. Identify the head (essentially the nucleus of the spermatid), acrosome, and tail regions. (The acrosome, which caps the nucleus anteriorly, contains enzymes involved in sperm penetration of the egg.) In the space below, draw a few sperm as viewed through a microscope.

Penis

Obtain a cross section of the penis. Scan the tissue under low power to identify the urethra and the cavernous bodies. Compare your observations to Figure 29.1c and Plate 45 in the Histology Atlas. Observe the lumen of the urethra carefully. What type of epithelium do you see?

Explain the function of this type of epithelium.

_____

_____

_____

Seminal Vesicle

Obtain a slide showing a cross-sectional view of the seminal vesicle. Examine the slide at low magnification to get an overall view of the highly folded mucosa of this gland. Switch to higher magnification, and notice that the folds of the vesicle protrude into the lumen where they divide further, giving the lumen a honeycomb look (Figure 29.3). Notice that the loose connective tissue lamina propria is underlain by smooth muscle fibers—first a circular layer, and then a longitudinal layer. Identify the vesicular secretion in the lumen, a viscous substance that is rich in sugar and prostaglandins.

Epididymis

Obtain a cross section of the epididymis. Notice the abundant tubule cross sections resulting from the fact that the coiling epididymis tubule has been cut through many times in the specimen. Using Figure 29.2b and Plate 44 in the Histology Atlas as guides, look for sperm in the lumen of the tubule. Examine the composition of the tubule wall carefully. Identify

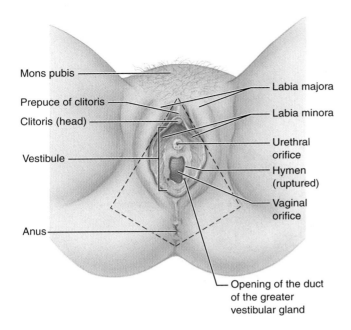

Mons pubis

Prepuce of clitoris

Clitoris (head)

Vestibule

Anus

Labia majora

Labia minora

Urethral orifice

Hymen (ruptured)

Vaginal orifice

Opening of the duct of the greater vestibular gland

FIGURE 29.4 External genitalia of the human female. (The region enclosed by dashed lines is the perineum.)

the *stereocilia* of the pseudostratified columnar epithelial lining. These nonmotile microvilli absorb excess fluid and pass nutrients to the sperm in the lumen. Now identify the smooth muscle layer. What do you think the function of the smooth muscle is?

_____

_____

_____

Gross Anatomy of the Human Female Reproductive System

The **ovaries** (female gonads) are the primary reproductive organs of the female. Like the testes of the male, the ovaries produce both an exocrine product (eggs, or ova) and endocrine products (estrogens and progesterone). The other accessory structures of the female reproductive system transport, house, nurture, or otherwise serve the needs of the reproductive cells and/or the developing fetus.

The reproductive structures of the female are generally considered in terms of internal organs and external organs, or external genitalia.

ACTIVITY 3

Identifying Female Reproductive Organs

As you read the descriptions of these structures, locate them on Figures 29.4 and 29.5 and then on the female reproductive system model or large laboratory chart.

External Genitalia

The **external genitalia (vulva)** consist of the mons pubis, the labia majora and minora, the clitoris, the urethral and vaginal orifices, the hymen, and the greater vestibular glands. The **mons pubis** is a rounded fatty eminence overlying the pubic symphysis. Running inferiorly and posteriorly from the mons pubis are two elongated, pigmented, hair-covered skin folds, the **labia majora,** which are homologous to the scrotum of the male. These enclose two smaller hair-free folds, the **labia minora.** (Terms indicating only one of the two folds in each case are *labium majus* and *minus,* respectively.) The labia minora, in turn, enclose a region called the **vestibule,** which contains many structures—the clitoris, most anteriorly, followed by the urethral orifice and the vaginal orifice. The diamond-shaped region between the anterior end of the labial folds, the ischial tuberosities laterally, and the anus posteriorly is called the **perineum.**

The **clitoris** is a small protruding structure, homologous to the male penis. Like its counterpart, it is composed of highly sensitive, erectile tissue. It is hooded by skin folds of the anterior labia minora, referred to as the **prepuce of the clitoris.** The urethral orifice, which lies posterior to the clitoris, is the outlet for the urinary system and has no reproductive function in the female. The vaginal opening is partially closed by a thin fold of mucous membrane called the **hymen** and is flanked by the pea-sized, mucus-secreting **greater vestibular glands.** These glands (see Figure 29.4) lubricate the distal end of the vagina during coitus.

Internal Genitalia

The internal female organs include the vagina, uterus, uterine tubes, ovaries, and the ligaments and supporting structures that suspend these organs in the pelvic cavity. The **vagina** extends for approximately 10 cm (4 inches) from the vestibule to the uterus superiorly. It serves as a copulatory organ and birth canal and permits passage of the menstrual flow. The pear-shaped **uterus,** situated between the bladder and the rectum, is a muscular organ with its narrow end, the **cervix,** directed inferiorly. The major portion of the uterus is referred to as the **body;** its superior rounded region above the entrance of the uterine tubes is called the **fundus.** A fertilized egg is implanted in the uterus, which houses the embryo or fetus during its development.

In some cases, the fertilized egg may implant in a uterine tube or even on the abdominal viscera, creating an **ectopic pregnancy.** Such implantations are usually unsuccessful and may even endanger the mother's life because the uterine tubes cannot accommodate the increasing size of the fetus. ●

The **endometrium,** the thick mucosal lining of the uterus, has a superficial **functional layer,** or **stratum functionalis,** that sloughs off periodically (about every 28 days) in response to cyclic changes in the levels of ovarian hormones in the woman's blood. This sloughing-off process, which is accompanied by bleeding, is referred to as **menstruation,** or **menses.** The deeper **basal layer,** or **stratum basalis,** forms a new functionalis after menstruation ends.

The **uterine,** or **fallopian, tubes** enter the superolateral region of the uterus and extend laterally for about 10 cm (4 inches) toward the ovaries in the peritoneal cavity. The distal ends of the tubes are funnel-shaped and have fingerlike

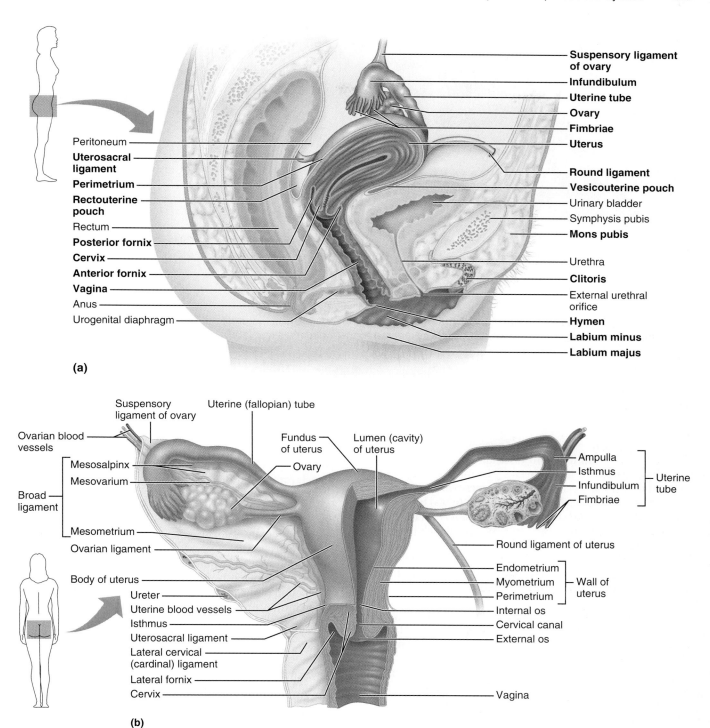

(a)

(b)

FIGURE 29.5 Internal reproductive organs of the human female. (a) Midsagittal section of the human female reproductive system. **(b)** Posterior view.

projections called **fimbriae.** Unlike the male duct system, there is no actual contact between the female gonad and the initial part of the female duct system—the uterine tube.

Because of this open passageway between the female reproductive organs and the peritoneal cavity, reproductive system infections, such as gonorrhea and other **sexually transmitted diseases (STDs),** can cause widespread inflammations of the pelvic viscera, a condition called **pelvic inflammatory disease (PID).** ●

The internal female organs are all retroperitoneal, except the ovaries. They are supported and suspended somewhat freely by ligamentous folds of peritoneum. The peritoneum takes an undulating course. From the pelvic cavity floor it moves superiorly over the top of the bladder, reflects over the anterior and posterior surfaces of the uterus, and then over the rectum, and up the posterior body wall. The fold that encloses the uterine tubes and uterus and secures them to the lateral body walls is the **broad ligament** (Figure 29.5b). The

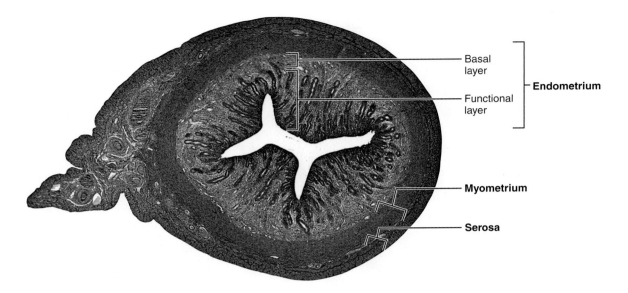

FIGURE 29.6 Cross-sectional view of the uterine wall. The mucosa is in the proliferative stage. Notice that the basal layer has virtually no glands compared to the functional layer (100×).

part of the broad ligament specifically anchoring the uterus is called the **mesometrium** and that anchoring the uterine tubes, the **mesosalpinx.** The **round ligaments,** fibrous cords that run from the uterus to the labia majora, and the **uterosacral ligaments,** which course posteriorly to the sacrum, also help attach the uterus to the body wall. The ovaries are supported medially by the **ovarian ligament** (extending from the uterus to the ovary), laterally by the **suspensory ligaments,** and posteriorly by a fold of the broad ligament, the **mesovarium.**

Within the ovaries, the female gametes (eggs) begin their development in saclike structures called *follicles.* The growing follicles also produce *estrogens.* When a developing egg has reached the appropriate stage of maturity, it is ejected from the ovary in an event called **ovulation.** The ruptured follicle is then converted to a second type of endocrine gland, called a *corpus luteum,* which secretes progesterone (and some estrogens).

The flattened almond-shaped ovaries lie adjacent to the uterine tubes but are not connected to them; consequently, an ovulated egg* enters the pelvic cavity. The waving fimbriae of the uterine tubes create fluid currents that, if successful, draw the egg into the lumen of the uterine tube, where it begins its passage to the uterus, propelled by the cilia of the tubal walls. The usual and most desirable site of fertilization is the uterine tube, because the journey to the uterus takes about 3 to 4 days and an egg is viable for up to 24 hours after it is expelled from the ovary. Thus, sperm must swim upward through the vagina and uterus and into the uterine tubes to reach the egg. This is an arduous journey, because they must swim against the downward current created by ciliary action—rather like swimming against the tide!

*To simplify this discussion, the ovulated cell is called an egg. What is actually expelled from the ovary is an earlier stage of development called a secondary oocyte.

ACTIVITY 4

Conducting a Microscopic Study of Selected Female Reproductive Organs

Wall of the Uterus

Obtain a cross-sectional view of the uterine wall. Identify the three layers of the uterine wall—the endometrium, myometrium, and serosa. Also identify the two strata of the endometrium: the functional layer and the basal layer. The latter forms a new functional layer each month. Figure 29.6 of the proliferative endometrium may be of some help in this study.

As you study the slide, notice that the bundles of smooth muscle are oriented in several different directions. What is the function of the **myometrium** (smooth muscle layer) during the birth process?

_____

_____

Sketch a small portion of the uterine wall in the space below. Label the functional and basal layers.

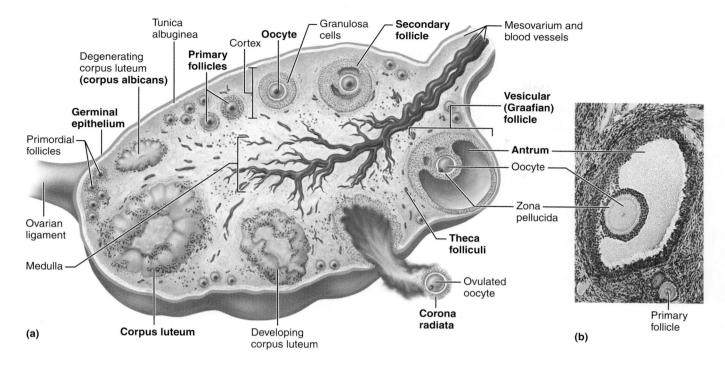

FIGURE 29.7 **Anatomy of the human ovary. (a)** The ovary has been sectioned to reveal the follicles in its interior. Note that not all the structures would appear in the ovary at the same time. **(b)** Photomicrograph of a mature vesicular (Graafian) follicle (60×).

Uterine Tube

Obtain a prepared slide of a cross-sectional view of a uterine tube for examination. Using Plate 48 in the Histology Atlas as a guide, notice the highly folded mucosa (the folds nearly fill the tubule lumen). Then switch to high power to examine the ciliated secretory epithelium.

Ovary

Because many different stages of ovarian development exist within the ovary at any one time, a single microscopic preparation will contain follicles at many different stages of development. Obtain a cross section of ovary tissue, and identify the following structures. Refer to Figure 29.7 as you work. (See also Plate 49 of the Histology Atlas.)

Germinal epithelium: Outermost layer of the ovary.

Primary follicle: One or a few layers of cuboidal follicle cells surrounding the large central developing ovum, or **oocyte,** the immature egg.

Secondary (growing) follicles: Follicles consisting of several layers of follicle (granulosa) cells surrounding the central developing ovum, and beginning to show evidence of fluid accumulation and **antrum** (central cavity) formation.

Vesicular (Graafian) follicle: At this stage of development, the follicle has a large antrum containing fluid produced by

the granulosa cells. The developing ovum is pushed to one side of the follicle and is surrounded by a capsule of several layers of granulosa cells called the **corona radiata** (radiating crown). When the immature ovum (secondary oocyte) is released, it enters the uterine tubes with its corona radiata intact. The connective tissue stroma (background tissue) adjacent to the mature follicle forms a capsule that encloses the follicle and is called the **theca folliculi.** (See also Plate 19 in the Histology Atlas.)

Corpus luteum: A solid glandular structure or a structure containing a scalloped lumen that develops from the ovulated follicle. (See Plate 20 in the Histology Atlas.) ▬

DISSECTION AND IDENTIFICATION:

The Reproductive System of the Cat

Don gloves and obtain your cat, a dissection tray, and the necessary dissecting instruments. After you have completed the study of the reproductive structures of your specimen, observe a cat of the opposite sex. (The following instructions assume that the abdominal cavity has been opened in previous dissection exercises.) ▬

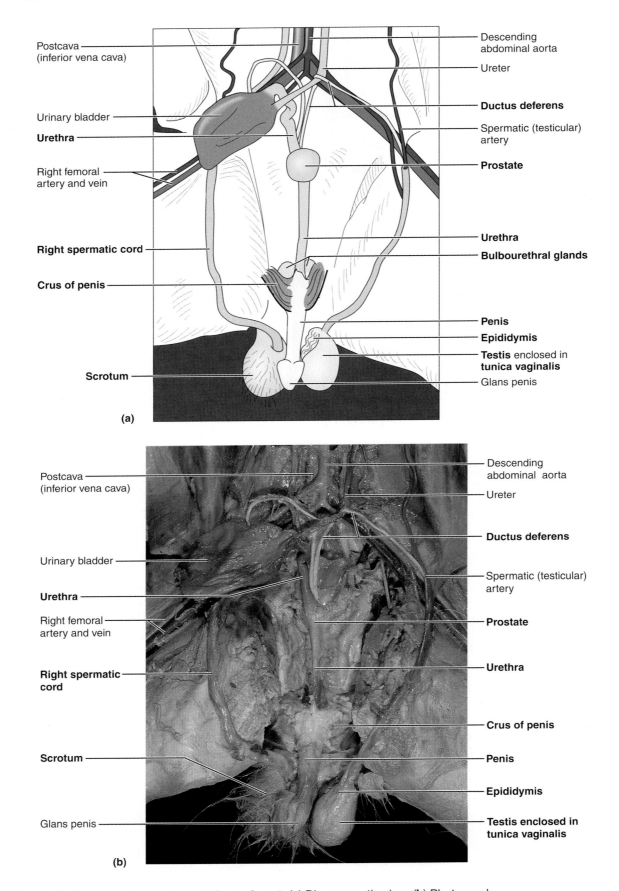

FIGURE 29.8 Reproductive system of the male cat. (a) Diagrammatic view. **(b)** Photograph.

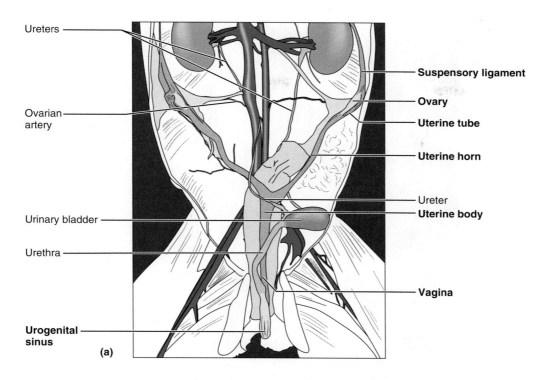

Ureters

Ovarian artery

Urinary bladder

Urethra

Urogenital sinus

Suspensory ligament

Ovary

Uterine tube

Uterine horn

Ureter
Uterine body

Vagina

(a)

FIGURE 29.9 Reproductive system of the female cat. (a) Diagrammatic view.

ACTIVITY 5

Identifying Organs of the Male Reproductive System

Refer to Figure 29.8 as you identify the male structures.

1. Identify the **penis** and notice the prepuce covering the glans. Carefully cut through the skin overlying the penis to expose the cavernous tissue beneath, then cross section the penis to see the relative positioning of the three cavernous bodies.

2. Identify the **scrotum,** and then carefully make a shallow incision through the scrotum to expose the **testes.** Notice that the scrotum is divided internally.

3. Lateral to the medial aspect of the scrotal sac, locate the **spermatic cord,** which contains the spermatic (testicular) artery, vein, and nerve, as well as the ductus deferens, and follow it up through the inguinal canal into the abdominal cavity. (It is not necessary to cut through the pelvic bone; a slight tug on the spermatic cord in the scrotal sac region will reveal its position in the abdominal cavity.) Carefully loosen the spermatic cord from the connective tissue investing it, and follow its course as it travels superiorly in the pelvic cavity. Then, follow the ductus deferens as it loops over the ureter and then courses posterior to the bladder and enters the prostate. Using bone cutters, carefully cut through the pubic symphysis to follow the urethra.

4. Notice that the **prostate,** an enlarged whitish mass abutting the urethra, is comparatively smaller in the cat than in the human, and it is more distal to the bladder. In the human, the prostate is immediately adjacent to the base of the bladder. Carefully slit open the prostate to follow the **ductus deferens** to the urethra, which exits from the bladder midline. The

male cat urethra, like that of the human, serves as both a urinary and a sperm duct. In the human, the ductus deferens is joined by the duct of the seminal vesicle to form the ejaculatory duct, which enters the prostate. Seminal vesicles are not present in the cat.

5. Trace the **urethra** to the proximal ends of the cavernous tissues of the penis, each of which is anchored to the ischium by a band of connective tissue called the **crus** of the penis. The crus is covered ventrally by the ischiocavernosus muscle, and the **bulbourethral gland** lies beneath it.

6. Once again, turn your attention to a testis. Cut it from its attachment to the spermatic cord and carefully slit open the **tunica vaginalis** capsule enclosing it. Identify the **epididymis** running along one side of the testis. Make a longitudinal cut through the testis and epididymis. Can you see the tubular nature of the epididymis and the rete testis portion of the testis with the naked eye? ▪

ACTIVITY 6

Identifying Organs of the Female Reproductive System

Refer to Figure 29.9 showing a dissection of the urogenital system of the female cat as you identify the structures described below.

1. Unlike the pear-shaped simplex, or one-part, uterus of the human, the uterus of the cat is Y-shaped (bipartite or bicornuate) and consists of a **uterine body** from which two **uterine horns** (cornua) diverge. Such an enlarged uterus enables the animal to produce litters. Examine the abdominal cavity and identify the bladder and the body of the uterus lying just dorsal to it.

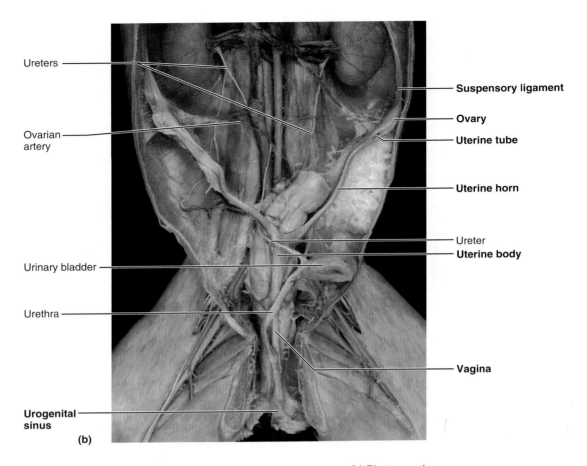

Ureters

Ovarian artery

Urinary bladder

Urethra

Urogenital sinus

Suspensory ligament

Ovary

Uterine tube

Uterine horn

Ureter
Uterine body

Vagina

(b)

FIGURE 29.9 (*continued*) **Reproductive system of the female cat. (b)** Photograph.

2. Follow one of the uterine horns as it travels superiorly in the body cavity. Identify the thin mesentery (the *broad ligament*), which helps anchor it and other reproductive structures to the body wall. Approximately halfway up the length of the uterine horn, it should be possible to identify the more important *round ligament,* a cord of connective tissue extending laterally and posteriorly from the uterine horn to the region of the body wall that would correspond to the inguinal region of the male.

3. Examine the **uterine tube** and **ovary** at the distal end of the uterine horn just caudal to the kidney. Observe how the funnel-shaped end of the uterine tube curves around the ovary. As in the human, the distal end of the tube is fimbriated, or fringed, and the tube is lined with ciliated epithelium. The uterine tubes of the cat are tiny and much shorter than in the human. Identify the **ovarian ligament,** a short thick cord that extends from the uterus to the ovary and anchors the ovary to the body wall. Also observe the *ovarian artery* and *vein* passing through the mesentery to the ovary and uterine structures.

4. Return to the body of the uterus and follow it caudad to the bony pelvis. Use bone cutters to cut through the median line of the pelvis (the pubic symphysis), cutting carefully so you do not damage the urethra deep to it. Expose the pelvic region by pressing the thighs dorsally. Follow the uterine body caudally to the vagina, and note the point where the urethra draining the bladder and the **vagina** enter a common

chamber, the **urogenital sinus.** How does this anatomical arrangement compare to that seen in the human female?

_____

_____

5. On the cat's exterior, observe the **vulva,** which is similar to the human vulva. Identify the slim **labia majora** surrounding the urogenital opening.

6. To determine the length of the vagina, which is difficult to ascertain by external inspection, slit through the vaginal wall just superior to the urogenital sinus and cut toward the body of the uterus with scissors. Reflect the cut edges, and identify the muscular cervix of the uterus. (Measure the distance between the urogenital sinus and the cervix.) Approximately how long is the vagina of the cat?

_____

7. When you have completed your observations of both male and female cats, clean your dissecting instruments and tray and properly wrap the cat for storage as described in the box on p. 220. ▪

NAME_____

LAB TIME/DATE_____

Anatomy of the Reproductive System

Gross Anatomy of the Human Male Reproductive System

1. List the two principal functions of the testis. _____

and _____

2. Identify all indicated structures or portions of structures on the diagrammatic view of the male reproductive system below.

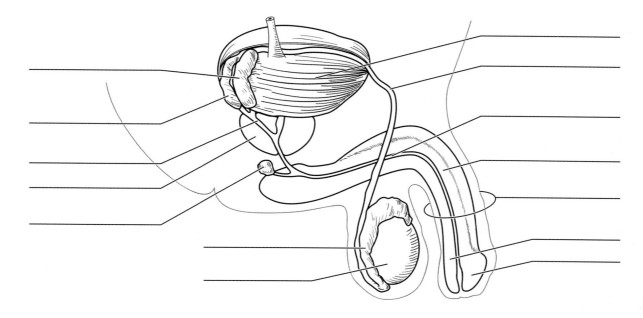

3. A common part of any physical examination of the male is palpation of the prostate. How is this accomplished?

(Think!) _____

4. How might enlargement of the prostate interfere with urination or the reproductive ability of the male?

_____

_____

5. Why are the testes located in the scrotum rather than inside the ventral body cavity? _____

_____

6. Match the terms in column B to the descriptive statements in column A.

Column A

_____ 1. copulatory organ/penetrating device

_____ 2. site of sperm/androgen production

_____ 3. muscular passageway conveying sperm to the ejaculatory duct; in the spermatic cord

_____ 4. transports both sperm and urine

_____ 5. sperm maturation site

_____ 6. location of the testis in adult males

_____ 7. loose fold of skin encircling the glans penis

_____ 8. portion of the urethra between the prostate and the penis

_____ 9. empties a secretion into the prostatic urethra

_____ 10. empties a secretion into the membranous urethra

Column B

a. bulbourethral glands

b. ductus (vas) deferens

c. epididymis

d. glans penis

e. membranous urethra

f. penis

g. prepuce

h. prostate

i. prostatic urethra

j. seminal vesicles

k. scrotum

l. spongy urethra

m. testes

7. Describe the composition of semen, and name all structures contributing to its formation. _____

_____

_____

8. Of what importance is the fact that seminal fluid is alkaline? _____

_____

9. What structures compose the spermatic cord? _____

_____

Where is it located? _____

10. Using the following terms, trace the pathway of sperm from the testes to the urethra: rete testis, epididymis, seminiferous tubule, ductus deferens.

_____ → _____ → _____ → _____

Gross Anatomy of the Human Female Reproductive System

11. Name the structures composing the external genitalia, or vulva, of the female.

_____

12. On the following diagram of a frontal section of a portion of the female reproductive system, identify all indicated structures.

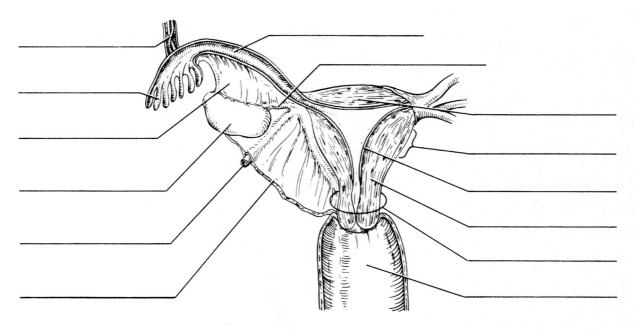

13. Identify the female reproductive system structures described below.

_____ 1. site of fetal development

_____ 2. copulatory canal

_____ 3. "fertilized egg" typically formed here

_____ 4. becomes erectile during sexual excitement

_____ 5. duct extending superolaterally from the uterus

_____ 6. partially closes the vaginal canal; a membrane

_____ 7. produces oocytes, estrogens, and progesterone

_____ 8. fingerlike ends of the uterine tube

14. Do any sperm enter the pelvic cavity of the female? Why or why not? _____

_____

15. What is an ectopic pregnancy, and how can it happen? _____

_____

_____

_____

16. Put the following vestibular-perineal structures in their proper order from the anterior to the posterior aspect: vaginal orifice, anus, urethral opening, and clitoris.

Anterior limit: _____ → _____ → _____ → _____

17. Name the male structure that is homologous to the female structures named below.

labia majora _____   clitoris _____

18. Assume a couple has just consummated the sex act and the male's sperm have been deposited in the woman's vagina. Trace the pathway of the sperm through the female reproductive tract.

_____

19. Define *ovulation.* _____

Microscopic Anatomy of Selected Male and Female Reproductive Organs

20. The testis is divided into a number of lobes by connective tissue. Each of these lobes contains one to four _____

_____, which converge on a _____ which, in turn, empties into a

tubular region at the testis mediastinum called the _____.

21. What is the function of the cavernous bodies seen in the male penis? _____

_____

_____

22. Name the three layers of the uterine wall from the inside out.

_____, _____, _____

Which of these is sloughed during menses? _____

Which contracts during childbirth? _____

23. What is the function of the stereocilia exhibited by the epithelial cells of the mucosa of the epididymis? _____

_____

24. On the diagram showing the sagittal section of the human testis, correctly identify all structures provided with leader lines.

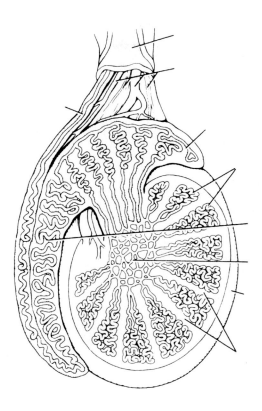

Dissection and Identification: The Reproductive System of the Cat

25. The female cat has a _____ uterus; that of the human female is _____ .

Explain the difference in structure of these two uterine types. _____

_____

_____

26. What reproductive advantage is conferred by the feline uterine type?

_____

_____

27. Cite differences noted between the cat and the human relative to the following structures:

uterine tubes or oviducts _____

_____

site of entry of ductus deferens into the urethra _____

_____

_____

location of the prostate ————————————————————————————————

——

——

seminal vesicles ———————————————————————————————————————

——

urethral and vaginal openings in the female

——

——

Surface Anatomy Roundup

M A T E R I A L S

- ☐ Articulated skeletons
- ☐ Three-dimensional models or charts of the skeletal muscles of the body
- ☐ Hand mirror
- ☐ Stethoscope
- ☐ Alcohol swabs
- ☐ Washable markers

O B J E C T I V E S

1. To define *surface anatomy* and explain why it is an important field of study, and to define *palpation*.
2. To describe and palpate the major surface features of the cranium, face, and neck.
3. To describe the easily palpated bony and muscular landmarks of the back, and to locate the vertebral spines on the living body.
4. To list the bony surface landmarks of the thoracic cage and explain how they relate to the major soft organs of the thorax, and to explain how to find the second to eleventh ribs.
5. To name and palpate the important surface features on the anterior abdominal wall, and to explain how to palpate a full bladder.
6. To define and explain the following: *linea alba, umbilical hernia,* examination for an inguinal hernia, *linea semilunaris,* and *McBurney's point.*
7. To locate and palpate the main surface features of the upper limb.
8. To explain the significance of the antecubital fossa, pulse points in the distal forearm, and the anatomical snuff box.
9. To describe and palpate the surface landmarks of the lower limb.
10. To explain exactly where to administer an injection in the gluteal region and in the other major sites of intramuscular injection.

Surface anatomy is a valuable branch of anatomical and medical science. True to its name, **surface anatomy** does indeed study the *external surface* of the body, but more importantly, it also studies *internal* organs as they relate to external surface landmarks and as they are seen and felt through the skin. Feeling internal structures through the skin with the fingers is called **palpation** (literally, "touching").

Surface anatomy is living anatomy, better studied in live people than in cadavers. It can provide a great deal of information about the living skeleton (almost all bones can be palpated) and about the muscles and blood vessels that lie near the body surface. Furthermore, a skilled examiner can learn a good deal about the heart, lungs, and other deep organs by performing a surface assessment. Thus, surface anatomy serves as the basis of the standard physical examination. For those planning a career in the health sciences or physical education, a study of surface anatomy will show you where to take pulses, where to insert tubes and needles, where to locate broken bones and inflamed muscles, and where to listen for the sounds of the lungs, heart, and intestines.

We will take a regional approach to surface anatomy, exploring the head first and proceeding to the trunk and the limbs. You will be observing and palpating your own body as you work through the exercise, because your body is the best learning tool of all. To aid your exploration of living anatomy, skeletons and muscle models or charts are provided around the lab so that you can review the bones and muscles you will encounter. For skin sites you are asked to mark that are personally unreachable, it probably would be best to choose a male student as a subject.

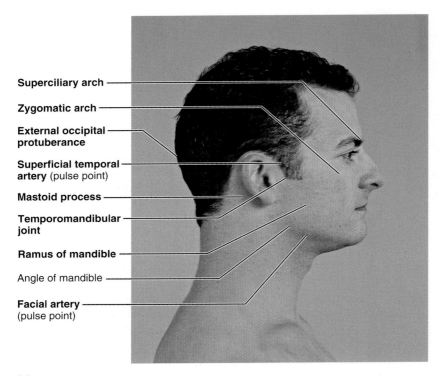

Superciliary arch

Zygomatic arch

External occipital protuberance

Superficial temporal artery (pulse point)

Mastoid process

Temporomandibular joint

Ramus of mandible

Angle of mandible

Facial artery (pulse point)

(a)

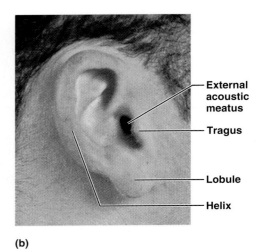

External acoustic meatus

Tragus

Lobule

Helix

(b)

FIGURE 30.1 Surface anatomy of the head. (a) Lateral aspect. **(b)** Close-up of an auricle.

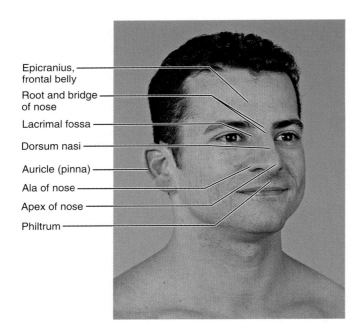

Epicranius, frontal belly

Root and bridge of nose

Lacrimal fossa

Dorsum nasi

Auricle (pinna)

Ala of nose

Apex of nose

Philtrum

FIGURE 30.2 Surface structures of the face.

A C T I V I T Y   1

Palpating Landmarks of the Head

The head (Figures 30.1 and 30.2) is divided into the cranium and the face.

Cranium

1. Run your fingers over the superior surface of your head. Notice that the underlying cranial bones lie very near the surface. Proceed to your forehead and palpate the **superciliary arches** (brow ridges) directly superior to your orbits (see Figure 30.1).

2. Move your hand to the posterior surface of your skull, where you can feel the knoblike **external occipital protuberance.** Run your finger directly laterally from this projection to feel the ridgelike *superior nuchal line* on the occipital bone. This line, which marks the superior extent of the muscles of the posterior neck, serves as the boundary between the head and the neck. Now feel the prominent **mastoid process** on each side of the cranium just posterior to your ear.

3. The **frontal belly** of the epicranius (see Figure 30.2) inserts superiorly onto the broad aponeurosis called the *galea aponeurotica* (Table 14.1, pp. 190 and 192) that covers the superior surface of the cranium. This aponeurosis binds tightly to the overlying subcutaneous tissue and skin to form the true **scalp.** Push on your scalp, and confirm that it slides freely over the underlying cranial bones. Because the scalp is only loosely bound to the skull, people can easily be "scalped" (in industrial accidents, for example). The scalp is richly vascularized by a large number of arteries running through its subcutaneous tissue. Most arteries of the body constrict and close after they are cut or torn, but those in the

scalp are unable to do so because they are held open by the dense connective tissue surrounding them.

What do these facts suggest about the amount of bleeding that accompanies scalp wounds?

_____

_____

Face

The surface of the face is divided into many different regions, including the *orbital, nasal, oral* (mouth), and *auricular* (ear) areas.

1.   Trace a finger around the entire margin of the bony orbit. The **lacrimal fossa,** which contains the tear-gathering lacrimal sac, may be felt on the medial side of the eye socket.

2.   Touch the most superior part of your nose, its **root,** which lies between the eyebrows (see Figure 30.2). Just inferior to this, between your eyes, is the **bridge** of the nose formed by the nasal bones. Continue your finger's progress inferiorly along the nose's anterior margin, the **dorsum nasi,** to its tip, the **apex.** Place one finger in a nostril and another finger on the flared winglike **ala** that defines the nostril's lateral border. Then feel the **philtrum,** the shallow vertical groove on the upper lip below the nose.

3.   Grasp your **auricle,** the shell-like part of the external ear that surrounds the opening of the **external acoustic meatus** (Figure 30.1). Now trace the ear's outer rim, or **helix,** to the **lobule** (earlobe) inferiorly. The lobule is easily pierced, and since it is not highly sensitive to pain, it provides a convenient place to hang an earring or obtain a drop of blood for clinical blood analysis. Feel the **tragus,** the stiff projection just anterior to the external acoustic meatus. Next, place a finger on your temple just anterior to the auricle. There, you will be able to feel the pulsations of the **superficial temporal artery,** which ascends to supply the scalp (Figure 30.1).

4.   Run your hand anteriorly from your ear toward the orbit, and feel the **zygomatic arch** just deep to the skin. This bony arch is easily broken by blows to the face. Next, place your fingers on the skin of your face, and feel it bunch and stretch as you contort your face into smiles, frowns, and grimaces. You are now monitoring the action of several of the subcutaneous **muscles of facial expression** (Table 14.1, pp. 190 and 192).

5.   On your lower jaw, palpate the parts of the bony **mandible:** its anterior body and its posterior ascending **ramus.** Press on the skin over the mandibular ramus, and feel the **masseter muscle** bulge when you clench your teeth. Palpate the anterior border of the masseter, and trace it to the mandible's inferior margin. At this point, you will be able to detect the pulse of your **facial artery** (Figure 30.1). Finally, to feel the **temporomandibular joint,** place a finger directly anterior to the external acoustic meatus of your ear, and open and close your mouth several times. The bony structure you feel moving is the *head of the mandible.* ▬

ACTIVITY 2

Palpating Landmarks of the Neck

Bony Landmarks

1.   Run your fingers inferiorly along the back of your neck, in the posterior midline, to feel the *spinous processes* of the cervical vertebrae. The spine of C_7, the *vertebra prominens,* is especially prominent.

2.   Now, beginning at your chin, run a finger inferiorly along the anterior midline of your neck (Figure 30.3). The first hard

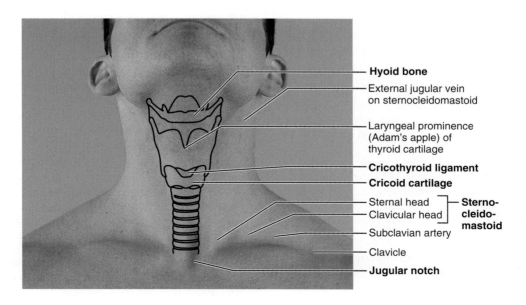

- Hyoid bone
- External jugular vein on sternocleidomastoid
- Laryngeal prominence (Adam's apple) of thyroid cartilage
- **Cricothyroid ligament**
- **Cricoid cartilage**
- Sternal head ⎤ **Sterno-**
- Clavicular head ⎦ **cleido-mastoid**
- Subclavian artery
- Clavicle
- **Jugular notch**

FIGURE 30.3 Anterior surface of the neck. A diagram of the underlying skeleton of the larynx is superimposed on a photograph of the neck.

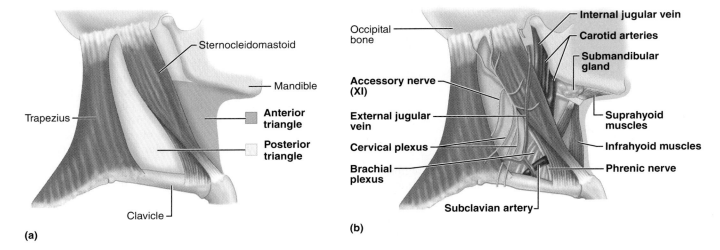

FIGURE 30.4 Anterior and posterior triangles of the neck. (**a**) Boundaries of the triangles. (**b**) Some contents of the triangles.

structure you encounter will be the U-shaped **hyoid bone,** which lies in the angle between the floor of the mouth and the vertical part of the neck. Directly inferior to this, you will feel the **laryngeal prominence** (Adam's apple) of the thyroid cartilage. Just inferior to the laryngeal prominence, your finger will sink into a soft depression (formed by the **cricothyroid ligament**) before proceeding onto the rounded surface of the **cricoid cartilage.** Now swallow several times, and feel the whole larynx move up and down.

3.   Continue inferiorly to the trachea. Attempt to palpate the *isthmus of the thyroid gland,* which feels like a spongy cushion over the second to fourth tracheal rings (see Figure 30.3). Then, try to palpate the two soft lateral *lobes* of your thyroid gland along the sides of the trachea.

4.   Move your finger all the way inferiorly to the root of the neck, and rest it in the **jugular notch,** the depression in the superior part of the sternum between the two clavicles. By pushing deeply at this point, you can feel the cartilage rings of the trachea.

Muscles

The **sternocleidomastoid** is the most prominent muscle in the neck and the neck's most important surface landmark. You can best see and feel it when you turn your head to the side.

Obtain a hand mirror, hold it in front of your face, and turn your head sharply from right to left several times. You will be able to see both heads of this muscle, the **sternal head** medially and the **clavicular head** laterally (Figure 30.3). Several important structures lie beside or beneath the sternocleidomastoid:

•   The *cervical lymph nodes* lie both superficial and deep to this muscle. (Swollen cervical nodes provide evidence of infections or cancer of the head and neck.)

•   The *common carotid artery* and *internal jugular vein* lie just deep to the sternocleidomastoid, a relatively superficial location that exposes these vessels to danger in slashing wounds to the neck.

•   Just lateral to the inferior part of the sternocleidomastoid is the large **subclavian artery** on its way to supply the upper limb. By pushing on the subclavian artery at this point, one can stop the bleeding from a wound anywhere in the associated limb.

•   Just anterior to the sternocleidomastoid, superior to the level of your larynx, you can feel a carotid pulse—the pulsations of the **external carotid artery** (Figure 30.4).

•   The *external jugular vein* descends vertically, just superficial to the sternocleidomastoid and deep to the skin (Figure 30.3). To make this vein "appear" on your neck, stand before the mirror, and gently compress the skin superior to your clavicle with your fingers.

Triangles of the Neck

The sternocleidomastoid muscles divide each side of the neck into the posterior and anterior triangles (Figure 30.4a).

1.   The **posterior triangle** is defined by the sternocleidomastoid anteriorly, the trapezius posteriorly, and the clavicle inferiorly. Palpate the borders of the posterior triangle.

The **anterior triangle** is defined by the inferior margin of the mandible superiorly, the midline of the neck anteriorly, and the sternocleidomastoid posteriorly.

2.   The contents of these two triangles are shown in Figure 30.4b. The posterior triangle contains many important nerves and blood vessels, including the **accessory nerve** (cranial nerve XI), most of the **cervical plexus,** and the **phrenic nerve.** In the inferior part of the triangle are the **external jugular vein,** the trunks of the **brachial plexus,** and the **subclavian artery.** These structures are relatively superficial and are easily cut or injured by wounds to the neck.

In the neck's anterior triangle, important structures include the **submandibular gland,** the **suprahyoid** and **infrahyoid muscles,** and parts of the **carotid arteries** and **jugular veins** that lie superior to the sternocleidomastoid.

•   Palpate your carotid pulse.

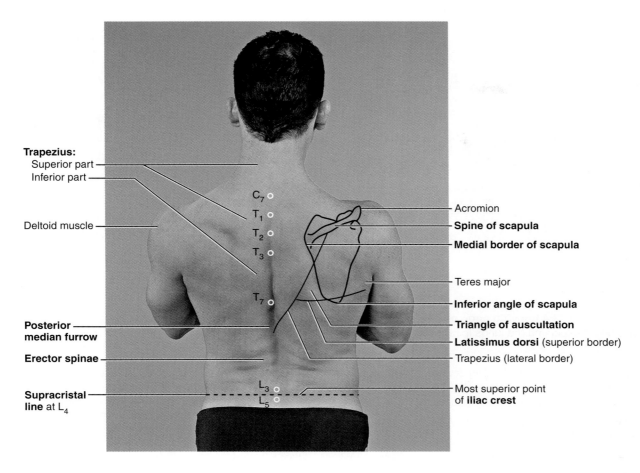

Trapezius:
Superior part
Inferior part

Deltoid muscle

C₇
T₁
T₂
T₃

T₇

Posterior median furrow

Erector spinae

Supracristal line at L₄

L₃
L₅

Acromion
Spine of scapula
Medial border of scapula

Teres major
Inferior angle of scapula
Triangle of auscultation
Latissimus dorsi (superior border)
Trapezius (lateral border)

Most superior point of **iliac crest**

FIGURE 30.5 Surface anatomy of the back.

A wound to the posterior triangle of the neck can lead to long-term loss of sensation in the skin of the neck and shoulder, as well as partial paralysis of the sternocleido-mastoid and trapezius muscles. Explain these effects.

_____

_____ ●

ACTIVITY 3

Palpating Landmarks of the Trunk

The trunk of the body consists of the thorax, abdomen, pelvis, and perineum. The *back* includes parts of all of these regions, but for convenience it is treated separately.

The Back

Bones

1. The vertical groove in the center of the back is called the **posterior median furrow** (Figure 30.5). The *spinous processes* of the vertebrae are visible in the furrow when the spinal column is flexed.

- Palpate a few of these processes on your partner's back (C_7 and T_1 are the most prominent and the easiest to find).

- Also palpate the posterior parts of some ribs, as well as the prominent **spine of the scapula** and the scapula's long **medial border.**

    The scapula lies superficial to ribs 2 to 7; its **inferior angle** is at the level of the spinous process of vertebra T_7. The medial end of the scapular spine lies opposite the T_3 spinous process.

2. Now feel the **iliac crests** (superior margins of the iliac bones) in your own lower back. You can find these crests effortlessly by resting your hands on your hips. Locate the most superior point of each crest, a point that lies roughly halfway between the posterior median furrow and the lateral side of the body (see Figure 30.5). A horizontal line through these two superior points, the **supracristal line,** intersects L_4, providing a simple way to locate that vertebra. The ability to locate L_4 is essential for performing a *lumbar puncture,* a procedure in which the clinician inserts a needle into the vertebral canal of the spinal column directly superior or inferior to L_4 and withdraws cerebrospinal fluid.

3. The *sacrum* is easy to palpate just superior to the cleft in the buttocks. You can feel the *coccyx* in the extreme inferior part of that cleft, just posterior to the anus.

Muscles The largest superficial muscles of the back are the **trapezius** superiorly and **latissimus dorsi** inferiorly

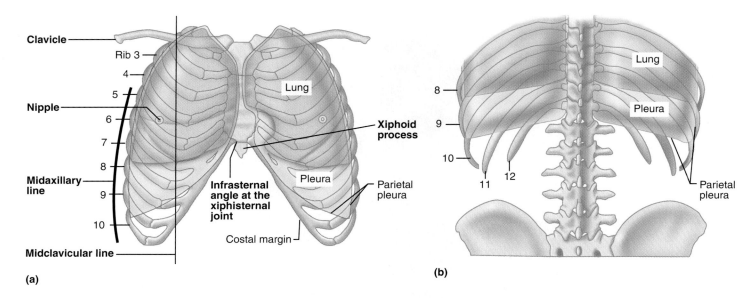

FIGURE 30.6 The bony rib cage as it relates to the underlying lungs and pleural cavities. Both the pleural cavities (blue) and the lungs (pink) are outlined. (**a**) Anterior view. (**b**) Posterior view.

(Figure 30.5). Furthermore, the deeper **erector spinae** muscles are very evident in the lower back, flanking the vertebral column like thick vertical cords.

1.   Shrug your shoulders to feel the trapezius contracting just deep to the skin.

2.   Feel your partner's erector spinae muscles contract and bulge as he straightens his spine from a slightly bent-over position.

The superficial muscles of the back fail to cover a small area of the rib cage called the **triangle of auscultation** (see Figure 30.5). This triangle lies just medial to the inferior part of the scapula. Its three boundaries are formed by the trapezius medially, the latissimus dorsi inferiorly, and the scapula laterally. The physician places a stethoscope over the skin of this triangle to listen for lung sounds (*auscultation* = listening). To hear the lungs clearly, the doctor first asks the patient to fold the arms together in front of the chest and then flex the trunk.

What do you think is the precise reason for having the patient take this action?

_____

_____

3.   Have your partner assume the position just described. After cleaning the earpieces with an alcohol swab, use the stethoscope to auscultate the lung sounds. Compare the clarity of the lung sounds heard over the triangle of auscultation to that over other areas of the back.

The Thorax

Bones

1.   Start exploring the anterior surface of your partner's bony *thoracic cage* (Figures 30.6 and 30.7) by defining the

extent of the *sternum.* Use a finger to trace the sternum's triangular *manubrium* inferior to the jugular notch, its flat *body,* and the tongue-shaped **xiphoid process.** Now palpate the ridgelike **sternal angle,** where the manubrium meets the body of the sternum. Locating the sternal angle is important because it directs you to the second ribs (which attach to it). Once you find the second rib, you can count down to identify every other rib in the thorax (except the first and sometimes the twelfth rib, which lie too deep to be palpated). The sternal angle is a highly reliable landmark—it is easy to locate, even in overweight people.

2.   By locating the individual ribs, you can mentally "draw" a series of horizontal lines of "latitude" that you can use to map and locate the underlying visceral organs of the thoracic cavity. Such mapping also requires lines of "longitude," so let us construct some vertical lines on the wall of your partner's trunk. As he lifts an arm straight up in the air, extend a line inferiorly from the center of the axilla onto his lateral thoracic wall. This is the **midaxillary line** (see Figure 30.6a). Now estimate the midpoint of his **clavicle,** and run a vertical line inferiorly from that point toward the groin. This is the **midclavicular line,** and it will pass about 1 cm medial to the nipple.

3.   Next, feel along the V-shaped inferior edge of the rib cage, the **costal margin.** At the **infrasternal angle,** the superior angle of the costal margin, lies the **xiphisternal joint.** Deep to the xiphisternal joint, the heart lies on the diaphragm.

4.   The thoracic cage provides many valuable landmarks for locating the vital organs of the thoracic and abdominal cavities. On the anterior thoracic wall, ribs 2–6 define the superior-to-inferior extent of the female breast, and the fourth intercostal space indicates the location of the **nipple** in men, children, and small-breasted women. The right costal margin runs across the anterior surface of the liver and gallbladder. Surgeons must be aware of the inferior margin of the *pleural cavities* because if they accidentally cut into one of these cavities, a lung collapses. The inferior pleural margin lies

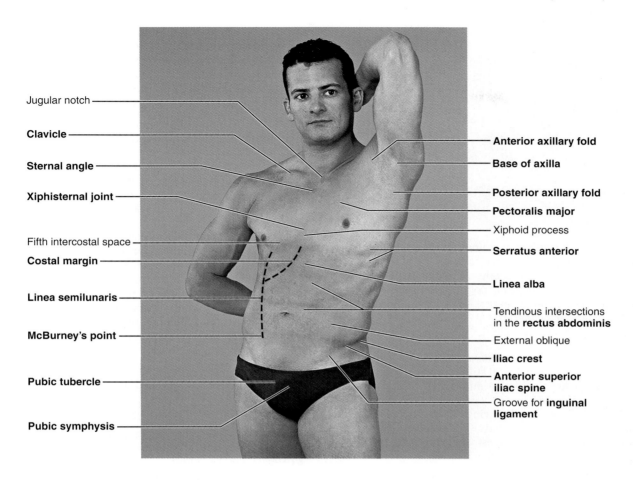

Jugular notch

Clavicle

Sternal angle

Xiphisternal joint

Fifth intercostal space

Costal margin

Linea semilunaris

McBurney's point

Pubic tubercle

Pubic symphysis

Anterior axillary fold

Base of axilla

Posterior axillary fold

Pectoralis major

Xiphoid process

Serratus anterior

Linea alba

Tendinous intersections in the **rectus abdominis**

External oblique

Iliac crest

Anterior superior iliac spine

Groove for **inguinal ligament**

FIGURE 30.7 The anterior thorax and abdomen.

adjacent to vertebra T_{12} near the posterior midline (see Figure 30.6b) and runs horizontally across the back to reach rib 10 at the midaxillary line. From there, the pleural margin ascends to rib 8 in the midclavicular line (see Figure 30.6a) and to the level of the xiphisternal joint near the anterior midline. The *lungs* do not fill the inferior region of the pleural cavity. Instead, their inferior borders run at a level that is two ribs superior to the pleural margin, until they meet that margin near the xiphisternal joint.

5.   The relationship of the *heart* to the thoracic cage is considered in Exercise 23. We will review that information here. In essence, the superior right corner of the heart lies at the junction of the third rib and the sternum; the superior left corner lies at the second rib, near the sternum; the inferior left corner lies in the fifth intercostal space in the midclavicular line; and the inferior right corner lies at the sternal border of the sixth rib. You may wish to outline the heart on your chest or that of your lab partner by connecting the four corner points with a washable marker.

Muscles   The main superficial muscles of the anterior thoracic wall are the **pectoralis major** and the anterior slips of the **serratus anterior** (Figure 30.7).

•   Using Figure 30.7 as a guide, try to palpate these two muscles on your chest. They both contract during push-ups, and you can confirm this by pushing yourself up from your

desk with one arm while palpating the muscles with your opposite hand. ▪

Palpating Landmarks of the Abdomen

Bony Landmarks

The anterior abdominal wall (see Figure 30.7) extends inferiorly from the costal margin to an inferior boundary that is defined by several landmarks. Palpate these landmarks as they are described below.

1.   **Iliac crest.** Locate the iliac crests by resting your hands on your hips.

2.   **Anterior superior iliac spine.** Representing the most anterior point of the iliac crest, this spine is a prominent landmark. It can be palpated in everyone, even those who are overweight. Run your fingers anteriorly along the iliac crest to its end.

3.   **Inguinal ligament.** The inguinal ligament, indicated by a groove on the skin of the groin, runs medially from the anterior superior iliac spine to the pubic tubercle of the pubic bone.

4.   **Pubic crest.** You will have to press deeply to feel this crest on the pubic bone near the median **pubic symphysis.**

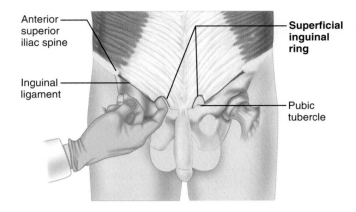

Anterior superior iliac spine

Inguinal ligament

Superficial inguinal ring

Pubic tubercle

FIGURE 30.8 Clinical examination for an inguinal hernia in a male. The examiner palpates the patient's pubic tubercle, pushes superiorly to invaginate the scrotal skin into the superficial inguinal ring, and asks the patient to cough. If an inguinal hernia exists, it will push inferiorly and touch the examiner's fingertip.

The **pubic tubercle,** the most lateral point of the pubic crest, is easier to palpate, but you will still have to push deeply. **Inguinal hernias** occur immediately superior to the inguinal ligament and may exit from a medial opening called the **superficial inguinal ring.** To locate this ring, one would palpate the pubic tubercle (Figure 30.8). The procedure used by the physician to test whether a male has an inguinal hernia is depicted in Figure 30.8. ●

Muscles and Other Surface Features

The central landmark of the anterior abdominal wall is the *umbilicus* (navel). Running superiorly and inferiorly from the umbilicus is the **linea alba** (white line), represented in the skin of lean people by a vertical groove (see Figure 30.7). The linea alba is a tendinous seam that extends from the xiphoid process to the pubic symphysis, just medial to the rectus abdominis muscles (Table 14.3, pp. 195–197). The linea alba is a favored site for surgical entry into the abdominal cavity because the surgeon can make a long cut through this line with no muscle damage and minimal bleeding. Several kinds of hernias involve the umbilicus and the linea alba. In an **acquired umbilical hernia,** the linea alba weakens until intestinal coils push through it just superior to the navel. The herniated coils form a bulge just deep to the skin.

Another type of umbilical hernia is a **congenital umbilical hernia,** present in some infants: The umbilical hernia is seen as a cherry-sized bulge deep to the skin of the navel that enlarges whenever the baby cries. Congenital umbilical hernias are usually harmless, and most correct themselves automatically before the child's second birthday. ●

1. **McBurney's point** is the spot on the anterior abdominal skin that lies directly superficial to the base of the appendix (see Figure 30.7). It is located one-third of the way along a line between the right anterior superior iliac spine and the umbilicus. Try to find it on your body.

McBurney's point is the most common site of incision in appendectomies, and it is often the place where the pain of appendicitis is experienced most acutely. Pain at McBurney's point after the pressure is removed (rebound tenderness) can indicate appendicitis. This is not a *precise* method of diagnosis, however.

2. Flanking the linea alba are the vertical straplike **rectus abdominis** muscles (see Figure 30.7). Feel these muscles contract just deep to your skin as you do a bent-knee sit-up (or as you bend forward after leaning back in your chair). In the skin of lean people, the lateral margin of each rectus muscle makes a groove known as the **linea semilunaris** (half-moon line). On your right side, estimate where your linea semilunaris crosses the costal margin of the rib cage. The *gallbladder* lies just deep to this spot, so this is the standard point of incision for gallbladder surgery. In muscular people, three horizontal grooves can be seen in the skin covering the rectus abdominis. These grooves represent the **tendinous insertions** (or **intersections** or **inscriptions**), fibrous bands that subdivide the rectus muscle. Because of these subdivisions, each rectus abdominis muscle presents four distinct bulges. Try to identify these insertions on yourself or your partner.

3. The only other major muscles that can be seen or felt through the anterior abdominal wall are the lateral **external obliques.** Feel these muscles contract as you cough, strain, or raise your intra-abdominal pressure in some other way.

4. Recall that the anterior abdominal wall can be divided into four quadrants (see Figure 1.7a). A clinician listening to a patient's **bowel sounds** places the stethoscope over each of the four abdominal quadrants, one after another. Normal bowel sounds, which result as peristalsis moves air and fluid through the intestine, are high-pitched gurgles that occur every 5 to 15 seconds.

• Use the stethoscope to listen to your own or your partner's bowel sounds.

Abnormal bowel sounds can indicate intestinal disorders. Absence of bowel sounds indicates a halt in intestinal activity, which follows long-term obstruction of the intestine, surgical handling of the intestine, peritonitis, or other conditions. Loud tinkling or splashing sounds, by contrast, indicate an increase in intestinal activity. Such loud sounds may accompany gastroenteritis (inflammation and upset of the GI tract) or a partly obstructed intestine. ●

The Pelvis and Perineum

The bony surface features of the *pelvis* are considered with the bony landmarks of the abdomen (p. 523) and the gluteal region (p. 528). Most *internal* pelvic organs are not palpable through the skin of the body surface. A full *bladder,* however, becomes firm and can be felt through the abdominal wall just superior to the pubic symphysis. A bladder that can be palpated more than a few centimeters above this symphysis is retaining urine and dangerously full, and it should be drained by catheterization. ▬

Palpating Landmarks of the Upper Limb

Axilla

The **base of the axilla** is the groove in which the underarm hair grows (see Figure 30.7). Deep to this base lie the axillary *lymph nodes* (which swell and can be palpated in breast cancer), the large *axillary vessels* serving the upper limb, and much of the brachial plexus. The base of the axilla forms a "valley" between two thick, rounded ridges, the **axillary folds.** Just anterior to the base, clutch your **anterior axillary fold,** formed by the pectoralis major muscle. Then grasp your **posterior axillary fold.** This fold is formed by the latissimus dorsi and teres major muscles of the back as they course toward their insertions on the humerus.

Shoulder

1.   Again locate the prominent spine of the scapula posteriorly. Follow the spine to its lateral end, the flattened **acromion** on the shoulder's summit. Then, palpate the **clavicle** anteriorly, tracing this bone from the sternum to the shoulder (Figure 30.9). Notice the clavicle's curved shape.

2.   Now locate the junction between the clavicle and the acromion on the superolateral surface of your shoulder, at the **acromioclavicular joint.** To find this joint, thrust your arm anteriorly repeatedly until you can palpate the precise point of pivoting action.

3.   Next, place your fingers on the **greater tubercle** of the humerus. This is the most lateral bony landmark on the superior surface of the shoulder. It is covered by the thick **deltoid muscle,** which forms the rounded superior part of the shoulder.

Intramuscular injections are often given into the deltoid, about 5 cm (2 inches) inferior to the greater tubercle (refer to Figure 30.17a, p. 529).

Arm

Remember, according to anatomists, the arm runs only from the shoulder to the elbow, and not beyond.

1.   In the arm, palpate the humerus along its entire length, especially along its medial and lateral sides.

2.   Feel the **biceps brachii** muscle contract on your anterior arm when you flex your forearm against resistance. The medial boundary of the biceps is represented by the **medial bicipital furrow** (see Figure 30.9). This groove contains the large *brachial artery,* and by pressing on it with your fingertips you can feel your *brachial pulse.* Recall that the brachial artery is the artery routinely used in measuring blood pressure with a sphygmomanometer.

3.   All three heads of the **triceps brachii** muscle (lateral, long, and medial) are visible through the skin of a muscular person (Figure 30.10).

Elbow Region

1.   In the distal part of your arm, near the elbow, palpate the two projections of the humerus, the **lateral** and **medial epicondyles** (Figures 30.9 and 30.10). Midway between the epicondyles, on the posterior side, feel the **olecranon process** of the ulna, which forms the point of the elbow.

2.   Confirm that the two epicondyles and the olecranon all lie in the same horizontal line when the elbow is extended. If these three bony processes do not line up, the elbow is dislocated.

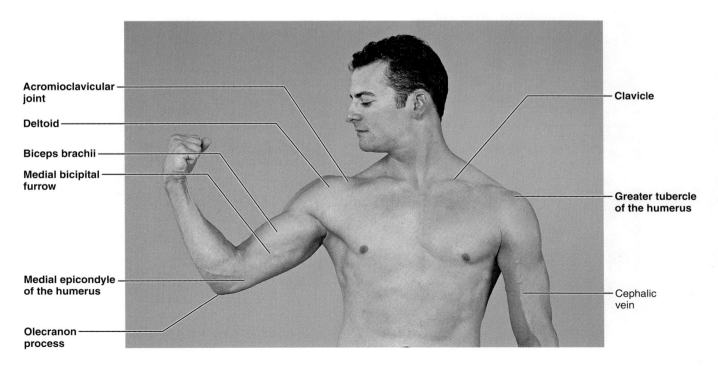

FIGURE 30.9 Shoulder and arm.

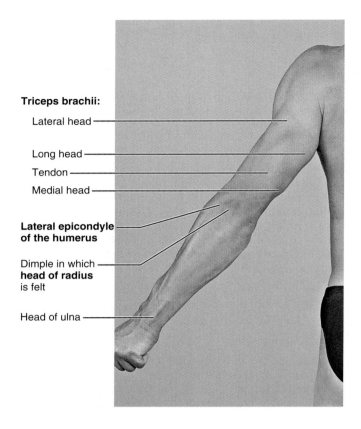

Triceps brachii:

Lateral head

Long head

Tendon

Medial head

Lateral epicondyle of the humerus

Dimple in which **head of radius** is felt

Head of ulna

FIGURE 30.10 Surface anatomy of the upper limb, posterior view.

3.   Now feel along the posterior surface of the medial epicondyle. You are palpating your ulnar nerve.

4.   On the anterior surface of the elbow is a triangular depression called the **antecubital fossa,** or **cubital fossa** (Figure 30.11). The triangle's superior *base* is formed by a horizontal line between the humeral epicondyles; its two inferior sides are defined by the **brachioradialis** and **pronator teres** muscles (see Figure 30.11b). Try to define these boundaries on your own limb. To find the brachioradialis muscle, flex your forearm against resistance, and watch this muscle bulge through the skin of your lateral forearm. To feel your pronator teres contract, palpate the antecubital fossa as you pronate your forearm against resistance. (Have your partner provide the resistance.)

Superficially, the antecubital fossa contains the **median cubital vein** (see Figure 30.11a). Clinicians often draw blood from this superficial vein and insert intravenous (IV) catheters into it to administer medications, transfused blood, and nutrient fluids. The large **brachial artery** lies just deep to the median cubital vein (see Figure 30.11b), so a needle must be inserted into the vein from a shallow angle (almost parallel to the skin) to avoid puncturing the artery. Other structures that lie deep in the fossa are also shown in Figure 30.11b.

5.   The median cubital vein interconnects the larger **cephalic** and **basilic veins** of the upper limb. These veins are visible through the skin of lean people (see Figure 30.11a). Examine your arm to see if your cephalic and basilic veins are visible.

Forearm and Hand

The two parallel bones of the forearm are the medial *ulna* and the lateral *radius.*

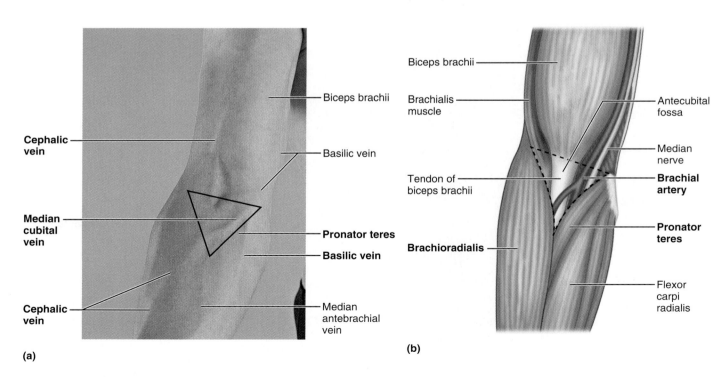

Biceps brachii

Cephalic vein

Basilic vein

Median cubital vein

Pronator teres

Basilic vein

Cephalic vein

Median antebrachial vein

(a)

Biceps brachii

Brachialis muscle

Antecubital fossa

Median nerve

Tendon of biceps brachii

Brachial artery

Brachioradialis

Pronator teres

Flexor carpi radialis

(b)

FIGURE 30.11 The antecubital (cubital) fossa on the anterior surface of the right elbow (outlined by the triangle). (a) Photograph. (b) Diagram of deeper structures in the fossa.

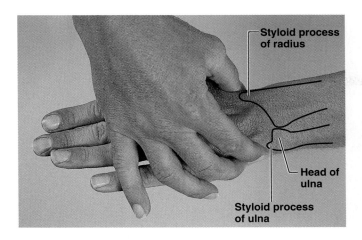

FIGURE 30.12 A way to locate the styloid processes of the ulna and radius. The right hand is palpating the left hand in this picture. Note that the head of the ulna is not the same as its styloid process. The styloid process of the radius lies about 1 cm distal to the styloid process of the ulna.

1.   Feel the ulna along its entire length as a sharp ridge on the posterior forearm (confirm that this ridge runs inferiorly from the olecranon process). As for the radius, you can feel its distal half, but most of its proximal half is covered by muscle. You can, however, feel the rotating **head** of the radius. To do this, extend your forearm, and note that a dimple forms on the posterior lateral surface of the elbow region (see Figure 30.10). Press three fingers into this dimple, and rotate your free hand as if you were turning a doorknob. You will feel the head of the radius rotate as you perform this action.

2.   Both the radius and ulna have a knoblike **styloid process** at their distal ends. Figure 30.12 shows a way to locate these processes. Do not confuse the ulna's styloid process with the conspicuous **head of the ulna,** from which the styloid process stems. Confirm that the styloid process of the radius lies about 1 cm (0.4 inch) distal to that of the ulna.

Colles' fracture of the wrist is an impacted fracture in which the distal end of the radius is pushed proximally into the shaft of the radius. This sometimes occurs when someone falls on outstretched hands, and it most often happens to elderly women with osteoporosis. Colles' fracture bends the wrist into curves that resemble those on a fork. ●

Can you deduce how physicians use palpation to diagnose a Colles' fracture?

_____

_____

3.   Next, feel the major groups of muscles within your forearm. Flex your hand and fingers against resistance, and feel the anterior _flexor muscles_ contract. Then extend your hand at the wrist, and feel the tightening of the posterior _extensor muscles._

4.   Near the wrist, the anterior surface of the forearm reveals many significant features (Figure 30.13). Flex your fist

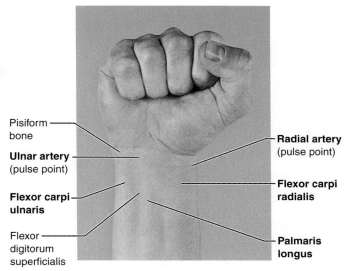

FIGURE 30.13 The anterior surface of the distal forearm and fist. The tendons of the flexor muscles guide the clinician to several sites for pulse taking.

against resistance; the tendons of the main wrist flexors will bulge the skin of the distal forearm. The tendons of the **flexor carpi radialis** and **palmaris longus** muscles are most obvious. (The palmaris longus, however, is absent from at least one arm in 30% of all people, so your forearm may exhibit just one prominent tendon instead of two.) The **radial artery** lies just lateral to (on the thumb side of) the flexor carpi radialis tendon, where the pulse is easily detected (Figure 30.13). Feel your radial pulse here. The _median nerve_ (which innervates the thumb) lies deep to the palmaris longus tendon. Finally, the **ulnar artery** lies on the medial side of the forearm, just lateral to the tendon of the **flexor carpi ulnaris.** Using Figure 30.13 as a guide, locate and feel your ulnar arterial pulse.

5.   Extend your thumb and point it posteriorly to form a triangular depression in the base of the thumb on the back of your hand. This is the **anatomical snuff box** (Figure 30.14). Its two elevated borders are defined by the tendons of the thumb extensor muscles, **extensor pollicis brevis** and **extensor pollicis longus.** The radial artery runs within the snuff box, so this is another site for taking a radial pulse. The main bone on the floor of the snuff box is the scaphoid bone of the wrist, but the styloid process of the radius is also present here. (If displaced by a bone fracture, the radial styloid process will be felt outside of the snuff box rather than within it.) The "snuff box" took its name from the fact that people once put snuff (tobacco for sniffing) in this hollow before lifting it up to the nose.

6.   On the dorsum of your hand, observe the superficial veins just deep to the skin. This is the **dorsal venous network,** which drains superiorly into the cephalic vein. This venous network provides a site for drawing blood and inserting intravenous catheters and is preferred over the median cubital vein for these purposes. Next, extend your hand and fingers, and observe the tendons of the **extensor digitorum** muscle.

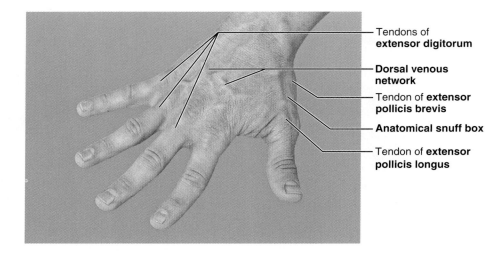

FIGURE 30.14 **The dorsum of the hand.** Note especially the anatomical snuff box and dorsal venous network.

7. The anterior surface of the hand also contains some features of interest (Figure 30.15). These features include the *epidermal ridges* (fingerprints) and many **flexion creases** in the skin. Grasp your **thenar eminence** (the bulge on the palm that contains the thumb muscles) and your **hypothenar eminence** (the bulge on the medial palm that contains muscles that move the little finger). ▬

Palpating Landmarks of the Lower Limb

Gluteal Region

Dominating the gluteal region are the two *prominences* (cheeks) of the buttocks. These are formed by subcutaneous fat and by the thick **gluteus maximus** muscles (Figure 30.16). The midline groove between the two prominences is called the **natal cleft** (*natal* = rump) or **gluteal cleft.** The inferior margin of each prominence is the horizontal **gluteal fold,** which roughly corresponds to the inferior margin of the gluteus maximus.

1. Try to palpate your **ischial tuberosity** just above the medial side of each gluteal fold (it will be easier to feel if you sit down or flex your thigh first). The ischial tuberosities are the robust inferior parts of the ischial bones, and they support the body's weight during sitting.

2. Next, palpate the **greater trochanter** of the femur on the lateral side of your hip. This trochanter lies just anterior to a hollow and about 10 cm (one hand's breadth, or 4 inches) inferior to the iliac crest. To confirm that you have found the greater trochanter, alternately flex and extend your thigh. Because this trochanter is the most superior point on the lateral femur, it moves with the femur as you perform this movement.

3. To palpate the sharp **posterior superior iliac spine** (see Figure 30.16), locate your iliac crests again, and trace each to its most posterior point. You may have difficulty feeling this spine, but it is indicated by a distinct dimple in the skin that is easy to find. This dimple lies two to three finger breadths

lateral to the midline of the back. The dimple also indicates the position of the *sacroiliac joint,* where the hip bone attaches to the sacrum of the spinal column. (You can check *your* "dimples" out in the privacy of your home.)

The gluteal region is a major site for administering intramuscular injections. When giving such injections, extreme care must be taken to avoid piercing a major nerve that lies just deep to the gluteus maximus muscle. Can you guess what nerve this is?

It is the thick *sciatic nerve,* which innervates much of the lower limb. Furthermore, the needle must avoid the gluteal nerves and gluteal blood vessels, which also lie deep to the gluteus maximus.

To avoid harming these structures, the injections are most often applied to the **gluteus *medius*** (not maximus) muscle superior to the cheeks of the buttocks, in a safe area called the

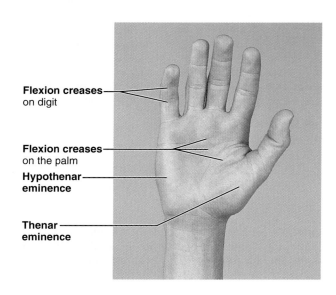

FIGURE 30.15 **The palmar surface of the hand.**

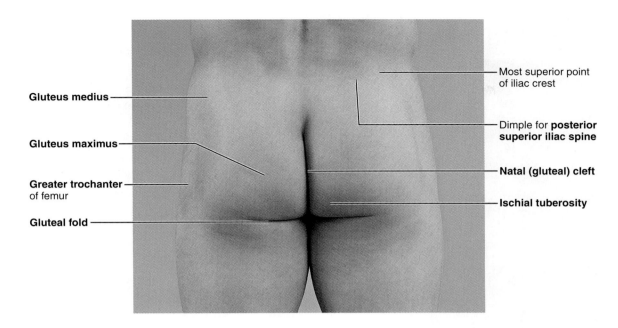

FIGURE 30.16 The gluteal region. The region extends from the iliac crests superiorly to the gluteal folds inferiorly. Therefore, it includes more than just the prominences of the buttock.

ventral gluteal site (Figure 30.17b). To locate this site, mentally draw a line laterally from the posterior superior iliac spine (dimple) to the greater trochanter; the injection would be given 5 cm (2 inches) superior to the midpoint of that line. Another safe way to locate the ventral gluteal site is to approach the lateral side of the patient's left hip with your extended right hand (or the right hip with your left hand). Then, place your thumb on the anterior superior iliac spine and your index finger as far posteriorly on the iliac crest as it can reach.

The heel of your hand comes to lie on the greater trochanter, and the needle is inserted in the angle of the V formed between your thumb and index finger about 4 cm (1.5 inches) inferior to the iliac crest.

Gluteal injections are not given to small children because their "safe area" is too small to locate with certainty and because the gluteal muscles are thin at this age. Instead, infants and toddlers receive intramuscular shots in the prominent **vastus lateralis** muscle of the thigh.

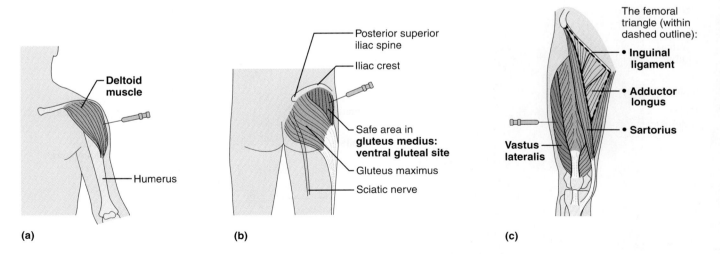

FIGURE 30.17 Three major sites of intramuscular injections. (a) Deltoid muscle of the arm. **(b)** Ventral gluteal site (gluteus medius). **(c)** Vastus lateralis in the lateral thigh. The femoral triangle is also shown.

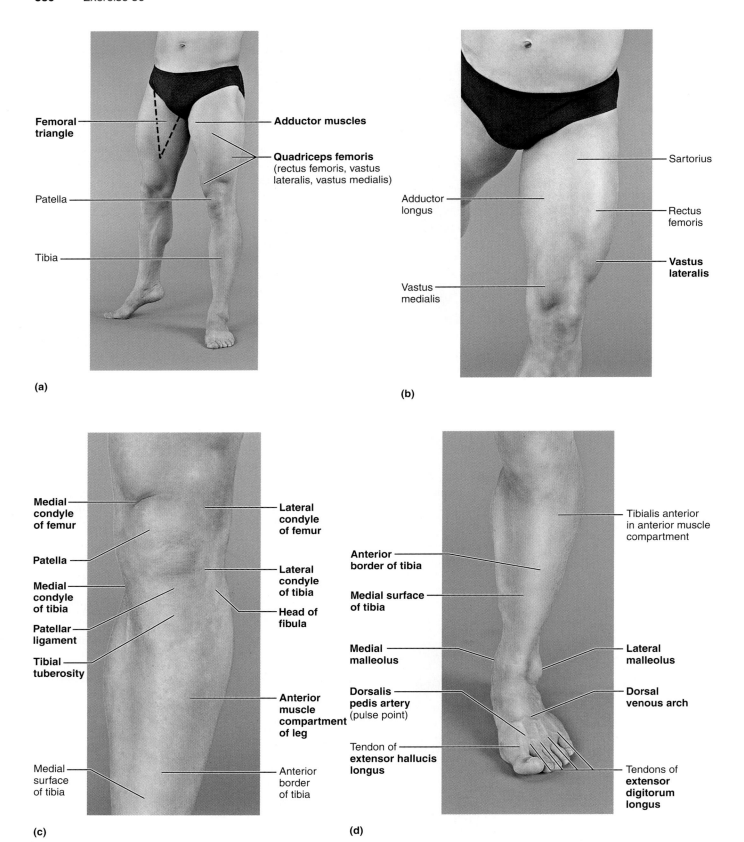

(a)

Femoral triangle

Adductor muscles

Quadriceps femoris (rectus femoris, vastus lateralis, vastus medialis)

Patella

Tibia

(b)

Sartorius

Adductor longus

Rectus femoris

Vastus lateralis

Vastus medialis

(c)

Medial condyle of femur

Patella

Medial condyle of tibia

Patellar ligament

Tibial tuberosity

Medial surface of tibia

Lateral condyle of femur

Lateral condyle of tibia

Head of fibula

Anterior muscle compartment of leg

Anterior border of tibia

(d)

Tibialis anterior in anterior muscle compartment

Anterior border of tibia

Medial surface of tibia

Medial malleolus

Dorsalis pedis artery (pulse point)

Tendon of **extensor hallucis longus**

Lateral malleolus

Dorsal venous arch

Tendons of **extensor digitorum longus**

FIGURE 30.18 Anterior surface of the lower limb. (**a**) Both limbs, with the right limb revealing its medial aspect. The femoral triangle is outlined on the right limb. (**b**) Enlarged view of the left thigh. (**c**) The left knee region. (**d**) The dorsum of the left foot.

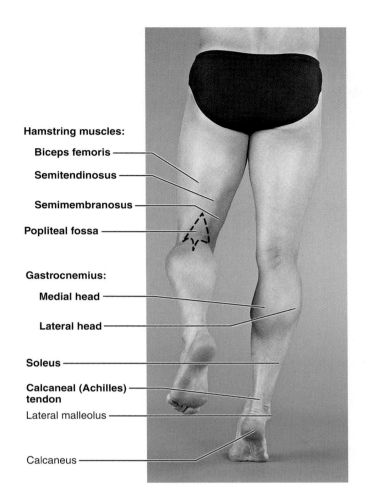

Hamstring muscles:

Biceps femoris

Semitendinosus

Semimembranosus

Popliteal fossa

Gastrocnemius:

Medial head

Lateral head

Soleus

Calcaneal (Achilles) tendon

Lateral malleolus

Calcaneus

FIGURE 30.19 Posterior surface of the lower limb. Notice the diamond-shaped popliteal fossa posterior to the knee.

Thigh

The thigh is pictured in Figures 30.18 and 30.19. Much of the femur is clothed by thick muscles, so the thigh has few palpable bony landmarks.

1.   Distally, feel the **medial** and **lateral condyles of the femur** and the **patella** anterior to the condyles (see Figure 30.18c and a).

2.   Next, palpate your three groups of thigh muscles—the **quadriceps femoris muscles** anteriorly, the **adductor muscles** medially, and the **hamstrings** posteriorly (see Figures 30.18a and b and 30.19). The **vastus lateralis,** the lateral muscle of the quadriceps group, is a site for intramuscular injections. Such injections are administered about halfway down the length of this muscle (see Figure 30.17c).

3.   The anterosuperior surface of the thigh exhibits a three-sided depression called the **femoral triangle** (see Figure 30.18a). As shown in Figure 30.17c, the superior border of

this triangle is formed by the **inguinal ligament,** and its two inferior borders are defined by the **sartorius** and **adductor longus** muscles. The large *femoral artery* and *vein* descend vertically through the center of the femoral triangle. To feel the pulse of your femoral artery, press inward just inferior to your midinguinal point (halfway between the anterior superior iliac spine and the pubic tubercle). Be sure to push hard, because the artery lies somewhat deep. By pressing very hard on this point, one can stop the bleeding from a hemorrhage in the lower limb. The femoral triangle also contains most of the *inguinal lymph nodes* (which are easily palpated if swollen).

Leg and Foot

1.   Locate your patella again, then follow the thick **patellar ligament** inferiorly from the patella to its insertion on the superior tibia (see Figure 30.18c). Here you can feel a rough projection, the **tibial tuberosity.** Continue running your fingers inferiorly along the tibia's sharp **anterior border** and its flat **medial surface**—bony landmarks that lie very near the surface throughout their length.

2.   Now, return to the superior part of your leg, and palpate the expanded **lateral** and **medial condyles of the tibia** just inferior to the knee. (You can distinguish the tibial condyles from the femoral condyles because you can feel the tibial condyles move with the tibia during knee flexion.) Feel the bulbous **head of the fibula** in the superolateral region of the leg (see Figure 30.18c). Try to feel the *common fibular nerve* (nerve to the anterior leg and foot) where it wraps around the fibula's *neck* just inferior to its head. This nerve is often bumped against the bone here and damaged.

3.   In the most distal part of the leg, feel the **lateral malleolus** of the fibula as the lateral prominence of the ankle (see Figure 30.18d). Notice that this lies slightly inferior to the **medial malleolus** of the tibia, which forms the ankle's medial prominence. Place your finger just posterior to the medial malleolus to feel the pulse of your *posterior tibial artery.*

4.   On the posterior aspect of the knee is a diamond-shaped hollow called the **popliteal fossa** (see Figure 30.19). Palpate the large muscles that define the four borders of this fossa: The **biceps femoris** forming the superolateral border, the **semitendinosus** and **semimembranosus** defining the superomedial border, and the two heads of the **gastrocnemius** forming the inferior border. The *popliteal artery* and *vein* (main vessels to the leg) lie deep within this fossa. To feel a popliteal pulse, flex your leg at the knee and push your fingers firmly into the popliteal fossa. If a physician is unable to feel a patient's popliteal pulse, the femoral artery may be narrowed by atherosclerosis.

5.   Next, palpate the main muscle groups of your leg, starting with the calf muscles posteriorly (see Figure 30.19). Standing on tiptoes will help you feel the **lateral** and **medial heads of the gastrocnemius** and, inferior to these, the broad **soleus** muscle. Also feel the tension in your **calcaneal (Achilles) tendon** and at the point of insertion of this tendon onto the calcaneus bone of the foot.

6. Observe the dorsum (superior surface) of your foot. You may see the superficial **dorsal venous arch** overlying the proximal part of the metatarsal bones (Figure 30.18d). This arch gives rise to both saphenous veins (the main superficial veins of the lower limb). Visible in lean people, the *great saphenous vein* ascends along the medial side of the entire limb (see Figure 24.8, p. 405). The *small saphenous vein* ascends through the center of the calf.

As you extend your toes, observe the tendons of the **extensor digitorum longus** and **extensor hallucis longus** muscles on the dorsum of the foot. Finally, place a finger on the extreme proximal part of the space between the first and second metatarsal bones. Here you should be able to feel the pulse of the **dorsalis pedis artery.** ▪

NAME_____

LAB TIME/DATE _____

Surface Anatomy Roundup

_____ 1. A blow to the cheek is most likely to break what superficial bone or bone part? (a) superciliary arches, (b) the philtrum, (c) zygomatic arch, (d) the tragus

_____ 2. Rebound tenderness (a) occurs in appendicitis, (b) is whiplash of the neck, (c) is a sore foot from playing basketball, (d) occurs when the larynx falls back into place after swallowing.

_____ 3. The anatomical snuff box (a) is in the nose, (b) contains the styloid process of the radius, (c) is defined by tendons of the flexor carpi radialis and palmaris longus, (d) cannot really hold snuff.

_____ 4. Some landmarks on the body surface can be seen or felt, but others are abstractions that you must construct by drawing imaginary lines. Which of the following pairs of structures is abstract and invisible? (a) umbilicus and costal margin, (b) anterior superior iliac spine and natal cleft, (c) linea alba and linea semilunaris, (d) McBurney's point and midaxillary line, (e) philtrum and sternocleidomastoid

_____ 5. Many pelvic organs can be palpated by placing a finger in the rectum or the vagina, but only one pelvic organ is readily palpated through the skin. This is the (a) nonpregnant uterus, (b) prostate, (c) full bladder, (d) ovaries, (e) rectum.

_____ 6. A muscle that contributes to the posterior axillary fold is the (a) pectoralis major, (b) latissimus dorsi, (c) trapezius, (d) infraspinatus, (e) pectoralis minor, (f) a and e.

_____ 7. Which of the following is not a pulse point? (a) anatomical snuff box, (b) inferior margin of mandible anterior to masseter muscle, (c) center of distal forearm at palmaris longus tendon, (d) medial bicipital furrow on arm, (e) dorsum of foot between the first two metatarsals

_____ 8. Which pair of ribs inserts on the sternum at the sternal angle? (a) first, (b) second, (c) third, (d) fourth, (e) fifth

_____ 9. The inferior angle of the scapula is at the same level as the spinous process of which vertebra? (a) C_5, (b) C_7, (c) T_3, (d) T_7, (e) L_4

_____ 10. An important bony landmark that can be recognized by a distinct dimple in the skin is the (a) posterior superior iliac spine, (b) styloid process of the ulna, (c) shaft of the radius, (d) acromion.

_____ 11. A nurse missed a patient's median cubital vein while trying to withdraw blood and then inserted the needle far too deeply into the cubital fossa. This error could cause any of the following problems, except this one: (a) paralysis of the ulnar nerve, (b) paralysis of the median nerve, (c) bruising the insertion tendon of the biceps brachii muscle, (d) blood spurting from the brachial artery.

_____ 12. Which of these organs is almost impossible to study with surface anatomy techniques? (a) heart, (b) lungs, (c) brain, (d) nose

_____ 13. A preferred site for inserting an intravenous medication line into a blood vessel is the (a) medial bicipital furrow on arm, (b) external carotid artery, (c) dorsal venous arch of hand, (d) popliteal fossa.

_____ 14. One listens for bowel sounds with a stethoscope placed (a) on the four quadrants of the abdominal wall; (b) in the triangle of auscultation; (c) in the right and left midaxillary line, just superior to the iliac crests; (d) inside the patient's bowels (intestines), on the tip of an endoscope.

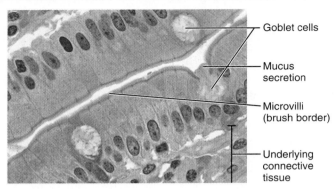

Goblet cells

Mucus secretion

Microvilli (brush border)

Underlying connective tissue

PLATE 1 Simple columnar epithelium containing goblet cells, which are secreting mucus (400×). (Exercise 5, p. 55)

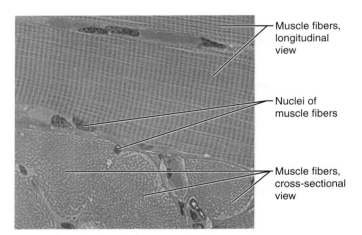

Muscle fibers, longitudinal view

Nuclei of muscle fibers

Muscle fibers, cross-sectional view

PLATE 2 Skeletal muscle, transverse and longitudinal views (400×). (Exercise 5, p. 68; Exercise 13, p. 177)

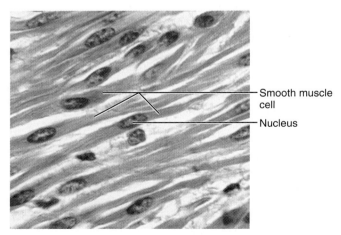

Smooth muscle cell

Nucleus

PLATE 3 Smooth muscle cells (650×). (Exercise 5, p. 68)

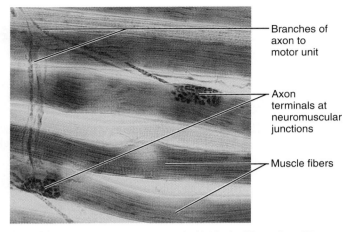

Branches of axon to motor unit

Axon terminals at neuromuscular junctions

Muscle fibers

PLATE 4 Part of a motor unit (150×). (Exercise 13, p. 179)

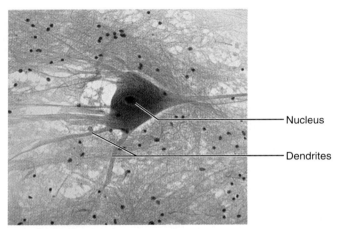

Nucleus

Dendrites

PLATE 5 Light micrograph of a multipolar neuron (200×). (Exercise 5, p. 67; Exercise 15, pp. 247, 248)

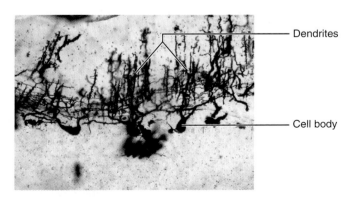

Dendrites

Cell body

PLATE 6 Silver-stained Purkinje cells of the cerebellum (125×). (Exercise 5, p. 67; Exercise 15, p. 250)

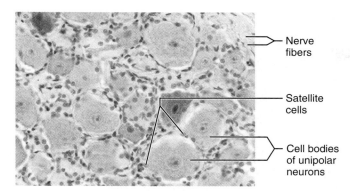

PLATE 7   Dorsal root ganglion displaying neuron cell bodies and satellite cells (200×). (Exercise 15, p. 250)

Nerve fibers

Satellite cells

Cell bodies of unipolar neurons

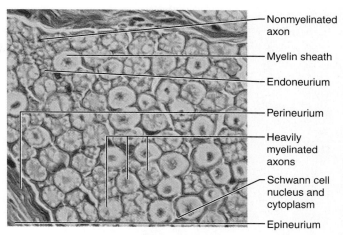

Nonmyelinated axon

Myelin sheath

Endoneurium

Perineurium

Heavily myelinated axons

Schwann cell nucleus and cytoplasm

Epineurium

PLATE 10   Cross section of a portion of a peripheral nerve (250×). Heavily myelinated fibers are identified by a centrally located axon surrounded by an unstained ring of myelin. (Exercise 15, p. 251)

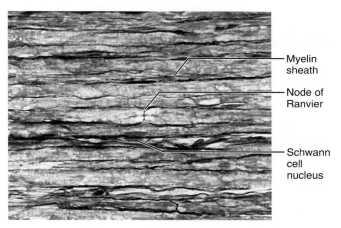

Myelin sheath

Node of Ranvier

Schwann cell nucleus

PLATE 8   Longitudinal view of myelinated axons (500×). (Exercise 15, p. 249)

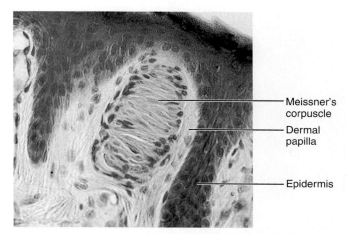

Meissner's corpuscle

Dermal papilla

Epidermis

PLATE 11   Meissner's corpuscle in a dermal papilla (275×). (Exercise 15, pp. 251, 252)

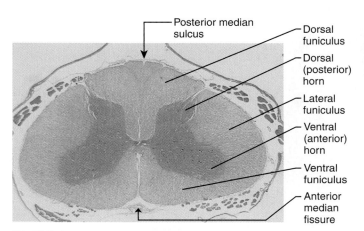

Posterior median sulcus

Dorsal funiculus

Dorsal (posterior) horn

Lateral funiculus

Ventral (anterior) horn

Ventral funiculus

Anterior median fissure

PLATE 9   Adult spinal cord, cross-sectional view (12×). (Exercise 17, p. 287)

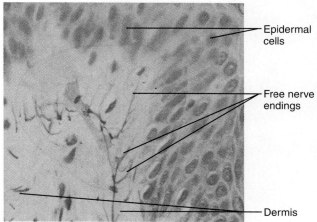

Epidermal cells

Free nerve endings

Dermis

PLATE 12   Free nerve endings at dermal-epidermal junction (400×). (Exercise 15, pp. 251, 252)

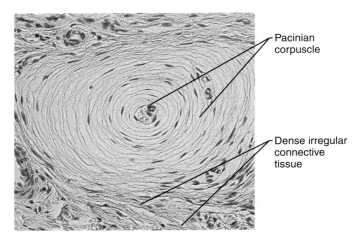

Pacinian corpuscle

Dense irregular connective tissue

PLATE 13 Cross section of a Pacinian corpuscle in the dermis (125×). (Exercise 15, pp. 251, 252)

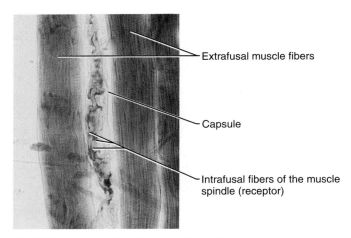

Extrafusal muscle fibers

Capsule

Intrafusal fibers of the muscle spindle (receptor)

PLATE 14 Longitudinal section of a muscle spindle (325×). (Exercise 15, p. 252)

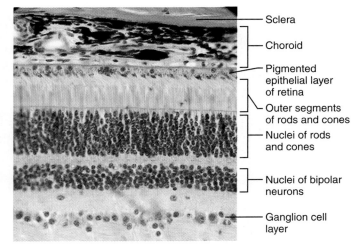

Sclera

Choroid

Pigmented epithelial layer of retina

Outer segments of rods and cones

Nuclei of rods and cones

Nuclei of bipolar neurons

Ganglion cell layer

PLATE 15 Structure of the retina of the eye (250×). (Exercise 18, p. 311)

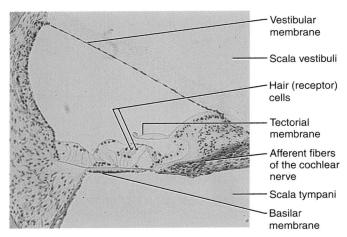

Vestibular membrane

Scala vestibuli

Hair (receptor) cells

Tectorial membrane

Afferent fibers of the cochlear nerve

Scala tympani

Basilar membrane

PLATE 16 The spiral organ of Corti (150×). (Exercise 19, p. 330)

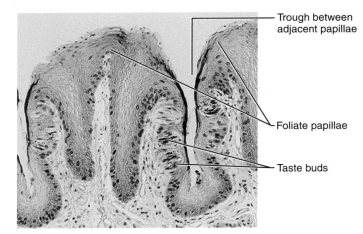

Trough between adjacent papillae

Foliate papillae

Taste buds

PLATE 17 Location of taste buds on lateral aspects of foliate papillae of tongue (150×). (Exercise 20, p. 343)

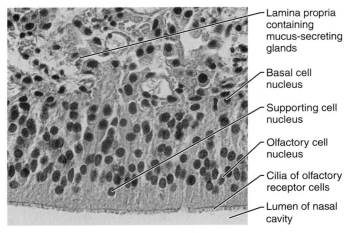

Lamina propria containing mucus-secreting glands

Basal cell nucleus

Supporting cell nucleus

Olfactory cell nucleus

Cilia of olfactory receptor cells

Lumen of nasal cavity

PLATE 18 Olfactory epithelium. From lamina propria to nasal cavity, the general arrangement of cells in this pseudostratified epithelium: basal cells, olfactory receptor cells, and supporting cells (350×). (Exercise 20, p. 342)

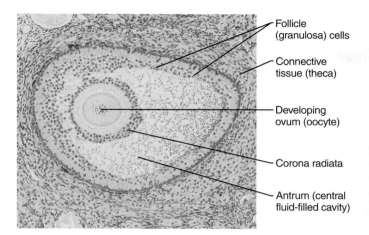

Follicle (granulosa) cells

Connective tissue (theca)

Developing ovum (oocyte)

Corona radiata

Antrum (central fluid-filled cavity)

PLATE 19   A vesicular follicle of ovary (140×). (Exercise 29, p. 507)

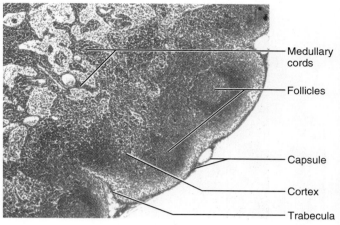

Medullary cords

Follicles

Capsule

Cortex

Trabecula

PLATE 22   Main structural features of a lymph node (15×). (Exercise 25, p. 432)

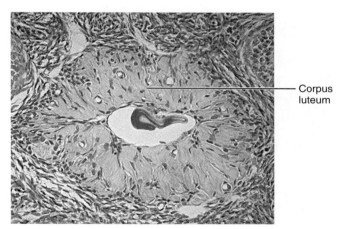

Corpus luteum

PLATE 20   Glandular corpus luteum of an ovary (125×). (Exercise 29, p. 507)

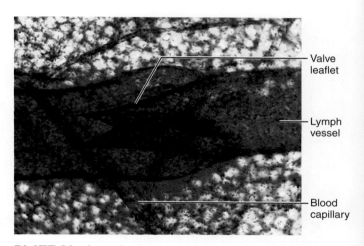

Valve leaflet

Lymph vessel

Blood capillary

PLATE 23   Lymphatic vessel (550×). (Exercise 25, p. 431)

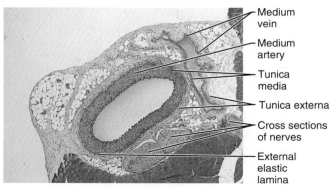

Medium vein

Medium artery

Tunica media

Tunica externa

Cross sections of nerves

External elastic lamina

PLATE 21   Cross-sectional view of an artery, a vein, and nerves (25×). (Exercise 24, p. 400)

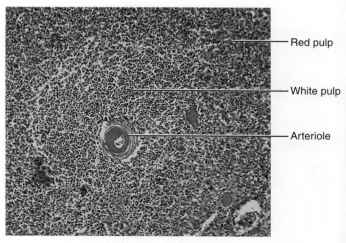

Red pulp

White pulp

Arteriole

PLATE 24   Microscopic portion of spleen showing red and white pulp regions (50×). (Exercise 25, p. 433)

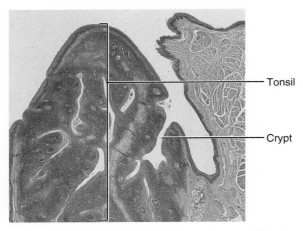

PLATE 25   Histology of a palatine tonsil. The luminal surface is covered with epithelium that invaginates deeply to form crypts (15×). (Exercise 25, p. 433)

- Tonsil
- Crypt

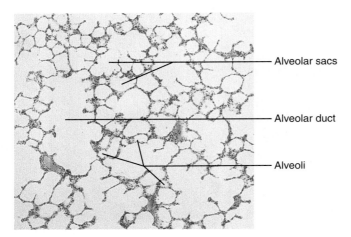

PLATE 26   Photomicrograph of part of the lung showing alveoli and alveolar ducts and sacs (25×). (Exercise 26, p. 445)

- Alveolar sacs
- Alveolar duct
- Alveoli

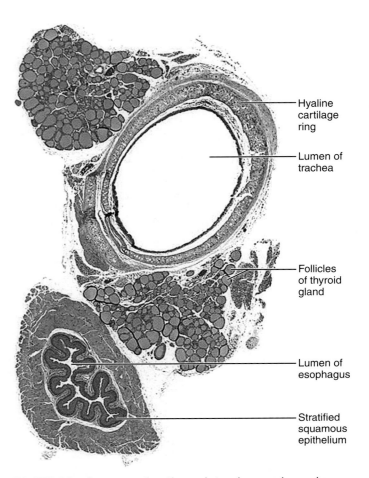

PLATE 28   Cross section through trachea and esophagus (10×). (Exercise 26, p. 445)

- Hyaline cartilage ring
- Lumen of trachea
- Follicles of thyroid gland
- Lumen of esophagus
- Stratified squamous epithelium

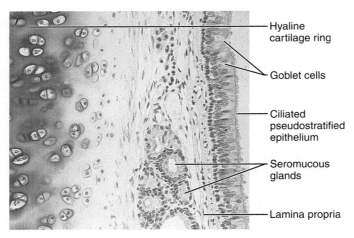

PLATE 27   Cross section through the trachea showing the ciliated pseudostratified epithelium, glands, and part of the supporting ring of hyaline cartilage (125×). (Exercise 26, p. 445)

- Hyaline cartilage ring
- Goblet cells
- Ciliated pseudostratified epithelium
- Seromucous glands
- Lamina propria

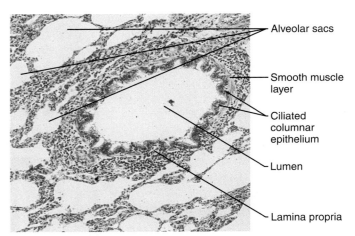

PLATE 29   Bronchiole, cross-sectional view (50×). (Exercise 26, p. 445)

- Alveolar sacs
- Smooth muscle layer
- Ciliated columnar epithelium
- Lumen
- Lamina propria

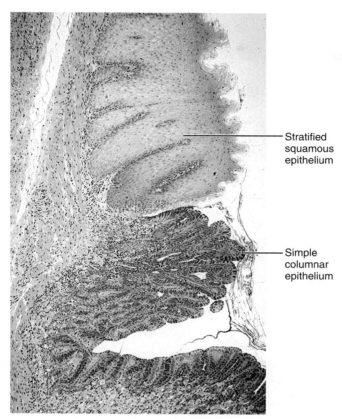

PLATE 30 Gastroesophageal junction showing simple columnar epithelium of stomach meeting stratified squamous epithelium of esophagus (50×). (Exercise 27, p. 462)

Stratified squamous epithelium

Simple columnar epithelium

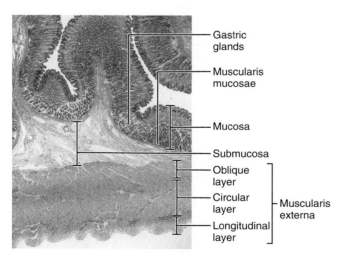

Gastric glands

Muscularis mucosae

Mucosa

Submucosa

Oblique layer

Circular layer

Longitudinal layer

Muscularis externa

PLATE 31 Stomach. Longitudinal view through wall showing four tunics (25×). (Exercise 27, pp. 457, 462)

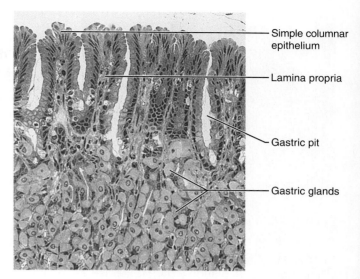

Simple columnar epithelium

Lamina propria

Gastric pit

Gastric glands

PLATE 32 Detailed structure of gastric glands and pits (175×). (Exercise 27, p. 462)

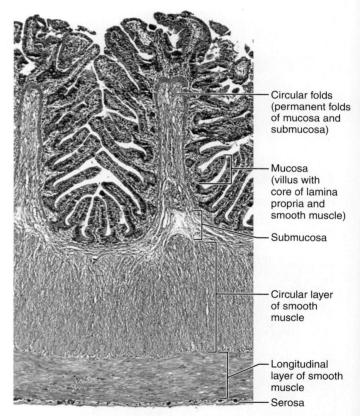

Circular folds (permanent folds of mucosa and submucosa)

Mucosa (villus with core of lamina propria and smooth muscle)

Submucosa

Circular layer of smooth muscle

Longitudinal layer of smooth muscle

Serosa

PLATE 33 Cross section through wall of small intestine showing circular folds and the arrangement of layers or tunics (35×). Villi of mucosa are large and obvious. (Exercise 27, p. 464)

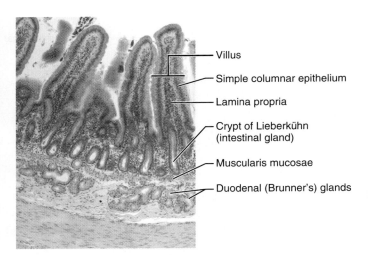

PLATE 34   Cross-sectional view of duodenum showing villi and duodenal glands (15×). (Exercise 27, p. 464)

- Villus
- Simple columnar epithelium
- Lamina propria
- Crypt of Lieberkühn (intestinal gland)
- Muscularis mucosae
- Duodenal (Brunner's) glands

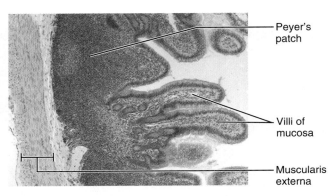

PLATE 35   Cross section through ileum, showing Peyer's patches (15×). (Exercise 27, p. 464)

- Peyer's patch
- Villi of mucosa
- Muscularis externa

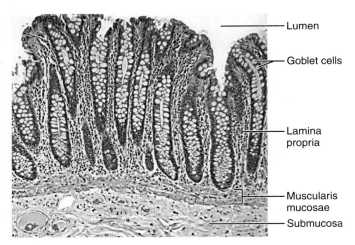

PLATE 36   Large intestine. Cross-sectional view showing the abundant goblet cells of the mucosa (35×). (Exercise 27, p. 466)

- Lumen
- Goblet cells
- Lamina propria
- Muscularis mucosae
- Submucosa

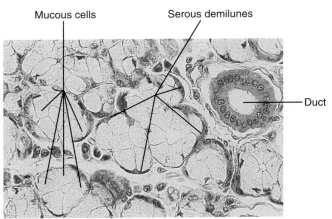

PLATE 37   Sublingual salivary glands (225×). (Exercise 27, p. 468)

- Mucous cells
- Serous demilunes
- Duct

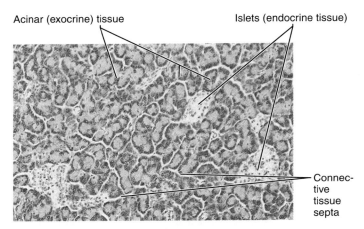

PLATE 38   Pancreas tissue. Exocrine and endocrine (islets) areas clearly visible (100×). (Exercise 21, p. 355; Exercise 27, p. 469)

- Acinar (exocrine) tissue
- Islets (endocrine tissue)
- Connective tissue septa

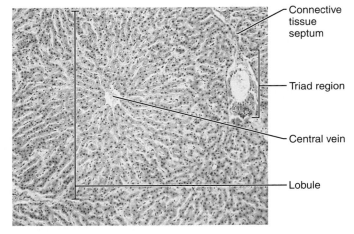

PLATE 39   Pig liver. Structure of liver lobules (35×). (Exercise 27, p. 471)

- Connective tissue septum
- Triad region
- Central vein
- Lobule

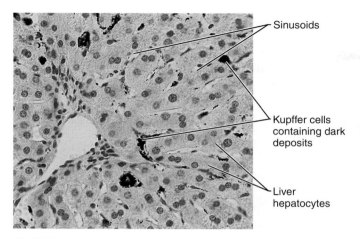

PLATE 40   Liver stained to show location of phagocytic cells (Kupffer cells) lining sinusoids (325×). (Exercise 27, p. 471)

Sinusoids

Kupffer cells containing dark deposits

Liver hepatocytes

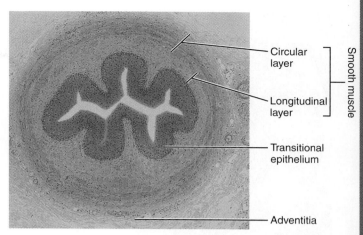

PLATE 43   Cross section of ureter (35×). (Exercise 28, p. 488)

Circular layer

Longitudinal layer

Smooth muscle

Transitional epithelium

Adventitia

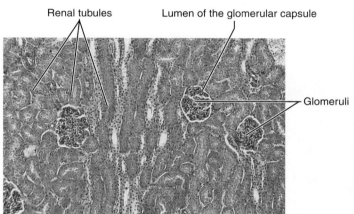

PLATE 41   Renal cortex of kidney (60×). (Exercise 28, p. 487)

Renal tubules

Lumen of the glomerular capsule

Glomeruli

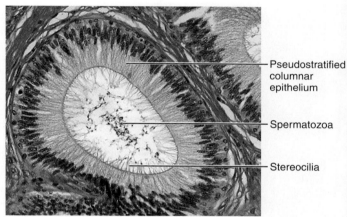

PLATE 44   Cross section of epididymis (165×). Stereocilia of the epithelial lining are obvious. (Exercise 29, p. 503)

Pseudostratified columnar epithelium

Spermatozoa

Stereocilia

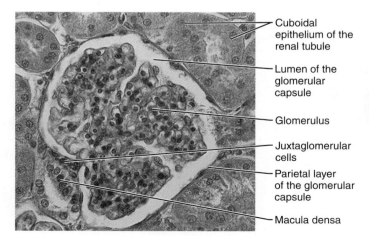

PLATE 42   Detailed structure of a glomerulus (300×). (Exercise 28, p. 487)

Cuboidal epithelium of the renal tubule

Lumen of the glomerular capsule

Glomerulus

Juxtaglomerular cells

Parietal layer of the glomerular capsule

Macula densa

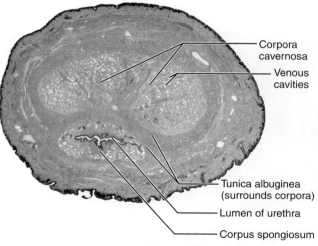

PLATE 45   Penis, transverse section (2.5×). (Exercise 29, p. 503)

Corpora cavernosa

Venous cavities

Tunica albuginea (surrounds corpora)

Lumen of urethra

Corpus spongiosum

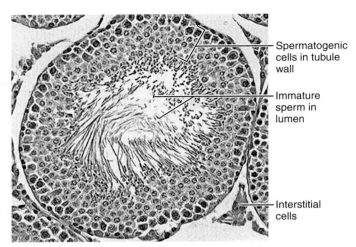

PLATE 46   Cross section of a portion of a seminiferous tubule (300×). (Exercise 29, p. 502)

Labels: Spermatogenic cells in tubule wall; Immature sperm in lumen; Interstitial cells

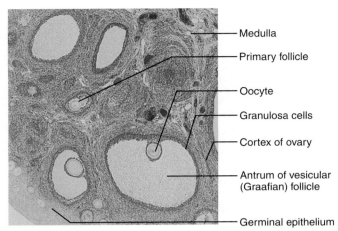

PLATE 49   The ovary, showing its follicles in various stages of development (45×). (Exercise 29, p. 507)

Labels: Medulla; Primary follicle; Oocyte; Granulosa cells; Cortex of ovary; Antrum of vesicular (Graafian) follicle; Germinal epithelium

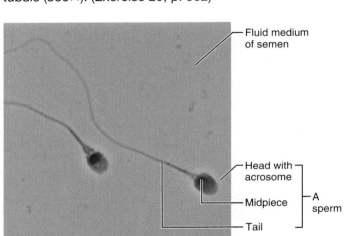

PLATE 47   Semen, the product of ejaculation, consisting of sperm and fluids secreted by the accessory glands (particularly the prostate and seminal vesicles) (1650×). (Exercise 29, p. 503)

Labels: Fluid medium of semen; Head with acrosome; Midpiece; Tail; A sperm

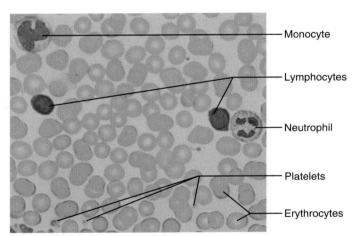

PLATE 50   Human blood smear (800×). (Exercise 22, p. 367)

Labels: Monocyte; Lymphocytes; Neutrophil; Platelets; Erythrocytes

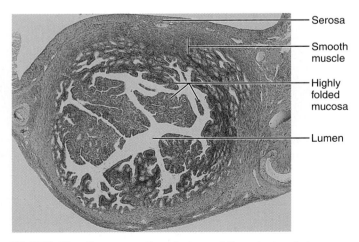

PLATE 48   Cross-sectional view of the uterine tube (25×). (Exercise 29, p. 507)

Labels: Serosa; Smooth muscle; Highly folded mucosa; Lumen

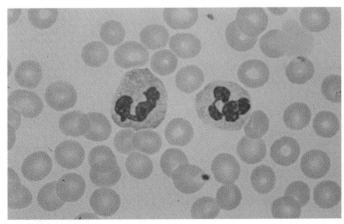

PLATE 51   Two neutrophils surrounded by erythrocytes (1500×). (Exercise 22, p. 367)

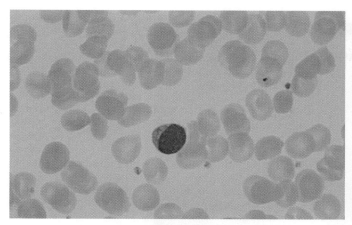

PLATE 52 Lymphocyte surrounded by erythrocytes (1125×). (Exercise 22, p. 367)

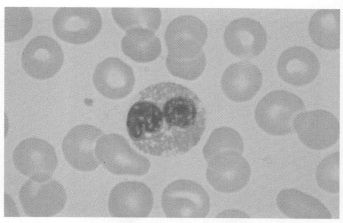

PLATE 54 An eosinophil surrounded by erythrocytes (1750×). (Exercise 22, p. 367)

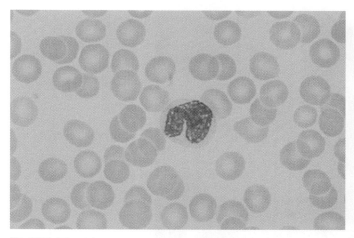

PLATE 53 Monocyte surrounded by erythrocytes (925×). (Exercise 22, p. 367)

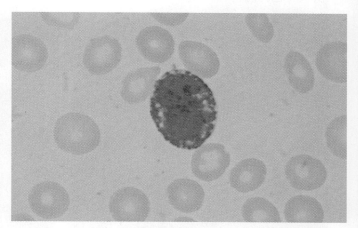

PLATE 55 A basophil surrounded by erythrocytes (1750×). (Exercise 22, p. 367)

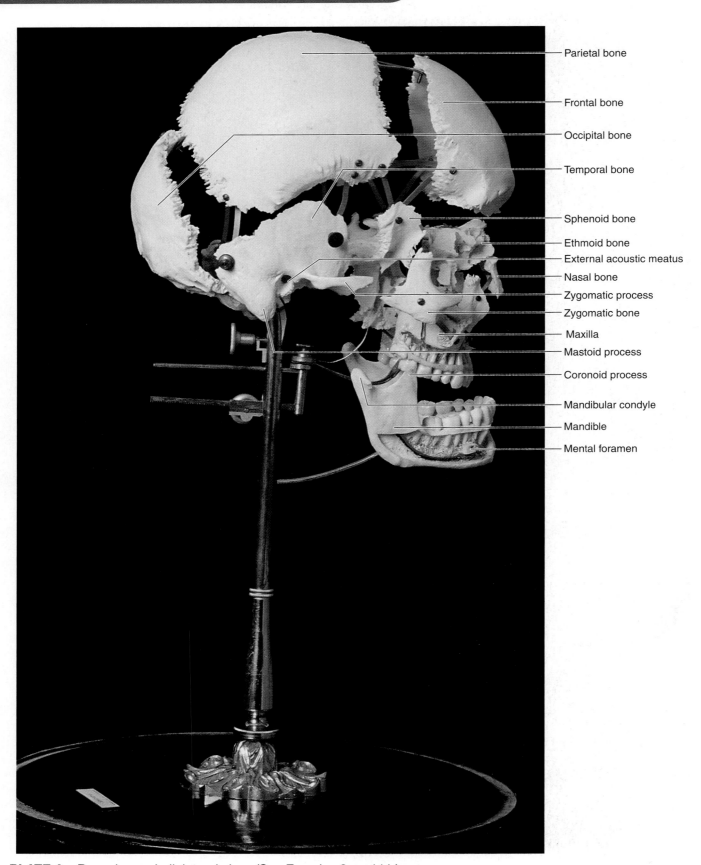

Parietal bone

Frontal bone

Occipital bone

Temporal bone

Sphenoid bone

Ethmoid bone

External acoustic meatus

Nasal bone

Zygomatic process

Zygomatic bone

Maxilla

Mastoid process

Coronoid process

Mandibular condyle

Mandible

Mental foramen

PLATE A   Beauchene skull, lateral view. (See Exercise 9, p. 111.)

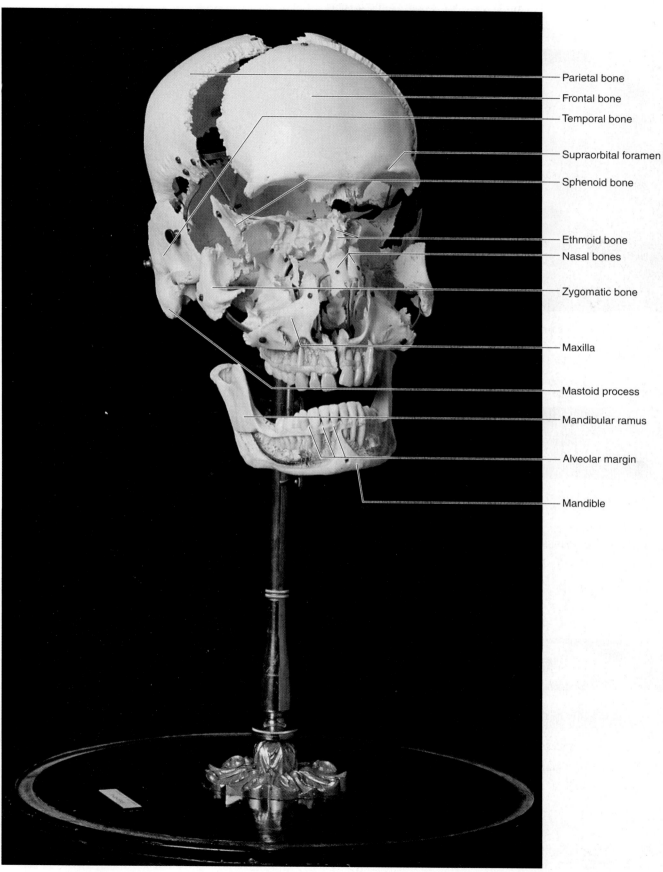

Parietal bone

Frontal bone

Temporal bone

Supraorbital foramen

Sphenoid bone

Ethmoid bone

Nasal bones

Zygomatic bone

Maxilla

Mastoid process

Mandibular ramus

Alveolar margin

Mandible

PLATE B   Beauchene skull, frontal view. (See Exercise 9, p. 111.)

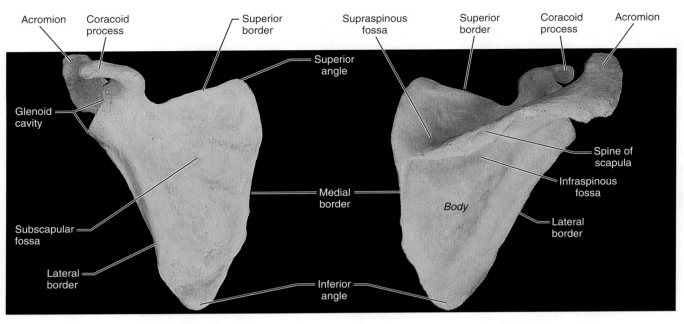

(a) Anterior view

Scapula

(b) Posterior view

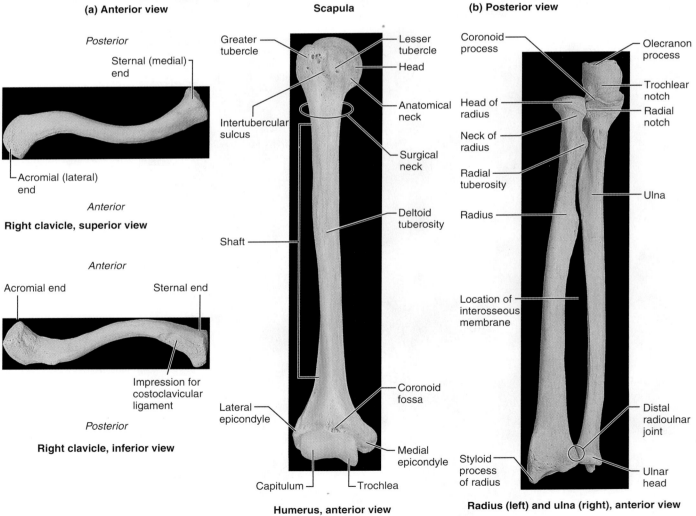

Right clavicle, superior view

Right clavicle, inferior view

Humerus, anterior view

Radius (left) and ulna (right), anterior view

PLATE C Photographs of selected bones of the pectoral girdle and right upper limb. (See Exercise 10, pp. 133–138.)

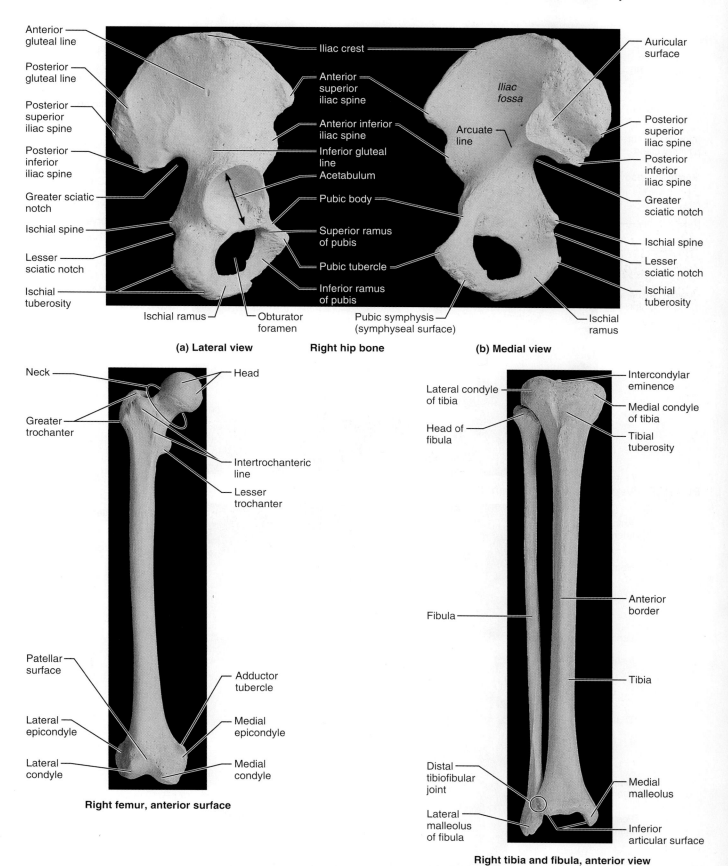

(a) Lateral view   **Right hip bone**   **(b) Medial view**

Right femur, anterior surface

Right tibia and fibula, anterior view

PLATE D   Photographs of selected bones of the pelvic girdle and right lower limb.
(See Exercise 10, pp. 139–144.)

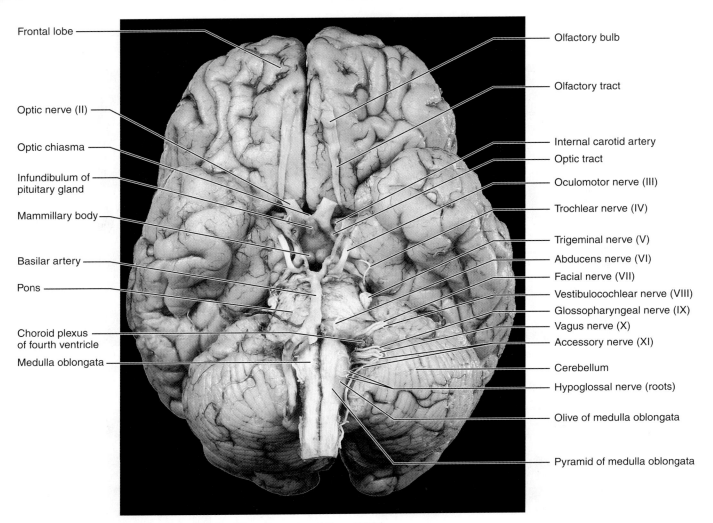

Frontal lobe

Optic nerve (II)

Optic chiasma

Infundibulum of
pituitary gland

Mammillary body

Basilar artery

Pons

Choroid plexus
of fourth ventricle

Medulla oblongata

Olfactory bulb

Olfactory tract

Internal carotid artery

Optic tract

Oculomotor nerve (III)

Trochlear nerve (IV)

Trigeminal nerve (V)

Abducens nerve (VI)

Facial nerve (VII)

Vestibulocochlear nerve (VIII)

Glossopharyngeal nerve (IX)

Vagus nerve (X)

Accessory nerve (XI)

Cerebellum

Hypoglossal nerve (roots)

Olive of medulla oblongata

Pyramid of medulla oblongata

PLATE E Ventral view of the brain. (See Exercise 16, p. 260.)

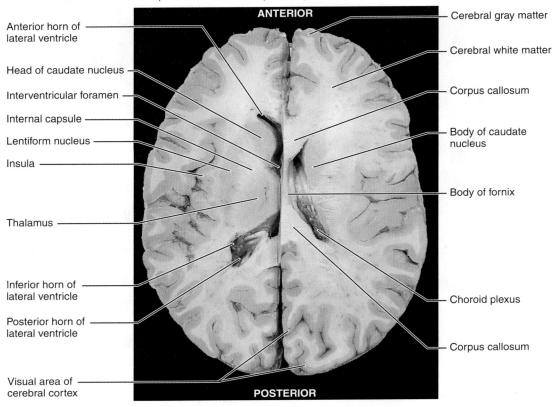

ANTERIOR

Anterior horn of
lateral ventricle

Head of caudate nucleus

Interventricular foramen

Internal capsule

Lentiform nucleus

Insula

Thalamus

Inferior horn of
lateral ventricle

Posterior horn of
lateral ventricle

Visual area of
cerebral cortex

Cerebral gray matter

Cerebral white matter

Corpus callosum

Body of caudate
nucleus

Body of fornix

Choroid plexus

Corpus callosum

POSTERIOR

PLATE F Transverse section of the brain, superior view. Left: on a level with the intraventricular foramen; right: about 1.5 cm higher. (See Exercise 16, p. 263.) (Lentiform nucleus-putamen and globus pallidus.)

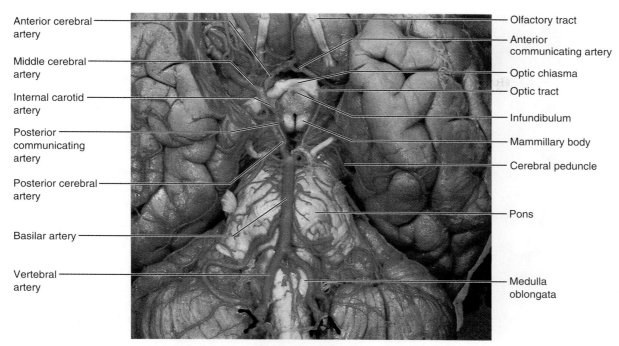

Anterior cerebral artery

Middle cerebral artery

Internal carotid artery

Posterior communicating artery

Posterior cerebral artery

Basilar artery

Vertebral artery

Olfactory tract

Anterior communicating artery

Optic chiasma

Optic tract

Infundibulum

Mammillary body

Cerebral peduncle

Pons

Medulla oblongata

PLATE G   Cerebral arterial circle (circle of Willis). (See Exercise 24, p. 411.)

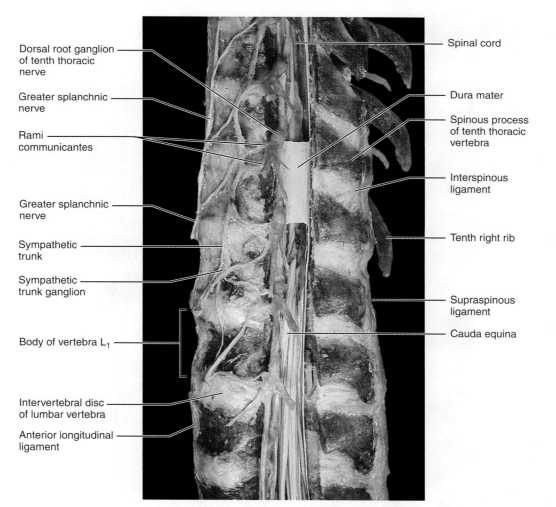

Dorsal root ganglion of tenth thoracic nerve

Greater splanchnic nerve

Rami communicantes

Greater splanchnic nerve

Sympathetic trunk

Sympathetic trunk ganglion

Body of vertebra L₁

Intervertebral disc of lumbar vertebra

Anterior longitudinal ligament

Spinal cord

Dura mater

Spinous process of tenth thoracic vertebra

Interspinous ligament

Tenth right rib

Supraspinous ligament

Cauda equina

PLATE H   Vertebral column and spinal cord, lower thoracic, and upper lumbar regions from the left. (See Exercise 17, p. 284.)

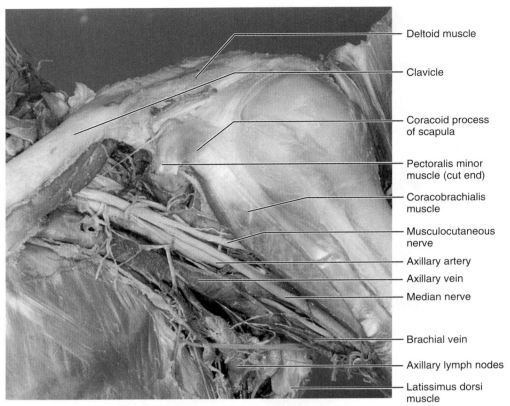

Deltoid muscle

Clavicle

Coracoid process of scapula

Pectoralis minor muscle (cut end)

Coracobrachialis muscle

Musculocutaneous nerve

Axillary artery

Axillary vein

Median nerve

Brachial vein

Axillary lymph nodes

Latissimus dorsi muscle

PLATE I Brachial plexus and axilla. (See Exercise 17, pp. 290–291.)

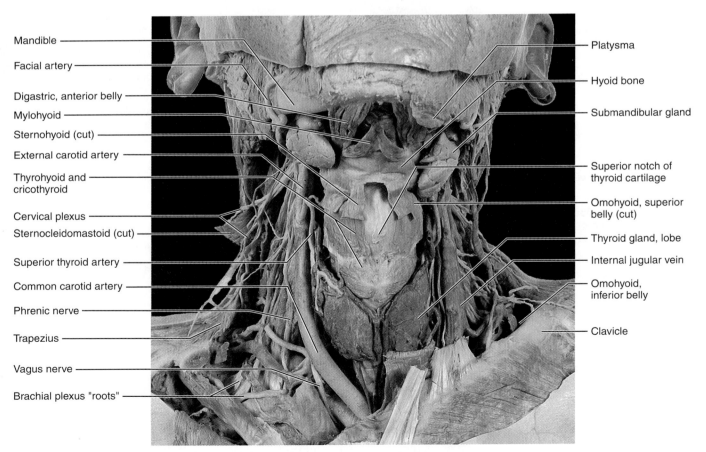

Mandible

Facial artery

Digastric, anterior belly

Mylohyoid

Sternohyoid (cut)

External carotid artery

Thyrohyoid and cricothyroid

Cervical plexus

Sternocleidomastoid (cut)

Superior thyroid artery

Common carotid artery

Phrenic nerve

Trapezius

Vagus nerve

Brachial plexus "roots"

Platysma

Hyoid bone

Submandibular gland

Superior notch of thyroid cartilage

Omohyoid, superior belly (cut)

Thyroid gland, lobe

Internal jugular vein

Omohyoid, inferior belly

Clavicle

PLATE J Muscles, blood vessels, and nerves of the neck, anterior view. (See Exercise 24, pp. 400–403.)

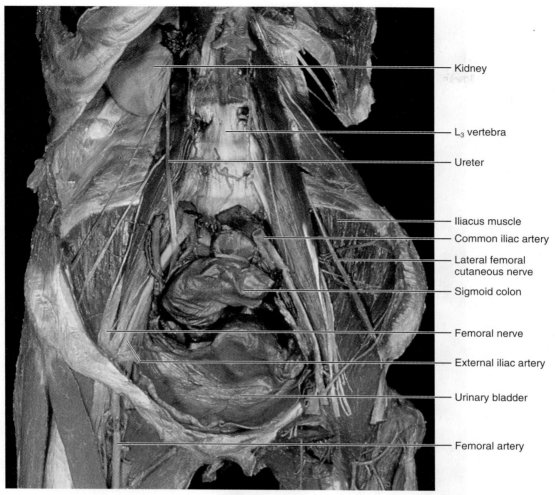

Kidney

L₃ vertebra

Ureter

Iliacus muscle
Common iliac artery
Lateral femoral
cutaneous nerve
Sigmoid colon

Femoral nerve

External iliac artery

Urinary bladder

Femoral artery

PLATE K   Lumbar plexus. (See Exercise 17, pp. 292–293.)

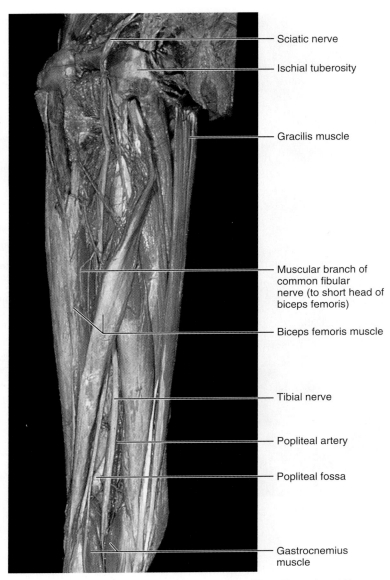

- Sciatic nerve
- Ischial tuberosity
- Gracilis muscle
- Muscular branch of common fibular nerve (to short head of biceps femoris)
- Biceps femoris muscle
- Tibial nerve
- Popliteal artery
- Popliteal fossa
- Gastrocnemius muscle

PLATE L   Course of sciatic nerve along posterior thigh and knee. (See Exercise 17, pp. 294–295.)

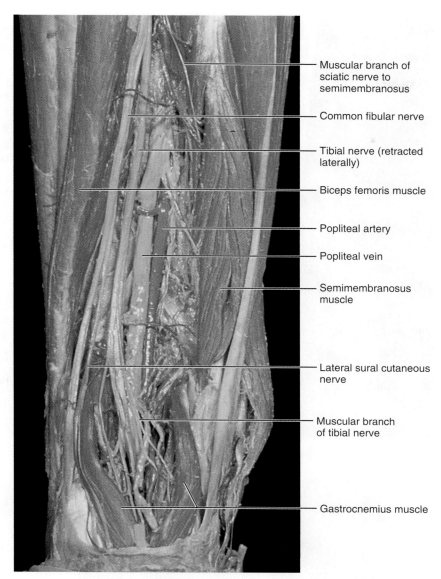

Muscular branch of
sciatic nerve to
semimembranosus

Common fibular nerve

Tibial nerve (retracted
laterally)

Biceps femoris muscle

Popliteal artery

Popliteal vein

Semimembranosus
muscle

Lateral sural cutaneous
nerve

Muscular branch
of tibial nerve

Gastrocnemius muscle

PLATE M   Deep branches of sciatic nerve in popliteal fossa. (See Exercise 17, pp. 294–295.)

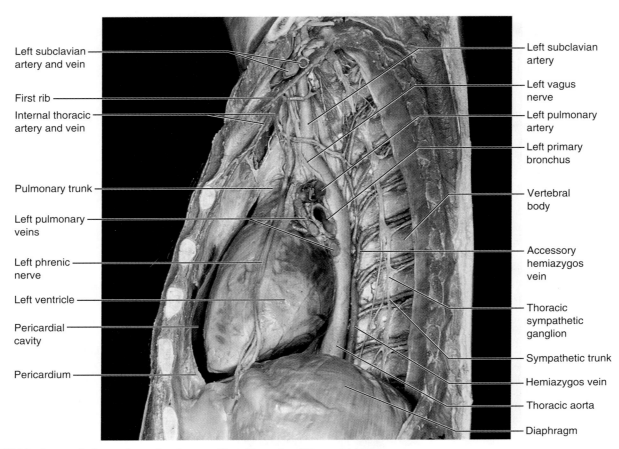

Left subclavian artery and vein

First rib

Internal thoracic artery and vein

Pulmonary trunk

Left pulmonary veins

Left phrenic nerve

Left ventricle

Pericardial cavity

Pericardium

Left subclavian artery

Left vagus nerve

Left pulmonary artery

Left primary bronchus

Vertebral body

Accessory hemiazygos vein

Thoracic sympathetic ganglion

Sympathetic trunk

Hemiazygos vein

Thoracic aorta

Diaphragm

PLATE N   Lateral view of mediastinum. (See Exercise 26, p. 444.)

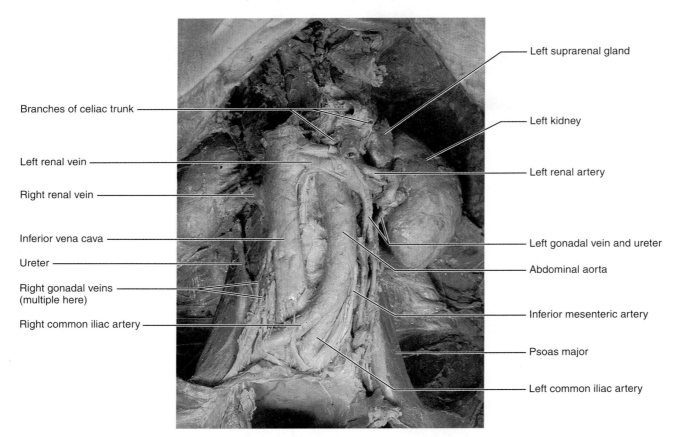

Branches of celiac trunk

Left renal vein

Right renal vein

Inferior vena cava

Ureter

Right gonadal veins (multiple here)

Right common iliac artery

Left suprarenal gland

Left kidney

Left renal artery

Left gonadal vein and ureter

Abdominal aorta

Inferior mesenteric artery

Psoas major

Left common iliac artery

PLATE O   Arteries in the abdominal cavity showing branches of the aorta. (See Exercise 24, p. 402.)

The Metric System

Measurement	Unit and abbreviation	Metric equivalent	Metric to English conversion factor	English to metric conversion factor
Length	1 kilometer (km)	= 1000 (10^3) meters	1 km = 0.62 mile	1 mile = 1.61 km
	1 meter (m)	= 100 (10^2) centimeters = 1000 millimeters	1 m = 1.09 yards 1 m = 3.28 feet 1 m = 39.37 inches	1 yard = 0.914 m 1 foot = 0.305 m
	1 centimeter (cm)	= 0.01 (10^{-2}) meter	1 cm = 0.394 inch	1 foot = 30.5 cm 1 inch = 2.54 cm
	1 millimeter (mm)	= 0.001 (10^{-3}) meter	1 mm = 0.039 inch	
	1 micrometer (μm) [formerly micron (μ)]	= 0.000001 (10^{-6}) meter		
	1 nanometer (nm) [formerly millimicron (mμ)]	= 0.000000001 (10^{-9}) meter		
	1 angstrom (Å)	= 0.0000000001 (10^{-10}) meter		
Area	1 square meter (m^2)	= 10,000 square centimeters	1 m^2 = 1.1960 square yards 1 m^2 = 10.764 square feet	1 square yard = 0.8361 m^2 1 square foot = 0.0929 m^2
	1 square centimeter (cm^2)	= 100 square millimeters	1 cm^2 = 0.155 square inch	1 square inch = 6.4516 cm^2
Mass	1 metric ton (t)	= 1000 kilograms	1 t = 1.103 ton	1 ton = 0.907 t
	1 kilogram (kg)	= 1000 grams	1 kg = 2.205 pounds	1 pound = 0.4536 kg
	1 gram (g)	= 1000 milligrams	1 g = 0.0353 ounce 1 g = 15.432 grains	1 ounce = 28.35 g
	1 milligram (mg)	= 0.001 gram	1 mg = approx. 0.015 grain	
	1 microgram (μg)	= 0.000001 gram		
Volume (solids)	1 cubic meter (m^3)	= 1,000,000 cubic centimeters	1 m^3 = 1.3080 cubic yards 1 m^3 = 35.315 cubic feet	1 cubic yard = 0.7646 m^3 1 cubic foot = 0.0283 m^3
	1 cubic centimeter (cm^3 or cc)	= 0.000001 cubic meter = 1 milliliter	1 cm^3 = 0.0610 cubic inch	1 cubic inch = 16.387 cm^3
	1 cubic millimeter (mm^3)	= 0.000000001 cubic meter		
Volume (liquids and gases)	1 kiloliter (kl or kL)	= 1000 liters	1 kL = 264.17 gallons	1 gallon = 3.785 L 1 quart = 0.946 L
	1 liter (l or L)	= 1000 milliliters	1 L = 0.264 gallon 1 L = 1.057 quarts	
	1 milliliter (ml or mL)	= 0.001 liter = 1 cubic centimeter	1 ml = 0.034 fluid ounce 1 ml = approx. $\frac{1}{4}$ teaspoon 1 ml = approx. 15–16 drops (gtt.)	1 quart = 946 ml 1 pint = 473 ml 1 fluid ounce = 29.57 ml 1 teaspoon = approx. 5 ml
	1 microliter (μl or μL)	= 0.000001 liter		
Time	1 second (s)	= $\frac{1}{60}$ minute		
	1 millisecond (ms)	= 0.001 second		
Temperature	Degrees Celsius (°C)		$°F = \frac{9}{5}°C + 32$	$°C = \frac{5}{9}(°F - 32)$

A.D.A.M. Interactive Anatomy Correlations

Appendix B lists correlations of Dissectible Anatomy images in the A.D.A.M. Interactive Anatomy (AIA) program with exercises in this manual. To start the AIA program, insert the AIA CD in your CD-ROM drive. Double-click the Interactive Anatomy 4.0 application icon located in the Interactive Anatomy folder on your hard drive. From the Introduction screen, click Dissectible Anatomy. From the open dialog box, click Open. To change anatomical views, click the View button drop-down menu in the toolbar, and select Anterior, Posterior, Lateral, or Medial. Click on the Structure List to launch the List Manager (Macintosh only) or choose from the list of available structures (Windows only).

Note that AIA also offers Atlas Anatomy and 3-D Anatomy. Take some time to explore these additional features of AIA.

After you click Open from the open dialog box, the following image appears:

Exercise 1
The Language of Anatomy

To illustrate a coronal plane
View: Anterior
Structure: Skull—coronal section

To illustrate a midsagittal plane
View: Medial
Structure: Skin

To illustrate a ventral body cavity
View: Anterior
Structure: Diaphragm

To illustrate serous membranes of the ventral body cavity
View: Anterior
Structure: Pericardial sac, Parietal peritoneum, Peritoneum

To illustrate a parietal pleura
View: Medial
Structure: Costal parietal pleura diaphragmatic

Exercise 7
Classification of Covering and Lining Membranes

To illustrate parietal pleural membranes
View: Anterior
Structure: Parietal pleura

Exercise 9
The Axial Skeleton

To illustrate bones of the cranium and face
View: Anterior
Structure: Skull

To illustrate bones of the cranium
View: Posterior
Structure: Bones—coronal section

To illustrate bones of the cranium and face
View: Lateral
Structure: Skull

To illustrate hyoid bone
View: Lateral
Structure: Hyoid bone

To illustrate paranasal sinuses
View: Anterior
Structure: Mucosa of maxillary, Frontal, Sphenoidal sinuses, Ethmoidal sinus

To illustrate a vertebral column
View: Anterior
Structure: Intervertebral disc

To illustrate a posterior vertebral column
View: Posterior
Structure: Intervertebral disc

To illustrate a vertebral column and intervertebral discs
View: Medial
Structure: Sacrum

To illustrate a sacrum and lumbar vertebrae
View: Posterior
Structure: Sacrum

To illustrate a bony thorax
View: Anterior
Structure: Ribs

Exercise 10
The Appendicular Skeleton

To illustrate a pectoral girdle
View: Anterior
Structure: Clavicle

To illustrate a pectoral girdle
View: Posterior
Structure: Scapula

To illustrate a humerus
View: Anterior
Structure: Humerus

To illustrate an ulna
View: Anterior
Structure: Ulna

To illustrate bones of the wrist and hand
View: Anterior
Structure: Bones of hand

To illustrate a female pelvis click on the Gender button and choose Female
View: Anterior
Structure: Bones—coronal section

To illustrate a male pelvis click on the Gender button and choose Male
View: Anterior
Structure: Bones—coronal section

To illustrate a femur
View: Anterior
Structure: Femur

To illustrate a tibia
View: Anterior
Structure: Tibia

To illustrate bones of the foot
View: Anterior
Structure: Bones of the foot

Exercise 12
Articulations and Body Movements

To illustrate a synovial joint of the knee
View: Anterior
Structure: Synovial capsule of knee joint

To illustrate a synovial joint capsule of the hip
View: Anterior
Structure: Synovial joint capsule of the hip

Exercise 14
Gross Anatomy of the Muscular System

To illustrate muscles of the face
View: Anterior
Structure: Orbicularis oculi muscle

To illustrate muscles of mastication
View: Anterior
Structure: Masseter muscle

To illustrate superficial muscles of the neck
View: Lateral
Structure: Platysma muscle, Sternocleidomastoid muscle

To illustrate deep muscles of the neck
View: Lateral
Structure: Strap muscles

To illustrate thorax and shoulder muscles
View: Lateral
Structure: Pectoralis major muscle, Serratus anterior muscle

To illustrate thorax muscles
View: Anterior
Structure: External intercostal muscles, Internal intercostal muscle

To illustrate abdominal wall
View: Anterior
Structure: Rectus abdominis muscle, External abdominal oblique muscle, Internal abdominal oblique muscle

To illustrate thorax muscles
View: Lateral
Structure: Latissimus dorsi muscle

To illustrate posterior muscles of the trunk
View: Posterior
Structure: Rhomboideus muscle

To illustrate muscles associated with the vertebral column
View: Posterior
Structure: Semispinalis muscle, Splenius muscle

To illustrate muscles of the humerus that act on the forearm
View: Posterior
Structure: Brachialis muscle

To illustrate anterior muscles of the forearm that act on the hand and fingers
View: Anterior
Structure: Flexor carpi radialis muscle, Palmaris longus muscle, Flexor carpi ulnaris muscle, Flexor digitorum superficialis muscle

To illustrate deep muscles of the forearm that act on the hand and fingers
View: Posterior
Structure: Abductor pollicis longus muscle

To illustrate muscles acting on the thigh
View: Anterior
Structure: Sartorius muscle

To illustrate quadriceps
View: Anterior
Structure: Rectus femoris muscle, Vastus lateralis muscle, Vastus medialis muscle, Vastus intermedius muscle, Tensor fasciae latae muscle

To illustrate muscles acting on the thigh and originating on the pelvis
View: Posterior
Structure: Gluteus maximus muscle, Gluteus medius muscle, Gluteus minimus muscle

To illustrate hamstrings
View: Posterior
Structure: Long head of the biceps femoris muscle, Semitendinosus muscle, Semimembranosus muscle

To illustrate superficial muscles acting on the foot and ankle
View: Posterior
Structure: Gastrocnemius muscle, Soleus muscle, Popliteus muscle, Tibialis posterior muscle

To illustrate muscles acting on the foot and ankle
View: Anterior
Structure: Tibialis anterior muscle, Extensor digitorum longus muscle, Extensor hallucis longus muscle

Exercise 16
Gross Anatomy of the Brain and Cranial Nerves

To illustrate a cerebrum
View: Anterior
Structure: Skull—coronal section

To illustrate a cerebrum
View: Lateral
Structure: Brain

To illustrate cranial nerves
View: Lateral
Structure: Cranial nerves

To illustrate a vagus nerve
View: Lateral
Structure: Vagus nerve {CN X}

To illustrate phrenic and vagus nerves
View: Anterior
Structure: Phrenic and vagus nerves {CN X}

Exercise 17
Spinal Cord, Spinal Nerves, and the Autonomic Nervous System

To illustrate a spinal cord
View: Posterior
Structure: Spinal cord

To illustrate deep nerve plexuses and intercostal nerves
View: Anterior
Structure: Deep nerve plexuses and intercostal nerves

To illustrate a brachial plexus and branches
View: Anterior
Structure: Brachial plexus

To illustrate a central nervous system and sacral plexus
View: Medial
Structure: Central nervous system and sacral plexus

To illustrate a sciatic nerve and branches
View: Medial
Structure: Sciatic nerve and branches

To illustrate a tibial nerve
View: Posterior
Structure: Tibial nerve and branches

To illustrate autonomic nerve plexuses
View: Medial
Structure: Autonomic nerve plexuses

To illustrate a sympathetic trunk
View: Anterior
Structure: Sympathetic trunk

Exercise 18
Special Senses: Vision

To illustrate muscles and external anatomy of the eye
View: Anterior
Structure: Muscles of the eye

To illustrate eye muscles
View: Lateral
Structure: Eye muscles—medial

Exercise 21
Functional Anatomy of the Endocrine Glands

To illustrate a pituitary gland
View: Lateral
Structure: Pituitary gland

To illustrate a thyroid gland
View: Anterior
Structure: Thyroid gland

To illustrate a suprarenal gland
View: Anterior
Structure: Suprarenal {Adrenal} gland

To illustrate a pancreas
View: Anterior
Structure: Pancreas

To illustrate ovaries click on the Gender button and choose Female
View: Medial
Structure: Ovary

To illustrate testes click on the Gender button and choose Male
View: Anterior
Structure: Testis

To illustrate a thymus gland
View: Anterior
Structure: Thymus gland

Exercise 23
Anatomy of the Heart

To illustrate a heart
View: Anterior
Structure: Heart

To illustrate fibrous pericardium
View: Anterior
Structure: Pericardiacophrenic vein

To illustrate visceral pericardium
View: Anterior
Structure: Epicardium

To illustrate heart chambers and heart valves
View: Anterior
Structure: Heart—cut section

To illustrate coronary arteries
View: Anterior
Structure: Coronary arteries

Exercise 24
Anatomy of Blood Vessels

To illustrate an aortic arch and branches
View: Anterior
Structure: Aortic arch and branches

To illustrate common carotid arteries
View: Anterior
Structure: Common carotid arteries

To illustrate major branches of the descending aorta
View: Anterior
Structure: Celiac trunk and branches

To illustrate a descending thoracic aorta
View: Anterior
Structure: Descending thoracic aorta

To illustrate an abdominal aorta and branches
View: Anterior
Structure: Abdominal aorta and branches

To illustrate an aortic arch and branches
View: Medial
Structure: Aortic

To illustrate veins draining into the vena cavae
View: Lateral
Structure: Venae Cavae and tributaries

To illustrate pulmonary circulation
View: Anterior
Structure: Pulmonary arteries

To illustrate arterial supply of the brain
View: Lateral
Structure: Aortic arch and branches

To illustrate hepatic portal circulation
View: Anterior
Structure: Portal vein and tributaries

Exercise 25
The Lymphatic System

To illustrate lymphatic vessels and lymphoid organs
View: Anterior
Structure: Lymph vessels

To illustrate a thoracic duct
View: Anterior
Structure: Thoracic duct

To illustrate axillary and cervical lymph nodes
View: Anterior
Structure: Axillary and cervical lymph nodes

To illustrate a thymus gland
View: Anterior
Structure: Thymus gland

To illustrate a spleen
View: Anterior
Structure: Spleen

To illustrate palatine glands and tonsils
View: Anterior
Structure: Palatine glands and tonsils

Exercise 26
Anatomy of the Respiratory System

To illustrate an upper respiratory tract
View: Medial
Structure: Nasal conchae

To illustrate an upper respiratory tract
View: Lateral
Structure: Mediastinal parietal pleura of right pleural cavity

To illustrate a larynx
View: Anterior
Structure: Thyroid gland

To illustrate an epiglottis
View: Anterior
Structure: Epiglottis

To illustrate lower respiratory structures
View: Medial
Structure: Right lung

To illustrate lower respiratory structures
View: Anterior
Structure: Trachea

To illustrate lungs
View: Anterior
Structure: Lungs

To illustrate lungs—coronal section
View: Anterior
Structure: Lungs—coronal section

To illustrate a right lung
View: Lateral
Structure: Right lung

To illustrate a parietal pleura
View: Anterior
Structure: Parietal pleura

To illustrate a diaphragm
View: Anterior
Structure: Diaphragm

To illustrate a trachea
View: Lateral
Structure: Trachea

Exercise 27
Anatomy of the Digestive System

To illustrate an oral cavity
View: Lateral
Structure: Esophagus

To illustrate tonsils
View: Anterior
Structure: Palatine tonsil

To illustrate salivary glands
View: Lateral
Structure: Parotid gland, Parotid duct, Deep salivary glands

To illustrate an esophagus
View: Lateral
Structure: Esophagus

To illustrate a stomach
View: Anterior
Structure: Stomach, Stomach—coronal section

To illustrate a stomach
View: Lateral
Structure: Stomach

To illustrate an ileum
View: Anterior
Structure: Ileum

To illustrate a duodenum
View: Anterior
Structure: Duodenum

To illustrate a transverse colon
View: Anterior
Structure: Transverse colon

To illustrate an ascending and descending colon
View: Anterior
Structure: Ascending colon, Descending colon

To illustrate a colon
View: Medial
Structure: Colon

To illustrate teeth
View: Anterior
Structure: Skull

To illustrate a bile duct, liver, and gallbladder
View: Anterior
Structure: Bile duct {Common bile duct}, Liver—coronal section, Gallbladder

To illustrate a pancreas
View: Anterior
Structure: Pancreas

Exercise 28
Anatomy of the Urinary System

To illustrate kidneys
View: Anterior
Structure: Kidney, Kidney—longitudinal section

To illustrate a ureter
View: Anterior
Structure: Ureter

To illustrate a urinary bladder
View: Anterior
Structure: Urinary bladder

To illustrate a female urethra click on the Gender button and choose Female
View: Medial
Structure: Urethra

To illustrate a male urethra click on the Gender button and choose Male
View: Medial
Structure: Urinary bladder and prostate, Urethra

Exercise 29
Anatomy of the Reproductive System

To illustrate testes click on the Gender button and choose Male
View: Anterior
Structure: Testis

To illustrate a penis click on the Gender button and choose Male
View: Anterior
Structure: Penis

To illustrate a uterus click on the Gender button and choose Female
View: Anterior
Structure: Uterus

To illustrate mammary glands click on the Gender button and choose Female
View: Anterior
Structure: Breast

Credits

Very special thanks to Leslie King of University of San Francisco, dissectionist for Exercise 2, Organs Systems Overview, Figures 2.1(a–d), 2.2, 2.3(a), 2.4(a), and 2.5 (b, c).

ILLUSTRATIONS

Exercise 1
1.1–1.3, 1.6, 1.7: Imagineering. 1.4, 1.5: Precision Graphics. 1.8: Adapted from Marieb/Mallatt, *Human Anatomy,* 3e, F1.10, © Benjamin Cummings, 2003.

Exercise 3
3.2–3.4, Activity 3: Precision Graphics.

Exercise 4
4.1, 4.2: Imagineering. 4.3: Tomo Narashima. 4.4: Adapted from Campbell, Reece, and Mitchell, *Biology,* 5e, F12.5. © Benjamin Cummings, 1999. Table 4.1: Precision Graphics.

Exercise 5
5.1, 5.3, 5.5–5.7: Imagineering. 5.2: Precision Graphics. 5.4: Kristin Otwell/Imagineering.

Exercise 6
6.1: Tomo Narashima. 6.2, 6.4, 6.5, 6.7–6.9: Imagineering.

Exercise 7
7.1, 7.2: Imagineering.

Exercise 8
8.1: Laurie O'Keefe. 8.2, 8.4, 8.5, Table 8.1: Imagineering. 8.3: Carla Simmons.

Exercise 9
9.1–9.3, 9.19: Nadine Sokol. 9.4, 9.5, 9.7, 9.8, 9.10, 9.12–9.17: Imagineering. 9.6: Nadine Sokol/Kristin Mount. 9.11: Kristin Mount.

Exercise 10
10.1–10.9, Table 10.1: Imagineering.

Exercise 11
11.2a, b: Nadine Sokol

Exercise 12
12.1, 12.5, 12.6: Precision Graphics. 12.3, 12.4, 12.7–12.10, Table 12.1: Imagineering.

Exercise 13
13.1, 13.2, 13.5: Imagineering. 13.3, 13.4: Raychel Ciemma.

Exercise 14
14.1: Adapted from Martini, *Fundamentals of Anatomy & Physiology,* 4e, F11.1, Upper Saddle River, NJ: Prentice-Hall, © Frederic H. Martini, 1998. 14.2–14.7: Imagineering. 14.18: Precision Graphics.

Exercise 15
15.1, 15.2, 15.5, 15.9b: Precision Graphics. 15.3, 15.6, 15.8, 15.9a: Imagineering. 15.7: Charles Hoffman.

Exercise 16
16.1, 16.2, 16.4, 16.5, 16.7a, 16.8a, b: Imagineering. 16.7b, 16.8c, 16.9, 16.11, 16.13: Precision Graphics.

Exercise 17
17.1–17.3, 17.5a, 17.6–17.11: Imagineering. 17.5b: Stephanie McCann. 17.12–17.14: Kristin Mount.

Exercise 18
18.1: Charles W. Hoffman. 18.2: Wendy Hiller Gee and Kristin Mount. 18.3–18.4, 18.8, 18.9: Imagineering. 18.7: Shirley Bortoli. 18.10, 18.11: Precision Graphics.

Exercise 19
19.1–19.3, 19.5, 19.7, 19.8: Imagineering. 19.4: Precision Graphics.

Exercise 20
20.1, 20.2: Imagineering.

Exercise 21
21.1, 21.2: Imagineering. 21.3: Precision Graphics. 21.4: Kristin Mount.

Exercise 22
22.1, 22.6, Table 22.1: Imagineering. 22.2, 22.3: Precision Graphics.

Exercise 23
23.1: Wendy Hiller Gee. 23.2, 23.3, 23.6, 23.10: Barbara Cousins. 23.4, 23.5: Imagineering. 23.8: Precision Graphics.

Exercise 24
24.1: Adapted from Tortora and Grabowski, *Principles of Anatomy and Physiology,* 9e, F21.1, New York: Wiley, © Biological Sciences Textbooks and Sandra Reynolds Grabowski, 2000. 24.2, 24.7, 24.14, 24.19: Imagineering. 24.3–24.6, 24.8–24.13: Barbara Cousins. 24.15: Kristin Mount. 24.17, 24.18: Precision Graphics.

Exercise 25
25.1a: Adapted from Marieb/Mallatt, *Human Anatomy,* 3e, F20.1, © Benjamin Cummings, 2003. 25.1b, c, 25.2, 25.3, 25.4: Imagineering.

Exercise 26
26.1–26.5, 26.9: Imagineering. 26.6: Precision Graphics.

Exercise 27
27.1, 27.18: Kristin Mount. 27.2: Adapted from Seeley, Stephens, and Tate, *Anatomy and Physiology,* 4e, F24.2, New York: WCB/McGraw-Hill, © McGraw-Hill, 1998. 27.3, 27.4: Cyndie Wooley. 27.5a: Kristin Otwell. 27.5c, d, 27.6, 27.8, 27.11, 27.12, 27.13, 27.15–27.17: Imagineering. 27.7, 27.9: Precision Graphics.

Exercise 28
28.1a, 28.2: Linda McVay. 28.1c, 28.3–28.5, 28.8: Imagineering. 28.6: Precision Graphics. 28.9: Kristin Mount.

Exercise 29
29.1, 29.2, 29.5, 29.7, 29.9: Imagineering. 29.4: Carla Simmons. 29.8: Kristin Mount.

Exercise 30
30.3–30.8, 30.11, 30.12, 30.18, 30.19: Imagineering. 30.17: Precision Graphics.

PHOTOGRAPHS

Exercise 1
1.1, 1.3: Jenny Thomas, Pearson Benjamin Cummings. 1.3a: Howard Sochureck. 1.3b: Science Photo Library/Photo Researchers. 1.3c: CNRI/ Science Photo Library/Photo Researchers. 1.7b: Custom Medical Stock.

Exercise 2
2.1, 2.2, 2.3, 2.4a, 2.5b–c: Elena Dorfman, Pearson Benjamin Cummings. 2.4b–c, 2.6: From *A Stereoscopic Atlas of Human Anatomy* by David L. Bassett. 2.5a: Dissection by Shawn Miller, photograph by Mark Nielsen and Alexa Doig. 2.7: Carolina Biological Supply/Phototake.

Exercise 3
3.1: Leica Microsystems. 3.5: Victor Eroschenko, Pearson Benjamin Cummings.

Exercise 4
4.1b: Don Fawcett, Science Source/Photo Researchers. 4.4: Ed Reschke.

Exercise 5
5.3a: G.W. Willis/Visuals Unlimited. 5.3b, e, f, h, 5.5d, i, 5.7c: Allen Bell, University of New England; Pearson Benjamin Cummings. 5.3c: Cabisco/Visuals Unlimited. 5.3d, 5.5a, b, e, g, j, k, 5.7b: Ed Reschke. 5.3g: R.G. Kessel and R.H. Kardon/Visuals Unlimited. 5.5c, h: Nina Zanetti, Pearson Benjamin Cummings. 5.5f: Ed Reschke/Peter Arnold. 5.6: Biophoto Associates/Photo Researchers. 5.7a: Eric Graves/Photo Researchers.

Exercise 6

6.2a: Dennis Strete/Fundamental Photographs. 6.3: Pearson Benjamin Cummings. 6.5b: Carolina Biological Supply/Phototake. 6.5d: Manfred Kage/Peter Arnold. 6.6a: Marian Rice. 6.6b: Elsevier. 6.7a: Cabisco/Visuals Unlimited. 6.7b: John D. Cunningham/Visuals Unlimited. Review Sheet: Marian Rice.

Exercise 8

8.3c and Review Sheet: Allen Bell, University of New England; Pearson Benjamin Cummings. 8.4: Ed Reschke.

Exercise 9

9.4, 9.5, 9.7: Ralph T. Hutchings. 9.9: From *A Stereoscopic Atlas of Human Anatomy* by David L. Bassett. 9.16: Dissection by Shawn Miller, photography by Mark Nielsen and Alexa Doig.

Exercise 10

Table 10.1: From *A Stereoscopic Atlas of Human Anatomy* by David L. Bassett.

Exercise 11

11.1: Jack Scanlon, Holyoke Community College, MA. 11.2: Ralph T. Hutchings.

Exercise 12

12.2, 12.7: From *A Stereoscopic Atlas of Human Anatomy* by David L. Bassett. 12.8d: L. Bassett/Visuals Unlimited. 12.10: Video Surgery/Photo Researchers.

Exercise 13

13.4b: John D. Cunningham/Visuals Unlimited.

Exercise 14

14.4b, 14.14b: From *A Stereoscopic Atlas of Human Anatomy* by David L. Bassett. 14.5, 14.8, 14.9: Dissection by Shawn Miller, photography by Mark Nielsen and Alexa Doig. 14.11f: Stephen Spector, Pearson Benjamin Cummings. 14.17: Centers for Disease Control and Prevention. 14.19–14.30: Shawn Miller (dissection) and Mark Nielsen (photography), Pearson Benjamin Cummings.

Exercise 15

15.2c: Triarch/Visuals Unlimited. 15.3: Don Fawcett/Photo Researchers. 15.4: Victor Eroschenko, Pearson Benjamin Cummings.

Exercise 16

16.2, 16.4, 16.6a, b, 16.7c, 16.10: From *A Stereoscopic Atlas of Human Anatomy* by David L. Bassett. 16.3: Leonard Lessin/Peter Arnold. 16.5: Pat Lynch/Photo Researchers. 16.11: Sharon Cummings, University of California, Davis; Pearson Benjamin Cummings. 16.12, 16.13b, 16.14: Elena Dorfman, Pearson Benjamin Cummings.

Exercise 17

17.1b, c, d, 17.8: From *A Stereoscopic Atlas of Human Anatomy* by David L. Bassett. 17.4: Victor Eroschenko, Pearson Benjamin Cummings. 17.7, 17.9: Ralph T. Hutchings. 17.12b: © Paul Waring/BioMed Arts Associates, Inc. 17.13: Elena. Dorfman, Pearson Benjamin Cummings. 17.14: Shawn Miller (dissection) and Mark Nielsen (photography).

Exercise 18

18.3b: From *A Stereoscopic Atlas of Human Anatomy* by David L. Bassett. 18.4b: Ed Reschke/Peter Arnold. 18.5b: Stephen Spector, courtesy of Charles Thomas, Kansas University Medical Center; Pearson Benjamin Cummings. 18.6: Elena Dorfman, Pearson Benjamin Cummings. 18.12a, b: Richard Tauber, Pearson Benjamin Cummings. 18.13: A.L. Blum/Visuals Unlimited.

Exercise 19

19.6a, b, c: Richard Tauber, Pearson Benjamin Cummings.

Exercise 20

20.1: John D. Cunningham/Visuals Unlimited. 20.2d: Carolina Biological Supply/Phototake.

Exercise 21

21.5a: Michael Ross/Photo Researchers. 21.5b, d: Victor Eroschenko, Pearson Benjamin Cummings. 21.5c: Carolina Biological Supply/Phototake. 21.5e: Benjamin Widrevitz, Natural Sciences Division, College of DuPage, Glen Ellyn, IL. 21.5f: Ed Reschke/Peter Arnold.

Exercise 22

22.4a, b, c, 22.5a, b, c, d: Elena Dorfman, Pearson Benjamin Cummings. 22.6b: Meckes and Ottawa/Photo Researchers. 22.7 and Review Sheet: Jack Scanlan, Holyoke Community College; Pearson Benjamin Cummings.

Exercise 23

23.2: *Color Atlas of Anatomy: A Photographic Study of the Human Body:* © Schattauer Publishing. 23.3b: From *A Stereoscopic Atlas of Human Anatomy* by David L. Bassett. 23.3c: Lennart Nilsson, *The Body Victorious,* New York: Dell, © Boehringer Ingelheim International GmbH. 23.7 and Review Sheet: Ed Reschke. 23.8a, b, 23.9c: Wally Cash, Kansas State University; Pearson Benjamin Cummings.

Exercise 24

24.1: Gladden Willis/Visuals Unlimited. 24.15: From *A Stereoscopic Atlas of Human Anatomy* by David L. Bassett. 24.16, 24.19: Shawn Miller. 24.20: Elena Dorfman, Pearson Benjamin Cummings.

Exercise 25

25.1: L. Bassett/Visuals Unlimited. 25.3b: Biophoto Associates/Photo Researchers. 25.4c: Mark Nielsen, Pearson Benjamin Cummings. 25.4d: LUMEN Histology, Loyola University Medical Education Network.

Exercise 26

26.1b, 26.5b: From *A Stereoscopic Atlas of Human Anatomy* by David L. Bassett. 26.5a: Richard Tauber, Pearson Benjamin Cummings. 26.7, 26.8: Shawn Miller (dissection) and Mark Nielsen (photography), Pearson Benjamin Cummings. 26.9b: University of San Francisco. 26.10a: Ed Reschke/Peter Arnold. 26.10b: Carolina Biological Supply/Phototake.

Exercise 27

27.5b: From *Color Atlas of Histology* by Leslie P. Garner and James L. Hiatt, © Williams and Wilkins, 1990. 27.6a, c, 27.14, 27.15b: From *A Stereoscopic Atlas of Human Anatomy* by David L. Bassett. 27.8d: LUMEN Histology, Loyola University Medical Education Network. 27.13: Science Photo Library/Photo Researchers. 27.16: Phototake. 27.17, 27.19: Shawn Miller (dissection) and Mark Nielsen (photography), Pearson Benjamin Cummings. 27.18: Elena Dorfman, Pearson Benjamin Cummings.

Exercise 28

28.1: Richard Tauber/Benjamin Cummings. 28.3a: From *A Stereoscopic Atlas of Human Anatomy* by David L. Bassett. 28.7: P.M. Motta and M.Castellucci/SPL/Photo Researchers. 28.8b: Shawn Miller (dissection) and Mark Nielsen (photography), Pearson Benjamin Cummings. 28.9: Elena Dorfman, Pearson Benjamin Cummings.

Exercise 29

29.2b: Pearson Benjamin Cummings. 29.2c: From *A Stereoscopic Atlas of Human Anatomy* by David L. Bassett. 29.3: Robert Wagner, University of Delaware. 29.6: Biodisc/Visuals Unlimited. 29.7: Ed Reschke. 29.8b: © Paul Waring/BioMed Arts Associates, Inc. 29.9: Shawn Miller (dissection) and Mark Nielsen (photography), Pearson Benjamin Cummings.

Exercise 30

30.1–30.3, 30.5, 30.7, 30.9–30.11, 30.13–30.16, 30.18, 30.19: Jenny Thomas/Benjamin Cummings. 30.12: Paul Waring/BioMed Arts Associates.

Histology Atlas
PLATES 1, 6 , 7, 21, 31, 34, 35: Nina Zanetti, Pearson Benjamin Cummings. PLATES 2, 4, 9, 10, 12–14, 16–19, 27, 29,

32, 37–43, 48–53: Victor Eroschenko, Pearson Benjamin Cummings. PLATES 3, 5: Biophoto Associates/Photo Researchers. PLATES 8, 20: Eroschenko's Interactive Histology. PLATE 11: College Biology Dept., Kilgore, Texas. PLATE 15: David B. Fankhauser, University of Cincinnati Clermont College. PLATE 22: LUMEN Histology, Loyola University Medical Education Network. PLATE 23: Ed Reschke/Peter Arnold. PLATE 24: Dept. of Health Technology and Informatics, Hong Kong Polytechnic University. PLATE 25: John Cunningham/Visuals Unlimited. PLATE 26: Marian Rice. PLATE 28: Delta-gen. PLATE 30: Roger C. Wagner, Dept. of Biological Sciences, University of Delaware. PLATE 33: G.W. Willis/Visuals Unlimited. PLATES 36, 46: University of Kansas Medical Center. PLATE 44: Michael W. Davidson and Florida State University, in collaboration with Optical Microscopy at the National High Magnetic Field Laboratory. PLATE 45: Harry Plymale. PLATE 47: M. Abbey/Visuals Unlimited. PLATE 54: Pearson PH College. PLATE 55: James O. Ballard.

Human Anatomy Atlas

PLATES A, B: Elena Dorfman, Pearson Benjamin Cummings. PLATES C–F, H, J, O: Ralph T. Hutchings. PLATES G, I, K–N: From *A Stereoscopic Atlas of Human Anatomy* by David L. Bassett.

Index